Le logotype d'ICME–7

Le logotype d'ICME–7 s'inspire d'une construction géométrique élémentaire des racines carrées successives qui est tout à fait dans l'esprit de la géométrie grecque – quoique la figure elle-même n'ait été retrouvée dans aucun document de l'époque. Il a été conçu par René J. Lemieux, de l'École des arts visuels de l'Université Laval, qui le décrit comme suit.

Formé d'unités triangulaires reliées optiquement entre elles et évoquant l'association de groupes et d'individus, le motif principal du logotype d'ICME–7 est un assemblage géométrique qui détermine sept filets blancs rayonnant à partir d'une forme circulaire suggérée. Cette diffusion de la lumière reflète le développement et la transmission des connaissances qui sont au coeur même de l'acte d'enseignement. Le motif s'appuie sur une signature typographique comprenant l'élément figuratif connu qu'est la feuille d'érable canadienne. La couleur bleue est la couleur institutionnelle du Québec.

The ICME–7 logo

The ICME–7 logo is based on an elementary construction of successive square roots that is in the spirit of Greek geometry – though the figure has never been found in texts of the period. The logo was designed by René J. Lemieux, of the École des arts visuels de l'Université Laval, who describes it as follows.

Formed from triangular units that are optically related and that evoke the association of groups and individuals, the principal motif of the ICME–7 logo is a geometrical configuration that defines seven white rays radiating from an implied circular form: the scattering of the white light carries the idea of the development and transmission of knowledge which is at the heart of the act of teaching. This motif is complemented by a typographical signature including the Canadian maple leaf, a well known figurative element. The blue color is the institutional color of the province of Québec.

Proceedings of the 7th International Congress on Mathematical Education

Actes du 7e Congrès international sur l'enseignement des mathématiques

Canadian Cataloguing in Publication Data

International Congress on Mathematical Education (7th : 1992 : Université Laval)

Proceedings of the 7th International Congress on Mathematical Education : Québec, 17-23 August 1992 = Actes du 7ᵉ Congrès international sur l'enseignement des mathématiques : Québec, 17-23 août 1992

    Includes bibliographical references.
    Texts in English and French.
    Held at Université Laval.

    ISBN 2-7637-7362-1

1. Mathematics – Study and teaching – Congresses. 2. Mathematics teachers – Training of – Congresses. 3. Mathematics – Data processing – Congresses. I. Gaulin, Claude, 1938-   . II. Title. III. Title : Actes du 7ᵉ Congrès international sur l'enseignement des mathématiques. IV. Title : Proceedings of the Seventh International Congress on Mathematical Education. V. Title : Actes du septième Congrès international sur l'enseignement des mathématiques.

QA11.A1I57 1992   510'.7   C94-940509-4E

Données de catalogage avant publication (Canada)

Congrès international sur l'enseignement des mathématiques (7ᵉ : 1992 : Université Laval)

Proceedings of the 7th International Congress on Mathematical Education : Québec, 17-23 August 1992 = Actes du 7ᵉ Congrès international sur l'enseignement des mathématiques : Québec, 17-23 août 1992

    Comprend des réf. bibliogr.
    Textes en anglais et en français.
    Tenu à l'Université Laval.

    ISBN 2-7637-7362-1

1. Mathématiques – Étude et enseignement – Congrès. 2. Professeurs de mathématiques – Formation – Congrès. 3. Mathématiques – Informatique – Congrès. I. Gaulin, Claude, 1938-   . II. Titre. III. Titre : Actes du 7ᵉ Congrès international sur l'enseignement des mathématiques. IV. Titre : Proceedings of the Seventh International Congress on Mathematical Education. V. Titre : Actes du septième Congrès international sur l'enseignement des mathématiques.

QA11.A1I57 1992   510'.7   C94-940509-4E

Proceedings of the 7th International Congress on Mathematical Education

*A*ctes du 7ᵉ *Congrès international sur l'enseignement des mathématiques*

QUÉBEC
17-23
August / *août*
1992

Edited by /
sous la direction de

Claude Gaulin
Bernard R. Hodgson
David H. Wheeler
John C. Egsgard

LES PRESSES DE L'UNIVERSITÉ LAVAL
Sainte-Foy, 1994

Cover illustration / *Illustration de la couverture*
  « Au pied du Château Frontenac, Vieux-Québec », pastel, 1992
  Collection du Département de mathématiques et de statistique,
  Université Laval
  Lucienne Zegray
  Canadian artist / *Artiste canadienne*

Cover design / *Conception de la couverture*
  Norman Dupuis

Photographs / *Photographies*
  Martin R. Hoffman, Brooklyn
  Service des relations publiques, Université Laval
  Office du tourisme et des congrès de la Communauté urbaine
  de Québec

Layout / *Mise en page*
  Éditions l'Ardoise, Québec

Les Presses de l'Université Laval
Cité universitaire
Sainte-Foy (Québec)
Canada G1K 7P4

CONTENTS

TABLE DES MATIÈRES

PREFACE

This book comprises the Proceedings of the 7th International Congress on Mathematical Education (ICME-7) which was held at Université Laval, Québec City, Canada, from August 17 to 23, 1992.

Every International Congress on Mathematics Education (ICME) is structured around a "scientific program," but mathematics education is not a science of the same character as mathematics or most of the other sciences. The definition of our field is fuzzier, it overlaps a number of other domains, and its achievements are less likely to achieve consensus. Furthermore, mathematics education is an applied science and its practices vary considerably with the social, economic, and cultural environments in which it takes place. An international meeting on mathematics education must therefore provide opportunities not only for the dissemination of what is currently known about the major problems, advances, and trends in the field worldwide, but also for interaction, and possibly confrontation, among participants whose views of the purposes and methods of mathematics education are radically different.

The sequence of quadrennial ICMEs has increasingly emphasized the intrinsic importance for mathematics educators of face-to-face debate and discussion. The ICME programs have increasingly incorporated these activities within the scientific sessions, not leaving them to the corridors and cafeterias. For example, the programs for the more recent congresses have included a substantial number of working groups whose mandate requires the leaders to encourage and facilitate the exchange of views among participants.

Following the usual procedures, the Executive Committee of the International Commission on Mathematical Instruction (ICMI) appointed an International Program Committee (IPC) to plan the scientific program of ICME-7. All the other aspects of the Congress organization were delegated to the host country, Canada, which established a National Committee for

ICME-7 with a number of subcommittees, including in particular a Local Organizing Committee and an Executive Committee. (Readers will find the memberships of all the committees listed on pages 448–453.)

At its first meeting in September 1989, the IPC discussed the general aims and structure of the program and arrived at a framework having much in common with that of previous ICMEs, but with a few significant innovations. The IPC invited four distinguished speakers to give plenary addresses representing important facets of mathematics education. The value of meeting in face-to-face groups for at least part of the time, exemplified by the "Action Groups" and "Theme Groups" in the programs of ICME–5 and ICME–6, was accepted by the Committee, though it decided to collapse the two strands into one. A central feature of the program thus became a set of twenty-two Working Groups, each meeting for four 90-minute sessions and scheduled simultaneously. These Groups, covering a broad range of practical and theoretical issues, were intended to provide participants with an up-to-date perspective on a particular topic, as well as an opportunity to work on some aspects in depth. To ensure international coverage, each Group was planned in detail by a team comprising a chief organizer, a local (Canadian) organizer, and four or five advisers from different countries.

In response to feedback from people who attended ICME–6 suggesting that participants would benefit from "more good lectures", the IPC extended invitations to forty-four speakers to present 45-minute papers on a broad range of subjects.

The detailed planning of seventeen Topic Groups, each meeting for two 90-minute sessions, was delegated to chief organizers appointed by the IPC. These Groups, somewhat different in character from Working Groups, were not required to provide time for face-to-face discussion and were chosen largely on the basis of proposals submitted to the IPC. The program made the usual provision for the official ICMI Study Groups – the International Group for the Psychology of Mathematics Education (PME), the International Study Group on the Relations between the History and Pedagogy of Mathematics (HPM), and the International Organization of Women and Mathematics Education (IOWME). Each was invited to organize four 90-minute sessions and report to the Congress on their on-going activities. For the first time at an ICME, three of the ICMI Studies (publications on special topics planned and compiled by ICMI) were presented.

The extent and rapidity of technological change is affecting mathematics, and education, and the daily lives of people in many countries of the world. Issues arising from these largely unintended shifts are dealt with in several components of the program, but the IPC felt the matter important enough to give it special attention. An intensive 3-hour "Miniconference on calculators and computers", open to all participants, was organized on the opening afternoon of the Congress. As the IPC hoped, this event not only put an important topic high on the Congress agenda, it also performed the useful social function of bringing participants together early in the Congress and involving them straight away in joint activities and discussion.

In the Congress announcements, a general invitation was extended to individuals to submit a proposal for a short presentation in the form of a poster, or a videotape, or an item of computer software. A majority of the proposals, namely 439, was accepted for inclusion in the program, and a *Book of Abstracts* was printed and distributed to all participants at the beginning of the Congress. In eliminating the usual category of short oral presentations, the IPC argued that, in a large international meeting, visual and/or written contributions were potentially more effective means of communication than 10-minute talks spoken very rapidly. An effort was made to raise the status of poster presentations and some small success was probably achieved judging by the large numbers of participants who visited and showed interest in the poster displays.

The scientific program of ICME-7 was rounded out with an impressive Canadian presentation and some national presentations (using videotape), displays and presentations of an important number of educational projects, workshops, exhibitions of books and other materials, and a variety of special meetings and other activities. It is a good question whether the crowded nature of the program, and the rather miscellaneous character of the selection process ("like a supermarket"), are productive features of the Congress or not, but it is probably true that a more streamlined affair, while perhaps more appropriate for some purposes, would give a less realistic and accurate view of the state of mathematics education worldwide.

This book of *Proceedings of the 7th International Congress on Mathematical Education* includes the texts of the four plenary lectures, reports of the various groups and of the mini-conference on calculators and computers, and an overview of other activities on the program – including social and cultural events. Abstracts of the 45-minute lectures delivered are also provided; the full text of twenty-seven of them appears in the companion volume *Selected Lectures from the 7th International Congress on Mathematical Education.*

The venue for the Congress was the campus of Université Laval, the oldest francophone university in America. Its excellent facilities for scientific and social meetings of all kinds – including plenary and subplenary sessions, working groups of various sizes, projects, workshops and exhibitions, poster sessions, the cultural evening and, of course, daily happy hours around the "big tent" – and for accommodation in students residences, were greatly appreciated by the 3 407 participants coming from 94 different countries.

The editors thank all the people – speakers, group leaders, organizers – who provided reports for these Proceedings. With the exception of the plenary lecturers, they were required to work within severe space constraints; they met deadlines and accepted reductions in their texts with courtesy and for-bearance. We also acknowledge the exceptional contribution of Thérèse Gadbois, Éditions l'Ardoise, Québec, who formatted the complete text and converted it to camera-ready form with great skill and patience. Finally, we wish to express our gratitude to Les Presses de l'Université Laval, in particular to Jacques Chouinard and Suzanne Allaire, for their excellent work and cooperation.

Claude Gaulin
Bernard R. Hodgson
David H. Wheeler
John C. Egsgard

December 1993

PRÉFACE

On trouvera ici les Actes du 7ᵉ Congrès international sur l'enseignement des mathématiques (ICME-7), qui s'est déroulé à l'Université Laval, à Québec (Canada), du 17 au 23 août 1992.

Chaque Congrès international sur l'enseignement des mathématiques (ICME) se construit autour d'un « programme scientifique » – quoique la didactique des mathématiques ne soit pas une science de même nature que les mathématiques ou la plupart des autres sciences. Sa définition est plus floue, elle chevauche plusieurs autres domaines et ses résultats font moins facilement consensus. De plus, la didactique des mathématiques est une science appliquée et sa pratique varie considérablement selon le milieu social, économique et culturel où elle s'applique. Une rencontre internationale sur l'enseignement des mathématiques doit donc fournir l'occasion non seulement de faire connaître la situation actuelle dans le monde concernant les problèmes, les progrès et les tendances dans ce domaine, mais également de susciter des échanges, voire des confrontations, entre des participants et participantes ayant une vision radicalement différente des buts et des méthodes de l'éducation mathématique.

Les congrès ICME ont lieu tous les quatre ans. D'une fois à l'autre, on a fait une place de plus en plus grande, dans le programme scientifique, aux discussions et aux débats face à face, au lieu de les laisser survenir spontanément dans les corridors et les cafétérias. C'est ainsi que le programme des derniers congrès ICME comprenait un nombre important de groupes de travail dont les responsables avaient pour tâche d'encourager et de faciliter les échanges de points de vue entre participants et participantes.

Conformément à l'usage, le Comité exécutif de la Commission internationale de l'enseignement mathématique (CIEM) a constitué un Comité international du programme (CIP), responsable du programme scientifique d'ICME-7. L'organisation de tous les autres aspects du congrès a été confiée au pays hôte, le Canada, qui a mis en place un Comité national et de nombreux sous-comités, dont le Comité d'organisation locale et le Comité exécutif d'ICME-7. (On trouvera la liste des membres des divers comités aux pages 448 à 453.)

Lors de sa première rencontre en septembre 1989, après avoir examiné les objectifs généraux et la structure générale du programme, le CIP en est arrivé à un cadre assez semblable à celui des congrès ICME précédents, mais toutefois avec quelques innovations majeures. Il a invité quatre spécialistes de renom à faire une conférence plénière sur des aspects importants de l'éducation mathématique. Conscient de l'intérêt que présentent les rencontres face à face comme celles qui avaient été organisées dans les « Groupes d'action » et les « Groupes thématiques » lors des congrès ICME-5 et ICME-6, le CIP a décidé de mettre au cœur du programme d'ICME-7 une série de vingt-deux « Groupes de travail » devant se dérouler en parallèle durant quatre séances de 90 minutes. Ces groupes, portant sur toute une gamme de questions théoriques et pratiques, furent conçus de manière à offrir aux participants une vue d'ensemble sur un thème particulier, tout en leur donnant l'occasion d'en approfondir certains aspects. Afin de garantir une représentation internationale, l'organisation de chaque Groupe de travail fut confiée à une équipe comprenant une personne responsable en chef, une autre, responsable locale (canadienne), ainsi que quatre ou cinq consultants de différents pays.

En réaction aux commentaires reçus après ICME-6 selon lesquels il faudrait prévoir davantage de « bons exposés » à ICME-7, le CIP a invité quarante-quatre personnes à présenter des conférences de 45 minutes sur des sujets variés.

Le CIP a aussi décidé de créer dix-sept « Groupes thématiques » – différents des Groupes de travail sous plusieurs rapports, les discussions face à face n'y étant pas essentielles et la plupart portant sur des thèmes ayant été suggérés au Comité du programme. Pour chacun, le soin de planifier deux séances de 90 minutes fut confié à une personne responsable en chef. Également, comme à l'habitude, on a prévu au programme la participation des trois Groupes d'étude officiels de la CIEM : le Groupe international de psychologie de l'éducation mathématique (PME), le Groupe international d'étude des relations entre l'histoire et la pédagogie des mathématiques (HPM) et le Mouvement international pour les femmes et l'enseignement des mathématiques (IOWME/MOIFEM). Chacun d'eux fut invité à planifier quatre séances de 90 minutes et à y faire rapport sur ses activités en cours. Le CIP a aussi mis au programme la présentation de trois des Études de la CIEM (publications sur des sujets spécifiques préparées par la CIEM) – une primeur dans les congrès ICME.

L'ampleur et la rapidité des changements technologiques affectent les mathématiques, l'éducation, de même que la vie quotidienne des habitants de nombreux pays. Le CIP a cru bon d'accorder une attention particulière aux problèmes résultant de tels changements en bonne partie imprévisibles, même si plusieurs autres activités prévues au programme s'y rapportaient. C'est ainsi qu'un « Mini-congrès sur les calculatrices et les ordinateurs » d'une durée de trois heures fut mis au programme de l'après-midi de la journée d'ouverture, à l'intention de tous les participants. Comme le souhaitait le CIP, cette activité a non seulement permis de mettre fortement l'accent sur un sujet important, mais elle a également facilité les contacts sociaux, en permettant aux participants de se rencontrer dès le début du Congrès et en les amenant à s'impliquer immédiatement dans des activités collectives et des discussions.

Dans les annonces du Congrès, une invitation a été faite à toute personne intéressée à soumettre une communication brève sous forme d'affiche, de bande vidéo ou de logiciel. La plupart des propositions reçues, soit 439 en tout, ont été acceptées pour présentation à ICME-7 et un *Recueil des résumés* a été remis à chacun des participants à son arrivée au Congrès. L'argument avancé par le CIP pour éliminer du programme les communications brèves orales est que, dans une grande rencontre internationale, les présentations visuelles ou écrites constituent un moyen de communication plus efficace qu'un exposé de 10 minutes débité à toute vitesse. À en juger par leur nombre et par l'intérêt des participants qui les ont visitées, les communications par affiche ont connu du succès à ICME-7 et les efforts pour rehausser leur statut ont porté fruit.

Le programme scientifique d'ICME-7 comprenait également une imposante présentation canadienne et quelques autres présentations nationales faites sous forme de bandes vidéo, la présentation sous diverses formes d'un nombre important de projets, des ateliers, des expositions de livres et de matériel didactique, ainsi que diverses réunions et autres activités spéciales. On peut se demander si un programme aussi chargé et la nécessité pour les participants de faire un choix parmi toute une variété d'activités – un peu comme au supermarché – sont des aspects productifs des congrès ICME. Il est probable, toutefois, que tout en étant préférable à plusieurs points de vue, un programme allégé offrirait forcément une vision moins réaliste et moins précise de la situation de l'éducation mathématique dans le monde.

Ce livre des *Actes du 7e Congrès international sur l'enseignement des mathématiques* renferme les textes des quatre conférences plénières, les rapports des divers groupes et du mini-congrès sur les calculatrices et les ordinateurs, ainsi qu'un aperçu des autres activités au programme – y compris les activités socioculturelles. Il contient également les résumés des conférences de 45 minutes qui ont été présentées. (On trouvera le texte complet de vingt-sept d'entre elles dans le volume *Choix de conférences du 7ᵉ Congrès international sur l'enseignement des mathématiques* qui accompagne celui-ci.)

Le Congrès s'est déroulé sur le campus de l'Université Laval, la plus ancienne université francophone d'Amérique. Les 3407 participants venant de 94 pays ont grandement apprécié les installations excellentes qu'offre cette cité universitaire pour l'organisation de réunions scientifiques et sociales de toutes sortes – y compris des séances plénières et sous-plénières, des groupes de travail de tailles diverses, des projets, des ateliers et des expositions, des communications par affiche, des événements culturels et, bien sûr, des réceptions sous la grande tente – de même que pour le logement dans les résidences universitaires.

L'équipe de direction remercie tous les responsables de conférences, de groupes et d'autres activités au programme qui ont préparé des rapports pour ce volume des Actes. À l'exception des auteurs de conférences plénières, tous ont dû se soumettre à des contraintes d'espace assez restrictives ; c'est avec beaucoup de compréhension qu'ils ont respecté les échéanciers et accepté des coupures dans leur texte. Nous voulons également souligner la contribution tout à fait exceptionnelle de Thérèse Gadbois, des Éditions l'Ardoise, à Québec, qui a fait preuve d'une habileté et d'une patience remarquables dans le travail de mise en page et de montage du texte final. Nous voulons enfin exprimer notre reconnaissance aux Presses de l'Université Laval, en particulier à Jacques Chouinard et à Suzanne Allaire, pour leur excellent travail et tout le concours qu'ils nous ont apporté.

Claude Gaulin
Bernard R. Hodgson
David H. Wheeler
John C. Egsgard

Décembre 1993

CODES OF COUNTRIES

CODES DES PAYS

AND	Andorra / *Andorre*
ARG	Argentina / *Argentine*
ARM	Armenia / *Arménie*
ATG	Antigua
AUS	Australia / *Australie*
AUT	Austria / *Autriche*
BEL	Belgium / *Belgique*
BGR	Bulgaria / *Bulgarie*
BHR	Bahrain / *Bahreïn*
BOL	Bolivia / *Bolivie*
BRA	Brazil / *Brésil*
BRN	Brunei Darussalam / *Brunéi Darussalam*
BWA	Botswana
CAN	Canada
CHE	Switzerland / *Suisse*
CHL	Chile / *Chili*
CHN	China / *Chine*
CIV	Ivory Coast / *Côte d'Ivoire*
COL	Colombia / *Colombie*
CRI	Costa Rica
CUB	Cuba
CZR	Czech Republic / *République tchèque*
DEU	Germany / *Allemagne*
DNK	Denmark / *Danemark*
DOM	Dominican Republic / *République dominicaine*
EGY	Egypt / *Égypte*
ESP	Spain / *Espagne*
EST	Estonia / *Estonie*
FIN	Finland / *Finlande*
FJI	Fiji / *Fidji*
FRA	France

GBR	United Kingdom / *Royaume-Uni*
GLP	Guadeloupe
GRC	Greece / *Grèce*
GTM	Guatemala
HKG	Hong Kong / *Hong-Kong*
HTI	Haiti / *Haïti*
HUN	Hungary / *Hongrie*
IDN	Indonesia / *Indonésie*
IND	India / *Inde*
IRL	Ireland / *Irlande*
IRN	Iran
ISL	Iceland / *Islande*
ISR	Israel / *Israël*
ITA	Italy / *Italie*
JAM	Jamaica / *Jamaïque*
JPN	Japan / *Japon*
KOR	South Korea / *Corée du Sud*
KWT	Kuwait / *Koweït*
LAT	Latvia / *Lettonie*
LBN	Lebanon / *Liban*
LCA	Ste-Lucia / *St. Lucie*
LIT	Lithuania / *Lithuanie*
LUX	Luxembourg
MAR	Morocco / *Maroc*
MEX	Mexico / *Mexique*
MOZ	Mozambique
MTQ	Martinique
MUS	Mauritius / *Ile Maurice*
MWI	Malawi
MYS	Malaysia / *Malaisie*
NAM	Namibia / *Namibie*
NGA	Nigeria / *Nigéria*
NLD	Netherlands / *Pays-Bas*
NOR	Norway / *Norvège*
NZL	New Zealand / *Nouvelle-Zélande*
PAK	Pakistan
PER	Peru / *Pérou*
PNG	Papua New Guinea / *Papouasie-Nouvelle-Guinée*
POL	Poland / *Pologne*
PRI	Puerto Rico / *Porto Rico*
PRT	Portugal
QAT	Qatar
RUS	Russia / *Russie*

SAU	Saudi Arabia / *Arabie Saoudite*
SGP	Singapore / *Singapour*
SLN	Slovenia / *Slovénie*
SVK	Slovakia / *Slovaquie*
SWE	Sweden / *Suède*
SWZ	Swaziland
THA	Thailand / *Thaïlande*
TUR	Turkey / *Turquie*
TWN	Taiwan / *Taïwan*
TZA	Tanzania / *Tanzanie*
UGA	Uganda / *Ouganda*
UKR	Ukrainia / *Ukraine*
URY	Uruguay
USA	United States / *États-Unis*
UZB	Uzbekistan / *Ouzbékistan*
VEN	Venezuela
VNM	Viet Nam
YEM	Yemen / *Yémen*
ZAF	South Africa / *Afrique du Sud*
ZWE	Zimbabwe

SCHEDULE

Day	Schedule
SUNDAY August 16	REGISTRATION (until 24:00). Inauguration of the Math Trail in Old Québec / Musée de la Civilisation especially open after 19:00
MONDAY August 17	09:00 Opening ceremonies; Plenary lecture (1); Honorary degrees award; Lectures; Miniconference on calculators and computers; 18:00 Happy hour; (after 19:00) Special meetings / Setting up of posters, projects, exhibitions, etc. / Film/video program
TUESDAY August 18	Working Groups (1); Lectures; Lectures; Topic Groups (1); Best time for viewing projects, workshops, exhibitions and posters / Canadian presentation; Study Groups (1) / ICMI Studies (1); Happy hour; Special meetings / Film/video program
WEDNESDAY August 19	Working Groups (2); Plenary lecture (2); Lectures; Lectures; Topic Groups (2); Best time for viewing projects, workshops, exhibitions and posters / Canadian presentation; Study Groups (2) / ICMI Studies (2); ICMI's General Assembly; Happy hour; 5 km Run/Walk; Special meetings / Film/video program
THURSDAY August 20	EXCURSION DAY
FRIDAY August 21	Working Groups (3); Plenary lecture (3); Lectures; Lectures; National video presentations / Special sessions; Best time for viewing projects, workshops, exhibitions and posters / Poster round tables / Special meetings; Study Groups (3) / ICMI Studies (3); Happy hour; FREE EVENING
SATURDAY August 22	Working Groups (4); Lectures; Special sessions; National video presentations / Special sessions; Best time for viewing projects, workshops, exhibitions and posters / Film/video program; Study Groups (4) / ICMI Studies (4) / Special meetings; Happy hour; Cultural Evening
SUNDAY August 23	Lectures; Plenary lecture (4); Closing ceremonies

Time scale: 08:30 – 09:00 – 10:00 – 11:00 – 12:00 – 13:00 – 14:00 – 15:00 – 16:00 – 17:00 – 18:00 – 19:00 – 20:00 – 21:00 – 22:00

GRILLE-HORAIRE

Jour	Programme
DIMANCHE 16 août	INSCRIPTION (jusqu'à 24:00) — Inauguration du sentier mathématique dans le Vieux-Québec / Ouverture spéciale du Musée de la civilisation après 19:00
LUNDI 17 août	Cérémonies d'ouverture · Conférence plénière (1) · Remise de doctorats honorifiques · Conférences · Mini-congrès sur les calculatrices et les ordinateurs · Réception · Réunions spéciales / Installation des posters, projets, expositions, etc. / Films et vidéos
MARDI 18 août	Groupes de travail (1) · Conférences · Conférences · Groupes thématiques (1) · Moment privilégié pour voir les projets, les ateliers, les expositions et les posters / Présentation canadienne · Groupes d'étude (1) / Études de la CIEM (1) · Réception · Réunions spéciales / Films et vidéos
MERCREDI 19 août	Groupes de travail (2) · Conférence plénière (2) · Conférences · Conférences · Groupes thématiques (2) · Moment privilégié pour voir les projets, les ateliers, les expositions et les posters / Présentation canadienne · Groupes d'étude (2) / Études de la CIEM (2) · Réception · Course/marche de 5 km · Assemblée générale de la CIEM · Réunions spéciales / Films et vidéos
JEUDI 20 août	JOURNÉE D'EXCURSION
VENDREDI 21 août	Groupes de travail (3) · Conférence plénière (3) · Conférences · Conférences · Présentations nationales par vidéo · Moment privilégié pour voir les projets, ateliers, expositions et posters / Films et vidéos / Tables rondes sur les posters / Réunions spéciales · Groupes d'étude (3) / Études de la CIEM (3) · Réception · SOIRÉE LIBRE
SAMEDI 22 août	Groupes de travail (4) · Conférences · Séances spéciales · Présentations nationales par vidéo · Moment privilégié pour voir les projets, les ateliers, les expositions et les posters / Films et vidéos / Réunions spéciales · Groupes d'étude (4) / Études de la CIEM (4) · Réception · Soirée culturelle
DIMANCHE 23 août	Conférences · Conférence plénière (4) · Conférences · Cérémonies de clôture

Heures : 08:30 · 09:00 · 10:00 · 11:00 · 12:00 · 13:00 · 14:00 · 15:00 · 16:00 · 17:00 · 18:00 · 19:00 · 20:00 · 21:00 · 22:00

PRESIDENTIAL ADDRESS

ALLOCUTION DU PRÉSIDENT

Miguel de Guzmán

Universidad Complutense, Madrid [ESP]

Monsieur le Maire de la ville de Québec,
Monsieur le Recteur de l'Université Laval
et autres dignitaires,
Chers collègues,
Mesdames, Messieurs,

En ma qualité de président de la Commission internationale de l'enseignement mathématique, au nom de son Comité exécutif et de son Assemblée générale, au nom de tous les participants à ce septième Congrès international sur l'enseignement des mathématiques et au nom de l'ensemble de la communauté mathématique – particulièrement de tous ceux qui sont engagés en éducation mathématique –, je désire exprimer mes remerciements les plus chaleureux au gouvernement du Canada, à ceux de la province et de la ville de Québec, ainsi qu'à l'Université Laval pour l'hospitalité qu'ils nous offrent et pour toute l'aide qu'ils ont apportée aux organisateurs de ce congrès.

A strong indication of the high esteem a country has of education, of mathematics, of mathematical education, and of culture in general is its eager disposition to cooperate to such an extent in the organization and funding of such a Congress, from which so many fruitful consequences are derived throughout the whole world concerning mathematical education. To the people of Canada and also to the different organizations in Canada and from other countries which have collaborated in and sponsored this magnificent event, our most hearty thanks and our warmest congratulations for their wonderful disposition towards culture and towards mathematics.

1

I wish also to express our warmest thanks to those inside the organization of the Congress, the Canadian team as well as the international team, who have made this Congress possible through their constant dedication for several years. I would like to mention in particular the names of Professors Bernard Hodgson, Claude Gaulin, David Wheeler, and David Robitaille. To all of you who have participated in the preparation of this event, so important and full of consequences for the whole mathematical community around the world, and especially to all the members of the different committees, I would like to say in the name of all of us: Please, be sure that we appreciate very warmly all the efforts you have made on our behalf and on behalf of the whole mathematical community. We congratulate you on your evident success in the preparation of this Congress.

I wish also to express my thanks to all participants, to all of you who have come here to share your educational experiences in one way or another, through your lectures, talks, posters, and participation in the different activities. All of us are here with a common wish, that of serving the mathematical community concerned with education in the most effective possible way, working together towards a betterment of mathematical education in all countries in the world, with the deep persuasion that this work will greatly influence the progress of human culture.

This Congress is a manifestation of the increasing vitality of the ICMI, due very significantly to the efforts of Professors Jean-Pierre Kahane and Geoffrey Howson, who have enriched its activity in many directions in the last decade – to mention just one, through the very influential idea of the ICMI Studies, of which quite a few have already been completed, with some still in preparation.

The present world circumstances impel us to keep working in the directions in which ICMI has been so successfully acting up to now and also to try to give a stronger impetus to one action which in the mind of our Executive Committee should be at this moment a firm priority, that is: SOLIDARITY IN MATHEMATICAL EDUCATION.

The United Nations Program for Development issued a few months ago an impressive Report on Human Development. With an extraordinary wealth of information, and after several years of study by a very competent team, it examines carefully the present problems of the distribution of human and material resources in the world. According to the report, the last decade has been characterized by a drastic enlargement of the gap between rich countries and poor countries, between rich people and poor people in the world.

Two pieces of information are quite conclusive:

- At this moment one can say that a fifth of the world population (the rich people) owns more than 80 per cent of the total material resources, while another fifth of the population (the poor people) owns less than 1.5 per cent of those resources.

- This situation of imbalance has been rapidly deteriorating in recent decades, and especially during the 1980s. In 1960, the richest fifth of the world population was 30 times richer than the poorest fifth. In 1980 it was 45 times richer, and in 1989 it was 60 times richer.

This could also be expressed in the following way: There was a family of five brothers. Everywhere it was proclaimed that they were equal in rights. But one of the brothers had made himself the owner of almost everything (80%) the family owned. And another brother had almost nothing (1.5%). Some time ago the rich brother was 30 times as rich as his poor brother. But now he is 60 times as rich... THIS IS OUR WORLD. THIS IS OUR INHUMAN DEVELOPMENT.

Of course, human development, educational and cultural opportunities, social structures, and so on are in a great measure conditioned by the economic situation, and so the disparity between poor people and rich people in these aspects is at least as great as the economic figures show.

From this rapidly deteriorating situation in the distribution of material and human resources in the world, we can infer several conclusions:

- The actions and the efforts performed by global institutions in the last decade have been intense and well applied in many cases, but clearly they have been totally insufficient.

- We need to think of imaginative new ways to try to improve this situation, which is becoming unbearably unjust. Otherwise, global conditions will become still worse than they are at this moment.

- We cannot rely only on what global organizations are trying to do. We cannot silence our consciences with the excuse that there are already organizations in charge of trying to remedy the injustice of this situation. WE NEED TO FOSTER IN US AND AROUND US A PERSONAL COMMITMENT. WE NEED TO TAKE AN ACTIVE AND PERSONAL PART TO IMPROVE THIS SITUATION. WHAT CAN WE DO?

Ours, of course, is an educational task. And this task is based on two fundamental pillars: human resources and material resources. Our personal involvement can take very many different forms:

- We can actively look for places in our own environment where our personal cooperation in education might be very much welcomed

3

and needed. There is a South in every North. There are many under-developed groups of people inside every country. Perhaps for too long we have been looking just for places where we could find some profit for our own development. The time might already have come to look for places where we could offer something of ourselves.

- For some of us the barriers of language with many of the countries in need of development in mathematical education do not exist. We may offer some of our time to cooperate with them. Perhaps we should take the initiative, not waiting to be called or asked or invited, but looking ourselves for places to go and for funds to finance our work in those countries – not imposing upon them our way of look-ing at their problems, but asking the people there, with an open disposition, where, when, and in what ways we could be of any help.

- Many of us who live and work in those countries with better economic conditions could and should personally offer some of our material resources in order to help others achieve better development in math-ematical education.

ICMI COULD HELP, ICMI SHOULD HELP, TO ARTICULATE THIS PERSONAL COMMITMENT. I am sure that there will be many people in many countries who would like to find concrete ways to act. ICMI, working together with the Committee on Exchange and Development of the Interna-tional Mathematical Union, could establish a panel to channel the offers and to receive the requests for help. All of you who would like to contribute with your ideas and with your personal time and effort to this solidarity programme are invited to get in contact with any of the members of the ICMI Executive Committee. To all the persons who can think of effective ways to contribute to the betterment of the educational conditions in math-ematics in particular regions or concrete groups of people in the world, I would like to ask: Please share your ideas with us.

Regarding the material resources needed for getting ahead with this SOLIDARITY PROGRAM, some of us in the Executive Committee have been working towards the initiation of what we have called a SOLIDAR-ITY FUND FOR EDUCATION IN MATHEMATICS and have tried to start collecting some funds from personal friends around us who have agreed to start collaborating with ICMI in this form. It is a pleasure to express our thanks to the persons from different countries who have generously con-tributed to this SOLIDARITY FUND, which has started with an amount of US$20 000. I have no doubt that many of you will wish to collaborate per-sonally to increase this amount through your own contributions or through your active participation to obtain funds from different sources, personal or institutional. This SOLIDARITY FUND will be administered for the mo-ment by the Treasurer and Secretary of ICMI, Professor Mogens Niss. All of you who wish to contribute to this SOLIDARITY FUND are invited to send their contributions to his address.

There are many other ways in which we can contribute. For example, perhaps many people coming here have thought that the registration fees of US$300 we all have paid for this Congress was far from being inexpensive. If many of you, who come from rather affluent countries, are inclined to think that this is expensive, imagine what may think many professors and teachers of mathematics from many countries where their monthly salary is below that amount. If you keep this situation in your mind, I am sure that many of you would agree to pay together with your own registration a portion of the registration fees of one less affluent person whose attendance at the Congress could be made possible in this way. Maybe we should introduce this not just as an option, but as a very reasonable and just solidarity tax. Achieving solidarity is not a matter of charity. ACHIEVING SOLIDARITY IS A MATTER OF JUSTICE.

For this Congress there has been a Grants Committee for helping participants coming from countries where the economic conditions are not good at all. About 90 participants have received some kind of support in order to attend it, all continents being represented. This has been possible thanks to the efforts of the Canadian International Development Agency, with funds coming also from UNESCO, the ICME-7 Organization, IMU, and ICMI. Altogether, 75 000 Canadian dollars have been distributed. I would like to express our most hearty thanks to all these sponsors and also to those in charge of the Grants Committee for the delicate and intense work they have done.

Yet we should try to reach still more ambitious goals. Perhaps, with the personal contributions we are suggesting, we shall be able in the future to have several hundreds of participants from many more countries who are in urgent need – much more than most of us – of opportunities for development and exchange like the ones this Congress is going to offer.

The Executive Committee of ICMI would like to submit the preceding idea to our Spanish colleagues who will be in charge of organizing the next International Congress, ICME–8, in Seville, in order to explore its feasibility. For that, we still have time.

We could also proceed in a similar way with the Proceedings of this Congress and with many other publications related to ICMI. Persons in a sufficiently good economic situation could very willingly pay a little more in order that the publications they find useful can reach persons, places, and centers in less affluent countries at a drastically reduced price. Otherwise, perhaps people in these countries will be totally unable to buy them. We should introduce a new style of life, a spirit of austerity – austerity not just for itself, but for sharing. Perhaps a new slogan would make sense: TAKE ONE, PAY TWO!

Of course, this SOLIDARITY PROGRAM and SOLIDARITY FUND, which are intended to be based primarily and above all on PERSONAL COMMITMENTS AND PERSONAL CONTRIBUTIONS of all people around the world, will have to be given some structure if it is going to be efficient. It will have to try by all means to take good care that personal resources and material resources go in fact to the places where they are really needed and most effective, exploring with diligence what are in each case the right ways to achieve this goal. As many of you know, this is not an easy task, since in some cases resources come with strings and restrictions, and in some others they are channeled through organizations whose honesty, impartiality, and integrity one can rightfully doubt.

This SOLIDARITY spirit is in complete agreement with the goals of the program proposed by the International Mathematical Union which has declared the year 2000 to be the WORLD MATHEMATICAL YEAR 2000.

As you may know, on the sixth of May 1992, IMU, together with UNESCO and other institutions, decided to declare the year 2000 the World Mathematical Year 2000. In the second objective of its programme, it decided to proclaim mathematics as one of the central keys for understanding the world and for the progress of our human culture. ICMI, our International Commission on Mathematical Education, together with the Commission on Development and Exchange of IMU, was charged with the task of fostering an adequate development of mathematical education in all countries of the world. One can be sure that such a development is going to become impossible unless we take some innovative and drastic measures, which include a personal commitment like the one our Executive Committee has agreed to promote within the entire mathematical community.

If this Seventh International Congress serves to launch such a solidarity spirit, first of all among its participants and through them in their particular communities, it will have done a great service to mathematical development in our world. Let us look forward to it.

To conclude:

Je déclare ouvert ce septième Congrès international sur l'enseignement des mathématiques.

I declare open this Seventh International Congress on Mathematical Education.

Queda inaugurado este Séptimo Congreso Internacional de Educación Matemática.

PLENARY LECTURES
CONFÉRENCES PLÉNIÈRES

TEACHERS OF MATHEMATICS

LES ENSEIGNANTS ET ENSEIGNANTES DE MATHÉMATIQUES

Geoffrey Howson

University of Southampton [GBR]

My title today immediately suggests two questions: *Why speak about mathematics teachers?* and *Why should a university professor choose to talk on that topic?* Let me deal, then, with these questions first.

Teachers are central to mathematics education. We may have particular personal concerns for, say, curriculum development, the impact of new technology, or research into learning. These, together with many other aspects of mathematics education, will be discussed and, I hope, illuminated at this Congress. Yet it is the individual teacher in the classroom and the body of teachers within a country on whom the well-being of mathematics education rests. However, at past Congresses, apart from some contributions on pre- and in-service training, little attention has been specifically paid to teachers, their problems and hopes.

The second question is more easily answered. My passport, issued in 1984 and not prepared especially for this meeting, describes my occupation not as a professor, a mathematician, a mathematics educator, an educationalist, a researcher, or a lecturer, but as a *teacher*.

Formerly, in England the word *teacher* was used to describe those who taught in primary or elementary schools. Those in grammar schools were not "teachers" but "masters" and "mistresses": they aspired to a higher social status. Similar verbal distinctions can be found in other countries, for example, between *Lehrer* and *Professor*. Such distinctions may not only be socially disturbing but can be professionally unfortunate. There is a suggestion, for example, that the requirement for professional, pedagogical training may not be shared.

To think of "teachers" being found only in primary/elementary schools is now old-fashioned. Yet barriers still exist between those in schools and the "lecturers" to be found in further and higher education. This has many ill-effects.

To believe that "mathematics education" and "teaching" are concerns only of schools splits the educational community, weakens the cause of mathematics education and leads to inadequate teaching at the tertiary level. Learning problems are still to be found, and there is a great need for curriculum development, past the age of 16. Vast numbers of students from the developed countries now proceed to higher and further education. Many study mathematics as either a major topic or, more likely, as a service subject. Yet tertiary level education, particularly that aimed at commercial, technical, and vocational students, receives little attention from "mathematics educators". Certainly, it is not well represented at this Congress. Again, *Everybody counts,* a report of the US National Research Council (1989, p. 13), claimed that American industry spends nearly as much each year on the mathematical education of its employees as is spent on mathematics education in the public schools of the USA. Here are other types of teachers and another important area of mathematics education which we are in danger of disregarding.

Mathematics education is a vital component of today's culture. We weaken our position and our possible social and political influence when we take too narrow a view of what this phrase can mean.

But, of course, even though there are many types of mathematics teachers and that our coming together provides us with strength through unity, it must be accepted that there are considerable differences between us so far as, for example, resources, expectations, demands, status, aims, and attitudes towards mathematics are concerned. It is important that we, as members of an international congress, realise and act upon this. We all operate within particular societies and subsocieties within very different social, economic, and political contexts. Let us look briefly at some examples of these differences, bearing in mind what *your* vision of a typical classroom or teaching situation is.

[*At this point a selection of slides illustrating mathematics education at primary, secondary or tertiary level in Southern and East Africa, China, England, the Gulf States and Japan was shown. These demonstrated a wide range of class sizes, from a university tutorial for three students to classes of well over forty; of classroom organization, ranging from small groups (some informally sitting on the floor) to classes rigidly aligned at their desks, co-educational and single-sex classes; and a great disparity in classroom resources and atmosphere, from colourful, well-equipped and welcoming classrooms to poorly endowed ones with insufficient desks for all the pupils in the class or, in one instance, furniture which had to be borrowed from the local church (the only class in that particular primary school which had any classroom furniture).*]

Even these few slides are sufficient to demonstrate very great differences in contexts and in teaching methods.

Class size and the resources provided within the classroom are two immediately obvious constraints on teachers. Both are, of course, dominated by economic considerations. Conditions vary enormously from country to country. Here are some data from the *1981 Second International Mathematics Study* (Travers and Westbury, 1989, p. 60).

Number of Students in Class (13+)

Country	Median	Mean	Standard Deviation
Hong Kong	44	43.3	4.3
Japan	41	39.4	6.4
England	27	25.4	8.2
USA	26	26.4	7.0
France	24	23.8	3.0
Finland	22	22.0	7.0
Luxembourg	19	19.0	5.8

In some of the developing countries student-staff ratios are, of course, much worse than any of those given here: primary classes of 100+ are not unknown.

How much money is available to provide resources for students?

Here the differences between countries are even greater and in recent years have increased rather than decreased.

World Bank data indicate that between 1970 and 1980 spending on education per student rose in the richest and middle income countries, but decreased by one third in the poorest countries. The ratio of expenditure on non-salary expenses per child between the richest and poorest countries was of the order of 300 : 1. For example, Bolivia, Malawi and Nepal spent about one US dollar per child per year on furniture, equipment and texts – that is they, in effect, could only provide copy-books for the pupils. China spent about 40 dollars per child – providing children with textbooks, often poorly printed, but little else. At the third level of 300 dollars per year in non-salary inputs, typical of OECD countries, then much more is possible and the role of the teacher changes dramatically. (See, e.g., Fuller and Heyneman, 1989; Heyneman, 1990.)

11

These differences in class sizes and available resources are but two factors to be noted when viewing these slides. Another obvious difference is the way in which the classroom or lecture room is organised.

Again, the range is great and includes:

• students taking part in a tutorial,

• pupils working in small groups around tables,

• pupils working at their desks in a "traditional" classroom arrangement,

• students sitting in a tiered lecture room.

Of course, the key differences here are the possibilities offered for student-teacher and student-student interactions. Different approaches to learning and teaching are implicit in the classroom organisation. The role of the teacher and the demands made of the teacher vary accordingly. The organisational, managerial demands, for example, are very great in the "small group" situation, far less so in the lecture room, although there, different problems of motivation, discipline and communication arise.

When we speak of mathematics teaching, we have, therefore, not only to think of a very wide range of possible students – certainly not just pupils in schools, but also of the very different circumstances in which teaching takes place. Moreover, the individual teacher may have little control in determining, for example, how even the classroom is organised. The constraints of class size, to say nothing of external pressures from, for example, parents, politicians or headteachers, can rule out certain options.

These might sound simplistic comments. Yet at former ICMEs, I have often seen these and other differences completely ignored. We all share a common interest in mathematics education – and I wish shortly to turn to what is common. However, we must remember that national characteristics and opportunities differ very widely. National aims for mathematics education, to say nothing of those held by individual teachers, and national characteristics of mathematics teaching are not always shared. A Congress such as this provides us with an opportunity to interchange experiences and thoughts with people from many other countries. Those interchanges will be less valuable, however, if we do not realise that our basic aims and the contexts in which we are putting ideas into operation are not necessarily shared. I do hope, therefore, that a feature of this Congress will be a willingness to take these differences into account and that opportunities are taken, for example, not only to describe innovations, but also to consider in more detail the philosophies which underpin them and the constraints which have helped fashion them.

Such heterogeneity is not necessarily bad, for there is much we can learn from the situations and practices of others. However, all of us must deplore the vast differences in the financial provisions which exist between nations and which appear to be becoming ever more pronounced. As one who, in the 1960s, spent much time in the so-called "developing countries", I particularly regret that many of the hopes of those days have disappeared: that the enthusiasm shown then has so often been replaced by despair and acceptance of inferior standards. Congress members from the richer countries, therefore, have a special duty to offer encouragement and, wherever possible, aid to those few delegates from the poorer countries who are present at this meeting. What we must avoid doing at this Congress is to give the impression that the only problems which affect mathematics education are those to be found in North America, Australasia and Western Europe.

Yet although there are many factors which separate us as teachers, whether they be financial, social, or the types of student we teach, we nevertheless should share much that is common.

We all have a common interest in defining our aims for mathematics education. Although there will be differing outcomes, the procedures proposed, and the issues and problems identified will have general interest. Indeed, this has already been recognised at ICMEs through, for example, consideration of such issues as "mathematics for all" and "gender".

We have also, I hope, a common concern for students, for adjusting to their strengths and weaknesses, for interesting, enthusing and motivating them, and for attempting to ensure that they achieve our and their aims. Similarly, we all have a common care for "mathematics" – however we choose to define that – and for its well-being. I hope we shall also be distinguished by our willingness

- to think about our tasks as teachers,
- to consider new procedures, and
- to have those procedures investigated, compared and assessed.

Again, all these aspects have been covered at previous ICMEs and will be further discussed at this meeting.

Where we have been less successful is in looking at other problems involving teachers and with which teachers are concerned. These relate both to teachers seen as a national body, as a national asset, and also to teachers as individuals. Our interests have often been mathematical or pedagogical in an imposed sense, that is, for example, we have discussed what school teachers should know, and what we see as the aims of pre- and in-service education, without a very large input from serving teachers. We have often ignored political and social issues and, I suspect, the feelings of teachers themselves.

Let us turn briefly to consider one or two such matters.

The problems of the recruitment and status of teachers have been recognised for many centuries. Juvenal in his *Satires* (Satire VII, 135ff) tells of the poor status of the teacher and deplores the way in which, nineteen hundred years ago, Roman society respected outward displays of wealth and extravagance, rather than learning and expertise.

This particular problem, in relation to schools, was recognised in England in the early nineteenth century by the Central Society of Education. It established a competition with the first prize of One Hundred Pounds – a large sum in those days, and more than twice the annual salary of many elementary school teachers – for the best essay on the need and methods for raising the profession of the educator in the eyes of the public. Five essays on the subject were collected together and published in 1839 (Lalor, et al., 1839). (By some strange coincidence, my copy of the work was first sold by a bookseller, Mr P. Sinclair, who had his shop at 11 Fabrique Street, Québec. Somehow it found its way back across the Atlantic and into an English secondhand bookshop.) The essays make sad, but familiar reading:

> The teacher... holds a low place in public estimation (p. 351).

> The profession of educator is not honoured... It is not generally felt, that [teachers] are the greatest benefactors of society. Their labours are [badly paid] and often grudgingly. [...] Most of them would have [been more financially successful] if they had applied the same amount of mental power and activity to... business. They are not socially recognised as equals, by those to whom they may be, intellectually and morally, far superior (p. 265).

The complaints are, then, all too familiar. What of the suggestions for improving matters?

One of the 1839 contributors suggested that action had to be taken on six fronts:

1. The Nation must establish a national scheme for "educating the [teacher]".

2. The Nation must improve, to the utmost practicable extent, the whole substance and system of education.

3. The Nation must raise the [salary] of the educator ... to one worthy of a liberal profession.

4. The Nation must demand [for educators] ... those distinctions which are bestowed on eminence in the other learned professions. [It was proposed, for example, that there should be degrees, indeed

doctorates, in didactics and that education faculties should be established in the universities and ranked equally with existing ones.]

5. "Every individual... must [show] that respect and deference to the profession to which it is so well entitled."

6. "The educator's own efforts must be unceasing." (pp. 409-410)

Such a list can be discouraging – just how far have we come to attaining what we should all see as reasonable aims for today: are we no further on?

Yet we must realise that what is so often dismissed within education as "reinventing the wheel", represents an attempt to answer a key educational question which will always have to be posed, but, nevertheless, asked within very different contexts. Questions about the training, status and pay of teachers cannot be answered in any objective, static fashion. It must, however, always be questioned whether contemporary assumptions are appropriate.

These questions are, indeed, being asked in certain countries. Sometimes, as in England, they are asked by politicians who already have their own, often highly inappropriate, answers. It is vital for the future well-being of mathematics that such issues become the concern of bodies such as ICMI. We cannot afford to act in a detached, apolitical manner. The problem of teacher recruitment, often made more difficult by demographic changes, is likely soon to become acute in many countries. Recently the problem has been eased in some countries by the economic recession which has brought into teaching many who, in other times, would have sought other employment. Whether these persons will stay in teaching, once (and if) economic prosperity returns, is not so obvious. Yet there is no denying that the age distributions of teachers in schools and universities provide cause for alarm. Here, for example, are data concerning mathematics teachers and researchers in the French secondary and higher education sectors. Note the unfortunate and alarming distributions, the high means and the small standard deviations.

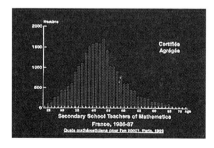

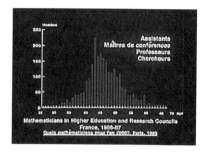

(Suggesting "desirable" distributions towards which a country might aim provides an interesting and non-trivial challenge.)

It is essential that we ensure that there are, and in the future will be, sufficient well-trained teachers entering educational systems. The problem is one which arises in every country. Of course, local conditions and responses to the problem will differ greatly. For example, in Japan teachers still have high status and there is strong competition for teaching posts. To take another example, there is concern in British Columbia, Canada that only 20 per cent of Grade 10 mathematics teachers are women (Robitaille, 1991, p. 52). Yet in Portugal less than 20 per cent are men. This is an area in which international data, experiences, and proposed solutions can and should be shared. I believe that ICMI should consider mounting an international study on the topic. The well-being of mathematics depends upon how effectively we respond to this challenge.

The publication of the 1839 book to which I have referred was a political act: it was no theoretical exercise. The time was one of a rapidly expanding educational system. The curriculum, the purpose of education and, in particular, the role and methods of the teacher were the subject of great discussion. The influences of, amongst others, Pestalozzi, Froebel, Arnold, and von Humboldt were being felt. New demands were being made of teachers. Moreover, it was realised that the status and training of teachers had to be improved in order to attract better-qualified persons to the profession. If this were not done, then hoped-for improvements could not take place.

A climate of opinion was formed in England which ensured that significant changes did occur. In February of 1839, the Minister in charge of internal affairs, Lord John Russell (grandfather of Bertrand Russell, the mathematician, philosopher and educator), argued that something must be done about "the insufficient number of qualified schoolmasters, the imperfect [method] of teaching which prevails in, perhaps, the greatest number of the schools; [the absence of any sufficient inspection] of the nature of the instruction given; the [need for teacher training establishments] and [the general] neglect of [education at a state level]." (Quoted in Maclure (1969), p. 43) The response was swift. Later that year both an embryonic Ministry of Education and an Inspectorate of Schools were created; the following year saw the establishment of the first of a chain of teacher training institutions.

We are, I believe, in a similar situation now. Education is bursting out of its old straitjacket. Education for all and tertiary education for a greater proportion of the population necessitate a comparable rethinking of aims and curricula. Employment demands have changed significantly: now we must respond to those of the second industrial revolution, that of the computer, rather than those of the first, prompted by the steam engine. Teachers have to consider new, and often conflicting, theories of education, new methods of organizing their work, and new technological possibilities. All these have combined to put them under enormous stress. Moreover, that stress has been made worse because now, unlike pre-1839 England, education is very much on the agenda of governments. The amount of money spent on education today is an appreciable part of national budgets everywhere. This fact, and public conceptions as to whether that money is being well spent or not, are major electoral issues. Everywhere, education is being given a high political status, simply because it affects so many voters. Increasingly there is a clash between short-term political expediency and the long-term planning which must underpin significant improvements in educational practice. Educational advances are not made overnight; they require years to come to fruition – years in which the original aims and processes are constantly having to be modified to cope with changing contexts.

Such changes as we have witnessed in the last thirty years have had an enormous effect on teaching at all levels. Increased access to education, attempts to overcome social and gender barriers, wider and deeper aims for teaching – moves away from limited rote-learning methods – have all increased the load on the individual teacher. The importation of market models into education with an emphasis on a mechanistic type of quality control, on measuring the output, and even on attempting to measure how much individual students or classes have gained during a particular timespan, mean that, in some countries, teachers now have to devote considerably more of their time to assessment and administration than was ever the case in the past.

Perhaps, I might give an example of how I have witnessed this change and of one way in which I have seen status conferred on schoolteachers. Thirty years ago I joined the School Mathematics Project which was just being established in Southampton, England. That Project was a schoolteachers' co-operative. Although it was given a home by a university and provided with an administrative framework outside the schools by its founder, Sir

Bryan Thwaites, it relied on teachers for its professional work. For some years now I have been the Chairman of the SMP, helping to provide it with the necessary administrative and financial support. Yet it is still school-teacher-driven. (See, e.g., Thwaites, 1972; Howson, 1987.)

That a Project should for thirty years generate the finances needed for its own survival and have considerable influence both in its own country and in many others is quite remarkable. (Here perhaps it should be added that although many often associate SMP only with classroom materials, it has also had considerable influence in the UK in the areas of assessment and in-service education.) The Project, like others of its kind, provides a great testimony to the professional competence of the teachers who have worked for it. Bringing schoolteachers together to work on curriculum development both recognises their professionalism and helps develop it still further. There is still a need for the teachers involved to seek external advice and to be made aware of research findings. However, if schoolteachers are to achieve the status we wish them to have then they must be allowed to develop and demonstrate true professionalism. Frameworks within which such professionalism can be nurtured and displayed must be created. Any other course of action may be economically more attractive, but will condemn schoolteachers to being merely inefficient transmitters of the work of others and will deny students contact with originality in the classroom.

It must be admitted, though, that demands on teachers have grown so much in the last thirty years that many of SMP's working practices have had to be changed. No longer can schoolteachers be expected to read and write in their spare time. All too often, they have no spare time! The teach-er's duties have expanded to fill much of the evenings as well as the days. Now key teachers have to be relieved of their normal duties to become full-time writers and planners. Such extra loading of teachers, *at all educational levels*, can only be for the worse.

This brings us face to face with key questions that must be considered in all countries: What is it legitimate to ask of teachers? What should be the role and responsibility of a teacher? To what extent do politicians, "mathematics educators" and teachers differ in their perceptions of this role?

Here let me quote from the ICMI Study, *School Mathematics in the 1990s* (Howson and Wilson, 1986) :

> It is very easy to go on adding extra loads on teachers, by giving them, say, greater responsibilities for curriculum design, choice of teaching methods, and student assessment. Clearly, these are all educationally desirable if the teachers' backs are strong enough to carry such weights. We remarked [earlier] that, so far as content was concerned, in many countries "less" was being demanded of students in the "hope" of achieving "more". Yet everywhere there seem to be increasing loads on teachers. Do we, then, run the risk of

"blaming the victim"? ... Proposals should not be formulated in terms of teachers we should wish to see in schools, but within the capabilities of those that are there. [Of course, the possibility of extending those capabilities lies at the heart of in-service education.] ... When looking ahead ..., it must never be assumed that teachers, themselves, have no role to play in analyzing their situation and finding a means of change. (p. 82)

There is a clash here between demanding a degree of autonomy for the teacher, and the need to ensure that those who do not have the requisite knowledge and preparation to exercise autonomy are not simply encouraged to make out as best they can. Hans Freudenthal once drew his readers' attention (Freudenthal, 1973, p. 162) to an advertisement that appeared in a French provincial newspaper:

Wanted: a swimming-teacher who can swim himself.

The advertiser was clearly seeking a degree of ability, knowledge and technical skill in the tutor. Similarly, these qualities must be present in teachers, at all levels, if they are to be set certain aims. For example, mathematics is now, rightly, being seen not only as a bank of knowledge and of techniques, but as an "activity". But it is all too easy for that activity to degenerate into the equivalent of splashing around in the water if the teacher does not have the ability to swim mathematically him- or herself.

The degree of autonomy to be given to teachers must, therefore, be a function of their preparedness, experience and training. Teachers should not be advised to cast aside the lifebelts provided by texts or other published schemes, unless it is clear that they can swim or that adequate tuition can be provided. Yet that does not stop us from asking serious questions about any scheme, or looking to see how it might be improved. For instance, one question I should ask about any scheme or curriculum proposal is "In what ways will the teacher be a better teacher of mathematics after adopting it?"

Autonomy, therefore, is a key, but by no means simple, issue. What of another that I have touched upon: status?

Of course, we all agree that teachers should be well paid and be more highly regarded by society. Yet there are enormous doubts raised about our ability significantly to improve the status of teachers. As I indicated earlier, it was never the case that *all* teachers enjoyed high status. It was only teachers of the academic élite who were so recognised. Now the expansion of educational opportunities and, in many countries, the coming of comprehensive schools and sometimes comprehensive higher education, have resulted in much larger and far more homogeneous teaching forces. In such circumstances it becomes more difficult to keep up professional standards and the rewards offered. Recent economic policies followed by countries world-wide have tried to reduce public expenditure and encourage "capitalist" approaches. These policies offer little encouragement to those who wish to see the status of teachers raised. Yet if that status falls further and teachers' professionalism is further devalued, then we shall become locked into a downward spiral of poor recruitment, low expectations, reduced effectiveness and even lower esteem. What is likely to happen to teaching forces in some of the countries of Eastern Europe, to mention but one problem area? What response can we, as mathematics educators, make to the problem of status? There is no obvious way ahead, and we can, if we wish, choose to ignore this particular problem. However, like the closely related issues of teacher supply, recruitment, and qualifications, it is an issue worthy of ICMI's specific consideration. Moreover, it is not an issue which affects mathematics alone. We must try to benefit from the support, experiences and ideas of other subject organisations.

So far, I have spoken about issues which affect teaching forces and problems at a national level. I should now like to turn very briefly to some issues which affect me as an individual teacher and give examples of problems which I experience. My guess is that they will be shared by many teachers at all levels.

Earlier I spoke about the *Satires* of the Roman Juvenal. In a famous passage he writes: *"Occidit miseros crambe repetita magistros"* (VII, 154). (That cabbage hashed up again and again proves the death of the wretched teachers.)

Am I alone in finding it hard to raise enthusiasm for teaching a particular topic for the nth time? Of course, no two classes are the same and one varies the approach, but despite the new recipe it's still cabbage again! How can teachers be helped to deal with this problem? Replacing the nutritious cabbage by the mathematical equivalent of two brussels sprouts, artistically displayed in the manner of *nouvelle cuisine*, may provide variety for the teacher but will not necessarily best serve the students' needs.

Another problem is the way in which one gradually grows away from the age, the interests, and even an understanding of the motivations and aspirations of one's students. Again, an increasing awareness of what is possible within a classroom, and attempts to attain deeper pedagogical aims, can lead to what at first glance seems to be less "effective" teaching. How do we help teachers (and politicians) to reconcile themselves to this?

Other problems are more frequently spoken about. There is that of *time*. How many teachers feel, like me, that they know only too well how their teaching could be improved and that, given more time, *they themselves* could make their teaching more effective? It is now generally accepted by educators that students should not be seen as empty vessels to be filled with knowledge. Similarly, teachers are not simply waiting for a fill-up of pedagogical know-how to be supplied by educators, advisers, or inspectors.

Again, to quote from *School Mathematics in the 1990s*:

A teacher who has to teach 5 or 6 classes a day has little time to reflect on his or her teaching, to prepare instructional materials, to inspect a variety of alternative approaches, or to work with colleagues in developing and renewing a coherent programme. A teacher who lacks a work space, equipment, a budget for purchasing materials or travelling, discretionary time for working with colleagues or students, cannot be expected to develop far as a "reflective practitioner". [As we have seen, this effectively limits what many teachers in developing countries can be expected successfully to do.] Meanwhile it is vital that administrators and researchers should pay more attention to [what causes] ... teachers to "close up", be unadventurous, and resort to giving *more* exposition and *more* drill, etc. To what extent are teachers actually affected by, say, the technical difficulties of managing heterogeneous classes, a lack of mathematical qualifications, the emphasis [now placed] on *measurable* achievements by students, the fear of being held accountable for student failure, and so on? (p. 80)

These questions are not easy to answer and do not refer only to school-teachers. Certainly we shall not get to grips with them *via* questionnaires and statistical correlations of student attainment with such factors as teacher's age, years of teaching experience, etc.

Yet successful in-service education largely hinges on an understanding of teachers' feelings and their, or rather our, perceptions of needs – for I do not exclude myself from those requiring help. And it must be stressed that although teachers may well know how they might improve their teaching, there will still be areas in which we need to be made more aware of possibilities to be considered.

I do not want to give the impression that this is a field in which there has been no worthwhile research. However, I do believe that there has been far too little.

Here it must be admitted that research work with teachers is not easy to arrange. There is a degree of suspicion concerning ends and means. Also, it is not easy to plan a research project to leave one with objectives that are both practicable and can lead to data and observations likely to prove of value.

In his survey, *Critical Variables in Mathematics Education* (published posthumously in 1979, and which takes the limited, "school" view of mathematics education), Ed Begle was extremely pessimistic:

My overall reaction to the mass of information about teachers which is available to us is one of discouragement. These numerous studies have pro-vided us no promising leads. We are no nearer any answers to questions about teacher effectiveness than our predecessors were some generations ago. What is worse, no promising lines of further research have been opened up. Evidently our attempts to improve mathematics education would not profit from further studies of teachers and their characteristics. Our efforts should be pointed in other directions. (Begle, 1979, pp. 54-55)

This passage in itself could form the basis for a lecture – if not several. How has the concept of teacher "effectiveness" changed over the years? To what extent was the lack of value of the work studied by Begle a criticism of research aims and designs? How does one interpret the last recommendation – to try new research procedures and to formulate new goals, or simply to ignore one of the most critical variables in mathematics education simply because research on it does not fit easily into the PhD paradigm?

Of course it is a matter of great concern to politicians that the teachers in their educational systems should become more "effective". However, which of us teachers would not himself, or herself, want to become more "effective"?

This observation leads me naturally to another great concern I have with the sociology of mathematics education. A colleague in the Education Department at Southampton complains if I begin an argument by saying "Speaking as a mathematician". She rightly insists that she too is a mathematician, although her job description is "educator". It is important that we remember this duality. There is a great danger, particularly in some of the richer, developed countries, that those concerned with mathematics education will be effectively partitioned into the three groups: mathematicians, mathematics educators, and teachers. Even worse, such a division will be seen as defining a social and intellectual hierarchy.

The importance and complexity of mathematics education is such that it is right that there should be full-time workers who do not engage either in teaching mathematics *per se,* or in mathematics research. Yet we must be aware of possible consequences. I have written elsewhere of the danger that parts of "mathematics education" will detach themselves from mathematics teaching in much the same way that "philosophy of mathematics' has drifted well away from "mathematics" itself. (Howson, 1991)

In the 1839 book to which I referred, the winner of the prize considered the benefits of connecting with each of the universities a professor of education. After some discussion the author eventually rejected this idea: "the means by which it might be made to work beneficially seem to be somewhat remote" (p. 117). I am not arguing that the writer was correct, indeed his view was a very limited one. Nevertheless, the difficulties he foresaw were real and are still with us. How does one win that parity of esteem with colleagues in other faculties? In some ways the answer is easy. The place of Entomology within a university is not in doubt, neither is that of History or Philosophy. It is, then, tempting for us to achieve comparability by assuming accepted norms: if insects can be studied, then so can teachers –

mathematics education has a history, and teaching mathematics a philosophy. The importance of such studies is not to be denied, but where does that leave the mathematics educator who wants to *serve* and *help* teachers, not just to study, count, or assess them? Perhaps it would be a useful check for all of us contributing to this Congress to ask of our contribution :

> How will/could it help teachers, under what conditions and within what timescale?

As I have stressed earlier, one aim of all innovations and developments should be to help make the teacher's job easier and more rewarding. We cannot go on for ever adding to the teacher's load. Although the primary aim of educational establishments is to foster the students' growth, unless they also supply worthwhile and satisfying employment to teachers, then they cannot succeed.

The relationship between mathematics educators and teachers leads us naturally to consideration of that between educators and mathematicians. This also is problematical, not only within particular institutions, but also on an international level. ICMI is a sub-commission of the International Mathematical Union. Some would like to see this link severed. Certainly, it is unfortunate if the link is seen as a hierarchical one – a parent with a less intellectually capable child. But there is no need for the relationship to be on those lines. If the intellectual complexities of mathematics education are properly explained and understood, and if we establish and observe our own professional norms, then there is no reason why we should not claim and obtain comparability of esteem. Yet our cause is unlikely to be advanced if we deliberately separate ourselves from the mathematicians. Progress in mathematics education depends upon the involvement of, indeed the increased coming together of, mathematicians, educators, and teachers. This means, of course, not only that all schoolteachers should have *some* experience of doing mathematics, however elementary, but that all mathematicians should acquire an attitude of enquiry towards teaching and learning.

This need brings me to the last of my points. Since the last Congress, held in Budapest, ICMI has lost three of its former Presidents: three outstanding mathematicians who did devote time and effort to mathematics education and to forging links between the various interested parties. Marshall Stone was the Chairman at the first ICMI meeting which I attended in 1958. He was very active in mathematics education at the school level in the 1950s and 1960s, and later contributed to the development of higher education in the third world. Hassler Whitney contributed at many ICMEs. He was a remarkably gifted man, opening up many new areas in mathematics, but also possessing any number of other talents. Although his body aged, he remained young at heart, and, in his last years, working with young children and their teachers gave him both considerable pleasure and a stimulus. Any history of twentieth century mathematics will dwell on the breakthroughs and insights of Stone and Whitney. It is good that they should have chosen to be associated so closely with the work of ICMI.

It is with no disrespect to these two, however, that I wish to talk somewhat longer about the third of these Presidents, Hans Freudenthal. Future historians of mathematics may have less to say about him than the other two, but he will still have a place in their writings, for he was an extremely distinguished mathematician. He was also a historian of mathematics, a mathematics educator, and a teacher – both of future mathematicians and of mathematics educators. His influence on mathematics education will be seen to be seminal.

First, we see how he successfully ranged over all the three fields that I have described and helped bind them together. Moreover, he showed his interest in mathematics education when he was still at the peak of his mathematical powers.

But what sets Freudenthal apart is the way in which he worked to establish mathematics education as a discipline: to provide it with professional norms, to display those norms in operation himself, to disseminate that which was good, to reject that which lacked intellectual rigour and failed to meet his standards, and, all the time, to ensure that contact was maintained with the concerns of the teacher and the learner.

Freudenthal master-minded the first ICME, held at Lyons under his presidency. He was responsible for launching *Educational Studies in Mathematics,* the first professional journal devoted to mathematics education. Within the Netherlands he established IOWO, a unique developmental and in-service training establishment. There also he fostered the professional careers and supervised an outstanding group of mathematics educators, several of whom will be contributing to this Congress. His books will be looked back upon as landmarks in the development of mathematics education. In particular, readers will marvel at *Revisiting mathematics education,* (Freudenthal, 1991) a product of his mid-eighties, which encapsulates and refines so much of his earlier work. Here is not the place to attempt even briefly to describe Freudenthal's thoughts on mathematics education. However, I should like you to note that a lecture on Freudenthal's work will be given later this week. (See abstract of Goffree's lecture on page 352.)

In closing this talk, I wish to draw your attention to two quotations. The first is by Freudenthal himself and sets goals for *all* teachers:

> Explore what is known about learning and about what can happen in a classroom and try to use this knowledge in your teaching.

Reflect on the means you use to teach mathematics.

Reflect on the nature of mathematical activity.

Determine upon a philosophy of mathematical activity and mathematics education and fit your instruction to this. (Bruggen and Freudenthal, 1977, pp. 230-231)

The other quotation is one which this week can well serve as his obituary. Those who have visited St. Paul's Cathedral in London may well recognise it. The epitaph refers to Sir Christopher Wren, architect of St. Paul's, one-time Professor of Astronomy and a Founder Fellow of the Royal Society:

Si monumentum requiris, circumspice. [If you would see his monument, look around.]

This Congress is a monument to Freudenthal. Let us try to ensure that this week would have given him pleasure and that he would have been happy with the level of intellectual rigour displayed. May we try like him to bring together mathematicians, mathematics educators, and teachers, through a common concern for mathematics, its learning and teaching, and with the shared aim of advancing mathematics education as a discipline.

NOTE

This paper includes some phrases and sentences which, because of the pressures of time, were omitted in the plenary lecture given at ICME–7.

REFERENCES

Begle, E.G. (1979). *Critical variables in mathematics education.* Washington: Mathematical Association.

Bonnet, S.A. et al. (1989). *Quels mathématiciens pour l'an 2000?* Paris: Association Cinquante Lycées.

Bruggen, J.C. van, & Freudenthal, H. (1977). Soviet studies in the psychology of learning and teaching mathematics. *Proc. Nat. Acad. Edn.,* (4).

Freudenthal, H. (1973). *Mathematics as an educational task.* Dordrecht: Reidel.

Freudenthal, H. (1991). *Revisiting mathematics education.* Dordrecht: Kluwer Academic Publishers.

Fuller, B., & Heyneman, S.P. (1989). Third world school quality: current collapse, future potential. *Educational Researcher, 18*(2), 12-19.

Heyneman, S.P. (1990). Education on the world market. *American School Board Journal,* 28-30.

Heyneman, S.P. (1990). Economic crisis and the quality of Education. *Int. J. Educational Development, 10*(2/3), 115-129.

Howson, A.G. (1991). Review of "The philosophy of mathematics education". *Mathematical Gazette,* 75, 471-473.

Howson, A.G. (Ed.) (1987). *Challenges and responses.* Cambridge, UK: Cambridge University Press, Cambridge.

Howson, A.G., & Wilson, B.J. (1986). *School mathematics in the 1990s.* Cambridge, UK: Cambridge University Press,.

Lalor, J. et al. (1839). *The educator: prize essays.* London: Taylor and Walton.

Maclure, J.S. (1969). *Educational documents: England and Wales 1816-1968.* London: Methuen Educational.

National Research Council. (1989). *Everybody counts: A report to the Nation on the future of mathematics education.* Washington: National Academy Press.

Robitaille, D.F. et al. (1991). *Mathematics '90: A status report on school mathematics in British Columbia.* Vancouver: Ministry of Education.

Thwaites, B. (1972). *The School Mathematics Project: the first ten years.* Cambridge, UK: Cambridge University Press.

Travers, K.J., & Westbury, I. (1989). *The IEA Study of Mathematics I: analysis of mathematics curricula.* Oxford: Pergamon.

BRINGING MATHEMATICAL RESEARCH TO LIFE IN THE SCHOOLS

SUSCITER LA RECHERCHE MATHÉMATIQUE DANS LES ÉCOLES

Maria M. Klawe

University of British Columbia, Vancouver [CAN]

INTRODUCTION

This paper is concerned with giving school children an understanding and appreciation of doing research in mathematics. My basic thesis is that this is something that needs to be done, and something that can be done. The arguments for why it needs to be done include making mathematics more enjoyable and meaningful for students, encouraging students to pursue careers in the mathematical sciences, and building societal awareness, appreciation, and support of the contributions of mathematical research. The techniques I propose for achieving this goal include giving children exposure to research mathematicians and their work, building connections between mathematical research and the activities children enjoy most, and having children do hands-on activities in which they explore accessible mathematical ideas and concepts. My ideas stem primarily from my experiences giving presentations in school classes on mathematics and being a mathematician. Much of the paper is devoted to concrete descriptions of presentations as well as the underlying philosophy behind them.

Since this is a paper motivated by my personal experiences, I will start by saying a few things about myself and my background to help place my ideas in context. Next, I discuss in more detail why I think it important to have school children (and their teachers and parents) understand and appreciate doing research in mathematics. I then describe the general framework I use to present mathematics and some specific examples of presentation modules I use in the schools. I also include a collection of miscellaneous tricks and tips I have accumulated while giving presentations.

The final section discusses how these ideas and strategies can be extended to have a broader impact, as well as a proposal for a complementary approach based on video games.

About Me

I am a research mathematician working at the interface of discrete mathematics and theoretical computer science. I also spend a significant amount of time on administrative matters, having been the Head of my department for the last four years and a manager in the IBM Research Division for the four years before that. I am the product of Canadian universities, primarily the University of Alberta. At this point I have spent roughly half my working life in an industrial research lab in California, and the other half in universities, mostly in Canada. I am married to a mathematician/ computer scientist, Nick Pippenger, and we have two children, a boy aged 10 and a girl 7. I have no formal training in mathematics education, though I have benefited greatly from discussions with teachers and specialists in mathematics education. I have been visiting schools for over 15 years, first as a speaker about careers in mathematics for women, then as a parent volunteer in my children's mathematics and science classes, and most recently as a participant in the Province of British Columbia's Scientists in the Schools program. This program matches volunteer scientists with interested schools, and covers the expenses for scientists to give school presentations throughout the province[1]. Through this and similar activities I spend about a day per month working with school children.

Rationale and Objectives

In North America there is widespread agreement among politicians and educators on the importance of increasing interest in careers in science and engineering, especially among women and under-represented minorities (see, e.g., George, 1991; National Research Council, 1989, 1990; Blackstone and Hamilton, 1989). In past decades many of the efforts were aimed at women and minorities, with fairness and equity as the primary reasons. Today, the primary justification is economic, with the realization that industrial competitiveness depends on the existence of a broad base of technical knowledge and skills within the population. There continues to be strong emphasis on women and minorities, partly because of the belief that there is a higher percentage of under-utilized talent in these populations.

In talking to high school students in both Canada and the United States I have found that many students view careers in science and engineering quite negatively. Students are frequently of the opinion that such careers are narrow, boring, demanding, difficult, not prestigious, not people-oriented, under-paid with respect to the degree of commitment and talent needed, and that these careers preclude having a satisfying family life. In addition they often blame science and engineering for creating the technology that led to problems with the environment. Student opinions of subject matter in school mathematics and science courses are not much better – boring, too difficult, and irrelevant are common criticisms. Mathematics is of particular importance for two reasons. First, the level of abstraction and the lack of knowledge about mathematicians and why mathematics is important makes mathematics more likely to be viewed as too difficult and/or irrelevant. Second, because of its integral role in most areas of science and engineering, fear, dislike and poor understanding of mathematics courses is a common barrier to pursuing a technical career. Obviously not all students dislike mathematics and science. Some high school students love these subjects and go on to pursue highly successful careers in these areas. The problem is that not enough students feel this way. Moreover, the peer culture is generally not supportive of students who work hard and/or do well in mathematics and science subjects. This discourages many from continuing their studies in these fields.

I spend time in the schools because having research mathematicians (and other scientists and engineers) communicate what they do, why they do it, and why they love doing it, can be an important part of the solution to the problem described above. I also do it because I enjoy the challenge of trying to make mathematics understandable to children, and I appreciate the new insights this effort brings me. Perhaps the biggest reason I do it is because it is such fun.

My goal is to leave all the students (not just the mathematically talented ones) with the following set of beliefs:

1. Doing mathematics can be a lot of fun.

2. Being a mathematician is GREAT in terms of interest, excitement, flexibility, and salary.

3. People that work hard become good at mathematics.

4. Using and creating mathematics is important for the future of our society.

Reaching all the students with my presentation is obviously important to achieving my objectives of making mathematics more enjoyable and meaningful for students, and the long-term building of societal appreciation for mathematical research. In addition I believe we will not see significant progress in attracting more good students to math, science and engineering until the peer support is there. Consider the difference in peer support for careers in mathematics and science versus professional sports careers. Both kinds of careers require a combination of many years of hard work, innate talent, and luck. Both offer many rewards. The chances of achieving and sustaining a successful career are greater in a scientific field than in professional sports, and one could reasonably argue that the productive scientist does more for society than the successful athlete. Yet most North American children admire and support peers who succeed at sports but fail to appreciate (and even scorn) those who succeed in mathematics and science. Another interesting comparison is the strength of peer support for choosing careers in medicine and law versus those in mathematics, science or engineering, despite the similarities in training requirements and chances of success.

There are several factors that may account for these differences in attitudes. First, North American culture glorifies careers in sports, medicine, and law. Consider, for example, the number of television shows and movies on sports heroes, doctors, and lawyers, compared to the number on mathematicians or other scientists. Second, children's opinions are influenced by their direct experiences. Children play sports (usually a pleasurable experience), go to doctors (whom they experience as being in a position of power and prestige), but rarely encounter mathematicians. Indeed, most children think of a mathematician as a person who does arithmetic all day. The third factor is the difference in earning levels of moderately successful professional athletes, doctors, and lawyers compared to mathematicians and scientists (though at the moment, particularly in Canada, the pay gap between lawyers and academic mathematicians and scientists is probably more perception than reality). As individual mathematicians, it is difficult for most of us to affect the first and third factors, i.e. to change the media image of mathematicians, or to substantially raise our salaries. However, it is within our power to affect the second, namely to give children direct experiences of what mathematical research and researchers are like.

PRESENTATION FRAMEWORK

Underlying Philosophy

The design of all components of my presentations are based on a number of beliefs and objectives. I try to make all elements as interactive as possible to sustain student involvement and interest. My basic format is to ask the class questions whose answers lead to the discovery of the information I want to communicate. When necessary I elaborate on student answers to cover additional points. I present a handful of modules on loosely related topics rather than concentrating on a single theme. This makes it easier to ensure that some elements emphasize the importance of mathematical research to other aspects of our society, while some emphasize the enjoyment aspects of mathematical exploration. I stress the interdisciplinary and people-oriented aspects of being a mathematician.

I relate as much material as possible to popular activities such as sports, video games, creative arts, adventure, and puzzles. For example, I often tell the students that I have thought a lot about what kids of their age do that is most like being a researcher in mathematics, and that I have finally come up with the answer. I ask them to guess, and then I tell them my answer – playing video games. This is generally a surprise to them and to their teacher. I ask them to think about what it's like to start playing a new video game. The answers I am looking for are that it's like exploring a new world full of puzzles and challenges; that the way one masters a new game is to figure out what combination of moves and tricks work in various situations and then to apply them to other situations; and that success depends not only on developing basic skills, but on thinking through problems, on experimenting, and on talking to other players and consulting books. Some of the basic skills one uses in being a mathematical researcher are different, but the rest of the process is very similar. In particular, the problem solving techniques, the exhilaration of success, and extended periods of intense concentration and absorption are amazingly alike.

There are many areas and aspects of mathematical research that cannot be presented in this manner. Fundamental and significant results often involve sufficiently sophisticated and abstract concepts that they are difficult to communicate to other mathematicians, let alone ten year-olds. Nevertheless, the image presented is accurate about a substantial fraction of mathematical research and researchers, and is analogous to the images school children have of other careers.

Format

Most of my presentations are from 75 - 90 minutes in length and are to classes of about 30 students aged 10 -12. Research in British Columbia has shown that this is the critical age range to reach students in terms of maintaining their interest in math and science (Blackstone and Hamilton, 1989). I also speak to audiences of other ages using the same material with minor adjustments. My audiences are usually very mixed with respect to mathematical interest and talent. My presentation consists of several parts: scene-setting questions, an auto-introduction, and two or three subject modules. A juggling lesson is often included for a brief change of pace at some point.

Scene-Setting Questions

I start my presentation by asking the class a series of questions of the form "How many people like x?" (and a few of the form "How many people absolutely hate x?"). Students express their opinions by raising their hands. As well as giving me valuable information about my audience, and setting

31

the stage for my presentation, this has the advantage of getting everyone immediately involved in the presentation since the questions are chosen so that each student will respond positively to at least one question. A typical series of questions is shown in Figure 1(a). After this I point out that every-one liked at least one of the things I mentioned, and that I'm going to show them that there's something like each of these things in being a research mathematician.

Scene-Setting Questions

How many people love mathematics?
How many people absolutely hate mathematics?
How many people think mathematics is OK but not great?
How many people love science?
How many people love doing art?
How many people love doing sports?
How many people love playing video games?
How many people love solving puzzles?
How many people love designing clothes?

Figure 1(a)

Who am I ?

Maria Klawe
Professor and Head, Dept. of Computer Science, UBC
Researcher
        discrete mathematics, theoretical computer science,
        computational geometry
Teacher
Mother
Slightly Crazy
Runner
Kayaker, Artist, ...

Figure 1(b)

Auto-Introduction

The goal of this section is to emphasize the "mathematician as human-being" view. I tell the class that I'm going to start by telling them something about myself because one of the reasons I am there is so that they get to meet a real live mathematician, and put up my introductory transparency (Figure 1(b)). We then explore each of the items on the transparency. Using this approach has two advantages. It saves the teacher from having to introduce me, and it allows me to make the introduction interactive. Here's how a typical session goes.

Maria Klawe: I start with my name, explaining that everyone in the world, except my children, calls me Maria because it's hard to both spell and pronounce my last name correctly (Klawe rhymes with Ave as in Ave Maria). Among other things this lets the children know that I want them to call me Maria.

Professor and Head of the Department of Computer Science at UBC: At this point I ask "Who knows what UBC is?" Usually several children know that UBC stands for the University of British Columbia, and this leads us into a discussion of what a university is. Typical questions I ask include: "what is a university, why do people go to universities, when do people go to university, and who here thinks they will go to university". I draw analogies between professors and teachers, my department and their school, the role of the Head and their principal. I also talk about the difference between undergraduate and graduate students.

Researcher (discrete mathematics, theoretical computer science, computational geometry): I ask what it means to do research? Typically answers begin along the lines of "to study things" or "to look things up in the library to find out more information about a subject". I respond "Yes, that's one part of doing research, but can someone tell me others?" I am looking for answers that incorporate the ideas of discovery, exploration, creation. I explain that we are going to explore some of the areas in computational geometry and discrete mathematics that I work in. I ask what geometry means. Generally someone tells me it has to do with shapes. I ask them to guess what computational geometry means, and of course someone correctly guesses that it must have something to do with computers and geometry. This gives me a chance to say something about it, i.e. computational geometry concerns mathematical tools to help computers do tasks that involve shapes.

Teacher: This part doesn't need much explanation since they know what it means to be a teacher. At most I talk about the difference between teaching a class and teaching someone to be a researcher as one does in supervising a graduate student.

Mother: I ask the class why I put this on the transparency. Some of my favourite answers are: "You are proud of your children." "Your children drive you crazy (in reference to the next entry on the transparency)." "You want us to know that you have children so that we will think you will know how to talk to us." "You are looking for a husband and you think that someone would be more likely to marry you if you've already shown that you can have children." I answer "yes, but it's not the reason" to all except the last, to which I say that I already have the most wonderful husband in the universe (it's true, too). I then explain that the reason is that I want to destroy a myth. I say:

"When I was your age (thirty years ago) there was a myth that girls (and women) couldn't do math and science. We now know that this myth was false, since there are many successful women mathematicians, scientists, and engineers. Now there is a new myth which is also false. The new myth is that women can't have both an ambitious career as a mathematician, scientist, or engineer, as well as enjoying and doing a good job as a mother. It's hard work to do both, but it's always hard work to be a good parent. In fact it's hard work to anything well, including being a child. Most of the women mathematicians and computer scientists that I know have children, and love being a mother as well as having their career. My own children are now 10 and 7 and I'm totally crazy about them, though they are, on occasion, unbelievably awful – but mostly they are unbelievably wonderful. The really important ingredients for success in combining motherhood and a career are having a husband who fully shares the responsibilities of being a parent, having a job that pays enough to afford good child-care, and having a job with enough flexibility to allow for spending more time with your children at critical times. Most careers in mathematics, science, and engineering are pretty good with respect to the last two criteria."

Slightly crazy: I tell the class they have already probably figured this one out, but if they haven't, they're sure to do so during the rest of the presentation.

Runner: I reveal the fact that I run marathons (which explains part of the slightly crazy entry). Sometimes I ask how long a marathon is, or how many people have participated in a race. This year I have been announcing that I won my age-group division in the Vancouver marathon. The level of applause that greets this piece of information continues to amaze me. The first time I mentioned this was at a presentation a few days after the race. I mentioned it because I was still consumed with excitement about my performance. After I saw how much that class loved it, I decided to make it part of my regular routine. Sometimes I use this opportunity to tell the students how physically uncoordinated I am, how bad I was at all sports when I was in school, and how incredible it is to me that I have become a competitive athlete after all these years. I make the analogy that people who think they are bad at mathematics may well have hidden mathematical talents.

Kayaker, Artist ... : I say little about these except that ocean kayaking and landscape painting are also things I love and that are important to me.

SUBJECT MODULES

The first module is the one I use to stress the role that mathematics and mathematicians play in other fields. The other modules focus on getting the students to enjoy exploring some mathematical ideas, and on broadening their appreciation of mathematics. For the most part I have merely sketched the material covered in each module, but occasionally some of the questions I ask and some typical answers are indicated.

Computer Animation

This module consists of showing a video of the Academy Award winning computer animation, *Tin Toy* (1988), and exploring how the baby (the central character in the movie) was created. The underlying mathematical theme is how spline curves and surfaces are used to model complex objects in computer graphics. There are several other elements woven into the presentation: why computers are useful in animation; how other types of knowledge and skills (e.g. physiology, kinesiology, artistic, play writing, computer science) are needed to make a successful computer-animated movie; the role of mathematics as a concise language for describing shapes and position; how complex objects are assembled from simple basic elements; the importance of modelling objects in the computer using small amounts of data; and analogies between two and three dimensions.

I start with a short introduction about the film, Tin Toy, which won the 1989 Academy Award in the Short Animated Feature category. Tin Toy was made by a team working at Pixar. (Has anyone heard of Pixar? (no) Lucas Film? (maybe) Star Wars, Indiana Jones, etc.? (definitely – this leads to the story of how Lucas Film pioneered special effects and how Pixar and Industrial Light and Magic were spun-off as separate companies)). I describe the key players on the Pixar team that created Tin Toy, and their education and training. John Lasseter is a traditional animator who began his studies with a four year fine arts program in animation and then went to work for Walt Disney (himself). Bill Reeves is one of the leading researchers in computer graphics. Bill did his undergraduate degree in Mathematics and his Ph.D. in Computer Science. Eben Ostby is a computer scientist and artist, and has studied both fields at university. I warn the class that Tin Toy is only five minutes long. I stress that they should keep in mind that Tin Toy is entirely computer generated and that while watching they should think about how it could have been done on a computer.

After the video we discuss how animations are done (a sequence of pictures with small changes between consecutive pictures), look at hand-drawn sequences for a stick figure waving its hand and a rotation of a cube, and discuss how I actually drew the sequences and how I could have saved time by using a computer drawing program. (The sequences are illustrated in Figure 2 but, like the rest of the figures in the paper, they were drawn on the computer because of the convenience with respect to word-processing.) I explain that in hand-drawing the stick-figure sequence I was able to use tracing to make the task easier. We note that using a copy-paste technique

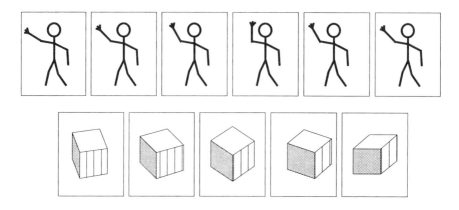

Figure 2

on the computer is easier still. For the cube rotation, I used a wooden block (I have the actual block there as a prop), and had to sketch each frame separately. We discuss why I couldn't use tracing for the cube sequence (all the shapes change). I explain that if we told the computer the position of each of the cube's corners, then the computer could easily calculate where the corners would move under a rotation and could thus draw a picture of what the cube would look like after each small rotation in the sequence.

We discuss how each object that we want the computer to draw must be represented by a model in the computer, how the position of a point is specified (coordinates), and how shapes such as line segments and circles are easy for the computer to work with since they can be uniquely specified using a small number of points. We talk about the basic shapes that are included in all computer drawing programs (e.g. rectangles, circles, polygons, etc.) and discuss why all programs have essentially the same set of shapes (they are commonly used, good building blocks, and fast for the computer to manipulate). We talk about why computers get slower when they manip-ulate complex objects (the calculations involve large numbers of points so they take more time). We talk about basic three-dimensional shapes (spheres, pyramids, rectangular blocks, cones, rings, cones) and discuss where such shapes were used in Tin Toy. We talk about how the stick figure is composed of lines and a circle, and discuss whether the baby is similarly composed of basic 3D shapes.

This leads into a discussion of how smooth shapes could be modelled in a computer. We start by exploring how a two-dimensional smooth-curve drawing of a ghost might be modelled. We discuss how using a freehand drawing tool would involve too many points (a point for each pixel on the computer screen). We look at the advantages (small number of points) and disadvantages (corners) of a straight-line approximation (I use an analogy with connect-the-dots drawing). This leads to the idea of using circular arcs instead of straight lines to connect points on the ghost line-drawing. I explain that computer models actually use another type of curve called a spline. A spline is like a circular arc in that it can be described with a small number of points, but it gives slightly smoother approximations.

Now we move to the actual technique that was used to model the baby. I pull out my well-worn doll (courtesy of my daughter's doll collection), and explain that what the Pixar team did was to buy a doll, and draw several thousand dots on the doll, putting more dots where more detail was needed. The Pixar team then used a three-dimensional analogue of a mouse to input the coordinates of each dot. The dots were then connected with (flat) triangles to form a faceted surface (I illustrate this with a surface constructed from Zaks), and finally each flat triangle was replaced by a curved triangular patch so as to get a smooth surface. At this point we observe that this only gives a stationary model of the baby, so we discuss some of the techniques used in the animation of the baby (e.g. observing and analyzing the motions of real babies, and the modelling of some facial muscles to get the facial expressions).

We next discuss what makes Tin Toy successful as a movie (characterization, plot, humour, graphics), and what skills were needed to make it. A good hands-on activity associated with this module is to pass out some simple smooth curve drawings (ghosts, etc.) and ask students to explore where to place 20 dots in order to give the best straight-line (connect-the-dots) approximation.

Tetris

In this module I present two topics based on the video game Tetris. The first explores whether there is a winning strategy when there is only a single type of piece, and is based on the M.Sc. thesis of J. Brzustowski (undated). The second concerns packing a set of pieces into a rectangle. It is based on a trick played by R. L. Graham in his invited lecture at the first ACM-SIAM Symposium on Discrete Algorithms in 1990. The primary objectives of this module are to explore how creating a mathematical formalism (finite state machine) helps to solve real-world problems (finding winning strategies for Tetris), and to examine easily understandable proofs that combine geometric reasoning with counting. In addition, students are exposed to the technique of forming generalizations and variants of a familiar object, and to how knowledge is gained by studying simplified versions.

I use a transparency to briefly define the game of Tetris and the names of the objects involved (see Figure 3(a)). My experience is that almost all students have had some experience playing Tetris, but the transparency is needed to establish common names for the elements of the game. We then

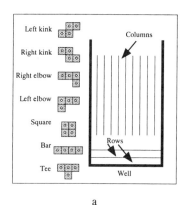 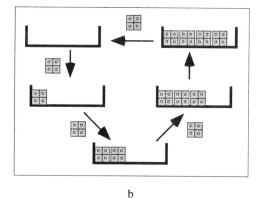

a   b

Figure 3

consider the problem of finding a winning strategy under the assumption that there is no time limit for choosing where a piece should be placed. The definition of a winning strategy is a strategy that allows one to play indefinitely without the well ever overflowing. We discuss how the game can be varied by limiting the pieces to a subset and by changing the number of columns and depth of the well.

We start with the case where the only type of piece is the square and the number of columns is even. Everyone agrees that there are winning strategies for this game. I put up a transparency illustrating such a strategy (Figure 3(b)). This introduces the notation (a graphical version of a finite state machine) we use to describe strategies. We discuss the case where the number of columns is odd. Everyone agrees that there is no winning strategy in this case. I ask them to explain why. Next we look at the case where the only piece is the left kink and the number of columns is 8. After some discussion we find a winning strategy. Now we explore what happens if the number of columns is 7. Trial and error convinces the class that there cannot be a winning strategy but they find it more difficult to explain why. I lead them to a proof from Brzustowski (undated) based on alternately colouring the columns of the well red and blue. Each left kink covers 2 red squares and 2 blue squares no matter where it is placed. Whenever a row is cleared the number of red squares removed is one more than the number of blue squares removed since there are 4 red columns but only 3 blue columns. Thus the number of occupied blue squares must accumulate, and the well eventually will overflow.

For the second topic we look at trying to pack all seven Tetris pieces into a 4 × 7 rectangle. After the students have tried long enough to be convinced that it might be impossible, we attempt to prove that it cannot be done. We start by trying to apply the colouring idea from the preceding paragraph. The students discover that alternately colouring rows or columns does not work, and eventually (with hints if necessary) arrive at the idea of colouring the rectangle like a checkerboard. Now, since all pieces except the Tee cover two squares of each colour, any placement of the 7 pieces must cover 15 squares of one colour and 13 of the other. As the rectangle has 14 squares of each colour, the packing is impossible. I leave the class with the problems of trying to pack all the pieces except the Tee into a 4 × 6 rectangle (fairly easy), and trying to pack all the pieces with an extra Tee into a 4 × 8 rectangle (harder). This module works best if each student has a set of pieces to manipulate.

The Spider Puzzle

In this module I present the class with a simply stated geometric puzzle involving a student who wishes to avoid being crawled on by a spider while asleep. We then, as a group, gradually discover the solution by sketching proposed solutions (and demonstrating their failures) on an overhead projector. The main objective of this module is to explore a mathematical problem requiring different problem-solving skills from those present in traditional school mathematics.

The spider puzzle is defined as follows. Jenny (I begin by asking for a volunteer who is afraid of spiders so I can give the student in the puzzle a name) is terrified of spiders. She knows there is a spider somewhere on the walls, floor, or ceiling of her bedroom, but does not know where. The spider is too small to be seen but can be felt and Jenny wants to avoid having the spider crawl on her during the night. The spider can crawl on any surface except water, and can also drop down on a vertical thread. It is so small that it can land on an arbitrarily small surface (except water). Jenny places each leg of her bed in a bowl of water (Figure 4(a) shows the two-dimensional version of this problem) which prevents the spider from climbing up the legs of her bed. However the spider can still drop down onto Jenny from the ceiling (Figure 4(b)). The problem is to figure out what Jenny should

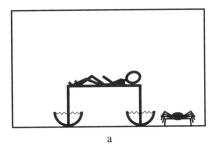
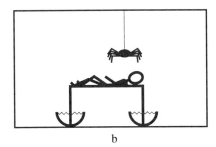

a   b

Figure 4

construct in her bedroom to protect her from the spider. The construction must obey the constraint that Jenny and the spider remain in the same connected component (I express this by saying that Jenny and the spider must still breathe the same air)[2].

I put a transparency of Figure 4(a) (drawn in permanent ink) on an overhead projector and ask the class for ideas (it helps to hand out a paper copy to each student so that they can try drawing solutions). As soon as someone has an idea for a solution I ask him or her to draw the solution (in washable ink) on the transparency. I then ask the class whether it is a valid solution, and if not, why not. Initial attempts tend to be along the lines shown in Figure 5(a). Students enjoy drawing routes the spider (Figure 5(b)) could use to get to Jenny on the transparency.

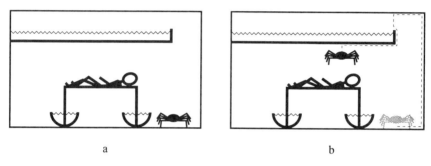

a   b

Figure 5

After the first few attempts fail, several silly suggestions are made (shoot the spider with a water gun, buy Jenny a scuba diving outfit and fill the room up with water, etc.). Eventually (sometimes after some hints) someone suggests an idea along the lines shown in Figure 6(a), and the

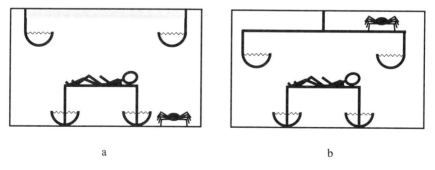

a   b

Figure 6

class realizes that the structure shown prevents the spider from reaching the shaded portion of the ceiling if the spider was not already there. At this point students usually start to have so many ideas and suggestions simultaneously that the best idea is to let students continue to work on the problem individually. Most students arrive at some variant of the solution shown in Figure 6(b) in a few minutes.

MISCELLANEOUS TIPS

Over the years I have assembled a number of minor tricks and strategies to help my presentations. Here are the ones I've found most useful.

Wear the right clothes: It really helps to wear clothes that the students identify with. For the last few years I have dressed in very bright colours and worn my fanciest running shoes.

Be prepared to cope with unavoidable delays in starting your presentation: Often it is necessary to wait for the arrival of part of the audience or a crucial piece of equipment. I use such periods to learn the names of the students in the audience. They like the interaction and knowing many of the names helps in soliciting answers to questions during the presentation.

Switch gears from time to time – a juggling lesson: I usually include a juggling lesson that purports to demonstrate the principle of mathematical induction, but primarily provides a break so that students who have lost the thread can tune in again. The demonstration also allows me to stress the fact that in mathematics as in athletics, practice and hard work can compensate for lack of innate talent.

Use props: the more outlandish the better.

Include hands-on activities: Like props, the more the better is the rule. Even for the juggling lesson, I get volunteers to come up and try out the basic steps.

Stick to simple audio-visual equipment: Canadian schools all have overhead projectors and VCRs, but the existence of other equipment (computers, etc.) is much less uniform.

Give your presentation in the classroom rather than an auditorium: The atmosphere is more intimate, the students expect to be involved and to interact, and are more comfortable.

Allow for enough time: 75 minutes is the absolute minimum if I want the class to participate effectively, especially in hands-on activities.

BROADENING THE IMPACT THROUGH
KITS AND VIDEO GAMES

Extensions

The impact of the approach presented in this paper could be increased in several ways. First, more materials for teachers to use in preparatory and follow-on activities surrounding presentations are needed. I would like to see mathematicians and teachers collaborate in creating such materials and in exploring how these types of presentations can be used to support the curriculum. The second is to get substantially more mathematicians (and other scientists) to regularly give presentations in the schools. Programs like B.C. Scientists in Schools are helpful in this regard since they make scientists and schools aware of the possibilities. They also facilitate the process by matching schools with scientists, by providing funds for travel and supplies, and by providing scientists with helpful information on preparing and giving school presentations. Even with such support, preparing a successful presentation involves a significant investment of time and thought, as well as a good deal of trial and error. We should develop kits containing videos, hands-on activities, props, etc., on a number of different mathematical subjects. Such kits could then be made available to prospective volunteers through workshops on building complete presentations around the kits.

Video Games

Video games are an excellent vehicle to use to increase the exploration of mathematical concepts by children. Children love playing video games for extended periods of time on a daily basis. The exploratory and interactive nature of video games is ideally suited to exploring mathematical concepts. There are already a number of games that are mathematical in nature, e.g. Tetris and its variants (Welltris, Hatris, Columns, Dr. Mario), Pipedream, Boxxle, etc.; adventure games, such as Mario Brothers III, seem to be more popular, perhaps because they are less abstract and present a wider variety of environments and challenges. A promising approach is the integration of mathematical exploration into adventure games. I suggest we develop adventure games in which the problems, puzzles, and reward systems are mathematical, though the goal, characters, and environment are not. In most adventure games the protagonist must accumulate various resources (money, food, special tools and powers, etc.) to progress through the game. Consider the examples below in which the player explores the relationships among perimeter, shape, and area while attempting to optimize the amount of resource obtained.

Upon discovering a treasure chest, the player is asked to position a slider on a scale to select the width and length of the base of the chest.

The length of the portion of the scale to the left of the slider determines the width of the base, and the length on the right determines the length of the base. The chest is then redrawn with the appropriate dimensions, and its lid springs open to reveal a single layer of coins arranged in a regular array. The player thus receives an amount of money proportional to the area of the base of the chest. Since the sum of the base's width and length is fixed, the player quickly learns that the slider should be set at the middle of the scale. This example can be improved (in terms of video game effectiveness) by introducing elements of skill and hand-eye coordination. For example, the player positions the slider by throwing a dart at the scale. As the player reaches higher levels in the game, the shooting of the dart is hampered by random obstacles that appear and disappear, obstructing a clear shot at the middle of the scale unless the player achieves the correct timing. Another example that focuses on area-exploration is to allow the player to draw a curve with fixed arc-length on a background consisting of a regular array of coins. The fixed length curve is represented by a rope that the player drags through the array of coins. The player is rewarded with the number of coins lying in the interior of the figure formed by adding the line joining the two endpoints of the rope. The idea that the reward is the number of coins in the interior can be graphically communicated to the player by an animation showing the coins roll out of the interior one at a time and stack themselves while a voice enumerates them. At higher levels in the game the underlying lattice of the coin array is altered causing the player to explore how the optimal shape changes. Another variant allows the player to throw two darts at a target. The lattice of the coin array is given by the two vectors from the centre of the target to the points hit by the darts.

It is easy to think of other mathematical concepts that can be explored in similar ways. Fractions lend themselves to puzzles based on filling shapes with pieces of other shapes. Addition and subtraction of positive and negative numbers can be handled in many ways. Consider balancing weights where anti-gravity weights are included, or swimming in streams with currents. It is more challenging to find games to illustrate the multiplication of positive and negative numbers, particularly the multiplication of two numbers that are both negative, but even this can be done (as suggested by Frank Tompa from the University of Waterloo) with games involving lenses that invert as well as magnify.

If done in isolation the creation of video games that explore mathe-matical concepts is unlikely to be enough to convince children of the joys and importance of learning mathematics. If the games are designed well, the children will be largely unaware of the educational component invol-ved. Thus it is important to provide complementary materials that build a bridge to the standard curriculum. Such materials would include clue books (e.g. "How to win at ...") that explain the mathematics needed to solve the puzzles and optimize the rewards. Practice modules in which the students can hone their skills at each set of concepts and puzzles are also needed. The practice module would provide students with a broader range of examples to explore on the given topic. Finally, sets of practice module experiments and game examples for sections of standard textbooks must be developed so that the students see the connection between the abstract techniques and concepts and their applications in the games.

Implementing this proposal will not be easy. Talented and experienced video game designers must be engaged in the project to ensure that the video games are successful as video games. Otherwise children will not play them. Initially it may be hard to convince game designers that the market is large enough to justify their time commitment. Another problem is the negative image of video games, particularly among parents and teachers. Contributing factors to this image include the frequent emphasis on violence, the lower appeal to girls, and the belief that playing video games wastes time and encourages aggressive and competitive behaviour. These issues can be addressed by ensuring that the video games are nonviolent and gender-neutral, and by doing a good job of communicating the educational benefits. In addition, advances in distributed computing enable the development of multi-person games in which players must cooperate to achieve their goals. Despite the inherent difficulties, the video game approach appears to be one of the most promising avenues for getting large numbers of children to enjoy math and science, and deserves serious investigation in the immediate future.

NOTES

1. For information contact Science World BC, 1455 Quebec Street, Vancouver, B.C. Canada V6A 3Z7.

2. I do not know the origin of this puzzle – I heard it from a computer scientist, Xioanan Tan, who was intrigued by the fact that her 11-year-old son was able to solve it almost instantaneously while many professional mathematicians took several hours to find the solution.

REFERENCES

Blackstone, P., & Hamilton, G. (1989). Gender equity in mathematics, science and technology: a survey of Vancouver Island schools. In *Breaking the barriers software and information kit for grades 3-7.* Victoria, Canada: Software Training Associates.

Brzustowski, J. (undated). *Can you win at Tetris?* M.Sc. Thesis, Department of Mathematics, University of British Columbia, Vancouver.

National Research Council. (1989). *Everybody counts: a report to the nation on the future of mathematics education.* Washington: National Academy Press.

George, D. (1991). *Values and participation in the physical sciences and engineering: a comparative study.* Ph.D. Thesis, Department of Psychology, University of Victoria, Canada.

National Research Council. (1990). *Reshaping school mathematics: a philosophy and framework for curriculum.* Washington: National Academy Press.

Tin Toy. (1988). A Pixar Film, directed by John Lasseter and William Reeves. Obtainable from: Direct Cinema Ltd., Los Angeles, CA 90069, USA.

ENSEIGNER LA GÉOMÉTRIE : PERMANENCES ET RÉVOLUTIONS

TEACHING GEOMETRY : PERMANENCES AND REVOLUTIONS

Colette Laborde

Université Joseph Fourier, Grenoble [FRA]

Choisir deux caractéristiques contradictoires est un procédé éprouvé de la rhétorique enseignée à l'école – du moins dans la tradition française – pour constituer un titre. Pourtant les mots ne sont pas là que pour des raisons formelles mais aussi parce qu'ils traduisent des complémentarités qui ont forgé aussi bien le développement de la géométrie que celui de son enseignement.

La permanence de la place importante qu'a occupée la géométrie dans les mathématiques n'est plus à souligner. Jusqu'au XVIIIᵉ siècle et au-delà, un mathématicien n'était rien d'autre qu'un géomètre comme en atteste l'article « Géomètre » de l'*Encyclopédie* de Diderot et d'Alembert[1]. Même si depuis lors, et peut-être parce que, de profonds bouleversements ont affecté la nature de la géométrie et sa place dans les mathématiques (Strässer, 1992), la prégnance de l'esprit de géométrie subsiste à tel point qu'à ce même congrès, il y a exactement vingt ans, dans la haute époque des mathématiques modernes, Thom (1972, p. 208) s'écriait que l'esprit de géométrie irrigue presque partout le champ immense des mathématiques et que chercher à l'éliminer constituait une erreur pédagogique considérable[2].

---

1. Je cite : « *géomètre, se dit proprement d'une personne versée dans la Géométrie ; mais on applique en général ce nom à tout mathématicien [...]* »

2. En anglais dans le texte : « *The spirit of geometry circulates almost everywhere in the immense body of mathematics, and it is a major pedagogical error to seek to eliminate it.* »

L'enseignement de la géométrie euclidienne a fait preuve d'une remarquable longévité dans de nombreux pays et a valu aux multiples auteurs des « remakes » des *Eléments* d'Euclide des succès de librairie dont devraient être jaloux nos auteurs actuels d'ouvrages scolaires, puisque la durée de certains d'entre eux a pu excéder un siècle.

Par révolutions, j'entends les changements, parfois spectaculaires malgré des signes précurseurs, qui ont ébranlé l'édifice institué de la géométrie ou de son enseignement, comme par exemple les géométries non euclidiennes, ou le mouvement des mathématiques modernes qui a chassé le géométrisme de l'enseignement de la géométrie. Mais j'entends surtout l'idée de trajectoire au sens de révolution des planètes, l'idée de mouvement inséparable de l'idée d'invariant géométrique puisque constitutive de l'élaboration des savoirs géométriques, comme l'écrit Lobatchevski dans son introduction aux *Nouveaux principes de géométrie* (1837) :

> En réalité dans la nature nous ne connaissons que le mouvement, c'est ce qui rend possible la perception de nos sens. Tous les autres concepts, par exemple ceux de la Géométrie, sont produits artificiellement par notre esprit et tirés des propriétés du mouvement et, pour cette raison, l'espace lui-même, pris à part, n'existe pas pour nous.

Plus encore, si l'on ne considère pas la géométrie pour elle-même mais du point de vue de son utilisation, les modèles géométriques ont souvent manifesté leur prégnance dans les problèmes de trajectoire, cinématique, mécanique ou relativité générale, mais aussi leur inadéquation ; ainsi dans ce dernier cas, le modèle fourni par la géométrie euclidienne ne permet-il pas de rendre compte pourquoi ces fameux êtres mythiques à deux dimensions habitués à vivre sur un écran à deux dimensions et transportés brusquement sur la surface d'une sphère immense (Einstein & Infeld, 1936), développant des moyens de communication qui leur permettent de parcourir des grandes distances, reviennent à leur point de départ lorsqu'ils vont toujours tout droit en avant.

C'est dans cette idée de *modèle* que la complémentarité entre permanence et révolution prend toute sa force. Le modèle fournit des éléments de permanence qui permettent de structurer la variabilité incontrôlée de domaines de réalité et de la maîtriser partiellement. Déjà la tradition relative à l'origine de la géométrie telle qu'elle est rapportée par Hérodote (Livre II, 109) contient cette image du caractère inaltérable du savoir géométrique face à l'instabilité due aux phénomènes naturels : la géométrie serait née chez les Égyptiens de la mesure des terrains qu'il leur fallait sans cesse renouveler à cause des crues du Nil. Mais la validité d'un modèle possède des limites ; bien souvent ce sont des révolutions (Kuhn, 1970) qui ont été à l'origine de la prise de conscience de ces limites face au conservatisme[3] scientifique qui a pu régner.

L'argument de mon exposé gravite autour de l'idée de modèle. Il cherche à lire la résolution de problèmes mathématiques par le mathématicien d'une part, par l'élève d'autre part, à la lumière de la modélisation et de l'expérimentation dans le modèle, à dégager les caractéristiques des modèles géométriques, à souligner le rôle dans l'expérimentation de la dimension supplémentaire de modélisation en géométrie que constitue le mouvement, dimension historiquement ancienne mais qui a trouvé une forme contemporaine de matérialisation dans les nouvelles technologies. Un paragraphe final est consacré à quelques réflexions sur l'enseignement issues du point de vue adopté, en plus de l'évocation permanente des questions d'enseignement tout au long de l'exposé.

MODÈLES ET MODÉLISATION

Un modèle offre une certaine lecture, une certaine interprétation d'un *domaine de réalité*. Ces notions de modèle et domaine de réalité sont volontairement prises ici dans une acception très large. Ainsi, on considérera que tout individu, confronté dans son existence quotidienne à de nombreux domaines de réalité, en élabore des modèles mentaux qui lui sont propres ; ces modèles lui permettent ensuite d'adapter ses comportements ou même de les automatiser. Certains modèles sont explicites et s'expriment alors dans divers supports d'expression (ou systèmes de signifiants) : dessins, schémas, langages naturels ou artificiels... On appelle souvent modèle le résultat même de cette expression. Parmi les modèles explicites, certains sont collectivement partagés. Un exemple banal est celui d'un plan de métro, qui constitue un modèle du domaine de réalité que constitue le réseau de transport en question. L'exposé ne concernera que les modèles explicites et collectivement partagés. Les modèles scientifiques entrent dans cette catégorie.

Du processus de modélisation, je retiendrai deux fonctions complémentaires, celle d'*abstraction* et celle de *représentation*. Une modélisation met en jeu une certaine abstraction du domaine de réalité concerné en ne retenant de ce dernier qu'un certain ensemble d'objets et de relations qui sont représentés dans le modèle. Le modèle ne rend compte que d'une partie

---

3. Je reprends ici un des termes employés par Einstein et Infeld poursuivant la fiction des êtres à deux dimensions ; je cite : « *S'ils sont conservateurs, si la géométrie euclidienne a été enseignée chez eux pendant des générations, quand ils ne pouvaient pas voyager au loin et que leur géométrie était conforme aux faits observés, ils feront certainement tous les efforts possibles pour lui rester attachés, nonobstant l'évidence de leurs mesures. Ils pourraient essayer de rendre les phénomènes physiques responsables de ce désaccord. Ils pourraient, par exemple, dire que les variations de la température déterminent une déformation des lignes et, par suite un écart de la géométrie euclidienne.* »

du domaine de réalité ; une diminution de complexité est ainsi assurée mais au prix d'une réduction. À chaque modèle est donc attaché un *domaine de fonctionnement* dans le domaine de réalité dépendant des objets et relations retenus pour la modélisation.

Ainsi, un plan de métro modélise-t-il le réseau matériel des voies et stations par un graphe de nœuds et d'arêtes liés par des relations d'appartenance et d'ordre. Si de sa lecture on peut trouver tous les chemins (c'est-à-dire les suites ordonnées de stations) d'une station à une autre, le plan ne donne en revanche aucune information sur le chemin à suivre à l'intérieur d'une même station pour changer de ligne, une station étant un objet primitif dans la lecture faite.

Un modèle fournit aussi une représentation du système d'objets et de relations retenus pour la modélisation ou encore, pour prendre une image plus parlante, une incarnation de ce système dans un support d'expression. Les plans de métro sont des représentations matérielles d'un système formel d'objets (points et lignes) liés par deux types de relations. Un même support peut être utilisé pour différents modèles : le dessin d'un graphe peut aussi bien représenter un plan de métro qu'un système de communication dans une communauté. C'est un autre aspect qui constitue aussi la force et la faiblesse des modèles. Parce qu'ils sont exprimés dans des supports déjà connus voire familiers, ils facilitent la compréhension par l'apport de sémantique inhérent au support même. Mais toute interprétation issue du support ne donne pas une information nécessairement valide sur le domaine de réalité. On peut ainsi délimiter un *domaine d'interprétation* à l'intérieur du support du modèle.

Une information déterminée à partir du plan de métro de Montréal sur le tracé réel des lignes serait certainement erronée dans la mesure où ses concepteurs ont cherché (pour des raisons de clarté ou pour forcer les lignes de métro à suivre les directions Est-Ouest et Sud-Nord si particulières à Montréal[4]) à rendre le plus possible rectiligne par morceaux le dessin des lignes. En revanche, le plan routier d'une ville donne des informations fiables sur le tracé des rues, l'angle de leurs intersections par exemple.

Le passage du domaine de réalité au modèle (qui correspond au processus que j'ai appelé lecture ou interprétation) se fait par la construction du système d'objets et de relations retenus pour la modélisation. Dans le cas de modèles scientifiques, il s'agit d'éléments théoriques dont l'élaboration se fait en interaction avec celle des modèles. On parle souvent du domaine

---

4. Toute personne ayant passé plus de 24 heures à Montréal sait que le choix des points cardinaux n'y est pas guidé par la logique solaire, mais par la volonté de ses habitants de faire coïncider les axes cardinaux avec les axes géométriques de l'île de Montréal. C'est un exemple de modèle géographique tyrannique.

de validité d'un modèle. Dans la description que je propose ici, le domaine de validité est celui de la théorie : dans quelle mesure permet-elle de décrire, d'expliquer et de prédire des faits du domaine de réalité ? On appréciera le rôle fondamental de la théorie qui donne sens au modèle, en déterminant ses limites tant du point de vue de sa validité que de ses domaines de fonctionnement et d'interprétation.

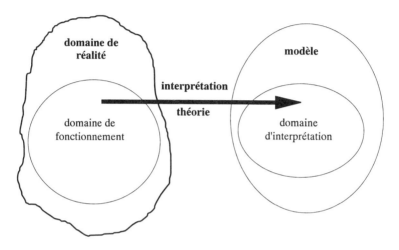

Figure 1

Alors que dans les sciences expérimentales les domaines de réalité sont pris dans le monde matériel, la situation peut paraître quelque peu confuse au sein même des mathématiques, domaines de réalité et modèles étant de nature identique. En effet, en mathématiques, un ensemble d'objets est pris comme domaine de réalité et peut être lu comme modèle d'une axiomatique. Le même ensemble donne lieu à des lectures différentes et c'est en cela que réside la force des mathématiques (cf. plus bas).

L'ensemble des points du plan euclidien peut ainsi être lu dans une lecture projective. L'interprétation qui en sera faite est le plan projectif. De cette modélisation, on ne peut attendre des informations sur les distances entre points ou les angles par exemple (les distances et les angles sont en dehors du domaine de fonctionnement). De même que le plan de métro de Montréal rend rectiligne le tracé des lignes, la lecture projective rend sécantes toutes les droites. On ne peut donc inférer que deux droites euclidiennes se coupent à partir d'un modèle projectif (limites du domaine d'interprétation). L'existence du domaine d'interprétation est particulièrement apparente dans les modèles plans d'objets de l'espace à trois dimensions (intersection de droites, longueur de segments, angles...).

Outre les interprétations différentes que l'on peut faire d'un même ensemble en mathématiques, une même axiomatique peut aussi se matérialiser par différents modèles. Une bonne illustration (en particulier à propos des domaines d'interprétation) en est fournie par les géométries non euclidiennes dont des modèles sont exprimés en termes de géométrie euclidienne.

Il y a plusieurs façons connues de modéliser l'axiomatique d'une géométrie hyperbolique, par exemple, le modèle de Klein-Beltrami et celui de Poincaré. Dans les deux modèles, le plan hyperbolique est formé des points intérieurs à un disque euclidien donné D de bord C. Dans celui de Klein-Beltrami, les droites sont les cordes ouvertes de ce disque, alors que dans celui de Poincaré, les droites sont les diamètres ouverts de D ou les arcs ouverts de cercle orthogonaux au cercle C. Dans les deux modèles, l'appartenance est représentée par l'appartenance euclidienne. Lire l'appartenance de façon identique à la géométrie euclidienne est donc licite dans les deux modèles. En revanche, lire la mesure des longueurs de façon identique à la géométrie euclidienne est illicite dans les deux modèles. On voit se dessiner les limites du domaine d'interprétation, qui par ailleurs n'est pas le même dans les deux modèles : on ne peut interpréter à l'euclidienne les angles dans le modèle de Klein-Beltrami alors qu'on le peut dans celui de Poincaré. On retrouve là ce que des mathématiciens appellent la conformité du modèle.

MODÈLES ET EXPÉRIMENTATION

Dans les sciences expérimentales, nul n'est à convaincre du rôle de l'expérimentation sur le domaine de réalité pour l'élaboration du modèle. Mais dans certains cas, le modèle même sert de lieu d'expérimentation pour étendre les connaissances sur le domaine de réalité. Les relations entre objet et image par une lentille peuvent ainsi être représentées par une modélisation géométrique connue.

Des manipulations dans ce modèle permettent d'anticiper les variations de l'image en fonction de certaines variations de l'objet (variation de la taille du segment objet AB, variation de la distance de l'objet à la lentille) ou de la lentille (variation de la distance focale). Ces manipulations peuvent aussi être considérées comme des expérimentations. Le modèle procure une plus grande facilité d'expérimentation que le domaine de réalité, mais il permet aussi des expérimentations impossibles dans le domaine de réalité (tel un passe-muraille, l'objet peut traverser la lentille dans le modèle, le modèle ne rendant pas compte des aspects matériels des objets). Le modèle fonctionne comme un *laboratoire d'expérimentation* du domaine de réalité. Il réalise une matérialisation de ce que Mach a appelé une expérience de pensée (*Gedankenexperiment*) ou encore d'une expérience imaginaire suivant les termes de Koyré (1966, p. 225-226) :

C'est là que l'imagination entre en scène. Allègrement elle supprime l'écart. Elle ne s'embarrasse pas des limitations que nous impose le réel. Elle réalise « l'idéal » et même l'impossible. Elle opère avec des objets théoriquement parfaits et ce sont ces objets-là que l'expérience imaginaire met en jeu. Ainsi, elle fait rouler des sphères parfaites sur des plans parfaitement lisses, et parfaitement durs, suspend des poids à des leviers parfaitement rigides et qui, eux ne pèsent rien ; fait émaner la lumière de sources punctiformes ; [...] Ce faisant, elle obtient des résultats d'une précision parfaite – ce qui ne les empêche pas, parfois, d'être faux, du moins par rapport à la *rerum natura* – et c'est pour cela, sans doute, que ce sont si souvent des expériences imaginaires qui sous-tendent les lois fondamentales des grands systèmes de philosophie naturelle, tels ceux de Descartes, de Newton, d'Einstein... et aussi de Galilée.

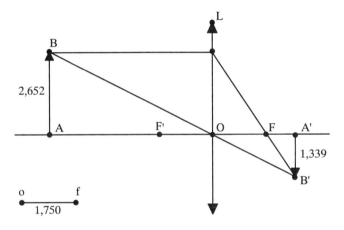

Figure 2

Un point de vue analogue d'expérimentation dans le modèle peut être pris en mathématiques (ce point de vue est en particulier défendu dans Chevallard, 1992). Un exemple classique est celui des démonstrations en géométrie euclidienne ne mettant en jeu que des relations d'incidence. Le domaine de réalité ou système initial est la géométrie euclidienne. Une méthode rodée consiste à utiliser une modélisation projective, à envoyer une droite bien choisie à l'infini et à interpréter par une modélisation euclidienne le nouveau problème qui s'avère alors être un problème connu. Voici un exemple de cette méthode pour le théorème de Pappus (P, Q et R sont alignés).

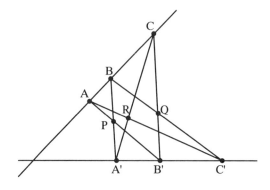

Figure 3

Après envoi à l'infini de la droite PQ, il suffit de montrer que R est aussi à l'infini, c'est-à-dire que BC' et B'C sont parallèles.

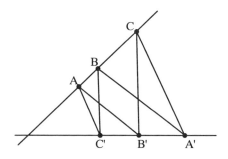

Figure 4

Le jargon usuel des mathématiciens, que j'ai repris à dessein dans l'expression *envoyer à l'infini,* révèle bien le caractère de manipulation sous-jacent au procédé.

L'empilement des modèles est un des éléments de cette démarche ex-périmentale particulièrement fécond pour l'avancée dans le problème. En effet, le changement de modèle met en évidence certains aspects plus cachés dans un autre support ou facilite des manipulations moins aisées dans le précédent modèle. L'inadéquation partielle entre modèles due aux limites des domaines de fonctionnement et d'interprétation n'est pas à prendre avec résignation ; il faut au contraire *se réjouir* de ce déséquilibre, source d'a-vancée dans la connaissance. Une adéquation parfaite entre deux modèles signifie certes que le deuxième modèle confirme le premier, mais aussi qu'aucun élément nouveau n'a été produit de cette uniforme platitude.

On retrouve la notion de déséquilibre, en tant que source de restructuration cognitive et de progrès subséquent, exprimée en particulier dans Piaget. C'est d'ailleurs, comme le souligne Douady (1986), une part importante du travail du mathématicien que de changer de point de vue et de mode d'expression, et cela s'est avéré très fructueux dans le développement des mathématiques.

LES MODÈLES GÉOMÉTRIQUES

On peut s'interroger sur les caractéristiques des modèles de nature géométrique qui ont rendu leur prégnance si forte en mathématiques. Le point de départ de ces modèles est sans doute ce qu'on a souvent appelé le « *géométrisme hellène* » (Michel 1950, p. 638 et suiv.), dont l'inventivité est certes due en partie à l'obstacle à une avancée purement algébrique que constituait pour les Grecs anciens leur numération engoncée dans le carcan de leur alphabet.

Dégageons, à l'aide d'un exemple de ce géométrisme hellène, les caractéristiques des modèles géométriques sur lesquelles s'appuient les procédés de résolution d'un problème algébrique. Le choix du domaine algébrique permet de mieux mettre en évidence par contraste le rôle du géométrique dans la solution. Nous prendrons la résolution de l'équation ax = b, problème énoncé dans le modèle hellène (probablement depuis l'époque pythagoricienne) sous la forme : « appliquer un rectangle égal à une figure rectiligne donnée sur un segment donné »[5], ou encore dans notre langage actuel « construire un rectangle dont on connaît le côté a et l'aire b »[6].

On se donne un segment AB de longueur a et un rectangle ACDE d'aire b. On construit alors F sommet du rectangle construit sur EAB. On appelle G le point d'intersection de la droite AF avec DC. On construit les rectangles ACGI et BCGH.

---

5. Il s'agit d'une « *parabole* » au sens ancien du terme (c'est-à-dire depuis l'époque pythagoricienne jusqu'à Apollonios de Perga). On désignait alors par parabole l'opération qui consistait à porter sur une droite donnée, en coïncidence avec un segment donné de cette droite, un parallélogramme (rectangle ou non) d'une surface égale à une surface donnée. Si l'application faisait apparaître un excès, on disait qu'il y avait « *parabole avec hyperbole* », si elle laissait un défaut, « *parabole avec ellipse* ». C'est lorsqu'ils furent rapportés aux sections coniques par Apollonios que les termes prirent leur sens actuel. Il y a cependant un lien sémantique entre les deux acceptions. À l'équation de la parabole correspond l'application de la surface y^2 sur le segment 2p. À l'équation de l'ellipse correspond une application avec défaut $x^2/a^2 = 1 - y^2/b^2$, à celle de l'hyperbole une application avec excès $x^2/a^2 = 1 + y^2/b^2$.

6. Pour des raisons de simplicité, je donne ici un cas particulier de la proposition I.44 des *Eléments* d'Euclide qui porte sur un parallélogramme et non un rectangle.

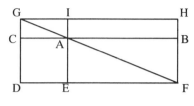

Figure 5

La diagonale FG coupe le rectangle GHFD en deux triangles rectangles d'aire égale. De chacun de ces deux triangles on retranche des triangles égaux (GIA et GCA, ABF et AEF). Les rectangles restant ACDE et BHIA ont donc une aire égale. Donc HB × a = b. Le rectangle cherché est BHIA. La longueur du segment HB ou encore celle de CG est le nombre b/a.

La solution repose sur l'égalité des aires des rectangles ACDE et BHIA (proposition I.43 des *Eléments*) qui elle même est obtenue par une manipulation en pensée du dessin (appelée « appréhension opératoire » par Duval, 1988) et l'*évidence sensible* de l'additivité des aires. Le dessin joue donc un rôle fondamental dans la manipulation et dans les évidences sensibles qu'il permet. Une caractéristique essentielle du modèle géométrique est son expression dans un support graphique à deux dimensions qui permet le recours à une perception globale (registre figuratif). Une deuxième caractéristique est la *généralité implicite* du procédé de solution qui ne dépend pas des dimensions du rectangle et du segment de départ (mais la question de l'existence de la solution n'est pas posée). On remarquera de plus que cette démarche est très différente de la démarche algébrique où l'on calcule comme si l'on supposait connue la quantité cherchée x ; le procédé géométrique construit au contraire cette dernière à partir des quantités connues.

Prenons un autre exemple, en remontant moins haut le cours du temps. On a pu dans le passé (il y a environ trente ans, sinon plus) apprendre à des élèves à résoudre sans le secours de l'algèbre des problèmes arithmético-algébriques à l'aide de représentations géométriques. Ainsi trouver deux quantités inconnues dont on connaît la somme et la différence se faisait par la représentation des deux inconnues par deux segments. La résolution du problème consistait à en *construire* le modèle graphique, c'est-à-dire un premier segment somme, juxtaposition des deux segments donnés, en dessous un deuxième segment différence ; on pouvait par une *manipulation* constater que la différence s'obtenait à partir de la somme en retranchant deux fois le plus petit des segments.

Cette manipulation toute géométrique se fait sans recours à une mesure et est indépendante de la taille des segments (généralité implicite). Le procédé ici est certes très semblable à celui de l'algèbre : manipulation de grandeurs inconnues comme si elles étaient connues mais il prend une forme totalement différente. En algèbre les inconnues sont des lettres tandis que les quantités connues sont des nombres. Il y a mélange de deux registres (i.e. de supports de représentation) de statut différent, le numérique et le littéral, et l'on opère comme si les deux registres étaient identiques. Le modèle géométrique n'a qu'un seul registre figuratif.

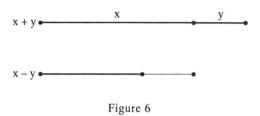

Figure 6

Il est intéressant de signaler que ces deux caractéristiques du modèle géométrique (recours à l'évidence sensible et généralité implicite) sont encore à l'œuvre dans des manuels d'enseignement pour des élèves de 11 à 15 ans pour établir, par exemple, la distributivité de la multiplication par rapport à l'addition, le procédé de multiplication des fractions ou des identités remarquables. Dans tous ces exemples semble sous-jacente l'intention de donner du sens à des écritures formelles par une interprétation géométrique. De même le recours à l'évidence sensible est un point d'appui dans la détermination de la convergence d'une suite $u_{n+1} = f(u_n)$ ou la comparaison d'une série à une intégrale.

DESSINS ET FIGURES DE LA GÉOMÉTRIE

Les représentations graphiques, qu'on appelle communément figures, jouent un rôle fondamental dans le raisonnement géométrique. J'en prendrais pour indice le fait qu'*a contrario* les tentatives variées de remplacement des raisonnements géométriques par des démarches d'autre nature se sont accompagnées de la suppression des figures. Ainsi, en 1788, Lagrange peut-il exprimer son contentement dans l'introduction à sa *Mécanique Analytique* :

> On ne trouvera point de Figures dans cet Ouvrage. Les méthodes que j'y expose ne demandent ni constructions, ni raisonnements géométriques ou mécaniques, mais seulement des opérations algébriques, assujetties à une marche régulière et uniforme.

On confond souvent la figure avec sa trace matérielle sur le papier. Mais l'on sait bien que le raisonnement ne porte pas seulement sur cette entité matérielle mais sur une entité plus générale (cf. l'exemple précédent de division de b par a). Si l'on adopte le point de vue de la modélisation, il est plus adéquat de distinguer *figure* de *dessin* comme cela a déjà été proposé, par exemple dans Parzysz (1988) et Laborde (1990). La figure est l'objet mathématique du modèle euclidien pris comme domaine de réalité, tandis que le dessin est une matérialisation de la figure sur le papier, le sable ou l'écran de l'ordinateur, un modèle tout comme le dessin du métro de Montréal, un modèle de la figure. Le support de matérialisation n'est pas anodin et conditionne le domaine d'interprétation. Une figure peut aussi être représentée dans d'autres supports, par exemple pour une figure plane, dans l'ensemble des couples de $\mathbf{R}^2$.

Certainement issu d'un processus de modélisation d'objets physiques de l'espace dans sa double dimension d'abstraction et de représentation – la géométrie ne s'est-elle pas constituée en partie comme modélisation de l'espace physique qui nous entoure, comme le rappelle Freudenthal (1971) ? – le système des dessins géométriques s'est constitué avec ses règles et ses conventions, devenues petit à petit implicites. Il s'ensuit que son interprétation pose de nombreux problèmes. Au-delà des bruits dus à la matérialité et l'éventuelle imprécision du tracé que tout mathématicien élimine de façon machinale pour ne plus travailler que sur un dessin infiniment précis (Arsac, 1989), les informations licites que l'on peut tirer du dessin ne sont pas déterminées par le seul dessin mais par un discours accompagnant le dessin (Duval, 1988). Certes le mathématicien sait de façon générale que la position du dessin dans la feuille est en dehors du domaine d'interprétation, que les congruences et les rapports lus sur le dessin peuvent faire partie du domaine d'interprétation mais non la longueur d'un segment donné considérée indépendamment des autres longueurs (dans le modèle de l'axiomatique d'Euclide, tous les dessins attachés à une figure se déduisent par similitude[7]). Certes des conventions plus ou moins explicites sont en vigueur : le dessin doit être le plus général possible, il doit éviter de favoriser des interprétations abusives et ne sembler indiquer que des propriétés vérifiées par la figure. Certes le mathématicien a recours à des marques supplémentaires sur le dessin (de congruence de segments ou d'angles, de perpendicularité), mais un dessin ne pourra jamais lui donner avec certitude le domaine d'appartenance d'un point (segment, droite, demi-droite, domaine du plan…), le dessin ne représentant qu'une instanciation particulière de la

---

7. Les dessins plans de figures géométriques avec mesures, c'est-à-dire dont les angles et les segments ont des mesures indiquées, utilisés par exemple dans l'arpentage, sont des modèles relevant d'une lecture différente d'une lecture purement géométrique euclidienne du domaine de réalité que constitue un espace physique. Il s'agit d'une géométrie avec mesures. Cependant la géométrie scolaire utilise aussi ce type de dessins (en général avant l'introduction de la démonstration), en partie avec l'objectif de faire constater par les élèves des propriétés géométriques à l'aide de mesures sur le dessin. Il s'agit donc d'une modélisation différente qui peut s'ériger en obstacle lorsque les élèves ensuite doivent passer à une géométrie de la démonstration ne reposant plus sur des mesures constatées empiriquement. On change sans le dire le domaine d'interprétation des dessins géométriques.

figure : un point représenté sur le segment AB, côté d'un triangle, appartient-il seulement au segment, ou à la droite AB toute entière, ou à une des deux demi-droites d'origine A ou B ?

Ces problèmes d'interprétation ont été ignorés pendant longtemps et l'idée d'une théorie géométrique spontanée découlant naturellement du sensible (en particulier chez les enfants) a pu être dominante et culminer au XVIIIe siècle sous l'influence du sensualisme (théorie du primat des sensations dans la construction des connaissances par l'individu) hérité de Locke et poursuivi par Condillac. On en trouve trace en France, pays où fleurissaient les ouvrages d'enseignement en cette période révolutionnaire, par exemple dans le célèbre discours introductif à la 4e édition des *Eléments de géométrie* de Lacroix (1804), idée qui avait été auparavant poussée à son extrême au point de devenir caricaturale chez La Chapelle (*Institutions de Géométrie*, 1765) :

> Des angles, des lignes, des cercles, ne sont faits que pour frapper les sens ; il n'y faut guère autre chose que les yeux & la main [...] L'objet de la Géométrie est bien autrement sensible que celui du Politique & de l'Astronome [...] Les Géomètres ne sauraient être plus près de leur objet qu'ils le sont, ils le voient et ils le touchent. On ne peut donc rien trouver qui soit mieux assorti au caractère des enfants qui veulent agir, voir, toucher que la science des Mathématiques, très visible, très maniable en ses éléments. Tracer une ligne, décrire un cercle, élever une perpendiculaire, mener des parallèles, tirer des tangentes, former des angles, les mesurer, les agrandir, les diminuer ; toujours de l'action, toujours de l'amusement, & par conséquent toujours du progrès.

Si cet optimisme naïf n'est plus de mise, un certain inductivisme continue cependant d'animer l'enseignement de la géométrie, qui se manifeste par des procédés d'ostension dans les manuels ou chez les enseignants (Johsua & Johsua, 1989) : il suffirait de montrer un ou des dessins pour que l'élève conceptualise la propriété géométrique visée. Un usage tout aussi incontrôlé des nouvelles technologies est susceptible de favoriser ces comportements qu'une caricature du numéro de juin 1992 du journal *Mathematiklehren* prend pour cible : un enseignant se tient debout près d'un moniteur de télévision sur lequel apparaît seulement un dessin, celui classique de la propriété de Pythagore (carrés portés par les côtés d'un triangle rectangle) filmé par une caméra à partir du même dessin déjà tracé au tableau et l'enseignant s'écrie dans une phrase dont la forme interrogative n'est que pure rhétorique : « Hat noch jemand Fragen ? »[8].

Les difficultés des élèves liées à l'interprétation des dessins en tant que modèles de figures ont néanmoins été dégagées depuis quelque temps. D'origine physiologique tout autant que conceptuelle, elles concernent

---

8. « Quelqu'un a-t-il encore des questions ? »

notamment la résistance à l'élimination des imperfections du tracé (une tangente à un cercle est vue comme confondue sur un petit segment avec le cercle), la non-reconnaissance de l'invariance de la figure pour des positions différentes du dessin (Zykova, 1969 ; Fisher, 1978 ; Arsac, 1989 ; Yerushalmy & Chazan, 1990), les phénomènes de typicalité (Cordier & Cordier, 1991) ou d'exemples prototypiques (Hershkowitz, 1990; Noirfalise, 1991) ; l'attraction perceptive de certains aspects du dessin entrave une analyse géométrique adaptée à la solution du problème en cachant par contraste des combinaisons de parties de la figure (Guillaume, 1937; Duval, 1988). Ainsi dans le dessin de la proposition I.43 des *Eléments*, l'œil est plus attiré par les sous-rectangles que par les triangles (les grands triangles surtout sont difficiles à voir), ce qui rend la démonstration de l'égalité des aires difficile pour des élèves de 11 à 15 ans (Mesquita, 1989).

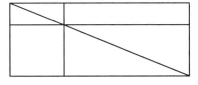

Figure 7

Certains principes de cette attraction sont formulés dans la *Gestalt-psychologie*, ou plus récemment dans les études sur la typicalité portant sur les traits saillants d'un objet qui en font un exemple plus représentatif qu'un autre d'une catégorie d'objets. Ainsi l'évidence sensible est facilitée (Duval, 1988) :

- si le regroupement de parties élémentaires du dessin utile pour la solution est convexe ;

- si ce regroupement est donné et non à trouver ;

- si une même partie élémentaire n'entre pas simultanément dans deux regroupements intermédiaires à comparer.

En un mot, le passage du dessin à la figure ne va pas de soi, les élèves en restant à une vue très empiriste de la géométrie, comme ont pu aussi le constater des recherches nord-américaines (par exemple, Hillel, Kieran & Gurtner, 1989; Schoenfeld, 1982).

Mais un apprentissage est possible. En effet, contrairement à une idée répandue, les activités visuelles résultant d'une interaction entre données physiologiques et cognitives, comme l'ont montré les théories psycho-génétiques (Piaget, 1973), sont susceptibles d'évolution et peuvent être l'objet d'un apprentissage. Bishop (1983) montre que ce qu'il appelle *ability for interpreting figural information* possède certes une composante person-nelle importante dépendant des expériences individuelles, mais est aussi l'objet d'influences culturelles et peut évoluer sous l'effet d'un apprentis-sage spécifique. L'activité de réorganisation visuelle est d'autant plus cruciale en géométrie que les dessins ne sont pas des formes élémentaires (telles un rond ou un trait) mais des assemblages complexes. Les problèmes ne satis-faisant pas aux conditions (données plus haut) facilitant l'évidence sensible permettent un tel apprentissage. Les problèmes nécessitant un changement de point de vue par rapport à celui de l'énoncé y participent également (Robert & Tenaud, 1988).

Exemple

Soit un triangle rectangle ABC, rectangle en A. Soit P un point de BC, I et J ses projections orthogonales sur AB et AC. Pour quelle position de P la longueur IJ est-elle minimum ?

La solution réside dans la reconnaissance du rectangle AIPJ non indiquée dans l'énoncé.

LE MOUVEMENT : UNE DIMENSION SUPPLÉMENTAIRE DE MODÉLISATION

L'idée du mouvement en géométrie n'est pas neuve puisque les géo-mètres grecs avaient mis au point divers procédés instrumentaux pour décrire des courbes définies mécaniquement, mais l'intervention du mouvement était alors « interdite en droit dans le raisonnement géométrique » pour des raisons qui tenaient plus de la métaphysique que de la science (Bkouche, 1991). Rompant avec la tradition grecque, le XVIIᵉ siècle a vu l'apparition explicite du mouvement pour établir une propriété géométrique ou effectuer une construction géométrique (Bkouche, *ibid.*). On en trouve de nombreux exemples à partir de ce siècle, dont celui de la génération cinématique de l'ellipse par un roulement sans glissement due à La Hire : tout point du plan attaché à un cercle roulant intérieurement sans glisser sur un cercle de rayon double décrit une ellipse, à l'exception des points du cercle intérieur qui décrivent un diamètre du grand cercle (hypocycloïde à deux points de rebroussement).

Cette idée s'est d'abord exprimée dans la géométrie scolaire par le coup de balai donné à la géométrie des *Eléments* d'Euclide et l'instauration de la géométrie des transformations (qui continue d'être la seule enseignée dans certains pays), bien des années, il faut le dire, après la théorisation par les mathématiciens de la géométrie comme l'étude des invariants de groupes de transformations, et bien des années aussi après une proposition audacieuse faite en France par Méray (*Nouveaux Eléments de Géométrie*, première édition, 1874[9]) d'enseigner la géométrie à partir du mouvement, alors que ce dernier n'avait sans doute pas connaissance du programme d'Erlangen[10] : le mouvement de translation permet d'introduire le parallélisme, le mouvement de rotation, la perpendicularité.

Si Méray s'est intéressé au mouvement des « *figures solides* » indéformables (p. 3, troisième édition), il évoque cependant (p. 7, *ibid.*) la notion de figure variable :

> Une déformation lente et sans rupture, d'un corps mou comme une pâte ferme, ou flexible comme un ressort, [...] nous montre une succession de plusieurs figures solides inégales, mais l'origine commune qui caractérise toutes ces figures, les ressemblances plus ou moins accentuées qui sont observables entre elles, permettent de voir dans le phénomène une même figure, que le déplacement de ses divers points dans l'espace fait varier dans sa forme.

Cette idée de mouvement plus général met en évidence la distinction figure/dessin : la figure apparaît comme l'invariant géométrique opposé aux variations du dessin à condition évidemment que le mouvement préserve les invariants de la théorie géométrique considérée (par exemple, les relations d'alignement et d'intersection en géométrie projective[11], les égalités d'angles et de rapports de longueur en géométrie euclidienne). Une nouvelle dimension est ajoutée au graphisme en tant que support d'expression des figures géométriques : le mouvement. De la même façon que les dessins géométriques procèdent d'une abstraction des objets de l'espace physique qui nous entoure, le mouvement dans lequel Lobatchevski voyait l'origine de nos sensations est maintenant intégré dans la modélisation. Mais comme dans tout processus de modélisation, c'est un mouvement construit, un *mouvement conçu en fonction de la théorie et contrôlé par elle.*

La sémantique des propriétés géométriques s'enrichit par le nouvel éclairage qu'apporte le mouvement. En effet, ces variations mettent en évidence des relations entre objets dont l'invariance ne peut pas apparaître dans un dessin statique, mais peut en revanche être mise en évidence dans une vue dynamique par contraste avec des éléments variables. Il est intéressant de constater que Clairaut dans ses *Eléments de géométrie* (1741), qui tranchent considérablement avec les « remakes » des *Eléments* d'Euclide de

---

9. Deuxième édition, 1903 ; troisième édition, 1906.

10. Il a d'ailleurs rejeté ensuite la confusion entre la notion de mouvement et celle de transformation proposée par les organisateurs de la réforme de 1902/1905 de l'enseignement de la géométrie en France (Bkouche, 1991).

11. Le procédé de raisonnement en géométrie projective, décrit plus haut, qui consiste à envoyer une droite à l'infini, peut aussi être considéré comme relevant d'un usage d'un modèle dynamique dans lequel le mouvement est idoine à l'axiomatique de la géométrie projective.

l'époque et dont l'objectif est « *d'intéresser et d'éclairer les Commençants* » (préface), utilise le mouvement pour « *faire voir comment on est parvenu à découvrir* » telle ou telle vérité. La propriété de la somme des angles d'un triangle[12] est ainsi introduite (première partie LXII) par l'idée que lors du déplacement de C sur le côté AC fixe, la variation de l'angle B est compensée par celle de C[13]. La méthode de démonstration qui consiste à mettre en jeu une parallèle à AC passant par B ne relève plus du *deus ex machina* mais devient un instrument délibéré de contrôle de la variation de la somme des angles B et C en les juxtaposant par la droite BC (tel un instrument de mesure en sciences expérimentales) ; elle perd son caractère magique, elle répond de façon rationnelle à une interrogation.

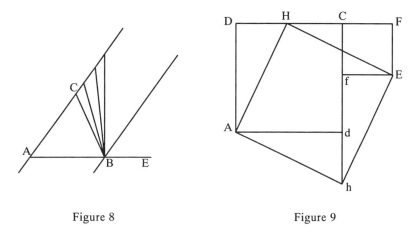

Figure 8 Figure 9

Le même procédé de mouvement est pris pour introduire la construction d'un carré d'aire égale à la somme des aires de deux carrés inégaux (seconde partie XVII), proposition qui débouche sur la propriété de Pythagore.

Clairaut propose de chercher un point H de DF tel que

1° en tirant les lignes AH & HE, & faisant tourner les triangles ADH, EFH, autour des points A & E, jusqu'à ce qu'ils aient les positions Adh, Efh, ces deux triangles se joignent en h ;

12. Cet exemple est commenté par Barbin (1991) pour illustrer l'utilité de l'étude par les élèves de textes historiques.

13. Je cite : « *Supposons, par exemple, que BC tournant autour du point B, s'écarte de AB, pour s'approcher de BE, il est clair que pendant que BC tournerait, l'angle B s'ouvrirait continuellement ; & qu'au contraire l'angle C se resserrerait de plus en plus ; ce qui d'abord pourrait faire présumer que, dans ce cas, la diminution de l'angle C égalerait l'augmentation de l'angle B & qu'ainsi la somme des angles des trois angles A, B, C serait toujours la même quelle que fût l'inclinaison des lignes AC, BC sur la ligne AE.* »

2° que les quatre côtés AH, HE, Eh, hA, soient égaux et perpendiculaires les uns les autres.

On s'aperçoit dans le mouvement que les deux triangles ne peuvent se joindre en h que si DH = CF.

La démonstration mathématique dont on connaît les difficultés d'enseignement universellement partagées est susceptible de prendre ainsi une autre dimension : ce n'est plus, comme trop souvent dans l'enseignement, une preuve qui vient après la connaissance mais en fait ne l'établit pas, comme l'écrit Wheeler (1990, p. 2), c'est une preuve qui explique (Hanna, 1990). Elle explique des phénomènes de compensation et une invariance que l'on constate et dont on cherche les raisons.

De plus, comme Hanna (1990, p. 11) le note, souvent le recours aux modèles géométriques peut être à la source d'une évidence visuelle qui ne constitue pas une preuve, mais qui débouche sur une preuve appelée en allemand *inhaltich-anschaulicher Beweis*. Le mouvement élargit le spectre possible des évidences. La démonstration de Clairaut sur la somme des angles d'un triangle montre que si le mouvement appelle une explication, il peut conduire en même temps à l'outil mathématique de l'explication.

Les possibilités numériques et graphiques offertes par l'informatique ont conduit à la conception de logiciels de géométrie proposant des systèmes graphiques dynamiques modélisant la géométrie, utilisant en particulier la fonctionnalité de *manipulation directe* dans laquelle l'utilisateur s'engage en étant acteur et régulateur du mouvement (Nanard, 1990). Donnons ici deux exemples contemporains de la potentialité de ces modèles.

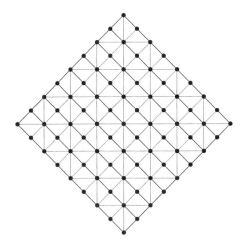

Figure 10 – Poumon idéal (u = 0)

La notion de dimension fractionnaire est particulièrement mise en évidence par la variation continue d'une fractale (par exemple celle modélisant une coupe plane de deux poumons dépendant du paramètre u mesure du demi-angle séparant les deux poumons) d'une surface de dimension 2 pour u = 0° à une ligne de dimension 1 pour u = 90°.

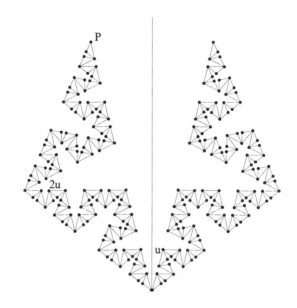

Figure 11 – Poumon pour u voisin de 10°

Figure 12 – Poumon de fumeur invétéré (u voisin de 90°)

Le problème de l'optimisation de l'empaquetage de dix cercles égaux dans un carré a reçu une meilleure solution (Mollard & Payan, 1990) grâce à l'outil d'expérimentation qu'a été le logiciel Cabri-géomètre®[14]. L'efficacité de l'expérimentation a tenu ici à la conjonction de deux éléments :

- la construction d'un modèle géométrique dynamique dans lequel les dix cercles pouvaient être déplacés en respectant les contraintes matérielles de non-chevauchement grâce à la variation continue en

---

14. Cabri-géomètre est une implémentation informatique de la géométrie euclidienne sous forme d'un micro-monde à manipulation directe (Laborde & Strässer, 1990).

manipulation directe de quelques points dont dépendaient géométriquement l'ensemble des cercles ;

- la puissance de calcul du logiciel qui donnait les mesures avec une grande précision.

Le caractère expérimental de l'activité mathématique est magnifiquement illustré par ce résultat, ainsi que la distinction expérimentation/observation. L'expérimentation est construite à l'aide de connaissances au sein d'un modèle. On ne peut qu'être impressionné par la force du modèle géométrique si l'on sait que la même amélioration a été simultanément apportée de façon indépendante par un modèle numérique exigeant deux heures de calcul de CRAY X-MP (de Groot, Peikert & Würtz, 1990).

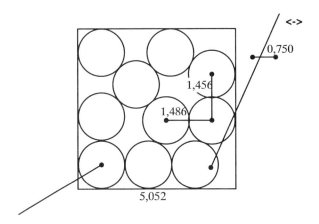

La figure représente la disposition des cercles avec les leviers à l'aide desquels on peut déplacer continûment l'ensemble des cercles et ajuster le carré.

Figure 13

CONSÉQUENCES SUR L'ENSEIGNEMENT DE LA GÉOMÉTRIE EN SCOLARITÉ MOYENNE

Modélisation et problèmes

On sait que les situations d'apprentissage en mathématiques font souvent appel à des problèmes pour lesquels le sens de la question posée en fait aux élèves nécessite l'emploi de la connaissance visée et non l'utilisation d'indications externes au savoir, comme par exemple lorsque les élèves cherchent à deviner les attentes de l'enseignant.

Les savoirs géométriques apparaissent comme efficaces dans des problèmes où ils permettent une modélisation moins coûteuse qu'une recherche empirique par tâtonnement longue ou même impossible. Ce sont historiquement les problèmes de calcul de distances inaccessibles[15] (tels ceux de la hauteur des pyramides que la tradition eudémienne attribue à Thalès, de l'évaluation de la distance entre deux lieux séparés par une rivière). La solution de ces problèmes qui portent sur le méso-espace ou le macro-espace[16] nécessite un modèle dans le micro-espace[17] qui peut prendre la forme d'un dessin sur une feuille de papier. Deux types de problèmes se posent :

- celui de la construction du modèle ;

- celui du calcul à l'aide du modèle de la distance cherchée.

Le premier type requiert l'abstraction de la situation des données à retenir pour la résolution du problème. Le second nécessite l'emploi de savoirs géométriques et des manipulations éventuelles (tracés auxiliaires par exemple, considération de parties du dessin) pour calculer la distance inconnue à l'aide d'éléments connus, distances et/ou angles. Si le deuxième type de problèmes apparaît dans l'enseignement des mathématiques,

---

15. Clairaut (*op. cit.,* préface) prend justement ce point de vue dans son ouvrage pour les Commençants en le distinguant nettement de celui des Traités d'arpentage : « *Enfin, comme j'ai choisi la mesure des Terrains pour intéresser les Commençants, ne dois-je pas craindre qu'on ne confonde ces éléments avec les Traités ordinaires d'Arpentage ? Cette pensée ne peut venir qu'à ceux qui ne considéreront pas que la mesure des Terrains n'est point le véritable objet de ce Livre mais qu'elle me sert seulement d'occasion pour faire découvrir les principales vérités géométriques.* »

16. On peut distinguer trois espaces dans lesquels les problèmes ne se posent pas de la même façon, parce qu'ils ne mettent pas en jeu les mêmes possibilités de contrôle (Brousseau, 1983) :

- le micro-espace, l'espace des objets que l'on peut déplacer sur une table ;

- le méso-espace, l'espace des objets entre 0,5 et 50 fois la taille de l'individu ; les déplacements y sont coûteux ;

- le macro-espace qui met en jeu des problèmes de repérage et d'orientation. La mesure d'une distance est plus coûteuse que celle d'un angle.

17. Il s'agit bien d'un modèle ; pour avoir des informations sur le macro- (resp. méso-) espace, on passe dans le micro-espace et on pratique l'expérience dans le modèle : il suffit de repérer à quel moment de la journée l'ombre du bâton est égale au bâton (d'après Hiéronyme de Rhodes rapporté par Diogène Laërce I, 37), au même moment l'ombre de la pyramide sera égale à sa hauteur. C'est dans ce passage du macro- (resp. méso-) espace au micro-espace que réside la puissance de la notion de modèle comme Apulée (*Florides* 18) devait l'écrire à propos de Thalès : « *Maximas res, parvis lineis reperit* ».

notamment à propos de la trigonométrie, le premier type est rare, les mécanismes de modélisation ne faisant pas l'objet d'un apprentissage en mathématiques[18], car trop souvent devenus transparents aux acteurs même de l'enseignement (Legrand 1990, p. 370).

Notons qu'on peut organiser le même type de problèmes en se cantonnant à l'espace de la feuille de papier et en posant des questions relatives à des mesures qui ne peuvent être obtenues directement sur le papier :

- problèmes de comparaison d'aires (tels celui de la proposition I.43 des *Eléments* d'Euclide – voir Capponi, 1988) ou de recherche d'extrema de grandeurs ;

- problèmes dans lesquels une contrainte artificielle est créée, comme par exemple :

    i) Trouver la bissectrice de deux droites dont l'intersection et son voisinage sont cachés sous une tache d'encre.

    ii) Trouver un moyen qui permet de calculer le périmètre de n'importe quel triangle tronqué comme celui donné ci-dessous, en ne disposant que d'une feuille de papier.

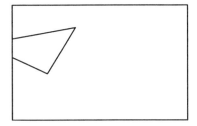

Figure 14

La difficulté de ce deuxième problème réside justement pour les élèves dans la confection d'un modèle du triangle tronqué, sous forme d'un triangle entier, de façon à pouvoir mesurer son périmètre. En effet, le modèle qu'ils essaient de construire est un modèle isométrique (Balacheff, 1988). Or le modèle isométrique peut fort bien ne pas rentrer dans la feuille de papier

18. En revanche, ils ont été l'objet de projets expérimentaux parfois de vaste taille, comme dans l'équipe de Gênes autour de Boero (1989) où les savoirs géométriques sont introduits comme outils de contrôle et de prédiction de phénomènes technologiques ou astronomiques, ou comme le projet « Applied problem-solving in middle school mathematics » de Lesh (1981).

fournic puisque le procédé doit fonctionner pour n'importe quel triangle tronqué. L'idée la plus primitive de modèle est celle de copie parfaite. Mais une qualité du modèle qui le rend opératoire est celle d'être plus manipulable que le domaine de réalité : un modèle est construit en général de façon à justement ne pas être une copie. Les élèves cherchaient par la confection d'un modèle isométrique à se rapprocher de la copie au lieu de chercher une modélisation différente dont ils maîtrisent les règles de passage direct et inverse entre l'objet et son modèle. Dans ce type de problème, les propriétés de la transformation géométrique réduction (appelée encore homothétie en français) prennent un sens : ce sont d'une part les propriétés qui conservent les relations entre éléments dans le passage de l'objet à son modèle (parallélisme, congruence d'angles, égalité de rapports de longueurs), d'autre part la relation qui permet de passer de la longueur d'un élément de l'objet à celle de son image dans le modèle. La même question, pour un énoncé dans lequel l'objet et son modèle sont donnés, nécessite certes l'utilisation de certaines de ces propriétés, mais le sens de ces dernières est complètement différent, car l'élève ne se pose pas le problème de trouver une transformation possédant ces propriétés. La transformation est déjà fournie, il suffit de la reconnaître et ses propriétés sont alors des règles qu'il faut savoir pour les appliquer.

Rôle des informations visuelles

Un problème appelle l'usage de savoirs géométriques si sa résolution ne consiste pas en une simple activité visuelle. Cependant les modèles que sont les dessins en géométrie mettent en jeu des informations visuelles qui, quoique ne fournissant pas directement la solution, jouent un double rôle dans la résolution de problèmes géométriques (Laborde, 1990) :

- en fin de résolution, lorsque l'élève pense avoir trouvé une solution, elles donnent des indications sur la validité de cette solution ; c'est un moyen de validation partielle ou d'invalidation ; ce dernier cas se produit par exemple dans les problèmes de construction, si le procédé élaboré par l'élève aboutit à un résultat perceptif en contradiction flagrante avec ce qu'il attendait ;

- pendant la recherche, l'exploration du dessin (ou des dessins) peut conduire l'élève à des conjectures et être à l'origine de démarches de solution, comme le souligne Fischbein (1987, p. 104) : c'est une source d'expérimentation.

Dans les deux cas, la visualisation n'est pas réduite à une appréhension perceptive mais entre en interaction avec des connaissances géométriques développées par l'élève. Dans la construction d'images de figures géométriques par une symétrie, l'élève s'attend à ce que la figure image ait une certaine ressemblance avec la figure objet, les longueurs et les angles ne doivent pas être trop différents, la nature de la figure doit être conservée (un triangle a pour image un triangle, un cercle a pour image un cercle, une figure fermée a pour image une figure fermée). L'activité visuelle repose sur des intuitions et des connaissances, qu'elles soient en actes (Vergnaud, 1988) ou explicites et résultats d'un apprentissage. Elle s'enrichit au fur et à mesure de l'enseignement, si ce dernier s'attache à la faire progresser par un apprentissage approprié en confrontant l'élève à des problèmes qui appellent un travail sur le dessin (Lemonidis, 1991).

Les nouveaux laboratoires de géométrie

Les nouvelles technologies présentent l'intérêt, comme il a déjà été dit, de modifier l'éventail des manipulations permises et d'élargir le champ des évidences sensibles. En cela, elles fournissent autant de nouveaux laboratoires par les modèles géométriques (ou autres) qu'elles proposent (Laborde, 1992). Les expériences imaginaires évoquées par Koyré (cf. plus haut) sont devenues réalités dans les micromondes (géométriques ou non) pour ordinateurs qui ne sont rien d'autres que des modèles de domaines de réalité.

Les fonctionnalités d'un micromonde de géométrie sont des outils potentiels d'expérimentation de différents types.

Action sur le dessin pour en modifier l'aspect
et faciliter une appréhension opératoire

La possibilité de rendre invisibles des éléments du dessin, ou au contraire d'épaissir les traits, facilite ces regroupements de parties de figures évoqués plus haut.

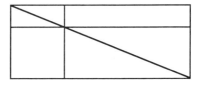

Figure 15

Obtention d'une multiplicité de dessins attachés à une même figure

La multiplicité et/ou la variation continue des dessins attachés à une figure offerte par les logiciels fournit un instrument d'invalidation de dessins tracés au jugé. Le dessin visuellement correct cesse de l'être dès qu'un de ses éléments varie parce qu'il n'a pas été construit à l'aide de propriétés géométriques. La distinction figure/dessin et celle corrélative construction/ tracé deviennent une réalité.

L'exploration dynamique d'une figure peut mettre en évidence des invariants ou l'absence d'invariants et conduire les élèves à se poser la question du pourquoi. Ainsi une classe de cinquième (élèves de 12-13 ans) s'est posé le problème de l'existence de deux angles obtus dans un triangle (Bergue, 1992) car elle n'arrivait pas en déplaçant continûment les sommets d'un triangle à obtenir deux angles obtus. Il y avait toujours compensation d'un angle par un autre (on retrouve exactement le ressort de la présentation de Clairaut). Dans le même esprit, on peut demander de trouver un triangle dans lequel deux bissectrices intérieures sont perpendiculaires.

Variation contrôlée du dessin

À partir de l'observation des modifications du dessin dans le *déplacement contrôlé* d'un de ses éléments, c'est-à-dire d'un déplacement laissant *intentionnellement* invariante une propriété géométrique donnée (par exemple, déplacement d'un point sur une droite ou un cercle, déplacement d'une droite parallèlement à elle-même), on peut inférer des relations de dépendance entre éléments et déboucher sur des conjectures (cf. exemple de Clairaut).

Ce serait tomber dans le même utopisme que celui du XVIIIᵉ siècle que de laisser croire que les élèves se transforment spontanément en expérimentateurs avertis dès qu'ils ont entre les mains un de ces nouveaux logiciels. Au moins trois types de conditions sont nécessaires à un usage non erratique mais authentiquement expérimental du logiciel (en ce que l'expérimentation est construite et se fait en interaction avec les connaissances) par rapport au domaine de savoir dont l'apprentissage est visé (ici la géométrie) :

i)   des conditions sur le logiciel :

  • la qualité du modèle numérique sous-jacent, la robustesse du moteur géométrique, afin d'éviter entre autres à l'interface des contradictions trop flagrantes avec la théorie géométrique (ces aspects sont discutés en termes de fidélité épistémique dans Wenger, 1987) ;

  • l'engagement direct de l'utilisateur qu'il permet, c'est-à-dire selon Nanard (1990) la possibilité d'agir directement et librement sur les représentations des objets et de pouvoir percevoir de façon immédiate leurs réactions ;

ii)   l'explicitation des limites du domaine de fonctionnement et du domaine d'interprétation du logiciel afin que déjà au moins l'enseignant qui l'utilise dans la classe organise son enseignement et conçoive les tâches destinées aux élèves en connaissance de cause ;

iii) des conditions sur l'organisation de l'enseignement : sur l'insertion du logiciel, sa dévolution aux élèves, la mise en place d'un nouveau contrat (ce que l'enseignant attend des élèves, les conditions de travail), le nouveau type de tâches proposées aux élèves.

MORALE

De nombreuses époques de la géométrie ont été évoquées et cet exposé aura effectué plusieurs révolutions, de la géométrie grecque aux nouvelles technologies. J'espère que s'en dégage la permanence du modèle et de l'expérimentation géométriques. On dit qu'une jolie formule aurait été prononcée par Lagrange alors qu'il s'était placé dans la situation embarrassante de chercher à démontrer le postulat d'Euclide sur les parallèles à une séance de classe de physique et de mathématiques de l'Institut (Borgato & Pepe, 1988) ; il se serait aperçu de sa méprise au milieu de son exposé et aurait mis son manuscrit dans sa poche en s'exclamant : « Il faut que j'y songe encore. » Je souhaiterais que tout enseignant de mathématiques se dise : « L'enseignement de la géométrie : il faut que j'y songe encore. »

NOTE

Tous les dessins géométriques de cette présentation ont été effectués avec le logiciel Cabri-géomètre®.

RÉFÉRENCES

Arsac G. (1989). La construction du concept de figure chez les élèves de 12 ans. In *Proceedings of the Thirteenth Conference of the International Group for the Psychology of Mathematics Education* (pp. 85-92). Paris: Éditions GR Didactique et acquisition des connaissances scientifiques.

Balacheff N. (1988). *Une étude des processus de preuve en mathématiques chez des élèves de collège.* Thèse d'État. Grenoble: IMAG, LSD2, Université Joseph Fourier, Grenoble.

Barbin E. (1991). The reading of original texts : how and why to introduce a historical perspective? *For the Learning of Mathematics, 11*(2), 12-13.

Bergue, D. (1992). Une utilisation du logiciel « Géomètre » en 5ème. *Petit x,* IREM de Grenoble, *29,* 5-13.

Bishop, A. (1983). Space and geometry. In R. Lesh & M. Landau (Eds.), *Acquisition of mathematics concepts and processes* (pp. 125-203). New York: Academic Press.

Bkouche, R. (1991). Variations autour de la réforme de 1902/1905. *Cahiers d'histoire & de philosophie des sciences, 34,* 180-213.

Boero, P. (1989). Mathematical literacy for all experiences and problems. In *Proceedings of the Thirteenth Conference of the International Group for the Psychology of Mathematics Education* (pp. 62-76). Paris: Éditions GR Didactique et acquisition des connaissances scientifiques.

Borgato, M.T., & Pepe, L. (1988). Una memoria inedita di Lagrange sulla teoria delle parallele. *Bolletino di*

Storia delle Scienze Matematiche, Vol. VIII, fasc. 1, 307-322.

Brousseau, G. (1983). Études de questions d'enseignement. Un exemple : la géométrie. *Séminaire de didactique des mathématiques et de l'informatique,* année 1982-3, *45,* 183-227. Grenoble: IMAG, LSD, Université Grenoble 1.

Capponi, B. (1988). Mesure et démonstration. Un exemple d'activité en classe de quatrième. *Petit x,* IREM de Grenoble, *17,* 29-48.

Chevallard, Y. (1992). Le caractère expérimental de l'activité mathématique. *Petit x,* IREM de Grenoble, *30,* 5-15.

Cordier, F., & Cordier, J. (1991). L'application du théorème de Thalès. Un exemple du rôle des représentations typiques comme biais cognitifs. *Recherches en didactique des mathématiques, 11*(1), 45-64.

Douady, R. (1986). Jeux de cadres et dialectique outil-objet. *Recherches en didactique des mathématiques, 7*(2), 5-31.

Duval, R. (1988). Pour une approche cognitive des problèmes de géométrie en termes de congruence. *Annales de didactique et de sciences cognitives, 1,* 57-74. Strasbourg: Université Louis-Pasteur et IREM.

Einstein, A., & Infeld, L. (1936). *L'évolution des idées en physique.* Paris: Champs, Flammarion.

Fischbein, E. (1987). *Intuition in science and mathematics : an educational approach.* Dordrecht: Reidel.

Fisher, (1978). Visual influences of figure orientation on concept formation in geometry. In R. Lesh & D. Mierkiewicz (Eds.), *Recent research concerning the development of spatial and geometric concepts* (pp. 307-321). Colombus, Ohio: ERIC.

Freudenthal, H. (1971). Geometry between the devil and the deep sea. *Educational Studies in Mathematics, 3*, 413-435.

de Groot, C., Peikert, R., & Wuertz, D. (1990). The optimal packing of ten equal circles in a square. *IPS Research Report* n° 90-12. Zurich: IPS, ETH-Zentrum.

Guillaume, P. (1937). L'appréhension des figures géométriques. *Journal de Psychologie,* XXXVᵉ année, n° 9-10, 675-710.

Hanna, G. (1990). Some pedagogical aspects of proof. In Creativity, thought and mathematical proof, *Interchange, 21*(1), 6-13.

Hershkowitz, R. (1990). Psychological aspects of learning geometry. In P. Nesher & J. Kilpatrick (Eds.), *Mathematics and cognition* (pp 70-95). Cambridge, UK: Cambridge University Press.

Hillel, J., Kieran, C., & Gurtner, J.L. (1989). Solving structured geometric tasks on the computer : the role of feedback in generating strategies. *Educational Studies in Mathematics, 20*(1), 1-39.

Johsua, M.A., & Johsua, S. (1987). Les fonctions didactiques de l'expérimental dans l'enseignement scientifique. *Recherches en didactique des mathématiques, 8*(3), 231-266.

Koyre, A. (1966). *Études d'histoire de la pensée scientifique.* Paris: Gallimard, 1973.

Kuhn, T. (1970). *La structure des révolutions scientifiques.* Paris: Champs, Flammarion, 1983.

Laborde, C. (1990). L'enseignement de la géométrie en tant que terrain d'exploration de phénomènes didactiques. *Recherches en didactique des mathématiques, 9*(3), 337-363.

Laborde, C. (1992). Solving problems in computer based geometry environments: the influence of the features of the software. *Zentralblatt für Didaktik der Mathematik, 92*(4), 126-133.

Laborde, J.M., & Strässer, R. (1990). « Cabri-géomètre » a micro-world of geometry for guided discovery learning. *Zentralbaltt für Didaktik der Mathematik, 90*(5), 171-190.

Legrand, M. (1990). Rationalité et démonstration mathématiques, le rapport de la classe à une communauté scientifique. *Recherches en didactique des mathématiques, 9*(3), 365-406.

Lemonidis, C. (1991). Analyse et réalisation d'une expérience d'enseignement de l'homothétie. *Recherches en didactique des mathématiques, 11*(2-3), 295-324.

Lesh, R. (1981). Applied mathematical problem solving. *Educational Studies in Mathematics, 12*(2), 235-264.

Lobatchevski, N. (1837). *Nouveaux principes de géométrie.* Mémoires de la Société Royale de Liège, 3ᵉ année, tome 2, 1900.

Mesquita, A.L. (1989). Sur une situation d'éveil à la déduction en géométrie. *Educational Studies in Mathematics, 20*(1), 55-77.

Michel, P.H. (1950). *De Pythagore à Euclide.* Paris: Société d'édition « Les Belles Lettres ».

Mollard, M., & Payan C. (1990). Some progress in the packing of equal circles in a square. *Discrete Mathematics, 84*, 303-307.

Nanard, J. (1990). *La manipulation directe en interface homme-machine.* Thèse de doctorat d'État. Montpellier: Université des Sciences et Techniques du Languedoc.

Noirfalise, R. (1991). Figures prégnantes en géométrie ? *Repères–IREM,* n° 2, pp. 51-58.

Parzysz, B. (1988). Knowing vs seeing, problems of the plane representation of space geometry figures. *Educational Studies in Mathematics, 19*(1), 79-92.

Piaget, J. (1973). *Introduction à l'épistémologie génétique : la pensée mathématique,* 2ᵉ édition. Paris: Presses Universitaires de France.

Robert, A., & Tenaud, I. (1988). Une expérience d'enseignement de la géométrie en Terminales C. *Recherches en didactique des mathématiques, 9*(1), 31-70.

Schoenfeld, A. (1982). Psychological factors affecting students' performance on geometry problems. In *Proceedings of the Fourth Annual Meeting of the North-American Chapter of the International Group for the Psychology of Mathematics Education,* University of Georgia, Athens, 168-174.

Strässer, R. (1992). Didaktische Transposition – eine « Fallstudie » anhand des Geometrie-Unterrichts. *Journal für Mathematik-Didaktik, 13*(2/3), 231-252.

Thom, R. (1972). Modern mathematics: does it exist? In G. Howson (Ed.), *Developments in mathematics education.* Proceedings of the Second International Congress on Mathematical Education (pp. 194-209). Cambridge, UK: Cambridge University Press.

Vergnaud, G. (1988). Frameworks and facts in the PME. In A. & K. Hirst (Eds.), *Proceedings of the Sixth International Congress on Mathematical Education* (pp. 29-47). Budapest: Janos Bolyai Mathematical Society.

Wenger, E. (1987). *Artificial intelligence and tutoring systems.* Los Altos, CA: Morgan Kaufman Publishers.

Wheeler, D. (1990). Aspects of mathematical proof. In: Creativity, thought and mathematical proof. *Interchange, 21*(1), 1-5.

Yerushalmy, M., & Chazan, D. (1990). Overcoming visual obstacles with the aid of the Supposer. *Educational Studies in Mathematics, 21*(3).

Zykova, V.I. (1969). The psychology of sixth grade pupils' mastery of geometric concepts. In J. Kilpatrick & I. Wirszup (Eds.), *Soviet studies in the psychology of learning and teaching mathematics* (Vol. 1, pp. 149-188). Stanford, CA: School Mathematics Study Group, Stanford University.

FRACTALS, THE COMPUTER,
AND MATHEMATICS EDUCATION

LES FRACTALS, L'ORDINATEUR
ET L'ENSEIGNEMENT DES MATHÉMATIQUES

Benoit B. Mandelbrot

IBM T. J. Watson Research Center and Yale University
Yorktown Heights, NY, and New Haven, CT [USA]

It is a great honor and a great pleasure to be asked to attend and close this Seventh International Congress on Mathematical Education. The fundamental importance of your work has always been very clear to me, and it has been very frustrating, and certainly not a good thing in itself, that the bulk of my working life went without the pleasures and the agonies of teaching. On the other hand, academic life being what it was, there is every evidence, in my case, that being sheltered from it has been a necessary condition for the success of my research. An incidental consequence is that some of the external circumstances that dominated my life may matter to the story I shall tell you, and it will be good to mention them, in due time.

But let me forget past frustrations; they are the last thing I should mention in front of this group of people. Seeing you all assembled in this lecture hall, after reading through the program of this Congress and taking a walk through the halls, I may perhaps be excused for experiencing a momentary feeling of deep accomplishment. Clearly, for better or worse, I have ceased to be alone in an observation, a belief, and a hope that keep being reinforced over the years.

The observation is that fractals – together with chaos, easy graphics, and the computer – enchant many young people, which, in turn, makes them excited about learning mathematics and physics. The belief is that this excitement can help make these subjects easier to teach to teenagers and to beginning college students. This is true even of those students who do not feel they will need mathematics and physics in their professions. This belief leads to a hope – perhaps megalomaniac – concerning the abyss which has lately separated the scientific and liberal cultures. It is a cliché, but one confirmed by my experience, that scientists tend to know more of music, art, history, and literature, than humanists know of any science. A related fact is that far more scientists take courses in the humanities than the other way around. So let me give voice to a strongly held feeling. Would it be extravagant to hope that, starting with this piece of mathematics called fractal geometry, we could help broaden the small band of those who see mathematics as essential to every educated citizen, and therefore as having its place among the liberal arts?

The lost unity of liberal knowledge is not just something that old folks gather to complain about; it has very real social consequences. The fact that science is understood by few people other than the scientists themselves has created a terrible situation. One aspect is that our life hinges on vital decisions about science and technology policy. But these decisions are all too often taken either by people so closely concerned that they have strong vested interests, or by people who went through the schools with no math or science. Thus, every country would be far better off if understanding and appreciation of some significant aspect of science could become more widespread among its citizens. This demands a liberal education that includes substantial instruction in math.

Fractals prove to have many uses in technical areas of mathematics and science. However, this will not matter in this talk. Besides, if fractals' usefulness in teaching is confirmed and proves lasting, it is likely to dwarf all their other uses.

No pictures will be shown in this text and I shall assume all of you to have a rudimentary awareness or knowledge of fractals, or will one day become motivated to acquire this knowledge elsewhere. My offering is my book, *The fractal geometry of nature* (1982), but there are many more sources at this point. Skipping the pictures will provide me at one stroke with space for diverse aspects of a basic and very concrete question about mathematics education: what should be the relations, if any, between (a) the overall development of mathematics in history, (b) the present status of the best and brightest in mathematics research, and (c) the most effective ways of teaching the basics of the field?

By simplifying (strongly but not destructively), one can distinguish three mutually antagonistic approaches to education. The first two are the "old" math, dominated by (a) above, and the "new" math, dominated by (b). But the approach I welcome would be resolutely pragmatic. It would encourage educational philosophy to seek points of easiest entry, and to cease to be encumbered, either by how mathematics research began, or by its present state.

Let me elaborate by a simile – which I have of course loaded in my favor!: think of the task of luring convinced nomads into hard shelter. One could tempt them into the kinds of shelters that have been built long ago, in countries that happened to provide a convenient starting point in the form of caves, or one could try to tempt them into the best possible shelters, those being built far away, in highly advanced countries where architecture is dominated by "structurally pure" skyscrapers. But both strategies would be most ill-inspired. It is clearly far better to tempt our nomads by something that interests them spontaneously. But such happens precisely to be the case with fractals, chaos, easy graphics, and the computer. Hence, if their effectiveness becomes confirmed, a working pragmatic approach to mathematics education may actually be at hand. We may no longer be limited to the old and new math. Let me dwell on them for a moment.

The "old math" approach to mathematics education saw the teacher's task as that of guiding the child or young person of today along a simplified sequence of landmarks in the progress of science throughout the history of humanity. An extreme form of this approach used to prevail when the sole acceptable textbook of geometry was Euclid's *Elements*.

A belief often invoked to buttress this approach asserts that the mental evolution of mankind was the product of historical necessity, and that the evolution of an individual must proceed in the same sequence. In particular, the acquisition of concepts by the small child is thought to follow the same sequence as the acquisition of concepts by humankind. I tend to believe that such is indeed the case, but only for concepts that children must have acquired before they start studying mathematics.

An acknowledged failing of old math was that the teacher could not conceivably move fast enough to reach modern topics. For example, the school mathematics and science taken up between ages 10 and 20 used to be largely restricted to topics humanity discovered in antiquity. As might be expected, teachers of "old lit" were subjected to the same criticism. A curriculum once reserved to Masters of Antiquity was gradually changed to leave room for the likes of Shakespeare and of increasingly modern authors; in the USA, it had to yield room to American Masters, not to mention multicultural programs.

These concerns about being comprehensive motivated efforts around the 1900s to enrich geometry with properly modern topics. But quite different were the motivations of the second broad approach to mathematics education. It was exemplified by the "new math" of the 1960s. Militantly anti-historical, it viewed the early history of mathematics research as irrelevant to its present development. And it viewed the state of mathematics in the 1960s, and the direction in which it was then evolving, as something of intrinsic value: the product of historical necessity, the closest we can get to an ideal, and therefore the model at every level of mathematics education.

We all know that "new math" died a while ago, victim of its obvious failure as an educational theory. The Romans used to say that "of the dead, one should speak nothing but good". But in the case of new math this would not be right because this unmitigated disaster ought at least teach us how to avoid a repetition. However, it is well-known that failure is an orphan (while success has many would-be parents – as we shall also see in a different example mentioned later on in this story). In less allusive words, new math deserves a serious debate, but the responsibility for this historical episode is not claimed by anyone, today. Take for example the French formalists who once flourished under the pen-name of Bourbaki (I shall have much more to say about them). They had nurtured an environment in which new math became all but inevitable, yet today they join everyone else in making fun of the outcome, especially when it hurts their own children or grand-children. This denial of responsibility is strikingly explicit in a one-hour story a French radio network devoted to the Bourbaki a few years ago. (Audio-cassettes may be available from the Société Mathématique de France.) One hears in it that the Bourbaki bear no more responsibility than the French "man in the street" (failure *is* indeed an orphan), and that they have never made a statement in favor of new math. On the other hand, having lived through the episode, I do not recall their making a statement against, and I certainly recall the mood of that time.

Be that as it may, it is not useful to wax indignant, but important to draw a lesson for the future. The lesson is that frontier mathematics research must not again be allowed to dominate mathematics education. At the other unacceptable extreme, needless to say, I see even less merit in the notion that one can become expert at teaching mathematics or at writing textbooks, yet know nothing at all about the subject. Quite to the contrary, the teachers and the writers must know a great deal about at least some aspects of mathematics.

Fortunately, I see mathematics as a very big house, and it offers teachers a rich choice of topics to study and transmit to students. The serious problem is: how to choose among those topics. My point is that this choice must not be left to people who have never entered the big house of mathematics. It must not be left, either, to the leaders of frontier mathematics research, nor to those who claim authority to interpret the leaders' preferences. Of course, you all know already which wing of the big house I think deserves special consideration. But let me not rush to talk of fractals, and stop to ask why this house deserves to be visited.

To help the transition, let me mention in passing a synthesis or compromise between the past and the present. Arithmetic and number theory have the special assets of having ancient roots, being one of the top fields in today's mathematical research, and including large portions that are independent of the messy rest of mathematics. Therefore this synthesis has been tried very widely in an attempt to fire youngsters' imagination. I am told it does marvels with children who had previously been branded as ambitious and mathematically gifted. Helping the very gifted and ambitious is an extraordinarily important task, both for the sake of those individuals, and for the sake of the future development of math and science. But (as has already been stated) math and science literacy *must* extend beyond the very gifted pupils.

Unfortunately, as we all know, this belief is not shared by everyone. How can we help it become more widely accepted? All too often, I see the need for math and science literacy referred to exclusively in terms of labor needs: the needs (already mentioned) of future math and science teaching and research, and those of an increasingly technological society. To my mind, however, this direct utilitarian argument fails on two accounts: it is not (or is no longer) politically effective; and it is not sufficiently ambitious.

First of all, sad to say, it has always been hard to explain why, if scientific literacy is valuable and remains scarce, the scientifically literate fail (overall) to reap the financial rewards of valuable scarcity. In fact, scientific migrant workers, like agricultural ones, keep pouring in from poorer countries. This year 1992 is especially unkind to the utilitarian argument since many engineers and scientists are becoming unemployed and must move on to fields that do not require their specialized training.

Even though this is an international meeting, allow me to center the following comments on the conditions in the USA. In its crudest form, very widespread only a few years ago, the utilitarian argument led many people to compare the United States unfavorably to countries where there are far more students in math or science, like the Soviet Union, France, or Japan. Similarly unfavorable comparisons compared foreign language instruction in the USA to that in other countries. The explanation in the case of the languages of Hungary or Holland is obvious: the Hungarians are not genetically or socially superior to the Austrians, but the Hungarian language is of no use elsewhere; hence, multilingual Hungarians receive unquestioned real-life rewards. Similarly, France and Japan provide unquestioned real-life rewards to those who do well in math, which is why school programs heavy in compulsory math are tolerated.

For example, many jobs in France that require little or no academic knowledge to be performed are reserved (by law) for those who pass a qualifying examination that tries to be objective, and ends up being heavy on math. The jobs are desirable, so there are many applicants; the exams are difficult, and the students are motivated to be serious about preparing for them.

Some of these jobs are among the best possible. For example, in many French businesses one cannot approach the top unless one started at the École Polytechnique. This is the school I went to (I first entered École Normale Supérieure, but left immediately). When Polytechnique was first organized for peacetime after Napoleon's fall in 1815, it selected and judged its students on the subjective grounds used in today's America, but ever since that time, the criteria for entrance and ranking have grown increasingly objective – that is, mathematical. One reason was the justified fear of nepotism and political pressure, another the skill of Augustin Cauchy (1789–1857), a great mathematician and a master at exerting self-serving political pressure.

A few years ago I could observe the result when I attended my forty-fifth class reunion. For a few freshly retired classmates a knowledge of science had been essential. But many had held very powerful positions to general acclaim, yet hardly remembered what a complex number is. They gave no evidence of an exceptionally strong love of science among Polytechnique alumni. (I do not know what to make of the number of articles the *Alumni Monthly* devotes to the paranormal.) But they could never have reached those powerful positions without having entered Polytechnique; to achieve that goal, one had to be a wizard at math, at least up to age twenty.

The United States of America also singles out an activity that brings monetary rewards and prestige that continue through a person's life – independently of the person's profession. This activity is sports. In France it is math. For example, one of my classmates became president of France, his goal since childhood; to help himself along, he chose to go to a college even more demanding than MIT.

For a long time France recognized a second path to the top: a mastery of Greek or Latin writers and philosophers. But by now this path has been replaced by an obstacle course in public administration. A competition continues between the two ways of training for the top, but no one claims that mathematics is important *per se*. You see how little bearing this French model has on the situation in the USA.

Needless to say, many French people have always complained that their society, and therefore their school system, demands more math than is sensible; other French people complain that the teaching of math is poor. And on a recent trip to Japan, I heard the same complaints. So my feeling is that the real problem may not involve embarrassing national comparisons.

Lacking the purely utilitarian argument, what could one conceivably propose to justify more and better math and physics? When I was young some of my friends were delighted to reserve "real" math to a small elite. But other friends and I envied the historians, the painters, and the musicians. Their fields also involved elite training, yet their goals seemed to have the additional virtue of striking raw nerves in other human beings, and to be well understood and appreciated by a wide number of people with comparatively minimal and unprofessional artistic education. Our goals, on the contrary, were becoming increasingly opaque, beyond a circle of specialists. Tongue in cheek, my youthful friends and I felt we would be far happier if a lucky strike would induce ordinary people to come closer to us without having to be bribed by promises of jobs and money, like French adolescents. Who can tell, a popular wish to come closer to us might even induce them to buy tickets to our performances!

When our demanding dream was challenged as ridiculous and contrary to history and common sense, we could only produce one historical period when something like our dream had been realized. This example – little known, especially outside France – concerns the first translation of Newton into French. Feminists, listen: the translator was Gabrielle Émilie le Tonnelier de Bréteuil, marquise du Châtelet-Lomont (1706–49). Madame du Châtelet was a pillar of High Society, and her salon was among the most brilliant in Paris. In her heyday it welcomed all the best people; Voltaire, for example, the most celebrated French writer of the time, was her intimate friend. Besides this case there are the letters that the great Leonhard Euler (1707–83) wrote to "German princes" on topics of mathematics. Thus a significantly broad scientific literacy was welcomed and conspicuously present in a century when it hardly seemed to matter.

Why is there such a difference between activities that appeal to many (like serious history), and those which appeal to no one, except the specialists? To try and explain this outrageous contrast, let me sketch yet another bit of history, by discussing a sharp contrast between knowledge patterned after astronomy and knowledge patterned after history.

The ancient perfecting Greeks and the medieval scholastics saw a perfect contrast between two extremes: the purity and perfection of the Heaven, and the hopeless imperfection of the Earth. "Pure" meant being subject to rational laws which involve simple rules yet allow excellent predictions of the motion of planets and stars. Many civilizations and individuals have had the belief that their lives are written up in full detail in a book and hence can in theory be predicted and cannot be changed. But the Greeks thought otherwise. They expected almost everything on Earth to be confusing. In particular, events that were in themselves insignificant could have unpredictable and overwhelming consequences. This became a favorite theme of many writers: Benjamin Franklin's *Poor Richard's alma-nac* (1757) puts it as follows:

> A little neglect may breed mischief.
> For lack of a nail, the shoe was lost;
> for lack of a shoe, the horse was lost;
> for lack of a horse, the rider was lost;
> for lack of a rider, the message was lost;
> for lack of a message, the battle was lost;
> for lack of a battle, the war was lost;
> for lack of a war, the kingdom was lost;
> and all because of one horseshoe nail.

From this perspective, it seems to me that belief in astrology, and the hopes that continue to be invested today in diverse would-be sciences, all express a natural desire to escape the terrestrial confusion of human events and emotions by putting them into correspondence with the pure predictability of the stars.

The beautiful separation between pure and impure (confused) lasted until Galileo. He destroyed it by creating a terrestrial mechanics that obeyed the same laws as celestial mechanics; he also discovered that the surface of the Sun is covered with spots and hence is imperfect. His extension of the domain of order opened the route to Newton and to science. His extension of the domain of disorder made our vision of the universe more realistic, but removed the Sun's surface for a long time from the reach of science.

After Galileo, knowledge was freed from the Greeks' distinction between Heaven and Earth, but it continued to distinguish between several levels of knowledge. At one end was "hard" knowledge, a science of order patterned after astronomy. At the other end, was "soft" knowledge patterned after history, i.e. the study of human and social behavior. (In German *Wissenschaft* is both *knowledge* and *science*; this may be one of several bad reasons why the English and the French often use *science* as a substitute for *knowledge*.)

Let me at this point remind you of the envy I experienced as a young man, when watching the natural hold on minds that is the privilege of psychology and sociology, and of my youthful dreams of seeing hard science somehow succeed in achieving a similar hold. Given the nature of science, until a few decades ago, this was an idle dream. Human beings (not all, to be sure, but enough of them) view history, psychology, and sociology as "alive" (as long as they are not scarred by mathematical modeling). Astronomy is not viewed as alive; even when the Sun and the Moon are personified, they become superhuman, godlike because of their regularity. In the same spirit, many students view math as cold and dry, something wholly separate from their spontaneous concerns, not worth thinking about unless they are compelled to. Scientists and engineers must know the rules that govern the motions of planets. But these rules have nothing to do with history, or with messy, everyday life, in which, let me repeat, the lack of a "nail" can lose a horse, a battle, a war, and even a kingdom.

Now we are ready for my main point, which must be the reason why you have asked me to your Congress. In recent years the sharp contrast between astronomy and history has collapsed. We are witness to the coming together of a new kind of science; not a new *species*, nor even (to continue in taxonomic terms) a new *genus* or *family*, but a token of a much more profound change. Towards the end of the 19th century, a certain seed was sowed by Poincaré; but practically no one paid attention, and the seed failed to develop until recently. It is only since the 1960s that the study of "true disorder" and complexity has come onto the scene. Two key words are *chaos* and *fractals*, but I shall keep to fractals. Again and again my work has revealed cases where simplicity breeds a complication that seems incredibly lifelike.

The crux of the matter is a geometric object that I first saw in 1979, took very seriously, and worked hard to describe in 1980. It has been named the *Mandelbrot set*. It starts with a formula so simple that no one could possibly have expected so much from it. You program this silly little formula into your trusty personal computer or workstation, and suddenly everything breaks loose. Astronomy described simple rules and simple effects, while history described complicated rules and complicated effects. Fractal geometry has revealed simple rules and complicated effects. The complication one sees is not only most extraordinary but is also spontaneously attractive, and often breathtakingly beautiful. Besides, you may change the formula by what seems a tiny amount, and the complication is replaced by something altogether different, but equally beautiful.

The effect is absolutely like an uncanny form of white magic. I shall never forget the first time I experienced it. I ran the program over and over again and just could not let it go. I was a visiting professor at Harvard at the time and interest in my pictures immediately proved contagious. As the bug spread, I began to be stopped in the halls by people who wanted to hear the latest news... In due time, *Scientific American*, in April 1985, published the story that spread the news beyond Harvard.

The bug spread to tens, hundreds, and thousands of people. I started getting calls from people who said they loved those pictures so much that they simply had to understand them: where could they find out about the multiplication of complex numbers? Other people wrote to tell me that they found my pictures frightening. Soon the bug spread from adults to children, and then (how often does this happen?) from the kids to teachers and to parents.

Lovable! Frightening! One expects these words to be applied to live, warm bodies, not to mere geometric shapes. Would you have expected kids to go to you, their teachers, and ask you to explain a mathematical picture? And be eager enough to volunteer to learn more and better algebra? Would you expect strangers to stop me in a store downtown, because they just have to find out what a complex number is? The fact that my Polytechnique classmates soon forgot all about math shows that it had not mattered to them as much as it should have.

Next, let me remind you that the "new math" fiasco started when a committee of my elders, including some of my friends, all very distinguished and full of goodwill, figured out among themselves that it was best to start by teaching small kids the notions that famous professors living in the 1950s viewed as being fundamental, and therefore simple. They wanted grade schoolers to be taught the abstract idea of a set. For example, a box containing five nails was given a new name: it became a set of five nails. As it happened, hardly anyone was dying to know about five-nail sets.

On the other hand, the initial spread of fractals among students and "ordinary people" was neither planned nor supported by any committee or corporation, least of all by IBM, which was the sponsor of my scientific work but had no interest in its graphic or "popular" aspects. This spread was one of the most truly spontaneous events I ever heard of or witnessed. People could not wait to understand and master the white magic and find out about those crazy Mandelbrot sets. The five-nail set was rejected as cold and dry. The Mandelbrot set was welcomed almost as if it were alive. Everything suggests that its study can become a part of liberal knowledge!

Chaotic dynamics meets the same response. There is no fun in watching a classical pendulum beat away relentlessly, but the motion of a pendulum made of two hinged sticks is endlessly fascinating. I believe that this contrast reveals a basic truth that every scientist knows or suspects, but few would concede. The only trace of historical necessity in the evolution of science may be that its grand strategy is not to begin with the most exciting questions but with the questions that are simple enough to be tackled at a given time. The lesson for the educator is obvious. Motivate the students by that which is fascinating, and hope that the resulting enthusiasm will create sufficient momentum to move them through that which is no fun but is necessary.

Let me now face some objections. Fractals, chaos, easy graphics, and the computer are having a rapidly increasing effect on the mathematics research profession. However it is no secret that – to put it mildly – they have not been immediately and universally popular. I shall argue momentarily that this hostility does not matter in itself, and I believe that it will decline. But its manifestations do raise interesting issues.

Some persons have declared themselves offended that mathematics should be represented to the wide public by fractals *et al.*, simply because they view this field as uncharacteristically easy and otherwise unrepresentative.

It is quite true that much about fractals appears "easy", almost "obvious" today. Indeed, it is easily explained, especially to children. But yesterday nothing was obvious, just the opposite. My writings have blamed mathematicians for having boxed themselves and everyone else in an intellectual environment where constructions now viewed as "proto-fractal" were once viewed as "pathological" and anything but obvious. This intellectual environment was proud of having broken the connections between mathematics and physics. Today there is a growing consensus that the continuity of the links between mathematics and physics is obvious, but the statements ring false in the mouths of those who denied and destroyed this continuity; they sound better in the mouths of those who rebuilt it.

As to the assertion that fractal geometry is easy, the term is simply ridiculous. In mathematics, some of my earliest observations about the Mandelbrot set remain as open conjectures; no one knows the dimensions of self-affine sets beyond the simplest, etc., etc. In physics, turbulence and fractal aggregates remain mysterious, etc., etc.

Finally, to say that fractals are "unrepresentative" may be an accurate description. However, as I have already argued, this is not a drawback but rather a very great strength from the viewpoint of education. If it is true that "math was never like that", it is also true that "this is more lifelike than any other branch of math".

One passionate objection to the computer as the point of entry into "real" mathematics is that, if the young replace solving traditional problems by computer games, they will never be able to understand the fundamental notion of mathematical rigor. This fear is based on an obvious chain of associations: the computer started as a tool of applied mathematics; applied mathematicians spurn rigor; *ergo*, the computer is the enemy of rigor.

I think with equal passion that the precise contrary is true: the computer is rigor's only true friend. True, a child can play forever with a ready-made program that draws Mandelbrot sets and never understand rigor, nor learn much of any value. But neither does the child who always does his mathematical homework with the teacher's answer book at his elbow. On the contrary, the notion of rigor is of the essence for anyone who has been motivated to write a computer program – even a short one – from scratch.

When I was a student a non-rigorous proof did not order me to try harder. Even worse, I soon realized that even my excellent teachers occasionally failed to notice clearcut errors in my homework and exams. We were told that Hilbert had listed all requirements for rigor, but that the list was above our heads. In the case of a computer program, on the contrary, being rigorous is not simply an esthetic requirement; in most cases, a non-rigorous program fails completely, and the slightest departure from absolute rigor makes it scream "error" at the programmer. No wonder that, as we shall see, the birth of the computer was assisted by logicians and not mathematicians. It is true that, on occasion, a non-rigorous program generates meaningless typography or graphics, or – worse – sensible-looking but wrong output. But those rare examples only prove that programming requires no less care than does traditional proof.

Moreover, the computer programmer soon learns that a program that works on one computer, with its operating system, will not work on another. He will swear at the discrepancies, but I cannot imagine a better illustration of the changeability and arbitrariness of axiomatic systems.

Many other concepts that used to be subtle and controversial before the computer was invented became clear afterwards. Thus, computer graphics refreshes a distinction between fact and proof, one that many mathematicians prefer not to acknowledge but that Archimedes described wonderfully in these words: "Certain things first became clear to me by a mechanical method, although they had to be demonstrated by geometry afterwards because their investigation by the said mechanical method did not furnish an actual demonstration. But it is of course easier, when the method has previously given us some knowledge of the questions, to supply the proof than it is to find it without any previous knowledge. This is a reason why, in the case of the theorems that the volumes of a cone and a pyramid are one-third of the volumes of the cylinder and prism (respectively) having the same base and equal height, the proofs of which Eudoxus was the first to discover, no small share of the credit should be given to Democritus who was the first to state the fact, though without proof."

The first two sentences might easily have been written in our time by someone describing renascent experimental mathematics, but Archimedes lived from 287 to 212 BC, Democritus from 460 to 370 BC and Eudoxus from 408 to 355 BC. (Don't let your eyes glaze over at the names of these ancient heroes. Please, keep on!)

A child (and why not an adult?) eventually becomes tired of seeing chaos and fractal games as white magic and draws up a list of observations he wants to really understand. To do so is to reach beyond the role of Democritus to the role of Eudoxus. Moreover, anyone's list of observations is bound to include several that are obviously mutually contradictory, stressing the need for a referee. Is there a better way of communicating another role for rigor and/or a role for further experimentation?

Another criticism of the computer is that it can only be concerned with discrete finite systems and cannot communicate the notions of limit and of continuity. Once again the precise contrary is true. It must be confessed, however, that the greatest benefits may well be found in advanced topics. Well beyond the level of the educational topics we are discussing, the computer has helped me sort out different kinds of limits and identified cases where the limit was thought to be important but proved not to be so.

I cannot spend any more time on the topic of the computer and rigor. Now I would like to recall that, early in this story, the words "historical necessity" were used twice: as applied to the long early history of mathematics, and as applied to the state of mathematical research in the 1960s. If the state of research in the 1960s had not been historically necessary, "new math" would have had no legitimacy, and neither will other new maths that may hit us in the future. The idea of historical necessity as applied to math, therefore, deserves to be criticized at length.

During the 1960s, I heard many a lecturer describe the flow of 20th century mathematics as that of a single majestic river whose course was not a historical accident but had been preordained by inner logic, and which would proceed inevitably and inexorably towards increasingly general, "structural", or "fundamental" notions – which happened to be increasingly abstract. As I recall these descriptions, they had none of the messiness of Earthly history, but much of the purity of the Heavens, as understood by the Greeks and sketched above.

Needless to say, the majestic flow in question was unflinchingly understood to be leaving aside many people (including myself), and innumerable topics that concerned either the foundations (logic) or applications. A message was communicated, to the effect that much of what looks like mathematics is *not really* mathematics, even though the distinction may not be obvious to the outsider. My position is starkly different. I see mathematics as a very broad enterprise that shelters many diverse topics, ranging from the very concrete to the very abstract. This view is well represented by a simile I heard used by Hermann Weyl (1885–1955). He compared mathematics to the delta of a great river, one made of many streams; they may vary in their width and the speed of the flow through them; nevertheless, all are always a part of the system, and no individual stream is permanently the most important. This simile represented the mood of mathematics at the time when Weyl wrote, close to the year 1900 – and also, for that matter, its mood near the year 1800. More importantly, mathematics has been changing so fast for a decade or so that I feel that Weyl's simile well represents the mood as we approach the year 2000.

But the resemblances between these snapshots taken centuries apart certainly do not imply that mathematics is outside ordinary history. The 20th century gave us an example of something starkly different: a rocky history and continuing conflict. Mathematics has not become ruled by its own determinism; it has not become separate from every other aspect of human knowing and feeling; it has on the contrary been profoundly affected by endless external vicissitudes.

I would like to stress that the words "profoundly affected by" must not be misunderstood as meaning "enslaved by". A field's importance to the overall human experience is reflected by the fact that internal logic *does* have an influence upon its development; in that sense, the development of mathematics is one of the triumphs of mankind. But this does not deny that strife has been present in mathematics since the Ancient Greeks, as we shall see when this story ends by mentioning the long-standing conflict between the traditions of Plato and Archimedes. In particular, like every individual human activity, mathematics is very much a participant in general history, politics, demography, and technology, and it is heavily influenced by the idiosyncrasies of a few key people. Let me give some examples from this century.

Around 1920, a group of Polish mathematicians collected around a very forceful man named Waclaw Sierpinski (1882–1969). They chose to concentrate on a field that was not practiced much in the reigning intellectual capitals, and founded a very abstract new branch often called *Polish mathematics*. They did not hide – in fact, they proudly proclaimed – the fact that their goal largely involved national politics: they wanted to avoid seeing the newly reestablished Poland become a mathematical satellite of Paris or Göttingen. Would anyone claim that Polish nationalism had anything to do with the historical determinism of mathematics? As Polish mathematics thrived, it became one of the important forces pushing towards abstraction at all cost. Yet, by a bitter irony, some of the notions it originated failed to become important in mathematics, but eventually became important to physics – through fractal geometry.

My second example concerns Godfrey Harold Hardy (1877–1947), a strong person as well as a strong mind. In Hardy's youth, British mathematics was dominated by an earlier form of mathematical physics that had little concern with continental rigor. During World War I, Hardy was an outspoken pacifist who recoiled from some of the practical uses of the old British mathematics. During another War, in a book titled *A mathematician's apology* (1941), he gave an impassioned account of his ideal of pure mathematics, a mathematics that could have no bad application for the simple reason that it could have no application of any sort. (By another bitter irony, his best example turned out, in due time, to be essential to cryptography.)

Could anyone claim that Hardy's militant anti-nationalism had anything to do with the historical determinism of mathematics?

From ideology, let us move on to demography. The 1910s have been very cruel to French mathematics. First, Henri Poincaré (1854–1912) died prematurely on the operating table, then millions of young people died in trench warfare, and finally – perhaps worst of all – millions returned broken in health or spirit to a country that did not dare make heavy demands on them. As a result, the young postwar French mathematicians of the 1920s found that the only available teachers were men who had already been old in 1914 and so did not go to war. Some have written movingly about the hardship of training without the usual parental supervision from slightly older advisors, and (as may have been expected) this hardship contributed to the emergence of several very strong personalities. In any event, the France of the late 1920s and the 1930s gave rise to an extremist movement calling itself Bourbaki. But would anyone claim that a sudden demographic imbalance in a country with a long and glorious mathematical tradition has anything to do with the historical determinism of mathematics?

Further, no one would claim that the specific historical determinism of mathematics is synchronous with the intellectual moods and fashions that rule society at large. But it happens that a very unusual mood prevailed early in this century, particularly in the 1920s. One especially visible and durable effect was the invention of the "International Style" in architecture. In Finland, the small country where it was born, modern architecture merged smoothly into what came before it, without discontinuity and without heavy dogmatism. But modern architecture became dogmatic in Germany with the Bauhaus and in France with Le Corbusier (1887–1965). The latter built few houses but made many sketches (for example, his ideal improvement of Paris evokes the present suburbs of Moscow). When I was young, Le Corbusier was billed as a great intellect to whom modern architecture owed its intellectual legitimacy. Indeed, he wrote a great deal, but I find little in his writings beyond sophomoric trash. It may be that "Bauhaus" was inevitable at a certain stage of the technology and economics of raising large buildings, but no one ever convinced me that they were an inevitable wave of the future. For reference later in this story, recall that the favorite vocabulary of Bauhaus included the words "structure".

How was mathematics affected by the above-mentioned politics, demographics, and general intellectual moods? I charge them all with being responsible for the fact that near the middle of our century mathematics behaved in ways totally at variance with its mood today and in 1900 or 1800. This atypical mathematics is conveniently denoted by the name it took in France, but the current that gave rise to Bourbaki also affected many countries other than France, Poland, and Britain. It strongly affected the

USA, but some countries were spared (for example Sweden), and there were strong counteracting forces in Germany and Russia. At its strongest, it benefited from another extraneous event: a period of unprecedented economic and academic growth and minimal social pressure on the sciences allowed the balance in the universities to be rapidly overwhelmed by recently produced PhDs, including many Bourbaki products.

To sum up, Bourbaki found its roots in one of the many components of the mathematics of 1875-1925, gathered strength during the second quarter of our century (the period to which the above examples refer), and took power around 1950. During the third quarter of the century it exerted an extraordinary degree of control. There was no disorder in mathematics, but the field was narrowed down to a truly extraordinary extent. At one time it seemed to reduce to little more than algebraic topology; at a later time, to number theory and algebraic geometry. These are extremely important fields, to be sure, but concentration on a single field was quite contrary to the historical tradition (mentioned early in this paper) that had led Hermann Weyl to the image of the delta of the Nile. Mathematics seemed to have reduced itself to basically a single stream at any given time. This happened to be the cliché description that Hermann Weyl (in a contrasting image) applied to physics.

I have never been indifferent to Bourbaki. Indeed, their shadow greatly affected my life, and my feelings towards the "new order" they represented were raw: fear, loathing and refusal to cooperate. These feelings moved me at age 20 when I entered and immediately left École Normale Supérieure in Paris (it was about to become – so to speak – the Bourbaki Party School), and then fourteen years later left the University for industrial research. (All this is described in my contribution to *Mathematical people*, Birkhäuser, 1985.)

The Bourbaki, as has already been implied, never paid attention to the historical accidents that contributed to their birth; they felt themselves to be the necessary and inevitable response to the call of history. Today, however, this call seems forgotten. One of their leaders, André Weil (born in 1906), recently published his autobiography (Birkhäuser, 1991); to my great disappointment he grandly passed by the opportunity to explain Bourbaki – as opposed to listing selected gossip about their history. He adamantly passed by a second opportunity when the *Gazette des mathématiciens* interviewed him shortly afterwards.

There is wide consensus that, like new math, "Bourbaki is dead". Who killed Bourbaki? Throughout its heyday, my friend Mark Kac (1914–1984) and many other open-minded mathematicians kept arguing vehemently, in speeches and articles, that Bourbaki had misread mere accidents for the arrow of history. But such criticism invariably lacks bite, and it had no effect. My own partisan opinion is that Bourbaki's fate was typical of many ideologies outside science. The founders could only insure their immediate succession; gradually, the ideological fervor weakened and the movement continued largely by force of habit. The resulting weakness did not become obvious to everyone until after the movement was knocked down by yet another event that had nothing to do with the historical determinism in mathematics. This event was the rebirth of experimental mathematics that followed (slowly, as we shall see) the advent of the modern computer.

Thus, the 1970s saw a technological development destroy the legitimacy of a movement whose birth in the 1920s was influenced by Polish and English ideology, a demographic catastrophe in France, and the general intellectual mood of the day, and whose success was hastened by a long spurt of economic growth.

Where did the computer come from? From mathematics understood in a broad sense. What relation is there between the advent of the computer and mathematics as narrowly reinterpreted by Bourbaki? None. The computer rose from the convergence of two fields that surely belong to mathematics but were spurned by Bourbaki, namely, logic and differential equations. We all know that one must never rewrite history as it might have proceeded if two crucial events had chanced to occur in the reverse order. But in this instance the temptation is strong to air the following conviction. Had an earlier arrival of the computer saved experimental mathematics from falling into a century of decline, Bourbaki might have never seemed to anyone to be an unavoidable development. Let me elaborate on the computer's roots.

Surprisingly, while "foundations of analysis" was one of their preferred terms, the Bourbaki had only contempt for the logical foundations of mathematics, as in the work of Kurt Gödel (1906–1978) and Alan Turing (1912–1954). In the 1930s, Turing had phrased his model of a logical system in terms of an idealized computer. His "Turing machine" had a very great influence on the thinking of those who developed the actual hardware.

However, the man who made the computer a reality was John von Neumann (1903–1957; Neumann János in the original Hungarian). He was not only a mathematician, but also a physicist and an economist, and his very great breadth of interests came to include a passion to find ways to predict the weather.

Thus the computer itself was born in the 1940s from a strange combination of abstract logic and the desire to control Nature. For a very long time, "core" mathematicians felt totally unconcerned, and viewed it with revulsion. Von Neumann, because of his work on the computer, ceased to be accepted as a mathematician and was made to resign from the Princeton

Institute for Advanced Study. But eventually the computer changed mathematicians' lives in a very profound fashion.

Those events bring up a question that is very old but has been asked especially sharply in the context of computers. What are, in a discovery, the respective contributions of the tool and of its user? Galileo wrote a whole book complaining bitterly about those who belittled his discovery of sunspots, those who said it was only due to his having lived during the telescope revolution. Take the chapter of mathematics called the global theory of iteration of rational functions, to which the Mandelbrot set belongs. Pierre Fatou (1878–1929) and Gaston Julia (1893–1978) are – quite rightly – praised for developing this chapter, and no one would dream of belittling their contributions as being due to their having lived during the age of Paul Montel. Montel was the mathematician who, in 1912, introduced Fatou's and Julia's key tool, the normal families of functions. Soon afterwards he was called into the Army, leaving behind Fatou (who was a cripple) and Julia (who had come back as a wounded war hero). Today, however, a new kind of tool is treated differently: some belittle work based on the computer as solely due to the workers having lived in the computer age. If it were so, we would be faced with a mystery. Why should experimental mathematics have attracted so few practitioners for many years after the maverick von Neumann saw that mathematics could benefit from the modern computer? The first major response came from a physicist, Enrico Fermi (1901–1954). A desire to understand nonlinear mathematics inspired him, together with J. Pasta and S. Ulam, to write a text (*Los Alamos Document LA-1940*, 1955) that was not published in its time, yet became very influential in physics. It was finally printed in the *Collected papers of Enrico Fermi*, 1962-5, Vol. 2, and reprinted in S. Ulam, *Sets, numbers and universes*, 1974. But von Neumann's and Fermi's lead was not followed by other mathematicians.

When I was new at IBM, which I joined in 1958, opportunities to use computers were knowingly and systematically offered to – and spurned by – every noted mathematician who could be coaxed into the building. Even the example of S. Ulam is interesting. Having contributed to an (already-mentioned) famous early paper on experimental mathematics, he might have been expected to become a herald of the new trend. Yet the preface he wrote in 1963 to a reprint of this paper asserts the following: "Mathematics is not really an observational science and not even an experimental one. Nevertheless, computations [were] useful in establishing some rather curious facts about simple mathematical objects."

The opinion that the tool is all that mattered is certainly not applicable in my case; explicit and visual geometry became essential to my work well before the computer era started and continued as I was bucking the Bourbaki tide.

Allow me to insert here some comments that may appear overly auto-biographical, but which I believe relevant. I may hold many advanced degrees but did not spend that much time in school; I lived in France during World War II when it was more important to keep body and soul together. I encountered a difficult test in 1944 when France was liberated. I had missed most of the special training that everyone viewed as essential for the examinations that were described early in this story. When expected to solve some problems by algebra, which I had not mastered at the required level of fluency, I solved them by geometry, which I loved and for which I had a "freakish" gift. The flipside is that those who solve problems the expected way and those who solve them in their own way become different persons. I had triumphed in the examinations, but my exclusive devotion to geometry made me, willy nilly, a misfit; fortunately, I was a well-tolerated misfit, even one who was increasingly well-regarded. I even held a professorship in mathematics in France at one time. But then I resigned, and immediately hit a long spell when no academic department – rich or poor – wanted me in its backyard, except as a visitor.

My good fortune was to land at a place where an enlightened manager took the risky gamble of supporting me. This was the IBM Research Division, well before its heyday. I was never to live in a garret, but I was absolutely alone. I could not even say I needed help in building the promising new discipline of fractal geometry: for a long time I had no idea I was building a new discipline. My feeling was that I was simply following a capricious but uncontrollable fancy.

Let me say a few words about attitudes towards solitude. For a long time, there were very few scientists. Some had a few peers scattered around to whom they could write, and others founded schools, but it was not unusual for a scientist to spend his whole life all by himself. But today schools have grown in size, and science is a very social enterprise that is deeply hostile to lone investigators who do not follow the leads of the profession.

Every profession sets a straight path for itself, but my path seemed always to be bending. The resulting intellectual solitude was a constant source of agony. On many occasions, I was even tempted to straighten out – to continue along some tangent, to hold on to the direction I happened to be going at the moment, and simply extend it in a straight line. I was tempted, but I held on to my crooked path.

Then my persistence was rewarded by a lucky break, which reunited me with geometry and led directly to fractals. The computer arrived and its scope was being slowly enriched to enable it to draw shapes. First, we had pen-tracing tables. Next, we could draw on laboratory cathode ray tubes and photograph what we saw. Then a prototype printing machine came into the IBM Research Center. It was not very good at printing but I saw instantly that it could be used to draw, and the assistant I had got at long last tamed it for that goal. The computer is a dry machine, but what we forced out of it was anything but dry.

Events started moving faster and faster. Finally, I realized that I was working out a gradually emerging new field and I had earned the privilege of giving it a name: I called it "fractal geometry". Helped by a few people, I wrote books; two were well received, and the third took off like wild fire. Early on I had found endless inspiration in a record of coin-tossing to be found in the famous probability textbook of William Feller. It is reproduced as Plate 241 in my book *The Fractal geometry of nature* (1982). Feller's random numbers were surely neither computer-generated nor computer-plotted, and no other textbook of probability felt such a figure was needed.

In the late 1960s, computer-assisted graphics became a critical tool in my work, but any achievements I could claim in the following ten years have paled compared to what I achieved in 1979–1980. Many people think (as I do) that mathematics took a sharp turn when the Fatou-Julia theory that has already been mentioned became again a wide-awake component of the mathematical mainstream. This event came about because the topic was thoroughly changed by the availability of a new tool, one that did not come from within mathematics (like the Montel theory), but from outside.

My observations and mathematical conjectures concerning the map $z \cdot z + c$ were presented in May 1980 at a special seminar at Harvard, then in November 1980 at a seminar in Bures near Paris, at the Institut des Hautes Études Scientifiques. The Bures seminar was widely attended, and it had a profound effect on the man who was at that time the leader of Bourbaki, Adrien Douady. He dropped all previous work and has ever since devoted himself fully to a set I had described to him, first at the Bures seminar, and subsequently at many private meetings. Soon after that, Douady and his student John H. Hubbard proposed for this set the term *Mandelbrot set* and the letter M.

At one time the early history of this set attracted a wealth of popular interest that may have come to the attention of some of you. I discuss the issue in the Foreword I wrote for a book by Heinz Otto Peitgen et al., *Fractals for the classroom,* Vol. I, 1991. The evidence, combined with dismissal of claims devoid of evidence, shows that no one had bothered to draw M before I first did. Far more important, no one viewed it as worthy of being examined; there is no competitor for the credit for the discovery of the first and most striking list of properties of M.

Before ending, I would like to bring the story back to a higher plane. Nearly all the events we have discussed in my story belong to the 20th century. We all know this has been a period of strife, and you may be tempted to conclude from my account that strife in mathematics is but a special case of a general phenomenon. But, once again, history provides a salutary background. Indeed, the various outside events (political, demographic, and technological) that deeply influenced mathematics in our century are best understood against the background of a very long conflict which goes back to Classical Greece, when mathematics and science were being formulated in nearly their present form, and when the notion of proof was being developed. The two sides of this conflict can be called pluralistic and utopian.

The pluralistic view is wonderfully expressed in the quote from Archimedes that I gave earlier in this story. The views of Archimedes deserve to be called pluralist because he acknowledges a proper balance between the role of proof and the role of experiment, including the role of the senses, as tools in the search for new mathematical facts. On the other hand, judging from the tone of the quote, it seems that Archimedes was already responding to some authoritatively stated contrary opinion. It must have been the utopian view held by Plato (427–347 BC), a man of very great power, both in intellect and in influence. Yes, it so happens that the curses I hear too often being cast today against the return of the eye to the hard sciences do little but echo Plato – without his sense of style. And the pluralists who welcome and praise the return of the eye, thinking of themselves as down-to-earth and modern, may not know much of Plato, yet are actively fighting his shadow.

If you have stayed on listening to me, you may wish to learn more about the Plato versus Archimedes story; you could begin with the already-mentioned Foreword I wrote for *Fractals for the classroom.*

Before ending, let me acknowledge what must have been obvious all along. I am a working scientist fascinated by history and education, but totally ignorant of the literature of educational philosophy. I hope that some of my thoughts will be useful, but fear that many will be found to be commonplace, or otherwise deserving to be credited elsewhere... but I must leave it to you to decide. One area where I claim no originality is the historical assertions: they are documented facts, not stories made up to fit a conclusion.

Now to conclude. The best is to quote myself and to ask once again: Is it extravagant to hope that, starting with this piece of mathematics called fractal geometry, we could help broaden the small band of those who see mathematics as essential to include every educated citizen and therefore to have mathematics take its place among the liberal arts? A statement of hope is the best place to close.

POSTSCRIPT

The rush of events urges me to add two comments, each concerned with one of the main themes of the preceding text.

Open-eyed readers of these *Proceedings* who also follow the press may have noticed a sudden and unprecedented flurry of articles concerned with the moods that prevail today in the mathematics research community. What a change! Not long ago, the very existence of such a community was almost a secret. Today, many of its members vie with each other and with journalists in expressing extreme and contradictory views of what is right and what is not. Of course (to quote Benjamin Disraeli as quoted by William Safire) traditionalists rush to "repudiate with indignation and abhorrence (the) new fangled theories" associated with the computer.

On this account, my advice to the teachers of mathematics is simple: read this material if you find it amusing, but do not take it seriously. First of all, the reporting tends to be inaccurate. Far more important, this material only serves to confirm one of the themes of the preceding paper: the current noise and furor – like nearly everything concerning the mathematics research community – have little to do with the needs of the mathematics educator.

Another of my themes is that replenishing the ranks of professional mathematicians is an essential goal, but it is neither sufficiently ambitious nor particularly difficult to fulfill. Far more important is the goal of helping the whole field survive, by teaching some mathematics to Everywoman and Everyman. Mathematics belongs to the humanities, everyone deserves to be acquainted with its spirit, and those who will not go far in this field deserve something. They should see their education end with something nice to remember, not with failure in Calculus I, II or III. On this account, I must draw your attention to the book *Fractals for the Classroom* (1991) – which I mentioned previously – and a forthcoming book by Michael Frame and David Peak, to be published by W.H. Freeman in 1994. The latter results from the undergraduate course "Fractal Geometry for non-mathematicians" recently given at Yale University, in which computer demonstrations were extensively used in the classroom and material was provided that related mathematics with nearly every student's field.

WORKING GROUPS

GROUPES DE TRAVAIL

LA FORMATION DE CONCEPTS MATHÉMATIQUES ÉLÉMENTAIRES AU PRIMAIRE

FORMATION OF ELEMENTARY MATHEMATICS CONCEPTS AT THE PRIMARY LEVEL

Responsable en chef / *Chief Organizer* : Helen Mansfield [AUS]
Responsable local / *Local Organizer* : Nadine Bednarz [CAN]
Consultants / *Advisory team members* : Terezinha Nunes [BRA / GBR],
Neil Pateman [USA]

L'évolution des recherches et des expériences portant sur la formation des concepts mathématiques élémentaires et réalisées au cours des dix dernières années est marquée par une *prise en compte de la dimension sociale* dans l'apprentissage.

Cette dynamique socio-cognitive, qui forme la toile de fond d'expériences réalisées en classe avec des enfants dans différents pays, puise ses fondements théoriques dans les *travaux de Vygotski* ou de *l'école socioconstructiviste.*

Il nous est apparu important de resituer dans un premier temps, à l'intérieur du groupe de travail, ces deux perspectives en mettant en évidence les fondements théoriques dont elles s'inspirent. Deux présentations ont permis d'atteindre cet objectif. L'une d'entre elles, *Synthesizing the individual and the social : sociocultural theory applied to the Mathematics Education of young children,* par Peter D. Renshaw [AUS], a mis en évidence les concepts centraux qui donnent sens aux activités développées par les psychopédagogues russes, à la suite des travaux de Vygotski. L'organisation des apprentissages en classe y repose sur une conception du développement dans lequel le social et l'activité apparaissent centraux. Cette conception de l'apprentissage renvoie par ailleurs à un système complexe où les rôles du savoir théorique, du savoir empirique et du langage ne sont pas ceux habituellement retenus dans l'enseignement. Les situations ont avant tout pour but l'appropriation de concepts théoriques à travers la réflexion théorique. Leur maîtrise précède l'apprentissage à agir sur les choses empiriques. Pour que l'apprentissage puisse avoir lieu, un lien entre les concepts spontanés et les concepts scientifiques doit pouvoir être établi. Des stratégies ont été élaborées dans cette perspective par Davidov dans ses expériences d'enseignement, stratégies qui encouragent un mécanisme de régulation partagée, dans lequel le langage joue un rôle essentiel comme outil de médiation.

La deuxième conférence d'introduction par Paul Cobb [USA], *Constructivism and Activity Theory : a consideration of their similarities and differences as they relate to Mathematics Education,* a repris les concepts clefs de la perspective socio-constructiviste, en comparant celle-ci à la théorie de l'activité développée par Davidov.

L'activité collective et les interactions en classe, tout comme dans la perspective vygotskienne, y jouent un rôle essentiel. Au-delà de cette similarité des deux courants de recherche, des différences importantes ont été mises en évidence par Cobb. Il en est ainsi de la conception même du processus d'apprentissage qui guide les interventions élaborées de part et d'autre. Pour Vygotski, les concepts scientifiques naissent d'un contact indirect avec l'objet et ne peuvent être acquis que par un processus allant du général au particulier. Ce point de vue va présider au choix et à l'organisation de l'activité d'apprentissage. « L'opposition entre le développement des concepts spontanés et celui des concepts scientifiques sert de base à l'activité d'apprentissage dans la psychologie soviétique, selon laquelle le processus d'élaboration des concepts scientifiques et théoriques doit être organisé d'après le schéma déductif. » (Davidov, 1972) Dans la perspective socio-constructiviste, les chercheurs réfèrent au contraire à un développement des concepts davantage contextualisé, laissant place à des différenciations possibles, et la construction de l'activité d'apprentissage va s'articuler sur les conceptions développées par les élèves (voir Garnier, Bednarz, Ulanovskaya, 1991).

La réaction de Leslie Steffe [USA] aux deux conférences d'introduction s'est attardée à la place du social dans la théorie piagétienne, contestant ainsi l'interprétation qu'en donnent souvent les socio-constructivistes. « The omission of interaction as a property of human beings is often attributed to the work of Piaget and its inclusion is often attributed to the work of Vygotski. However, Piaget's work can be legitimately understood as a socio-cultural approach although those who concentrate specifically on socio-interaction interpret Piaget as taking an almost exclusive biological approach to genetic epistemology. » Par la suite, cette analyse a fait l'objet de discussions à l'intérieur du groupe de travail et certains participants ont resitué les fondements de l'école socio-constructiviste, pour laquelle l'expérience sociale intervient à titre de constituant même des dynamiques individuelles. Ainsi, pour l'école de psychologie sociale génétique, « les instruments cognitifs que l'enfant élabore sont autant de structurations de la représentation du champ social qu'il est amené à élaborer lors d'interactions sociales » (Mugny, 1985). En cela, les chercheurs de ce champ s'écartent de la position individualiste piagétienne relativement au développement cognitif.

La discussion s'est par la suite orientée sur quatre sous-questions abordées partiellement par chacun des deux conférenciers de départ : 1) Que recouvrent les concepts et comment s'élaborent ces concepts chez les jeunes enfants ? 2) Quelles influences les environnements sociaux et culturels ont-ils sur la formation de concepts élémentaires au niveau primaire ? 3) Quel curriculum mettre en place pour les jeunes enfants, quels choix doit-on poser face au contenu et à l'élaboration de stratégies didactiques en classe visant une formation « optimale » des concepts mathématiques par les jeunes enfants ? 4) Quel rôle jouent le langage et le symbolisme dans cette forma-tion de concepts élémentaires par les jeunes enfants ?

THÈME 1

Gérard Vergnaud [FRA] a introduit le premier de ces thèmes par le biais de la théorie des champs conceptuels. Les deux questions suivantes ont alors fait l'objet plus spécifique de discussions : Quels sont les méca-nismes qui interviennent dans le développement conceptuel, et quels sont ceux qui peuvent contribuer au changement conceptuel ? La réflexion amorcée par Gérard Vergnaud, par le biais des concepts de schèmes et théo-rèmes en acte, a été ici alimentée par d'autres contributions : Siegbert Schmidt [DEU], Werner Weiser [DEU], Carolyn Maher [USA], Emanuila G. Gelfman [RUS], Michael Mitchelmore [AUS], Adalira Saenz-Ludlow [USA], Irit Peled [ISR], Kathryn Irwin [NZL], Luisa Maria Morgado [PRT], Peter Bero [SVK]. Les points suivants ont alors fait l'objet de discussions. Le terme « mécanismes » a été interprété de multiples façons, le groupe s'entendant toutefois sur le fait qu'il réfère à une construction plus générale que celle de stratégie.

Trois aspects concernant les mécanismes intervenant dans le dévelop-pement conceptuel ont été mis en évidence à partir des idées engendrées par le groupe.

- Le premier aspect concerne les mécanismes internes qui sont à la base de l'organisation de la pensée de l'enfant et de la conceptua-lisation. La notion d'abstraction réfléchissante a été considérée comme un exemple important de tel mécanisme interne.

  La notion de modèle implicite (Fischbein, 1985) a également été considérée dans cette perspective comme ayant une influence sur le développement conceptuel de l'enfant.

- Le second aspect mis en évidence relativement aux mécanismes intervenant dans le développement conceptuel a trait à l'influence des médiateurs sociaux. Les participants ont ainsi montré leur accord avec le fait que les concepts ne s'élaborent pas isolément. Ces médiateurs sociaux réfèrent aux interactions sociales dans la construction des concepts mathématiques par les enfants, et à une institutionnalisation nécessaire des connaissance mathématiques au sein du processus d'apprentissage (Brousseau, 1986).

• Le troisième aspect qui a été discuté en relation avec les mécanismes intervenant dans le développement conceptuel a trait à l'importance du contexte et à la nature de la tâche proposée. L'expérience sociale est ici envisagée sous les aspects signifiants attachés aux contenus des tâches et situations. Cette nature sociale de la situation présentée aux sujets rejoint la préoccupation de certains didacticiens sur le contrat didactique qui lie l'intervenant, les élèves et le savoir au sein d'une situation pédagogique (Brousseau, 1986 ; Schubauer-Leoni, 1986).

THÈME 2

Terezinha Nunes [BRA / GBR] a introduit le deuxième thème en s'interrogeant sur le rôle des particularités culturelles et sociales dans la construction des connaissances mathématiques par les enfants.

Les deux questions suivantes ont alors fait l'objet plus spécifique des discussions relativement au thème 2 : Comment les interactions entre enfants en classe contribuent-elles à l'apprentissage mathématique des enfants ? Comment les connaissances et raisonnements prennent-ils forme et se différencient-ils dans des contextes culturels différents ?

La réflexion amorcée par Nunes a été ici alimentée par d'autres contributions : Louise Poirier [CAN], Verdiana G. Kashaga-Masanja [TZA], Anne Reynolds [USA], Joanna Higgins [NZL], Kathryn Crawford [AUS], Swapna Mukhopadhyay [USA].

Le groupe s'est entendu sur différentes significations possibles associées au terme *contexte culturel* à la lumière des communications présentées :

• la culture des pairs, différente de celle de l'adulte (elle domine quand le professeur est absent et disparaît quand le professeur entre) ;

• la culture associée à différentes origines ethniques ;

• la culture des enfants telle que révélée par leurs histoires ;

• d'autres contextes culturels ont aussi été identifiés, tels ceux rattachés au milieu socio-économique, à la culture de la classe, de l'école...

Cette idée d'une diversité culturelle est souvent mal acceptée. Pourtant le concept d'un contexte culturel idéal n'est peut-être ni nécessaire ni désirable. La culture n'apparaît pas non plus comme quelque chose de statique, et la façon dont l'école est perçue diffère d'une culture à l'autre.

Dans ces contextes culturels, comment les connaissances et raisonnements prennent-ils forme ?

Généralement, et ce à l'intérieur de n'importe quel contexte culturel, il semble y avoir un fossé entre ce qui est attendu et ce qui est atteint, en ce qui a trait aux connaissances et raisonnements mathématiques. La question suivante a alors été posée : Qu'est-ce qui dans une culture (ou un contexte culturel) fait que les connaissances et raisonnements mathématiques apparaissent si difficiles ou si simples à développer ?

Enfin, l'impact très grand de la *culture scolaire* a été mis en évidence : au fur et à mesure que les enfants avancent (d'un niveau scolaire à l'autre), la culture scolaire devient très persuasive. (En se conformant à la culture scolaire, ils apprennent avant tout à adapter leurs réponses et solutions.)

THÈME 3

Le troisième thème abordé par le groupe a eu trait au curriculum mathématique pour les jeunes enfants. Deux interventions, celle de Martin Hughes [GBR], *Teachers' beliefs about concept formation and curriculum decision-making in early mathematics,* et de Robert Wright [AUS], *Concept development in early childhood mathematics : teachers' theories and research,* ont introduit le thème. Les deux questions suivantes ont alors fait l'objet de discussions : Comment se prennent les décisions quant au contenu à mettre en place dans une classe de jeunes enfants, et comment ces décisions reflètent-elles les croyances des enseignants sur la façon dont les concepts se forment chez les enfants ? Comment des stratégies en classe peuvent-elles être développées de façon à conduire à une meilleure formation de concepts mathématiques par les jeunes enfants ? Plusieurs contributions sont venues enrichir la discussion : Joy Scott [AUS], Fran Ciupryk [AUS], Toyoko Yamanoshita [JPN], Mary Faire [NZL], Günter Krauthausen [DEU], George Malaty [FIN], Piet Human [ZAF], Tony Herrington [AUS], Ceri Morgan [GBR].

La nécessité d'un curriculum national flexible a été mise de l'avant par le groupe ainsi qu'une nécessaire médiation des manuels et du matériel par les enseignants. La façon dont ce contenu est structuré et présenté est une indication des croyances de l'enseignant sur la façon dont les enfants apprennent. Une perspective différente a aussi été mise de l'avant face aux décisions à prendre sur le curriculum, celle qui consiste à identifier non pas un contenu mais davantage un ensemble de situations riches, en mettant en évidence les concepts qu'elles pourraient permettre de développer. Le groupe a enfin relevé l'importance de travailler non seulement sur la théorie mais également sur des unités spécifiques d'enseignement dans un groupe de travail lors d'un prochain congrès ICME.

La détermination au jour le jour du contenu et des approches a été considérée comme une caractéristique dominante de la façon dont se prennent les décisions dans la classe. La mise en place de nouvelles perspectives d'enseignement exige donc un changement important de la part des enseignants et un support dans la présentation de situations qui motivent un engagement actif de la part des enfants.

THÈME 4

Le thème 4 portait sur le rôle du langage naturel et du symbolisme dans la formation de concepts élémentaires. Celui-ci a été introduit par deux présentations : *The role played by language in the development of mathematical thought in young children* par Nadine Bednarz [CAN], et *The role of symbolism in the formation of elementary concepts* par Zbigniew Semadeni [POL].

Plusieurs contributions (Lena Licón Khisty [USA], Gillian Boulton-Lewis [AUS], Lyne Outhred [AUS], Adela Jaime [ESP], Jean-Marie Labrie [CAN], Jane-Jane Lo [USA]) ont permis là encore d'éclairer les deux questions qui étaient posées : Comment le développement conceptuel peut-il s'articuler sur le symbolisme développé par les enfants ? Quel rôle joue le langage dans les interactions de jeunes enfants avec d'autres enfants, lorsqu'ils essaient d'articuler leurs propres réalités mathématiques ?

La première partie des discussions a mis en évidence les nombreux problèmes que soulèvent l'utilisation du symbolisme dans les manuels et l'enseignement des mathématiques. Plusieurs exemples ont permis d'illustrer les difficultés que cette utilisation provoque chez les élèves. Le fait que cette sur-symbolisation s'accompagne souvent d'un appauvrissement de la langue naturelle comme support à l'enseignement a également été mis en évidence.

Certaines interventions ont enfin fait ressortir le rôle du langage naturel et du symbolisme élaboré par les enfants dans la construction de concepts mathématiques.

Une telle approche, qui s'inscrit dans une perspective socio-constructiviste et trouve son ancrage dans les travaux de Vygotski, implique une réflexion sur la nature des situations didactiques proposées aux enfants. Celles-ci doivent mettre en place une véritable communication fonctionnelle entre les enfants, dans laquelle le langage et le symbolisme vont jouer un rôle essentiel.

NOTE

Ce rapport a été préparé par Nadine Bednarz, en collaboration avec Helen Mansfield. Un certain nombre de communications présentées dans le cadre de ce groupe de travail seront publiées en 1994 par Kluwer Academic Publishers (Dordrecht, Pays-Bas), sous le titre *Mathematics for tomorrow's young children: International perspectives on curriculum.*

RÉFÉRENCES

Bauersfeld, H. (1988). Interaction, construction and knowledge: Alternative perspectives for mathematics education. In D. Grouws and T. Cooney (Eds.), *Perspectives on research on effective mathematics teaching* (pp. 27-46). Hillsdale, NJ: Erlbaum.

Brousseau, G. (1986). *Théorisation des phénomènes d'enseignement des mathématiques.* Thèse de doctorat d'État, Université de Bordeaux 1.

Cobb, P., Wood, T., & Yackel, E. (1991). A constructivist approach to second grade mathematics. In E. von Glasersfeld (Ed.), *Radical Constructivism in Mathematics Education* (pp. 157-176). Dordrecht: Kluwer Academic Publishers.

Davidov, V.V. (1972). Les types de généralisation au cours de l'apprentissage. [en russe] Moscou: Pedagogika. Traduction anglaise: Davidov, V.V. (1990). *Types of generalization in instruction.* Reston, VA: National Council of Teachers of Mathematics.

Davidov, V.V. (1988). Problems of developmental teaching. *Soviet Education, 30*(8), 6-97 and *30*(9), 3-83.

Doise, W., Mugny, G., & Perret-Clermont, A.N. (1975). Social interaction and the development of cognitive operations. *European Journal of Social Psychology, 5*, 367-383.

Fischbein, E., Deri, M., Nello, M.S., & Marino, M.S. (1985). The role of implicit models in solving verbal problems in multiplication and division. *Journal of Research in Mathematics Education, 16*(1), 3-17.

Garnier, C., Bednarz, N., & Ulanovskaya, I. (1991). *Après Vygotski et Piaget: perspectives sociale et constructiviste. Écoles russe et occidentale.* Bruxelles: De Boeck-Wesmael.

Glasersfeld, E. von (1990). Environment and communication. In L.P. Steffe & T. Wood (Eds.), *Transforming children's mathematics education* (pp. 30-38). Hillsdale, NJ : Erlbaum.

Lave, J. (1988). *Cognition in practice: Mind, mathematics and culture in everyday life.* Cambridge, UK: Cambridge University Press.

Mugny, G. (éd.) (1985). *Psychologie sociale du développement cognitif.* Berne : Peter Lang.

Perret-Clermont, A.N. (1980). *Social interaction and cognitive development in children.* London: Academic Press.

Piaget, J. (1966). *Psychology of intelligence.* Littlefield, NJ: Adams.

Renshaw, P.D. (1992). The psychology of learning and small group work. In R. Maclean (Ed.), *Classroom oral language* (pp. 90-94). Deakin, Victoria, Australia: Deakin University Press.

Schubauer-Leoni, M.L. (1986). *Maître – Élève – Savoir : Analyse psychosociale du jeu et des enjeux de la relation didactique.* Thèse de doctorat ès sciences de l'éducation, Université de Genève.

Vergnaud, G. (1990). La théorie des champs conceptuels. *Recherche en didactique des mathématiques, 10*(2/3), 133-170.

Vygotski, L.S. (1978). *Mind in society: the development of higher psychological processes.* Cambridge, MA: Harvard University Press.

Vygotski, L.S. (1985). *Pensée et langage.* Traduction de Françoise Sève. Paris : Éditions sociales.

Working Group 2 / *Groupe de travail 2*

STUDENTS' MISCONCEPTIONS
AND INCONSISTENCIES OF THOUGHT

CONCEPTIONS ERRONÉES ET
INCOHÉRENCES DE PENSÉE DES ÉLÈVES

Chief Organizer / *Responsable en chef* : Shlomo Vinner [ISR]
Advisory team members / *Consultants* : Kathleen Hart [GBR], Marie-Paule Lecoutre [FRA], Jens Holger Lorenz [DEU], Patricia Wilson [USA]

Each of the four sessions of the working group was dedicated to a different subtheme. Each session started with some introductory remarks which were supposed to trigger a discussion. Then the group split into four subgroups (three in English and one in French) for more "intimate" discussions. The subthemes were: 1) "The cognitive aspects of inconsistencies", introduced by Shlomo Vinner [ISR]; 2) "Misconceptions and how they are related to inconsistencies", introduced by Kathleen Hart [GBR]; 3) "Inconsistencies and misconceptions in the history of mathematics", introduced by Israel Kleiner [CAN]; 4) "Implications of misconceptions and inconsistencies for learning and teaching", introduced by Patricia Wilson [USA]. This report summarizes the main issues which were brought up in the introductory remarks of each session and in the discussions that followed them.

THE COGNITIVE ASPECTS OF INCONSISTENCIES

From a formal logical point of view, a person is considered to be inconsistent if he or she believes in two different statements p and q from which a statement r and its negation can be derived. Take for instance, a classical example from Erlwanger (1973) where a boy, making up his own rules for writing common fractions as decimals and vice versa, believes that $4/11 = 1.5$ and also $11/4 = 1.5$. To the interviewer it is quite clear that the boy is inconsistent. Formally, however, it takes a few steps to obtain a contradiction. Namely, by the symmetry and the transitivity of the equality relation it can be derived from the above that $4/11 = 11/4$. On the other hand, it is well known that $4/11 \neq 11/4$ and the last two statements are contradictory. Note that a person can be inconsistent and at the same time unaware of it. As a matter of fact, this is the case with the boy in the story. Of course, if people are unaware of their own inconsistencies one cannot expect them to change their beliefs. The question is about situations in which people *do* become aware of their inconsistencies. What do they do then? Both cognitive research and common experience show that there is more than one possible reaction. Sometimes people do not care at all about holding opinions which lead to a contradiction. Some people might be bothered a little bit by this fact, but will still sleep quite well when bedtime comes. Other people will not have any peace of mind until they "repair" their cognitive structure in such a way that it stops being inconsistent.

Another question which should be asked is whether there is a tendency for the mind to eliminate sources of inconsistencies. If there is such a tendency, how can we explain the fact that inconsistencies are so common and so frequent? This can be easily explained by compartmentalization. Compartmentalization occurs when two cognitive elements in somebody's mind which are supposed to be related to each other fail to connect. If you notice in the morning, in your kitchen, that you need to buy some fruit and you forget about the coffee – that is compartmentalization. In some contexts it might lead to inconsistencies. What remains to be explained now is the phenomenon of two different cognitive elements in somebody's mind which are supposed to be related yet are not. But this already belongs to the domain of memory research, which is clearly beyond the scope of this working group.

MISCONCEPTIONS AND HOW THEY ARE
RELATED TO INCONSISTENCIES

Sometimes misconceptions occur when people try to assimilate or to interpret new ideas by means of existing schemes which are not suitable for this purpose. For instance, a child, in an algebraical context, assigns numerical values to letters according to their place in the alphabet. This, of course, leads to inconsistencies. However, if we encourage children to check their answers and to reflect on them, they might abandon their misconceptions and adopt the correct ideas which are necessary for the continuation of their learning. The above child, when asked to explain the formula $V = D \times E \times F$ laughed and said it was wrong because "V isn't the 120th letter of the alphabet". Sometimes teachers inadvertently set a child on the way to error by giving a simplified explanation, as had the teacher of Simon, who when asked to do $600 - 236$ said: "When you cross out the 0, it goes directly to 9." Interviewer: "Does it?" Simon: "Yes". Interviewer: "So from nothing I suddenly have 9?" Simon: "Yes, because it is the highest number you can go up to, that's the way I do it."

There are also cases where textbook authors and teachers lack mathematical understanding; this can also lead to misconceptions and inconsistencies. In the minds of many students, symbols do not match concepts and so they manipulate concepts in a meaningless manner. This is another source of misconceptions and inconsistencies, though in their own eyes, very often, the students are consistent. It is suggested that a concrete experience as a preparation to mathematical concepts might help the students to deal with inconsistencies when they occur. It is also recommended that teachers ask students for explanations of their solutions. Quite often students can get the right answers for the wrong reasons.

Misconceptions commonly occur when students have to move from one domain to a new domain. They try to apply the laws of the old domain to the new domain and they fail. It happens when students move from the domain of whole numbers to the domain of fractions, from the domain of non-negative numbers to the domain of negative numbers, and from the domain of real numbers to the domain of complex numbers. Wrong analogies are the cause of many misconceptions and incorrect rules, but one has to remember that analogies are also a very important factor in learning. We do not want to inhibit every use of analogy by our students. Thus we should not despair when we confront a student inferring from $a = b \Rightarrow ac = bc$ (a correct rule) that also $a < b \Rightarrow ac < bc$ (an incorrect rule). With the current situation of teaching and learning mathematics, where the emphasis is on procedures and not on concepts, we should expect many misconceptions which result from memory failures and wrong analogies. The students, unfortunately, do not have the tools to check their answers and to reflect on them. Moreover, one of the tools by means of which students can become aware of their inconsistencies is mathematical proof. This topic, however, has been almost eliminated from the curriculum in many countries or has been reserved for highly selected populations only.

The following question was raised: Is it possible to (almost) exhaust the list of misconceptions in a certain mathematical domain or will we always discover new ones? The general impression is that almost the same misconceptions occur again and again. On the other hand, when computers and computer graphics become an integral part of students' learning environments, it is reasonable to expect new types of misconceptions with which we are not yet familiar.

INCONSISTENCIES AND MISCONCEPTIONS IN THE HISTORY OF MATHEMATICS

Not only have students been guilty of misconceptions and inconsistencies, but so have mathematicians, in fact famous mathematicians, throughout history. So students should not feel embarrassed when making

mistakes – they are in good company. Teachers might gain a better appreciation of students' difficulties from witnessing mathematicians of the first
rank struggle with ideas which today are commonplace and obvious. Moreover, just as misconceptions and inconsistencies in the history of mathematics
were, in general, a stimulus for the further development of mathematics
rather than an empediment to its growth, so student's misconceptions and
inconsistencies should be viewed by teachers as opportunities for clarification and for learning rather than as dead ends. We would like to point out
some historical misconceptions in order to illustrate the above claim:
1) The Pythagoreans in ancient Greece believed that the ratio between the
lengths of any two segments can be expressed by a fraction. This belief
came to be contradicted by one of their major discoveries, namely, the fact
that the ratio between a diagonal and a side in a square cannot be expressed
by a fraction. It is reasonable to assume that this contradiction hindered for
a while some mathematical progress that could otherwise have been made.
2) When negative numbers were first introduced there was a tendency for
some mathematicians to reject them. One of the reasons given was the following: the laws of negative numbers imply that $1/-1 = -1/1$ but how can it
be that the ratio between a large quantity and a small quantity (namely 1
and -1) is equal to the ratio between a small number and a large number?
What caused the misconception here was the belief that numbers represent
quantity. This belief is shared by many students when starting to learn about
negative numbers and it gives them a lot of trouble until they abandon it.
3) In the 18th century the correspondence defined by the rule $f(x) = x$ for
$x > 0$ and $f(x) = -x$ for $x \le 0$ was not considered as a function because a
function should be expressed by one formula. Again, many students today,
at various stages, share the same idea.

In spite of the above, we do not advocate discussing historical difficulties with beginners. These might increase their confusion rather than
ease it.

IMPLICATIONS OF MISCONCEPTIONS AND
INCONSISTENCIES FOR LEARNING AND TEACHING

The most important contribution of inconsistencies is the cognitive
conflict that is produced when the learner must consider conflicting ideas.
Piaget has referred to this conflict as striving to reach equilibrium. There is
a critical dilemma involved in using the powerful learning idea of a cognitive conflict as a teaching tool: A cognitive conflict is personal. No person
can create a cognitive conflict for another person. Traditionally we have
attempted to resolve this dilemma with partial solutions, but we need to be
more aggressive with better solutions. Partial solutions, for example,
were: 1) To offer imaginative problems. 2) To ask stimulating questions.
3) To value multiple solutions. 4) To discuss solution processes. Better

solutions might be: 1) Let students pose their own problems. 2) Let students pose stimulating problems. 3) Let students critique their own solutions. 4) Let students reflect on their own solutions.

It is suggested that the following questions deserve further research:

- How can a teacher help a student create cognitive conflict?

- How should a teacher react to a conflict that he or she sees?

- How can a teacher create a classroom atmosphere that motivates and values cognitive conflicts?

All the above suggests a sort of a program for further investigation in the domain of students' misconceptions and inconsistencies of thought.

The reader who did not attend the sessions of the working group can use *Children's strategies and errors* (1984) as a reference for misconceptions, and a special issue of *Focus on Learning Problems in Mathematics* (1990) on inconsistencies as a reference for inconsistencies.

NOTE

This report was prepared by Shlomo Vinner, in collaboration with Kathleen Hart, Israel Kleiner, Marie-Paule Lecoutre, Walter Sanders, Vicki Schell and Patricia Wilson. Since the work of the Group was based on discussions of problems, issues and ideas in the domain, and not on papers presented to participants, detailed proceedings will not be produced. A list of Group participants can be obtained from: Patricia S. Wilson, Mathematics Education Department, University of Georgia, 105 Aderhold Hall, Athens, GA 30602, USA.

REFERENCES

Booth, L.R. (1984). *Algebra: children's strategies and errors.* Windsor, Berks., UK: NFER-Nelson.

Erlwanger, S.H. (1973). Benny's conceptions of rules and answers in IPI Mathematics. *The Journal of Children's Mathematical Behaviour, 1,* 7-26.

Focus on learning problems in mathematics (1990): Special issue *12*(3/4).

Hart, K.M. (1984). *Ratio: children's strategies and errors.* Windsor, Berks., UK: NFER-Nelson.

Working Group 3 / *Groupe de travail 3*

STUDENTS' DIFFICULTIES IN CALCULUS

DIFFICULTÉS DES ÉTUDIANTS ET ÉTUDIANTES EN CALCUL DIFFÉRENTIEL ET INTÉGRAL

Chief Organizers / *Responsables en chef* : Michèle Artigue [FRA], Gontran Ervynk [BEL]
Local Organizer / *Responsable local* : Marie-Jane Haguel [CAN]
Advisory team members / *Consultants* : Roberto Baldino [BRA], Mary Barnes [AUS], Habiba El Bouazzaoui [MAR], Tommy Dreyfus [ISR]

The main aim of the working group was to support the improvement of the teaching of calculus, furthering an integration of research results with classroom practice. The goal of its activities was to develop and support reflection and discussion about the objectives of teaching in the field, about students' difficulties, about all aspects of existing or ongoing teaching experiments, about the impact of new technologies, about the present status of calculus courses and their influence on students' assessment, taking into account the situation in different countries and the expectations of different audiences.

The *plenary address* by David Tall [GBR], in the first session, focused on documented students' difficulties in calculus, on empirical evidence rather than unsupported intuitions. Calculus can mean a variety of different things, from informal calculus to formal analysis, and more recent approaches, including non-standard analysis and the use of computers. There seems, however, to be inherent difficulties which cause problems no matter how it is taught. The limit concept, for instance, creates a number of cognitive conflicts of various kinds. It requires the learner to reconcile old and new by re-constructing a new coherent knowledge structure, but it is easier for the student to keep conflicting elements in separate compartments and never let them be brought simultaneously to the conscious mind. Several corrective strategies have been proposed: to avoid early reference to the language of limits; to make the student confront the discrepancies; to concentrate on procedural aspects; alternatively, to start with formal definitions; to take profit from a non-standard approach, etc.

Other difficulties include students' inadequate mental images of functions; difficulties in translating real-world problems into calculus formulations; in selecting and using appropriate representations; in handling quantifiers; in algebraic manipulation – or lack of it; student preference for procedural methods rather than conceptual understanding. Remedial hypotheses include active learning; building up intuitions suitable for later formalisation; interactive computer graphics; computer programming; symbolic manipulation software.

Progress over the next four years will profit from more empirical evidence, from more reflection on the evidence, and from theories of learning more appropriate for practical teaching.

SUBGROUP 1

Identification, analysis, and treatment
of student difficulties in learning calculus

Organizer: Ed Dubinsky [USA]

Maggy Schneider [BEL] presented an epistemological obstacle related to the abuse of Cavalieri's principle. She showed that this obstacle could explain errors made by students calculating areas and volumes. Roberto Baldino [BRA] identified different kinds of difficulties encountered by students and connected these problems to students' facility with algebra, geometry, and trigonometry. Miriam Amit [ISR] raised the question of formal versus informal methods in determining the derivative of a function. She observed that students tend to distort theorems, that teachers and textbooks segment topics, and that students confuse the "everyday" meaning of symbols with their use in mathematics. Jim Kaput [USA] argued that the problems of calculus cannot be solved where they occur, but they could be by introducing calculus concepts in the K-12 curriculum, the essential issue of calculus being the mathematization of change.

The discussion focused on the notion of epistemological obstacle; the relationship between technical skills and conceptual understanding; obstacles arising in going from intuitive to formal calculus; methods of teaching, such as the historical approach, offering students lots of examples, provoking cognitive conflict and motivation.

SUBGROUP 2

Teaching conceptions and strategies for calculus

Organizer: Marc Rogalski with Marc Legrand [FRA]

Marc Legrand [FRA] proposed a strategy to make students of age 18 work as mathematicians do. The teacher organizes scientific debates about conjectures, mathematical concepts, etc. In this approach formal activities don't come at the end of the teaching process but may be needed from the beginning as tools of precision and reliability. Nicolas Rouche [BEL] advocated a genetic approach with students of age 16. "Mental tools" are constructed to organize a field of phenomena arising from geometry and physics through real problems, similar to those encountered in the history of calculus. The objective is to experience a "theory in construction"; new concepts are built only when needed. In Ricardo Nemirovsky's [USA] conception the roots of calculus are in the basic intuitions of common experience including variation/change. He introduces concepts as dynamic patterns intuitively describing physical change; from there students develop their own concepts. Don O'Shea [USA] sees calculus as a tool for the exploration of rich and complex real phenomena, with intensive use of computers for simulations and approximations. In the Five Colleges "Calculus in Context" Project the main ideas of beginning calculus emerge from contexts in the physical, social, and life sciences.

During the discussion, the subgroup analyzed and compared the specific choices and the conditions for the success of these strategies. Four common opinions emerged:

- It takes a long time to teach and learn calculus.
- Calculus must be linked with the study of real phenomena.
- Calculus must go beyond the learning of "rules and procedures" to the level of "ideas and concepts".
- The training of teachers is a crucial point in changing the teaching of calculus.

Other questions arose: the possibility of introducing a concept of derivative without the limit concept; the connection between limit, derivative, and the concept(s) of infinity; the status of proof; the role of geometry in the introduction of the limit concept.

SUBGROUP 3

Calculus for non-specialists

Organizers: John & Annie Selden [USA]

Joan Hundhausen [USA] saw the main difficulties as retention and transfer. She suggested designing many problems for student practice with transfer, working on modeling, visualization, and real world interpretation of mathematical results. Clifford Smith [ZAF] emphasized the variety of students in his classes and asked how much one can do in a limited time (a 16-week semester). The ensuing discussion centered on content and students' difficulties. Some questions: how to cope with the time pressure? Should one bother to prove theorems? How does one teach problem solving? What computational skills do students really need? Some answers: one can present epsilon-delta definitions in terms of machine tolerances. One can begin with a problem and work towards a technique to solve it. One can encourage students to generate analogous problems in their field of special-isation.

The second day, Sandy Norman [USA] gave examples from research on students' learning. They come to us with limited views and with cognitive obstacles, but they do know many things which make sense from their per-spective. Mary Barnes [AUS] said the main problem is that non-specialists do not see the relevance of the calculus to what they perceive as their interests. She urged a focus on the modeling of real life situations and asked what parts of the calculus should be left out. In the discussion two ways emerged to deal with non-specialist (including business) students: 1) a tra-ditional techniques course, which considers only polynomials and rational functions, and 2) a more qualitative course which includes trigonometric, exponential and logarithmic functions, incorporates graphing and other technology, and emphasizes interpretation of results. But there was no general agreement in favor of either.

SUBGROUP 4

Technology in the teaching of the calculus

Organizer: David Tall [GBR]

William Davis [USA] spoke of his experience using *Mathematica*, showing examples of students' work in problem solving. Even weak students managed to achieve *some* success. Joe Wimbish [USA] drew on his experi-ences with liberal arts students using *Derive* and *Maple*. Students using the computer seemed to enjoy engaging in mathematical argument, realizing that there is more to mathematics than just "getting the right formula". On the debit side, they also believe that using computers is somehow "cheating". Paul Roder [GBR] reported how specially designed software could be used in class discussion. He showed how visual ideas of local straightness could be introduced prior to more formal ideas. Peter Jones [AUS] spoke of using a graphic calculator, the lecturer leading discussion and the students using it for exploration, learning, and in examinations, but its use was less than optimal. Only a small percentage of students could relate information in different representations: algebraic, numerical, graphical.

In discussion the initial focus was on differences in success. Wimbish remarked that the difficulties reported by Jones were also found in his course when individuals were examined, but conflicts were considerably fewer when students were assessed in groups. Some students have a strong algebraic bias and this affects their ability or willingness to integrate different representations. The new technology must be used in a way which is appropriate for a technology-rich society. Mathematicians may be less willing to change than students are. It was suggested that the graphical approach is *qualitative*, leading to conceptual insight; the numerical is *quantitative*, giving accurate computations where required; and the symbolic is *manipulative*, allowing concepts to be manipulated at a higher theoretical level. Different roles played by representations may be related to different abilities.

SUBGROUP 5

Renovation in the curriculum of calculus courses

Organizer: Ted Eisenberg [ISR]

John Mack [AUS] reported about innovations in Australia and some neighbouring countries (Singapore, Indonesia, New Zealand). His impression is that there have not been significant recent changes in the methods of teaching, learning, or assessing calculus except in New Zealand. Keith Schwingendorff [USA] listed 11 innovations in the USA stimulated by grants from the National Science Foundation. He focussed in detail on the Purdue Calculus Reform Project based on theoretical groundwork by Ed Dubinsky. Charlene Beckmann [USA] stated that in spite of a profusion of reform activity, research focusing on student understanding is regrettably sparse. She gave details of projects at Oregon State University and Grand Valley State University which include a research component to assess validity. These studies provide evidence to support the value of graphing calculators. Elisabeth Busser [FRA] reported about successive reforms in the calculus curriculum at the secondary level in France from 1980 on, based on the principles: focus on fundamental problems and methods in the calculus, restricted use of formalization in favor of an interaction between algebraic, numerical, and graphical approaches.

In discussion it became clear that "solving the calculus curriculum problem" is a major concern worldwide. But different countries take differents routes. The USA is very technology-minded, more so than other countries. Two philosophies of change seem to exist. One is radical and says: "throw out the entire program and rebuild it from scratch". The other takes advantage of the new technology without discarding the existing programs, and restructures the teaching according to epistemological, cognitive, and technological considerations.

The venue of the Congress: the campus of Université Laval

Le campus de l'Université Laval, lieu du congrès

Plenary session in the covered stadium

Séance plénière au stade couvert

The daily «happy hour» near the big tent

Le « 5 à 7 » quotidien près de la grande tente

Poster presentations

Communications brèves par affiches

Panel presentation during group work

Table ronde dans le cadre de travaux de groupe

Plenty of activity during a workshop
Un atelier très animé

Mathematical activities for young and older people
Activités mathématiques pour jeunes et moins jeunes

Project presentations

Présentation de projets

Two French exhibitions

Deux expositions françaises

Honorary degree conferred on Professor Pollak by Université
Laval. From left to right: Michel Gervais, Rector; Henry
Pollak, recipient; Claude Gaulin, chair of the Local Organizing
Committee for ICME-7

*Doctorat honorifique
décerné au pro-
fesseur Pollak par
l'Université Laval.
De gauche à droite :
Michel Gervais,
recteur ; Henry
Pollak, récipien-
daire ; Claude
Gaulin, président du
Comité d'organisa-
tion locale d'ICME-7*

*Doctorat honorifique
décerné au professeur
Kahane par l'Université
Laval. De gauche à
droite : Michel Gervais,
recteur ; Jean-Pierre
Kahane, récipiendaire ;
Bernard R. Hodgson,
président du Comité
national d'ICME-7*

Honorary degree conferred on Professor Kahane by Université
Laval. From left to right: Michel Gervais, Rector; Jean-Pierre
Kahane, recipient; Bernard R. Hodgson, chair of the National
Committee for ICME-7

Le savoir-compter

A special exhibition about
mathematics in primary
schools in Québec in the
19th century

*Exposition spéciale sur les
mathématiques à l'école
primaire au Québec au
XIXᵉ siècle*

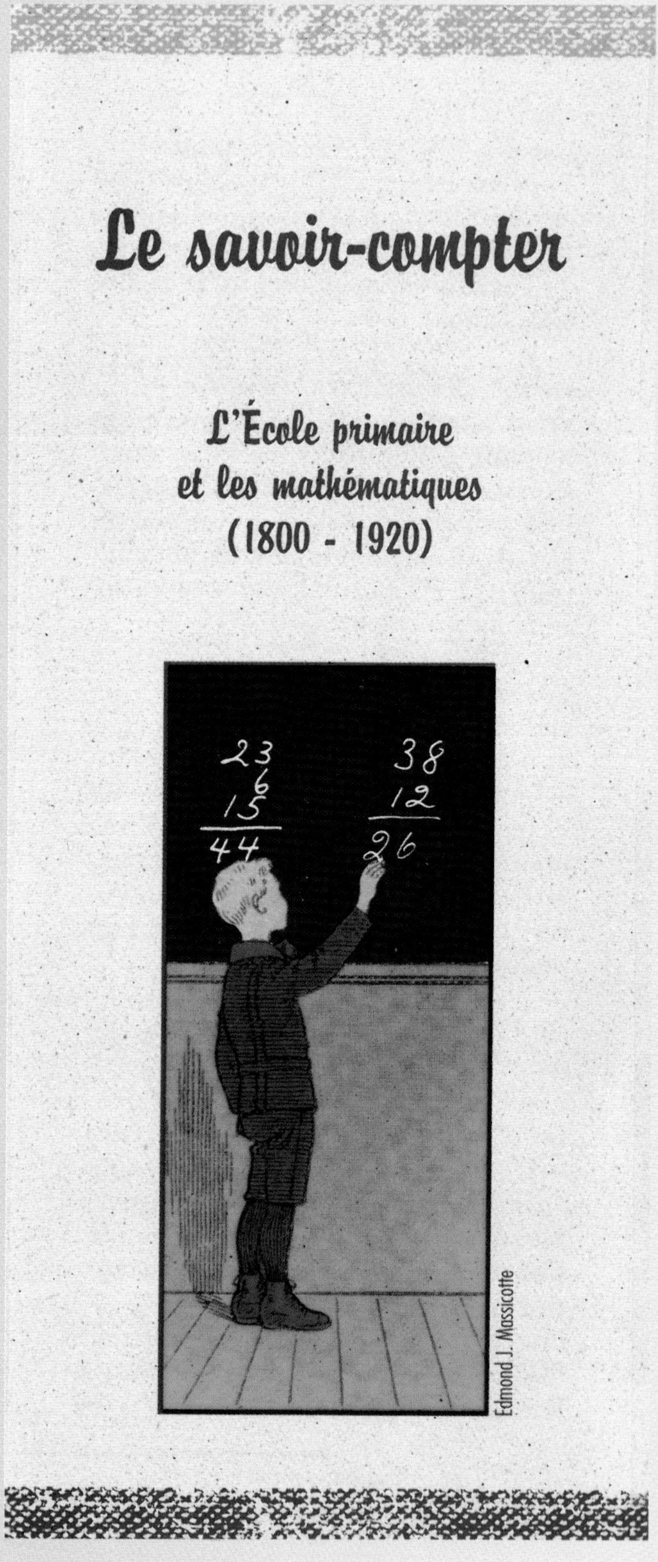

L'École primaire
et les mathématiques
(1800 - 1920)

Edmond J. Massicotte

Opening of the
cultural evening
*Ouverture de la
soirée culturelle*

The «Math Trail» in Old Québec:
mathematics from the environment

*Le « sentier mathématique »
dans le Vieux-Québec : à la
découverte des mathématiques
dans l'environnement*

The 5 km run/walk
*La course/marche
de 5 km*

David H. Wheeler, chair of the
International Program Committee,
receives congratulations from
Miguel de Guzmán, president of
ICMI; on his left: Mogens Niss,
secretary of ICMI

*David H. Wheeler, président
du Comité international du
programme, reçoit les félicitations
de Miguel de Guzmán, président
de la CIEM ; à sa gauche : Mogens
Niss, secrétaire de la CIEM*

Gonzalo Sánchez, president of the Spanish Federation of Mathematics
Teachers Associations, invites all participants to attend ICME-8
in Sevilla in July 1996

Gonzalo Sánchez, président de la Fédération espagnole des associations de
professeurs de mathématiques, convie tous les participants et participantes
au congrès ICME-8, à Séville, en juillet 1996

SYNTHESIS AND FINAL REPORT

Tommy Dreyfus [ISR]

Probably the most striking novel idea is that learning calculus should be seen as a very long term process rather than as a sequence of one to four courses taken over a two-year period. This process could be, somewhat artificially, split into three phases: intuitive, pragmatic and formal. The intuitive one starts as early as elementary school, stresses notions related to change and is informal in nature, with concepts being in formation rather than completely clarified. The pragmatic one is appropriate for high school, could (but need not) be based on real world applications and modeling, and is characterized by a "natural mode of functioning", where truth and falsity are established mainly on the basis of positive and negative examples. The formal phase introduces rigor and proof into calculus. The transitions between these phases can be expected to present serious obstacles to the student, e.g. in the transition from the pragmatic to the formal phase the status of a "true statement" changes radically.

Cooperative learning is ubiquitously stressed. At all levels, from elementary school to university courses in analysis, the value of debate between students is stressed.

Questions have been raised but not answered. Should (and can?) ideas be learned before, at the same time, or after the appropriate symbol manipulation? To what extent is manipulation still necessary?

Content is another central issue, with about as many participants favoring the traditional content as there are advocating a thorough revision. Several projects based on non-traditional methods and/or content report encouraging success with weak students. Questions concerning the evaluation of student achievement in non-traditional settings (group work, computer work, visual work) have been raised repeatedly but essentially left unanswered. Finally, everybody agrees that change in teachers is crucial but that, on the whole, calculus teachers, mainly professional research mathematicians, are conservative and resistant to changing their ways and the content of their instruction.

NOTE

A 121-page report of Working Group 3 proceedings has been compiled and sent to the participants. Further copies can be obtained from: Gontran Ervynk, K.U. Leuven Campus Kortryk (KULAK), 8500 Kortryk, Belgium, Fax: (32) 56 22 89 20, E-mail: fzaae01@blekul11.bitnet

Working Group 4 / *Groupe de travail 4*

THEORIES OF LEARNING MATHEMATICS

THÉORIES D'APPRENTISSAGE
DES MATHÉMATIQUES

Chief Organizer / *Responsable en chef* : Pearla Nesher [ISR]
Local Organizer / *Responsable local* : Douglas Owens [CAN]
Advisory team members / *Consultants* : Nicolas Balacheff [FRA],
Erik de Corte [BEL], Leslie P. Steffe [USA], Hans-Georg Steiner [DEU]

More than 200 people participated in the work of the group in the four sessions devoted to working groups. It was, therefore, necessary to split into three subgroups working in parallel. The plenary session met on the fourth session, to synthesize the group's work of the previous three sessions. Each subgroup was supposed to concentrate on the contribution of specific theories to the learning of mathematics, and their relation to the other theories. In fact, each subgroup dealt with similar theories, trying to synthesize the various approaches expressed in the subgroup. We will present, first, the subgroups' work as reported by the subgroups' organizers, and then proceed to the plenary session.

SUBGROUP 1

Sociological and anthropological perspectives
on mathematics learning

Organizer: Paul Cobb [USA]

During the first subgroup session, Jorg Voigt [DEU] and Geoffrey Saxe [USA] presented plenary papers to lay the groundwork for subsequent discussion. Voigt argued for the relevance of a symbolic interactionist perspective on social interactions during mathematics instruction. Saxe outlined a framework for analyzing emerging goals that takes account of cultural, social, and cognitive processes. Prepared reactions by John Richards [USA], Analúcia Schliemann [BRA], and Erna Yackel [USA] served to clarify issues raised by the subgroup plenary speakers.

During the second and third sessions, the subgroup met in two small groups to consider the relationships between: 1) Classroom social processes and mathematical cognition (presentations made by Ellice Forman [USA] and Bert van Oers [NLD]), and 2) Cultural practices and mathematical cognition (presentations made by Kathryn Crawford [AUS] and James Stigler [USA]). The remaining time in the second and third sessions was given over to panel discussion.

Emerging issues

- It became apparent that researchers working within different theoretical perspectives were using the same terms in different ways. These terms include activity, activity setting, context, task, goal, meaning, negotiation, internalize, and learning. In general, researchers working within the Vygotskian Activity Theory and socio-linguistic traditions question whether there is anything inside individuals that develops and instead typically focus on the influence of participation in social and cultural practices in mathematical learning. In contrast to these attempts to develop socio-cultural theories of learning, for researchers who take a constructivist perspective, cognition is in the head of the individual rather than in participating in cultural practices.

- A variety of definitions of learning were proposed that reflect these different theoretical positions. For example:

  a) Increasing participation in, integration into, or inculcation into a community of practice.

  b) Qualitative change in actions.

  c) Cognitive reorganization or developmental change in cognitive structures.

- There were similar differences in the way that mathematical language was characterized. From one perspective, mathematical signs and symbols are carriers of meaning that students appropriate. From another perspective, they express and communicate their mathematical thinking.

- One issue of immediate concern is the relevance of the various perspectives for mathematics education. The issue is the pragmatic one of what the different perspectives can offer as we clarify goals and develop explanations.

- The theoretical differences also indicate that it is important for researchers to clarify the basis on which they infer students' goals, interpretations, etc.

- Despite these differences, there was general agreement that it is important to consider the way in which the relationship between individual and social or cultural processes is both constraining and enabling. Constraints come to the fore when we focus on the conflict between students' cultural background and classroom mathematical practices. The enabling aspect is apparent when we attempt to account for the superior mathematical performance of, say, Japanese students over American students by referring to aspects of culture.

- The importance of analyzing the processes by which mathematical meanings are negotiated in the classroom was also generally accepted. These analyses make it possible to distinguish between intended tasks and instructional activities, those that are realized in the classroom.

- There was some disagreement on the usefulness of the classic macro/micro distinction. For example, some researchers stress the influence of general cultural beliefs and values on mathematical learning. Others contrast what goes on inside the classroom with what goes on outside, and argue that students are necessarily in a bi-cultural situation.

- The issue of what teachers should know about social and cultural issues was considered. For example, it seems important that teachers anticipate possible conflicts between their expectations and assumptions and those that reflect students' culturally diverse backgrounds. Further, it would be helpful if teachers develop an awareness of interactional processes that subvert their best intentions.

SUBGROUP 2

The contribution of constructivism to the learning of mathematics

Organizer: Gerald Goldin [USA]

The focus on the first day was on the philosophical perspectives offered by constructivism in several varieties on mathematics, mathematical learning and teaching, and the theory of mathematical education. There were three formal presentations:

- Ernst von Glaserfeld [USA] provided an overview of radical constructivist epistemology, stressing the theme that the experimental world is irrevocably subjective; that experimental reality is necessarily constructed; and that ulterior reality is inherently unknowable, and, it makes no sense to speak on "representation" of something inaccessible. To constructivists mathematics is seen as a consequence of human constructivism and agreements, not as external certainty.

- Dagmar Neuman [SWE] presented joint work by Ference Marton [SWE] and herself, describing how the empirical methods phenomenography lead to some differences with constructivism in the context of children using "double counting" strategies in early arithmetic.

- Paul Ernest [GBR] discussed and compared aspects of information processing theory, trivial constructivism (von Glaserfeld's term), radical constructivism, and social constructivism; he contrasted "absolutist" and "fallibilist" nature of mathematics.

The formal presentations followed a lively discussion in which the characterization of "trivial constructivism" was vigorously challenged, alternate interpretations of Piaget, Polanyi, and others were raised, and the student-centered focus of teachers (an old idea) was seen as central to the educational implications of constructivism.

The second day offered a series of presentations from the perspective of cognitive theory that takes learning as a constructive process.

- Nicolas Herscovics [CAN] addressed the interface between constructivism, cognition, and developmental theory, describing several models of understanding that can describe children's developing concepts of early arithmetic.

- George Booker [AUS] presented the construction of mathematical conventions, distinguishing inculcation from acculturation, and leading into developing cognitive representations in the content of the learning of fractions.

- James Kaput [USA] presented joint work by Gerald Goldin [USA] and himself, which was a joint perspective on the idea of representation in learning and doing mathematics; then,

- Gerald Goldin offered a synthesis of the three presentations. The emphasis was on major contrasts with some of the first day's perspectives: first, that the notion of "representation" should not be rejected, but on the contrary is a fundamental and powerful construct; second, that internal and external representations should both be admitted into the theory. It was argued that just as behaviorism erred in rejecting internal constructs, radical constructivism errs in rejecting external constructs, and that an adequate theory of mathematics education should admit both. Again a lively discussion was aroused in which (among other points) the difference between "scheme" and "schema" was stressed, interaction between children was discussed, and the external/internal distinction was debated.

On the third day, the discussion continued:

- Michael Otte [DEU] contrasted radical constructivism and radical empiricism, focusing on what turns a mental event into knowledge.

- Carolyn Maher [USA] presented joint work with Robert Davis and Alice Alston [USA]. Her presentation involved a short videotape of four children discussing a combinational problem, trying to convince each other of various strategies.

- Jere Confrey [USA] provided an overview of several key issues in constructivism, including: the "voice" of the child and the perspective of theory, she also renewed the critique of the concept of representation. Finally,

- Claude Janvier [CAN] drew implications for teacher education and stressed that constructivism does not "tell us what to do" and that constructive learning must occur independently of instruction. Considerable discussion followed, as to how strongly constructivist theory actually has implications for teaching, and to what extent the implications might (also) go in the opposite direction (implications of classroom practice for theory).

SUBGROUP 3

Cognitive science theories and their contribution to the learning of mathematics

Organizer: Brian Greer [GBR]

Most of the discussion of the subgroup may be subsumed under the general theme of the need to develop theories of mathematical cognition in general, and of particular aspects such as memory, imagery, and conceptualization. Clearly, such theories cannot be developed independently of conceptions of mathematics, mathematics education, the nature of learning, and the nature of teaching. A broad consensus among mathematics educators nowadays characterizes mathematics as a human activity, inseparable from human values, judgements, and goals, and including the solving of practical problems, but also the pleasures of intellectual exploration. A major goal of mathematical education is that children should be able to solve nonroutine problems – to become adaptive rather than merely routine experts, in Hatano's phrase.

Consistent with these conceptions, all the contributors emphasized the richness and complexity of mathematical thinking in comparison to the externally expressed products of such thinking. Joost Klep [NLD], for example, drew a sharp distinction between thinking as having a train of thought (non-linear), and lines of argument as expressed. Another recurrent theme was the conventional suppression of real-life considerations within the context of school mathematics, as in the example cited by Robert Davis of the student who cut a balloon in half in order to share five balloons between two people. Among the influential psychological theories of the recent past, Piagetian theory continues to be a major source of inspiration, as seen in Gérard Vergnaud's [FRA] theory of conceptual fields and Pat Thompson's [USA] ideas on imagery. Giyoo Hatano [JPN] argued that general cognitive theories of the acquisition of knowledge systems are potentially relevant (recognizing that knowledge acquisition involves restructuring, that the process of knowledge acquisition is subject to both cognitive and cultural constraints, that knowledge is usually domain-specific, and that knowledge acquisition is structured in context).

If information-processing theories are to be elaborated to encompass the richer conception of mathematical cognition, a necessary step will be the rejection of what Cobb has called "psychological formalism", and the acceptance that most of our reasonings are not algorithmic. Robert Davis [USA] argued for computers as a source of useful metaphors (but not for the simulation of cognitive processes).Vergnaud's theory of conceptual fields reflects the long-term nature of conceptualization within coherent domains in mathematics. The most obvious example concerns number. The elaboration of number from the natural numbers to $e^{i\pi} + 1 = 0$ corresponds to most of the course of civilization. David Carraher [BRA] pointed out that 6-year-olds can perform certain perceptually-based proportional reasoning tasks whereas 14-years-olds typically have difficulty with numerical propositional reasoning. A pedagogical strategy is the sowing of seeds for later development as early as possible.

The extension of schemes to wider and wider domains involves both continuity and discontinuity; the necessary conceptual restructuring often constitutes a cognitive obstacle for students. The long development within the individual has parallels in historical development; consequently, researchers are increasingly turning to analysis of the historical record. Thus, Carraher reported an approach to introducing rational numbers based on the Euclidean conceptualization of proportion. Another fundamental theme was the growth of knowledge in actions (both bodily and imaginative) and the role of reflective abstraction. Any contemporary theory of cognition needs to take account of the new repertoire of actions supportable by computer software. Moreover, software can often allow much more direct representations of mental operations, giving opportunity for the child to "follow its own train of thought" (Klep), to experience a "dialectic between intention, action, and expression" (P. Thompson).

From the discussion, therefore, emerged a rich conception of mathematical cognition embedded in human practices and correspondingly rich descriptions of thinking processes. And Greer concluded: "There is supposed to have been a cognitive revolution starting in 1956. I would like to suggest that the real cognitive revolution is now under way."

THE PLENARY SESSION

First, all participants of the working groups heard short reports by the subgroups' organizers that, in essence, were the above reports. The plenary speakers then attempted to synthesize the various ideas expressed in the three days' work.

- Pearla Nesher [ISR] in opening the session raised the question: is such a synthesis possible? For example, do very same terms really mean the same in various theoretical frameworks? She quoted different definitions for "scheme" taken from radical constructivists, constructivists, and information processing theorists to demonstrate her point.

- Alan Schoenfeld's [USA] main focus was on the creation of an overarching frame to include the various topics discussed in the subgroups. He stressed that human behaviour is goal-driven; attempts to understand people's mathematical learning must focus on why they do what they do (their goals), what they do (their behaviour), and their understandings of the world around them (their conceptions). Unification across the subgroups comes when one realizes that all of these have individual and social dimensions: individuals have goals, for example, but the way those goals are shaped depends on both one's local environment and the culture within which one lives. Examining all these factors: (goals, behaviour, conceptions) × (individual, local environment, culture), is necessary for a full view of learning.

- Les Steffe [USA] said that rather than thinking of learning theories as hypothetical deductive systems that are applied to mathematics learning in that way, we should be thinking about formulating models of mathematics learning which contain elements that are not anticipated *a priori*. The theoretician can do no better than to become a close listener, not only to learn what the mathematics of children might be like, but also how to bring it forth, to sustain it, and to modify it. A model of mathematics learning, then, should be about a teacher's interactive mathematical communication with children. The teacher (or theoretician) must "step outside" her actual interactions with children and become what Maturana has called a superobserver. Research on mathematics learning is not different from living; rather it is a part of living and its goal is to improve the quality of life in mathematics classrooms.

• Willibald Dörfler [AUT] raised in his presentation the question of the usefulness of theoretical terms like mental objects, mental entities, cognitive constructions, representations, and others. Is it a new form of psychological Platonism? He then presented his doubts about the ecological validity of this approach to explain mathematical thinking. Based on his subjective introspection, he claimed that he could not trace something like a mental object. Moreover, he elaborated on several examples, starting with large natural numbers, and ending with spaces of functions and other advanced examples, and presented arguments against the possibility of having images or mental representations of such objects. Finally, he suggested an approach that considers mathematics education as a process of socialization which should lead to appropriate systems of beliefs, attitudes, and convictions of which students and teachers should become conscious and aware. Within such a mathematical socialization the notions of metaphoric projection, image thinking, and image schemata will be key terms as mechanisms for creating mathematical understanding.

Working Group 5 / *Groupe de travail 5*

IMPROVING STUDENTS' ATTITUDES AND MOTIVATION

L'AMÉLIORATION DES ATTITUDES ET DE LA MOTIVATION DES ÉLÈVES

Chief Organizer / *Responsable en chef* : Gilah C. Leder [AUS]
Local Organizer / *Responsable local* : Erika Kündiger [CAN]
Advisory team members / *Consultants* : Laurie Hart [USA],
Jacques Nimier [FRA], Erkki Pehkonen [FIN], Eduard Poznjiak [RUS]

The main aim of the working group was to offer a forum for discussing the following:

- Theoretical frameworks for the development and improvement of students' attitudes and motivation.

- Empirical studies which focus on students' attitudes and motivation.

- Teaching ideas and strategies which have proved successful in the mathematics classroom.

Participants met together for the first and part of the final session, and split into two groups for the remainder of the time. This structure maximized opportunities for questions and discussion. One group had a strong focus on teaching ideas, the other concentrated more on experimental, research, and theoretical issues. A brief synopsis of the main points made in each of the presentations follows.

SESSION 1

The longer students have been exposed to school mathematics, the less favourable become their attitudes and motivation to the subject, according to Erika Kündiger [CAN]. If we accept that the motive to achieve can be learned then teachers can make a difference by teaching so that students can learn, showing the relevance to students of long and short term projects, and making work interesting. Specific strategies for motivating students are described by contributors to later sessions. Erkki Pehkonen

[FIN] began his presentation by giving examples of different definitions of attitude. His preferred model included feelings, beliefs, and behaviours. His assertion that changes in beliefs and feelings are prerequisites for changes in behaviour was strongly challenged during question time. Measurement of attitudes was the topic addressed by Gilah Leder [AUS]. Approaches used in previous research – Thurstone, Likert, and semantic differential scales, inventories and checklists, preference rankings, projective techniques, enrollment data, clinical and physiological measures, classroom observations, and interviews – were described. Data from a recent study revealed that students' responses on different self-report measures were generally consistent with each other and with data obtained through classroom observations.

SESSION 2 (A)

Greisy Winicki [ISR] argued that using mathematical problems in an historical setting is an excellent way of introducing some history of mathematics into the classroom, arouses students' curiosity for learning mathematics and enriches their construction of mathematical concepts. Drawing on data gathered from grade 8 and grade 9 students she provided experimental support for these assertions. The relationship between conceptions of school mathematics and social strata was discussed by Bernard Charlot [FRA]. The sample comprised students (females and males), aged 11-15, of different socio-economic backgrounds. Using written and interview data, three main themes were traced: students' perceptions of the usefulness of mathematics, students' beliefs about the importance of mathematics, and the impact of the teacher in shaping students' attitudes to mathematics. A study with the multiple aims of validating an attitudes to fractions instrument, surveying attitudes towards fractions at the end of compulsory schooling, and assessing whether certain curriculum innovations improved students' attitudes was reported by Joaquin Giménez [ESP]. Different dimensions of attitudes towards fractions were identified. Background variables such as father's and mother's level of education and location of the home – rural or urban – affected students' attitudes. The curriculum changes introduced seemed to have a positive affect on students' attitudes. An instrument devised to assess the attitudes and beliefs of students towards various dimensions of mathematics was described by Charlene Morrow [USA]. Characteristics both of the Summer Math program being monitored and of the students who had attended in past years were reported. This information allowed a more meaningful interpretation of the attitudinal changes obtained through participation in the program.

SESSION 2 (B)

Using problems, open-ended where possible, to motivate students in mathematics was the theme of Alexander Soifer's [USA] presentation. As an example he cited a problem posed four decades ago by an 18-year-old: What is the smallest number of colors with which we can color the plane in such a way that no color contains a monochromatic segment of length 1? Materials that allow students to experience the "joy of creation, depth and beauty of ideas, flight of fantasy, and unexpected elegance of reasoning, which are so characteristic of mathematics" should be made more readily accessible. Diana Sharville [GBR] described the assessment materials and strategies (practical, oral, aural, and written) used in the SMP Graduated Assessment Scheme, aimed at students in the lower 40% of the ability range. Assessment materials are set by an examination board. Marking, however, is done by accredited teachers at the students' school. This approach enables immediate feedback to be given to students. Increased motivation and achievement, as well as fewer behavioural problems, are indicators of the scheme's success. A course devised to improve the attitudes to mathematics of a group of preservice teachers was reported by Maria de Lurdes Serrazina [PRT]. By encouraging students to work collaboratively, to generate and substantiate their solutions to problems, to become familiar and comfortable with different material – calculators, attribute blocks, geoboards, polyhedrons, for example – students' views of mathematics became more favourable. When asked to reflect on the mathematics course they had just completed, students commented particularly on its emphasis on teaching for understanding rather than encouraging rote learning as they had experienced in their earlier schooling. Practical ways of motivating students, "a neglected art", were presented by Alfred Posamentier [USA]. Areas covered included presenting a challenge, telling a pertinent story, arousing students' curiosity, ways of identifying students' motivation, assessing and influencing the classroom atmosphere, decorating the classroom, and ways of overcoming students' and teachers' mathematics anxiety.

SESSION 3 (A)

Barry Onslow [CAN] argued that parents' as well as students' attitudes must be addressed if innovative programs are to be successful. By using case studies of two mothers involved in a Family Math program in Ontario, Canada, he illustrated ways in which the program changed their beliefs about and attitudes to mathematics. More generally, positive outcomes included parents making mathematics kits for the library, asking for more sessions, and a better appreciation by parents of strategies used by teachers in their classrooms. Children of parents unwilling to attend the program are likely to be increasingly disadvantaged. The effect of question context on students' motivation in mathematics was examined by Prue Purser [NZL]. Using a sample of grade 10 students, preferences for context (real life v. abstract) and area of mathematics (problem solving, geometry and graphs) were explored. Students' assessment of their mathematics ability and liking of mathematics were also obtained. Gender differences in confidence about doing well in mathematics, particularly on problems set in an unfamiliar context, were noted.

Concern about discipline problems in mathematics classes prompted the studies into students' achievement in and attitudes towards mathematics reported by Ngai Ying Wong [HKG]. Interest in mathematics, perceived difficulty of mathematics, self-concept, academic self-concept and attitudes towards mathematics were found to be strong predictors of students' success. Parents' educational background and time spent by students doing homework were not. Although there were no gender differences in achievement, males scored more positively than females on a number of affective variables.

SESSION 3 (B)

Ways of addressing math anxiety were described by Louise Lafortune [CAN]. Helpful steps include asking students to think about their reactions in situations that make them anxious, examining the reasons for *math* anxiety, considering ways of improving the classroom atmosphere through introducing appropriate activities such as relaxing before new mathematics work is begun, using math warm-ups, demystifying mathematics and alleviating test anxiety by allowing students to redo their tests. The importance of using real-life problems to motivate at-risk students in particular was the theme of the presentation given by A.V. Johnson II [USA]. Examples found to be successful included working out the tax to be paid on money earned in an actual part-time job and deciding on the best vs the cheapest way to travel. It has been estimated that we learn 10% of what we read, 20% of what we hear, 30% of what we see, 50% of what we see and hear, 70% of what we discuss with others, 80% of what we experience personally, and 95% of what we teach others. These approximations suggest what strategies we should adopt in the classroom to maximise student learning. Practical ways of motivating students by helping them to love and understand mathematics were described by John Egsgard [CAN]. He stressed the importance of helping students to be successful by introducing students to simple concepts and gradually building on these. He also advocated using frequent tests, real-life situations where possible, displaying student work in the classroom, and making challenging mathematics posters, puzzles and games readily accessible to students.

SESSION 4 (A)

L. Taylor [USA] used a Vygotskian framework for her model of mathematical attitude development. Within it, attitude is defined as a multicultural construct that involves an interaction between thinking, feeling, and acting. She argued that in this broad definition affect is only one part of attitude. Case study data supported her assertion that family, socialisation, schooling experiences, and relationships with mentors are also important determinants of attitudes. In her presentation Josette Adda [FRA] contrasted "typical" attitudes of students with those of mathematicians. For example, students often aim for success in a test, work within severe time constraints, work on problems with known answers, hide their faults, and often rely on the teacher rather than their own resources. Mathematicians long for discovery, know that worthwhile work often requires patience, are happy to work in an atmosphere of suspense, exploit and learn from their mistakes, and rely on their own judgement. Current schooling and curriculum practices do not encourage students to engage in scientific discovery and inquiry.

SESSION 4 (B)

A protocol for gathering mathematical metaphors was given by Dorothy Buerk [USA]. The questions and prompts used (e.g., "pretend that you have to describe mathematics to someone. List all the words or phrases you can think of that you could use", "write a paragraph beginning: For me math is most like a(n) ... ") have been most successful in getting 16-18 year old students to think and write about their feelings towards mathematics in a classroom setting. Maryvonne Hallez [FRA] described an interdisciplinary program, linking history, art, physics, natural sciences, French, music and mathematics, devised for students aged 11 and 12. Practical exercises, historical and scientific references from different countries, art books, and field trips are examples of methods used to encourage different worthwhile and motivational mathematical activities. Devising activities that will challenge all, yet not frustrate any student in a heterogeneous class was the topic addressed by Shmuel Avital [ISR]. The following task, set for students in grade 3, conveys the flavour of this session. "Make a table in which you classify the integers by the number of times they appear in the multiplication table. Try to use tables that go up to 15 × 15." "Explore what property is common to all integers in a particular class."

SUMMARY

Collectively, the presentations, questions, comments and discussions provided a variety of practical ideas for improving students' attitudes and motivation in mathematics. The importance of allowing students to experience activities common for mathematicians (e.g. ill-defined problems,

problems which cannot be solved quickly, problems which have more than one answer) was emphasised. The important role played by the teacher in shaping the students' learning environment was stressed. The influence of parents on students' attitudes and beliefs about mathematics was another common theme. The similarities of problems faced by teachers in different countries and different educational settings were particularly striking. Less consensus was found, however, about the most effective way of measuring attitudes and motivation realistically in a classroom setting. Maximising opportunities for realistic dialogue between researchers and practitioners, and between those in different countries grappling with similar concerns, were seen as high priorities.

NOTE

The papers presented in this working group by Lyn Taylor, Barry Onslow and Ngai-ying Wong have been published in a special issue, edited by G. Leder, of *Mathematics Education Research Journal, 4*(3), 1992, a publication of the Mathematics Education Research Group of Australia.

Working Group 6 / *Groupe de travail 6*

PRESERVICE AND INSERVICE
TEACHER EDUCATION

FORMATION INITIALE ET PERFECTIONNEMENT
DES ENSEIGNANTS ET ENSEIGNANTES

Chief Organizer / *Responsable en chef* : John Dossey [USA]
Local Organizer / *Responsable local* : Lars Jansson [CAN]
Advisory team members / *Consultants* : Claude Comiti [FRA], Graham
Jones [AUS], V. G. Kulkarni [IND]

Working Group 6 met over a four-day period with opening and closing days devoted to plenary sessions and other days devoted to 12 discussion subgroups focusing on distinct aspects of teacher education. Over 300 Congress attendees participated in some portion of the working group.

The opening plenary session featured Mary Lindquist [USA]. She spoke about the radical changes in teaching and teacher education needed to implement the National Council of Teachers of Mathematics *Curriculum, evaluation, and teaching standards*. These changes require teachers to take leadership roles for what is taught in the schools and to change the way in which that mathematics is taught. Part of this change process will require the construction of support networks of administrators, parents, and local business and professional groups. Both teachers and those in support roles must come to see that what students learn is fundamentally connected with how they learn it. In a like manner, beliefs concerning the nature of mathematics must change to include the view that all students (no matter what race, gender, or social class) can, and must, learn mathematics. If one considers the life of a teacher, 2500 days of that life are spent as a school student, 750 in an undergraduate preservice teacher education program, and as much as 5500 days teaching in a school classroom. Real change cannot be accomplished by university training. Effective reform must involve a broad systemic change involving the school curriculum, preservice education, seeing that equity is reflected in the teaching population, increasing the overall support for mathematics education in the public arena, increasing a life-long professional development programs, and increasing the esteem of teacher educators in institutions of higher education.

DISCUSSION SECTIONS

Days 2 and 3 of the working group were devoted to the work of twelve separate discussion/reporting groups. The topics ranged from the nature of content and methods courses, to gender/belief issues in teacher education, to integrating curriculum, technology, and change itself in teacher education programs. These sessions saw the presentation of over 50 papers reflecting research, theoretical models, and current program efforts. Throughout these sessions several themes consistently rose to the surface. Central to these discussions was the sense that the problem of changing teaching practice is cyclical. Students experience "direct" instruction in school. Preservice programs try to institute more open approaches to teaching and learning. However, when novice teachers return to school settings in clinical and beginning teaching, they enter situations that tend to reward "direct" instruction. Teacher education and teaching practice in schools must move forward together in a symbiotic fashion if change is to be initiated and achieved in practice.

Reform in teacher education programs must address the *preparation* of teachers for change, the *involvement* of teachers in the change process, *support* for teachers as they cope with the problems inherent in change, *consolidation* of new ideas into improved programs, and *extension* of both teacher skills and program features as the change takes hold. Over and over again, teacher participants talked of the need for understanding and support by co-workers, parents, and the business/professional community. Models for the development of such support sessions were shared based on programs in the United Kingdom, Israel, and the United States. Central to discussions was the need for a model for how curriculum reform should be instituted in a K-12 school system. It was not clear whether change should bubble up from the bottom, filter down from the top, or emerge across the full continuum. However, there was solid agreement that the change process should involve teachers at all levels of experience both to inform by tradition and to share new ideas from teacher education programs.

Another area of concern dealt with the structuring of clinical experiences in teacher education. While some were involved in school-based teacher education programs, they felt that such programs have a natural built-in conservatism. They also raised questions about how teachers should be selected as mentors, how the activities in the school might be better coordinated with the content program on the university campus, and how to deal with issues involving control and decision making in the school mathematics program.

University-based programs have analogous problems. How can the program be better articulated with programs in schools? In particular, how can school-based observations be planned to focus on a particular activity when the campus-based educator has little control over the school program, and, in fact, many different schools may be involved in the clinical experiences. How can campus-based discussions be better articulated with the current activities of the school classroom? What is the value of a cohort group of students that moves through a teacher education program together? On this issue there was concern about an unnatural leveling that occurs in a cohort group, while at the same time such groups might bring about more discussion and support during the years of education and teaching.

Another universal problem was the inability to assist novice teachers to become solid teachers of problem solving. Until teachers begin to see themselves as problem solvers, there is probably little hope that they will, in turn, see their students as potential problem solvers and feel that they have the confidence to guide their students in more open and authentic problem solving situations in the classroom. Questions arose about the roles that teachers' own school experiences, textbooks, classroom contexts, school organization, and other features play in the development of student problem solving skills.

Several noted concerns about the development of preservice teachers' ability to institute cooperative learning in their classrooms, to model and initiate journal writings as a mode of self-reflection among their students, and to design and implement active investigations to connect the classroom study of mathematics with real world uses of the same mathematics. How can preservice programs both provide students with an adequate base in these methods, and assure that these students also have a solid basis in mathematics, the school mathematics curriculum, and their interaction in the school classroom? One commonly held view was that many of these problems' solutions are bound up in the beliefs and attitudes of preservice and inservice teachers. In particular, their views of the nature of mathematics and how it is "best" taught. The identification of and self-reflection on a teacher's beliefs ought be a central feature of teacher education programs in mathematics. It is only through activities promoting such introspection that we can help teachers come to reach their potential and to help their students do the same. Activities involving responding to vignettes of classroom teaching, discussing the contents of video clips of classroom teaching, writing journal entries describing belief-based issues in teaching, and discussing gender, ethnicity, and age-based views in open discussion are ways of transcending beliefs and bringing improvement to both teaching and the curriculum. Specific materials that support these activities need to be developed for mathematics educators working with teachers of all levels.

One discussion group focused on the development of teachers' abilities to function in multicultural settings. The issues discussed here included: who decides what is the best approach for all students, how do mathematics educators recruit qualified and interested candidates for multicultural settings, how can political hurdles be circumvented in order to bring good mathematics to all students, and how can we be assured that all teachers and students can have equal access to instruction, materials, and opportunities? While many possible solutions to microproblems were discussed, the macroproblem of dealing with multicultural issues looms large and must be addressed at both the preservice and inservice levels.

Assessment, while the direct topic of one discussion group, was an issue in almost all of the groups. The assessment discussion group looked at ways in which alternative assessments and supportive instructional programs might be incorporated into the teaching of preservice elementary teachers. A program, at Indiana University, allows not only for the preservice teachers to experience the various assessment techniques, it also allows the graduate students in mathematics education teaching the course to obtain first-hand experience in using authentic assessment methods in their own teaching. Initial experience shows that both the students and the graduate assistants involved in the teaching both like the process and its outcomes. Other topics discussed in this group dealt with ways of measuring students' attitudes and beliefs about mathematics and its teaching. In order to make change, baseline data is needed to see the current status of teacher feelings and conceptions.

Another topic receiving a good deal of discussion was the development of specialists for teaching mathematics at the K-5 level. Two programs developed for educating such teachers were presented and discussion centered on the changes needed in school structure to accommodate such a program and the changes needed in university programs in order that these teachers receive appropriate instruction in both mathematics and age-related pedagogical methods. Both programs have been successful in creating such teachers and networks for their support once they leave the university programs. Of perhaps more importance than any one topic, the sessions of WG6 provided those in attendance with the opportunity to discuss their programs and those of their international colleagues. The interchanges provided ideas for change, encouragement to continue in difficult circumstances, and reactions for further reflection on research and curriculum development.

WG6 closed with a plenary address by Claude Comiti [FRA]. She spoke on the current changes in mathematics teacher education taking place in France. The central focus of her presentation was the creation of university institutes for teacher training known as Instituts Universitaires de Formation des Maîtres (I.U.F.M.). This movement began with a new law in 1989 mandating reform in teacher education. Three I.U.F.M. programs were begun in the fall of 1990 at Grenoble, Lille, and Reims. The fall of 1991 saw the creation of institutes in the remaining 25 educational districts within France. Like reforms in many other countries, these programs are five years in length and attempt to better link research and practice in the education of prospective teachers. It is hoped that this will lead to a coherence between levels and theory and practice that has been missing in previous conceptualizations. The general format for the programs consist of 3 years of content-based education in mathematics at the university, followed by 2 years of professional training in mathematics and mathematics education at the I.U.F.M. The latter two years consists of work in general pedagogical matters; continued formation of the candidates' knowledge in mathematics, its history and philosophy; additional mathematics content courses; and considerable classroom-based experience in mathematics classes. Hopefully this revised program will bolster what teachers know and are able to do. Like the recommendations from the *Teaching Standards* in the opening session, heavy emphasis is being placed on the school experience and constant reflection on classroom practice and the system-wide change of the components of a total mathematics education program. This attempt to link theory/research/ practice is guided by mathematics educators active in all three phases of the discipline. It is hoped that the same type of introspective, and professionally aware, view can be engendered in the program's students through a culminating professional project report required of all graduates. Many issues remain to be resolved in the development and formalization of the I.U.F.M. programs at the various universities involved. Already the programs have invigorated mathematics education and increased public awareness of the need for increased mathematics education for teachers. However, great disparities remain among the 28 campuses involved in staff and resources, recognition by the university departments, and time to carry out the activities needed to bring the plan into full action.

NOTE

Proceedings containing the papers presented to the participants will be published during 1994. Information can be obtained fron: John Dossey, 4520 Mathematics Department, Illinois State University, Normal, IL 61790-4520, USA, Fax: (1) 309 467-2759, E-mail: jdossey@ilstu.bitnet

Working Group 7 / *Groupe de travail 7*

LANGUAGE AND COMMUNICATION
IN THE MATHEMATICS CLASSROOM

LANGAGE ET COMMUNICATION DANS LA CLASSE

Chief Organizer / *Responsable en chef* : Heinz Steinbring [DEU]
Local Organizer / *Responsable local* : William Higginson [CAN]
Advisory team members / *Consultants* : Maria Bartolini-Bussi [ITA],
Athanassios Gagatsis [GRC], Nobuhiko Nohda [JPN],
Anna Sierpinska [CAN]

Mathematical knowledge can be conceived as a ready-made product or as a living "organism" with a great variety of self-referential relationships growing through reorganizations, enrichments, and generalizations. There is here a first analogy to "language" as being both a syntactical structure for denoting objects of the real world and a cultural/social means to construct new objects in the real world and to express one's own personal experiences.

If mathematical knowledge is a living organism, the perspective on the "learning environment" of mathematical knowledge changes dramatically: similarly to the acquisition of a language, the introduction to mathematical knowledge can be regarded as an introduction to a culture. However, one major problem is that students often lack a meaningful mathematical language to enter this culture; they are often speechless mathematically. In many classrooms, communication is asymmetric, restricted to a language based on a set of pre-determined technical terms which are defined by the teacher or some obscure conventions. If there is anything that gives meaning to these terms, often it is just the schematic patterns of classroom communication, "rituals" which have nothing to do with the mathematics to be taught or learned.

Papers prepared for this working group contained analyses of actual classroom communication as well as proposals of learning environments in which the classroom communication could be so improved as to allow students to enter the culture of mathematics. The proposed learning environments were built around concepts such as "neo-Socratic method", "focusing pattern", "journal writing", "report writing", "discussing journal entries", "coursework", "reading using hermeneutical methods", "formatting a mathematical argument", "small group discussion", "whole class discussion". Several theoretical frameworks were proposed to make sense of the different kinds of learning environments: the "constructivist perspective, "Leont'ev's activity theory", methods of "transcript analysis", "Wittgenstein's concept of language games", "linguistic analysis of figures of speech", "interactionist approaches", "ethnographical ideas", "analysis of written discourse", "hermeneutics", "semantic distance", "a tetrahedral model of communication".

The two *introductory plenary talks* at the first session focused on the teacher's and the students' role in communication. Bernadette Janvier [CAN] spoke on "What are the interventions of the teacher educator that indeed have an impact on the formation of future teachers and their teaching practices?" The teacher educator will be more willing to favor confrontation of conflicting understandings and phases of destabilization in the students if he or she has an attitude that is open to continuous feedback coming from his or her classroom practice and research. The teacher educator's interventions have to be refined in view of their value for the expected effects on the students. Second, Susan E. B. Pirie [GBR] spoke about "Pupils, language and mathematics – is there any connection?" Mathematics can be communicated through ordinary language, mathematical verbal language, formal language, unspoken but shared assumptions, and quasi-mathematical language. What are the implications of this variety of means of communication for students' understanding of mathematical concepts? Different symbolic forms can carry a multiplicity of interpretations that to the mathematician are "the same", but to the learner seem entirely unrelated.

SUBGROUP 1

Presenters: Albrecht Abele [DEU]; Maria Bartolini-Bussi [ITA] (organizer); Maria-L. Cestari [NOR]; Clive Kanes [AUS]; Hermann Maier [DEU]; Falk Seeger [DEU]; Dianna Siemon [AUS]

Discussions centred around theoretical frameworks and methodologies of research. Several "false dichotomies" were identified.

- The problem of relations between micro- (e.g. lesson) and macro-structures (e.g. long term processes) was discussed. Wittgenstein's philosophy of language (language games) and Leont'ev's activity theory were used as frameworks for discussion. Dialectical relationships between the two levels have been stressed considering that not only the framework to interpret the microstructure but also the epistemological significance of micro-events can exclude certain macro-level possibilities.

- The actor/observer paradox has been considered as a problem not only of methodology but also of theory. A solution could be found within a framework of participatory observation .

- The theory/practice dichotomy was also discussed.

The presence of dichotomies both in the papers and discussions raised the problem of coherence of theories in the educational field. Are we really aiming at constructing a coherent theory or are there obstacles to this goal that are intrinsic to the concept of educational theory itself?

SUBGROUP 2

Presenters: Martha Civil [USA]; Megan Clark [NZL];
Bernadette Janvier [CAN] (organizer); Rainer Loska [DEU];
Candia Morgan [GBR].

Discussions focused on teacher training and ways of improving communication in the mathematics classroom. The following points were made.

- In order to improve communication, the teacher must intervene at some point. The question is: when and how? With what aim in view?

- Possible causes of problems of communication and some means of remediation.

  a) Lack of motivation to communicate, if

   - the communication is not given a precise and explicitly-stated goal;

   - the problem on which the communication takes place is not endorsed by students as their own;

   - the problem is not mathematically challenging.

The choice of the initial question or problem about which communication was considered very important.

  b) The management of communication in the classroom often requires that the usual didactical contract be changed. It was agreed that this change should be made explicit by the teacher.

  c) An unfriendly context in the problem to be discussed may impede understanding and communication. However, do unfriendly contexts always play a negative role?

  d) The cultural heterogeneity of the class.

  e) Internal causes: cognitive, linguistic, emotional.

- Didactical tools of improvement of communication in the classroom.

    a) The neo-Socratic method.

    b) "Jeux de message", situations of formulation and communication (reference to Brousseau's theory of situations).

    c) "Coursework", a kind of assignment practiced in UK. In this case, the student "communicates" in writing to the teacher; the teacher responds by assessing the communication. However, current practices of assessment and criteria used therein are highly controversial .

- It was stressed that prospective teachers should not get the impression from our courses that a "constructivist style" teaching means a lack of control over the constructed meanings.

* Questions raised but not discussed: Are communication situations always good for all groups of students (e.g. adult, handicapped)? The male/female difference in the role of language: are different messages received when the same words are used by male/female teachers or students?

SUBGROUP 3

Presenters: William Atweh & Tom Cooper [AUS]; Jean-Philippe Drouhard & Yves Paquelier [FRA]; Götz Krummheuer [DEU] (organizer); Koichi Kumagai, Nobuhiko Nohda & Hideyo Emori [JPN]; Terry Wood [USA].

The subgroup focused on social patterns and constraints in mathematical communication. Two main strands of theoretical approaches determined the discussion: construction of meaning within a social process of interaction versus transmission of pre-given mathematical knowledge via communication. While the former used concepts like interaction, negotiation, and the interactive constitution of meaning, the latter expressed itself by using the concept of communication within a sender-receiver model and the idea of identifying perturbations in this transmission. Also the kind of empirical research and the theoretical re-conceptualization of empirical phenomena was inextricably bound to these different theoretical frameworks.

Those interested in interactional constructions partly tried to identify patterns of classroom interactions: "focusing pattern", "interactional patterns of different mathematical levels" and "formats of argumentation". They were focusing on micro-sociological aspects or concepts like the reaccomplishment of gender and social class, while the others focused rather on the macro-aspects of mathematical classroom processes. The discussion was stimulated by the presentation of pictorially represented models of relevant theoretical concepts. These models appeared simplistic and could easily be misinterpreted, but they were functional in pointing to conceptual relations in the underlying theory.

SUBGROUP 4

Presenters: Maria A.V. Bicudo [BRA]; Frances R. Curcio & Alice F. Artzt [USA]; Athanassios Gagatsis, T. Patronis & D. Spanos [GRC]; A.V. Marafioti Garnica [BRA]; Martin R. Hoffman & Arthur B. Powell [USA]; Ann Oaks & Barbara Rose [USA]; Susan E.B. Pirie [GBR] (organizer); Constance Smith & Judi Fonzi [USA].

Discussions centered around two activities related to texts: understanding texts and producing texts to improve understanding. The main themes were: hermeneutical methods of understanding texts; theories of "measuring" or identifying an understanding of an expression or a problem; various forms of writing as a vehicle to understanding.

- It was proposed to extrapolate hermeneutic methodologies to the study of transmission of meaning between the deliverer and the receiver (to encompass sayer and listener) and not to limit the discussion to reader/text interactions.

- There was a wide-ranging discussion related to the use of hermeneutical methods and techniques. It was proposed that the definition of "dictionary" be broadened to encompass any authority on the meaning of terms. Benefits were discussed that follow from consulting with someone who knows, particularly as symbolism increases the strength and precision of what is being said. An analogy was proposed related to reading a software manual to obtain clarification vs asking someone who has experience with the software for an explanation.

- A readability test was proposed but the situation was seen as more complex than that allowed. Problems arose which touched upon the fact that pupils might not understand what they tell us they have understood, that the syntax as well as the meaning of words causes problems, and that the strategies proposed do not seem well suited to bilingual students.

- The ambiguity of a written symbol like 3/4 was put forward, meanings of it ranging from 3 divided by 4, to 3 pieces of one quarter, to 3 out of four pieces. This provoked comments to the effect that even ordinary language is not universal among students from different backgrounds, and small group discussion was seen as a way for students to become familiar with each other's interpretations and to diminish the notion of "right" and "wrong" meanings.

- Much discussion centered on the need for the contextual mediation of meaning.

- Another big question was related to the use of writing as a vehicle to understanding. The notion of "expressive" writing was evoked and various kinds of such writing were discussed, e.g. journal, biographies, focus-in-class narratives, explanations, notes and process writing.

- Graphs as a tool for communication was another theme. Three levels of comprehension of graphs were distinguished: reading the data (literal), reading between the data (interpretative, interpolation), reading beyond the data (predicting and extrapolation).

- The role of assessment of students was also discussed. The subgroup focused on social patterns and constraints in mathematical communication. Activities in communication events were mentioned as being as a major problem. Also the question was raised as to the effect of joint writing on the teachers' practice.

- The last point of the session centered around "what is good communication?"

The subgroup's enthusiasm was tempered by the issue of the constraints imposed on classrooms by standardized testing and it was realized that a way must be found to avoid conflicts between "what and how to measure" and "what and how we would like to teach".

SUBGROUP 5

Presenters: Meraj Aksu [TUR]; Ferdinando Arzarello [ITA] (organizer);
Luciana M. M. Chamie & Maria A. V. Bicudo [BRA]; Maria Kaldrimidou &
Andrea Ikonomou [GRC]; Mollie McGregor [AUS]; Giancarlo Navarra [ITA];
Marek Pisarski [POL].

The main interest of this subgroup lay in the problems of understanding the language of mathematics. An important point was that the teachers' interpretation of a mathematical idea and its representation as an algorithm, a diagram or a graph, etc., may not resemble the students' interpretation or representation. Models, diagrams, colors, are not "transparent" and may not be helpful. The question was posed: could students be allowed to invent and use their own symbolism? The teacher could then lead them to realize the need for universal conventions, so that they can communicate with others.

The contrast between the natural and formal language was discussed. Models, images and metaphors generated from natural language processes may be unsuitable for mathematical reasoning. They may generate serious

144

misunderstandings and misconceptions. The algebraic language, for example, has symbolic functions that are missing or are developed in a completely different manner in ordinary language (e.g. ideographic, trans-formative). Pupils do not seem to learn to manage these symbolic functions very well. Moreover, symbols and diagrams often do not become "thinking tools" for students, but remain mere "knowledge containers" that they can be used to control mechanical processes but are not helpful in solving non-routine problems.

As a result of discussions two metaphors were constructed: the "theater metaphor" and the "joke metaphor". Interaction in the classroom is like a theater where actors feature some characters: students and teachers are both actors and spectators and must act after having clarified the difference of roles. This metaphor brings forth an important question: teachers cannot give the meaning directly; they must "act" it. How? In addition, understanding a mathematical statement or situation is like understanding a joke. A joke does not make its point explicitly; neither do mathematical statements about their meanings. To understand a joke or mathematics, one is expected to connect and select the right things to laugh at or make sense of. Otherwise the joke is missed or the meaning of the mathematical statement is lost. The question now is how to make students "laugh at the right moment" in the mathematics class? This metaphor connects learning mathematics with living in a culture: if you are not a member of the culture or if you do not know the culture, you will not understand "what the people are laughing at".

NOTE

This report was prepared by Anna Sierpinska and Heinz Steinbring.

Working Group 8 / *Groupe de travail 8*

INNOVATIVE ASSESSMENT OF STUDENTS IN THE MATHEMATICS CLASSROOM

INNOVATIONS DANS L'ÉVALUATION DES ÉLÈVES EN MATHÉMATIQUES

Chief Organizer / *Responsable en chef* : Júlianna Szendrei [HUN]
Local Organizer / *Responsable local* : Thomas Schroeder [CAN]
Advisory team members / *Consultants* : Gillian Close [GBR],
Derek Foxman [GBR], Mogens Niss [DNK], Luis Rico Romero [ESP]

About 120 delegates from many countries in this working group began from the premise that assessment, in all educational systems, is here to stay, whether we like it or not. However, the mathematics curriculum in many countries is changing to meet new objectives, adapting to increased knowledge about how children learn, and encompassing a broader range of teaching styles. Traditional methods of assessment, such as pencil and paper tests with multiple choice questions, do not meet the requirements of these curriculum changes and so corresponding innovations in assessment must take place. The group aimed to make recommendations for further studies and to encourage educators and researchers to explore new methods for assessing mathematical abilities.

Pre-Congress papers were available for the group's sessions in a booklet produced with the assistance of the Tamás Varga Memorial Foundation in Budapest.

At the first plenary session, Júlianna Szendrei [HUN] introduced some possible topics into which to subdivide the theme, and ran through the main issues as she saw them. In the first lecture Bennie Adams [USA] addressed one of Szendrei's paradoxes of assessment: assessment in mathematics seems easy, but in reality is problematic. He saw judging children's understanding of elementary concepts as particularly difficult, while Szendrei had seen judging higher-level mental processes as problematic.

The whole group then split into subgroups which worked through the two following sessions. Convenors summarized the discussions in their subgroup at the fourth and final session.

146

SUBGROUP 1

Paradoxes of assessment

Organizers: Bennie Adams [USA], Peter Petocz [AUS]

A small subgroup of six people chose discussion rather than papers. The following were identified as paradoxes of assessment:

- Relationship between assessment and objectives: which one comes first?

- If we assess all areas, not just skills/techniques, but also communication, research, organization, attitudes, etc., are we assessing mathematics – or everything?

- Assessing convergent abilities (e.g. solving an equation) can be very objective, but that is not really assessing mathematics ability. To assess broader abilities (e.g. ability to tackle an open-ended project) becomes more subjective, rather like the work of an art critic.

- While implementing assessment programs, the teacher is confronted with one of the same tasks that he/she is to assess: problem solving. How do teachers design such assessment tasks without previous experience?

- Should we assess formally or spend our energies on teaching/learning?

- What proportion of time and effort do we put into assessment? Is a situation with no assessment at all possible/desirable?

- Can assessment ever help or hinder learning? How can we modify assessment to maximize helping and minimize hindering?

- Do we change what we are assessing (rather like the Heisenberg uncertainty principle)?

SUBGROUP 2

Assessment of attitudes and dispositions

Organizers: Klara Tompa [HUN], Mogens Niss [DNK]

The main work of this subgroup of about 16 was discussion and sharing ideas; there were only two presentations. Ching-Lin Hu [CHN] described a "synthetical assessment" which emphasized assessment of the mathematical potentialities of students, the two main components of which consist of mathematical capacities and psychological aspects. This kind of assessment has mobilized the enthusiasm of middle school students. The second presentation concerned an investigation into pupils' conceptions of mathematics and mathematics teaching by Erkki Pehkonen [FIN] and Klara Tompa [HUN]. These two papers served as a good starting point to discuss many of the difficulties present when planning international or national assessments of attitudes, beliefs, or conceptions. Many questions emerged:

- Why ask children? What is the purpose of asking them? (Why not ask decision-makers, teachers, parents, as well as pupils themselves?)

- Is a questionnaire the right tool for investigating such a subjective, sometimes hidden field of personality? (There is more than one tool, including self-assessment methods, interviews.)

- What kinds of statistics allow obtaining something valid or relevant out of data gathered by questionnaire? (Example: factor analysis.)

- How can we ensure in an international study that our tools, our questionnaires, mean the same in all participating countries? (There are translation problems and cultural differences.)

- How do attitudes relate to achievement?

During the second session there were fruitful discussions about motivation (including the motivation of teachers), math anxiety (how to help pupils rather than assess them), attitudes towards problems (everyone favored a multiple approach rather than the sole use of questionnaires), and problem facing (stress was placed on the responsibility of assessors not to affect what is being measured).

SUBGROUP 3

Assessment of problem solving abilities

Organizers : Tom Schroeder [CAN], Norman Webb [USA]

Two of the four papers described external assessment systems of central educational agencies. Max Stephens [AUS] reported on the model for mathematics assessment used in Victoria, Australia, which has four components – extended investigations; challenging problems; multiple-choice knowledge and skill tasks; and analysis tasks. Cleo Campbell [USA] reported on an American school district's assessment program which is based on learning outcomes and emphasizes performance tasks. The other two papers discussed analyses of tasks. Kevin Collis [AUS] used a psychological model, SOLO, focusing on modes of functioning. Thomas Schroeder [CAN] presented a realistic, non-routine problem given to students in interviews to describe and evaluate elements of their problem solving abilities.

The following themes were addressed by participants:

1. Innovative assessment. Many innovations employ "performance" tasks or "authentic assessment" tasks involving students solving realistic problems or carrying out mathematical modeling. Some are quite extensive and demanding of students' time.

2. Scoring and interpretation of student's work on such tasks. Most of the innovative tasks that were presented were designed to permit multi-dimensional analysis and interpretation of students' work entailing several different aspects of valued mathematical performance. In some cases, the tasks lead to a single aggregated score or mark, e.g. the Victorian program is part of a university-entrance selection system. In other cases, the components of students' performance are kept separate for purposes of diagnosis or instructional decision-making.

3. Implementation of innovative assessment programm and change in assessment practices generally. In some cases, innovation in assessment was seen as following curriculum change, in some others as leading curriculum change. In either case, expectation changes and a new assessment and evaluation consensus is needed.

Some other issues emerged.

- Teachers' expectations do not always match what students do. To avoid teachers' preconceptions and to ensure the quality of assessment tasks, tasks could be based on research (e.g. a theory such as Collis's) and/or carefully piloted (e.g. Schroeder's tasks).

- Assessment has various purposes which need to be made explicit. For example, a description such as "external assessment" may or may not be integral to the curriculum taught.

- The feasibility of authentic or performance tasks is doubtful because of their cost in time and effort. One way to make them acceptable is to point out that investigative projects, challenging problems, and analysis, provide information for external purposes while at the same time engaging students in learning mathematics.

Not much was said about research on assessment. What are valid assessment tasks, and what meaning can be given to assessment experiences? Some members of the group voiced an interest in having more time at the next Congress for small group discussions where people could discuss specific issues. Overall, there still seems plenty of room for more innovation in innovative assessment.

SUBGROUP 4

Diagnostic assessment

Organizers: Derek Foxman [GBR], Luis Rico Romero [ESP]

Several aspects of diagnostic assessment were involved in the presented papers wich related to various levels of education systems. Roland Olstrope [SWE], with 14-16 year olds, has made use of comments on students' homework set on topics taught about a month before. He insisted on frequent diagnosis, feedback to the pupil, and pupils knowing what the objectives of teaching are. Ewaugh Finney Fields [USA] described the tests used on a mathematics assessment and placement program offered to highly motivated but academically marginal students at her university. John Izard [AUS] reported on his analysis using an item-response model of the results Claude Gaulin, Júliana Szendrei and Maria do Carmo Vila have obtained by administering a probability concept test developed in England to 1100 students from three countries (Hungary, Brazil and Québec). This illustrated how test scores could be interpreted in terms of the type of task students do. Paul Donaldson [AUS] asked his tertiary curriculum math students to make diary entries after each tutorial, providing a record of what had been covered, a means of communication, and an organizing tool for both students and lecturer.

Two presentations related to diagnosing educational systems rather than individual studies. Helena Sunzunegui de Iglecia [ARG] described a pilot study where test items from the IEA's second maths study (SIMS) were administered to 182 13-year-old students in a range of Argentinian schools. The results were considered low and several possible reasons given. Derek Foxman's data were from the Second International Assessment of Education Progress (IAEP–2). He used England's comparative results to show how international studies could provide information on, for example, the potential of different areas of the curriculum, the profile of above and below average topics, and the consistency of gender differences across countries.

The subgroup attempted to construct a framework for describing levels and methods of diagnosis. Assessment takes place to provide participants in education with information for action. There are two broad purposes for assessment: formative and summative. Diagnostic assessment is part of the teaching/learning process and so is formative assessment. All assessment, however, provides some diagnostic information. The detail or "depth" of diagnosis depends on the focus of the assessment:

	Students		Teachers
Depth	Overall level of achievement	↔	Program evaluation
of	Profile of strengths and weaknesses	↔	Diagnosing individuals
Diagnosis	Particular concepts/skills/ processes/attitudes		

The subgroup believed that one could use a range of diagnostic tools, both open and closed tasks, and both incidental evidence and formal purposive diagnostic situations.

To improve diagnosis, the discussion suggested roles for:

- Researchers to research students' misconceptions; to research observational and questioning techniques for the classroom; to carry out further analyses of test results to identify tasks students can do, rather than compare scores; to carry out surveys of performance nationally and internationally, including error analyses;

- Test developers to develop new tests and tasks with diagnostic potential, using research findings;

- Teachers to use a variety of diagnostic situations and tasks to monitor individuals and class progress, to respond rapidly to diagnostic information, and to share information with colleagues.

SUBGROUP 5

Assessment policy

Organizer: Gillian Close [GBR]

Two presentations (Margaret Brown [GBR], and Gill Close with Richard Browne [GBR]) focused on details of the National Curriculum assessment in UK. This included assessments made by teachers during their teaching and tests provided by central government, designed by a team directed by Gill Close. Leonor Cuhna Leal [PRT] described the relative benefits of various modes of assessment including two-stage tests, reports, and oral presentations. Tom Romberg [USA] described the large "testing industry" based on multiple-choice tests, and summarized policy problems in effecting assessment style changes.

The following questions emerged during the discussions:

- How is shared understanding of criteria achieved? Understanding must be shared between teachers within and across schools, with test writers, with pupils and at a more general level, with decision-makers, parents, and other users. Factors in shared understanding were identified, such as tests, exemplary assessment materials, training, moderation, and self-assessment.

- Teacher assessment or national/local tests? Many members favored teacher assessment against externally-imposed tests which do not assess agreed and shared curriculum goals. In the UK there was some evidence that national tests of the National Curriculum criteria could have a supportive influence on the curriculum when the tests were designed by educators in conjunction with teachers. External tests *per se* are not necessarily bad, but certain kinds of tests can harm the curriculum. The short question format, a narrow range of skills and concepts tested, and a lack of emphasis on problem-solving skills, are often at fault.

- Self-assessment? All members agreed that this is an essential part of assessment. Sharing and negotiating understanding of criteria between pupils, and between teacher and pupil, can only help learning. It increases ownership and responsibility for learning. Decision-makers and teachers need to be encouraged to include a self-assessment component in assessment schemes.

- Aggregation of separate aspects of attainment? The tension between the need to give very detailed diagnostic feedback to pupils, slightly aggregated information to parents and future teachers, and summary information of perhaps one score per pupil to school, local, and national decision makers was discussed. The group did not want assessment to focus only on the summary form of information. It saw the need to report more detailed attainment, e.g. on algebra, geometry, and problem solving.

- Moderation of teacher assessment? Everyone wanted some way of comparing teachers' assessments on common criteria and of supporting teachers in coming to agreed assessments of pupils' work. Decision-makers needed to make sufficient time available for meetings between teachers and moderators in order to keep the reliability and validity of assessment as high as possible.

- Breadth of teacher assessment? Everyone agreed that teacher assessment provide much broader information than any external test. There is a need to increase the respect for teacher assessment held by decision-makers, parents, and other users. In some countries, such as Germany, teachers are held in sufficiently high regard by society so that their assessments of pupils are not checked or supplemented by compulsory external assessments.

• Influence on national policy? Consensus between all the interested parties in mathematics education is needed if politicians and other decision-makers are to be influenced. In the USA the linking of school teachers, mathematics education lecturers and researchers, mathematicians in business and higher education, and parents has been important in establishing the NCTM Standards and in gaining nation-wide support for them.

Working Group 10 / *Groupe de travail 10*

MULTICULTURAL AND MULTILINGUAL CLASSROOMS

CLASSES MULTICULTURELLES ET MULTILINGUES

Chief Organizer / *Responsable en chef* : Patrick Scott [USA]
Local Organizer / *Responsable local* : Thomas O'Shea [CAN]
Advisory team members / *Consultants* : Elisa Bonilla [MEX], Lloyd
Dawes [AUS], Gilbert Cuevas [USA], Martha Villavicencio [PER]

The first session was plenary with many participants presenting posters describing their work in multicultural/multilingual classrooms, or materials designed for such classrooms. The next two sessions were discussions in the subgroups indicated below. The final session was plenary with reports from the subgroups and accompanying discussion.

SUBGROUP 1

Curriculum, resources, and materials for multicultural/multilingual classrooms

How can different cultures in one classroom be recognized and taken into account and what role should ethnomathematics play in multicultural and multilingual classrooms? Students might write a paper about their cultural background, using topics from the history of mathematics about people from their culture, or by using the library or family resources. They might review movies related to mathematics (example: *Stand and deliver*) or write about people from their own particular life experiences. By working across the curriculum using interdisciplinary procedures more material in the syllabus is covered and creative methods can be utilized. In the education of student teachers discussions should be held about the problems they might encounter with students who are underprepared in mathematics. They could also discuss ways in which they might teach underprepared students from different cultures. Other techniques which might be used in multicultural classrooms are the use of manipulatives, technology, collaborative or cooperative learning.

154

What is multicultural mathematics and how is it implemented? An aspect of multicultural mathematics is the historical developments of mathematics in different cultures (e.g. the Mayan numeration system). Another aspect could be prominent people in different cultures who use mathematics (e.g. an African-American biologist, an Asian-American athlete). Mathematical applications can be made in cultural contexts (e.g. using fractions in food recipes from different cultures). Social issues can be addressed via mathematics applications (e.g. use statistics to analyze demographic data). Multicultural mathematics materials can be integrated into the regular instructional program, and personalized activities can be arranged that are related to different cultures and draw on students own experiences.

What are the issues to which we need to be sensitive? Cultural-related differences in learning styles can present challenges. For example, Asian students are sometimes reluctant to ask a question in class and some American Indian students are reluctant to look teachers in the eye because it is considered rude. However, there should be caution in attempting to meet the specific needs of a particular group of students as generalizations can be misleading and potentially damaging. There is a wide range of abilities and learning styles within any group of people. Teachers need to be sensitive to the learning styles of all students in their classrooms regardless of their ethnic group. There is often teacher and student resistance to emphasizing cultural differences. Immigrant students may have learned different mathematics content or been in classrooms with different teaching styles. Teachers need to be aware that different algorithms are used for the basic arithmetic operations. Multilingual textbooks might present ideas in multiple languages or use icons (word-free symbols) for some kinds of problems and directions.

What multicultural mathematics is appropriate for majority culture classrooms? While multicultural perspectives should be infused throughout the curriculum for all students, trivialization of both the multiculturalism and the mathematics must be avoided. Textbooks and curriculum materials need to reflect multicultural perspectives. Commercial materials will change only as teachers become persistent in requesting changes.

SUBGROUP 2

Teacher education for mathematics in multicultural/multilingual classrooms

Multicultural perspectives are appropriate for all students. One misconception addressed by the group was that African mathematics is just for black students, South American mathematics for Hispanic students, etc. In a pluralistic society, all students need to be exposed to multicultural aspects of mathematics as part of having them interact with students from a variety of cultures. Multicultural aspects of mathematics should be blended throughout the mathematics curriculum irrespective of minority culture. It was agreed that such an approach would lead to a broader view of the role of mathematics as a cultural phenomenon, and enhance the view of mathematics as a systematic body of knowledge.

What multicultural mathematics should be taught? The group agreed that multicultural mathematics should not be taught as a form of mathematical oddity, or as a relief from the real mathematics of the curriculum. Topics such as symmetry and its application in a variety of cultures, the development of number in various cultures, were cited as examples that could be integrated into the regular curriculum.

The following are some implications for teacher education: to accomplish the curricular goals identified above, changes are needed in teacher education programs. Multiculturalism should be embedded within the teacher education curriculum, and not taught as a separate strand. In this way, multiculturalism is not trivialized. Also, by using present-day real-life situations to reflect cultural diversity among students, mathematics is not trivialized. One approach to restructuring the mathematics curriculum is to focus on the diverse algorithmic techniques used around the world, for example, the different methods for subtracting whole numbers.

SUBGROUP 3

Multicultural/multilingual classrooms for the 21st century

The group acknowledged the cultural origins of mathematics. A number of issues affecting outcomes were noted, including racism, conflicting values, and the role of parents. The gap between the third world and industrialized nations is increasing, not decreasing. The impact of global migration on all countries and the world-wide economic situation make defining concrete solutions of mathematics curriculum for the 21st century a complex task. It was noted that Sweden and Germany were experiencing unprecedented immigration from non-native speakers for which the education systems were ill-prepared. The language support available in countries like Australia has been developed over a long time. The difficulties of poorer countries in dealing with the effects of migration – incoming and, sometimes, the loss of talented people – are even greater.

The possible need to "reconstruct" mathematics if more equitable outcomes are to be achieved was discussed. The group accepted that while it may be helpful if some aspects of the formal mathematical culture did change (e.g. the language and values associated with mathematics), this will only happen from within. A model was developed that takes into account that students enter school with mathematical knowledge that is mainly informal. It can be considered ethnomathematics in that it is culturally and socially defined. That informal mathematics touches the formal mathematics culture. Within the model, the minimum expectation should be that everyone can learn and appreciate the power of mathematics.

Goals for students include mathematics for everyday life, for citizenship, for employment, and as a profession (love). Only in the last case was it seen that the student needs to access fully formal mathematics culture, although it would be an objective that all students appreciate the power and the beauty of mathematics. The mathematics needed for everyday life is culturally and socially defined. It was noted that someone living in Papua New Guinea may be able to use traditional ways of measuring land if they stay in their village. Universal conventions may be needed away from the village or in dealing with visitors. The curriculum must take account of this. It was also noted that all aspects of the mathematics curriculum must take account of calculators as they are beginning to impact on poorer nations as well as on wealthier ones. Mathematics for citizenship was seen to be that mathematics needed for someone to be an effective participant in community and political decision-making. The importance of statistics in this was noted. It was also argued that the mathematics curriculum needs to play a more active part in helping people make informed political decisions and that students need to be able to use mathematics in developing just and democratic societies. Mathematics for employment was seen as being defined by the type of employment. The curriculum for the 21st century should be constructed in such a way so that linguistic and cultural impediments do not prevent students from life-long learning that enables them to use mathematics personally, as a citizen and for employment. And those with a love and talent for mathematics should have pathways to the universal mathematics culture.

There is a need for effective leadership, respect for culture, and authentic assessment. Effective leadership was seen as essential in forming community and political views of education in establishing goals which foster mathematics learning. Account must be taken of cultural views of education including attitudes to achievement in mathematics, its perceived economic role, the effect of parental views of mathematics and the level of parental education. The knowledge the child brings to the classroom (mathematical, linguistic, social, etc.) is powerful and the mathematics curriculum must build on that existing base. Associated with learning is the need for accountability and authentic assessment which should support, but not drive, the curriculum.

SUBGROUP 4

Language and culture in the mathematics education
of indigenous groups

There was general agreement on the need to preserve cultural values. The need to uncover one's cultural roots was stressed. One illustration of this was the learning of mathematics through the use of the ancient Bolivian flute, the zampona, which serves as a means of uncovering diverse mathematical relations that the construction and use of this instrument entails. Another illustration was an investigation of Bishop's "six universal activities" (counting, locating, measuring, designing, playing, and explaining) in the highlands in the south of Mexico with the aim of using them in curriculum development for the primary school of one Mixe community.

The importance of teaching and learning mathematics in the first language was discussed. Participants explained about situations, past and present, where speaking the first language is a matter of embarrassment, or an occasion for punishment. Hence the pressure to reinforce cultural values, particularly in regard to first language. The need to support teachers was a central issue. Often, it was said, teachers are resistant to change, they are particularly resistant to teaching in the first language. Mostly their resistance seems to stem from the fact that they did not do their schooling in their first language and thus do not see the necessity for it. On the other hand, the efforts made in some communities to teach in their first language right up through the tertiary level were put forward. Particularly members of the Welsh [GBR] and Inuit [CAN] communities explained the need to establish teacher education programs in students' first language and how they have accomplished this. Although there was agreement on the need to promote bilingualism, there was not necessarily agreement on how to attain it. Mastering the first language and then going on to the second was one suggestion, with the learning of mathematics starting with the first language. However, learning both languages simultaneously and teaching mathematics simultaneously in both languages was also suggested.

Adding mathematical words to languages was considered. Much time was spent on the lack of certain mathematical words in particular languages. This came out strongly as another central issue for this subgroup. Various examples were offered. Three methods were suggested for the incorporation of new words: 1) adapt existing words (which is acceptable as long as the mathematical meaning appears to be "close enough" to the everyday use), 2) borrow words from another language (like most languages have done for terms that refer to computer science), or 3) invent words (like French, in particular, has done for terms that refer to computer science). As to the question of how to make new words acceptable to teachers and the community, the benefits of engaging the elderly, who are often very knowledgeable about the language, and widely respected, were highlighted. There are also some Maori [NZL] communities which have a language commission that helps in these matters.

NOTE

An *Annotated bibliography of multicultural issues in mathematics education* is available from Patricia S. Wilson, Mathematics Education Department, University of Georgia, 105 Aderhold Hall, Athens, GA 30602, USA.

Working Group 11 / *Groupe de travail 11*

THE ROLE OF GEOMETRY
IN GENERAL EDUCATION

LE RÔLE DE LA GÉOMÉTRIE
DANS LA FORMATION GÉNÉRALE

Chief Organizer / *Responsable en chef* : Rina Hershkowitz [ISR]
Local Organizer / *Responsable local* : John Del Grande [CAN]
Advisory team members / *Consultants* : M.A. (Ken) Clements [AUS],
Josep M. Fortuny [ESP], Konrad Krainer [AUT], Stefan Turnau [POL]

GLOBAL OVERVIEW

The group activity opened with a plenary session, in which the aims of the group work were presented, as well as the various approaches and domains which make geometry so important and attractive on one hand, and its teaching and learning in the classroom so problematic on the other. Work in the other three sessions took place in seven different subgroups.

The plenary lecture was given by Paul Goldenberg [USA], who gave a colorful and thoughtful answer to the question: "Why geometry?" (Goldenberg et al., 1992). His main arguments were:

- Geometry can connect well with students, and they with it. The many hooks include art, physical science, imagination, biology, curiosity, mechanical design, and play.

- Geometry also connects richly with the rest of mathematics. By a kind of transitive property that we would like the curriculum to try to realize, geometry may help us attract more students, and a more diverse group of students to mathematics.

- Within mathematics, geometry is particularly well placed for helping people develop important habits of mind that, if learned with that elusive thing called transfer, have valuable applications outside of mathematics as well. In particular, geometry is an ideal intellectual territory within which to perform experiments, develop qualitative, visually-based reasoning styles, and use these to spawn constructive arguments as well.

160

- Geometry, broadly conceived, is also ideally placed to help students expand their conception of mathematics itself.

While Goldenberg described "the heaven" of what should and could be done to give geometry its rightful role in education, Rina Hershkowitz [ISR] described and analyzed "the earth": the reality of teaching and learning geometry in the classroom. In addition she tried to show how the seven subgroups might make substantial contributions towards bridging the gap between the two.

- The situation of school geometry is especially complicated, precisely because it is at the crossroads between tradition and new, rich, creative developments.

- Because of the heavy traditional inheritance from Euclid, it is still very common to find mostly two kinds of school geometry courses:

  i) A deductive Euclidean-type course at the secondary level;

  ii) A "pre-formal" course for elementary schools, presenting some narrow Euclidean aspects of geometry as the science of space.

- In the typical deductive Euclidean course, the process of inductive discovery of geometrical patterns, formulated as conjectures, which is at the heart of mathematical activity, is almost completely neglected. However, the recent development of geometrical software has created a powerful learning environment for inductive pattern discoveries in geometry. Subgroup 5 worked on this.

- There is evidence (Hershkowitz, 1990) that many learners do not have the logical maturity to make proofs, nor the awareness of the necessity for "formal proofs", which are the main goal of a deductive course. This raises a question that was the main topic for Subgroup 4: What kinds of geometrical reasoning students can develop and how?

- Changes in society and in technology, and especially the microcomputer's graphic power, have had a great impact on curriculum development perspectives; the presentation of phenomena has changed from tables and formulas heavy with numbers and symbols to a dynamic visual presentation using computers. To understand, analyze, and predict, we have to engage in some form of visual thinking. Unfortunately the typical deductive course almost completely lacks the visual search for patterns, and in the pre-formal course this search is usually dull, requiring mainly abstract logical thinking not appropriate for the elementary school level. This question of changing the traditional elementary geometry of "spartan shapes" (Goldenberg et al, 1992) was featured in all the subgroups as well as in the plenary lecture.

- Geometry itself has undergone a very rich and creative development; new content areas, and geometrical applications, based on different geometrical approaches have been developed, and these should find expression in the curriculum.

For many years there has been a lack of agreement about the core curriculum – *what* and *how* to teach in geometry courses – which has led to the "neglect geometry syndrome". This is expressed in an impoverished geometry education for prospective teachers, a very narrow school geometry curriculum, very poor teaching materials, little time devoted to geometry in schools, and very poor student performance on geometrical items in national and international surveys. Only recently do statements about geometry (NCTM, 1989; Steen, 1990) seem to contain some common features.

Above all there is agreement that school geometry has to take a broad view of content, approaches, classroom activities, techniques, age of students, etc., and cannot be built up in a "clean" linear hierarchical order.

SUBGROUP 1

Geometry as a part of education in early childhood (3 to 8 years old)

Organizer: M.A. (Ken) Clements [AUS]

Three major themes were discussed: Young children making sense of space; the social construction of space in early childhood; and curriculum development in early childhood geometry.

Overall, the presenters helped to define the territory covered by the term "early childhood geometry". John Del Grande [CAN] described his research with grade 2 children in which it was shown that grade 2 children's spatial abilities can be improved through a nine weeks geometry intervention. Other presenters focused on the nature of spatial thinking associated with activities and games. In some of these sessions those present were actively involved in physical activities designed to illustrate points being made by the presenter. It was recognized that geometry curricula for early childhood need to be defined or redefined as a result of the impact of technology. New rather than revised curricula are needed. It was also recognized that cultural considerations should be paramount in any re-definitions of early childhood curricula. Not only do different cultures have different spatial conventions, but the language of space often differs radically from culture to culture. Clements summarized some of the literature on cultural differences in spatial thinking, and the aspect of language was emphasized by Nerida Ellerton, Assia Levita & Kay Owens [AUS]. Frantisek Kurina [CSR] presented a fascinating paper on developments in early childhood geometry curricula in the Czech Republic. The standard theoretical bases of early childhood space deriving from the pioneering work of Piaget and Inhelder, and the van Hieles, were called into question in the paper by Robyn Zevenbergen [AUS], who argued that spatial concepts need to be seen as socially constructed and largely influenced by curricula. They are not primarily a function of maturation, and should not be associated with stages or levels.

SUBGROUP 2

Different aspects and roles of visualization in geometry

Organizers: Martin Cooper [AUS], Iman Osta [LBN], Joop van Dormolen [NLD]

In the discussion the difference between visualization and external visual representation was gradually clarified, visualization being seen as linked with internal activities including cognition, the formation of images, imagination and the development of an understanding of geometrical relationships. The real world was seen as an important source of informal geometrical ideas. The following scheme was gradually developed:

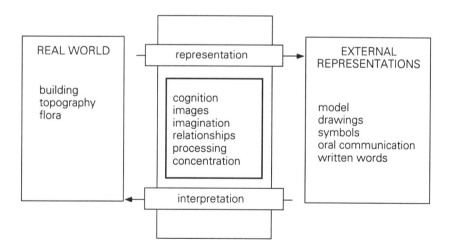

Visualization is connected with mental operations – it is something in one's mind. Incoming signals can be visual, oral or tactile. It appears that for different levels of geometry, different components of the model act as triggers of visualization for informal aspects of geometry, the real world being an important catalyst; for more formal geometry, external representations play a greater role as starting points. It was suggested that maybe geometry has a double status: while a concept itself refers to general and abstract objects, its external representation must be expressed by a specific configuration using concrete and particular objects.

SUBGROUP 3

Processes of geometric concept formation

Organizers: Guershon Harel [USA], Larry Sowder [USA], Stefan Turnau [POL], Avrum I. Weinzweig [USA]

A common theme of the presentations and discussion in this subgroup was the importance of informal or exploratory work in concept formation. Several examples of such informal work illustrated the intent, with the examples ranging from paper strips to 3-D objects to computer work. Wide-ranging discussions included several comments on proof; there was a feeling that proofs should arise out of experimental/informal work. The importance of going from visualization and representation to the abstract for the construction of mathematical concepts was stressed.

SUBGROUP 4

Geometry and mathematical reasoning structures

Organizers: Arthur F. Coxford [USA], Josep M. Fortuny [ESP], Angel Gutiérrez [ESP]

The work of this subgroup was developed around three main components of the teaching/learning processes:

- The recognition and analysis of types of students' geometrical reasoning. Verbal and graphical reasoning were identified as two parallel styles of thinking. On the one hand, a problem solving context which is designed to foster the ability to create formal proofs, produced a predominance of verbal reasoning. On the other hand, a problem solving context based on 3-dimensional manipulations, produced a predominance of graphical reasoning.

- The role of instruction in the development of students' geometrical reasoning. The improvement of students' reasoning comes mainly from their classroom experiences, and therefore motivation should be a component of the teaching activity. Several suggestions were presented, with specific examples, for such motivation. From another point of view, theoretical frameworks, like the van Hiele model, should guide the teachers' activity in the classroom, since they help them assign appropriate tasks to the student and to understand their answers. Attention was also paid to the role of computers as appropriate tools for representing and modeling the geometrical concepts and their network of properties and relationships.

- The assessment and evaluation of students' geometrical reasoning. Different curricular systems show two ways of assessment, one in which students are asked to prove formally a given geometrical statement, and the other, through open-ended problems and research projects, in which the students produce their own generalizations and are asked to justify them. The discussion focused on the advantages and disadvantages of each one.

SUBGROUP 5

Computers and conjecturing in secondary school geometry

Organizers: Daniel Chazan [USA], Michal Yerushalmy [ISR]

The teaching of geometry has been enriched by the development of a lot of computer software which allows teachers to pose inquiry problems for students, and students to explore their own problems. As pointed out by Steve Brown [USA], our choice of problems reveals much about ourselves, our views of students and what we value. He raised many questions about the different but complementary roles played by the teacher and the student as problem posers. To stimulate dialogue the subgroup examined problems given to students; eleven different pieces of software were involved. As Jean-Marie Laborde [FRA] pointed out, all of these problems had in common a desire to have students become mentally engaged with geometry as active inquirers. In most of the programs, students are asked to explore in "scientific" ways. Laborde began to sketch principles common to the design of these programs. A total of eight research and development projects were discussed and the group concluded its work by discussing future research and development agendas, and ways in which new work might build on prior work in the field.

SUBGROUP 6

Geometry through its history

Organizer: John Fauvel [GBR]

The main topics discussed were:

- Geometry through historical stories. This discussion focused on fairly gentle interactions in which the teacher encourages children's interest through telling or showing stories about geometrical practice or theory in the past.

- Geometry through instruments: it concentrates on what can be learned from geometrical instruments, especially past surveying instruments (like astrolabes, backstaffs, and dials) which can be easily built and demonstrated in the classroom. It was clear from talks and discussions that there is a powerful source here of interdisciplinary, cross-curricular work which consolidates student understanding of geometry (trigonometry, in particular).

- Geometry through historic texts. The use of old geometry texts for teaching geometry in the classroom was explored. The work focused on examples of texts, methods, and approaches developed in Japan, and in France by members of IREMs.

SUBGROUP 7

Geometry and other areas of life

Organizers: Konrad Krainer [AUT], George W. Bright [USA], John G. Harvey [USA]

Konrad Krainer gave an introductory talk on global aspects of geometry and other areas of life, above all stressing a complex view of separating and linking theory and practice in geometry instruction, illustrated by some examples. Günther Graumann [DEU] discussed some practice-oriented teaching units and pointed out their importance for general education. Alicia Villar [URY] demonstrated that projective geometry yields many possibilities for students to work with applications.

- Geometry and nature, culture, sports, games, etc. George Bright gave an overview of geometry in informal settings, especially referring to games. Susan Williams [USA] reported on research on the game *Tetris*. Three other presentations were concerned with geometry in arts and craft: Villar described students' studies of the golden rectangle, Florence Klimas [USA] reported on development of quilt squares and Virginia Usnick & Phyllis Miller [USA] reported on using art to teach mathematical ideas.

- Geometry and science, techniques, computers, etc. Richard Lehrer [USA] discussed the ways that LOGO can assist children to develop spatial sense.

CONCLUDING REMARKS

The combined contribution of the plenary session and the subgroups brought up several common themes and beliefs.

- The belief that visualization takes many forms, including intuitive and analytical thinking, global and local reasoning, dynamic representations and interpretations, etc. Visualization is the basis for visual activity *per se*, for geometry, for mathematics in general, for science, art, and so on. It can and should be developed for a wide age range, from the very young to the relatively mature.

- The belief that it is necessary to create connections and hooks in both directions – from geometry outwards and vice versa.

- The belief that the impact of technology must find expression in changes in content, approaches, methods and thinking processes in the teaching and learning of geometry. Seen in a historical context this is an almost obvious statement. In the past, the creative and didactic geometrical environment responded to the available instruments. Using the microcomputer, the student can "see" with his eye, and with his mind's eye, the invariants of a shape undergoing dynamic transformation.

REFERENCES

Goldenberg, E.P., Cuoco, A., & Mark, J. (1992). *Making connections with geometry.* Paper presented by Paul Goldenberg to Working Group 11 at ICME-7.

Hershkowitz, R. (1990). Psychological aspects of learning geometry. In P. Nesher & J. Kilpatrick (Eds.), *Mathematics and cognition* (pp. 70-95). Cambridge, UK: Cambridge University Press.

National Council of Teachers of Mathematics. (1989). *Curriculum and evaluation standards for school mathematics.* Reston, VA: NCTM.

Steen, L.A. (1990). *On the shoulders of giants: new approaches to numeracy.* Washington: National Academy Press.

Working Group 12 / *Groupe de travail 12*

PROBABILITY AND STATISTICS
FOR THE FUTURE CITIZEN

PROBABILITÉ ET STATISTIQUE
POUR L'ADULTE DE DEMAIN

Chief Organizers / *Responsables en chef* : Mary Rouncefield [GBR],
James Schultz [USA]
Local Organizer / *Responsable local* : James Swift [CAN]
Advisory team members / *Consultants* : Manfred Borovcnik [AUT],
Jordan Stoyanov [BGR], Kirsten Vännman [SWE], Michimasa Kobayashi
[JPN]

The presentations in this well-attended working group covered a wide range of topics, and at two sessions participants also had time in three subgroups talking about gender issues, the situation in developing countries, and teaching statistics to non-numerate students.

The first session of the group was concerned with the role of technology in teaching probability and statistics. David Moore [USA] talked about videos. Videos are useful for distance learning and as a classroom supplement can make statistics seem real by showing it in use, and can display high quality dynamic computer graphics. They can be used to stimulate interest, to introduce a simulation, to explain a difficult topic, and to provide case studies for analysis. Their weaknesses include their expense, lack of personal interaction with other people, and lack of active experience. Videos tend to be non-linear in their presentation, there is less attention to detail than might occur with an instructor, and note-taking is sometimes difficult. Peter Holmes and Mike Hammond [GBR] described a development project on using databases and spreadsheets in teaching data-handling to pupils aged 11-16. In the first year the project concentrated on teaching within mathematics, and in the second on teaching data-handling across the curriculum. The third year will focus mainly on inservice work and dissemination of materials and results. Students of this age generally find it motivating to work with computers and quickly learn how to do so, selecting appropriate parts of software and ignoring unfamiliar features. Spreadsheets and databases enable students to work with large sets of real data and are valuable in developing data-handling skills. In most of the project's activities the students themselves enter their data or secondary data. However, if the data set is large, data files might need to be prepared in advance. Examples of activities produced for the project are measuring how far toy cars travel when rolled down a ramp, and studying global temperature changes over the past 160 years. Brian Hudson [GBR] talked about a curriculum development project he had directed. A major part of it involved developing a suppplement to an existing cross-curricular package on economic awareness and environmental education. The supplement provided materials for the mathematics classroom for pupils aged 14-16. Written material was supported by data files containing statistics on energy consumption from 1950 to 1988 for several countries. The aim of the project was to encourage collection of data in the local community. Hudson suggested that a model of investigation suitable for large data sets was: 1) set context, 2) pose questions, 3) analyze data, 4) interpret results.

The first session ended with a general discussion on the use of computers in statistics education. Participants were reminded that a large part of the world has no access to computers, and even where they are available access may be limited. However, technology includes graphic and programmable calculators, and hand analyses can help understanding. Although spreadsheets are satisfactory for some problems, it is valuable for students of 16 and over to learn about and use statistical packages. There was discussion about the possibility of students exchanging data, and the contribution they might make to data bases, and a warning that collection of data is a time-consuming activity. The use and criticism of secondary data is also important. There are sometimes problems if statisticians go outside the mathematics classroom and into other data areas. Analysis of real data cannot be separated from political questions. It is important that students draw their own conclusions from data amd learn to criticize each other. One way of doing this is to encourage essays based on the analysis of small data sets, although students tend to be surprised if asked to write or speak in mathematics classes.

The second session was concerned with cross-curricular issues and applications of statistics. Annie Morin [FRA] talked about statistics and probability for today's French citizen. Statistics can be found everywhere, on television and in newspapers. She showed data relating to the collection and sale of scallops, and data relating to road accidents, both of which have been used in French schools. She suggested that, as a minimum, students leaving full-time education at the age of 16 should be able to handle data, read and understand graphs and other diagrams and tables, and be familiar with percentages. It is important to train students to be critical and open-minded and to introduce them to the ideas of causality and risk. Rheta Rubenstein [CAN] talked about the University of Chicago School Mathematics Project with which she and James Schultz were involved. This integrates statistics into a one-year course on functions for students 16 and 17 years old. Three topics where links can be made are graphs, transformations, and modeling. Shape and spread are features of both mathematical and statistical graphs. Being able to compare and contrast graphs is an important skill. Both functions and data can be transformed by translation and change of scale, and the effects of transformations on data can be demonstrated via dot plots and boxplots. This lays the foundation for transformations of the normal distribution. A major application of both functions and statistics is to model real situations and here the differences between statistical and mathematical methods become less distinct. Teaching statistics and functions together uses time well, reduces the amount of learning, and makes mathematics more accessible. Megan Clark [NZL] talked about how the context of problems affects students' performance. She presented results relating to two first-year statistics courses at Victoria University in Wellington, New Zealand: course "X", recommended for mathematics, physical sciences, and engineering students, and course "Y", recommended for biological sciences, social sciences, commerce, and medical students. The same topics were taught in both courses, but comparison of grades suggested it was easier for females to do well on course Y. An analysis of examination results over five years showed that abstract questions were unpopular. Males tended to perform better than females on the machinery and money problems in course X. There were more "people problems" in course Y and here the males, many of whom had dropped mathematics at an earlier stage, tended to try the same questions as the females. Questions on analysis of variance, chi-square, and regression, set in the context of data, were popular and done well by all, with females outperforming males. In 1991 students on course Y were given an assignment in which they were asked to do either a problem involving data on a hostility test or one on the strengths of concrete. Apart from context the two problems were identical. Half were given the assignment with the problem on hostility levels placed first, half with this problem placed second. Students tended to answer the first part presented, but females were more likely to answer the second part if the first part was about concrete. Megan Clark emphasized that it is important to set problems in a variety of contexts, with some likely to appeal to females and ethnic minorities. Glyn Davies [GBR] talked about a project on data-handling in the National Curriculum in the U.K. He suggested that data-handling should be practical, investigational, real, purposeful, appropriate, cross-curricular, and enjoyable. An example is recording where litter is found on a plan of the school. Points made in

170

discussion were that curriculum design is difficult, an adult's model for what works with children might be wrong, and children do not always get the learning experience intended. In teaching probability, avoid referring only to 6-sided dice, provide experience with randomness, use simulation (but not too soon), do not place stress on combinatorics or axioms, and do not build statistics on probability.

In the third session, presentations were concerned with the teaching of probability and statistics in some developing countries. Andi Nasoetion [IDN] spoke about statistics at school level in Indonesia. Indonesia consist of more than 1300 islands, less than half of them populated. Twenty-five percent of the population over the age of 25 has had no schooling, and only 1% has had any higher education. Approaches to teaching have had to change in response to increased participation. Quantitative literacy can be presented through data analysis, and memorizing formulas can be avoided. Girls from rural areas do less well than those from urban areas. The belief that the "soft" sciences do not require mathematics results in subject streaming in schools according to the perceived level and amount of mathematics – yet those who perform poorly in mathematics need more time learning mathematics, not less. One of the biggest problems facing education in Indonesia is organization, partly because of the country's geography, but teachers do have one day free a week when they meet for discussion. Aziz Lazraq [MAR] talked about opening up opportunities in probability and statistics. Probability and statistics are not taught at school level in Morocco apart from an introductory probability course in the last year for science students. The only statistics undergradute course includes no computing and its graduates have difficulty in obtaining jobs. However, there is a high demand for graduates from the 25 BSc courses in computer science and all include at least one statistics module. There are also four MSc courses in computer science with a strong emphasis on probability and statistics. Lazraq made the following recommendations: 1) give computer training, both in the development of software and the use of existing packages, 2) use real-life examples, 3) increase the awareness of statistical techniques amongst persons employed in industry. Parul Deoki [FJI] described some problems in teaching probability at the University of the South Pacific. This is a regional university serving twelve developing island nations which have their own educational systems, languages, and cultures. Students have to adjust to instruction in the foreign language: English, spoken with non-standard accents. Some of the remote islands do not have electricity, which limits the modes of instruction of distance learning courses. Some students are unfamiliar with cards and dice, and some even have difficulty in distinguishing between the outcomes "head" and "tail" in tossing a coin. Their prior beliefs and superstitions affect the learning of probability. Some students need a lot of extra help. Saleha Habibullah [PAK] talked about statistics in her country. Statistics is not taught at school but there are courses at FA/FSc level (grades 11-12), BA/BSc level (grades 13-14) and MA/MSc level (grades 15-16). The FA/FSc syllabus covers some descriptive statistics, probability, estimation, tests of hypotheses, regression, correlation, association, index numbers, and time series. The BA/BSc syllabus is similar with some topics treated in greater detail, plus analysis of variance, curve fitting, and vital statistics. Until recently practical work consisted of long numerical examples to be solved with calculators, but a new scheme requires students to perform experiments. Teaching statistics in Pakistan is directly affected by the economic situation and indirectly by the country's social and cultural climate.

The last session of the group was on current and future trends and strategies in the teaching of probability and statistics. Jan de Lange [NLD] talked about developing a critical attitude. He gave examples of how politicians and others interpret and manipulate graphs. He suggested that students might be asked to explain how to use a data set to justify two conflicting views such as "the defence budget is increasing" and "the defence budget is decreasing". The talk given by Gail Burrell [USA] was based on her experience with the Quantitative Literacy Project. In a data-driven curriculum connections can be made with algebra, geometry, trigonometry, and functions. Two successful data sets are school dropout rates in different states of the USA, and the age and price of cars. The former gives rise to discussion about how dropout rates are measured. Changes in dropout rates from one year to another can be plotted as dot plots, which gives practice in ordering integers; comparing states with increases and states with decreases motivates negative numbers. Scatter diagrams of ages of cars vs prices are instructive. Although an eyeball line and a median fit might be obtained, a line assumes constant depreciation, which is inappropriate. This leads on to ideas of curve fitting and transforming data. Children should always think about the numbers before they start number-crunching. Peter Wilder [GBR] concentrated on modeling with probability. Historically, mathematicians had found probability difficult, partly because it is not easy to test conjectures by experiment. Modern technology enables pupils to build computer models of random processes and compare the results with their predictions, perhaps later restructuring their model. Modeling reveals students' beliefs. Wilder described some of his work with students on some well-known counter-intuitive problems in probability where it is necessary to identify clearly both the conditioning event and the target event. Manfred Borovcnik [AUT] talked about intuitive strategies for teaching probability and statistics. The difficulty of finding answers to problems by trial and error, and the gap between intuition and mathematics, makes teaching difficult. Strategies to improve the situation include giving concrete examples, making the theory simpler, and relating teaching to intuition. He thought more use of computers, more interviews with students, and the use of analogies would help, and that it is intuitions which are the key to probability.

NOTE

This report was written by Flavia Jolliffe [GBR].

Working Group 13 / *Groupe de travail 13*

THE PLACE OF ALGEBRA IN
SECONDARY AND TERTIARY EDUCATION

LA PLACE DE L'ALGÈBRE DANS L'ENSEIGNEMENT
SECONDAIRE ET POST-SECONDAIRE

Chief Organizer / *Responsable en chef* : Carolyn Kieran [CAN]
Advisory team members / *Consultants* : Anthony Gardiner [GBR],
Anna Sfard [ISR], Bert Waits [USA]

The first three of the working group sessions each began with a keynote presentation: (Anna Sfard [ISR]: "The development of algebra: confronting historical and psychological perspectives"; Alan Bell [GBR]: "Putting purpose into school algebra"; Bert Waits [USA]: "The influence of technology on the teaching and learning of algebra" (paper coauthored with John Harvey and Franklin Demana [USA]). Participants then split into three subgroups according to their level of interest (prealgebra, secondary, tertiary) to discuss how the ideas of the keynote presentations might be applied at the level of their subgroup. The fourth session opened with a plenary reaction by Abraham Arcavi [ISR] to the three previous keynote presentations and discussions, and was then followed by a discussion period involving participants and keynote speakers.

Anna Sfard, who provided a retrospective on the history of the development of algebra and then showed how this history can be used as a source of insight on the learning and teaching of algebraic concepts, focused on some recurrent phenomena in the development of abstract ideas. She looked at turning points in the formation of algebraic thinking: the transition from arithmetic to rhetorical and syncopated algebras, the introduction of algebraic symbolism, and the emergence of abstract algebra. These turning points were examined not only for the mechanisms which put such developments into motion but also for the nature and the source of the cognitive difficulties which invariably surface whenever a crucial step forward is to be made. The point of departure for this pattern-finding is her theoretical model according to which the formation of mathematical knowledge is a more or less cyclic process – a process in which transitions from one level to another follow some constant course. In this particular scheme, mathematics is viewed as a hierarchy in which what is conceived operationally, namely as a computational process, on one level is reified into an abstract object, or conceived structurally, on a higher level. Sfard's psychological observations were reinforced with data coming from a wide range of empirical studies.

Alan Bell's presentation focused on ways in which we should redirect the teaching of school algebra. He began by pointing out that research on the learning of algebra identifies two kinds of difficulty: a) local errors and misconceptions, including notational errors such as $3^2 = 6$, or xy for x + y, and false canceling as in $(2x + 1) / (2x + 7) = 1/7$; and b) global or strategic failures, such as the inability to reason with algebra, or to recognize the difference between an equation and an identity. The former type of error can be treated by the methods of Diagnostic Teaching (Bell et al., 1985); the latter requires a restructuring of the algebra curriculum, in which manipulative skills take second place (though still an important place) to authentic algebraic activities – these being global activities which display the meaning and purpose of algebra. Such activities involve the main algebraic strategies of: generalizing, working with functions and formulas, forming and solving equations. For example:

1. Show that the sum of a number of four digits and the number formed by reversing the digits is always divisible by 11.

2. (The following chart of pizza prices asks students to explore the relations between diameter and cost, and to discuss what is good value.)

Size	Diameter of pizza plate	Cost
Mini	20 cm	$4.00
Small	25 cm	$5.00
Medium	27.5 cm	$7.50
Large	30.5 cm	$8.60
Family	38 cm	$10.50

3. Show that, if $2s = a + b + c$, $s(s - a) + (s - b)(s - c) = bc$.

Example 3 is suggested as one which is *not* in itself such an authentic activity (though it may be a valid component of a larger activity). The remainder of Bell's presentation discussed some examples of tasks, including pupils' own work, which have been used in the classroom to develop pupils' awareness and abilities under the three headings above.

Bert Waits emphasized how technology can change (in certain countries or areas, has already changed) the teaching and learning of algebra. Algebra can now be viewed more broadly as a language of representation, rather than simply as the process of paper and pencil computations and algorithms.

Low cost scientific calculators are tools that make numerical representations and numerical problem solving readily accessible to algebra students. For example, an exact algebraic solution to the equation $\cos x = x$ is not possible while a simple numerical recursion ($x_{n+1} = \cos x_n$) provides an easy solution using scientific calculators. Inexpensive pocket graphing calculators are tools that make computer-generated geometric representations, graphical analysis, and visualization readily accessible to algebra students. For example, magnifying (by a zoom-in) the graph of $y = x^3 - x^2 + x - 5$ at the x-intercept provides an accurate solution to the equation $x^3 - x^2 + x - 5 = 0$, not possible or not practical with paper and pencil methods alone. Use of computer symbolic algebra systems like Derive make complicated, tedious symbolic manipulations, like finding the exact solution to $x^3 - x^2 + x - 5 = 0$ over the field of complex numbers, routine. Thus, in the future, much less time needs to be spent on paper and pencil algorithms. More time can be spent in algebra on problem solving skills, exploring connections among multiple representations, "what if" investigations, structure, and applications.

The *prealgebra discussion subgroup,* which was led by Liora Linchevski [ISR] assisted by Shmuel Avital [ISR] , Orit Zaslavsky [ISR], and Pat Perks [GBR], defined prealgebra as the stage of transition between the environment of arithmetic and that of formal algebra. Participants agreed that prealgebra is the continuation of arithmetic in the sense that it deals mainly with numbers but asks different questions about those numbers. Using the three keynote presentations as a framework for their discussions, prealgebra group participants focused on various mathematical ideas, experiences, and situations that can be introduced through arithmetic in order to facilitate children's understanding of the meaning, significance, and use of symbolic representations and later on of algebraic manipulations. For example, it was agreed that algebraic ideas and procedures could be executed without the explicit use of letters. Another issue examined was the place of modeling word problems as a possible route for combining meaningful situations with the beginnings of algebraic manipulations. The keynote presentation on the role of technology stimulated a discussion of how calculators, at the prealgebra stage, could play a central role in providing pupils with opportunities to construct arithmetic patterns, to explore and check mathematical ideas, and to reach and express generalizations.

The *secondary algebra discussion subgroup,* which was led by M. Kathleen Heid [USA], assisted by Jerry Johnson, Sharon Senk, and Rose Mary Zbiek [USA], focused first on the following issues related to the Sfard presentation: the need to distinguish between algebraic thinking and algebra (as well as their respective histories and the contexts surrounding them); the question of whether reification can be orchestrated or accelerated; what might be the next stage in the history of algebra and whether students do/ should/must pass through the three stages described by Sfard (generalized numerical computations, universal computations, and abstract structure); and whether it is advisable for students to be taught how to *do* algebra first and understand its meaning later. Issues related to the Bell presentation that were subsequently discussed included: the importance of not divorcing symbolic algebra and geometric (or visual or graphical) algebra; the role of the study of structures in the secondary school algebra experience; and, because of the advent of technology, the need for more research on how much paper-and-pencil work is required for students to understand algebra. The Waits presentation on technology led to discussions of a new vision of school algebra as a realm of mathematical exploration, as well as of the need for research to focus more globally on issues of choice of tool rather than solely on graphical representations, and on questions such as: What classes of functions should students study and why? What relative roles do reasoning, evidence, and formal proof have once technology enters the classroom?

The discussion of the *tertiary discussion subgroup,* led by Ed Barbeau [CAN], ranged over a variety of issues. There was agreement with the historical framework provided by Sfard and with the notion that algebra students somehow have to create this development in themselves. The difficulties in attaining ownership illustrated in the Bell presentation persist into the post-secondary level. The group was essentially persuaded by the arguments in favor of technology found in the Harvey, Waits, and Demana paper, although it was noted that their examples did not deal so much with algebra as with its application to analysis. Participants expressed the need to examine how technology can enhance the sort of strategic thinking lying behind the display of algebraic expressions or the way they should be thought about. Other points of discussion included the difficulties faced by tertiary algebra students: many are put off by the formalism of definitions, axioms and logical deduction; others cannot handle entities with the appropriate flexibility; they often arrive in college with lack of skill and experience, and are undermined by misconceptions and imprecision. Technology can help through computer packages such as CAYLEY that permit the manipulation of complicated examples, the making of conjectures, and the checking of understanding. For algebra as a service for other sciences, it is not easy to hit the appropriate level of abstraction, as some broader understanding seems to be essential for effective application. In any case, it was emphasized that algebra is a sufficiently important component of the tertiary curriculum that much more attention to the problems of teaching and learning is warranted.

Abraham Arcavi's keynote address at the closing session of the working group synthesized and integrated the three previous addresses and the discussions that they stimulated.

1. What are the main lessons from the historical evolution of the ideas in algebra which are applicable to our understanding (and improving) of algebra learning? This question was analyzed on the basis of Sfard's distinction between the operational and the structural nature of mathematical ideas. The concerns raised referred mainly to: Whose history? To what extent can we defer meaning without falling into mere drill and practice? Is the history of the ideas as they evolved in the best minds of their time a good source for enriching our understanding of student learning?

2. What are the main ideas of algebra to be reflected in a school algebra course? Bell suggested the following: generalizing, forming and solving equations, and working with functions and formulas. The main issues raised by the discussion referred to the following: the need for a more general view of algebra beyond its symbolic aspect, the question of how algebra connects to the real world (or, in other words, do we really need algebra to get along?), and the need to accompany curriculum projects with careful observation of students.

3. The potential of technology in the teaching and learning of algebra was addressed by Waits. The main concerns regarding the increasing role of technology in mathematics classrooms referred to: the preparation of teachers (including their beliefs about mathematics and teaching), the possibility that technology could further distance the Third World from the rest of the world, the emergence of new learning difficulties inherent to the new tools, and the redefinition of some classics of instruction like symbol manipulation in favor of new themes (like symbol sense).

NOTE

This report was prepared by Carolyn Kieran, in collaboration with A. Arcavi, E. Barbeau, A. Bell, M.K. Heid, L. Linchevski, A. Sfard, Y. Shefi, and B. Waits.

Papers and discussions of the Working Group WG13 will appear in the book: Kieran, C. (Ed.) *The place of algebra in secondary and tertiary education.* Submitted for publication.

REFERENCES

Bell, A.W., Onslow, B., Pratt, K., Purdy, D., & Swan, M.B. (1985). *Diagnostic teaching: teaching for long term learning* (Report of ESRC Project 8491/1). Nottingham, UK: University of Nottingham, Shell Centre for Mathematical Education.

Sfard, A., & Linchevski, L. (in press). The gains and the pitfalls of reification – the case of algebra. *Educational Studies in Mathematics*.

Working Group 14 / *Groupe de travail 14*

MATHEMATICAL MODELING
IN THE CLASSROOM

MODÉLISATION MATHÉMATIQUE EN CLASSE

Chief Organizer / *Responsable en chef* : Trygve Breiteig [NOR]
Local Organizer / *Responsable local* : Brendan Kelly [CAN]
Advisory team members / *Consultants* : Gabriele Kaiser-Messmer [DEU],
Jan de Lange [NLD], Zalman Usiskin [USA]

Mathematical modeling in the classroom has been a topic of discussion at all ICMEs since ICME-2, occasionally appearing under the titles "applications of mathematics" and "links between mathematics and other subjects". State-of-the-art reports may be found in Pollak (1979) and Bell (1983). Recent working group summaries may be found in Lesh (1986), Niss (1988) and Blum (1988). Also related to the affairs of this working group are the International Conferences on the Teaching of Mathematical Modelling and Its Applications (ICTMAs), whose sessions are summarized in Berry et al. (1984, 1986, 1987), Blum et al. (1989), and Niss et al. (1991).

At this conference, the working group met for four sessions. The opening and closing sessions were plenary meetings. In the two intermediate sessions the group participants, whose number vacillated between 100 and 130, chose one of four subgroups.

The *opening session,* which consisted of three introductory lectures, dealt with two overall themes: What is mathematical modeling? What is being done? Werner Blum [DEU] gave an overview of the topics to be discussed. He began by reviewing the arguments for the inclusion of mathematical modeling as an essential part of mathematics teaching. Then he described the role of mathematical modeling in present-day mathematics curricula and in everyday mathematics teaching practice, and gave reasons why modeling usually plays only a minor role in the classroom. He closed by identifying various recently-developed materials and resources for teaching mathematical modeling. Ron Lewis [CAN] exemplified what a teacher can do with a specific area of modeling, in this case involving fractals.

He described his experiences with a unit involving fractals he has developed over several years in his secondary school. This unit begins with the problem of the length of a coastline and proceeds through the introduction of mathematically regular fractals such as the snowflake curve. Jan de Lange [NLD] described his experiences with problem-oriented curricula at the secondary level. Although in general such curricula are considered to be a success, major difficulties have arisen dealing with the teacher's role as facilitator rather than explicator, the teaching and learning of the structure of mathematics along with basic skills, and the assessment of students.

The *Primary subgroup* was led by Leen Streefland and Heleen Verhage [NLD]. The participants felt that with primary children, mathematical models need to be developed first before they can be applied. Koeno Gravemeijer [NLD] sketched the following sequence:

$$\boxed{\text{situations}} \rightarrow \boxed{\text{models of...}} \rightarrow \boxed{\text{models for...}} \rightarrow \boxed{\text{formal mathematics}}$$

This distinction in the concept of modeling, reflected by almost all contributors, indicates a change of perspective in the learning process. Concrete phenomena in this framework support both the process of modeling as well as the construction of the models by the learners. Dagmar Neuman [SWE] noted that children use their fingers to indicate numbers when modeling simple subtraction problems, and that these ideas gave them access to basic number patterns. Despina Potari [GRC] reported on children's construction of a village, first by making plans on paper, finally realizing them in a scale model, in the process developing fundamental measuring and geometric concepts in two and three dimensions. Terezinha Nunes [GBR] pointed out that the representations a child has at hand will influence the structure of the solution in problem solving. She referred to experiments which show that using a model is not automatic and so must be developed by learners in the teaching-learning process. Koeno Gravemeijer [NLD] showed the power of the "empty number line" representation. Mieke Abels [NLD] reported on experiences with a pair of number lines (one of which is elastic) in teaching percents, beginning with the context of ratios of vinegar and oil in a salad dressing. Leen Streefland [NLD] argued that besides the problem situation and presentation for the pupils, certain actions in the context are important, too. The context might become a situation model in the background for the pupils' schematizing. Max Bell [USA] argued for plausible and clear specifications for teaching applications and mathematical modeling if those emphases are ever to compete successfully with the traditional basics of computation.

The *Lower Secondary subgroup* was led by Alan Rogerson [AUS]. Eight invited speakers made presentations. Alan Rogerson reported on the International Mathematics in Society Project, which since 1980 has been producing thematic materials for students of ages 11-16. Tetsuo Matsumiya, Akira Yanagimoto, and Yuichi Mori [JPN] described a case study of modeling in the classroom based on the mathematics of a track and field sport. Gail Burrill [USA] described a stimulating modeling project based on analyzing subjective ratings of various makes of cars. Paulo Abrantes [PRT] outlined some of the work being done in Portugal using thematic sequences, open problems, and project work to more effectively teach mathematics. John Gillespie [GBR] showed excerpts from computer interactive videos he has been developing at the Shell Centre to stimulate open modeling by students. Lucia Grugnetti [ITA] spoke on the highly socially relevant problems that were being used in Cagliari, Italy, to introduce mathematical modeling. Manmohan Arora [BHR] reported on the educational situation in general in India, pointing out the severe constraints in developing countries governing any implementation of modeling and applications-oriented curricula. Angela Pesci [ITA] raised general questions of the importance of motivation in modeling, the emphasis that should be placed on the conceptual development of mathematics, and the distinction that should be made between deductive and inductive reasoning. In the general discussions, Corinne Hahn [FRA] described her innovative modeling approach to teaching mathematics in a business school, while Julian Williams [GBR] spoke about the enactive and relevant-to-student activities developed in the Mechanics in Action project.

The *Upper Secondary subgroup* was led by Gabriele Kaiser-Messmer [DEU]. Sue Burns [GBR] described reasons to include modeling in a modern curriculum and gave examples of case studies based on authentic problems suitable for the classroom. Jonathan Choate [USA] demonstrated how modeling along with appropriate software can be used to study a variety of real-world phenomena. Tibor Nemetz [HUN] described the Hungarian income tax as an authentic example for the classroom which promotes a slow and careful introduction into the modeling processes. In the discussion that ensued, the following points were raised: the difficulty of meeting student interests even with authentic examples; the role of technology and its accessibility for all students; modeling as a possible tool for uncovering student misconceptions about mathematics. Yoshiki Nagayama [JPN] made a presentation on origami, the Japanese art of paper-folding, in which he emphasized the elementary geometrical transformations involved. Maria Salett Biembengut [BRA] described mathematical modeling as a new way of teaching and exemplified this using a variety of problems related to bees. Robert Money [AUS] gave an overview of the situation in Australia concerning the role and relevance of modeling examples in school and described different modeling materials and courses developed so far. Ann Kitchen and Julian Williams [GBR] described the Mechanics in Action Project, in which mathematical modeling plays an important part and which uses different forms of assessment procedures. The discussion dealt primarily with the different ways of assessing modeling examples and courses, as well the general difficulties entailed in this assessment.

The Tertiary subgroup was led by John Berry [GBR]. Heinrich Abel [DEU] described a mathematics course for engineers designed around a series of modules with videotapes and supporting textbooks as the instructional medium. Ted Graham [GBR] described the mathematics component of a preparatory course for engineering students which uses the DERIVE symbolic manipulator software to help students explore models containing mathematics beyond that which students have previously encountered. Following these presentations, the subgroup split itself into working groups, which generated a set of 13 "favorite problems" as examples of the kinds of problems which can stimulate mathematical modeling in the classroom, covering the following contexts: knots in ropes; street light placement; crop-spraying; bacterial concentrations; towing icebergs to arid lands; cutting a sausage; track and field start positions; rocket launches "straight up"; fair division among more than 2 people; runs of cards after shuffling; beer level and the center of gravity of a beer can; pricing doughnuts and raffles so as to optimize money taken in. Alistair Carr [AUS] then shared experiences in teaching modeling-based courses and discussed the problems of their design, implementation and assessment. Chris Haines [GBR] described his work with John Izard [AUS] on the formulation of descriptors to provide objective assessment criteria.

The subgroup then again divided into working groups, which discussed peer and self-assessment. A variety of issues emerged, such as: How does one achieve some consistency in grades and assessment when self-assessments are applied? How does an instructor factor out the unequal contributions of various group members when the quality of a team project is assessed and grades are to be assigned to individual team members? Some potential solutions to these quandaries were suggested.

The *Closing Plenary* session consisted primarily of three talks regarding the future of mathematical modeling in the curriculum. Solomon Garfunkel [USA] began by assuming that the classroom of the future will have the computer-based technology of the information age and a curriculum whose core is applications and modeling. Under these assumptions, two questions are unresolved: What mathematical themes and contexts can provide a coherent development of basic concepts that can be internalized by students? At what point should differentiation between science and non-science bound students begin? He described a recent proposal of the Consortium for Mathematics and Its Applications (COMAP) to deal with these questions in grades 9 to 11. Gabriele Kaiser-Messmer [DEU] gave an overview of what we know and what we need to learn about mathematical modeling in the classroom. Successful approaches include: extensive periods in which students are actively engaged in all phases of the modeling process; a balance between informal context-centered and formal mathematically-oriented approaches; a significant number of authentic problems from outside mathematics; and new methods of assessing modeling activities in addition to coursework. Needed are research – particularly longitudinal studies – into the obstacles to teaching and learning mathematics via modeling, and the integration of modeling into pre-service and inservice teacher education. Zalman Usiskin [USA] spoke of the diversity of notions about mathematical modeling, including the notion that applied mathematics is an inferior type of mathematics, or fundamentally different from pure mathematics, or parallels pure mathematics, or that it *is* mathematics, the latter conception being the one probably shared by most in this working group. The future of mathematical modeling in elementary and secondary classrooms depends to a great extent on which of these notions prevail.

The session ended with a question-and-answer period in which various issues were addressed, including the fundamental question of the integration of mathematical modeling as a continuing expectation in the everyday mathematics curriculum of students.

Summary: To create and handle mathematical models is part of both societal work and scientific work. It plays an important role in the development of students' mathematical concepts. The group has analyzed and advocated its inclusion into curriculum, and focused on how this raises special issues and challenges. One main output of this group may be the awareness of the complexity and the problems of teaching and learning modeling and applications, and the avoidance of easy solutions.

NOTE

The papers from the working group summarized in this report can be found in the following book: Breiteig, T., Huntley, I. & Kaiser-Messmer, G. (Eds.) (1993). *Teaching and learning mathematics in context.* Chichester, UK: Ellis Horwood.

REFERENCES

Bell, M. (1983). Materials available worldwide for teaching applications of mathematics at the school level. In M. Zweng et al. (Eds.), *Proceedings of the Fourth International Congress on Mathematical Education* (pp 252-267). Boston: Birkhäuser.

Berry, J. et al. (Eds.) (1984). *Teaching and applying mathematical modelling.* Chichester, UK: Ellis Horwood.

Berry, J. et al. (Eds.) (1986). *Mathematical modelling methodology, models and micros.* Chichester, UK: Ellis Horwood.

Berry, J. et al. (Eds.) (1987). *Mathematical modelling courses.* Chichester, UK: Ellis Horwood.

Blum, W. (1988). Report on Theme Group 6: Mathematics and other subjects. In A. & K. Hirst (Eds.), *Proceedings of the Sixth International Congress on Mathematical Education* (pp. 277-291). Budapest: János Bolyai Mathematical Society.

Blum, W. et al. (Eds.) (1989). *Applications and modelling in learning and teaching mathematics.* Chichester, UK: Ellis Horwood.

Breiteig, T., Huntley, I., & Kaiser-Messmer, G. (Eds.) (1993). *Teaching and learning mathematics in context.* Chichester, UK: Ellis Horwood.

Lesh, R., Niss, M., & Lee, D. (1986). Report on Theme Group 6: Applications and modelling. In Carss, M. (Ed.), *Proceedings of the Fifth International Congress on Mathematical Education* (pp. 197-211). Boston: Birkhäuser.

Niss, M. (1988). Report on Theme Group 3: Problem solving, modelling and applications. In A. & K. Hirst (Eds.), *Proceedings of the Sixth International Congress on Mathematical Education* (pp. 237-252). Budapest: János Bolyai Mathematical Society.

Niss, M., Blum, W., & Huntley, I. (Eds.) (1991). *Teaching mathematical modelling and applications.* Chichester: Ellis Horwood.

Pollak, H. (1979). The interaction between mathematics and other school subjects. In *New Trends in Mathematics Teaching* IV (pp. 232-248). Paris: UNESCO.

Working Group 15 / *Groupe de travail 15*

UNDERGRADUATE MATHEMATICS
FOR DIFFERENT GROUPS OF STUDENTS

MATHÉMATIQUES DE NIVEAU POST-SECONDAIRE
POUR DIFFÉRENTS GROUPES D'ÉTUDIANTS
ET D'ÉTUDIANTES

Chief Organizer / *Responsable en chef* : Daniel Alibert [FRA]
Local Organizer / *Responsable local* : Harvey Gerber [CAN]
Advisory team members / *Consultants* : Barbara A. Jur [USA],
Adaremi O. Kuku [NGA], Susanti Linowih [IDN], Peter Nüesch [CHE],
John W. Searl [GBR], Martha Siegel [USA]

The first of four sessions began with an address by Margaret Cozzens [USA], who presented some of the important problems of the field. Then the group separated into four subgroups, each one managed by two members of the organizing team.

The subgroup on *Mathematics for non-specialists in the science field* was organized by Martha Siegel and Peter Nüesch. The following ideas were discussed:

- This task is in some ways more difficult (higher demand on mathematics) and in some ways easier (better-motivated students) than for other specialists.

- The formal approach is not adequate for this task; methods and concepts should be kept distinct.

- Mathematics courses are taught better by mathematicians and should be taught by mathematicians. The mathematics so taught should be used by the professors (who are not mathematics professors) in their later courses. Mathematics has to accompany the student from entry until graduation.

- The mathematical sophistication of research papers in these fields is high (as it is in economics). One goal of mathematics instruction is to enable the graduate to read her/his literature if she/he is not capable of writing mathematics in a sophisticated manner.

- The computer is a basic tool in all mathematics instruction. Syllabuses set up before computers were readily available need revision. Also, professors have to change their attitudes.

- Discrete mathematics has to be introduced.

Analysis (including numerical analysis), linear algebra, probability and statistics, discrete mathematics – all these four branches should be taught in a separate, parallel, but overlapping way. There is a compromise of too many minicourses (2 + 1 per week for one semester) and only one math course (taught according to the "bible", that is, engineering mathematics). Math is more than a nuisance to get over as quickly and painlessly as possible. Give mathematics its due.

The subgroup on *Service courses for non-scientists* was organized by B.A. Jur and Susanti Linowih. Discussions centered on five aspects of mathematics education for business students.

- *Secondary school:* Though it was reported that students say they do see the connections between their secondary school mathematics and their business courses, inadequate secondary preparation was a concern for the subgroup. It was linked to widespread need for remedial programs and special tutorials, to the anxiety, dislike, and difficulty some students associate with their college mathematics, to the threat of lower standards, and to some faculty unhappiness about having to teach students with weak backgrounds. The subgroup felt secondary students should become proficient in basic algebra.

- *Calculus and statistics:* Another report showed the percentage of American business programs requiring some calculus has increased and a study at Purdue indicated, with some surprise, a greater need for integral and multivariate calculus. Calculus was also seen as helping develop complex problem-solving skills in a new context. The subgroup recommends further investigations on this topic. It agreed that statistics education must include descriptive statistics, estimation, correlation and regression, and that it would also be desirable to cover hypothesis testing, χ^2, ANOVA, index numbers, time series, and non-parametric methods.

- *Computers:* Though access to computers may be limited, computer issues were not a major problem for the subgroup which generally felt it is more important to take the time needed for developing the understanding of concepts rather than to spend much time using computers for manipulation or number crunching. Of course, appropriate packages should be used as needed in advanced courses.

187

- *Staffing math courses for business:* The subgroup agreed faculty teaching such courses needed to be interested in teaching them (even though they differ greatly from the mathematical theorem/proof courses many professors prefer) and there were some indications that this is indeed happening more often. Faculty teaching mathematics for business may initially need some advice or training, and should be encouraged to dialog with business faculty. These courses do need monitoring and those who teach them well should be commended. There was concern that if mathematicians do a poor job with these courses, they will be deleted or taken over by other departments.

- *Ways to determine the need for curriculum revision on an ongoing basis:* Continue to survey students – several presenters reported having found some interesting information when such surveys were done. Establish communication with business educators and perhaps the business community, possibly including surveys or advisory committees. Keep aware of developments in technology that might suggest innovations in teaching mathematics for business.

The subgroup on *Research into tertiary mathematical education* was organized by John Searl and Daniel Alibert. There is no coherent body of research about mathematical education at the tertiary level. While the considerable amount of research which has focused (rightly) on the mathematical development of young children and adolescents offers insights into the learning of advanced mathematics, there has been no program devoted to the special needs of maturing students. As the student passes from secondary to tertiary education, the mathematical demands made upon him or her become more sophisticated. The mathematics moves from an intuitive style to a more formal approach. There is a more rapid transition from particular contextualized examples to abstract mathematical theory. The nature of formal proof is not well understood and the need for such proofs is not appreciated by all students. At the same time there is a sharp change in the learning situation. Instead of having a teacher to direct and control their studies, students find themselves having to organize their own learning.

The change from secondary to tertiary education demands from the students a deeper and more reflective understanding of the mathematics they have learned at school and upon which subsequent mathematical development depends. This process can be helped by an approach which requires the students to identify the abstract properties of mathematical objects and operations that allow specific problems to be solved. These properties often constitute the axioms of a general mathematical structure. Thus students move from a particular case to the general in a reflective mode of thought and construct the abstract structure for themselves.

The change from school to college also requires the students to assimilate a new body of ideas, often over a short period of time. This process can be helped by the appropriate use of technology. Research in this field has been very encouraging but the need for students to feel in control of the technology was underlined. Because the technology removes the chore of calculating it can provide opportunities for investigative approaches to problems. Such approaches may generate and encourage creativity and initiative in the students.

There are many difficulties associated with the evaluation of innovative programs to enhance the quality of learning at the tertiary level. Large scale surveys may give information, for example, about trends in undergraduate mathematics throughout the world, but they do not provide insight into the learning of mathematics. It is not usually possible to validate programs by the control versus experimental group model. A method which may offer some useful information is that of illuminative evaluation. This enables the researcher to identify more clearly the misunderstandings, mis-skills and misconcepts of individual students, and to illuminate the learning environment for the instructor.

The subgroup *Mathematics for specialists, teachers or researchers* was organized by Adaremi O. Kuku and Harvey Gerber. Problems and issues raised are:

- There is a general concern about the quantity and quality of undergraduate mathematics specialists at universities. Indeed the public image of mathematics hinders many of the liveliest minds from entering the subject.

- Universities need to ensure that their courses encourage interest in, appreciation of, and enjoyment of mathematics.

- However, the current standard methods of teaching and assessment do not adequately reflect the nature of the subject, or allow an adequate professional development of students.

The goals for an undergraduate training for specialists in mathematics include:

- The encouragement of independence, creativity, and self-confidence in students (particularly abilities in problem posing and solving, in conjecturing, in proving, and in modeling concrete situations).

- The encouragement of technical development, as well as an appreciation of professional issues such as:

  i) the place of mathematics in the scheme of things;

ii)   the notion of value in the subject;

iii)   the methods of working in the subject, such as thinking, learning, planning, writing, reading, talking, calculating, evaluating, communicating;

iv)   some appreciation of contemporary research developments, problems, and issues;

v)   the roles of concepts, definitions, calculations, algorithms, and computation in mathematics.

The realization of the goals listed above depends crucially on the assessment process, which should be sufficiently diversified in order to assess adequately the achievement of all these goals.

REFERENCES

Parlett, M., & Hamilton, D. (1972). *Evaluation as illumination: a new approach to the study of innovative programs.* Centre for Research in Educational Sciences, University of Edinburgh.

Cobb, G. (1991). Teaching statistics: more data, less lecturing. *Undergraduate Mathematics Education (UME) Trends, 3*(4).

Horgan and Walsh, J.A. (1990). Applications of statistics in accountancy.

Proceedings of The Third International Conference on Teaching Statistics. Dunedin, New Zealand.

Jur, B.A. (1990). *Trends in mathematics service courses for business.* Paper presented at the MAA meeting in Louisville.

Tall, D.O. (Ed.) (1991). *Advanced mathematical thinking.* Dordrecht: Kluwer Academic Publishers.

Working Group 16 / *Groupe de travail 16*

THE IMPACT OF THE CALCULATOR ON THE ELEMENTARY SCHOOL CURRICULUM

L'IMPACT DES CALCULATRICES SUR LE CURRICULUM DES ÉCOLES PRIMAIRES

Chief Organizer / *Responsable en chef* : Hilary Shuard † [GBR]
Local Organizer / *Responsable local* : Lorna Morrow [CAN]
Advisory team members / *Consultants* : Donna Berlin [USA],
Renée Caron [CAN], Alwyn Olivier [ZAF], Maria Rubies [ESP]

The group received and discussed 23 presentations by contributors from Australia, Canada, France, Germany, South Africa, Sweden, the United Kingdom, and the United States. Three sessions were conducted in small groups. The liveliness and commitment of the group members made the sessions very successful.

Among the major topics of presentations were:

• curriculum development projects which make use of calculators;

• the use of the calculator in the classroom and across the school;

• attitudes toward calculator use;

• the development of children's thinking; and

• the development of teaching styles.

Several *major issues* were identified, and are discussed below. The quotations are all from written materials distibuted by presenters.

The most important issue was not overtly discussed, but became clear from the styles of working described by different presenters. Different projects and different teachers use calculators in different ways; the style of calculator use depends on the philosophy of mathematics teaching adopted by the project or the teacher. Some presenters took the view that children need to be taught particular concepts and skills. Other presenters wanted children to investigate and explore mathematical ideas for themselves.

The calculator provides a powerful tool for either approach to mathematics. Some projects provide worksheets on which children fill in answers to pre-determined problems; sometimes lesson notes are also provided. The following is an example of a largely pre-determined problem from the Hamilton Project (George Knill [CAN]).

"Determine the pattern and complete the table.

Odd Numbers Sum				Sum	
			1	1	1( )
		3 +	5	8	2( )
	7 +	9 +	11	27	3( )
13 +	15 +	17 +	19		
— +	— +	— +	— + —		
— + — +	— +	— +	— + —		

Describe the pattern in your own words."

In the British projects such as CAN (Calculator-Aware Number) and the Calculators in Primary Mathematics Project, the approach is less structured. Laurie Rousham [GBR] reported: "Initially it was difficult for teachers to control content in math sessions as the children increasingly saw this as their prerogative. Although children as young as six would spend whole mornings investigating something of interest to them, on other days they would not, and they were often less interested in teacher-initiated directions."

How is the calculator used in the elementary classroom? Is it only a tool for obtaining quick answers, and for checking answers obtained by other methods? Presenters stated that the checking of answers is the most frequent use of calculators in elementary classrooms. Other uses of a calculator were shown in the presentations. These included: helping children to concentrate on the solution of a problem without becoming lost in the calculation, making accessible problems which would be impossible without the calculator, using the calculator to explore mathematical patterns and concepts, and exploring features of the calculator itself. An example of a problem which would not be possible without a calculator was given by Franklin Demana [USA].

"The population of a small village was 400 in 1980, and it is growing at the constant rate of 2% per annum. When will the population be 550?"

How can teachers be equipped to take advantage of these more interesting uses of the calculator, which are unknown to many teachers?

How can the calculator be used with other materials, such as manip-ulatives, computers, and textual materials? John Sutton [USA] had surveyed the uses of calculators in published texts, and noted how unimaginative were the exercises provided, for example:

A sample of a 5th grade "read the calculator display" activity:

"Use this key sequence to change 6 7/8 to a decimal.

Press 7 ÷ 8 + 6. What does the display show?"

In what ways should children be expected to calculate nowadays? All participants agreed that children need to gain facility in mental calculation. Hartwig Meissner [DEU] stated a student's experience: "For many problems in mental arithmetic I do not need the calculator. I am as safe as the calculator, but I am quicker in my head than in pressing the keys."

A fundamental question is whether the traditional pencil-and-paper algorithms should continue to be taught. Among the projects which gave presentations, only CAN has given up teaching the traditional pencil-and-paper algorithms. All other projects seem to expect these methods to continue alongside the calculator, at least for the time being. Perhaps mathematics educators feel that teachers and parents will be resistant if children are not taught the traditional methods. Teachers may be worried about what mathematics they should teach if the algorithms are no longer required. Ingvar Persson [SWE] found that "investigation shows that during 60-75% of the time used for mathematics in school, students are doing algorithmic calculations with pencil and paper."

What other changes in content is the calculator bringing to the elementary curriculum? It seems to make available an earlier treatment of more abstract and complex numerical topics, and problem solving methods such as 'trial and improvement'. Real data, rather than simplified data, can now be used. Said Hilary Shuard: "Among the changes are the much earlier use of large numbers, decimals and negative numbers. CAN children are also much more willing to investigate mathematical problems, and to think out their own methods. In many classes, an investigational approach has spread from number to other parts of mathematics, and to other curriculum areas."

Elementary teachers often seem to be reluctant to use calculators in their own classrooms. Peter Howard [AUS] gave the results of an enquiry in which teachers were asked whether they believed that calculators should be used in elementary classrooms. They were then asked how often they themselves used calculators in their classrooms. Of 147 Australian teachers surveyed, "85% strongly supported the introduction of calculators into the primary years, but only 32% responded that they were currently using calculators." Howard also found that a majority of kindergarten teachers did not see the calculator as relevant for their class. However, Susie Groves [AUS] provided several examples of uses of the calculator for very young children. These included the following: *"Happy families* is an activity which has been used at grade 1, where the calculator is only used as a recording device. Children enter a number of their choice between 1 and 99. They then group themselves around the room in their "families" (i.e. with others in the same group of ten). Children first order themselves within their families, and then across the whole grade. *Number line-up.* This involves a group of children entering numbers of their choice into their calculators and then sorting themselves into ascending order. Grade 1 and 2 children frequently include negative or very large numbers in this activity."

Teachers who have not used calculators in the classroom have expectations about the consequences of calculator use. Meier [USA] has surveyed 263 American teachers. She found that: "The biggest concerns of teachers with regard to calculator usage in the mathematics classroom fell into four categories:

- Students not knowing basic facts and/or being dependent on the calculator.
- Lack of availability for all students.
- Misunderstanding of the uses of calculators by parents and teachers.
- Lack of consistent practices and policies in their school district.

The most commonly cited benefits were:

- Ability of students to self-check work.
- Increasing problem solving opportunities.
- Motivating students/improving student attitudes.
- Incorporating technology and "real world" methods.

It is often thought that parents are opposed to the use of calculators in the elementary classroom. How true is this? Some members thought that parents were usually supportive if they were properly informed about the reasons for calculator use. However, one survey compared how parents and teachers perceived the importance of various mathematical topics in the elementary classroom. Basic facts, manipulatives and computation were thought to be the most important topics, but John Sutton [USA] said: "In comparison to any and all of the other topics, in almost every instance, both parents and teachers felt calculators were not very important, especially in grades 1 to 4." He also spoke on the question of who should provide children with calculators. Should it be the school or the parent? "In a study conducted in over 80 classrooms with over 2000 students in grades K-8 during the 1987-8 school year, over 96 percent of the students surveyed indicated they had a calculator in their home and that they had access to it." Should all children in a class be expected to have the same model of calculator? What functions are needed on a calculator for the elementary grades? Who should decide whether a calculator should be used for a particular activity, the teacher or the child?

What is the relation of the calculator to tests and other assessments? Should tests include "calculator required" items? Should calculators be allowed in standardized tests, at this stage in history, when some schools use calculators and others do not?

Some projects were able to provide data on the comparative performance on standardized tests of children who were accustomed to using calculators and those who were not. Gary Bitter and Mary Hatfield [USA] say: "One third of the eighth-grade students were taught by a teacher committed to integrating calculators into mathematics instruction, as confirmed by observational data. This teacher's students performed significantly better on all Iowa Test of Basic Skills mathematics tests, both with and without the calculator." Laurie Rousham added: "In an external, county-wide mathematics test of 36 items (not all number) eight-year-old children in the four CAN schools outperformed other Suffolk children of the same age in twenty-eight items and had lower facility rates in seven. On the 7 items of underperformance, CAN children's facility rate was a mean of 2.9 percentage points lower than the non-CAN group, whereas on the 28 items where they performed better it was a mean of 10.8 points higher (CAN facility rate 74.1%; non-CAN 44%)."

REFERENCES

Australian Association of Mathematics Teachers / Curriculum Development Centre (1987). *A national statement on the use of calculators for mathematics in Australian schools.* Canberra: Curriculum Development Centre.

Bitter G.G., & Hatfield M.M. (1992). Integration of the Math Explorer Calculator into the mathematics curriculum: *The Calculator Project Report.* Arizona State University.

Victoria College, Burwood, Australia. *The Calculators in Primary Mathematics Project Newsletter*.

California State University – Fullerton (1991). *Calculators and Mathematics Project (CAMP-LA)*, Books 1 to 4 (Grades K-8).

National Council of Teachers of Mathematics (1989). *Curriculum and evaluation standards for school mathematics*. Reston, VA: NCTM.

National Council of Teachers of Mathematics (1992). *Calculators in mathematics education*. Reston, VA: NCTM.

Shuard H., Walsh A., Goodwin J., & Worcester V. (1991). *Calculators, children and mathematics*. Simon & Schuster. [Video with same title also available from Simon & Schuster.]

Working Group 17 / *Groupe de travail 17*

TECHNOLOGY IN THE SERVICE OF THE MATHEMATICS CURRICULUM

LA TECHNOLOGIE AU SERVICE DU CURRICULUM DE MATHÉMATIQUES

Chief Organizer / *Responsable en chef* : Klaus-D. Graf [DEU]
Local Organizer / *Responsable local* : Denis Therrien [CAN]
Advisory team members / *Consultants* : Enrique C. Alzati [MEX],
Nicolina A. Malara [ITA], Evgenia Sendova [BGR],
Ole Skovsmose [DNK], Kiyoshi Yokochi [JPN], Nurit Zehavi [ISR],
Jochen Ziegenbalg [DEU]

The intention of Working Group 17 was to investigate some of the empirical, social, and philosophical backgrounds to its theme. An opening plenary session was dedicated to the philosophy of critical mathematics education, including the role of technology. Then the group divided into four subgroups according to educational levels. A general impression from the working group is that enormous progress has been going on in mathematics educational technology and that there is world-wide agreement about the necessity to introduce computers into mathematics education. This combines with large financial problems. Also, the need for more exact research is obvious.

At the *opening plenary session,* Ole Skovsmose [DNK] spoke on "Technology and critical math education". He explained that normally technology in the classroom is associated with the question: how can one use computers to assist mathematics education? Technology can be seen as a fundamental social-structuring principle because mathematics and computer-aided mathematics are strongly affecting society. Examination grades, IQs, and the income tax system, are examples. He reported about a Danish project, "Mathematics education and democracy in a high-tech society: family support in a micro-society", in which mathematics was introduced as a design tool and the computer was used when it became necessary to keep an overview on a large amount of data. Critical questions were asked with regard to changes in society stemming from the influence of mathematical and algorithmic

197

modeling. The talk ended with a discussion of the importance of different types of knowledge related to solving the problems studied by the project: mathematical, technological, and reflective knowledge. A lively discussion occurred about the general feasibility of the methods and about the required teacher training.

The *primary level subgroup* presentations showed the importance of the non-standard facilities of the computer (beyond what can be done in reasonable time with paper and pencil) in helping children gain an understanding of mathematical ideas. Hirokazu Okamori and Tomoko Yanagimoto [JPN] discussed the application of computers to the study of ratio for a variety of problems (including time as a variable). Immo O. Kerner [DEU] explained how counting and fundamental arithmetical operations can be studied in primary mathematics education by using the power of the computer to produce tables (for addition, etc) in any quantity, before turning to the well-known algorithms.

Although most presentations in the *lower secondary level subgroup* were focused on computers, Barry Kissane [AUS] considered the use of programmable pocket calculators. Françoise Ollivier [FRA] stressed the help offered to the teacher by the overhead projector, and to designers of materials by video and graphics software. The discussion concerning computers focused on:

- the use of adequate software for special elements of the curriculum;

- the analysis of the difficulties of pupils in the use of certain software or in programming activities.

The *software* considered was the following:

- Spreadsheets for the study of applied problems (J. Hammond [AUS]) and the use of data bases (Dave Miller [GBR]); traditional problems such as linking algebra with arithmetic (Enrica Lemut [ITA]; Miller); elaboration of numerical data from given functions / formulas (J. M. Barnes [CAN]).

- Didactically efficient software to face a delicate aspect in the teaching of geometry: the link between space and the plane (Lemut).

- Cabri-géomètre for a dynamic study of the elements of Euclidean geometry which fosters the formulation of conjectures (Heinz Schumann [DEU]).

- Graphics software for the dynamic study of classes of functions with particular reference to the links: tables ↔ graphs ↔ formulas ↔ tables (Hartwig Meissner [DEU]; M. Borba [BRA]; Mary Barnes [AUS]).

- Logo for the visualization and study of axial and central symmetries (E. Gallou-Dumiel [FRA]).

By analyzing the behavior and the papers of pupils solving problems on the computer, difficulties of various kinds (linguistic, cultural and planning) have been highlighted. It has been observed how these difficulties can be amplified or – on the contrary – remain concealed without adequate intervention by the teacher. (Enrica Lemut, Maria Reggiani [ITA])

Problems similar to those experienced in Western countries also exist in China. It is clear to researchers from there that experiences which come from the practice should be explored intensively, that the technological conditions should be improved and that powerful teams should be established to undertake studies. (Rui-Fen Tang [CHN])

In the *upper secondary level subgroup,* the role of software over three decades was characterized in this way: the 70s was the time of games in instruction, the 80s was the time of integrating software into curriculum, the 90s is the time when curricula will be redesigned because of the existence of technology. (Nurit Zehavi [ISR])

Teachers reported how software like MACSYMA gives rise to new ways of teaching. (Douglas Butler [GBR]; Jim Claffey [AUS]) Roles and activities of many students have undergone changes by being exposed to software. They effected major changes in the software, thus turning from passive users of software to pioneers. (Sharon Dugdale [USA]) Many found new solution strategies and they became more graphically oriented. (Hannah Perl [ISR]) Many act like mathematical explorers. (Jenny Sendova [BGR]) In some places, mathematical modeling has been discovered as a technique in school, being applied in physics, art, biology and physical activities. (Shoichiro Machida, Hideyuki Kurihara & S. Moriya [JPN]) Changes in the math curriculum were reported from Italy, where a computer science component with PASCAL was introduced in all secondary schools. (Maria Tereas Moffino [ITA]) Also, real and large problems (like the butterfly problem) can be put in the curriculum now. (Dale Burnett [CAN])

The new technologies have reached schools in countries with special problems, like China, South Africa, and the third world countries. In China computers are being used in instruction for drawing graphs, demonstrating concepts, coaching, mimicking teacher behavior, making question banks and playing games. (Guan Chen Zhi [CHN]) Problems are being caused by the first world dumping their obsolete equipment and software in the third world without preparation or local input. There is an enormous need for effective teacher training and consideration of local conditions when using modern technology. (Paul E. Laridon [ZAF])

In the *tertiary level subgroup*, great efforts to improve the quality of mathematics instruction at universities and other tertiary level schools were reported. A project in Scotland gives special attention to reorganizing instruction as a whole, creating a computerized tutorial system for calculus consisting of components like lectures, worked examples, motivating examples and tests. A particular feature of this system is a stringent evaluation component in the test section making multiple choice tests dispensable. (Cliff Beevers [GBR]) At the National Central University in Taiwan, computer use is integrated in many fields like calculus, linear algebra, differential equations, number theory, etc. Programming exercises are viewed as complementing traditional mathematical problem solving techniques. Students who completed this program showed a strong capacity for making conjectures and attempting to prove them. (Yang Hua [TWN]) Graphics calculators are becoming important tools at this level, e. g. in precalculus. In the discussion special attention was given to the problem of linking these calculators to computers. (Gregory D. Foley [USA])

Great importance has to be given to the conceptual side of mathematics vs the manipulative side at university level. A careful evaluation of a case study at Trenton State College demonstrated that working on the conceptual side was greatly enhanced by the use of graphical display techniques. (Robert F. Cunningham [USA])

The importance of modern and effective tools became very clear through a report on the introduction of microcomputers into the educational system of Turkey. Lack of resources and tools still is one of the main problems. (Yasar Ersoy [TUR]) Information technology also plays an important role in math applications. This was underlined by a report about the German-U.S.A. project "Industrial Applications of Mathematics for Engineering Students". Together with mathematics the project contains a variety of aspects to be considered in modern education for the professional world: bilateral, bilingual, multimedia, linguistic capabilities (technical vocabulary). (Heinrich Abel [DEU]) Finally the subgroup attempted to look ahead to the year 2000. Reasons for curriculum changes will be the continuation of new developments in information technology, mathematics, sciences, etc. Pedagogy will ask for intelligent computer-aided systems allowing active learning by experiments, exploration, conjecturing as well as conceptual emphasis, visualization and de-emphasis of some formal skills. (Gerhard König [DEU])

CLOSING SESSION

It is the duty of today's mathematics educators to continue to spread mathematical knowledge from all over the world as it has always been done in the old Chinese, Arabic, Western, and other worlds. Kiyochi Yokochi and Shin Watanabe [JPN] made a presentation: "Mathematics education using computers in Japan and China: study exchanges between Japan and China". The growth of computer use in Japanese mathematics education since 1976 reveals the great importance of early cooperation between universities and schools. From the beginning computer use covered all levels from kindergarten to university. The material situation in China is not as good. However, there has been a lively interest in computers for school since about 1982. Regular teacher training courses, including courses on developing software with Japanese and Chinese lecturers, were established, leading to immediate activities in Chinese schools. Meanwhile computers can be found in most Chinese city schools and computer use is established in some curricula. Study exchanges on mathematics education using computers is continued through the Japan-China Mathematical Education Conferences held each year in Japan or China.

NOTE

The proceedings of the Group, edited by K.-D. Graf, N.A. Malara, N. Zehavi and J. Ziegenbalg, will be published as a university print of about 200 pages in 1993 at a price less than ten dollars. Information can be obtained from: Klaus-Dieter Graf, Kurstraße 5, 1000 Berlin 38, Germany; Fax: (30) 838 75109; E-mail: graf@inf.fu-berlin.de

Working Group 18 / *Groupe de travail 18*

METHODS OF IMPLEMENTING CURRICULUM CHANGE

MÉTHODES D'IMPLANTATION DE CHANGEMENTS DE PROGRAMMES

Chief Organizer / *Responsable en chef* : Hugh Burkhardt [GBR]
Local Organizer / *Responsable local* : David Alexander [CAN]
Advisory team members / *Consultants* : Andy Begg [NZL], Beatriz D'Ambrosio [USA], Christine Keitel [DEU], Eizo Nagasaki [JPN], Jim Ridgway [GBR]

During the first meeting of the working group, Hugh Burkhardt [GBR] provided an overview of the topics and outlined the working structure of the group. The dynamics and types of curriculum change with their associated models were referred to. The ways in which models of change differ were listed: central direction vs growth from a localized development; the scale of change; the complexity of change (profound or superficial); the pace, the source; the pressures and rewards; the support, the feedback mechanism in the implementation model. The members of the organizing panel added their comments.

The members of the group then selected the type of system they wished to consider:

- a *centralized* system with strong national control of curriculum;

- a *"third world"* system with severe economic constraints;

- a *"distributed"*system based on local control with strong national influences.

Six subgroups of approximately twelve members each resulted. One concentrated on the "third world" system, two on centralized systems, and three on "distributed" systems. The subgroups were then asked to imagine their role to be that of making recommendations to a Ministry of Education on how to implement curriculum change in mathematics education. The focus was to be on methods of implementation, not on the precise nature of the proposed changes.

The subgroups met for a short time on the first day, all of the second and third days, and part of the fourth day. During the last hour of the fourth day, Hugh Burkhardt and David Alexander [CAN] summarized for the entire Group the reports of the subgroups. While the subdivision into subgroups based on the type of system provided a context for discussions, the differences in the results of the discussions were minimal. The principal points are summarized in the following.

The main focus of change must be individual teachers, but support must be provided in a variety of ways. Peer support is important – it is easier for a pair of teachers in a school to implement a change than for an individual to work in isolation. The provision of a feedback mechanism that allows the change to be modified as it is implemented is important in developing the involvement of teachers. Administrators (principals, department heads, superintendents, etc.) need to recognize the demands that change places on teachers and give adequate support in providing time for teachers to reflect on their practice individually and in conjunction with others.

The administrators must have sufficient understanding of the nature of the change undertaken so that they will not impose conditions which make it more difficult for teachers to implement the change. Parents should be made aware of the change and efforts should be directed to persuading as many of them as possible to support the teachers' efforts. Assessment strategies, particularly system-wide strategies, should be changed as necessary to be supportive of the curriculum change rather than acting to discourage it.

The development of monitoring strategies which can influence the change as it progresses is important, as is careful consideration of the rate of change demanded and its relationship to a teacher's need to feel "safe" in the use of some strategies. One of the subgroups considered the problems of change at the tertiary level. The subgroup recognized the importance of persuading individual faculty members of the need for change, but noted that department chairs through the tenure/promotion/merit award systems could influence the success or failure of individual efforts.

The subgroups focusing on "third world" systems were particularly impressed with ICMI's potential to take the lead in the consideration of problems relating to curriculum change in the Third World. Based on their experiences and discussions over the four sessions they made the following recommendations:

That an ICMI Study Group be formed on "Implementing Curriculum Change". The Study Group should:

- identify examples of good practice for curriculum change in mathematics education throughout the world;

- provide a support system for change initiatives in diverse cultures by providing information and acting as a consultative body for curriculum change proposals;

- identify sources of funds which might partially support curriculum change initiatives in the Third World.

That ICMI should act to:

- increase the participation of mathematics educators from Third World countries in ICMI conferences;

- increase the participation of teachers of mathematics from *all* countries in ICMI conferences;

- organize a Miniconference for Classroom Teachers at ICME-8 to broaden the sharing and learning of the participants and legitimize "grass roots" initiatives.

While the four sessions did not provide sufficient time for the groups to make an in-depth study of the topic or produce generic plans for curriculum change, the high level of attendance throughout the sessions and the intensity of the discussions suggest that the topic and the format achieved the goal of the organizers in providing a basis for participants to share experiences and gain insights through that sharing which will inform and enhance their own implementation of change.

REFERENCES

Burkhardt, H., Fraser, R., & Ridgway, J. (1990). The dynamics of curriculum change. In I. Wirszup & R. Streit (Eds.), *Developments in school mathematics around the world,* Vol. 2. Reston, VA: National Council of Teachers of Mathematics.

Fullan, M. (1980). *The meaning of educational change.* New York: Teachers College Press.

Howson, A.G., Keitel, C., & Kilpatrick, J. (1981). *Curriculum development in mathematics.* Cambridge, UK: Cambridge University Press.

Various articles in J. Malone, H. Burkhardt, & C. Keitel (Eds.), *The mathematics curriculum: towards the year 2000,* the report of an ICME-6 theme group. Perth, Australia: SMEC, Curtin University of Technology.

Working Group 19 / *Groupe de travail 19*

EARLY SCHOOL LEAVERS

MATHÉMATIQUES POUR LES ÉLÈVES QUI QUITTENT TÔT LEURS ÉTUDES

Chief Organizer / *Responsable en chef* : Carlos Vasco [COL]
Local Organizer / *Responsable local* : Richard Pallascio [CAN]
Advisory team members / *Consultants* : Afzel Ahmed [GBR], Ed Jacobsen [FRA]

PRESENTERS

Carlos Vasco [COL]: Introduction. Dione Lucchesi de Carvalho [BRA]: *Mathematical education of illiterate adults.* Richard Pallascio [CAN]: *Instrumental mathematics and contextualization.* Ed Jacobsen [FRA]: *Survival in mathematics education (in school and in life).* Afzal Ahmed [GBR]: *Transferable numerical skills.* Anthula Natsoulas [USA]: *Basic numeracy for school learning.* Iris Carl [USA]: *Equity and equality: We should do more than just mouth the words.*

Two short presentations were made at the beginning of each of the first three sessions, followed by an hour discussion. This was possible because of the size of the group which averaged about 20 participants. The discussions moved from an initial emphasis on potential early school leavers and the ways to prevent them from leaving the formal educational system, to an emphasis on goals and strategies for providing additional educational opportunities for those who had left the formal system at some point. The last session was devoted to a discussion of principles, concepts, goals and strategies from the last point of view. The text which follows is a summary of these discussions.

CONCEPTS OF NUMERACY

Various definitions of numeracy have been proposed: (1) Skills of numerical and spatial thinking required for daily living in society. (2) Informed numeracy involves knowing when to use math, what math to use, how to do math, and how to use the results provided by the mathematics.

(3) Deployment of simple mathematical processes and skills in the tackling and solving of real life problems and tasks. (Shell Centre, Nottingham). (4) Mathematical skills that enable people to cope with the practical demands of everyday life (Cockroft Report). (5) Ability to reason intelligently with qualitative information (James Fey).

The reverse, innumeracy, has been defined by John Allen Paulos as the inability to understand and criticize numerical and statistical data, which leads people to fall into all sorts of scams and deceptions.

PRINCIPLES

Every student has the right to acquire (in or out of school) mathematical knowledge that is useful as universal knowledge; hence *every* student must have access to the full mathematics curriculum. All teachers have the duty to accept the former principle, in spite of the difficulty of identifying mathematical properties in the students' procedures, and of negotiating with them the acceptance of their knowledge as valuable.

Objects and materials involve different levels of representation, and require knowledge of rules appropriate to their structure, which is often of symbolic nature.

The construction of mathematical knowledge is a long and slow process, and it is an eminently social activity, mediated by language.

Contextualization should take into account the use of standard and non-standard representations of the thinking process, as well as the individual's cultural and social environment rather than thwarting it. Contextualization should not mean leaving students immersed in their social/cultural situations and strategies, but lead the way to de-contextualizing them, making them more abstract, general and complex, and thus more widely applicable, enabling students to mathematize in a more scientific way.

The types of mathematical thought a citizen will need are now changing. There are increasing demands of the workplace for more mathematical knowledge. A minimum core curriculum for all is desirable if it is rich enough to be compatible with the above principles, and if care is taken that the minimum does not become the maximum for the majority of students.

There is a need for different ways to teach mathematics because of the presence of calculators and computers.

Affect and self-esteem are very important.

TWO QUESTIONS

(1) Why should a student learn math?

Among reasons one can mention the acquisition of career-related skills, of attitudes and knowledge which will result in an informed member of society and an educated citizen.

(2) What should he or she learn?

Mathematics as problem solving. Mathematics as communication. Mathematics as reasoning. Mathematical connections. Basic operations with whole numbers, fractions and decimals, statistics and probability, geometry and algebra.

GOALS

General goals

Empower people to respond to demands of society as it develops technologically.

Ability to think, ask questions and assess answers, cooperate, communicate, make decisions, improve self-discipline; imagination, resourcefulness, independence.

Teach math skills, and skills to learn mathematics.

Achieve mathematical reasoning by formulating hypotheses, selecting proof elements, constructing arguments, extracting conclusions, mastering the mathematical pathway.

Help students survive in life after school. Help keep students in school.

Make students aware of resources and instruments available to them from their cultural and experiential background, making explicit their connection to mathematics and decontextualizing them.

While at school, get students to see mathematics as a tool for solving many kinds of problems.

Value mathematics communicate and reason mathematically to develop confidence for doing math, and become math problem solvers.

Acquire reading comprehension skills to understand texts with mathematical content across the curriculum and in daily life.

Develop mathematical language.

Develop problem solving strategies.

Expand world view of the role of mathematics.

Specific goals

Be fluent with mental calculations and estimations.

Ascertain when an exact answer is needed and when an estimate is more appropriate.

Decide which mathematical operations are appropriate in particular contexts.

Use a calculator or computer correctly, confidently, and appropriately.

Develop an ability to verify mental or calculator results.

Interpret and use tables, diagrams, graphs, statistical techniques and spreadsheets to organize, analyze, and present information.

Interpret and validate quantitative results presented by others.

Formulate specific questions from vague problems.

Select effective problem solving strategies.

STRATEGIES

At policy-making level

Coordinate policies and activities with other agencies, especially employers, associations of principals, supervisors, teachers, organized minority groups, etc.

Change assessment and prevent it from driving the curriculum to the teaching of routine calculation skills. The assessment should include practical projects, research projects, portfolios and open questions.

At teacher education level

Improvement of mathematical knowledge of teachers.

Get teachers to accept that the mathematical knowledge of their students is also valid.

Encourage teachers to appreciate the value of errors as possible generalizations out of limited experiences or as coming from different interpretations.

At classroom level

Approach a same content from all the mathematical aspects related to it.

Approach same content at different levels of complexity and with different types of representation, including those used by mass media: tables, graphics, etc.

Consider students' mistakes as raw material, useful in the process of knowledge construction.

Let rigor be an effect of the activity, arising from the need to communicate, and not as a previous condition.

Let evaluation be an integration of all the productive moments of a process in which students evaluate themselves, the groups evaluate themselves and each student, and the teachers evaluate the adequacy of the activities, topics, content, methods and evaluations.

Pay more attention to everyday language.

The emphasis in learning activities should be put on the operation carried out and not on the objects.

Take into account not only social relations generated in society, but also those generated in the school system.

Projects with contextualized activities in such a way as to promote an instrumental conception of mathematics. (Example: Space experiment about tomato growth in spaceship led students to compare speed in solving tangram puzzles in silence vs listening to Heavy Metal music: their hypothesis was that they could work better with silence.)

Require involvement of parents and extensive participation of teachers (see John M. Peterson, "Remediation is no remedy", in *Educational Leadership*, March 1989).

Implicit and explicit applications and connections with other areas of life and the school curriculum: ask what they saw on TV, newspapers, and what they would like to understand better.

Use of a cooperative learning environment.

Learning activities characterized by high expectation and high status for participants.

Calculators and computers as integral part of the math classroom.

Develop strategies that come from real contexts.

Integrate everyday mathematical procedures with school mathematical knowledge.

Operations on concrete cultural objects, like money, should be preferred. But if the students' daily life doesn't offer a sufficiently rich source of materials, teachers can take other cultural objects from their reserves.

Use their own profession, trade, etc., to start the mathematics curriculum. (Example: For adults in urban settings, use decoration, budget, rent, charge accounts, paychecks.)

Prepare for standardized tests only a short time before them, and realize that students then perform as well or better than when they are "taught to the test" for a long period.

NOTE

A more extensive report can be found in the booklet *Proceedings of the Working Group WG19 on mathematics for premature school-leavers,* edited by Carlos E. Vasco and Richard Pallascio. Copies are available for CAN$6.75 from: CIRADE, C.P. 8888, succ. A, Montréal (Québec), Canada H3C 3P8. Fax: (1) 515 987-4636.

Working Group 20 / *Groupe de travail 20*

MATHEMATICS IN DISTANCE LEARNING

MATHÉMATIQUES DANS LES PROGRAMMES D'ENSEIGNEMENT À DISTANCE

Chief Organizer / *Responsable en chef* : Gordon Knight [NZL]
Local Organizer / *Responsable local* : Jean-Paul Ginestier [CAN]
Advisory team members / *Consultants* : Leong Fook [MYS],
Edwin Dickey [USA], Joy Davis † [GBR]

The Working Group had its origins at ICME-6 when distance education was a subgroup of Action Group 7 on *Adult, technical and vocational Education*. A recommendation of that group was that distance education should have its own place in the program of ICME-7. When the decision was made to include this working group in ICME 7 the advisory team agreed that:

i)   as far as possible, the group would concentrate on questions relating to the teaching and learning of *mathematics* in distance education rather than on more general questions;

ii)   the principal feature of all the sessions would be *discussion* rather than presentation.

The group was small enough (about 25 people) to remain together for discussion and the sessions were each organized around a different aspect of mathematics in distance education. It was hoped to run a session in parallel with Session 2 for participants from less developed countries, but there were too few in this category to make this possible. Session coordinators led the sessions with oral presentations leading to discussion question. Other participants were asked to make written presentations which were distributed and referred to during discussions.

SESSION 1

Written material

Coordinator: Gordon Knight [NZL]

In many distance education systems, written materials are the only means of transmission between teacher and student. Even those systems which rely very heavily on other technologies usually employ a significant amount of written material.

- A modular approach in which the material to be learned is broken into sections each containing a structure of objectives, presentation, worked examples, exercises and tests was illustrated in written papers by Leong Fook [MYS], Felicia McFarlane [LCA] and Chantal D'Halluin & Bruno Vanhille [FRA]. This kind of structure is described in detail in an article by Bääth (1983) in a list of ideas for the construction of distance education courses.

- A topic which was raised more than once during the working group was the relationship of cultural factors to mathematics in distance education. Apart from the general relationship between mathematics education and culture which applies to any mode of teaching, and the obvious differences between countries in the availability of technology, there seem to be cultural questions relating specifically to distance education. Distance education has been influenced very strongly by models developed in western industrialized societies by institutions such as the Open University in Great Britain. There is an increasing awareness (Guy, 1990) that the thinking behind this development contains ideologies which may be inappropriate for other cultural settings, and perhaps even for different cultural groups within Western society.

- A balance between formal and informal language, which is very much a part of mathematics teaching in a face-to-face situation, is much more difficult to achieve in written material. Mathematicians seem reluctant to put in writing anything which might be seen by their colleagues, or superiors, as not precisely correct. Informal writing also takes a lot of space and, in a mode which is often constrained by resource considerations, may be seen as inefficient. Supplementary material with audio or video tapes has been used as a means of overcoming this problem.

- For many years the emphasis in distance education study material in mathematics has been on the student learning by completing a significant number of exercises. Recent research (Ward and Sweller, 1990) is challenging this view and suggesting that suitably structured

212

worked examples provide a more efficient method of teaching and learning. This has obvious implications for the development of courses and warrants further research in the distance learning mode.

SESSION 2

The role of technology

Coordinator: Edwin Dickey [USA]

As a basis for the discussion, Dickey prepared Table 1 illustrating the impact of various forms of technology on instructional factors relating to students, teachers and mathematics.

Audio technology, whether one-way by broadcasts or audio cassette tapes, or two-way by telephone, are relatively low cost. However, the importance of symbolic representations in mathematics means that the technology is used principally to supplement written material.

- Video technology, usually by TV broadcast or videotape, is a rapidly growing medium in distance learning. Many users who are working with groups of students with this technology, and with one way audio, use facilitators working with the group. This increases interaction between members of the group and, to some extent, between the teacher and the group. A major advantage is that the learners have the power to control the pace of instruction. They can fast-forward over familiar material, pause to work out a problem, or rewind to see and hear an explanation again. These are not, of course, facilities available to the face-to-face student in a lecture or classroom situation.

- Interaction can be enhanced for one-way video by combining it with two-way audio. Often called live, interaction television, this type of video delivery of instruction is used by many universities and increasing numbers of school districts in the United States. Student-to-teacher interaction is usually by the telephone to the studio and then broadcast to all sites.

- Two-way video combined with two-way audio is the most interactive medium available but the increase in delivery cost and complexity of equipment required is considerable.

- Through the use of a modem, computers may be used to transmit information through telephone lines. Though currently limited to the transmission of text, developments which allow the transmission of graphics, sound, and even slow-scan video are beginning. Pierre Jarraud [FRA] presented a written paper on his experiences of using

TABLE 1 — The Impact of Various Distance Education Delivery Models on Student, Instructor & Math Factors

Delivery Models

	Audio Only		One-Way Audio and Video				Two-Way Audio / One-Way Video	Two-Way Audio / Two-Way Video	Computer Mediated	On-Campus Traditional
	One Way	Two Way	Broadcast or Cable	Broadcast or Cable with Facilitator	Tape	Tape with Facilitator				
STUDENT FACTORS										
Interaction Potential	Low	Medium	Low	Medium	Low	Medium	Medium	Medium	Medium	Medium
Convenience	Medium	Low	Low	Low	High	Medium	Low	Low	High	Low
Outreach	High	High	High	Medium	High	Medium	Medium	Medium	Medium	Medium
Inter-Student Learning Potential	Low	Low	Low	Medium	Low	Medium	High	High	Medium	High
INSTRUCTOR FACTORS										
Course Development Effort	High	High	High	High	High	High	Medium	Medium	Medium	Medium
Course Delivery Effort	Low	Low	Low	Medium	Low	Medium	High	High	High	High
Repeated Course Offering Effort	Low	Low	Low	Medium	Low	Medium	High	High	High	High
MATH FACTORS										
Ability to Depict Math Symbols	Low	Low	High	High	High	High	High	High	Low	High
Ease of Utilizing Technology	Low	Low	High	High	High	High	High	High	Medium	Medium

electronic mail as a means of communication between student and teacher. Eugene Koltz [USA] described his recently-begun Geometry Forum, an electronic bulletin board devoted to all forms and levels of geometry, available to users of the Internet. The work of Frode Rönning [NOR] involving computer-mediated learning through a graphical user interface with electronic mail was described. Bert Zwaneveld [NLD] described StudioNet, a Dutch Open University project for studying mathematics with network-mediated support.

- Telefax can obviously speed up the communication between teacher and student which has traditionally been by postal system. Laser videodisks, CD-ROM and many other supplemental technologies will have an increasing role to play in distance education in the future.

- The potential to use any of these technologies clearly varies considerably from country to country, but as the technology becomes increasingly affordable and available, the imperative to use it grows. Technology is providing examples of learning at a distance which are *more* effective than traditional face-to-face learning.

SESSION 3

Communication with students

Coordinator: Pamela Surman [AUS]

In a session entitled "It isn't the medium, it's the message", Surman raised questions concerning the purpose of communication between teachers and students in distance education. She suggested that the development of effective learning behaviors which lead to the empowerment of students was the principal objective.

- Communication has two major factors, tutor-support, which is between the tutor and an individual student, and the learning materials, whether these use the written word as the medium or other technologies.

- As far as tutor-support is concerned, one of the most important features to recognize in distance education is that it depends much more than face-to-face teaching on good administrative structures. Efficiency in the delivery of study material, marking and return of assignments, and the availability of tutorial help is paramount if the student is to grow in confidence and use the study time available effectively. Inevitably systems sometimes break down and the ability to resolve administrative problems sensitively and quickly is a very important attribute of the distance educator.

- Tutors need to provide a "safe haven" for students by giving individualized, personal feedback aimed at giving encouragement and building confidence and self-esteem in students.

- Learning materials need to be student-based. That is they must be designed for the learner to learn from rather than the teacher to teach from. In addition to presenting the mathematics content to be learned, the materials need to address the learning processes themselves. Distance educators are becoming increasingly aware of the role of metacognition in learning.

- Metacognition involves knowledge of the task requirements and the learners own cognitive resources. It also involves knowledge of how to accomplish the task, to monitor progress and to review and evaluate personal knowledge or success.

- Texts which address metacognition "talk about themselves", show the reader how the structure of the text will aid comprehension and learning, give guidelines for students to monitor their comprehension and retention, and give procedures to follow if comprehension is not occurring.

- Learning-style inventories, attitude tests, personal contracts, impact surveys and learning diaries have all been found useful tools for metacognitive development.

SESSION 4

Research

Coordinator: Gordon Knight

In a survey of distance education and mathematics education journals, Gordon Knight found that there were very few articles relating to mathematics in distance education and only a small proportion of these had a research base. There is a large, and growing, body of research into more general features of distance education but little relating to the learning and teaching of mathematics.

- A number of areas in which research was needed were identified by the group:

  - gender and technology;

  - metacognitive skills and computers;

  - relationship between learning styles and means of delivery;

  - concept mapping;

- distance students' views of mathematics;

- the needs of special groups of students; returning adults, teachers, school students, etc.;

- the hidden curriculum of distance education;

- culture and mathematics in distance education;

- environmental factors.

There was not time for a full discussion of research methods, but mention was made of action research as a particularly appropriate model for the development of distance education courses in mathematics (Mousley and Rice, 1990).

CONCLUSIONS

The major disappointment of the group was that there were very few participants from less-developed countries, although a number had expressed interest in response to the earlier announcements of the Congress. Many such countries are looking to distance education as a means of tackling problems of teacher and adult education. It is imperative that those engaged in this enterprise in mathematics have an opportunity to discuss their difficulties. ICMI is the obvious body through which this might occur, perhaps by financial support for participants to ICME–8 and by an ICMI Study on the topic of mathematics education in less-developed countries.

On a much more positive note the participants saw the working group as a nucleus from which international co-operation in distance education in mathematics would grow. It was agreed that the group would keep in contact through an informal newsletter. This would provide a means of sharing information concerning publications, research, projects and people. It might also provide a means of communication with mathematics distance educators who were unable to come to the Congress. Kenneth Hardy (Carleton University, Department of Mathematics and Statistics, Ottawa ON, Canada KIS 5B6) agreed to be initial editor of the newsletter.

The participants felt that the group had been successful and that there should be another working group on the topic at ICME–8. Perhaps the last word should go to Chantal D'Halluin and Bruno Vanhille who wrote:

"En conclusion, il semble que les contraintes de communication imposées par l'enseignement à distance soient une véritable richesse pour une nouvelle approche pédagogique."

REFERENCES

Bääth, J.A. (1983). A list of ideas for the construction of distance education courses. In D. Stewart, D. Keegan & B. Holmberg (Eds.), *Distance education: international perspectives.* New York: St. Martin Press.

Guy, R. (1990). Research and distance education in the Third World cultural contexts. In T. Evans (Ed.), *Research in distance education 1.* Geelong, Australia: Deakin University Press.

Mousley, J, & Rice, M. (1990). Pedagogical evaluation and change: Teaching and research in mathematics distance education. In T. Evans (Ed.), *Research in distance education 1.* Geelong, Australia: Deakin University Press.

Ward, M., & Sweller, J. (1990). Structuring effective worked examples. *Cognition and Instruction*, 7, 1-39.

Working Group 21 / *Groupe de travail 21*

THE PUBLIC IMAGE OF
MATHEMATICS AND MATHEMATICIANS

L'IMAGE DES MATHÉMATIQUES,
DES MATHÉMATICIENS ET
DES MATHÉMATICIENNES DANS LE PUBLIC

Chief Organizer / *Responsable en chef* : Thomas Cooney [USA]
Local Organizer / *Responsable local* : Jean J. Dionne [CAN]
Advisory team members / *Consultants* : Luciana Bazzini [ITA],
Fred Goffree [NDL], Fou-Lai Lin [TWN], Elizabeth Oldham [IRL]

The discussion in the working group focused on four themes related to the public image of mathematics and mathematicians: images held from within the field of mathematics education, images held or conveyed from outside the field of mathematics education, issues related to studying images of mathematics, and programs for influencing people's images of mathematics. Each of these themes was the focus of a particular session. In general, the four sessions consisted of brief paper presentations followed by extensive discussions on issues raised by the paper presenters. This report highlights issues raised by the paper presenters that were subsequently addressed by the group participants. The list of papers presented is given at the end of this report.

IMAGES OF MATHEMATICS FROM WITHIN
MATHEMATICS EDUCATION

There was considerable discussion in this first session about the beliefs of teachers and students and how those beliefs influence the process of mathematics education. Elizabeth Oldham [IRL] suggested that students' beliefs may be well formed by the time they are 10-12 years old and therefore we should study the beliefs of teachers of this age group. Kelly and Oldham found that the teachers they studied would sometimes use the rhetoric of problem solving but interpret problem solving as solving standard problems involving pre-determined "right answers". They indicated that the views of preservice teachers were dominated by their concern to pass the "Leaving

219

Certificate" examination. Oldham indicated that practicing teachers saw mathematics as difficult, abstract, and logical. Further, the hierarchical character of the discipline was stressed in that "knowing the basics" must be accomplished before additional topics could be studied. Examinations were frequently mentioned as exerting considerable influence in shaping students' images of mathematics – a view expressed by Oldham whose practicing teachers held this view.

- Fou-Lai Lin, Men-Fong Huang, and Tien-Chen Chu [TWN] described what they called *exam math*; Taiwanese students' views of mathematics as computation, problem routinization, and memorization were shaped largely by the continual taking of examinations. In Taiwan, 75% of the students admitted to a good national university come from a few star provincial senior high schools. Thus entrance tests to both the top senior high schools and then to the good universities play a very large role in shaping life in the classroom. The authors described the teaching of mathematics as consisting of "Posing the problem, providing the most elegant solution, and ordering students to memorize the solution process". Thus learning, as described by Lin, Huang, and Chu, consists primarily of acquiring "a lot of different types of problems, paired with elegant solutions" in an effort to prepare for examinations. The discussion from other participants indicated that the notion of *exam math*, to varying degrees, reflected circumstances in their countries as well.

- Roberta Mura [CAN] conducted a survey on mathematicians' images of mathematics and found that they tended to hold a formalistic view of mathematics although a single philosophical perspective failed to capture most of their views. Mura concluded that changing teachers' images of mathematics may be difficult because of the often formalistic view of mathematics conveyed at the university level.

IMAGES OF MATHEMATICS FROM OUTSIDE
MATHEMATICS EDUCATION

The emphasis during this session was on the influence of culture and society in shaping people's images of mathematics. Ubiratán D'Ambrosio [BRA] pointed out the role society can play in influencing students' images of mathematics. Fulvia Furinghetti [ITA] illustrated how different views of mathematics are depicted in literature ranging from the role of mathematics in describing physical reality to the study of geometry (Euclid's *Elements* in particular) as an exercise in "pure deduction". She also discussed how mathematics is often represented in the movies. For example, in the film, *Radio days*, Woody Allen asks a classmate to recite mathematical formulas in an effort to show what a disagreeable character the classmate really is. There was considerable discussion about the way mathematics is conveyed in different types of media. Cartoons were shown that suggested a negative or limited view of mathematics. D'Ambrosio indicated how newspaper headlines often belie the mathematical meaning they intend. In general, the view was expressed that teachers must work to overcome the often negative image of mathematics that confronts students in a variety of settings.

- Toshiakira Fujii [JPN] discussed the images held by Japanese parents. He found several contrasts between the opinions of parents and those of students. For example, 91% of the parents thought that mathematics was a difficult subject at which to succeed if once you failed while only 66% to 71% of the students agreed, depending on their age level. With respect to the question of whether mathematics could be learned if it was taught efficiently, 92% of the parents agreed but only 70% to 79% of the students agreed depending on their age level. While 91% of the parents held the view that mathematics is a subject in which you get a single answer clearly, only 57% to 79% of the students agreed. In response to the question of whether mathematics is useful in solving social problems, only 30% of the parents agreed. The students' responses were interesting in that approximately 63% of the fourth and sixth graders agreed but this percentage decreased dramatically as only 25% of the eighth graders agreed and only 12% of the tenth graders agreed. The participants discussed how the increasing level of abstract mathematics as the students progress through the grades probably contributed to this view.

- From still another perspective, Marie-Françoise Jozeau [FRA] described a project in which her students studied early units of measure of the metric system in a context in which culture inflenced the nature of that development. It was not only an experience in learning about a mathematical topic (measurement) but also in considering the historical contexts in which measurement units are developed and applied.

ISSUES RELATED TO STUDYING
IMAGES OF MATHEMATICS

The focus during this session was on philosophical and methodological issues in studying teachers' beliefs. Paul Ernest [GBR] characterized the public's image of mathematics as cold, abstract, theoretical, ultra-rational, primarily masculine, largely remote and inaccessible to all but the most talented albeit important to society. He maintained that this public image may be the single most important issue of concern for those promoting reform in mathematics education. In contrast to an absolutist view – a view that encourages the image of mathematics as cold, abstract, and inhuman – Ernest described fallibilism in which mathematics is seen as the outcome of social processes.

- It was generally agreed that the teaching of mathematics is typically based on an absolutist view of mathematics with an emphasis on computational outcomes and the manipulation of symbols. The apparent gap between the absolutist view and a fallibilistic view that most current reform efforts embrace was addressed by Alba Thompson [USA]. Thompson suggested that inservice programs frequently encourage teachers to use manipulatives, in part to foster a broader view of mathematics. Yet teachers often fail to make the connection between the actions performed on objects or diagrams, the verbalization of those actions, and their representation in mathematical notation thus missing the larger issue about what constitutes mathematics. Thompson concluded that, "The restructuring necessary to create an entirely new image requires that a teacher experience numerous occasions to become aware of and question his deeply rooted ideas and unexamined assumptions about what it means to know, learn, and teach mathematics."

- Stephen Lerman [GBR] pointed out that since we are interested, generally speaking, in a teacher's philosophical perspective about mathematics, our research methodologies should be eclectic enough to account for these perspectives. Lerman described a case study of a teacher who exhibited a formalistic orientation in her thinking about mathematics. Lerman suggested that "action research" is a particularly appropriate methodology as researcher and practitioner work together to unpack and repack conceptions of mathematics and its teaching.

- The use of qualitative methodologies was exhibited by Melvin Wilson [USA] who studied three secondary preservice teachers' conceptions of function. The methodology involved extensive interviewing, observing the students' participation during a course in mathematics education, and analyzing their written responses to questions. Wilson's approach permitted him access to the teachers' thinking about mathematics, the teaching of mathematics, and the understanding of functions in particular.

DISCUSSIONS ON POSSIBLE RESEARCH AGENDAS GENERATED THE FOLLOWING QUESTIONS

- What images of mathematics are held by teachers at various levels, mathematicians, students, and those outside the field of mathematics education, e.g. the working public?

- How are these images developed and how can they be changed?

- How are these images related to student attitudes and achievement?

- To what extent should research on teachers' beliefs focus on specific content areas versus mathematics more generally?

- What theoretical perspectives and research methodologies best support this research?

INFLUENCING OUR IMAGES OF MATHEMATICS

To begin the fourth session, Raymond Wells [USA] described the role technology plays in shaping various aspects of a mathematician's life, including communication, mathematical computation, mathematical experiments, and mathematical modeling and simulation – thereby contributing to our image of mathematics. For example, computer software allows the mathematician to handle sophisticated computations easily. A related question discussed by Wells was, "If a computer is used for making a calculation in the proof of a theorem, does this constitute a valid proof of the theorem?" Wells made the case that the proof of a theorem is a *cultural* assertion, that is, a product of our continuously developing mathematical heritage.

- Dudley Blane [AUS] described the *Mathematics Trails* program which is designed to impact on students' and parents' images of mathematics. This program provides settings in which parents and students work cooperatively to create and solve problems related to or involving the environment. The emphasis of the program is on linking mathematics to the environment, thereby shaping students' and parents' images of mathematics. Such an approach is seen as a way to increase students' motivation to learn mathematics, to boost their confidence in creating and solving problems, and to facilitate the teachers' ability to connect mathematics to the real world.

- Another approach to influencing images of mathematics that also involved parents was described by Yolanda de la Cruz and Virginia Thompson [USA]. Their *Family Math* program addresses the image of mathematics held by parents who often think of mathematics as a very difficult and mysterious subject that requires drill and practice and memorizing to learn. In this program, parents and their children work in cooperative settings to solve problems and engage in mathematical explorations. Participants, parents in particular, not only indicated that they learned a considerable amount of mathematics – and had fun doing it – but that they also saw mathematics in a different light. These outcomes were described in a study involving both Latino families and South African Blacks.

223

- Thomas Cooney [USA] described experimental curricular materials for secondary preservice teachers that integrate mathematics and pedagogy using the topic mathematical functions. The overall objective of the materials is to help preservice teachers develop a conceptually sound basis for teaching functions and to impact on their image of mathematics so that they see mathematics from a fallibilistic perspective.

SUMMARY

There were many issues raised throughout the four sessions. Perhaps most important was the view that people's images of mathematics play a significant role in shaping the activities of mathematics education. There was the general feeling that teachers, students, and parents hold too limited a view of mathematics. The question then becomes, "How should the field take this circumstance under consideration?"

NOTE

Papers delivered to this Group can be obtained by writing to the authors directly. Other information can be obtained from: Thomas J. Cooney, 105 Aderhold, University of Georgia, Athens, GA 30602, USA. Fax: (1) 404 542 4551; E-mail: tcooney@moe.uga.edu

TITLES OF PRESENTED PAPERS

Blane, D. *Changing the image of mathematics through using the environment.*

Cooney, T. *Influencing secondary mathematics teachers' images of mathematics.*

D'Ambrosio, U. *The influence of culture in shaping images of mathematics.*

De La Cruz, Y. & Thompson, V. *Influencing views of mathematics through family math programs.*

Ernest, P. *Images of mathematics: a philosophical perspective.*

Fujii, T. *Images of mathematics held by Japanese parents.*

Furinghetti, F. *Images of mathematics outside the community of mathematicians.*

Jozeau, M.-F. *Developments outside the field of mathematics education that influence our image of mathematics.*

Kelly, L. and Oldham, E. *Images of mathematics among teachers: perceptions, beliefs, and attitudes of primary teachers and student-teachers in the Republic of Ireland.*

Lerman, S. *From reflection to research: some methodological issues in studying teachers' images of mathematics.*

Lin, F.L., Huang, M.-F., and Chu, T.-C. *The influence of examinations in shaping students' images of mathematics.*

Mura, R. *Images of mathematics held by mathematicians.*

Thompson, A. *The public image of mathematics and mathematics education reform.*

Wells, R. *The role of technology in mathematical research.*

Wilson, M. *Prospective secondary teachers' images of mathematics, mathematics teaching, and mathematical functions.*

Working Group 22 / *Groupe de travail 22*

MATHEMATICS EDUCATION
WITH REDUCED RESOURCES

ÉDUCATION MATHÉMATIQUE
AVEC DES RESSOURCES LIMITÉES

Chief Organizer / *Responsable en chef* : Elfriede Wenzelburger † [MEX]
Local Organizer / *Responsable local* : Eva Puchalska [CAN]
Advisory team members / *Consultants* : Lee Peng Yee [SGP],
Desmond Broomes [BRB], Paulus Gerdes [MOZ]

The group was concerned with questions related to the relationship between mathematics learning and resources and successful programs and projects intended to make mathematics education available to students in developing countries. A set of recommendations was developed and a directory was set up as the first step in a communication network between participants.

There were nine presentations by individual members of the working group, which had a total of twenty participants from thirteen countries (Australia, Bolivia, Canada, Dominican Republic, Japan, Malawi, México, Nigeria, South Africa, Spain, U.S.A., U.K., and Uruguay).

Alicia Villar [URY]: *Mathematics for everybody*. The relationship between the economic situation and mathematics achievement according to a study done by CEPAL (Comisión Económica para América Latina y el Caribe) was pointed out. The conclusions in the case of Uruguay are alarming. The need to bring mathematics within the reach of everybody was stated, together with the need to improve teacher training.

Jerome K. Turner [CAN]: *Complementarity, ethnomathematics and primary education in Bhutan*. Experiences in the Himalayan country Bhutan were presented and a medium of instruction for elementary school was examined which has a meaningful relationship to the cultural world in which Bhutanese children live: the world of their songs, games, and play activities. It is crucial for successful mathematics teaching to include such activities. Teachers play a central role in the process.

Elfriede Wenzelburger [MEX]: *Electronic calculators: an inexpensive but efficient teaching resource.* Electronic calculators are an inexpensive but efficient teaching resource for concept development and problem solving. An important factor in the adequate use of calculators is the skill of the teachers. Teacher education should include courses on calculator use. An experience with Guatemalan teachers was presented.

Alan Bishop [AUS]: *Mathematics with daily life objects.* The idea of discovering mathematics in simple easily-available objects was presented. This allows us to integrate well known objects of daily life, which are part of a specific culture, into the teaching-learning resources. This active approach needs well-prepared teachers who are able to monitor such discovery activities.

Walter Green [AUS]: *The Philippines-Australia Science and Mathematics Education Project.* At the request of the Philippines Government, Australia is assisting with the implementation of a secondary education development program. With PASMEP, equipment, teacher training, as well as curriculum and management support, are being provided to upgrade the quality and effectiveness of science and math education at the senior secondary level in the Philippines.

Indira Chako [NGA]: *Teacher education in Nigeria.* Experiences with teacher training programs in Nigeria were presented. The requirement for teacher certification imposed by the government puts pressure on universities to offer programs which increase the quantity but not the quality of certified teachers. Low salaries, insufficient mathematical background, and an ever-increasing student population were detected as the main problem, as well as badly-equipped schools.

Sarah González [DOM]: *Moving from negative assessment to positive development in the developing world.* The results of an assessment which was a small-scale replication of the Second International Mathematics Study were taken into account in launching various inservice teacher training programs in 1986. These are still going on. Follow-up assessment have shown an improvement in student's learning and a change in the pattern of teaching strategies of teachers.

Pat Hiddleston [MWI]: *The refugee situation in Malawi.* Refugees from Mozambique have been entering Malawi for many years but the flow has increased greatly since 1986. The refugee population in 1992 is estimated at almost 1 000 000, with 50% under 15 years old. It was recognized by the Malawi Government that there was a need for an education program to be set up and schools established. There are now 10 camp schools with 360 classrooms. All refugee education is free and all materials are provided free, though everything is in very short supply. Six subjects are taught, among them mathematics. The mathematics textbooks have recently been written for a new Mozambique primary syllabus and are in Portuguese. While these are good they are in very short supply. Although the work of the Malawian authorities assisted by international organizations is commendable, there are many shortfalls and problems. There is a need for many more classrooms, teacher training, and educational materials of all kinds.

Mary Harris [GBR]: *School, Math and Work Project.* The difference between mathematics in schools and mathematics in work was pointed out. While school mathematics is something to be done alone, out of context, with simplified numbers and simplified problems which admit only right or wrong answer with a given accuracy, mathematics in work situations is done socially, in context with real data and problems whose results are negotiable with an accuracy which depends on circumstances.

GENERAL CONCLUSIONS FROM THE PRESENTATIONS

In the context of reduced resources, the main resources are the teachers and the cultural environment of students. Creative teachers can discover the mathematics which is present in even simple objects and make the best use of local customs, potentially useful for teaching mathematics. Simple solar-powered calculators may make a difference in trying to bridge the huge technology gap between developed and developing countries. In the case of international cooperation projects, mutual understanding and a deep respect for the cultural values of the countries involved is a crucial factor for success. Also the disposition of all involved to learn from each other. A well-prepared creative teacher with an active teaching approach who integrates elements and objects of a given culture can go a long way in mathematics teaching at the elementary level. A major problem may be the lack of mathematical knowledge detected among teachers in many countries.

The group recommended setting up a network of interested persons in order to help support the projects described. The group considered it especially important to help teachers develop their own resources. The title of the Working Group might better have been "Mathematics in developing countries" since is not really clear what "reduced resources" means – reduced from what? The cooperation of developing countries which face similar problems should be fostered. The help of international agencies should be sought to start calculator projects in some countries.

NOTE

Initial plans for this group were made by Fidel Oteiza [CHL], who had been appointed Chief Organizer by the International Program Committee but at the last minute was not able to attend ICME–7.

REFERENCES

Turner, J.K. (1992). Complementarity, ethnomathematics and primary education. In Bhutan. *Canadian and International Education, 21,* 1.

Wenzelburger, E. (1992). *Uso de calculadoras en la enseñanza de la matemática.* Mexico: Grupo Editorial Iberoamerica.

Luna, E., González, S., & Wolfe, R. The underdevelopment of educational achievement: mathematics achievement in the Dominican Republic grade eight. *Journal of Curriculum Studies, 22*(4), 361-376.

Green, W. *The Philippines-Australia science and mathematics education project (PASMEP).* Obtainable from: SAGRIC International and Pty Ltd., 70 Hindwarsch Square, Adelaide, South Australia 5000.

Hiddleston, P. *The refugee situation in Malawi.* Obtainable from: University of Malawi, Box 280, Zomba, Malawi, East Africa.

Working Group 23 / *Groupe de travail 23*

METHODOLOGIES IN RESEARCH
IN MATHEMATICS EDUCATION

MÉTHODOLOGIES DE RECHERCHE
EN DIDACTIQUE DES MATHÉMATIQUES

Chief Organizer / *Responsable en chef* : Norbert Knoche [DEU]
Local Organizer / *Responsable local* : Joel Hillel [CAN]
Advisory team members / *Consultants* : Paolo Boero [ITA],
Jeremy Kilpatrick [USA]

Each of the four sessions dealt with a different topic. Session 1 was a general introduction to methodologies of research in mathematics education, Session 2 examined methodologies for gathering data, Session 3 considered methodologies for analyzing data, and Session 4 synthesized the work of the preceding sessions and explored unresolved issues of methodology. Session 1 contained two plenary lectures followed by discussion in three subgroups. Sessions 2 and 3 each began with a plenary lecture. Then the group divided into subgroups to hear one of three papers and to discuss both the paper and the lecture. Session 4 began with an overview of the issues and a summary of the work in Sessions 1 to 3. A panel discussion by the chairs of the subgroups raised issues for the plenary discussion that concluded the session.

Mathematics education has always seen itself as an interdisciplinary field that, along with its close connection to mathematics, works with ideas from other academic disciplines such as history, philosophy, psychology, anthropology, and sociology. Because the nature of the questions in a field conditions the methods used to investigate them, empirical researchers in mathematics education have understandably tried to borrow from the methods used in its reference disciplines, especially psychology and sociology. To what extent are the problems investigated in empirical research in mathematics education comparable to the research problems in the reference disciplines? And to what extent therefore can the research methods of those disciplines be used in our investigations? These questions were central to all the lectures and discussions.

What type of question is characteristic of research in mathematics education? In his lecture "What should mathematics education research be about?" Frank Lester [USA] used four questions to characterize research in our field: "What was?" "What is?" "What would happen if?" and "What should be?" Paolo Boero [ITA], in his lecture "Methodological choices concerning research in mathematics education: internal constraints and limitations," asked that research produce:

- a manner of viewing phenomena, which concerns the relationships between teachers, pupils, and knowledge;

- knowledge about mathematics teachers;

- knowledge about pupils' conceptions and individual learning processes;

- knowledge and reflections about the contents to be taught; and

- comparative studies about different curricula and studies about the effects of short- and long-term innovations.

In discussing the methods used in empirical research in education, one often distinguishes so-called method- or model-controlled research (using confirmatory data analysis) from research based on case studies or on observation and interview techniques (using exploratory data analysis). An intense discussion has recently begun on the value of these two types of research. This discussion increasingly tends to favor case studies and to reject methods that rely on mathematical statistics. To some extent this view also applies to models used in investigations in psychology and sociology.

The reasons for this attitude lie partially in the mathematical framework of the statistical models and partially in the problems investigated in our field. One of the strongest arguments against the use of statistical models in educational research is that such models compel the researcher to describe and evaluate the process under investigation by means of variables, more precisely by dependencies between variables. The available methods for evaluating these models are based on mathematical assumptions about the variables and their probability distributions that are not ordinarily met by the data of educational measurement.

Researchers in mathematics education contend that the learning process may be too complex to be described by variables, and certainly to be evaluated by investigating separate variables. This argument arises especially when one argues for a holistic approach to learning theory, as Boero did: "The separation of variables, which may be useful in psychological research, is meaningless in much of the research on learning processes. [...] Analyses of "whole" phenomena are not reducible to separate studies of the variables involved." A second argument against traditional statistical models is that learning is a process that takes place in individuals. How can the sampling methods used in confirmatory studies have any significance in learning studies, since it is characteristic of such methods that they do not take into account the individual? Olive Chapman [CAN], in her paper "Narrative inquiry in mathematics education," made the following observation:

> The current literature and trends in mathematics education suggest a growing disillusionment with the traditional, formalistic view of mathematics and a recognition of mathematics as a human activity, framed in personal cultural and historical contexts. [...] Research methods in mathematics education can no longer be restricted to those that are rooted in an empirical framework. Such methods usually strip away or de-emphasize social context, personal meaning, culture and history. [...] A shift to include research methods that retain personal or social contexts is necessary.

An example of such an investigation was given by Beth Southwell [AUS] in her paper "The stimulated recall methodology in research on problem solving." One way to combine case studies and quantitative methods was shown in the paper by Maria Carmen Batanero and Juan Díaz Godino [ESP], "A methodology to study the student's interaction with the computer." Both papers raised questions as to the validity of case studies and to what extent the findings can be transferred to other situations, especially to classroom situations. The question of how the usefulness of research findings depends on the methods used for data gathering and data analysis was discussed in the lecture by Norbert Knoche [DEU] "Methods of data analysis in educational research":

> It is not difficult to see that this question is not limited to case studies. It is a problem of exploratory studies as well as a problem of confirmatory data analysis. It is a problem of model-guided research as well as of case studies. It is the problem to acknowledge that all findings, independently of whether they stem from quantitative or qualitative methods of data gathering and data analysis, are interpreted findings. There is no method by which one gets a direct handle to the internal processes of thinking and learning, and with each method the reality is always an interpreted reality, interpreted at least by the researcher.

In his paper "Syntactically based methods of theory testing," David Kirshner [USA] contrasted studies of expert knowledge through think-aloud protocols with methods of syntactic research. A research method based on graph theory that can be used for case studies as well as for sampling procedures was discussed by Walther L. Fischer [DEU] in his paper "Formal concept analysis as a research tool in mathematics education." The idea is to represent cognitive knowledge mathematically as a so-called formal context, that is, a triple (G, M, I), where G is a set of objects, M a set of attributes corresponding to the elements of G, and I a binary relation (gIm means object g has attribute m). Fischer gave examples of questions that could be investigated by his method, including planning, designing, and evaluating instructional units and sequences.

To answer the question as to the extent to which exploratory and confirmatory studies can contribute to the development of knowledge about learning processes, it is necessary to understand the different aims and fields of application of these two methods of empirical research. Confirmatory data analysis tries to describe reality by a suitable probability model, to estimate the parameters of such a model, and to investigate hypotheses. One makes use of confirmatory data analysis when models and hypotheses are given. Exploratory data analysis is used in a contrary situation. Not models or hypotheses are given but data. The aim is to explore structures to generate hypotheses and perhaps to develop models. Despite the different aims and methods, a strict separation seems neither necessary nor reasonable. The results of exploratory studies influence the development of models of thinking and learning and thereby the use of statistical models in confirmatory studies. On the other hand, methods of confirmatory data analysis are used in exploratory studies. Qualitative as well as quantitative methods of data gathering and analysis, exploratory and confirmatory data analysis, are not alternatives but should be regarded as mutually supportive methods.

A description of the dependance of methods on the questions to be investigated and a discussion of the possibilities of complementary use were a main feature of Marie-Jeanne Perrin-Glorian's [FRA] lecture "Place de l'ingénierie didactique parmi les méthodologies de recherche en didactique des mathématiques en France," in which she discussed the tasks, aims, possibilities, conditions, constraints, and limits of didactic engineering:

> Les différents types de méthodes quantitatives ou qualitatives peuvent apporter des informations complémentaires et sont plus ou moins adaptées à la nature et au moment de la recherche. [...] Ce qui gouverne le choix d'une méthodologie, c'est l'origine du problème et l'état d'avancement du problème.

> [The different types of quantitative or qualitative methods can furnish complementary information and are more or less adapted to the nature and time of the research. [...] What governs the choice of a methodology is the source of the problem and its state of progress.]

The concept of didactic engineering in her lecture provoked an intense discussion of whether this term is adequate or even appropriate. It was argued that didactic engineering aims at studying teaching as it is and ought to be. It is essentially based on the confrontation between the a priori analysis of initial data (analysis that is problem-dependent and pupil- and classroom-independent) and the a posteriori analysis of the experimental data, observations and validation. There is a kind of dialectic tension between these two types of analysis. The discussion revolved around the question:

Is the term "engineering" ("the art of executing a practical application of scientific knowledge" according to Webster's dictionary) appropriate to our research? From the point of philosophy of science, didactic engineering seems to be, on the one hand, a methodology to create research methods using methodological tools and, on the other hand (and on a different level), a kind of research method itself.

In his paper "Assessment of classroom data," William M. Fitzgerald [USA] raised a general but important problem of today's educational research. He criticized the dominant forms of assessing learning and instruction in our field as too static in that investigations often start when instruction has ended. He asked that instruction and assessment be more closely related, that assessment be used to lead and direct instruction rather than simply to follow and report its results.

In this report we have tried to summarize the main aspects as they arose in the several contributions. The diversity of the themes that were considered were summarized by Jeremy Kilpatrick in his lecture "Problems of research methodology." In this lecture and in the subsequent panel discussion of William Ebeid [EGY], Lucia Grugnetti [ITA], and Joel Hillel [CAN], further questions and problems were discussed. These included the role of theory, paradigm, and ideology in research; the tension between eclecticism and interdisciplinarity; the nature and scope of *didactique des mathématiques*; problems in reporting case studies; and problems of redundancy across research studies. Studies reported in the working group demonstrated that quantitative and qualitative research methods are not only compatible but mutually beneficial.

REFERENCES

Artigue, M. (1990). Ingénierie didactique [Didactic engineering]. *Recherches en didactique des mathématiques*, 9(3), 281-307. Grenoble: La Pensée Sauvage. [English version published in 1992 in R. Douady & A. Mercier (Eds.), *Research in didactique of mathematics: Selected papers* (pp. 41-66). Grenoble: La Pensée Sauvage.]

Artigue, M., & Perrin-Glorian, M.-J. (1991). Didactic engineering, research and development tool: Some theoretical problems linked to this duality. *For the Learning of Mathematics*, 11(1), 13-18.

Brousseau, G., Davis, R.B., & Werner, T. (1986). Observing students at work. In B. Christiansen, A.G. Howson, & M. Otte (Eds.), *Perspectives on mathematics education* (pp. 205-241). Dordrecht: Kluwer Academic Publishers.

Howson, A.G., & Wilson, B.J. (1986). *School mathematics in the 1990s* (Ch. 7: Research). Cambridge, UK: Cambridge University Press.

Jaeger, R.M. (Ed.) (1987). *Complementary methods for research in education.* Washington: American Educational Research Association.

Romberg, T. (1992). Perspectives on scholarship and research methods. In D.A. Grouws (Ed.), *Handbook of research on mathematics teaching and learning* (pp. 49-64). New York: Macmillan.

235

TOPIC GROUPS

GROUPES THÉMATIQUES

MATHEMATICAL COMPETITIONS

CONCOURS MATHÉMATIQUES

Chief Organizer / *Responsable en chef* : Edward J. Barbeau [CAN]

Competitions have grown considerably in extent and variety within the past few years, to the extent that they have become a part of the educational process too significant to ignore in many countries. They involve, not only written papers for single competitors, but also team events and mathematical rallies which foster excitement and cooperation. They range from Olympiads for the most talented to competitions for hundreds of thousands of students, and have spawned journals for students, books for enrichment, correspondence programs and mathematics camps. Some of this diversity was reflected in the presentations at ICME-7.

The two sessions were devoted to the presentation of ten-minute papers in the categories: Junior student activities; Talent identification; and Research and pedagogy. Peter O'Halloran [AUS] and Ron Dunkley [CAN] were in the chair.

In the first session, George Lenchner [USA] described the Mathematical Olympiad for Elementary Schools (now in its fourteenth year). During the school year, there are five tests of five problems for about 75 000 students mainly in Grades 4-6, about half of whom are girls. There are awards that recognize individual participations and achievement. Louis-Philippe Gaudreault [CAN] spoke on the Mathémathlon, operating in the province of Québec; it is designed to foster interest and competence among Grade 3-6 pupils and increase the teacher's ability to handle problem-solving situations. The students prepare during the winter for tests at the local, regional and national levels. In 1991, 181 688 students from 6981 classes were involved. Le Kangourou de mathématiques in France was described by Claude Deschamps [FRA]. Modeled on the Australian Mathematics Competition, it is written at three levels for students in the 11-12 years, 13-14 years and 15-16 years age groups. In 1992, there were 320 000 participants, but it is a matter of concern that most students in the higher levels come from larger cities. Nikolai Konstantinov [RUS] described the

239

Tournament of the Towns in which teams from cities in Russia, Bulgaria, Australia and other countries write problem papers, with some collaboration permitted. He described the regime of papers, the scoring system that allows for differences of population size, and gave a sample problem.

The audience then heard three papers that dealt with the identification and fostering of mathematical talent by George Berzsenyi [USA] who spoke on the International Mathematical Talent Search, Bruce Henry [AUS] who spoke on the Mathematical Challenge for Young Australians program, and John Webb [ZAF] who ran a talent search and training program in his country. The International Mathematical Talent Search, modeled on a similar venture in the USA, is publicized through the journal *Mathematics and Informatics*; during the year, participants receive four sets of five problems to work on for six weeks. These are marked centrally and students receive a newsletter that discusses the solutions. The Australian program has three stages. In the "challenge" stage, about 12 000 students receive six problems which they have three weeks to solve. 6000 students pass to the "enrichment" stage, in which the students and their teachers receive material to work through. The final stage is the Telecom contest, in which about 500 students do five problems in three hours. The talent search in South Africa was instigated by that country's entry into the International Mathematical Olympiad. John Webb referred to the task of building trust in a multiracial society and fostering mathematical interest that goes beyond the Olympiad.

In the second session, the focus was on research and pedagogy. The problem seminar of Valladolid in Spain, described by Francisco Bellot-Rosado [ESP] was established in 1988 for 16-18 year-old students, who meet once a week for two hours. Harold and Betty Reiter [USA] analyzed the responses to questions in the 1991 and 1992 American High School Mathematics Examination, and discussed questions in which reponses of males and females differed. Ali Rejali [IRN] described what can be learned from the data collected from the Iranian competitions. Ian Brown [GBR] studied motivation for problem solving among both successful and un-successful students in an inner London competition. Pak-Hong Cheung [HKG] addressed the question of teaching students to solve problems in a more effective way. This requires not only an understanding of heuristics but a suitable belief system and familiarity with strategies and proof techniques. Tony Gardiner [GBR] found that he was becoming increasingly involved in competitions as the most effective means of reaching young students in Britain. He described the recent growth and effectiveness of contests in his country, mentioning in particular the Norwich Union Model-ling Project. The session concluded with a presentation on the undergraduate mathematics club Mu Alpha Theta by Carol McGill [USA] and on the University of Minnesota Talented Youth Program by Harvey Keynes [USA].

An additional session chaired by Peter Taylor [AUS] was held under the auspices of the World Federation of National Mathematics Competitions and dealt with more specialized aspects of organizing competitions. Juan Manuel Conde [ESP] discussed the correspondence training program for students preparing for national and international olympiads. Peter O'Halloran [AUS] traced the growth of the Asian-Pacific Mathematics Olympiad, a low-expense operation with students writing in their own locality. Mark Saul [USA] described the four events for 15-member teams who come together from all over the United States for the American Regions Mathematics League, while Walter Mientke [USA] gave an illustrated talk on the hierarchy of papers that make up the American Mathematics Competition. Svetoslav Bilchev [BGR] discussed a strategic approach to problem solving in which students try to solve related easier problems. Garnik Tonojan [ARM] gave an account of the development of elementary geometry from antiquity to the present. Finally, Alexander Soifer [USA] discussed some examples of problem creation and development.

Topic Group 2 / *Groupe thématique 2*

ETHNOMATHEMATICS
AND MATHEMATICS EDUCATION

ETHNOMATHÉMATIQUE
ET ÉDUCATION MATHÉMATIQUE

Chief Organizer / *Responsable en chef* : Ubiratán D'Ambrosio [BRA]

The group met in two sessions of 90 minutes each. In the first session a panel comprising Gloria Gilmer [USA], Mary Harris [GBR], Abdulcarismo Ismael [MOZ] and Gelsa Knijnik [BRA] gave views on ethnomathematics from different perspectives. Gilmer emphasized the role of the ethnomathematics approach in the mathematical education of minorities in the USA. By trying to recover practices which belong to their heritage, minority students can feel that mathematics is closer to their cultural history. They feel more confident and their self-esteem is enhanced. Harris referred to her work in England with adults coming for an educational experience which must relate to their work, and showed how the diversity of practices which are characteristic of ethnomathematics generates a favorable atmosphere for their learning. Ismael reported on the joint efforts of mathematicians, historians of mathematics, and mathematics educators to recover the origins of mathematical practices and theorizations in Africa. He referred to publications in several countries of Africa, and in particular to one edited by Paulus Gerdes, in Mozambique, specifically on ethnomathematics. Knijnik reported on several experiences with the ethnomathematical approach in Latin America, particularly on the pioneering work of Eduardo S. Ferreira with Amazonian Indians and a research related to land occupation, under the Land Reform Law in Brazil, which revealed a geometry developed by peasants with no formal schooling thus rediscovering practices found in Egyptian antiquity. These presentations took approximately 60 minutes; the other 30 minutes were devoted to remarks, comments and questions by the participants.

The second session consisted of a review of those communications to ICME-7 presented in the form of posters which were related to ethnomathematics. The reporters were Patrick J. Scott [USA], Vinicio Villani [ITA],

242

Rheta Rubenstein [CAN], Patra Techapiwat [THA] and George G. Joseph [GBR]. The panelists spoke briefly on their own work and reported on the posters which drew their attention. Scott, as editor of the Newsletter of the International Study Group on Ethnomathematics, was able to identify areas where ethnomathematical approaches have been particularly active. Villani reported on the efforts going on in Italy to train mathematics educators from Somalia to teach mathematics in their native languages, an important aspect of an ethnomathematical orientation. Rubenstein introduced a matricial methodology to deal with differences in a multicultural classroom. Techapiwat reported on efforts by the Thai educational system to recover the history of traditional mathematics in Thai culture. Joseph sketched his non-eurocentric version of the history of mathematics as related to mathematics education.

An overall view of the two sessions gives the clear impression that ethnomathematics is gaining space as a special field of research in both the history and the philosophy of mathematics. The historical aspect of ethnomathematics, besides calling for going beyond the current excessive eurocentrism, opens the way to a new vision of the European history of mathematics, mainly through a new look at the Middle Ages and the Renaissance. That becomes clear if one analyzes for example the role of artisans and of the popularization of mathematics in the 17th and 18th centuries. As was pointed out by some of the participants and discussants, ethnomathematics is "the art or technique (*tics*) of explaining, understanding, and coping with reality (*mathema*) in different cultural environments (*ethnos*)". It thus provides a methodology which confronts the hiatuses occurring in both the history and the teaching of mathematics, and can be used to overcome the barriers which are caused by them.

Topic Group 3 / *Groupe thématique 3*

MATHEMATICS FOR WORK: VOCATIONAL EDUCATION

MATHÉMATIQUES DU TRAVAIL ET ENSEIGNEMENT PROFESSIONNEL

Chief Organizer / *Responsable en chef* : Rudolf Strässer [DEU]

The group started from a dictionary-definition of work as the "exertion directed to produce or accomplish something / by which one earns a living". Therefore, mathematics for work has (in most cases) a non-mathematical context and purpose, and is related to employment and money. Vocational education "involves ... the study of technologies and related sciences and the acquisition of practical skills and knowledge related to occupations in various sectors of economic and social life" (UNESCO). Consequently, vocational education in mathematics may imply learning, in the workplace as well as in school or university, which is related to economic and social development.

The group distinguished two levels (qualified workers vs graduates/ professionals) and, for the first session, concentrated on "Vocational mathematics: teaching future qualified workers". Torben Steeg and Julian Williams [GBR] in a presentation on "The integration of mathematics within units of work in preparing vocational training" and John Searl [GBR] on "Teaching vocational mathematics: differences between the classroom and the workplace" highlighted problems and potentials of integrating work-related teaching units into general education – not least by offering meaningful contexts for mathematics to motivate students usually opting out of mathematics. Annie Bessot [FRA] in a talk on "Geometry for work: the case of building vocations" identified epistemological differences between scholarly geometry ("establish truth!") and spatial abilities relevant in the building sector ("be efficient!"). She analyzed in detail problem solving strategies in a situation which is fundamental for the reading of technical drawings in the building sector. Habiba el Bouazzaoui [MAR] presented a general analysis of "Mathematics in vocational education curricula in Morocco" and questioned the appropriateness of the curricula to the needs (particularly the economical needs) of society. There are cases where mathematics obviously functions more as a means of selecting future workers than as part of their qualification. Jim Ridgway and Don Passey [GBR] analyzed "the mathematical needs of engineering apprentices" and pointed to sharp contrasts between the beliefs of employers (basic skills are fundamental and easily transferred) and empirical studies of apprentices' experience which showed the necessity of setting school mathematics into the work context. Apprentices believed that self-confidence was an additional prerequisite of a successful apprentice. The entrance tests used by one employer failed to predict apprentice performance, whereas state examinations of general school mathematics were a good predictor. The overall issue of this first session was the way mathematical knowledge is involved in vocational contexts – showing that it is wrong to analyze the vocational use of mathematics in purely mathematical terms. A more appropriate approach may be to take pieces of mathematics as situated in vocational knowledge, with the consequent need to study the integration of both mathematics and vocational situations. Such an integrative approach may produce a fair description of "vocational uses of mathematics".

The second session of the topic group dealt with "Mathematics for work: teaching future graduates and professionals". It started with a presentation by Michael Cornelius [GBR] on "Mathematical problems experienced by graduates starting work", showing that difficulties with mathematics prevail even with university graduates. John Usher and Ken Brown [GBR] reported on "Industrial enhancement of problem-based learning", describing a university course to develop communication, interpersonal and group problem solving, and project management skills, as examples of skills desperately needed by graduates in industry and commerce. Assessing the group interaction was seen as a difficulty in this setting. Heinz Lohse [DEU] spoke on "Data analysis and statistics in professional training and practice" and presented an explorative study, lately conducted at the Technical University of Dresden, showing certain gaps between university training in Germany and the "needs" of industry and commerce, e.g. in terms of quality control and testing. Maria Dolores Ugarte Martinez [ESP] commented on "Mathematics in agricultural and chemical engineering: a Spanish perspective" by describing the mathematics curricula of some Spanish universities in engineering (particularly in agricultural and chemical engineering) and contrasting it to the technological development. In the subsequent discussion the cooperation of universities, professional bodies, and government was mentioned as a way to cope with the situation. An issue common to the last two presentations was the urgent need to adapt university training for professionals to the changing demands arising from technology.

A general discussion addressed the possibility of generating a resource book of work-related mathematics problems (an item bank), but also mentioned difficulties with classifying and making available the collected examples. Different types of sandwich-courses (from a weekly mix of two days at the college and three days at work to yearly alternations of work and college attendance) were brought forward as a way to integrate work and mathematics. Experiences in France, Germany and the United Kingdom were referred to. In his concluding remarks, Rudolf Strässer [DEU] stressed four major issues in mathematics for work: to adapt the teaching of mathematics at engineering/university level to the developments in technology (including the growing use of computers); to develop research methods that are appropriate for the exploration of the vocational use of mathematics – taking into account the integration of mathematics into vocational situations; devising ways to cope with the complementarity of situated knowledge (mathematics integrated in vocational contexts) and the chance of using the "same" piece of mathematics in a variety of contexts; to find ways to cope with the abuse of "vocational" mathematics, e.g. as a tool to select applicants for a job.

NOTES

More detailed information on the presentations made in Topic Group 3 can be obtained from Rudolf Strässer, Fax: (49) 521 106 2991, E-mail: rstraess@dave.hrz.uni-bielefeld.de

REFERENCES

Harris, M. (Ed.) (1991). *Schools, mathematics and work*. London: The Falmer Press.

Potari, D., & Searl, J.W. (1989). Creating a learning environment for 16+ mathematics. *Journal Inst. Math. Appl., 8*(2), 56-68.

Strässer, R., Barr, G., Evans, J., & Wolf, A. (1989). Skills versus understanding. *Zentralblatt für Didaktik der Mathematik, 21*(6), 197-202.

Usher, J.R., Simmonds, D.G., and Earl, S.E. (1991). Industrial enhancement through problem-based learning. In D. Boud & G. Feletti (Eds.), *The challenge of problem-based learning* (pp. 225-233). Kogan Page.

Topic Group 4 / *Groupe thématique 4*

INDIGENOUS PEOPLES AND MATHEMATICS EDUCATION

LES PEUPLES AUTOCHTONES ET L'ÉDUCATION MATHÉMATIQUE

Chief Organizer / Responsable en chef : Bill Barton [NZL]

This topic group met for two 90-minute sessions. About 50 people attended each session. The group provided a forum for indigenous people to report on their efforts to obtain an appropriate mathematics education. It also promoted discussion about language, systemic obstacles and the politics of such mathematics education.

The first session was opened by Nellie Palliser Moorhouse on behalf of a group presentation by the Inuit of Canada. Participants were welcomed to Canada and the conference on behalf of the Inuit. Then some of the history of Inuit education and mathematics language development was recounted. It was noted that French or English cannot be adequately translated into Inutitut. Thus it was necessary to develop a mathematical language from Inutitut vocabulary. Pasha Puttayuk described the use of different body parts as units of length. The next two presenters spoke in Inutitut, translated by Nellie Moorhouse. Susie Emudluk explained the structure of number words and the use of suffixes in relation to the way objects are arranged. "One" and "two" are special cases because the language contains singular, dual and plural indicators. This is why teaching begins with the word for three. Sarah Grey Scott described the formation and function of the Teacher Education courses which have been under Inuit control since 1975. They are credited by McGill University. There have been 51 graduates. Courses are mostly held during the summer and the principal language of instruction is Inutitut. During the school year the students are full-time teachers and must use the materials and methods learnt during the year. The language of instruction in schools is Inutitut until Grade 2, and French or English after that.

The Maori group from Aotearoa-New Zealand replied to the welcome with elder Sonny Riini speaking in Maori and the group singing a traditional chant. Tony Trinick presented a background to Maori education and explained how current educational paradigms were being challenged. Maori believe that mathematics should be taught holistically, that it is dependent on culture, and that it is accessible to all Maori people. Maori mathematics education aims at the same outcomes as the national curriculum, but also aims to retain the Maori language. Maori wish to include contemporary practice while retaining a Maori world-view. After 140 years of colonial education Maori language is under threat. In response, the Maori people have developed an indigenous preschool movement (Te Kohanga Reo), full Maori primary schools (Kura Kaupapa Maori), and area secondary schools, all of which operate under Maori values and which use Maori as the only language of instruction. There are also bilingual and immersion programs.

Salimata Doumbia [CIV] explained that traditional teaching in her country is by word of mouth in transferred proverbs, stories, songs and games. These contain all subjects combined together. She gave examples of several types of games and songs, and noted that the mystical connotations of numbers were still alive. Indigenous games are now in competition with pastimes from other countries, and the latter have had the effect of devaluing the traditional ones. Also relevant is the unharmonious passage of society from traditional to modern, and the Islamization of Africa which forbids some games.

The second session began with Gail Jaji [ZWE] explaining recent research done with David Metwa. This exploratory study of Zimbabwean childrens' beliefs about indigenous mathematics found that children believe that traditional mathematics exists and is legitimate, but that it is too elementary to be regarded seriously. These children also felt that mathematics could be taught in the Shona language but that it would thus be harder to learn. It was suggested that these beliefs would inhibit children bringing their culture into the mathematics classroom. Another study explored the impact of traditional understanding of number on school mathematics. It indicated that there is a loss of number sense as a result of westernization. The vernacular language (which is a place value language) is no longer used for counting or expressing number ideas.

Gareth Roberts gave an introduction in Welsh to his presentation of the situation in Wales where the indigenous language is used as the language of instruction into tertiary institutions as part of a deliberate policy to revive the Welsh language. He suggested two reasons for teaching in Welsh: English instruction may be an alienating factor producing poor mathematics performance by Welsh students; and language and pattern are interrelated (as demonstrated in Welsh poetry). Thus instruction in Welsh has the potential to enrich the mathematics curriculum. Sun Mingfu reported on a comparative study of Han and Tibetan children. He concluded that culture was an important factor and suggested that examples from Tibetan culture should be used, and that texts and teaching methods which are more suitable for the Tibetan context should be found. Martha Villavicencio [PER] spoke about the bilingual programmes in Peru, Ecuador and Bolivia, noting their relationship to the socio-political context in each country, and the similarities and differences betweeen groups. Programs began in the 1970s and a contemporary program called EAMCOS was described.

The resulting discussion centered around the low numbers of indigenous people present and the need for them to be present to speak for themselves. The meeting called for the ICME organizers to assume a greater responsibility in future in facilitating the attendance of people from indigenous groups. Another issue mentioned was the loss of their language by indigenous groups.

NOTE

A document was made available to participants prior to the Congress and a post-Congress publication has also been prepared. The two publications together contain all the presented papers (most in both French and English) and six accompanying papers (by Barton, Bishop, Davidson, Gerdes, Langdon and Rogerson). The combined edition can be obtained for US$10 by writing to Bill Barton, Auckland College of Education, P.B. 92601, Auckland, NEW ZEALAND-AOTEAROA.

The CO acknowledges the assistance of Lise Paquin [CAN] in arranging contacts with indigenous individuals and groups.

Topic Group 5 / *Groupe thématique 5*

THE SOCIAL CONTEXT OF MATHEMATICS EDUCATION

LE CONTEXTE SOCIAL DE L'ÉDUCATION MATHÉMATIQUE

Chief Organizer / *Responsable en chef* : Alan J. Bishop [AUS]

First session theme: *What are the influences of the social context on mathematics education*? Alan Bishop in his lead paper referred participants to research analyses which indicated three significant levels of social influence. At the cultural level, the research on ethnomathematics raises questions about the nature of the mathematical knowledge existing in any society, both inside and outside schools. At the societal and political level, we can recognize the different structures of formal, non-formal, and informal, mathematics education, which then face us with the issues of what mathematics should be represented in the formal, intended, curriculum. At the level of the educational institutions, we are becoming more aware about the issues of interpersonal influence, which affect both teachers' and learners' mathematical knowledge and their attitudes towards mathematics learning.

In the ensuing discussion groups, participants raised the following points:

- the language used for teaching is a major factor in all social issues, particularly in multilingual societies;

- the three levels referred to vary in importance in different societies, depending for example, on the range of social classes in the society, or on the degree of industrial and economic development of the society;

- a "Western" view of mathematics is often just imposed through education, thus relegating other views of mathematics to a second class level;

- the role of the public media is crucial in shaping public opinion about these issues, both overtly and covertly;

- parents play a significant mediating role with their children, particularly in relation to their expectations of achievement and attitude;

- adult learners need to be considered as well as young people;

- how should we train teachers to be more aware of these social issues?;

- examinations and assessment need much more attention, particularly in view of their role in shaping expectations;

- more importance should be placed on the society's values for education generally and for mathematics education in particular;

- teachers need much more advice on teaching mathematics with multicultural groups of students;

- non-formal education plays a very significant role in some societies, for example in Taiwan and Japan where children take out-of-school lessons, and it exerts an influence on formal education.

(The discussion leaders were Bernadette Denys [FRA], George Gheverghese Joseph [GBR], Murad Jurdak [LBN], Frederick Leung [HKG], Fou-Lai Lin [TWN] and Jan Thomas [AUS].)

Second session theme: *How should mathematics educators address the issues of social context?* Virginia Thompson [USA] in her lead paper addressed three significant areas where mathematics educators could, and in her view should, play a stronger role in the social process. Firstly, in the area of content, they should be influencing decisions about curriculum at both national and local levels, particularly concerning appropriate concepts and techniques, seeking ways to include societal uses of mathematics, and developing connections with personal knowledge, with cultural knowledge, and with other subjects. Secondly, in the area of assessment, they need to develop ranges of procedures appropriate to monitoring mathematical power in all students, such as written and oral presentations for projects and investigations, portfolios, open ended tasks and self-assessment. Thirdly, in relation to learning environments, they should be developing integrated teaching approaches, collaborative learning, the use of heterogeneous class groupings, and creating plentiful opportunities for written and oral communication.

The issues raised by Virginia Thompson for discussion included: How can we influence policy towards more appropriate curricula, how do we ensure adequate input from all social groups? What are the criteria for valid activities that reflect the cultural and societal aspects we want represented in the curriculum? How do we ensure access to all these classroom activities for all students? How can we communicate the reasons for change to teachers, students, parents, and the community as a whole?

In the discussion groups the following points arose:

- in trying to integrate students of different ethnic and social backgrounds, the major components of success are respect for all students and their cultures, and the joint efforts of teachers, students, parents and the community to work out solutions to complex educational problems;

- we should try to create teaching approaches which have "open beginnings" to allow students space to define their own interests and to set their own context for problems;

- there is a need to translate and interpret "national" documents in local contexts – who should do that?;

- the importance of accepting and using students' home language, knowledge and skills in class;

- adapt curricula to the learning styles and perceived needs of the classroom group;

- use applications which encourage the students to get involved in their community;

- as a teacher, be well informed about the social group you are dealing with, as well as being broad in your mathematical knowledge;

- make students aware of how the values they learn in mathematics classes impinge on other sets of values outside the classroom, and with which they may conflict;

- to what extent is a goal such as "mathematical empowerment" meaningful and achievable for all students?

(The discussion leaders for the second session were Josette Adda [FRA], William Ebeid [EGY], Dagmar Neuman [SWE], Geraldo Pompeu [BRA], Norma Presmeg [USA], John Volmink [ZAF] and Claudia Zaslavsky [USA].)

REFERENCES

Bishop, A, Hart, K., Lerman, S., & Nunes T. (1993). *Significant influences on children's learning of mathematics.* Paris: UNESCO.

Keitel, C., Bishop, A., Damerow P., & Gerdes, P. (Eds.) (1980). *Mathematics, education and society.* Paris: UNESCO.

Topic Group 6 / *Groupe thématique 6*

THE THEORY AND PRACTICE OF PROOF

LA THÉORIE ET LA PRATIQUE
DE LA PREUVE MATHÉMATIQUE

Chief Organizers / *Responsables en chef* : Gila Hanna [CAN],
Niels Jahnke [DEU]

The first session consisted of a panel discussion, while the second session took the form of four separate discussion groups.

SESSION 1

Panel discussion on the theory and practice of proof

After an introduction by Gila Hanna [CAN] and Niels Jahnke [DEU] the moderator, Peter Hilton [USA], first read a statement on the role of proof written by Yu. Manin [RUS], who was unfortunately unable to attend the Congress. Mariolina Bartolini Bussi [ITA] and Josette Adda [FRA] discussed students' apprehension of the nature and role of proof within a mathematical development. They both considered proof in geometry and noted the existence and importance of the continuum of "proof-types" ranging from the empirical to the theoretical.

Erich Wittmann [DEU] distinguished between demonstration and proof, the former often having a very concrete nature. He argued for introducing demonstrative reasoning as soon as the first grade. Philip Davis [USA] saw proof as part of the "evidence" a mathematician accumulates in building confidence in a given mathematical proposition, and ridiculed the idea that there is some kind of objective certainty peculiar to mathematics which is attainable only through the mechanism of proof. Judith Grabiner [USA] developed the very convincing thesis that criteria for the acceptability of mathematical arguments have varied from one historical period to another, citing, among several examples, Euler's expansion of the exponential function.

Peter Hilton summarized the various contributions of the panelists, identifying certain common themes and convergent trends. After a brief exchange of views among the panelists, which revealed much common concern, significant agreement, and no dramatic dissent, the meeting was opened to questions and discussion.

SUBGROUP 1

Empirical research

Organizers: Nicolas Balacheff [FRA], Nitsa Movshovitz-Hadar [ISR]

Empirical research on the teaching and learning of proof depends strongly on the choice of a theoretical framework, a methodology, the ways in which these two are related, and the questions asked. Some questions to consider are: What is a mathematical proof? What is the relationship in the mind of a student between proof and other means of validation? What are the social functions of mathematical proof? What are its functions as a tool in mathematics?

Daniel Chazan [USA] reported on research aimed at understanding what "to prove" means to students. Amos Ehrlich and Boaz Shanny [ISR] explored the nature of proof as a content to be learned. Gilbert Arsac [FRA] described the evolution of students' conceptions of proof in the context of social conflicts organized to favour a debate of validation and the recognition of its specific rules. Yasuhiro Sekiguchi [JPN] emphasized the need to relate proofs and refutations, especially in such social interaction. Bachir Keskessa emphasized the role of the didactical contract in the way students construct conceptions of proving in mathematics.

After a fruitful debate, it was felt that the problem of "teaching mathematical proof" should be reformulated as the problem of "teaching proof in mathematics".

SUBGROUP 2

Historical aspects of proof

Organizers: John Fauvel [GBR] and Israel Kleiner [CAN]

The session had two parts: five presentations of 10 minutes each, followed by a lengthy discussion. First John Fauvel [GBR] outlined the development of geometrical proof as a component of British mathematical education, drawing attention to perceptions of the ancient Greek origins as well as to debates about the use and value of proof in Euclidean geometry. Man-Keung Siu [HKG] then spoke about methods and conceptions of proof in ancient China. Judith Grabiner [USA] discussed the role of proof and rigour in eighteenth-century mathematical developments. Reuben Hersh [USA] spoke about the ways in which the computer has influenced the practice and conception of mathematical proof. Finally, Israel Kleiner [CAN] considered analytic versus synthetic approaches to proof, focusing on the fusion in the 20th century of algebraic and geometric ideas.

Participants made brief comments on pedagogical implications of historical developments, emphasizing the importance for mathematics educators of sharing ideas about this crucially important yet controversial theme of proof in the schools.

SUBGROUP 3

Recent developments and new ideas in the didactics of proof

Organizers: Francine Abeles [USA] and Michael Neubrand [DEU]

There were two themes: the impact of computing on the didactics of proof and the more classical issues involved in proving theorems. Albrecht Abele [DEU] emphasized the social processes in achieving group consensus among primary school children. Calvin Jongsma [USA] exhibited a system by Jaskowski and Fitch of "natural deduction" as a simple method for explaining, understanding, and constructing mathematical proofs. Michael Neubrand [DEU] pointed out that one can observe certain social patterns in the discussions of proofs which are still in the process of being accepted by the mathematical community, and drew some didactical conclusions. Francine Abeles [USA] discussed the role of computer programming, specifically Prolog, in evolving the strategies necessary to construct a mathematical proof. Philippe Bernat [FRA] showed his program, Chypre, which allows the construction of network-like proof formats in geometry. An advantage of a network approach is that students can explore a problem top-down, bottom-up or from the middle. Kathleen Kippen [CAN] presented a paper by J.H. Hoover and Piotr Rudnicki [CAN] on Mizar MSE, a proof-checker for predicate logic that is used in a first-year logic course for students of computing.

SUBGROUP 4

Teacher training and proof

Organizers: Michael de Villiers [ZAF] and Fulvia Furinghetti [ITA]

After a short introduction by the organizers there were six presentations:

- Peter Baptist [DEU]: "Elegant or inelegant? On the beauty of proofs".

- Sylvie Coppe [FRA]: "Processus de vérification chez les élèves de 1re en situation de résolution de problèmes".

- David Henderson [USA]: "Proof as a convincing argument that answers – why?"

- Peter Hilton and Jean Pedersen [USA] : "Strategies of proof and exposition".

- Dexter Luthuli [ZAF]: "The proof of Euclidean geometry riders viewed as an exercise in mathematical creativity".

- Bram van Asch [NLD]: "To prove, why and how?"

The following important points were raised: 1) Teacher training should discuss the "aesthetic qualities" of different proofs. 2) Good proofs should explain the meanings of the concepts involved, but different people may have different meanings requiring different explanations. 3) Teacher training should discuss the various purposes of proof, and proofs should not be limited to geometry. Prospective math teachers ought to discuss and compare different approaches to particular problems, e.g. algebraic and geometric approaches. 4) Proof should not be seen as an end-product. 5) Prospective teachers ought to be exposed to a variety of useful strategies for facilitating proof and exposition, e.g. choice of appropriate notation, consideration of particular but not special cases, systematic reorganization.

REFERENCES

Balacheff, N. (1987). Processus de preuve et situations de validations. *Educational Studies in Mathematics, 18*(2), 147-176.

Benson, J., Hilton, P., & Pedersen, J. (1993). *College preparatory mathematics*. New Almaden, CA: Pedersen Publishing Co.

De Villiers, M. (1990). The role and function of proof in mathematics. *Pythagoras, 24,* 17-24.

Furinghetti, F., & Paola, D. (1991). On some obstacles in understanding mathematical texts. In F. Furinghetti (Ed.), *Proceedings of the Fifteenth Conference of the International Group for the Psychology of Mathematics Education.* Assisi, Italy.

Hanna, G., & Winchester, I. (Eds.) (1990). *Creativity, thought and mathematical proof.* Toronto: OISE Press.

Topic Group 7 / *Groupe thématique 7*

MATHEMATICAL GAMES AND PUZZLES

JEUX ET PUZZLES MATHÉMATIQUES

Chief Organizer / *Responsable en chef* : Tibor Szentivanyi [HUN]

The sessions were chaired by the chief organizer who at the beginning of the first meeting characterized the main features of recreational mathematics as well as its role and importance in teaching mathematics. On both days there were demonstrations too, e.g. a selection of 3D geometrical forms were shown (Origami polyhedrons created by paper foldings) and some selected models from the collection of Andy Liu [CAN] were presented. A characteristic feature of both sessions was the contest between participants for the printed mathematical brain teasers which were distributed by the chairman and which could be won only by asking a good question. As a result of this a cheerful game evolved and there was a continuously high level of interest.

In the following summary the presentations are reviewed in the order in which they occurred:

Ole Bjorkqvist [FIN]: *Problem solving using geometry games.* The software presented is intended to be used in problem-solving activities at a relatively advanced level (secondary or tertiary mathematics education). It consists of a set of games, each one offering a geometric pattern of dots that are either light or dark. The common object of all the games is to make all the dots dark. The rules for changing the colour of the dots vary, however, from one game to another, and these have to be discovered by the player. The games are designed to make possible a progression from relatively easy games to games requiring careful mathematical analysis, often transferring possible solution strategies from one game to another. Some of the mathematical concepts involved are geometric configurations, symmetry, modular arithmetic, and matrices.

Gillian Hatch and Christine Shiu [GBR]: *Using mathematical games in the classroom.* The speakers examined how the social experience of playing games can be drawn on and made use of in the mathematics classroom.

257

Playing games involves the acceptance of a structured and rule-bound context which is in itself analogous to certain aspects of mathematics. Games also have a goal (solution) which provides a defined endpoint to the activity. This creates a time-frame natural to the children which allows them to proceed through the game at their own pace thus allowing appropriately extended contact with the ideas. Playing games naturally involves mathematical language. Negotiating permitted moves or procedures, and agreeing about their effects, provide intrinsic opportunities for children to develop and use mathematical language in order to predict, justify, convince, and evaluate. Teachers often find it very illuminating to "eavesdrop" on the language used in a mathematical game. This suggests that games can be used as a context for the authentic assessment of children's mathematical thinking. The presenters' focus is now on the potential effectiveness of using specific games, some of which are designed purely to support the development of mathematical processes, others of which are intended to incorporate the learning or rehearsal of defined mathematical content as they are played.

Akihior Nozaki [JPN]: *A universal algorithm for proving arbitrary staments.* In this talk Nozaki started with a simple algorithm by which he claimed he could prove any statement, true or false. The problem is to point out what is wrong with the algorithm. The trick lies in the irrational use of self-reference, which is very hard to find for many students. It may be an interesting puzzle for instructors how to evaluate various wrong answers of students.

Kuniko Ikari [JPN]: *Paper folding to make different geometrical shapes.* The speaker presented several Origami foldings which could support teaching mathematics in the classroom. She showed how to make a few forms, breaking down the whole process into simple steps. The presentation was accompanied by printed sheets with detailed figures on the basis of which one could follow the whole process.

Rüdiger Thiele [DEU]: *Mathematical games and their history.* As an introduction the speaker asked the question: what should we understand by a mathematical game? To answer this, he started with examples, first analyzing Tlachtli (a pre-Columbian ball game), then NIM, and finally dice-games, showing different aspects. At the conclusion of this part of the lecture he suggested: a game proceeds according to a set of rules. We regard a game as "mathematical" when the players can perceive and/or influence the course of the game on the basis of mathematical considerations. Discussing the history of games, Thiele expressed his views: games arose with mankind; on the other hand they arose out of cultic rituals. Most of the rules of antique games cannot be traced, they have disappeared completely. Even so there are a few collections, e.g. the book of King Alonso (10th century) who collected and described 1283 games. At the end of his presentation the speaker showed some examples — not only rule-stressing games like chess, solitaire, and NIM, with their strict logico-mathematical structures — that could be the subject of mathematical attention. Games of chance have a close connection with mathematics. He especially discussed board games, including Rithmomachia from about A.D. 1030, and finally dice-games and their planar versions.

Toshiko Kimura [JPN]: *The enjoyment of math lessons*. This was a presentation which induced almost all the participants in the session to become active. The speaker showed five polyhedra – tetrahedron, hexahedron, octahedron, dodecahedron and icosahedron – that she had made herself. The polyhedra were made using Origami principles, following suggestions developed by the Association of Mathematical Instruction (A.M.I.) in Japan. The polyhedra are the basis for popular lessons in Japanese schools. The speaker showed the complete process of making two of the polyhedra and the instructions were distributed amongst the participants.

Andy Liu [CAN]: *Two polyform puzzles*. The speaker explained that he is co-inventor and co-developer of two puzzles: "The Birds and the Bees", a joint invention with Michael Keller [USA], based on the (3,4,6,4) Archimedian tiling of the plane, and "The Chasagon Puzzles", a joint invention with Chas Gantt [USA], based on a tiling of hexagons and hexagons punctured by parallelograms. Liu discussed the history and background of tiling. Starting from the three regular shapes: equilateral triangle, square, and regular hexagon, he explained the generation of polyiamonds, polyominoes, and polyhexes. He then introduced two puzzles using multiforms with rounded edges, "Kwazy Quilt" and "Roundominoes". Finally, he showed the set of multiforms he had developed for recreational purposes based on the (3,4,6,4) tiling, having "atomic number" not exceeding 4 and "weight" not exceeding 17. This gave a set of 28 pieces: 14 symmetric pieces and 7 mirror-image pairs (which must remain so in a solution).

Diane Lavoie, Guy Godmaire and René Auclair [CAN]: *CIBLE*. "CIBLE" is a mathematical game, developed especially for the purpose. It stimulates students to research and examine the facts, raising their intellectual interest. Its aim is to find new research directions by creating the concept of the four arithmetic operations, and by developing algebraic factorization in different ways. The route-to-follow through the game is especially designed for teachers whose principal subject is mathematics, independently of the level of school they teach in (middle school, high school, university, or part-time instruction). Along the route the players may ask for pedagogical help: this may be from one specific tool up to symbolic representation.

Topic Group 8 / *Groupe thématique 8*

TEACHING MATHEMATICS
THROUGH PROJECT WORK

L'ENSEIGNEMENT DES
MATHÉMATIQUES PAR PROJETS

Chief Organizer / *Responsable en chef* : Jarkko Leino [FIN]

Project work is not a new method in education, not even in mathematics teaching. However the traditional way of teaching mathematics emphasizes the structure of mathematics from the start, with the consequence that the hierarchy of mathematical concepts and operations has a dominant role. Concepts are linked with each other according to the logic of mathematics teaching and learning. Teaching mathematics through projects has another philosophy which may seem to be contradictory to the traditional one. Hence projects as an ingredient of mathematics teaching may seem unusual to experts in didactics of mathematics and to researchers as well.

The group dealt with the topic from many different points of view and for different levels of teaching. Some of the papers presented referred to the importance and philosophy of the project method, others to its effects on learning, pedagogy, evaluation, or experiments in good practice. We will survey the papers to extract the essence of the topic.

Using the project method is an attempt to make knowledge dynamic, meaningfully constructed for some purpose by the learner, and organized on his prior experiences and knowledge. Knowledge is not isolated from the learner's world, his reality. This kind of ideal learning process is very close to the nature of mathematics as a discipline (Jarkko Leino [FIN]). Recent ideas, based on research, have emphasized the very nature of mathematical inquiry and the modes of generating knowledge that are characteristic of mathematics and meaningful to the learner.

Richard Pallascio [CAN] emphasized the meaning of the word project: to become free of the present moment, to appeal to one's own experience, to "project" oneself. A project is simultaneously a projection and an answer to ideals which we can feel internally. Pallascio favored integrative projects and fostering students' initiatives in project work. Students have to learn to use mathematical reasoning by formulating hypotheses, selecting proof elements, constructing arguments, extracting conclusions, mastering the mathematical pathway.

Paulo Abrantes [PRT] approached project work from the viewpoint of modeling. He emphasized the following characteristics: (a) A project is an extended piece of work where students' attention and interest are focused on a problem for a long time. (b) A variety of activities is involved, such as formulating and solving problems, computations, practical work, discussions, visits, reports, computer sessions, to be carried out individually or in group and class work. (c) Students experience working on a problem "from the beginning to the end". (d) Students take initiatives, have autonomy, and create products with a different dimension. (e) The method has an impact outside the classroom, arising out of extensions to the work, multiple contacts, and the nature of the outcomes. This increases the possibility of communicating mathematical activities to other students and teachers, to parents, etc.

John Berry [GBR] emphasized different aspects of so-called applied mathematics in all mathematics learning. The three main factors in mathematics learning are concepts, skills, and contexts. Context is essential also in mathematics teaching. In the U.K. the new methods of mathematics teaching, as embodied in *SMP 11-16* and *Enterprising mathematics*, start with real situations and contexts, followed by mathematical concepts, applications, and extentions.

Margareth Drakenberg [SWE] studied students' strategies and errors in understanding fractions by interviewing them about what they actually do and how they explain their thinking. The study indicated a great variety of solving strategies, many of which are incorrect. Most of the students had no idea about what they were actually doing, manipulating symbols as meaningless marks on a paper. Her conclusion was that a radical change in instruction was badly needed.

Christopher Haines [GBR] and John Izard [AUS] had experimented with project methods in tertiary education. They noticed that mathematical modeling rather than the presentation of complete models led to more developmental learning through project work in mathematics and related areas. Projects and investigational work encourage the student to think independently and to show initiative in ways which lead to greater levels of achievement and course satisfaction, in parallel with the development of individual and group communication skills. They developed value-added measures for incorporation in rating and assessment schemes. Such schemes must reflect the dynamic nature of varying inputs of student work.

Christopher Ormell [GBR] focused particularly on the pedagogy of project work. From the viewpoint of pedagogy there are two kinds of developmental targets with different characteristics: (a) realizable practical projects and (b) unusual feasibility studies. In the former category are, say, plans to carpet or heat a school, build a dog kennel or a covered walkway, organize a trip or a social event, etc. This is often called "using math to make things happen". In the latter category are, say, proposals for a pavement from the bus stop to college, or a cable-car system between campuses. The two types are really, in the educational context, aiming to make quite different appeals. Project pedagogy offers several important lessons: (a) One can't take any project for granted. (b) When a project is a success, the sense of magic it generates depends on a variety of factors: the degree of internal social harmony within the group of students, the degree to which the students trust and identify with the teacher. (c) Last year's magic may be this year's cold potatoes. The theme of a project needs to capture the imagination of the group. (d) The students need to possess a set of mathematical skills at a certain minimum level of competence before they begin.

Leila Pehkonen [FIN] presented a 6th grade project in which the students had to acquire information about orange juice of six different types. The price, volume, packing material, the country of origin, and the lists of content were studied. The data (frequencies, etc) obtained by the students were then analyzed and presented in diagrams, interpreted, discussed, etc.

Assessment strategies in project work should be extended to cover knowledge, understanding, skills, and personal qualities not assessed by traditional tests, such as the development of initiative, taking responsibility for learning, and applying problem solving strategies. Haines and Izard attempted to include these aspects. One promising approach was to use a form of checklist so that examiners do not omit important issues while assessing work.

Only a few examples of projects can be mentioned here: (a) a plan for the "ideal" classroom; (b) building a panel of mosaics; (c) studying the habits of students as mineral water consumers; (d) building a model of a stadium; and (e) building ancient instruments for sea navigation.

The way to evaluate project work came up many times in discussions. This sub-topic could offer a basis for discussions at the next ICME.

The following are the full titles of papers presented to the group:

Abrantes, P. *Project work in school mathematics for pupils aged 12-15: an experience in Portugal.*

Berry, J. *Experiences of project work in England.*

Drakenberg, M. *Strategies and errors in children's understanding of fractions.*

Haines, C., Izard, J. *Learning mathematics through project work: value-added implications for student progress.*

Leino, J. *The importance of project work in teaching mathematics.*

Ormell, C. *On the pedagogy of the project.*

Pallascio, R. *Project work: a method of reaching the level of rational knowledge in elementary school mathematics.*

Pehkonen, L. *Project work in practice: a case of 6th grade mathematics.*

NOTE

The papers presented to the group are published in the following 65-page book: Leino, J. (Ed.) (1992). *Mathematics teaching through project work.* Research report 27, Department of Teacher Education in Hämeenlinna, University of Tampere.

The cost is US $12 plus postage and the book can be ordered from: University of Tampere, Sales Office, P.O. 617, 33101 Tampere, Finland. Fax: (358) 31 157 150.

Topic Group 9 / *Groupe thématique 9*

MATHEMATICS IN THE CONTEXT
OF THE TOTAL CURRICULUM

LES MATHÉMATIQUES DANS LE CONTEXTE
D'UN CURRICULUM TOTAL

Chief Organizer / *Responsable en chef* : John Mack [AUS]

The purpose of this group was to explore issues arising from major developments in mathematics education in the past decade and which are already producing two significant outcomes:

i)   the mathematics education community has been successful in increasing public and government awareness of the importance of a broadly-based mathematics education, at all levels, in national plans to develop and restructure whole societies towards more effective and productive economies in this new technological age;

ii) new goals in many mathematics curricula are embracing a broader range of mathematical content, specific problem solving, modeling and other applications and a commitment to a greater level of conceptual understanding, with agreed ranges of assess-ment tasks checking on achievement, than ever before.

Yet, in general, we still have, and expect to have, much the same types of people teaching, or entering teaching, as we have had. In particular, the burden for achieving the new goals listed above will rest largely with classroom teachers, whether or not the professional mathematics education communities are able to provide support to them. Also, there is little evidence that much serious thinking about the general goals and structure of "universal education" and its relationship to mathematics education has yet occurred. In many countries, curriculum structure and school organization still closely resemble those deriving from a hundred years ago, when universal education stopped at age 12 and high schools were intended for a small group proceeding to university. Now, most (if not all) are expected to continue in schooling until 16 and even to 18, with many continuing to higher education, and a key goal of early education is to prepare everyone for an adult life in which further education and training will occur continually.

In this context, the significance of mathematics as a key skill or component in the understanding of how to approach many tasks in adult life and work has been emphasized – it is "more relevant than ever before" – yet a common criticism of mathematics by students is its irrelevance to their lives. This apparent contradiction is strengthened if one examines the current use of school mathematics in all other subject areas at the senior high school level. Usually, apart from some areas of science, no secondary mathematics is used.

This topic group presented its 60-70 participants with examples illustrating cooperative school-based activities linking mathematics with other curriculum areas in mutually reinforcing ways, thus helping to combat beliefs about its irrelevance. It also provided opportunities for exchanges of information on these and other school-based or more systemic initiatives intended to break down subject barriers and foster more opportunities for task-based and across-curriculum learning experiences.

To stimulate discussion, the CO invited teachers, selected world-wide, to prepare short papers and speak briefly to them. Some 30 pages were available as a background paper and the presentations based on those are summarized below.

K-6 (AGES 3-12) LEVELS

Dawn Bartlett and Penny Skinner [AUS] discussed aspects of mathematics teaching in the context of a totally integrated curriculum (the situation in Australia), offering opportunities to structure learning experiences and record progress under headings such as "social development", "investigation and communication", "work habits", etc, in which mathematical concepts and skills are developed as part of a general growth in learning. Bartlett indicated how easily sophisticated mathematical ideas may arise, unrecognized, in even the earliest stories and language experiences and lead to later confusions if not explored and developed.

7-10 (AGES 12-16) LEVELS

Diana Sharvill [GBR] identified practical problems that arise in introducing (as now required by a new curriculum policy) cross-curricular activities. Often, "new" methods and skills in mathematics are not communicated to other teachers, resulting in their using different ones with students and further eroding other teachers' confidence in mathematics when changes are pointed out. It is still common for other teachers to (wish to) use mathematical models before they are discussed in mathematics and this also can cause confusion. On the positive side, data collection, analysis and representation is common across many subject areas and could be usefully employed as a common thread tying mathematics to other areas, especially so if agreed common notations and terminologies were established. Also, project-based coursework and assessment is appropriate and valuable as a vehicle for a number of learning experiences linked with mathematics and its application to another area. Leonor Cunha-Leal [PRT] described MAT789, an experimental school-based program in which projects initiated by mathematics resulted in a number of collaborative experiences involving art, design, history and science, for example. The attitudes of students, parents, mathematics teachers and other teachers have been monitored; this is important to future work in a system where the national curriculum requires each school to allow program time for "integrated" curriculum activities.

11-12 (AGES 16-18) LEVELS

Gill Robinson and Gordon Knight [NZL] discussed the principles behind and implementations of a non-traditional course allowing thematic treatment (topics include land surveying, investment, children's learning of mathematics) and including a major project as part of its formal assessment, which students usually choose to do cooperatively with another subject area. Despite the success of this project, organizing inter-disciplinary teaching inside any school organized by traditional curriculum areas remains virtually impossible. Kumiko Adachi [JPN] demonstrated some of the practical student-centred activities used to explore important mathematical ideas (e.g. music abounds with examples of exponential growth).

TEACHER EDUCATION COURSES

Lorraine Harker and Anne Carrington [AUS] described courses for early childhood, primary and secondary trainee teachers, each of which integrates mathematics with another curriculum area (science, sports education), developed as alternatives to traditional courses.

Most of the second session consisted of free discussion of issues and problems raised the previous day. Many stressed the problems arising because separate curriculum areas have not attempted to inform each other of changes in content, method, practice or assessment, with the result that from secondary school on, only the learners fully experience the curriculum. Particularly with new stress on "whole task competence" and "problem-solving", it is increasingly likely that, unless project work and other extended tasks are shared cooperatively across curriculum areas, there will be a student overload of work coupled with a failure to achieve required goals in separate subjects. Despite the organizational difficulties and the commonly expressed concern, that "mathematical knowledge receives lower priority when it is shared with another subject", there was reasonable agreement that the collection, representation and analysis of data presented itself as an ideal area for developing and coordinating mathematical ideas across the curriculum, as well as providing a basis for important later graphical and analytical representations and their applications.

A number of participants stressed the importance of teachers' confidence in their understanding of mathematics as underpinning the successful use of contextual learning experiences, which may otherwise (especially for ages 4-10) become vehicles for avoiding the teaching of mathematics. Carlos Vasco [COL] remarked that in Colombia, where integration across the curriculum had recently become official policy for ages 5-9, teachers anxious about their mathematical competence had indicated a willingness to do exactly that! Thus, both preservice and inservice teacher education programs must seek ways of relating mathematics to "real world" and other subject area contexts. James Smith [USA] described a successful graduate inservice course promoting the integration of mathematics and science teaching K-12.

In summary, whether there be an official policy promoting across-curriculum work or simply if a school or schools are willing to experiment, some useful practical steps are to work with, say, two or three areas only, bring teachers together to establish mutual respect for each other's expertise and recognition of weaknesses, examine the curriculum content and goals in order to identify possible starting points for cooperative activity and especially look for learning tasks where this can be exploited. On a broader level, exchanging representatives on subject teacher associations or on curriculum planning activities can be strategically useful, as is the development of inservice work "across the curriculum".

NOTE

Further information on the discussions in Topic Group 9 can be obtained from John Mack, Fax: (61) 2 692 4534, E-mail: mack_j@ maths.su.oz.au

Topic Group 10 / *Groupe thématique 10*

CONSTRUCTIVIST INTERPRETATIONS OF TEACHING AND LEARNING MATHEMATICS

VISIONS CONSTRUCTIVISTES DE L'ENSEIGNEMENT ET DE L'APPRENTISSAGE DES MATHÉMATIQUES

Chief Organizers / *Responsables en chef :* John A. Malone and Peter C. S. Taylor [AUS]

The topic group met on two occasions, each of 90 minutes duration. Between 250 - 300 registrants attended each session. The chief organizers each acted as chairperson at one of the two sessions.

Four keynote presentations each of 20 minutes duration were made. Leone Burton [GBR] ("Implications of constructivism for achievement in mathematics") and Ken Tobin with Diane Imwold [USA] ("Reconceptualizing, deconstructing and reconstructing routines for the teaching and learning of mathematics") spoke at the commencement of the first session, while Evelyne Barbin [FRA] ("The epistemological roots of a constructivist interpretation of teaching mathematics") and Neil Pateman [AUS] ("Can constructivism underpin a new paradigm in mathematics education?") spoke at the second.

These presentations were summarized and analyzed for 15 minutes by a discussant (Jere Confrey [USA] in session 1 and Stephen Lerman [GBR] in session 2). Each session was concluded by 30 minutes of questions and discussion from the floor. Other contributions were made by Kathleen Cauley [USA], Gail Fitzsimmons [AUS], Lena Lindenskov [DNK], John Muldren [AUS], Judith Mousley [AUS], Leslie Steffe [USA], Peter Sullivan [AUS].

THEMES FROM THE LEAD PAPERS

Constructivism: a theory of mathematical knowing/learning

Knowledge is constructed, individually and collectively, rather than transmitted, so the ownership of learning is located in the learners and not in the teacher. To construct requires the learner actively to engage, and is

268

usually more effectively done through interdependence – that is working collaboratively – than in isolation. There are three ways of conceiving of mathematical objects and their knowledge. According to the *realist* conception, we discover mathematical objects, these objects pre-exist in reality. According to the *idealist* conception, we invent mathematical objects, these objects apply to reality. According to the *constructivist* conception, we construct the mathematical objects, these objects structure reality; reality is not given, it also is a human construction.

Implications for teaching and learning

Constructivist implications for the classroom demand a move away from lists of content, or lessons defined by particular outcomes, towards the view of the learning of mathematics as a complex interaction of existing knowledge, beliefs and skills, experiences, challenges and opportunities for resolution. We must build into the activities that we offer learners the opportunity to interpret, to negotiate meaning, to be challenged and thereby to construct some new understanding of their own which might, or might not, be matched by the understandings of other learners in the same class.

The view that constructivism represents a method of teaching, although understandable, diminishes the power of constructivism as a set of intellectual referents for making decisions in relation to actions. The teacher's role is to mediate the learning of students; two critical components of this role are to monitor learning and concentrate on providing constraints so that student thinking will be channelled in productive directions. As a mediator the teacher needs to ensure that students are provided opportunities for quality learning experiences to provide a solid base for learning with understanding. In the classroom, teachers should provide opportunities for students to represent their knowledge in a variety of ways throughout the lesson by writing, drawing, using symbols, and assigning language to what is known. Student thinking also needs to be stimulated by providing time to think.

Implications for the syllabus

A constructivist view of the syllabus requires a shift from a knowledge-based view of mathematics to an interpretative base of which reflection is a necessary part. At best, this leads to a view of the syllabus as possible learning outcomes rather than content input. And it requires learner reflection to provide the teacher with the necessary information about what has been understood. The result is not that the syllabus must be discarded, but that the assumption that all children learn the same thing in the same order at about the same age should be discarded.

Implications for students

Learners are expected to collaborate, to listen, to discuss, to reflect, to challenge, to negotiate and renegotiate meaning. Central to a constructivist approach is the expectation that learners will have partial, as well as complete understanding, and that sharing their articulations will be a necessary part of building their knowledge and skills. The class can only run successfully if the students accept responsibility for their part in the work of the class. There is a sense in which the students are constructivists too, in that they understand their role as to make meaning for themselves and to share their meanings, then assess the status of their knowledge and make changes accordingly.

Implications for assessment

A constructivist approach to assessment can only be rooted in the mathematics that learners are building and using. Work and qualities of this kind can only be assessed in the classroom and such assessment needs to be made over an extended period.

Constraints to constructivist classroom reform

Teacher beliefs are a prime reason for teachers continuing to act as they have done traditionally. In other words, teachers act in specific ways in given contexts because particular contemplated actions are deemed most appropriate when all circumstances are considered. Beliefs can take the form of language, images, metaphors, and combinations of these knowledge forms.

Overcoming constraints

If teachers are to change their practices in classrooms, therefore, it is essential that they change their beliefs. That is, they must understand why particular actions are preferred over others and why their extant beliefs are no longer considered viable. When considered from a constructivist point of view, the emphasis is on the teacher as a learner, a person who will experience teaching and learning situations and give personal meaning to those experiences through reflection, at which time extant knowledge is connected to new understandings arising from experience and social interaction with peers and teacher educators. The idea that teachers have a responsibility first to call into question the relevance of prepackaged curricula to the students in their classes and so to engage in some form of curriculum development, and further, that it is possible for them to think of themselves as researchers of their own classrooms, are not commonly held. The constructivist teacher is an agent of change, interested in the transformative possibilities of her practice, rather than the transmissive functions so heavily emphasised by the delivery metaphor still pervading education.

NOTE

Keynote addresses, contributors' papers, discussants' notes and a record of the open discussion will be published early in 1993 in a monograph of the proceedings of the topic group. Information on these proceedings can be obtained from the chief organizers.

REFERENCES

Davis, R. B., Maher, C.A., & Noddings, N. (Eds.) (1990). Constructivist views on the teaching and learning of mathematics. *Journal for Research in Mathematics Education.* Monograph No.4. Reston, VA: NCTM.

Schoenfeld, A.H. (1992). Radical constructivism and the pragmatics of instruction. *Journal for Research in Mathematics Education, 23*(3), 290-295.

Von Glasersfeld, E. (1987). *The construction of knowledge.* Seaside, CA: Intersystems Publications.

Von Glasersfeld, E. (1991). *Radical constructivism in mathematics education.* Dordrecht: Kluwer Academic Publishers.

Wheatley, G. (1991). Constructivist perspectives on science and mathematics learning. *Science Education, 75*(1), 9-21.

Topic Group 11 / *Groupe thématique 11*

ART AND MATHEMATICS

ART ET MATHÉMATIQUES

Chief Organizer / *Responsable en chef* : Rafael Pérez Gómez [ESP]

The main presentations of this topic group are referred to in the following report. The chief organizer spoke about "Learning mathematics from the Alhambra at Granada". The mosaics which are such a prominent feature of the Alhambra give us an opportunity to introduce a great many subjects into the mathematics classroom – polygons (shapes and angles), semiregular tessellations, dihedral kaleidoscopes, 3-D space coverings and space fillings, symmetry, etc. The work can be introduced by mean of slides showing views of the building itself, or by wallpaper, tiles, or other art media. Cefarino Ruiz Garrido [ESP] made a presentation on "Sculpture and geometry". This century has seen the intervention of geometry in the struggle between concrete and abstract in sculpture: the concrete representation of a geometrical object can be at the same time an abstract work of art. Other developments include arranging for sculpture to move, as in "mobiles", and the use of transparent materials so that the inner structure of the sculpture can be directly perceived. Garrido showed many slides of sculptures by Spanish and Spanish-American artists. Ronnie Brown [GBR] talked about the mathematics of knots with reference to the sculptures of John Robinson under the title "Mathematical themes in John Robinson's universe".

Vera W. de Spinadel [ARG], in "Mathematics for design", argued the need for a change of approach if mathematics is to play an appropriate role in the education of designers. The service courses for students of the natural sciences, mainly analytic geometry and calculus, are not necessarily those best suited for students of design. A set of courses which would supply a better mix of calculation techniques, problem solving skills, and food for the imagination, would be: Information science; Geometry of forms; Graph theory; Critical path methods; Derivatives and integrals: Probability and statistics. "Learning from buildings", a talk by Claudi Alsina [ESP], suggested that existing buildings are a rich resource for mathematics education, giving rise to the topics:

- geometry: shapes, symmetry, proportions;

- visualization: observations, representations, projects;

- measures: human measures; building measures, object measures;

- functions: empirical data, measure functions, cost functions;

- graphs: communications, transformations.

All these items can be found in a study of real buildings, not just very special and spectacular buildings like the Washington Pentagon, or a Brunelleschi dome, but also quite ordinary everyday buildings, which can supply us with endless problems about heat, light, height, the rise/tread ratios of steps, the speed of elevators, the sizes of furniture, and so on. Many examples were presented in the course of the talk.

Topic Group 12 / *Groupe thématique 12*

GRADUATE PROGRAMS AND THE FORMATION OF RESEARCHERS IN MATHEMATICS EDUCATION

PROGRAMMES DE MAÎTRISE ET DE DOCTORAT ET FORMATION DE CHERCHEURS EN DIDACTIQUE DES MATHÉMATIQUES

Chief Organizer / *Responsable en chef* : Hans-Georg Steiner [DEU]

Mathematics education is increasingly becoming an academically established and recognized field. In several countries there exist university programs to educate and promote young researchers towards a masters' or doctoral degree in mathematics education. In other countries that is just beginning and there is a strong need for advice and support, which may be provided through international cooperation as it is presently furthered, e.g. by the Erasmus Program of the European Community. Many countries do not yet have any related academic programs and are looking for models to get started. In some countries, such as Germany, there is little tradition in demanding particular coursework for a doctoral degree and the specific achievement just consists in writing a thesis (under the guidance of a professor). The growing complexity of the field and an increasing number of doctoral students from foreign countries may however make well-defined preparatory courses indispensable.

These problems and other topics have been a matter of analysis and debate among the participants of international conferences of the open International study group on Theory of Mathematics Education (TME) (for related TME goals, see Steiner, 1988). It was decided to broaden the basis of the debate by collecting, studying, interchanging and distributing information, by stimulating international discussion on different models and by outlining future perspectives. Meanwhile a first TME-survey has been made. The final version of the survey (see Batanero et al., 1992) and reports on selected examples of masters' and doctoral programs were the central components of Topic Group 12.

The *first session* was introduced by H.-G. Steiner [DEU] who talked about basic components in the formation of researchers in mathematics education, followed by reports by Colette Laborde [FRA] on doctoral programs in mathematics education in France and by Juan Díaz Godino [ESP] on the doctoral program at the University of Granada. In the *second session,* Thomas A. Romberg [USA], reported on the doctoral program in mathematics education at the University of Wisconsin at Madison. This was followed by reports from Elfriede Wenzelberger † [MEX] on a master's degree program at the National Autonomous University of Mexico, and by João Ponte [PRT] on a master's degree program at the University of Lisbon. Wenzelberger and M. Carmen Batanero [ESP] then presented the international TME-Survey. Both sessions provided time for discussion. All papers have been published in Steiner (1993).

With respect to basic components, Steiner identified core domains of mathematics education, main reference disciplines within an interdisciplinary approach, important types of knowledge and experience, forms and structures of formation, having in mind not only master's and doctoral programs but also the continued formation of researchers who are already working in the profession. Laborde reported that there are presently four doctoral programs in France, three of them run by cooperating units of up to four universities. All consist in one year of introductory work ending with the Diplôme d'études approfondies (DEA) and a three-year phase of work preparing a thesis. The overall prerequisite for all programs is a degree in mathematics (after four years of university study). Core domains of theoretical courses are mathematical knowledge (epistemology), learning processes, and the functioning of the didactical system. A part of the formation is devoted to research methodology. Díaz Godino explained how the doctoral program at Granada was started from scratch after the Department of Didactics of Mathematics had been established according to the 1984 University Reform Law. In the beginning only three of the 21 university teachers found themselves in the position to lecture and supervise work within the program. Therefore it was of great help to have a guest component, with lecturers and advisors from France, Great Britain, USA, Germany, Israel, and other Spanish universities for which financial support came and is still coming from different sources, including the Erasmus Program of the European Community. The content of the doctoral program includes methodological components (research design, data analysis), fundamentals (epistemology, theory of mathematics education, didactics of school subjects, curriculum development, evaluation), and related subjects (psychology, philosophy, history, etc.).

Romberg indicated that there are two different doctoral programs at Madison, one in the education department and one in the mathematics department. In the latter a kind of apprenticeship model is being practiced. Most doctoral students are simultaneously active as research assistants on some research projects. No formal course work is required. The master's degree is a prerequisite and every participant has to be a full-time student. Wenzelberger reported that the project "Master in Mathematics Education" at the National Autonomous University of Mexico goes back to 1978 and became a self-contained program in 1981, that during the first period about 50 students had taken the courses but none had finished writing a thesis. Recent changes in the overall program have caused very positive developments. Courses are subdivided into three domains: mathematics, pedagogy, and didactics of mathematics. Research programs are used as sources for the work on theses. Ponte explained the philosophy behind the master's program at the University of Lisbon which goes back to 1985. In their presentation of the TME-Survey, Batanero and Wenzelberger demonstrated some of the main outcomes of the survey relating to the general characteristics of programs, faculty members, students, contents, role and nature of research, specific lines and topics of research.

In discussion the following points were made:

- The requirements of teaching experience are ambivalent and, as post-graduate students, teachers often have difficulties changing their intentional point of view into a research viewpoint.

- For the formation of researchers there is a lack of textbooks in which the state-of-the-art in research is presented in a sufficiently unified way; joint efforts should be made to develop such textbooks.

- The introduction to research methodology is considered to be crucial, and the role of developmental work and its methodology is viewed as equally important as analytical research.

- Jobs for researchers and developers in mathematics education are no longer confined to the domains of school or university but exist in many places within the new societal learning structures related to the transfer of mathematical knowledge via professional software into various domains of life and work.

REFERENCES

Batanero, M.C., Díaz Godino, J., Steiner, H.G., & Wenzelburger, E. (1992). *An international TME-Survey: Preparation of researchers in mathematics education.* IDM-Occasional paper 135. Bielefeld: Institut für Didaktik der Mathematik, Universität Bielefeld.

Steiner, H. G. (1988). Theory of mathematics education and its implications for scholarship. In: H.G. Steiner & A. Vermandel (Eds.), *Foundations and methodology of the discipline mathematics education (Didactics of mathematics)*. Proc. 2nd TME-Conference, Bielefeld (FRG), July 15-19, 1985. Antwerp: Dept. of Didactics and Criticism, Antwerp University.

Steiner, H. G. (Ed.) (1993). Theory of mathematics education (TME): Graduate programs and the formation of researchers in mathematics education. Proc. Topic Group 12 at ICME-7, Québec, Canada, and additional papers. IDM-Occasional paper. Bielefeld: Institut für Didaktik der Mathematik, Universität Bielefeld.

Topic Group 13 / *Groupe thématique 13*

TELEVISION IN THE MATHEMATICS CLASSROOM

L'UTILISATION DE LA TÉLÉVISION DANS LA SALLE DE CLASSE

Chief Organizer / *Responsable en chef* : David Roseveare [GBR]

The main presentations to the group are summarized briefly and followed in each case by some of the questions arising in discussion.

Colette Pelé [FRA]: The Centre National de Documentation Pédagogique in Paris produces films conceived by teachers which are sold for secondary classroom use on video-cassette. *Trigonométrie* is an animated film showing a (toy) train running around a circular track, establishing labels $\pi/2$, π, $3\pi/2$, 2π, etc., at appropriate points. Unwrapping the labelled track into a straight line provides a situation for class discussion and explanation. The film also shows the graph of $x \rightarrow \sin x$ as well as real-life images illustrating trigonometrically-related transformations. The translation/ rotation of a cartoon figure completes this extract. A (cartoon) story of Achilles and the Tortoise was also shown and the presentation ended with videotape showing videodisc usage. Pelé briefly reported on: attitudes of pupils and teachers; feedback; extensions to the materials.

Questions:

- Do all classrooms have the required equipment? No! There is a variety of levels of provision.

- Would the animations not be better on computer? Maybe not better, but different!

- Is software published with the videos? No, but see the work done by some of the IREMs in France.

Paul Laridon [ZAF] presented a film called *Mathematics no problem* from a TV project for the black majority in South Africa. (See the reference given below for objectives and methodology.) An excerpt concerning tessellation was designed to look relaxed, not set in a formal classroom so as not to be threatening to teachers. Another extract contained a setting illustrating the "social milieu" philosophy: here, the need to measure a calf. The current status of the project is that TV production is almost finished; 20 programs have already been broadcast. Most programs have been reported as well-received. They are supported by a national newspaper. Laridon said that TV can be an agent for change by moving away from the "transmission" model of teaching/learning. Drama is essential to the portrayal of a constructivist approach. TV must aim for popularity to compensate for the density of mathematics and to attract pupils. Teachers must feel they have a stake in the medium.

Questions:

* Do we want to consider "whole course delivery" by TV?

* To what extent is the teacher diminished as an authority figure?

Experience in British Columbia (Canada) suggests that classroom teachers will not use videos because "they are too inefficient". But "talking heads" (unadorned lectures) such as the programs transmitted by Knowledge Network are successful. Television is used most effectively when it tries to solve learning problems, rather than teaching problems, which suggests that "lectures" would be less effective. TV is generally not good at detail.

Betsy McNeal [USA] spoke of a Children's Television Workshop (CTW) series called *Square One*. This series was devised specifically for 8-12 year olds watching at home, but it is useful in classrooms. Entertainment is employed to capture an audience; to promote positive attitudes towards mathematics; to encourage the use of problem solving processes; to expose a broad range of mathematics. Each program is a 30 minutes "magazine" with no single mathematical theme. It uses various TV styles, including game shows, spoof detective serials, "commercials". The programs are not just entertainment but provoke and involve follow-up. A study showed that, after 30 consecutive unsupervised viewings, students had gained a variety of problem solving strategies; broadened their conception of mathematics; become more interested in process than answer; and become more willing to pursue complex problems. CTW assists teachers by offering legal off-air recording, program guides, and Teachers' Guides. CTW staff attend teachers' conferences. Future possibilities for Square One include a textbook "surrounding" the TV; BBC co-production; re-packaging the existing Square One library. CTW is also discussing making segments separated by new linking material that suggests, but does not require, stopping the tape.

Question:

* Is the use of Square One in schools counter-productive because it is intended to be different from school?

279

Richard Phillips [GBR] showed The World of Number videodisc produced for the National Curriculum Council of England and Wales. It aims to support math teaching (particularly number attainment targets) at NC Key Stages 3-4 (Secondary). The project (3 × 12" double-sided laser-vision discs, software for a PC286, print material) ended in June 1992. The design team have maintained an "open-eyed" approach: there is much still to learn about multi-media. Development is focused on the production of a resource finely-tuned to classroom activities: 12 trial schools played an active part in development; 11-16 year olds speak on the discs wherever possible. The content includes: *Number games*, via milk bottle arrangements; *Mechanisms*, using an on-screen "toolbox" to plot points on animated linkages; *On the move*, marks drawn on video footage of traffic to calculate car speeds; *Perspectives*, four screen "windows" differently portraying the same (geometrical) information; *Who stole the decimal point?*, an adventure game; *Ways of calculating*, e.g. organizing a table-tennis league, trying to induce reflection on process, comparing own method with that shown on screen.

Questions:

- How much has this technology penetrated UK schools? Not much.

- How is this better than the IVIS/Newcastle disc? We copied a lot from them! Are other discs being worked on?

- How many children were in trial groups? Usually small groups, taking turns.

- How user-friendly is it? This is a very open resource (no hinting) but there is a worksheet.

- Why only a one-monitor system? This was specified by NCC. (One participant maintained that the future will be "one screen".)

Questions circulated by the chief organizer:

- Would participants like a regular informal TV/maths newsletter? (95% would.)

- Would they be prepared to write for it? (50% would.)

Other points arising in discussion:

- A major concern today is to avoid obsolescence; what uses remain for videotapes? Flexibility is the key: video can be used as pure tape, or as GOTO with barcode.

- Should there be only one delivery machine? Need for recording, not only for pure playback systems.

- Is the "ideal" video designed for individual pupils or for teachers to show to the whole class? The group included only three or four classroom teachers.

NOTE

This report is based on notes by John Jaworski [GBR].

REFERENCES

Les films mathématiques du CNDP. Order form and leaflet from: Équipe Maths-CNDP, 31, rue de la Vanne, 92120 Montrouge, France.

Mathematics No Problem, a recent SABC/BOPTV project leaflet available from Paul Laridon.

Square One TV, basic information leaflet (English/French) from Children's Television Workshop.

Children's problem-solving behavior and their attitudes towards mathemat-ics: a study of the effects of Square One TV. Volume V: Executive Summary, Children's Television Workshop, New York, 1991.

Square One TV, Teacher's Guide, Volumes I-IV, Children's Television Workshop, New York, 1987, 1988, 1989, 1990.

Phillips, R. (Feb. 1992). Gazing in at the Bright Lights, *Times Educational Supplement,* p. 40.

Topic Group 14 / *Groupe thématique 14*

COOPERATION BETWEEN THEORY AND PRACTICE IN MATHEMATICS EDUCATION

COOPÉRATION ENTRE THÉORIE ET PRATIQUE EN ÉDUCATION MATHÉMATIQUE

Chief Organizer / *Responsable en chef* : Falk Seeger [DEU]

We currently love to say that pupils and students in the mathematics classroom construct their knowledge. Is it not equally common sense to accept also that teachers construct their knowledge, and with it they construct not only a repertory of professional techniques but a way of being in the social world of the mathematics classroom? If teachers are viewed as constructing their ways of being in the world, there is no way for research to try to tell them what to do and why to start doing something or stop doing something else. "Theory" and "practice" can no longer be understood as competing to give the "real" picture of what goes on in the classroom: they do reflect upon and speak about the same processes and structures, but with different voices, from different perspectives, using different modes of reflection. What is needed, then, in the cooperation between theory and practice, is a dialogue where the different voices are listening to each other. The two sessions of Topic Group 14 highlighted the obstacles and difficulties involved in this dialogue. Basically, three types of problems were discussed in the contributions: problems resulting from the difference in the perspectives of teachers and researchers; problems connected with a changing view of teacher professionalization; problems connected with the concept of the teacher as researcher.

THE DIFFERENT PERSPECTIVES OF THEORY AND PRACTICE, OF RESEARCHERS AND TEACHERS

Teaching activity and research activity, obviously, deal with the same class of phenomena but with different objects and objectives:

- The apparent conflict between discovering patterns of teaching and learning as the object of research activity and changing these patterns as the object of teaching creates the urgent need to reconcile these two objectives on the basis of non-standard models of the research-application-research cycle. The paradigm of action-research is often seen as a way to reconcile the object and interest of research with the object and interests of teaching, because here change is becoming a salient motive for research while discovery is becoming a major interest of practitioners.

• Reconciling the objects of research and teaching is difficult because the corresponding activity systems produce and reproduce totally different time frames. It has been argued that it is precisely the different time perspective that is responsible for most of the difficulties in the cooperation between theory and practice. On the one hand, the attention of research is directed towards reconstructing after the fact what has happened, while teaching practice focuses on producing the conditions for future events. On the other hand, research is interested in short-term changes that follow experimental or quasi-experimental intervention, while teaching practice builds on the experience that the important patterns in the classroom change only at a slow, long-term rate.

• The dialogue between theory and practice is difficult because of the fact that in each realm a different mode of reflection is habitually used. There is e.g. a fundamental difference between reflecting while or after observing and reflecting while or after acting, which leads to the difficult task to put in relation the perspective of the observer and the perspective of the actor. Actor and observer hold different "modes of reflection" that are differently "centered": while the perspective of the actor is centered in the field, what happens in the situation is familiar and self-evident, the perspective of the observer is decentered from what happens in the situation which appears unfamiliar and hard to understand. The two perspectives are non-compatible but at the same time they are complementary in relation to their peculiar blind spot. If this point of view is reasonable then there can be no nearly complete picture of the classroom situation if one does not try to gain a re-centered perspective on the situation. This can be accomplished only in the dialogue between actor and observer.

• The last point is not only crucial for the problem of the observer in research in mathematics education but also directs attention to a conflict that can lead to serious misunderstandings between teacher educators and prospective teacher of mathematics. While observing lessons of prospective teachers, the mathematics educator's analysis focuses on reconstructing in retrospect what "really" happened.

In contrast, the prospective teacher's view is directed proactively towards "possible" situations.

THE ROLE OF PROFESSIONAL STANDARDS

Some of the reasons that make the cooperation between theory and practice difficult seem to lead back to the different professional standards the teaching community and the research community adhere to.

At least the following two issues deserve attention:

- Prospective teachers face the formidable task of learning to act and to reflect upon their action as a prerequisite to entering the profession. Here, one of the most important issues is seen in the conflict between the criteria for successful teaching held by the mathematics educator and the criteria the prospective teacher feels the need to fulfil. While the criteria of successful teaching of mathematics educators are primarily related to mathematical content and mathematics, the prospective teacher feels that developing his or her professional activity is primarily related to matters of conviviality and the smooth functioning of the social life of the classroom.

- There seems to be an apparent conflict between the way prospective teachers are being introduced into the social world of the classroom and their simultaneous appropriation of the standards of the profession. Professional training for prospective teachers often does not take care of the complex changes the person of the teacher experiences. What is needed here is not more research on instructional techniques, but an inquiry about how to listen to what prospective teachers have to say.

THE TEACHER AS RESEARCHER

It is often expressed that the concept of the "teacher as researcher" avoids at least some of the difficulties of the dialogue between theory and practice. This approach has indeed created some new insights and results to improve mathematics teaching and learning on a local and regional level. However, the more general problems of theory and practice remain unsolved. Specifically, two issues have to be mentioned:

- If a teacher acts as a researcher, the problems of theory and practice are shifted from the inter-individual to the intra-individual plane. This does not usually mean that they have disappeared.

- The difficulty of receiving funding for research done by teachers points to the more general problem of the reluctance of funding agencies to give money for research in mathematics education. At least in some countries, funds are given only to the classical disciplines. Unfortunately, the unique approach of mathematics education research in combining basic and applied research often does not seem to fit the criteria of such agencies.

NOTE

A more detailed report is available from: Falk Seeger, Institut für Mathematik, Universität Bielefeld, Postfach 100 131, 33502 Bielefeld, Germany; Fax: (521) 10 65 84 44; E-mail: fseeger@post.uni-bielefeld.de

Topic Group 15 / *Groupe thématique 15*

STATISTICS IN THE SCHOOL
AND COLLEGE CURRICULUM

STATISTIQUE DANS LE CURRICULUM DU SECONDAIRE ET DU POST-SECONDAIRE

Chief Organizer / *Responsable en chef* : Richard Schaeffer [USA]

Initial presentations and discussions in Topic Group 15 centered on recent trends, in both content and pedagogy, in the teaching of statistics at the school and college level. The focus then branched out to include the teaching of statistics to practitioners in research and industrial settings.

At the school level, statistics is becoming integrated into the core mathematics curriculum and is no longer an isolated course for the few. According to David Moore [USA], "statistics should be studied in the schools not primarily for its own sake, but rather because working with data is an excellent means of building and reinforcing essential mathematical constructs." Statistics consists of analyzing and describing data, producing data, and inference from data, and the topics should receive relative emphases in that order. The main thrust should be data analysis taught through an exploratory approach that emphasizes graphical displays.

Producing data through planned studies (sample surveys and randomized comparative experiments) is at the heart of statistical practice and should receive more attention than is usually the case in introductory courses. One should not attempt a systematic presentation of formal inference at the school level since this is a difficult and much debated topic. Data ("numbers with a context") provide a concrete basis for development of mathematical ideas and serves as a way to connect the mathematics to the lives of the students.

Probability should not form the basis for discussing statistics at the school level. Manipulatives should be used to provide experiences with randomness and to demonstrate the fact that rules of probability apply only to the long run. Then, simulation can be introduced. Combinatorials and axioms should not be part of the discussion at this level.

In teaching concepts of data and chance, new material must be added to the standard mathematics curriculum but the teacher must develop a change of attitude as well. Mathematics is to be learned from the questions that arise out of studies involving real data.

The notion of motivating students with real data carries over to the college curriculum. Saleha Naghmi Habibullah [PAK] reported that project-based teaching and learning of statistics has met with great success in Lahore. Projects designed and carried out by the students motivate and even excite students about statistics and its uses. These student projects have led to inter-collegiate competitions and exhibitions of statistical work that are well received throughout the college communities. Although difficult to get started, this approach to introductory statistics seems worth the effort.

Those who serve as statistical consultants in research institutions and industry must teach as well, and similar ideas to those listed above still apply. According to Anne Hawkins [GBR], a consultancy should be a means of in-house statistical education. Such situations provide small groups of highly motivated "students" who have many misconceptions about statistics and a variable (usually low) level of statistical literacy. These opportunities should be used to educate practitioners in the language of statistics, in principles rather than specifics (too much emphasis on P-values), and thinking intelligently about quantitative problems rather than memorizing facts.

The notion of teaching the practitioners has been used with great success in Japanese industry, as reported by Yoshinori Iizuka [JPN]. These industries are "managed by facts", and all personnel are educated in the statistical way of looking at things. This educational process emphasizes statistical sense rather than techniques, application ability rather than systematic knowledge, and problem-oriented rather than technique-oriented learning. Since problems come from the real work of the learner, students are enthusiastic.

Clearly, statistics will continue to play a major role in the mathematical education of students at all levels, serving as a motivator and illustrator of mathematical ideas at one level, and a valuable tool in its own right at another. Continuing attention must be paid to effective teaching of the subject.

NOTE

The CO acknowledges the assistance of Jim Swift [CAN] and Jean-Pierre Carmichael [CAN] in addition to those persons mentioned in the above report.

REFERENCES

Hoaglin, D.C., & Moore, D.S. (Eds.) (1992). *Perspectives on contemporary statistics.* Washington: Mathematical Association of America.

Landwehr, J., & Watkins, A. (1986). *Exploring data.* Palo Alto, CA: Dale Seymour Publications.

Moore, D.S. (1990). Uncertainty. In L.A. Steen (Ed.) *On the shoulders of giants: new approaches to numeracy* (pp. 95-137). Washington: National Academy Press.

Topic Group 16 / *Groupe thématique 16*

THE PHILOSOPHY OF MATHEMATICS EDUCATION

PHILOSOPHIE DE L'ÉDUCATION MATHÉMATIQUE

Chief Organizer / *Responsable en chef* : Paul Ernest [GBR]

Epistemological and philosophical issues are central to mathematics education. As René Thom said at ICME-2: "All mathematical pedagogy, even if scarcely coherent, rests on a philosophy of mathematics." Topics illustrating this include constructivism, problem solving and investigational pedagogies, curriculum theories, teacher beliefs, applications of the Perry Theory and Women's Ways of Knowing, ideologies of mathematics education, ethnomathematics, multicultural and anti-racist mathematics, work on gender, values and mathematics, and the epistemological foundations of research paradigms. Behind this is a "Kuhnian revolution" in the philosophy of mathematics. The Euclidean paradigm of mathematics as an absolute, incorrigible and rigidly hierarchical body of knowledge existing independently of human concerns is being challenged. Instead, many seek a philosophy that accounts more fully for mathematics, including the practices of mathematicians, its history and applications, its place in human culture, including issues of values, education and learning. Davis and Hersh (1980), Kitcher, Lakatos and Tymoczko (1985) propose new quasi-empiricist paradigms for the philosophy of mathematics. Parallel developments in the sociology of knowledge, e.g. Bloor and Restivo (1985), mathematics education, e.g. Ernest (1991), and poststructuralist and postmodernist thought, propose social constructivist accounts of mathematics. All have important implications for mathematics education.

With the above in mind the sessions of Topic Group 16 aimed to offer the opportunity for interested persons to make contact with current developments, theories and controversies.

The speakers were: Stephen I. Brown [USA], Kathryn Crawford [AUS], Paul Ernest [GBR], Ernst von Glasersfeld [USA], David Henderson [USA], Reuben Hersh [USA], Christine Keitel [DEU], Sal Restivo [USA], Anna Sfard [ISR], Ole Skovsmose [DNK], Thomas Tymoczko [USA].

The following key issues were raised.

What is the philosophy of mathematics education? It concerns the subject (mathematics), the teacher and teaching, the learner and learning, and the social context. Each gives rise to a characteristic set of philosophical problems and issues, including the philosophy of mathematics, aims and theories of teaching, the use of mediating cultural artifacts (textbooks, computers), theories of learning, and the relationships between these as realized in the social milieu.

How is the philosophy of mathematics relevant to education? In practice it influences the mathematics classroom especially via assessment. The use of ticks and crosses, and the impression that every question has a single correct answer (which the teacher possesses), communicates an absolutist epistemology to the learner.

Teacher beliefs (personal philosophies of mathematics) profoundly affect their classroom practices. Research results suggest that preservice teachers hold views of mathematics interpretable as absolutist or fallibilist, which intimately relate to their views of teaching and learning (e.g. transmission or constructivist, respectively).

Metaphors for mathematics include: rigidly structured "Eiffel Tower", near-eternal mountain, or continually growing, self-renewing forest. What do these metaphors presuppose and entail?

Mathematical objects may be real to mathematicians, but are accessed through decidedly human psychological means (imagery and intuition). The question therefore is not "Do the objects of mathematics exist?", but "How can we best offer students entry into "math worlds"?"

Mathematical symbolism enables the mathematician to manipulate the objects of mathematics. However, too often learners mimic the movements of mathematicians but are in fact empty-handed. Symbolic mathematics is meaningless unless conceptually underpinned.

Radical constructivism argues that symbols and texts have no inherent meaning other than that constructed for them by the reader. "Sharing of meaning" is not possible. Improved meshing of meanings is all that is possible. This view of interpretation has far-reaching consequences, e.g. for the notion of proof, and for the teaching of arithmetic.

The fallibilist branch of *hermeneutics* recognizes that the interpretative cycle never arrives at ultimate meanings, for it can never leave the knower's own realm of cognitive constructs (paralleling radical constructivism).

A radical sociology of mathematics sees mathematical forms, objects, symbols and theorems as collective objects and world views, embodying "math worlds". Their social histories reveal them to be materials and resources constructed around social interests. But can this social account dispense with the experiential world of the individual subject, constructed by its own intellectual endeavors?

Critical mathematics education: Mathematics education justifies and reproduces mathematics, a central shaping force in modern society. Mathematical thought abstractions generate realized abstractions embodied in artifacts and social patterns including supermarket check-outs, test scores, voting systems, assembly lines, bureaucratic structures, social institutions, etc. Our mathematized society leads not only to economic power and freedom but also to tight constraints on people's lives.

We need a *critical perspective of the mathematics curriculum* as conditioned by the social function of mathematics in society, with mathematics reforms interrogated to see whose interests they serve, and their relations with power, social structure, ideology and values. We need alternative concepts for mathematics education based on the social function of mathematics, and ways of acting together in the light of this knowledge.

The aims of mathematics education are to empower learners to understand and act on their environment, to be able to make competent and autonomous judgments through mathematics. Does this agree with its social role?

Ideologies of mathematics education: Is there a parallel between dichotomies such as fallibilist versus absolutist philosophies, constructivist versus passive reception theories of learning; facilitating, problem-oriented versus authoritarian theories of teaching? How do ideologies of mathematics education mediate power and serve the reproduction of inequalities?

Problems: Is the concept of problem inseparable from that of solutions? What about the problem as a project for the future, which involves uncertainty and risk? Problem posing offers ownership of problems and empowerment of learners.

What implicit assumptions do different theories and philosophies contain? What assumed model of a human being? Radical constructivism assumes the knowing subject has consciousness, memory, and a desire for order in its experiential world. The philosophy of mathematics education is about examining the underlying assumptions of the field.

NOTE

A more complete report of the talks presented in Topic Group 16 has been published in the *Philosophy of Mathematics Education Newsletter*, Number 6, 1992. A book, *Mathematics, philosophy, and education*, is planned which will include the full texts of the talks plus additional material. Information can be obtained from: Paul Ernest, University of Exeter School of Education, Exeter, Devon, EX1 2LU, UK; Fax: (44) 392 264 736; E-mail: ernest.p@exeter.ac.uk

REFERENCES

Philosophy of Mathematics Education Newsletter. Obtainable from: P. Ernest, University of Exeter, School of Education, Exeter EX1 2LU, U.K.

Brown, S.I., & Walter, M. (1990). *The art of problem posing.* Hillsdale NJ: Erlbaum.

Davis, P.J., & Hersh, R. (1980). *The mathematical experience.* Boston: Birkhauser.

Ernest, P. (1991). *The philosophy of mathematics education.* London: Falmer.

Restivo, S. (1985). *The social relations of physics, mysticism and mathematics.* Dordrecht: Reidel.

Skovsmose, O. (1985). Mathematical education versus critical education. *Educational Studies in Mathematics, 16,* 337-354.

Tymoczko,T. (1985) *New directions in the philosophy of mathematics.* Boston: Birkhauser.

Von Glasersfeld, E. (1991) *Radical constructivism in mathematics education.* Dordrecht: Kluwer Academic Publishers.

Groupe thématique 17 / *Topic Group 17*

LA DOCUMENTATION PROFESSIONNELLE DES ENSEIGNANTS DE MATHÉMATIQUES

PROFESSIONAL LITERATURE FOR MATHEMATICS TEACHERS

Responsable en chef / *Chief Organizer* : Jeanne Bolon [FRA]

Si la recherche en mathématiques ou sur les problèmes éducatifs est l'objet de bon nombre de publications bien répertoriées et bien diffusées parmi les chercheurs, les enseignants ordinaires en restent le plus souvent à une documentation restreinte, mal structurée et d'efficacité variable. Des exemples de différents pays ont été présentés.

Daniel Gilis [FRA] a montré comment la France dispose de conditions particulièrement favorables en matière d'infrastructures et de systèmes informatiques et télématiques, à la suite de choix gouvernementaux (années 1970 et 1980). Cela concerne toutes les sphères d'activité (économique, sociale, culturelle, éducative, etc.). Sur le terrain de l'éducation et de l'enseignement mathématique, on trouve des organismes officiels (par exemple le Ministère de l'éducation nationale, les Instituts de recherche sur l'enseignement des mathématiques, le Centre national de la recherche scientifique, l'Institut national de la recherche pédagogique) ou privés (par exemple, l'Association des professeurs de mathématiques de l'enseignement public). Les utilisateurs potentiels sont les enseignants, les formateurs d'enseignants ou les chercheurs. Une analyse de l'offre documentaire a été faite.

Pour Gerhard König [DEU], le souci de rendre compte de l'ensemble des publications mondiales fait tout l'intérêt de banques de données telles que « Zentralblatt für Didaktik der Mathematik (International Reviews on Mathematical Education) Mathematical Didactics Database ». La recherche documentaire peut être faite en allemand ou en anglais. Les sujets couverts sont :

- l'enseignement des mathématiques de l'école élémentaire à l'université et l'éducation des adultes ;

- les mathématiques élémentaires et leurs applications ;

- les mathématiques récréatives et les expositions populaires ;

- l'enseignement assisté par ordinateur et les technologies de l'information ;

- les thèmes principaux en pédagogie et psychologie en rapport avec l'enseignement des mathématiques et des sciences.

Une recension des principales bases de données au plan international a été fournie.

En France, à l'occasion de changements de programmes dans l'enseignement en collège (élèves de 12 à 15 ans), le Ministère de l'éducation nationale a chargé les Instituts de recherche sur l'enseignement des mathématiques d'essayer les nouveaux programmes et de rédiger des documents de soutien pour les enseignants, en moins d'un an. Les publications (*Suivi scientifique*), mises au point dans l'urgence, ont reçu un bon accueil des professeurs, des formateurs et des inspecteurs, malgré des défauts patents (activités trop riches, manque de cohérence, etc.). Pour Robert Delord [FRA], les professeurs, souvent découragés par la lecture de productions de certains chercheurs ou spécialistes, ont besoin d'« écrits intermédiaires » réellement accessibles, dont les caractéristiques sont à rechercher avec le concours de tous, praticiens, chercheurs, spécialistes.

Au Pérou, en dépit d'une situation économique difficile, des ouvrages documentaires pour les enseignants sont parus récemment (culture générale mathématique et pédagogique pour les enseignants de l'école primaire et secondaire, éducation mathématique bilingue). Mais, pour Teresa Arellano [PER], ces parutions restent confidentielles. Dans l'enseignement secondaire, les enseignants utilisent les mêmes ouvrages (d'une édition à l'autre, peu de changements), le plus souvent comme textes de référence. Les élèves disposent rarement de manuels, faute de ressources des familles. Les quelques livres novateurs n'ont pas été réédités, car les enseignants les jugent trop difficiles (manque de temps pour étudier le livre, voire préparer sa classe). En revanche, les recueils d'exercices et problèmes, baptisés « Pratiques », sont utilisés (surtout dans les établissements privés). Pour l'école primaire, des documents circulent, grâce aux enseignements de didactique (cours d'été, instituts pédagogiques) ou encore par le biais de programmes expérimentaux (éducation bilingue, quartiers populaires, éducation rurale andine). Pour la majorité des enseignants et du grand public, peu importe les taux élevés d'échec des élèves. Il y a d'autres urgences : survivre.

Au Chili, 900 écoles ont été sélectionnées (les plus pauvres du pays) pour un programme d'amélioration de la qualité et de l'égalité de l'enseignement. Les enseignants de ces écoles ont reçu une formation (mathématique et pédagogique) par ateliers sur la résolution de problèmes. Ils ont reçu du matériel scolaire et des documents d'accompagnement. Ismenia Guzmán [CHL] a étudié un échantillon de productions écrites d'enfants de 7-8 ans (répartis sur les douze régions du pays). Il ressort que la formation donnée a eu peu d'impact, malgré l'intérêt déclaré des enseignants pour les pratiques actives de recherche. La grande majorité d'entre eux imposent une voie pour résoudre le problème, voire modifient le problème en croyant le rendre plus facile. Très peu d'enseignants autorisent des voies de recherche diverses, qu'ils ne savent probablement pas gérer. Ces remarques, entre autres, montrent quelques points sur lesquels les ateliers de formation et les guides pédagogiques devront insister à l'avenir.

En Suisse romande, la documentation est abondante, les manuels officiels sont gratuits, les centres de documentation et bibliothèques sont nombreux et bien fournis, des formations complémentaires sont offertes, en cas de réformes en particulier. Pour François Jaquet [CHE], l'inadéquation entre l'offre de documentation et la demande des maîtres est patente. Les responsables des innovations proposent des documents, des actions de formation ou des expérimentations inspirés des résultats de la recherche en didactique des mathématiques. Or la majorité des enseignants accède difficilement au langage et à la terminologie de la recherche. Les maîtres s'intéressent à ce qui facilite leur tâche (solutions des exercices, fiches complémentaires pour élèves rapides ou lents, anciennes épreuves, etc.) ou aux méthodes permettant d'améliorer les apprentissages dans les domaines traditionnels de la maîtrise des apprentissages (entraînement des opérations, cours programmés, activités de révision des techniques de calcul, etc.). Pour eux, l'acquisition des connaissances nouvelles se fait par « petits pas », selon la structure rationnelle des notions mathématiques. L'Institut romand de recherche et documentation pédagogique (Neuchâtel) dresse actuellement l'inventaire des obstacles et, simultanément, élabore des propositions de stratégie.

Quelques adresses

Suivi scientifique, IREM de Lyon, Université Claude-Bernard, F–69622 Villeurbanne Cedex, France.

ZDM – MATHDI, Fachinformationszentrum Karlsruhe, D-7514 Eggenstein-Leopoldshafen 2, Allemagne.

Institut romand de recherche et documentation pédagogique (IRDP), Case postale 54, CH-2007 Neuchâtel, Suisse.

RÉFÉRENCE

Gilis, D., & Athenour, C. (1991). Que peuvent apporter l'outil télématique et les banques de données à l'enseignement et à la recherche en didactique des disciplines? *Recherches en didactique des mathématiques, 10*(2-3).

STUDY GROUPS

GROUPES D'ÉTUDE

AN HISTORICAL PERSPECTIVE ON LEARNING, TEACHING, AND USING MATHEMATICS

UNE VISION HISTORIQUE DE L'APPRENTISSAGE, DE L'ENSEIGNEMENT ET DE L'UTILISATION DES MATHÉMATIQUES

Sessions Organizers / *Responsables des séances* : Florence D. Fasanelli [USA] (chair), Evelyne Barbin [FRA], Israel Kleiner [CAN], V. Frederick Rickey [USA]

The main purpose of the International Group for the Relations between the History and Pedagogy of Mathematics (HPM) is to encourage teachers at all levels to use the history of mathematics in their classrooms to motivate and instruct their students. Accordingly, the four sessions at ICME-7 were organized around three themes:

- the history of mathematics and pedagogical problems;
- the history of mathematics as a cultural approach to solving problems;
- historical problems in the classroom.

Each session had two speakers addressing one or more of these issues and a discussant who had been asked to comment on the papers with regard to these themes, while at the same time ensuring that each of the primary, secondary, and tertiary levels of education were covered. In this way implications for teaching could be drawn for each level of teaching mathematics.

In the first session, Otto Bekken [NOR] outlined how he used history in the college classroom to enlighten students on the topic "Abel and uniform convergence". Through the reading of portions of the original papers the students came to understand why rigor is necessary in mathematics. The historical appoach is valuable here because the concept of uniform convergence is quite hard for students of analysis to understand, whereas Bekken's approach allows a deeper involvement with the original discovery. John Fauvel [GBR] used an historical example to show how students can be helped to incorporate mathematical ideas into everyday life skills. In his presentation, "Empowerment through modeling: the abolition of the slave trade", he showed how a mathematical idea, a diagram in this case, could be used to promote political purposes. Thomas Clarkson (1760-1846), Senior Wrangler at Cambridge University in 1783, and an anti-slave trade campaigner, used a diagram to express his ideas. If students are to become powerful communicators then they must learn to interpret the many kinds of diagrams that are so prevalent in our newspapers today. Evelyne Barbin [FRA], in reaction, noted that mathematical concepts sometimes have laborious births (why was uniform convergence introduced at just this time by Abel?) and raised the question of what kind of history is useful for teachers. She also asked how a historical approach could be used in the classroom to explain the role of error in mathematics. History also shows that the concept of rigor changes over time. We must help our students to understand the role of mathematics in our culture.

In the second session, Jan van Maanen [NLD] and Michèle Grégoire [FRA] looked at ways in which historical approaches to the development of mathematics could be used in the education of new learners. Van Maanen gave two examples (bisecting angles and computing logarithms) to show how "New mathematics may profit from old methods", i.e. how students and teachers can evaluate and better understand current mathematical methods by studying old ones. The historical approach shows that mathematical standards are chosen by the mathematical community, and that those standards do change. The approach also shows that mathematics is a dynamic field with links to general culture (this exercise is done in conjunction with teachers of language and history). In these exercises the students are inspired by being in direct contact with the masters. Grégoire discussed "History of mathematics for the classroom: the volume of a pyramid" in order to show how mathematical ideas arise from the imagination of individual mathematicians. By studying the development of the formula for the volume of a pyramid as presented in Legendre's *Géométrie* (1794), the curiosity of students was awakened and the formula de-mystified. The students wanted to know where the formula came from, not just how to use it. In his reaction to these ideas, Niels Jahnke [DEU] asked several provocative questions. Should the history of mathematics be used differently in teaching teachers than in teaching students? Can history be used at all levels of instruction or is it more applicable at university level? (Examples at the elementary level are particularly needed.) Can history clear away the cloud of technical details that surrounds mathematical ideas, and make them clearer to us? What can we realistically expect to gain from using history? We hear reports of success using history, but what about our failures? Can we by sharing them help other teachers? Should we include the blind alleys that mathematicians went down or should we present a rational reconstruction of history?

The third session focused on the pedagogical difficulties that an awareness of the developmental difficulties revealed by analysis of the historical evolution of mathematical concepts and ideas can illuminate. George Booker [AUS] examined the practical and philosophical obstacles to the development of the various forms of the fraction concept across time and different cultures. He showed how certain approaches were more favored by different conceptions of the nature of number and the practical means of allowing for divisibility of wholes into smaller parts. In particular, the difficulties in reconciling approaches to decimal and common fraction notions that are observed among new learners were seen to have historical precedents, while even the rejection of fractions as such by many learners could be contrasted with the philosophical difficulties the Greek mathematicians gave themselves by declaring unity indivisible. In showing these origins of the fraction concept, he showed how the use of an historical learning sequence clearly reveals the inherent difficulties that students face, while also suggesting ways that a teacher might use to overcome or even avoid them. The rich source of examples in the historical origins of the concepts and processes contrasts strongly with the very narrow and limited models traditionally used to "teach" fraction ideas. Man-Keung Siu [HKG] presented the complicated history of "Integration in finite terms, from Liouville's work to the calculus classroom of today", and explained why we must present these ideas in the elementary calculus classroom. Presenting ideas in historical context can help to convince students that mathematics is not simply a matter of following a collection of preformed ideas akin to recipes in a cookbook, but is more concerned with the interconnectedness of ideas from different areas. This conception of mathematics is rarely given in class, and a topic like Liouville's approach to integration can be given to provide students with insight into the calculus. Students need to know that there is an algorithm which will tell which functions are integrable in finite terms, and which then provides the integration of those that are integrable. The elegance and power of this procedure also raises the question which integrating techniques we should be teaching today. In reacting, Frank Swetz [USA] noted that we must present our objectives in using history very clearly. While the historical approach brings out the cumulative nature of mathematics, our objectives in a history of mathematics class may be very different from those in a class which is focusing on the mathematical content *per se*. While we cannot discuss topics such as integration in finite terms without giving the historical context, we need to ask ourselves whether we can always profitably adopt the historical learning sequence. We need to ensure that the approach we do adopt is a truthful, rather than a mythical, reconstruction of the evolution of ideas and approaches.

In the fourth and final session, V. Frederick Rickey [USA] argued for "The necessity of history in teaching mathematics". If we do not use history in our classrooms then we cannot pass the mathematical culture on to our students, and so are derelict in our duties. A list of ways of using history was presented, and then an example of how a mathematical error could be used to aid students' understanding (the error was in Cantor's first proof that the line and the plane have the same cardinality). He suggested that HPM should work hard to convert colleagues to the cause, must prepare and publish materials for the classroom (the French IREM group is currently doing the best job of this), and must start to communicate by e-mail. Maggy Schneider [BEL] presented "Reactions of pupils facing the concept of "indivisible" and paradoxes arising from undue use of this concept". By considering the method of Cavalieri the student is forced to come to grips with the idea of infinity and with the dilemma of indivisibles. By carefully observing the comments the students make, we can come to understand the epistemological difficulties they are having and thus take steps to help them gain a good understanding of these difficult ideas. Israel Kleiner [CAN], reactor, in discussing the ideas put forth in the concluding papers, noted that cognitive conflicts are not to be avoided but to be viewed as opportunities. Students are in good company when they make errors; all the great mathematicians have made them. He also highlighted the need to show how mathematics is created by persons working in a particular culture. Leading students (and it is one of our responsibilities) to see this, and to appreciate its significance, is extremely important as it gives us the opportunity to influence them to be future goodwill ambassadors for mathematics. At the same time, realistic goals for the mathematical education of students will allow us to achieve more mathematical understanding and motivation towards the subject. We must therefore be careful and judicious in our use of history; in particular, our objectives in using history should influence how we teach mathematics.

In summary, the very spirited and large audiences for these sessions showed that there is strong interest in the ways in which the teaching and learning of mathematics can be enhanced by consideration of the many different influences on us that the history of people, of cultures, and of mathematics itself, have had.

NOTES

- It is expected that the proceedings of the ICME-7 sessions, and of many of the presentations at the satellite meeting in Toronto, will be published early in 1993 by the Mathematical Association of America.

Details will be found in the newsletter of HPM which is published four times a year. Copies can be obtained by writing to the editor and asking to be added to the mailing list: Victor J. Katz, Department of Mathematics, University of the District of Columbia, 4200 Connecticut Ave. N.W., Washington, D.C. 20008, U.S.A.

• HPM has an active advisory board that oversees the implementation of its general aims, and which arranges meetings at national and international conferences of mathematicians, mathematics educators, and historians of mathematics. HPM is a diverse group with many interests spanning several disciplines, and this adds considerably to its insights and impact. The chair of HPM, elected in August 1992 for a four-year term, is John Fauvel of the Open University in Great Britain.

• The French "Groupe d'épistémologie et d'histoire des mathématiques" prepared a special report entitled *Stories of problems: history of mathematics* for ICME-7. It is available in the original French or in an abbreviated English-language version.

IOWME – International Organization of Women and Mathematics Education / *MOIFEM – Mouvement international pour les femmes et l'enseignement des mathématiques*

GENDER AND MATHEMATICS EDUCATION

GENRE ET ÉDUCATION MATHÉMATIQUE

Sessions Organizers / *Responsables des séances* : Gabriele Kaiser-Messmer [DEU], Patricia Rogers [CAN]

The work of the International Organization of Women and Mathematics Education was organized in two strands: (a) different theoretical models for addressing gender differences in mathematics, and (b) cross-cultural issues. Each strand began with a panel discussion after which participants met in small groups. The proceedings of the sessions will be published. What follows is a summary of the major issues discussed.

THEORETICAL MODELS FOR ADDRESSING GENDER DIFFERENCES IN MATHEMATICS

Panel discussion

Several models for addressing gender differences in mathematics education have been proposed and developed, mainly in Western countries. In the first panel, moderated by Gila Hanna [CAN], the following perspectives were represented: the *intervention* perspective, which locates the problem in the student; the *segregation* perspective, in which the interaction between girls and boys is often the primary focus; the *discipline* perspective, in which the nature of mathematics itself is problematized; and the *feminist* perspective, in which a critique of the gendered nature of teaching and learning mathematics leads to an examination of the use of power and authority in the mathematics community. There are significant overlaps between these perspectives. Nonetheless, panelists were asked to address those features of their chosen perspective which, for them, are essential.

Teresa-Anne Mashego [ZAF] introduced the intervention perspective by examining the effects on mathematics anxiety, creativity, and enthusiasm during problem solving of de-sensitization therapy and self-image thinking.

The segregation perspective was explored by Charlene Morrow [USA] who argued for all-female mathematics classes in the light of recent data which confirms that women educated in women's colleges are more likely to gain advanced degrees in mathematics and science than those educated in a coeducational setting. Sharanjeet Shan-Randhawa [GBR] explored the discipline perspective. She expressed the belief that a female way of teaching mathematics should be based on raising issues of equality and justice, for example, life-opportunities, racism and the environment, which are of immediate concern to all students. The feminist perspective was elaborated by Sue Willis [AUS] who argued that gender reforms in school mathematics should make explicit the process by which gendered patterns of participation and achievement in mathematics are produced and naturalized in both girls and boys. In her view, a comprehensive and critical understanding of the role of mathematics in constructing privilege is essential to deconstructing myths about gender appropriate behaviour.

Small group discussions

Two groups discussed the intervention perspective. Three contributions emphasized intervention strategies which have focused on significant adults who in turn may intervene in the lives of girls and women to influence their participation in mathematics. A series of workshops, whose design is based on recent research into women's attitudes, was described by Hélène Kayler, Louise Lafortune and Claudie Solar [CAN]. Barbro Grevholm [SWE] described a national network of women who, through conferences and workshops, encourage each other to share knowledge and information and collaborate on joint projects. A slightly different approach was described by Cornelia Niederdrenk-Felgner [DEU]. She has been involved in developing teacher-training materials which aim to make teachers more aware of gender-related problems and encourage them to reflect on their own teaching behaviors. By contrast, Pamela Shaw [AUS] described experiences in a remedial mathematics course for adults studying statistics in which the focus was on developing mathematical problem-solving skills as well as improving attitudes towards mathematics; she stressed the importance and benefits of evaluating such courses.

The segregation perspective concentrated on two summer programs for girls only: SummerMath at Mount Holyoke (James Morrow [USA]) and the Metro Achievement Program in Chicago (Denisse Thompson [USA]). While they differ in content and focus (SummerMath is restricted to mathematics and computer studies and Metro Achievement focuses on the whole person), both programs encourage and support girls to assume leadership roles and adopt behaviors not normally realized in mixed gender groups.

Two groups emphasized the discipline perspective. In one group, ideas were discussed for including topics in the curriculum which, it is believed, open up the study of mathematics to more girls. For example, Mary Barnes [AUS] proposed the use of small group investigative work in calculus as well as the inclusion of real-world applications related to the interests of girls. Joanna Higgins [NZL] discussed the use of games in the teaching of mathematics at the elementary level. In another group, Leone Burton [GBR] asked whether there is a female mathematics or a feminist mathematics and what its epistemology might look like. Lynn Friedman [USA] presented findings of recent studies which tried to clarify conditions which foster success for women in graduate school.

The feminist perspective was taken in three groups. Both Joanne Rossi Becker and Judith Jacobs [USA] developed a vision of teaching mathematics from a feminist perspective. They explored how mathematics itself and how it is presented could be changed to promote mathematical activity by females rather than how females should be changed in order to succeed at mathematics. Roberta Mura [CAN] attempted to uncover the feminist thought underlying all perspectives discussed in these sessions. Marja Meeder [NLD], while arguing for curriculum changes similar to those proposed above, criticized the direct, explicit approach in tackling gender issues in mathematics education. Instead, she described an implicit, indirect approach which, she argued, reaches a wider audience. Two presenters, Carole Lacampagne [USA] and Marjolijn Witte [NLD], described the influence of "mathematics culture" and of an absolutist notion of mathematics, showing how these place constraints on the (permitted) actions of learners in the classroom.

CROSS-CULTURAL ISSUES

Panel discussion

Panelists in this second strand were invited to engage in a question/ answer panel session, moderated by Christine Keitel [DEU], in which issues raised by theoretical approaches to addressing the gender imbalance in mathematics education were examined from a less Eurocentric stand-point. Six panelists from across the world were asked to begin by describing the situation in their own countries. From this and the ensuing discussion, several themes emerged.

Neela Sukthankar [PNG] and Hanako Senuma [JPN] each described the low status of women in their societies and the consequent effects that traditional sex roles have on women's expectations and their prospects for engagement in mathematics and science education. For example, in Papua New Guinea, where most of the national population live in rural areas, good schooling is difficult to find. This is further compounded by the custom, which persists today even among well-educated families, of sending male children to expensive international schools while the female children attend cheaper schools with poorer learning conditions. However, the positive aspects of sex-segregated schooling were stressed by Saleha Naghmi Habibullah [PAK] who suggested that further research is necessary to explore the advantages and disadvantages of coeducational schooling, especially in less industrialized countries. Finally, and this point was made forcefully, it has to be recognized that, in countries where daily survival is a primary concern, gender issues may well be less important.

Gender differences in mathematical performance were emphasized by several panelists. John Searl [GBR] reported that, while differences in England favor boys, no significant differences have been observed between girls and boys in Scotland. However, in Hawaii, as reported by Paul Brandon [USA], girls perform at higher levels than boys, with the gap between the performance of white boys and girls being smaller than the gap between the performance of boys and girls of colour. Brandon speculated about the possible role played by the peer culture of the immigrant and native Hawaiian student populations. Another pattern was introduced by Sharleen Denise Forbes [NZL]. She described how gender differences in performance have lessened for non-Maori New Zealanders, mainly of European decent, but have not changed for the indigenous population. This raises the question whether and how strategies which have been developed by the dominant culture in a society to increase the participation and performance of women in mathematics can effectively be applied to address differences for the minority groups.

Small group discussions

Discussion of the issues raised in the panel was continued in small groups facilitated by the panelists as well as by additional contributors. Several issues emerged.

Gender differences in performance favoring boys were reported by BerinderJeet Kaur [SGP]. Margaret Morton and Barbara Reilly [NZL] described the influence on gender differences in performance in calculus of several educational factors such as type of school and number of courses taken. The relationships between spatial skills, gender and mathematical performance were explored by Lindsay Anne Tartre [USA].

The situation in a less developed country was described by Pat Hiddleston and Myness Mkandawire [MWI]. They confirmed the important influence of traditional gender role expectations on determining whether females will have a good school education in the first place and then, more so, on whether they will be permitted to participate in mathematics courses. They too emphasized the positive influence of girls-only schools for higher mathematical achievements by girls.

The influence of cultural expectations on the mathematical attitudes of girls as well as on their performance was explored in several contributions. Cultural pressures on girls to avoid high mathematical achievements in Western societies were analyzed by Gilah Leder [AUS] who based her critique on the fear of success construct. She assessed the fear of success imagery by analyzing the ways in which outstanding females and males are portrayed in the print media. Gurcharn Singh Kaeley [PNG] described how females' dominant role in several matrilineal communities of the Island States of the South Pacific encourages them to out-perform males in mathematics. He argued, however, that even in the patrilineal communities of this part of the world, the cultural norms do not create gender differences in mathematics.

Gender distinctions within the world of work as well as within the educational system were pointed out by Mary Harris [GBR] who challenges traditional gender-biased perceptions by describing home and factory-made textiles as the results of mathematical activity. A more general radical point of view was emphasized by Betty Johnston [AUS] who questioned the high value accorded to quantification, rationality, and abstraction in our scientific and technological worlds. She evaluated the ways in which particular forms of measuring are linked to conceptions of mathematics and mathematical work, and explored how this is knotted into social relations and social structures, especially for women.

The issue of race was raised by SharanJeet Shan-Rhandawa [GBR] who views racism and sexism as partners in oppression. She has developed a female perspective in her teaching through which she attempts to build harmony and balance with the natural world.

Many people contributed to the four sessions. In addition to those named in the body of this report, the following participants chaired the small group discussions and submitted the discussion summaries on which this report in part is based: Agneta Aukema-Schepel [NLD], Tasoula Berggren [CAN], Carol Fry Bohlin [USA], Roy Bohlin [USA], Maggie Haynes [NZL], Laura Coffin Koch [USA], Beth Southwell [AUS], Pamela Surman [AUS], Lynn Taylor [USA], Heleen Verhage [NLD].

REFERENCES

Burton, L. (Ed.) (1990). *Gender and mathematics: an international perspective.* London: Cassell Educational Limited.

Fennema, E., & Leder, G. (Eds.) (1990). *Mathematics and gender.* New York: Columbia Teachers College Press.

Hanna, G., & Mertins, K. (1991). *Research on gender in mathematics, science and technology: an annotated bibliography, 1980–1990.* Paris: UNESCO.

Lafortune, L., & Kayler, H. (1992). *Les femmes font des maths!* Montréal: Éditions du Remue-Ménage.

Leder, G., & Sampson, S. (1989). *Educating girls: practice and research.* Sydney: Allen and Unwin.

PME: International Group for the Psychology of Mathematics Education /
Groupe international de psychologie de l'éducation mathématique

REPORT OF ACTIVITIES

RAPPORT D'ACTIVITÉS

Sessions Organizers / *Responsables des séances* : Kathleen Hart [GBR]
(president), A.J. (Sandy) Dawson [CAN], Nerida F. Ellerton [AUS],
Gerald A. Goldin [USA], Angel Guttiérez [ESP], Claude Janvier [CAN],
Barbara Jaworski [GBR], Stephen Lerman [GBR], Fou-Lai Lin [TWN],
Helen Mansfield [AUS], Rosamund Sutherland [GBR],
Jan van den Brink [NLD]

The sessions began with an overview by the President of the general
characteristics and achievements of PME. The International Group for the
Psychology of Mathematics Education (PME) meets every year in a different
country. This year its 16th meeting took place in Durham, New Hampshire,
U.S.A. The conferences are attended by about 300 members and the
organization's newsletter is sent to about 900 people who are past or present
members. The focus of all meetings is research and the constitution defines
the major aims of the organization as:

- To promote international contacts and the exchange of scientific
  information in the psychology of mathematics education.

- To promote and stimulate interdisciplinary research in the aforesaid
  area with the cooperation of psychologists, mathematicians, and
  mathematics teachers.

- To further a deeper and better understanding of the psychological
  aspects of teaching and learning mathematics and the implications
  thereof.

The conference sessions are of the following types: research reports
with discussion, working groups, discussion groups, plenary lectures, panel
discussions, poster sessions, and short oral presentations. The proceedings
of each meeting provide valuable reference material for researchers and
their students. The field is wide open since it is relatively new and methods
of research are often borrowed from other disciplines. The membership is
composed mainly of psychologists, mathematics educators, and mathematics

teachers. The focus of interest of each of those groups is slightly different but the learning of mathematics is at the core. Some of the members have been using research findings to assist curriculum development and the writing of effective materials for children. It is apparent that we still do not know a lot about children's and teachers' understanding of mathematics. We should be trying to find out more in order to provide teachers with evidence to show that adopting new teaching ideas produces results.

The strengths of PME lie in its international nature and the participation of people who are experts in their field. Members discuss, criticize, and amplify each other's work. They build on the results of others' research to extend a hierarchy, use a test, or provide data from a different culture.

The working groups play an important part in PME and reports from these groups occupied the remaining three sessions of the PME presentations.

Three working groups study different topic areas of the mathematics curriculum. The *Ratio and Proportion* group has (until relatively recently) separated proportional reasoning from fractional manipulation because these have appeared to require different understandings. The child often employs informal methods, which the teacher needs to know. The qualitative methods of the researcher, particularly interview techniques, can be adopted for use in the conventional classroom. The *Algebra* group aims to characterize the shifts that appear to be involved in developing the algebraic mode of thinking, and to investigate the role of symbolizing in this development. Other concerns of the group are the role of meaning in algebraic processing, the potential of computer-based environments, and the implications of research for teaching. The *Geometry* group has also in the past dealt with the role of computer environments in the learning and teaching of geometry. At ICME–7 their report concerned the influence of PME on a major piece of geometry research. This was based on the Van Hiele theory and over the years there has been considerable interaction between researchers concerning the hierarchies formed to comply with the theory and subsequently tested with children. The *Classroom Research* working group hopes that researchers will be inspired by teachers' instructional methods; their work is research *in* the classroom, *on* the classroom, *about* the classroom, and *of* the classroom. They listen to authors of articles, view videotapes (usually of children working on some mathematical topic) and read transcripts, then discuss the implications and immediately record their comments.

PME has three working groups concerned with teacher education. For their ICME-7 presentation, they gave the participants a brief written description of an incident involving an experienced mathematics teacher and a new teacher in a school. Members of the audience were asked to discuss the vignette with each other and to react as teacher educators. The leaders of the three groups (*Psychology of Mathematics Teacher Development, Teachers as Researchers in Mathematics Education,* and *Research on the Psychology of Mathematics Teacher Development*) then described their particular emphasis in interpreting the vignette.

The last two groups to present their work were those concerned with *Advanced Mathematical Thinking* and *Representation.* The former takes as its brief the creation of a domain of study of the processes underlying the learning of mathematics at an advanced level, choosing the age of 16 years as a pragmatic lower limit for their concerns. At PME meetings they have discussed mathematical and psychological processes relevant to advanced mathematical thinking, mathematical creativity, the concept of proof, and possible differences in kind between elementary and advanced mathematics. Their main conclusions have appeared in the book *Advanced Mathematical Thinking* edited by David Tall [GBR], and published by Kluwer. The role of representation in mathematics learning is of very great importance and the working group on *Representation* has considered at its meetings: internal and external representations, systems of representation in mathematics, definitional issues, types of representations (static vs. dynamic, imagistic vs. notational, etc.), characteristics of the media within which representations are embodied, and related theoretical issues. The group is particularly interested in effective systems of external representation and of internal representation and what properties make them powerful.

NOTE

Information about PME and copies of the proceedings of past meetings can be obtained from the Executive Secretary of PME, Joop van Dormolen, Kapteynlaan 105, 3571 XN Utrecht, The Netherlands.

ICMI STUDIES

ÉTUDES DE LA CIEM

THE INFLUENCE OF COMPUTERS AND INFORMATICS ON MATHEMATICS AND ITS TEACHING

L'INFLUENCE DES ORDINATEURS ET DE L'INFORMATIQUE SUR LES MATHÉMATIQUES ET LEUR ENSEIGNEMENT

Chief Organizer / *Responsable en chef* : Bernard Cornu [FRA]

In 1985, the International Commission on Mathematical Instruction chose "The Influence of Computers and Informatics on Mathematics and its Teaching" as the topic of its first study. A conference was held in Strasbourg, France (1985), and the study was then published as a book (Cambridge University Press, ICMI Study Series, 1986). After some years, ICMI and UNESCO wished to edit an updated version of the original book, and asked Bernard Cornu [FRA] and Anthony Ralston [USA] to edit the new version. This version brings the topics up to date, and incorporates new topics. It is published by UNESCO (1992) and can be obtained from UNESCO, Science and Technology Education Section, ED/EDV, 7 Place de Fontenoy, 75700 Paris, France; Fax: (33) 1 40 65 94 05.

SESSION 1

Integrating calculus and discrete mathematics

The presentation by Maria Mascarello [ITA], was based on her paper with Bernard Winkelmann: "Calculus teaching and the computer; on the interplay of discrete numerical methods and calculus in the education of users of mathematics", in the new version of the book. In teaching calculus to mathematics users, the concepts of continuous analysis sometimes appear difficult, and are insufficient in applications to obtain numerical results. Furthermore some calculus models have a discrete basis, as in the social or biological sciences. However the transition from the major part of the classical models to concrete numerical results cannot be accomplished in general without continuous analysis.

- Calculus teaching should include the direct treatment and study of discrete models.

- As for classical continuous models, if calculus cannot be used to obtain numerical results directly, except in special cases, it must however guide the use of numerical methods.

From a presentation by a "practitioner", Hugh Neill [GBR]:

- The ability to design and/or modify algorithms contributes greatly to mathematical understanding.

- The use of the programmable, graphics calculator, with its increasingly accessible programming languages, enables all students to turn their algorithms into programs. It gives students greater ownership of the subject.

- An indication was given of a possible way that programming can be introduced to students by automating a boring interactive process.

- The identical nature of the algorithms for calculating area and for solving differential equations was used as an illustration of the way that the calculator, as a discrete tool, can provide helpful information about continuous mathematics.

From a panel discussion, with Klaus-D. Graf [DEU], Hugh Neill, Erich Neuwirth [AUT], David Tall [GBR]:

- Do we need calculus/continuous mathematics for all at school; in particular, do we need limits? One answer was: yes, because of its efficiency. As an example, a problem can be solved by computer-assisted approximation of the sum of a power series. If calculus gives us a simple function like $(3x)/(1 - x)$ as a limit of this sum, the solution can be found far more efficiently. Another answer was: yes, because of the power of continuous mathematics to prove the correctness of discrete mathematics solutions. One statement stressed the need in general to show the students how one problem can be attacked by means of continuous and discrete mathematics, including random processes. Example: the mathematical modeling of different types of population growth by differential equations on the one hand, and probabilistic experiments on the other.

- The use of discrete numerical procedures offers a good entry to concepts of continuous calculus before or in parallel with a more formal development.

- Discrete and continuous methods remain complementary approaches which are both vital to mathematics. Discrete methods, through programming and, more importantly, the graphic calculator, give a quantitative approach which the pupil can carry out personally and then view the results either quantitatively (numerically) or qualitatively (graphically). However, continuous methods, through the use of functions and formulae, allow manipulative methods, using symbols, which give powerful solutions whenever they are applicable.

SESSION 2

The role of algorithmics in teaching mathematics

From the presentation "What are algorithms? What is algorithmics?" by Stephen B. Maurer [USA]: An algorithm is a systematic method for solving a class of problems, often involving iteration or repeated reduction to a previous case. Algorithmics is systematic, creative thinking about algorithms. Part of being systematic is having a sufficiently precise language for humans to describe algorithms – algorithmic language.

Algorithms are old but algorithmics is new. Maurer gave several examples of algorithms, from Euclid's method for finding gcd's to alternative approaches for evaluating $a(b + c + ... + z)$ on a hand calculator.

One reason to study algorithmics is that algorithms are pervasive in the modern world. As for reasons intrinsic to mathematics education, algorithmics allows for a fresh view on traditional material and gives students new opportunities for creativity.

From the presentation of a "practitioner", Elmar Cohors-Fresenborg [DEU]: In a 5-year curriculum project in 50 grade-7 classes, we have combined the introduction of computers with the introduction of the mathematical concept of functions. Our main aim was rather to construct mental models in the pupils' minds than to teach merely mathematical facts and train skills. We based our curriculum on a theory of Inge Schwank about the resonance between external representations and the cognitive structures of pupils. There exist individual preferences: predicative thinking emphasizes a preference for thinking in terms of relations and judgements, functional thinking emphasizes thinking in terms of courses and modes of action. Using the world of computers as a metaphor for understanding mathematics in an action-oriented way, we enabled especially functionally-oriented pupils to understand the formal aspects of school algebra more deeply.

From a panel discussion, with Jonathan Choate [USA], Philip Lewis [USA], Jacques Stern [FRA]:

- Algorithmics, especially difference equations, leads directly into modeling.

- One could do less algorithmics than Maurer proposed, e.g. the study of efficiency doesn't always arise naturally, and verification of algorithms is as hard for students as traditional proofs are. One could do more algorithmics than Maurer proposed, e.g. treat data structures as well as algorithms and do searching and sorting.

- The particular algorithms we use as examples today may become outmoded, but the basic ideas of algorithmics are likely to last.

- The general problem of the computability of a problem should be mentioned early.

- We should really define algorithms as specified procedures for processing information. This is much wider than only dealing with mathematical objects.

- The teaching of algorithms should not be restricted to mathematical examples; searching and sorting are also important. Even with no computer one can give simple examples of algorithms: looking up in a dictionary, sorting in alphabetical order.

- Mastering the teaching of algorithms will require teachers to have a basic understanding of several fields of theoretical computer science: logic, complexity theory, algorithm design. We might have to give up some other parts of the usual curriculum for teachers.

- Studying algorithmics keeps us from losing the "functionally-oriented" students who don't initially respond well to traditional algebraic formulations.

NOTE

The CO acknowledges the help of Maria Mascarello [ITA] and Stephen B. Maurer [USA] in organizing the program for this Group.

REFERENCE

Cornu, B., & Ralston, A. (Eds.) (1992). *The influence of computers and informatics on mathematics and its teach-* *ing,* Science and Technology Education, Document Series, 44. Paris: UNESCO.

THE POPULARIZATION OF MATHEMATICS

LA POPULARISATION DES MATHÉMATIQUES

Chief Organizer / *Responsable en chef* : Henry O. Pollak [USA]

A seminar on "The popularization of mathematics" was organized in Leeds, England, in September, 1989, by the International Commission on Mathematical Instruction (ICMI) and the results of the seminar were published as a book (Cambridge University Press, ICMI Study Series, 1990). The purpose of these three sessions on the topic during ICME-7 was to bring some of the highlights of the Leeds meeting to a larger audience, and to take a look at what has been happening around the world on this topic since. The richness of the Group's activity cannot be properly reflected in a few lines, so this report will be personal and idiosyncratic, with apologies to those whose work will not be as fully represented as it should. In particular, the many exciting excerpts from television programs and mathematical films which were shown in Québec obviously cannot be recaptured in print.

The newest work represented in these sessions seems to have taken place in Europe. Thus Jean-Pierre Kahane [FRA], in his opening presentation, "Vulgarisation mathématique, quoi de neuf?", summarized a number of recent activities, many of them European. In France there have been exhibitions at the Palais de la Découverte and elsewhere, and public debates on mathematics and art, mathematics and reality, and other themes. The European Mathematical Congress at the Sorbonne in July 1992 worked a great deal on "mathematics and the general public". The name of Jean-Michel Kantor [FRA] is especially prominent in this connection. Kantor spoke to the group on "Les maths sympas grâce à la télé" and showed a major mathematical film on video which he had made.

Returning to Kahane's presentation, he also took a look into the future. He suggested that mathematicians are not necessarily well-prepared to take the required steps in popularizing mathematics: we may not know how to write, or speak, or listen, in this milieu, and we may have to enlarge our personal view of mathematics. Any large-scale activity of popularization will also require the active participation of teachers.

A third French contribution to the theme was made by Gilles Cohen [FRA]. He is extraordinarily active in this area, heading the Fédération française des jeux mathématiques et logiques, which has 10 000 members, and running national and international competitions which, over the previous three years, had involved 120 000 people at seven levels, from primary school children to adults.The Fédération is responsible for a series of books, "Jeux mathématiques et logiques", published by Hatier, and a collection of pocket books, "Jeux en poche", from Éditions Pole. The Fédération puts on a road show on mathematical games, and a summer school, and has produced a television series. There is a special competition for young students who are afraid of mathematics! By August 1992 there were competition participants in 21 different countries, with a formal support organization in six of them. A plethora indeed!

Michele Emmer's [ITA] presentation was titled "Planning a mathematics museum", though he spoke about many of the activities concerned with popularizing mathematics in Italy, not only the new museum of mathematics in Pisa. He has written extensively on the history of mathematics, a subject about which he has also made a number of movies. Next year, in celebration of the book on the five Platonic solids, there will be an exhibition in Florence, and another in Venice where the first Greek Euclid was published.

Celia Hoyles [GBR], under the title "Televising mathematics: popularization or distortion?", pointed out that the purposes of popularization included extending the visibility of mathematics, increasing its cultural attractiveness, and getting away from its "school-boundedness" – that is, the view that mathematics is only what it appears to be in school. The Yorkshire Television series "Fun and games", in which she had played a major part, had ordinary people participate in non-trivial mathematics. They were able to find complex, beautiful, intriguing, counter-intuitive strategies for various puzzles and games, all without rehearsal. The show aired in prime time for four years. It used no formal language and no algebra, was fast-paced and full of action.

Once again, the audience in Québec was able to see several extracts from these delightful programs. Readers of this report are recommended to seize any opportunity of seeing them.

A very enjoyable form of popularization is the mathematics trail, which was presented, as at Leeds, by Dudley Blane [AUS]. A "mathematics trail" is a self-guided walk, starting off from a brochure which offers ideas and questions to help walkers formulate and discuss some interesting mathematical problems along the way. Any setting is appropriate for a mathematics trail: it can take place downtown in a city, in a shopping mall, a zoo, a major government building, a recreated historical town, the countryside. Blane laid the first trail in Melbourne, Australia, and has since then inspired many other trails in Australia and other countries. (A trail was prepared in the old city of Québec at the time of the Congress. *See page 403 in this volume.*) Walking a math trail is not orienteering, it is not competitive and there are no grades. You can tell the idea is successful because participants return bringing their families, they are happy to show their answer sheets and be interviewed, and students have been known to design trails for their parents to walk! A zoo is a particularly popular site. Questions which involve the weight and speed of animals are great fun. You can, for example, use footprints to estimate weight, and you can decide, in comparing yourself to various animals, whether you would more likely be their predator or their prey!

Florence Fasanelli [USA] spoke on mathematics in the mall – not a shopping mall, but the Washington Mall. There is a lot of beautiful mathematics, as well as science, that can come to mind as you walk around the Capitol Mall in Washington. Start at the Capitol. How large did Columbus think the earth was? What goes on in the Whispering Gallery? How is apportionment carried out? Consider the geometry to be found in the National Gallery, the skylights, the floors, and the paintings. What does the Foucault pendulum in the National Museum of American History lead you to think about? How were the stars in the American flag arranged when there were different numbers of states? Fasanelli gave just a taste of the many mathematical investigations suggested by walking the Washington Mall.

"Square One: math in a popular medium" was the title of Joel Schneider's [USA] presentation. "Square One" is a project devoted to informal mathematics education on a large scale. It is a television series distributed by the Public Broadcasting Network in the United States; its primary audience is 8-12 year olds watching at home in the late afternoon. Close to a million people watch the show every day. Each show consists of 6 - 12 comedy/variety segments in a magazine format. Typically, they parody other familiar television formats. A very popular part of each "Square One" show is the segment called "Mathnet", which features two mathematicians working in a police department and using their mathematical knowledge and skills to fight crime. The aim of "Square One" is to develop and maintain positive attitudes towards mathematics, to model effective problem solving, and to display a broad spectrum of mathematics. In one series of parodies of familiar commercials, we are told, "This segment was brought to you by Probability (or Combinatorics, or Geometry, or Statistics, or ...), a Division of Mathematics. It isn't just arithmetic!"

Thinking about the content of the presentations brings up several interesting points. Any of the forms of popularization – whether it be television, lectures, museums, books, newspapers, radio, etc. – can succeed only as long as it holds its audience. The program can be turned off, the book closed, the museum quitted, the newspaper used to wrap fish – and there is no teacher to object. This logic gives the attractiveness of the medium considerable weight in the inevitable tug-of-war between education and entertainment as presentations are developed. As any form of popularization succeeds – and the speakers presented not only some delightful efforts but also impressive evidence of their success – it is inevitable that the media of popularization will be asked to take a role in the formal as distinct from the informal educational system. For example, we can expect to see the increasing use of television segments in mathematics teaching at the primary and middle school levels, and beyond these levels as the breadth of our understanding of popularization allows.

Kahane closed his presentation by thinking about the International Year of Mathematics in the year 2000 – which is when ICME-9 should take place! We may expect by that time to see much regional action on popularization, and appeals to various media, such as films, books, exhibitions, and public debates. We could work with other scientists and help produce expository papers and books as well as sources of information for the media to draw upon. Above all, by then we will have become much more reflective and informative about our beloved mathematics.

ASSESSMENT IN MATHEMATICS EDUCATION AND ITS EFFECTS

L'ÉVALUATION EN ÉDUCATION MATHÉMATIQUE ET SES EFFETS

Chief Organizer / *Responsable en chef* : Mogens Niss [DNK]

This series of four sessions was devoted to presenting the aims, the scope, and the outcome of a recent ICMI Study on assessment. The sessions were organized with the assistance of Thomas A. Romberg [USA] (Session 2), Claudi Alsina [ESP] (Session 3), and Hugh Burkhardt [GBR] (Session 4).

As with previous ICMI Studies, this one too is based on three corner-stones: a discussion document (ICMI, 1990) written by the Program Committee for the Study, which was appointed by the Executive Committee of ICMI and chaired by the author of this report; the work of an invited international Study Conference held in Calonge, Spain, 11-16 April 1991; and a considerable number of papers, most of which were included in the pre-proceedings of the conference.

The tangible outcome of the Study is two books (see references), each one focusing on particular aspects of assessment. *Cases of Assessment in Mathematics Education* concentrates on presenting and discussing concrete assessment philosophies and practices, some of which are innovative or experimental, that are implemented in existing educational systems. In *Investigations into Assessment of Mathematics Education* the emphasis is on identifying and analyzing general and principal aspects of assessment in mathematics education. The two books can be read independently.

A representative coverage of the entire Study was not attempted in these four sessions at ICME-7. Instead, the endeavour was to present a selection of key issues and contributions that could constitute an overview of the state-of-the-art and current trends in assessment in mathematics education for a general audience, with attention being paid to important research contributions, crucial, non-rhetorical issues (genuine controversies and dilemmas) and different positions.

THE ACTIVITIES AND THE CONTENT OF THE FOUR SESSIONS

All the sessions of the Group were plenary sessions having an estimated average audience of about 200 delegates. The first three concentrated on presentations whereas the fourth was entirely devoted to discussion.

SESSION 1

Aims, main themes, issues and findings

Aims, main themes, issues and findings, was opened by an overview (see Niss, 1992b), given by the CO, of the Study and its place in the ICMI Study Series. First, a distinction between *assessment* and *evaluation* that pertains to the entire Study was introduced. Assessment is taken to concern the judging of the mathematical capabilities, performances, and achievements of *students*, whereas evaluation is reserved for the judging of educational and instructional *systems*, e.g. curricula, programs, teachers, and institutions. The present Study deals chiefly with assessment.

One main reason and motive for mounting a study on assessment was the observed increasing mismatch and tension between the state of and trends in mathematics education, and current assessment practices. Mismatch and tension result from the fact that in recent years mathematics education has developed strongly as regards ideals, goals, theory, and practice, whereas prevalent assessment concepts and practices have changed comparatively little.

We need to subject assessment in mathematics education to investigation, because

- the roles, functions, and effects of assessment are not well understood;

- there are divergent aims and conflicting interests involved in contemporary assessment modes;

- it is difficult to devise satisfactory, valid and reliable, assessment modes;

- the difficulties encountered are of a fundamental and universal nature and call for treatment from an international perspective.

Altogether, the main aim of the Study is to *assess assessment*, critically and constructively. The following observations form its prerequisites:

- Assessment in mathematics educations exists, and is here to stay, regardless of any well-justified reservations we might have about the current exercise of it.

- Assessment serves a variety of purposes (not necessarily compatible).

They fall into the three categories:

- The provision of information, to the individual student, the teacher, and the system (institutions, authorities, employers, parents).

- The establishment of a basis for decisions and actions concerning students' learning, teachers' teaching, the system's selection, filtering, and placement of individuals.

- The shaping of social reality for students, teachers, and institutions.

Assessment involves a multitude of different terms. Without aspiring to clarify all of these, it might be useful to keep the following constitutive components of assesment in mind:

- The subject of assessment (Who is assessed?)

- The objects of assessment (What content and abilities are assessed?)

- The items of assessment (What kinds of output are assessed?)

- The occasions of assessment (When does assessment take place?)

- The procedures and circumstances of assessment (What happens where, and who does what?)

- The judging and recording of assessment (What is emphasized, and what is recorded?)

- The reporting of assessment outcomes (What is reported to whom?)

The main presentation in the first session was "What does to assess mean?", by Antoine Bodin [FRA] (see Niss, 1992b). He attempted to identify and discuss the insufficiencies and weaknesses in current assessment procedures in mathematics education while at the same time taking stock of the prospects and promises opened by research in progress. To that end he suggested the following (personal) definition:

> To assess means to organize (or to inspect) some situations in such a way as to enable us to gather information which, when it has been processed, can reveal something reliable about the knowledge of an individual or a group.

On that basis, and utilizing results from his several years of detailed research on the assessment of French secondary school students (the EVAPM studies), Bodin gave concrete examples of the difficulties encountered when attempting to interpret consistently students' actual mathematical knowledge. Among his findings was that students' behaviour neither respects the usual taxonomies of objectives nor *a priori* analyses of difficulties, and that the contexts of the questions asked strongly influence the responses observed.

These and other findings led him to conclude that established ways of assessing knowledge not only suffer from a lack of validity but also, perhaps more surprisingly, from a lack of reliability.

Instead, Bodin emphasized the need to focus more on the meaning of the information gathered. In that respect he suggested a typology of meaning comprising three levels, of representation, communication, and object, respectively. A corresponding notion of assessment would go beyond the distinction between formative and summative assessment and focus on diagnostic assessment.

SESSION 2

Critical and analytical aspects of assessment

The first presentation, with the title "An international view of mathematical assessment" (see Niss, 1992b), was given by Jim Ridgway [GBR]. Taking his point of departure in seven snapshots of the different roles and functions of assessment as encountered in different categories of countries, Ridgway established a list of the uses of assessment, including (among others): explanation and maintenance of social division; qualification and access to higher education or to a career; certification of achievement or competence; enhancement or reduction of personal status and self-esteem; provision of feedback to students or parents; definition of the curriculum.

He suggested that a closer analysis of the uses and functions of assessment should take various levels into account such as: societal, industrial, family, student, teacher, departmental, school, curriculum development, inspectorial service, political, and international levels. As to the psychology of assessment, Ridgway emphasized that the choice of measures should reflect one's theory of what the phenomena of interest are. He found that established assessment procedures rooted in the psychometric tradition tend to be too little concerned with conceptual issues and aims and too much with technical issues, which may have detrimental effects. As he put it: "weighing a pig repeatedly does not increase its weight". Ridgway concluded by briefly outlining three activities through which assessment of mathematics in any country can be described and examined: a list of criteria for judging assessment schemes; identifying the key layers (agents) within the educational system; analysis of current assessment profiles.

Under the title "Paradigms, problems, and assessment" (see Niss, 1992b), Peter Galbraith [AUS], focused on how perceptions of assessment in mathematics education are intimately related to and vary with underlying general philosophical and ideological paradigms. He particularly mentioned and characterized three such paradigms: the conventional, the constructivist, and the critical. Each paradigm offers different answers to four substantive questions for mathematics education: What is there to know? How is the known constructed? How do we know when something about mathematics is known? How do we find out what is known? Assessment concepts and practices are functions of the answers to these questions, in particular the latter two.

With this general framework as a background, Galbraith examined some particular examples and their relations to underlying paradigms: generalized achievement testing, school assessment policy, formal versus contextual knowledge, assessment of problem solving, investigations and modeling, and mathematics: preserver of inequalities? This led him to conclude by asking: "What "givens" should be challenged and their status changed to "problematicals" through an analysis of underlying assumptions and belief systems?"

Thomas Romberg concluded the session by briefly summarizing a paper by Stieg Mellin-Olsen [NOR], "A critical view of assessment in mathematics education: Where is the student as a subject?" (see Niss, 1992b). This paper draws attention to the learner as a subject in the context of assessment rather than as an object, as is ordinarily the case, and discusses ways of implementing such a view of the learner in educational and assessment practice. Mellin-Olsen suggests that practical hermeneutics be introduced for that purpose. In practical hermeneutics, conversations with a student are taped and transcribed and submitted to an explicit interpretational activity which – and this is an important point – involves the student. By using this method assessment is also transformed into an interpretational activity that allows for the inclusion of the student's own learning goals.

SESSION 3

Cases of innovative/experimental assessment

This session offered three presentations of innovative/experimental cases of assessment conducted within three different kinds of educational framework. Under the heading "The range of performance assessed" (in Niss, 1992a, under a different heading) Max Stephens [AUS] presented the assessment scheme adopted by the state of Victoria for upper secondary school mathematics. In this scheme students are assessed on four different sorts of items, called CATs (Common Assessment Tasks). CAT 1 deals with an extended investigative project on a centrally set theme; CAT 2 contains challenging problems; CAT 3 is a multiple-choice test on standard skills and applications, whereas CAT 4 comprises four structured problems leading from routine to non-routine questions.

Chris Little [GBR] presented some secondary school assessment initiatives of the School Mathematics Project (SMP) (see Niss, 1992a). He made the point that it is possible to devise valuable, challenging, and innovative tasks for large-scale assessment within the boundaries of established, non-experimental curricula. To illustrate his point Chris Little gave examples of a variety of types of tasks included in the SMP program including written examinations, coursework assessment, open-ended tasks, oral assessment, etc.

The examples presented by Leonor Cunha Leal and Paulo Abrantes [PRT] refer to an innovative, small-scale curriculum project MAT789 for Grades 7-9 (see Niss, 1992a). Assessment in this project takes various forms, including two-stage tasks (inspired by Dutch experiences), essay-type questions and short reports, as well as extended project work assessment, and examples of all of these were presented. As a result of this innovative work a positive change in the classroom atmosphere in relation to assessment was observed.

SESSION 4

Issues, points, positions – intriguing or controversial?

Issues, points, positions – intriguing or controversial? was a discussion session in which quite a few members of the audience took part. It was organized and introduced by Hugh Burkhardt. On his suggestions the discussion dealt with the following issues:

- Political/social issues ("minimal" vs "beautiful", "private" vs "public", "standardized" vs "individual choice").

- Curriculum issues (task types – including design principles, in particular regarding curriculum balance and curriculum value – scoring schemas, analytical vs creative emphases).

- Technical issues (criteria, levels and tasks – including empirical development of tasks; modes of assessment; differentiation; costs; reliability).

REFERENCES

Commission Internationale de l'Enseignement Mathématique (ICMI) (1990). Assessment in mathematics education and its effects: Discussion document. *L'Enseignement Mathématique*, 2ᵉ série, 36, fasc. 1-2, 197-206.

Niss, M. (Ed.) (1992a). *Cases of assessment in mathematics education: An ICMI Study*. Dordrecht: Kluwer Academic Publishers.

Niss, M. (Ed.) (1992b). *Investigations into assessment in mathematics education: An ICMI Study*, Dordrecht: Kluwer Academic Publishers.

MINICONFERENCE

MINI-CONGRÈS

MINICONFERENCE ON CALCULATORS AND COMPUTERS

MINI-CONGRÈS SUR LES CALCULATRICES ET LES ORDINATEURS

Chief Organizers / *Responsables en chef* : Rosemary Caddy [GBR], Eric Muller [CAN]

The Miniconference occupied the first afternoon of the program. Plenaries, workshops, and many of the presentations used calculators, computers and their projection devices, either in a laboratory setting or as they might be used in a class situation. Other presenters discussed their experiences of the uses of calculators and computers in mathematics education. All raised questions of their impact and importance in the teaching and learning of mathematics. Participants were given a Miniconference supplement to the main Congress program booklet from which they selected their afternoon activities. To allow individuals to participate in small groups all activities had limited registrations. The reports of the five strands of the Miniconference follow.

MC1: 5-11 YEAR OLD STUDENTS / *ÉLÈVES DE 5 À 11 ANS*

Chief Organizers / *Responsables en chef* : Jan Stewart, Rita Crust [GBR]

The activities offered opportunities to experience some of the most successful applications of using technology with young children from around the world.

The afternoon began with a plenary lecture by Glen Kleiman [USA] titled "Technology: the good, the bad and the ugly". Employing a series of anecdotes and practical demonstrations, he steered participants through the many changes that have occurred in computer and video use over the past twelve years. He drew attention to the computer's powerful and revolutionary potential, to some possible misuses of the technology, and to the realities that must be addressed if the good uses are to have their proper impact on schools, students, and mathematics teaching.

For the remaining part of the afternoon participants attended one workshop and two presentations. Presentations and workshops emphasized the practical implementation of ideas and, in the workshops, participants were given the opportunity to work "like children" in simulated classroom situations. Topics ranged from graphic calculators to "drawing balls"; from artificial intelligence systems to microworlds; from the problem of integrating technology into a national curriculum to the success of individual projects. The presenters were: Hartwig Meissner [DEU], Jean César [FRA], Istvan Lenart [HUN], Anne Berit Fugelstad [NOR], Berit Blomberg, Barbra Grevholm and Ann-Margret Johansson [SWE], Joost Klep [NLD], Rina Cohen [CAN], Patricia Baggett, Donna Berlin, Gary Bitter, Elizabeth Bjork, Andrzej Ehrenfeucht, Robert Gilbert, Myles Gordon, Chris Hancock, John Olive and Arthur White [USA], and Stan Dolan and Hilary Shuard † [GBR].

MC2: 11-16 YEAR OLD STUDENTS / *ÉLÈVES DE 11 À 16 ANS*

Chief Organizers / *Responsables en chef* : Richard Phillips,
Rosamund Sutherland [GBR]

The workshops and presentations aimed to offer a glimpse of the diversity of computer and calculator uses in the mathematics classrooms throughout the world. Software ranged from large, open-modeling software such as spreadsheets, Cabri, and Logo (some of which was designed for the mathematics classroom and some for commercial purposes) to smaller more specific software – for example Doorzien and Alcor designed for the Netherlands National Curriculum. The diversity of ways of working included the use of the computers and calculators with whole classes and work with small groups of students.

The workshops focused on "hands on" activities with delegates taking on the role of students. They centered on a number of classroom activities and consisted of: "Exploring Logo" (Pat Drake, Tony Harries, Sylvia Johnson [GBR]); "Using spreadsheets in mathematics learning" (Joâo Pedro Ponte, Joâo Filipe Matos, Fernando Nuñes, Madelena Santos, Projecto Minerva [PRT]); "Cabri-géomètre" (Bernard Capponi [FRA]); "One micro with a class" (Malcolm Swan [GBR]); "Computer adventure games" (Heather Scott, Daniel Pead [GBR]); "Investigative software from the Netherlands" (Monica Wijers, Aad Goddijn [NLD]); "Collaborative work with a graphic calculator" (Teresa Smart [GBR]); "Problem solving with a graphic calculator" (Linda J. Wagner [USA]).

The presentations were grouped into sessions on how the computer and the calculator have been used in the classroom (Gareth Buckland, Dave

Pratt [GBR], Enrica Lemut [ITA], David Green [GBR]); sessions on the effects of the computer on students' reasoning (Shoichiro Machida [JPN], Patrick W. Thompson [USA], H. Sakondis [GBR], Júlianna Szendrei [HUN]); sessions which discussed the mathematical potential of computer environments (Gurudas Bajani [IND], Benoît Coté [CAN], Fernand Lemay [CAN], Katsuhiko Sato [JPN]); sessions on national policy issues (Jerry P. Becker [USA], David Green [GBR], Jim Ridgway [GBR], Tsuneo Uetake [JPN]).

The plenary session involved the audience in computer-based activities and gave them a feel for how children can work at the computer. It was led by some of the presenters listed above. Ridgway started and used the metaphor of a marriage between information technology and mathematics education to raise a number of important issues. Sutherland then introduced the audience to two 14 year old pupils, a girl from Sweden and a boy from England, who were successful at writing a variable procedure to draw the letter Q (for Québec). The audience also took part in a mathematical problem solving activity (Pyxidium) posed by Phillips in which individuals asked for data from the computer and then used this data to make conjectures. Also in the plenary session, Smart used a graphic calculator on an overhead projector to pose a series of problems. This provoked a debate on the relative merits of buying many calculators or fewer computers. Throughout the session the issue of equal access to computers and calculators for all students was addressed. Finally the need for more opportunities for teachers to learn about and use computers, and for more research on the ways in which students use computers and calculators to express, explore and learn mathematical ideas was stressed.

REFERENCES

Capponi, B., & Sutherland, R. (1992). Learning trigonometry in a French classroom. *Micromath, 8*(2), 32-33. Association of Teachers of Mathematics, UK.

Phillips, R. (1988). Four types of lesson with a microcomputer. *Micromath, 4*(1), 35-38 and *4*(2), 7-11. Association of Teachers of Mathematics, UK.

MC3: 15-18 YEAR OLD STUDENTS / *ÉLÈVES DE 15 À 18 ANS*

Chief Organizer / *Responsable en chef* : James T. Fey [USA]

The software, curriculum materials, and instructional strategies demonstrated and discussed in the sessions are eloquent proof that calculators and computers offer impressive opportunities to change the goals and predominant teaching/learning patterns in mathematics for students in this age range. Increasingly powerful graphing calculators and computer numeric, graphic, and symbolic software are being applied to create courses that reduce attention to routine symbol manipulation, enhance concept development, and extend problem solving in algebra, trigonometry, and calculus. Geometry tools that help students create, measure, and transform Euclidean figures, fractals, knots, and graphs provide exciting new ways to help students reason about visual patterns.

Perhaps the most impressive aspect of the situation is the striking improvement in ease of access to that technology. Calculators and pocket computers of real power are now available at quite modest prices. Computer software has been engineered to make it easy to use by students with only modest computer skills.

While further curricular and hardware/software developments are certainly forthcoming, it seems clear that the situation is right for finally realizing the potential of technology in the broad spectrum of school mathematics programs.

Jean-Marie Laborde [FRA] and Bert Waits [USA] were the plenary speakers in this section. Other presenters were: André Boileau, Maurice Garançon [CAN], Lars-Eric Bjork [SWE], Sue Burns, Sue Ahrens [GBR], Douglas Butler [GBR], Jim Claffey [AUS], Jonathan Choate [USA], Marcelo Borba, Eric Smith [USA], Sharon Dugdale [USA], Alfino Flores [USA], Nurit Hadas, Alex Friedlander [ISR], M. Kathleen Heid [USA], David McArthur [USA], Kenneth Ruthven [GBR], Heinz Schumann [DEU], Kiyoshi Yokochi, Akihiko Miyake, Katsuhisa Kawamura, Shoichiro Machida, Shin Watanabe, Ikutaro Morikawa [JPN], Daniel Chazan [USA], Gregory D. Foley [USA], Brian Hudson [GBR], Ron S. Lewis [CAN], Victor Minachin [RUS], Bernadette Perham, Arnold Perham [USA], Hannah Perl [ISR], Geoffrey Roulet, Lynda Colgan [CAN], Judah Schwartz, Michal Yerushalmy [USA], Clifford Smith [ZAF], Dan Teague [USA]

REFERENCES

Yerushalmy, M. (1990). Using empirical information in geometry: students' and designers' expectations. *Journal of Computers in Mathematics and Science Teaching*, 9(3), 23-37.

Schumann, H. (1991). Interactive theorem finding through continuous variation of geometric configurations. *Journal of Computers in Mathematics and Science Teaching*, 10(3), 81-105.

MC4: MATHEMATICS UNDERGRADUATES / *ÉTUDIANTS ET ÉTUDIANTES DE NIVEAU UNIVERSITAIRE SE SPÉCIALISANT EN MATHÉMATIQUES*

Chief Organizer / *Responsable en chef* : Anthony Ralston [USA]

Since there is relatively little use of technology for advanced undergraduate courses, this strand dealt mainly with technology in lower division undergraduate mathematics.

The plenary session offered two talks, nicely balanced between discrete mathematics and calculus. The first, by Steven S. Skiena [USA], discussed "Combinatorica", a system for doing combinatorics and graph theory which is built on top of "Mathematica". The second, by Beverly West [USA], discussed new approaches to teaching differential equations using a dynamical systems approach. Both talks relied heavily on computer-based demonstrations.

The four workshops covered a diverse set of topics. Two focused on the use of technology in teaching calculus, Marvin L. Brubaker, L. Carl Leinbach [USA] used the symbolic mathematical system Derive, while Harley Flanders [USA] used Microcalc. In the third workshop, Frank Demana [USA] used pocket computers (really sophisticated graphing calculators) to illustrate the teaching of a variety of calculus and other topics. In the fourth, Ed Dubinsky [USA] focused on pedagogical issues in an age of technology, in particular on how computers could be used to help students construct abstract concepts. A feature of this workshop was a video presentation of the ideas presented in action.

In the paper sessions, presentations on the use of technology for teaching calculus predominated (Edmund A. Lamagna [USA], Tom Dick [USA], Bart Braden [USA], Phoebe Judson [USA], Lawrence Sher [USA], W.E. Boyce, Joseph Ecker [USA], David A. Smith, L. C. Moore [USA], Jack Bookman [USA], James Horley [USA], Bill Davis [USA]). This is where most of the action is with technology in the teaching of undergraduate mathematics. Some presenters used computer demonstrations; others relied on the safer overhead projector technology. The remaining papers covered diverse topics. Two (Herbert Möller [DEU], Paul Zorn [USA]) discussed the teaching of analysis and one each discussed geometry (Gene Klotz [USA]) and Fourier series (Maria Teresa Galizia, Maria Mascarello [ITA]). The remaining four papers focused on considerations broader than a particular area of mathematics. One discussed the general issue of the use of graphing calculators in undergraduate mathematics (Peter Jones, Monique Boers [AUS]). Another (Katherine Pedersen [USA]) discussed the problem of how to assess students' work when dealing with a technology-intensive environment. A third (Cliff E. Beevers [GBR], D. A. James [USA]) discussed

335

the factors that affect the success of computer-assisted learning in university mathematics and the fourth (Gerald J. Porter [USA]) considered the inter-active mathematics text project whose aim is to enhance student learning through texts which integrate computer usage with traditional text.

Technology was extensively used in this strand. Surprisingly – perhaps luckily – with the exception of a couple of quite minor glitches, all went well. The participants seemed to appreciate the opportunity to visualize dynamically the topics being discussed by the lecturers.

REFERENCES

Cornu, B., & Ralston, A. (1992). *The influence of computers and informatics on mathematics and its teaching.* Paris: UNESCO.

Hubbard, J., & West, B. (1991). *Differential equations: a dynamical approach.* New York: Springer-Verlag.

Skiena, S. (1990). *Implementing discrete mathematics: combinatorics and graph theory with Mathematica.* Menlo Park, CA: Addison-Wesley.

Wolfram, S. (1988). *Mathematica: a system for doing mathematics by computer.* Menlo Park, CA: Addison-Wesley.

Char, B. et al. (1991). *First leaves: a tutorial introduction to Maple V.* New York: Springer-Verlag.

MC5: TEACHER EDUCATION / *FORMATION DES ENSEIGNANTS ET ENSEIGNANTES*

Chief Organizer / *Responsable en chef* : Connie Widmer [USA]

The challenge which technology proposes for teacher educators was demonstrated by Jon Coupland [GBR] in the plenary session. Within just the last decade, software for the classroom has progressed from asking for the answer to 3 + 4 to producing graphical representations of complex equations and involving the student in relatively unrestrained interactive learning situations. Technology thus has a special role to play in making a wide range of learning opportunities available for students.

Workshop leaders: George W. Bright, Patricia Lamphere [USA], Thomas C. O'Brien [USA], Sheila Sconiers, Beverly Jones [USA], James Schultz [USA], Philippe Clarou [FRA], Warwick Evans [GBR], Alwyn Olivier [ZAF], David Pagni, Marea Channel, Zelda Gold, Elisabeth Javor, Vicki Newman, Shirley Roberts [USA]; and paper presenters: Sunday A. Ajose [USA], Janet Duffin [GBR], Peter Baptist [DEU], James R. Leitzel [USA], Sarah B. Berenson [USA], Doug Clarke [AUS], David A. Thomas [USA], Dominique Guin [FRA], William Higginson [CAN], Juanita Copley [USA], Janice L. Flake [USA], Evgenia Sendova [BGR], Larry L. Hatfield [USA], Judith E. Jacobs [USA], Charles Lovitt [AUS], Edwin McLintock

[USA], Hirokazu Okamori, Masahiko Suzuki, Tomoko Yanagimoto [JPN], Frank Steen [USA], Nurit Zehavi [ISR], Frans H. J. van Galen [NLD], Mary M. Hatfield [USA] further developed this theme in presentations centered on teaching and learning strategies appropriate to the use of calculators, computers, and interactive media. The presenters, from 11 countries, identified many similarities in the problems and possibilities faced in teacher education, including the need for modeling appropriate uses of technology for prospective and inservice teachers, for realigning the curriculum and assessment in light of the availability of technology, and for constantly being attuned to new possibilities presented by advances in technology. Workshops involved the participants in the use of computer software which allows students to experience and construct important mathematical ideas and processes and in the use of calculators as an instructional medium for graphical representations and as an aid in performing and analyzing computations. Paper presentations addressed these and other issues, including spatial visualization, approaches to learning geometry, software design, uses of hypercard and fractals in the classroom, and the need for preparing teachers to deal with ethical issues surrounding the use of technology.

REFERENCES

Leitzel, J.R. (Ed.) (1991). *A call for change: recommendations for the mathematical preparation of teachers of mathematics*. Washington: Mathematical Association of America.

Shuard, H. et al. (1991). *Calculators, children and mathematics*. Great Britain: Simon & Schuster.

Fey, J.T. (1989). Technology and mathematics education: a survey of recent developments and important problems. *Educational Studies in Mathematics, 20*(3), 237-272.

Fey, J.T. (1989). Teaching mathematics for tomorrow's World. *Educational Leadership, 7*(1), 18-22.

ABSTRACTS OF LECTURES

RÉSUMÉS DE CONFÉRENCES

CONTRIBUTION DE L'APPRENTISSAGE DE LA GÉOMÉTRIE À LA FORMATION SCIENTIFIQUE

Gérard Audibert

Institut Universitaire de Technologie, Nîmes [FRA]

Cette conférence a pour but de répondre à la question suivante : « La géométrie est-elle actuellement essentielle à la formation scientifique des élèves ayant entre 11 et 18 ans ? » Elle comprend quatre parties où sont analysés quatre aspects de la géométrie : la géométrie, discipline de service ; la géométrie, discipline proche des activités spontanées des élèves ; la géométrie et la formation scientifique ; la géométrie et le dessin.

1. La géométrie est une discipline de service dans la plupart des activités professionnelles ou scientifiques. Elle joue ce rôle par exemple pour la mesure des terrains et des solides, la géographie, la cristallographie, le bureau d'étude, la robotique. Nous constatons que la géométrie de l'espace et la structure euclidienne y sont des outils privilégiés.

2. La géométrie est propice à des activités spontanées des élèves à condition d'en valoriser trois aspects essentiels : l'activité matérielle, la recherche de problèmes, les démarches de pensée. Nous observons en particulier que l'activité la plus importante en géométrie pour nos élèves consiste à dessiner des objets, que les problèmes sont efficaces dans la mesure où les énoncés sont courts, qu'ils utilisent un symbolisme rudimentaire et un vocabulaire simple et enfin que la géométrie fait appel aux démarches de pensée les plus riches et les plus fondamentales parmi celles qui sont nécessaires à la formation scientifique.

3. L'enseignement de la géométrie utilise des processus intellectuels riches et variés contribuant à la formation scientifique des élèves. Nous reconnaissons ces processus à travers les mots clefs suivants : symbolisme, formalisme, abstraction, structures, raisonnement, propriétés, démonstration, images mentales, concepts. Nous en examinons quelques-uns à propos d'exemples comme l'exhaustivité, l'image mentale, ou les rapports entre déplacements et matrices.

4. Le dessin et plus généralement les graphismes jouent un rôle important dans les sciences ; de là à la représentation graphique, il n'y a quelquefois qu'un pas. Le dessin est aussi une des clefs de l'activité géométrique. Ainsi le dessin géométrique va contribuer de façon importante à la formation scientifique. Nous examinons quelques aspects formateurs du dessin : sa matérialité, son rôle dans la résolution de problèmes, le calcul et la formation des images mentales.

Le texte de la conférence développe des arguments justifiant l'affirmation suivante : la géométrie est actuellement essentielle à la formation scientifique des élèves ayant entre 11 et 18 ans.

DIAGNOSTIC TEACHING

Alan Bell

Shell Centre for Mathematical Education,
University of Nottingham [GBR]

The Diagnostic Teaching Project had its origin at the time when research was beginning to uncover some widely held and deeply rooted misconceptions in key areas of mathematics. Its aim has been to develop a way of teaching, in a broadly Piagetian framework, which makes use of the results and methods of this research, which is robust in classroom use, and which secures effective long-term learning.

The key aspects of this method are the identification and exposure of pupils' misconceptions and their resolution through "conflict-discussion". Conceptual diagnostic tests also play a part both in helping pupils to become aware of their misconceptions and enabling the teacher to observe progress.

The teaching materials for a particular topic begin with a rich situation, containing various items of information, with an invitation to consider what further information can be found out from what is given. Following this initial exploration there is a focus on a few particular questions which contain important conceptual obstacles. The questions are deliberately posed in such a way as to allow misconceptions to come to the surface, if they exist, and thus to create a conflict which can be discussed and resolved. The third phase of the teaching cycle consists of exercises with built-in feedback of correctness.

The lecture emphasized the implications of the work for the treatment of the various curriculum areas studied, which are: decimal numeration, operations in contextual problems involving quantities and decimal numbers (rates), directed numbers, fractions and geometric reflections.

A typical example of the teaching experiments, on geometric reflections, compared the learning of two parallel classes, one taught by the diagnostic method, the other using a well known series of individualized booklets. It showed the marked superiority for retention which has been the characteristic of all our experiments with the diagnostic method. Between pre- and post-tests both classes made good progress, but by the time of the delayed test, two months later, the booklets class had lost much of its previous gain, while the diagnostic group had retained almost all that they had learnt.

The final section of the lecture offers some general reflections, drawing on the experience of the project, on current teaching practice, and on which aspects most need changing.

References

Bell, A.W. (1993a). Principles for design of teaching. *Educational Studies in Mathematics, 25*(1), 5-34.

Bell, A.W. (1993b). Some experiments in diagnostic teaching. *Educational Studies in Mathematics, 24*(1), 115-137.

Swan, M.B. (1983). *Teaching decimal place value: a comparative study.* Nottingham: Shell Centre for Mathematical Education.

READING, WRITING, AND MATHEMATICS: RETHINKING THE "BASICS" AND THEIR RELATIONSHIP

Raffaella Borasi and Marjorie Siegel

University of Rochester, NY [USA]

Attempts to integrate reading and writing in mathematics instruction have been limited by the pervasiveness of the transmission model in schools. This paper argues that conceptualizing knowledge, teaching, and learning as the construction of meaning through a process of *inquiry*, rather than as the transfer of discrete facts and techniques from expert to novice, can help educators rethink the basics – reading, writing, and mathematics – and their relationship. This shift from the transmission model to the inquiry model reflects the new directions set by recent calls for reform in mathematics education, as well as the new theories of reading and writing as meaning-making processes developed in the field of language education. As a result, new ways for using reading and writing to support mathematics learning in inquiry-oriented classrooms can be envisioned.

Recent research on "writing to learn mathematics" and "reading to learn mathematics" suggest that a wide range of texts as well as reading and writing activities could be employed in mathematics instruction. However, it is not only *what* students read and write but *how* and *why* they do so, that most differentiates the use of reading and writing in an inquiry classroom from the traditional view of the basics. In the context of inquiry, reading and writing are always purposeful and generative processes that help learners construct and reflect on their understanding with the support of peers. In this way, reading, writing, and talking become intertwined with mathematical activities as students move through a specific inquiry, so as to support the process of exploring the domain investigated, formulating questions, learning necessary concepts and techniques, carrying out the research, reflecting on the product and process of inquiry, communicating the results of the inquiry, and setting new directions for future inquiry. At the same time, creating a learning environment that supports inquiry in a mathematics classroom will require students to come to value the new assumptions of knowledge, learning, and teaching associated with doing inquiry. Reading and writing can contribute to the creation of such an environment by helping students make explicit their beliefs about mathematics, support classroom discussion of new social norms, and implicitly establish new patterns of classroom discourse which give students' voices a central place in the curriculum. In summary, reading and writing become integral to mathematics teaching and learning when conceptualized as inquiry and not simply a technical addition to the curriculum.

TEACHERS USING VIDEOTAPES AS REFERENCE POINTS TO ASSESS THEIR STUDENTS

John L. Clark

Toronto Board of Education [CAN]

In 1987, the Toronto Board of Education mandated the development of standards of student achievement to be used by teachers in assessing students and reporting their progress to parents. These standards are now known as *Benchmarks*. Prior to 1987, the Board did not have a system-wide testing program. Each school was responsible for the development of its own assessing and reporting procedures in cooperation with its parent community.

The *Benchmarks* are based on interviews of a representative sample of students at ages 8, 11, and 13. Each student was required to perform a wide variety of tasks in arithmetic, measurement, and geometry. Problem solving, the use of manipulative materials, and student explanations were integrated throughout the tasks. A majority of the students' performances were videotaped for further analysis and the performances were rated using holistic scoring. The results of the interviews have been published in the form of three libraries called *Benchmark Libraries* consisting of videotaped and printed information about student learning and achievement at each of the three age levels.

The plan for implementating *Benchmarks* is long-term, school-based, and involves teachers working collaboratively. Teachers are expected to shape the use of the *Benchmarks* and gradually integrate them into their daily practices. Unlike traditional testing programs, the use of *Benchmarks* is under the control of the teachers and principal of each school. The procedures for reporting students' progress to parents using *Benchmarks* will be developed by the local school in consultation with its parent community and supported by centrally developed guidelines.

Difficulties encountered in implementation have been teachers' resistance to change, traditions of teachers working in isolation, and beliefs about assessment. The strengths demonstrated by the Benchmark Program are: the enhancement of teachers' assessment skills, the use of *Benchmarks* by teachers to evaluate their own classroom programs, greater collaborative work among teachers, the increased involvement of parents, better communication from schools to parents about the goals of the mathematics curriculum, broader and more systematic reporting of students' progress to parents, and more equitable forms of assessment.

References

Clark, J. L. (1992). The Toronto Board of Education's benchmarks in mathematics. *The Arithmetic Teacher: Focus issue. 39* (6), 51-55.

Larter, S. (1991). *Benchmarks: The development of a new approach to student evaluation.* Toronto: Board of Education.

THE CHALLENGE OF SECONDARY SCHOOL MATHEMATICS

David Clarke

Australian Catholic University (Victoria) – Christ Campus
Oakleigh [AUS]

An intensive longitudinal study of a number of children, over a period which included transition from primary to secondary school, provided insight into the structure of mathematical behavior and the process whereby new experiences, new instructional approaches, and new social environments sustain, facilitate or restrict an individual's learning of mathematics.

A structure has been suggested for student mathematical behavior (Clarke, 1985). If the differences in students' mathematical behaviors are to be explained, such explanations must involve the realization of the essential individuality of the learning process and recognition of the complexity of the web of behaviors being studied (Clarke, 1992).

Four factors were identified as central to the challenge of secondary mathematics. These were:

- conceptions of mathematical competence;
- the mathematics classroom as social context;
- the individuality of mathematical behaviour;
- the experience of transition as discontinuity.

A general theory of transition is proposed, which takes its structure from three key aspects of the transition process: Discontinuity, Challenge and Adjustment.

The most significant finding of this study – and its most emphatic statement concerning the commencement of secondary school mathematics – is that the social and academic adjustments required by transition are inextricably linked and, in many ways, mirror each other. Attempts to facilitate student development must acknowledge this (Clarke, 1987).

References

Clarke, D.J. (1985). The Impact of secondary schooling and secondary mathematics on student mathematical behaviour. *Educational Studies in Mathematics 16*(3), 231 - 251.

Clarke, D.J. (1987). The interactive monitoring of children's learning of mathematics. *For the Learning of Mathematics, 7*(1), 2 - 6.

Clarke, D.J. (1992). *Finding structure in diversity: The study of mathematical behavior.* Paper presented to the 1992 Research Pre-session of the National Council of Teachers of Mathematics Annual Conference, Nashville, USA, April 30 - 31, 1992.

MATHEMATICIANS AND MATHEMATICAL EDUCATION IN ANCIENT MAYA SOCIETY

Michael P. Closs

University of Ottawa [CAN]

The Maya peoples of Southern Mexico and Central America have a long history. Their earliest identified village is dated around 1000 B.C. and their latest independent kingdom was not subdued until A.D. 1697. Maya civilization flourished from around A.D. 300 to 900, an era known as the Classic Maya period. This is the time when many of the ancient Maya cities containing stone pyramids, temples, and palace complexes were built. Perhaps the most exciting feature of Maya civilization was their system of hieroglyphic writing, completely unrelated to developments in the Old World. During the Classic period, Maya rulers regularly erected stone monuments carved with inscriptions celebrating the glories of their reigns. Other ancient texts have been found on ceramic vessels, numbering in the thousands, and in books, of which only four have survived. All these ancient texts were prepared by scribes who required training and education in their profession. In particular, there was a need for some mathematics education. It is of interest to examine the indigenous traditions in this area.

From early ethnohistoric reports and surviving artifacts, we can obtain an outline of the school curriculum followed by the Maya scribes. We are also able to know something of their school system and its position in Maya society.

Scenes of scribal activity occur in one of the pre-Columbian Maya codices. It is clear from these scenes that mathematical activity was regarded as something distinctive. There are also several portrayals of scribes on Classic Maya pottery, most dating from around A.D. 750. This material shows that mathematical specialists were differentiated from ordinary scribes. In addition, the pre-Conquest ethnohistoric data, as well as the Classic period pictorial data on the vases, indicate that there were scribe

347

lords, scholars who presided over the educational establishment in positions of power and prestige.

There are at least two classroom scenes on ancient ceramic vessels. One of these shows a mathematics lecture. Another interesting scene illustrates mathematicians at work on astronomical texts. Finally, there is a unique self-portrait of a female mathematician whose name and title are recorded in hieroglyphics.

There is reason to believe that an ancient Maya school complex has been discovered in recent archaeological excavations at the ancient Maya site of Copán in Honduras. During these same excavations, the tombs of two scribes have been uncovered.

Reference

Closs, M. P. (1986). The mathematical notation of the ancient Maya. *Native American Mathematics* (edited by Michael P. Closs), 291-369. Austin: University of Texas Press.

THE SPIRAL OF THEODORUS

Philip J. Davis

Brown University, Providence, RI [USA]

The logo of ICME–7 (which is an exploded version of a spiral I shall call the Spiral of Theodorus) was discussed historically, methodologically, and in the light of a certain non-linear system of difference equations which serves to generalize it. A variety of solutions of the basic matrix difference equation, both discrete and continuous, were shown and commented on. The system is wide open both for computer explorations as well as for theoretical developments.

The material in this talk is developed in considerable depth in the book:

Philip J. Davis, *Spirals: from Theodorus to chaos,* A.K. Peters, Ltd., 281 Linden St., Wellesley, MA 02181, USA, 1993.

This book has theoretical contributions by Walter Gautschi, Purdue University and Arieh Iserles, Cambridge University, UK.

FERMAT, GOLDBACH, WARING

Jean-Marc Deshouillers

Université de Bordeaux [FRA]

Les grands problèmes mathématiques ont en commun d'être des moteurs pour la recherche, ainsi que des instruments de mesure des progrès accomplis. En outre, la plupart d'entre eux ont des énoncés facilement compréhensibles. Le but de la conférence était de présenter les résultats récents concernant les problèmes de Fermat, Goldbach et Waring en expliquant comment ils s'insèrent dans la recherche mathématique contemporaine. (La compréhension de la quasi-totalité de l'exposé ne requiert pas de connaissances mathématiques autres que celles enseignées dans les lycées et collèges.)

LES MATHÉMATIQUES COMME REFLET DE LA CULTURE D'UNE ÉPOQUE

Jean Dhombres

Université de Nantes [FRA]

C'est précisément parce que les mathématiques constituent une composante fondamentale de la culture, dans ses modes d'expression, dans ses ressorts cachés et dans ses représentations, que leur enseignement soulève tant d'intérêt, tant de passion, mais aussi tant de difficultés. Culture et non technique puisque, tout comme la musique, la mathématique n'est pas réductible à un solfège.

Au lieu de chercher l'expression des mathématiques dans la culture générale – leur rôle donc le façonnage d'un *habitus* de pensée et de vivre – c'est dans leur cœur même que je propose de lire des modes culturels d'une époque, retournant ainsi le questionnement traditionnel et choisissant le monde baroque des XVIe et XVIIe siècles pour ne pas parler en général. Mais en associant mathématique et baroque, en visant une époque bien déterminée de l'histoire, je vise aussi et simultanément une science. Et j'associe cette science à l'histoire d'une façon particulière puisque, l'adjectif baroque annonçant, je veux évoquer un style. Dans ma ligne de mire, il y donc une forme, des résultats, des raisonnements, décrire des objets, faire du nouveau ou refaire de l'ancien dans l'ordre mathématique.

J'ai choisi deux thèmes précis, la formule de sommation d'une série géométrique qui court de Viète à Leibniz en passant par Torricelli, Fermat et Grégoire de Saint-Vincent à propos duquel je veux parler plus longuement, et la quadrature de l'hyperbole. Ma démarche relève d'une quête épisté-mologique sur les procédures et les imaginations par lesquelles fut, une fois, posé puis approprié ce qui est devenu un patrimoine scientifique, patrimoine nécessairement banalisé et réduit par la pratique scolaire. C'est en cela, je l'espère, que ma démarche peut entrer dans le champ d'investigation du didacticien des mathématiques. L'enseignant évoque-t-il suffisament l'insertion des formes de pensée au sein d'une culture qui n'est plus la nôtre?

De la géométrie algébrique dont il va être question, en un sens bien différent de celui aujourd'hui adopté, j'entends faire une unité stylistique, c'est-à-dire que je me refuse à la réduire à ces deux composantes, géométrie et algèbre, car un ou des hommes incarnés dans l'histoire la pensèrent de cette façon unitaire. Le « comment » de l'origine de la géométrie algébrique n'est donc nullement la géométrie algébrique toute prête, telle qu'on l'enseigne et la pratique aujourd'hui. Ce « comment » est l'atteinte d'une conscience initiale qui fut en même temps une intuition d'essence et détermina un horizon.

IMAGERIE ET RAISONNEMENT DANS L'APPRENTISSAGE ET LA RECHERCHE MATHÉMATIQUE

Tommy Dreyfus

Center for Technological Education, Holon [ISR]

Beaucoup de situations, en mathématiques, peuvent être abordées d'une façon algébrique, visuelle ou verbale. Bien que les mathématiciens utilisent souvent des raisonnements visuels et bien que le rôle de l'imagerie dans le raisonnement mathématique se soit accru considérablement durant les dernières années, nos étudiants, en général, se tournent très vite vers des formulations algébriques. Cette algébrisation (trop) rapide a pour conséquence une perte d'occasions de trouver des solutions, d'apprécier le côté esthétique des mathématiques et de comprendre en profondeur.

Cette tendance à l'algébrisation est due à l'éducation que l'on reçoit et à celle que l'on donne. Cette éducation supprime la visualisation, en lui accordant peu de valeur en mathématiques. Et ceci, malgré le fait que la plupart des didacticiens lui donnent une importance considérable dans les processus d'apprentissage, malgré le grand nombre d'illustrations que l'on trouve dans les livres d'enseignement, et malgré l'existence de recherches de haut niveau sur la visualisation. Les raisons principales en sont les suivantes :

- en général, l'activité visuelle dans l'enseignement est considérée et présentée comme auxiliaire et non pas comme mathématiquement valable ;

- le statut du raisonnement visuel, en mathématiques et dans l'enseignement des mathématiques, est de beaucoup inférieur à celui du raisonnement algébrique.

Pour remédier à cette situation, nous pouvons agir à différents niveaux. En tant que mathématiciens, nous devons renforcer le statut du raisonnement visuel ; nous devons créer des arguments visuels, apprendre à juger de leur validité et leur accorder la même valeur que nous accordons aux arguments verbaux et algébriques.

En tant qu'enseignants, nous devons employer le raisonnement visuel fréquemment, non seulement dans la solution de problèmes mais aussi à des moments cruciaux dans les démonstrations ; nous devons donner à nos étudiants beaucoup d'occasions de résoudre des problèmes de manière visuelle et de discuter de la validité de leurs arguments visuels ; enfin, nous devons leur donner de bonnes notes pour des solutions visuelles correctes.

En tant que chercheurs en didactique des mathématiques, nous devons considérablement élargir notre compréhension des processus cognitifs et mathématiques liés au raisonnement visuel ; nous devons examiner la validité mathématique et la validité didactique des diverses représentations visuelles de concepts et de processus de raisonnement.

Référence

Dreyfus, T. (1991). On the status of visual reasoning in mathematics and mathematics education. In F. Furinghetti (Ed.), *Proceedings of the Fifteenth conference of the International al Group for the Psychology of Mathematics Education* (Vol. I, pp. 33-48). Assisi, Italy.

FROM SHARING TO FRACTIONS

Joaquin Giménez

Universidad Rovira y Virgili, Barcelona [ESP]

This lecture presented many examples designed to facilitate the shift from discrete to continuous quantities, including a few examples suggested by current events like the 1992 Olympic Games in Barcelona and the anniversary of the first encounter between Europe and America. The dialectical role that contexts like sport and the knowledge of native Americans can play in primary education was also discussed.

HANS FREUDENTHAL: WORKING ON MATHEMATICS EDUCATION

*Fred Goffree **

National Institute for Curriculum Development, Enschede [NLD]

In contributing to mathematics education there are perhaps three ways to enter: from a general interest in education; from examining and speculating about the specific features of teaching and learning mathematics; and from an interest in the development of an improved mathematical education. There is enough to work on here to fill full-time jobs for many people, but Hans Freudenthal made substantial contributions apparently "on the side". It is not easy to put into words what he achieved, and the full extent of his work will probably never be known. As a close colleague for twenty years, I was aware of the difficulties I would encounter in attempting to do justice to the work of this remarkable man.

I made a selection of articles, papers, newspaper cuttings, notes, and books as a basis for this paper. In the first part I sketched Freudenthal's activity chronologically from the end of the Second World War to the early

---

* Lecture delivered by Huub Jansen [NLD]

seventies. Here we can discern in their initial forms some of the "building blocks" that Freudenthal would use to construct a theory "of and for" mathematics education: viz. the structure of the subject matter, the problem of thinking, mathematics as an activity, richness of context, mathematizing, the discontinuities of learning processes, raising levels of achievement, the value of reflection.

In the following part, chronology had to be set aside because Freudenthal was involved in so many fields on so many different levels. He approached research, in education and in mathematics education. He criticized general educational research with its statistical methods and lack of interest in individuals. He began to participate personally in research if it was close to children in classrooms and from a perspective of development.

Two core themes from his work were looked at in detail: *learning mathematics,* and *developing mathematics education.* Didactical concepts from an earlier period were completed and developed into key notions of a *science of mathematics instruction.* His last book dealt with a variety of "conceptual tools": the phenomenological approach, mathematization in all its forms, context, (re)inventing under guidance, levels of learning processes, paradigms of learning, reflection, insight, anticipated learning and learning by reflection, entwining learning strands, mathematical attitude. And many more besides.

TEACHING MATHEMATICS AND PROBLEM SOLVING TO DEAF AND HARD OF HEARING STUDENTS

Harvey Goodstein

Gallaudet University, Washington, DC [USA]

Only recently has the approach to teaching deaf students using ASL (American Sign Language) as "first language" and English as "second language" gained momentum. After years of learning "mathematics" with an emphasis on rote memory, and computation with limited experience in mental computation, reasoning, and measurement, deaf students generally have extreme difficulties in solving verbal and non-verbal problems at all levels, even through high school and college. There were three parts to this presentation. First, examples of such learning difficulties were presented, based on observations made at schools and "mainstreamed" programs serving deaf students, nationally. Second, some explanations for difficulties in teaching and learning mathematics and problem solving, relative to deaf students, were presented. Here, one such explanation is related to communication: nearly 90 percent of deaf students have hearing parents most of whom have had no previous exposure to deafness. Not because of deafness *per se,* but because of restrictive communication at home, the great majority of deaf students enter school with poor skills in ASL and English. Not many teachers are fluent in ASL; thus the communication environments are far from ideal even in schools and programs serving deaf students. Another explanation is related to teachers' background and expectations: the majority of teachers of deaf students at the elementary through secondary levels have weak mathematics background, poor problem solving skills, high math anxiety, and poor attitude toward mathematics. As a group, they find it most convenient to teach with emphasis on rote memory and computation instead of teaching for understanding and mastery of concepts involved. The third part dealt with the suggested learning/teaching strategies within the desired bilingual/bicultural (or multilingual/multicultural) learning environment involving ASL and English. Arguably, before deaf students can even communicate and reason mathematically in a precise or formal fashion (in English), they have to first overcome the three significant obstacles, sequentially if not concurrently: 1) learning how to communicate naturally via ASL; 2) learning and understanding the mathematics concepts and properties involved, verbally and manipulatively; and 3) reading and writing about these concepts and properties while learning English as a second language. Writing journals or "learning logs" is helpful in inducing students to express aloud their mental images of certain mathematical concepts or relations. These learning and teaching strategies have their parallels in bilingual/bicultural programs designed for other learners of English as a second language.

SOME TRENDS IN COMBINATORICS

Ronald L. Graham

Bell Laboratories, Murray Hill, NJ [USA]

The "probabilistic method" is a powerful technique pioneered by Paul Erdös used for proving the existence of various "nice" objects in combinatorics, graph theory, number theory, geometry, etc. Essentially, one defines an appropriate probability measure on the space of objects under study, and then shows that the set of desired objects has positive measure, and so, must exist. However, the method gives no information as to how such objects might actually be constructed.

Recently, significant progress has been made in addressing this fundamental issue. A variety of techniques have been introduced for giving specific constructions for certain classes of objects (e.g. graphs) which had previously only been known to exist by non-constructive methods.

In addition, it has been discovered that many of the random-like properties of graphs (and other structures as well) are inextricably linked to one another, so that, in fact, if a family of graphs possesses any of the "quasi-random" properties then it must necessarily possess all of them. Since it is typically easy to verify that certain of these quasi-random properties hold, this gives an effective way for constructing and analyzing explicit graphs that behave in many ways like random graphs.

ORIGIN AND EVOLUTION OF MATHEMATICAL THEORIES: IMPLICATIONS FOR MATHEMATICAL EDUCATION

Miguel de Guzmán

Universidad Complutense, Madrid [ESP]

The main problem is: When trying to introduce others to a concrete subject, what is the attitude one should foster? My main contention is that the crucial inspirations and insights in the work in a particular field come very often from familiarity with and deep knowledge of the evolution of the theory from its beginning, and of the thinking style in that particular area. This is acquired by learning about its motivations, the global circumstances (historical, social, personal) of its origin, the right ways of asking questions in that field, etc.

A knowledge of the history of mathematics and of the particular subject can offer us:

- a human vision of science and of mathematics;
- a frame in which all the elements appear in their right places;
- a dynamic vision of the evolution of mathematics;

- a view of the intertwining of mathematical thought and culture in human society;

- a more profound technical comprehension;

- a sense of the peculiar life of each mathematical theory.

The second part of the paper was devoted to substantiating these affirmations by exploring a case study, the field relative to the differentiation of integrals, from which many interesting lessons can be learned.

LE CALCUL INFINITÉSIMAL

Bernard R. Hodgson

Université Laval, Québec [CAN]

Les *infinitésimaux* ont connu un sort variable au fil des âges, tantôt utilisés avec profit par un Archimède, un Leibniz ou un Euler en raison des simplifications conceptuelles et techniques qu'ils introduisent, tantôt bannis par un Berkeley ou un Russell parce que non rigoureux, voire incohérents. Il y a un peu plus de trente ans, Abraham Robinson a découvert comment certains outils de la logique mathématique permettent de construire un corps de nombres *hyperréels* grâce auquel le calcul différentiel et intégral peut être développé de façon rigoureuse dans un contexte infinitésimal : cette légitimation *a posteriori* permet au mathématicien d'aujourd'hui de revenir en toute sérénité aux méthodes si fécondes faisant intervenir explicitement l'infiniment grand et l'infiniment petit.

Quoique fructueuses dans leurs applications en recherche, les méthodes de l'analyse non standard n'ont peut-être pas eu, sur le plan pédagogique, l'impact que certains prévoyaient. Diverses expériences sont cependant en cours actuellement, visant à renouveler l'enseignement de base en analyse par l'approche infinitésimale. Les fondements de ce *calcul infinitésimal* moderne reposent sur une introduction axiomatique de nombres infiniment petits (et infiniment grands), de façon à en permettre la présentation à un stade élémentaire en évitant les difficultés techniques reliées à une construction formelle (modèles non standard, ultraproduits). Il convient de distinguer ici deux variantes de ce calcul infinitésimal.

Dans l'approche de Keisler (*Elementary Calculus : An Infinitesimal Approach*), les hyperréels sont introduits, à l'aide de quelques axiomes appropriés, en tant qu'extension du corps des réels. Cette vision est très près du modèle de Robinson et a été utilisée fructueusement depuis plus de quinze ans dans divers contextes pédagogiques pour un enseignement complet du calcul. Une approche plus récente repose sur l'axiomatique IST (*Internal Set Theory*) de Nelson, qui diffère de la précédente par la présence, au sein même des ensembles de nombres habituels (**N**, **R**), de nombres « idéaux » non distinguables, avant IST, des nombres « standard ». Cette dernière approche fait actuellement l'objet d'une activité importante, en particulier en France, et suscite une littérature abondante. Elle fournit un cadre propice pour l'élaboration d'une théorie de différenciation des *ordres de grandeur*.

Diverses raisons peuvent être avancées pour tenter d'expliquer l'impact pédagogique apparemment restreint du calcul infinitésimal jusqu'ici (pré-occupations informatiques, inertie, obstacles philosophiques ou didactiques). Mais il semble clair que l'enseignement de l'analyse change, et certains des points de vue véhiculés dans une approche infinitésimale y sont sans doute pour quelque chose.

COMPUTER-BASED MICROWORLDS: A RADICAL VISION OR A TROJAN MOUSE?

Celia Hoyles

University of London [GBR]

In the talk I discussed the following questions:

- What is the potential of computer-based microworlds for mathematics learning?

- Why are mathematics educators interested in the design and development of microworlds?

- Is there a mismatch between theory and practice, between aspiration and implementation, and if so why?

When we started working in Logo mathematics in the early 80s, we held as our goal the evolution of a mathematical culture, a change in the relationship between teachers, pupils and mathematics. I discussed how the meaning of the word "microworld" has changed and argued that it made best sense to view a microworld as a *process* rather than an object: microworld activity is characterized by active involvement of students within motivated and motivating project work whose goals around a knowledge domain had been negotiated with the teacher. Through microworld interactions, students generate situated or mediated abstractions of a mathematical nature.

It is clear that the impact of computers on school life has not matched the original vision. Why has the Trojan horse turned into a Trojan mouse? We need to recognize that school activity exists in a culture of its own where learning has to coexist alongside other agendas: management, accountability, selection, and the "curriculum". I identified four processes by which any innovation is transformed as it moves into schools – "pedagogizing", compartmentalizing, incorporating, and neutralizing – and I discussed "incorporating" in some detail (see Chevallard, 1985).

Finally, I noted that many developments in the USA have tried to "preserve" innovation from "misuse" by teachers by producing "curriculum packages" which "deliver" the curriculum. These metaphors carry a clear message: a top-down transmission model of learning, which attempts to bypass teachers and keep children on well-defined tracks. In contrast, at the *level of software/curriculum design,* we need more expressive computational media tuned for the development of mathematical knowledge; more carefully designed and creative activities with rich avenues to explore; and more precise analyses of pedagogy and the way the computer structures, and is structured by, the classroom culture. At the *level of the teacher,* we need to provide opportunities for them to express their own mathematical ideas with software; to support attendance at *substantial* inservice courses which maintain a mathematical rather than a technical focus, and to make available ample hardware and easy access to technical and educational assistance.

References

Chevallard, Y. (1985). *La transposition didactique du savoir savant au savoir enseigné.* Grenoble: La Pensée Sauvage.

Hoyles, C., & Noss, R. (Eds.) (1992). *Learning Mathematics and Logo.* Cambridge, MA.: MIT Press.

DIFFERENT WAYS OF KNOWING: CONTRASTING STYLES OF ARGUMENT IN INDIAN AND WESTERN MATHEMATICAL TRADITIONS

George Gheverghese Joseph

University of Manchester [GBR]

A generally accepted view among historians of mathematics is that Indian mathematics was algebraic in inclination, empirical in practice and lacking in the notion of proof, in contrast to Greek mathematics which was geometric, anti-empirical, and insistent on rigorous proof. At a deeper level, what is often absent from a discussion of the contrasting mathematical traditions is an awareness of more fundamental differences in cognitive structures and in methodological conceptions regarding the nature and ways of establishing mathematical truths. By highlighting the central role of a "non-idealized" geometry in the study of altar construction in ancient India, and the role of *upapattis* (or demonstrations) associated with the Pythagorean theorem, found in commentaries on the work of the Indian mathematician/ astronomer Bhaskaracharya (b. AD 1114), this lecture aimed to bring into a sharper focus the general discussion of different styles of mathematical arguments and their possible relevance for the classroom. This paper was an extension of the discussion on the methodology of Indian mathematics contained in my book *The crest of the peacock; non-European roots of mathematics* (Penguin Books, London, 1992).

MATHEMATICS EDUCATION IN THE GLOBAL VILLAGE: THE WEDGE AND THE FILTER

Murad Jurdak

American University of Beirut [LBN]

The nineties promise to be the decade of transition to the information age. Today's technology of communication and the linkage of countries in one global economy make it necessary and desirable for all nations to make the transition together. However, this transition is unlikely to be even across industrialized and developing countries because of social, economic, and cultural differences.

More than any other school area, mathematics is at the forefront of this transition. The mathematical literacy of the information-based society is bound to be higher in standard, wider in scope, and qualitatively different from the existing one. The focus of the information-age mathematical literacy will be the development of such critical abilities as problem solving, communication in mathematics, higher-order reasoning skills, and the attitude to continue to learn new and different mathematics.

More than any time before, disparities in the 1990s in mathematics education between industrialized and developing countries are not a matter of degree but also of kind. In the first half of the twentieth century, the colonial powers and the countries under their patronage shared the same kind of mathematics education including curricula, textbooks, teaching methods, and even language of instruction. With the advance of "modern mathematics", many of the newly independent countries adapted mathematics programs imported from developed countries. The nineties are witnessing a sharp divergence in mathematics education. Whereas industrialized countries are contemplating and implementing deep changes in all aspects of mathematics education to achieve a qualitatively different mathematics literacy, developing countries cannot afford the human and material resources to make such changes.

Bridging the gap between the mathematical literacy of the information age and the traditional mathematical literacy in the developing countries does not seem to be easily attainable in the near future because of economic, social, and cultural constraints and barriers. The developing countries are forced to put on hold quality-improvement interventions of the kind required for attaining the information-age mathematical literacy because they have to cope with problems of quantitative growth.

Mathematics education will act as a wedge sustaining and reinforcing the division among countries along social, economic and cultural lines, and excluding whole communities from participating in the global economy. The neutral, indigenous, or the technological transfer approaches thus far have not provided an adequate response to this problem. International cooperation is needed to formulate and support internationally acceptable guidelines for sustainable development in mathematics education to empower all nations to cope with the demands of the information-age mathematical literacy.

BONUSES FROM UNDERSTANDING
MATHEMATICAL UNDERSTANDING

Thomas E. Kieren

University of Alberta, Edmonton [CAN]

There have been many recent studies of mathematical understanding. The bonus arising from such understandings has been a vocabulary for differentiating various kinds of understanding behavior, providing teachers and students with tools to discuss mathematical understanding. Some studies have linked understanding to the epistemological obstacles faced by learners, leading to an analysis of concepts in terms of change-points in the knower's understanding.

Susan Pirie and I observe the growth of mathematical understanding as a continuing, dynamic, multi-levelled, non-monotonic process. Such growth, for the observer, starts with a person's primitive knowing. Growth is played out over three levels or modes of informal activity, and three levels or modes of formal activity. At the heart of the former are the making, changing, and using of images. At the heart of the latter are developing, using, and generalizing about formal procedures. To be said to be showing understanding at any level, a person must both be able to act and reflectively express such action. One key mechanism in the growth of mathematical understanding is "folding back". A person at any level faced with a difficulty can fold back to a less sophisticated, less formal, understanding activity. But a person folding back is now engaged in such activity while informed by more sophisticated knowledge. Thus more formal mathematical understanding activity, unless it is a disjoint understanding, necessarily enfolds and unfolds from local image-based understanding.

What are the bonuses from such an understanding of mathematical understanding? We believe that it provides a teacher or a researcher with a new way of seeing mathematical activity. First, one can more fully observe, appreciate, and foster the varied understanding activities of students. One can appreciate both the value of, the potential sources of, and the necessary changes in a student's image of a mathematical idea. And one can more adequately trace and understand how a student's informal mathematical activity becomes formal. One can see growth in understanding not simply as indicated by a difference in test performance, but as a continuing pathway in a space of mathematical experience. From such a view, mathematical understanding is not seen as the acquisition of a few students, but as an ongoing process, within an environment, engaged in by all students.

References

Davis, R.B. (1992). "Understanding" understanding. *Journal of Mathematical Behavior, 11*(3), 225-241.

Pirie, S.E.B, & Kieren, T. (1992). Watching Sandy's understanding grow. *Journal of Mathematical Behavior, 11*(3), 243-257.

THE COLLABORATIVE CONSTRUCTION OF THE MATHEMATICS CURRICULUM USING TEACHER-CONSTRUCTED PROBLEMS

Magdalene Lampert

Michigan State University, East Lansing, MI [USA]

A mathematics curriculum can be a list of topics to be taught in logical order or a web of connected ideas that emerges from students' work on problems. The latter view is one that is embraced by current reforms, and this paper is a study of what it might mean to *teach* from this perspective. Problems can be constructed by the teacher improvisationally to both respond to students ways of thinking and take them into important mathematical territory. In this approach, curriculum is collaboratively constructed in interactions between teacher and students in the context of student work on teacher-constructed problems. Elements of the classroom ecology can be deliberately designed to enable both teacher and students to influence what is "covered".

We have been working on such designs in our fifth grade classroom and studying the results of these efforts. In the research reported here, one element of this design that is examined is the routine of students working problems, doing mathematical "experiments", and writing their reasoning in bound notebooks. Contents of these notebooks are shared among students and they are collected, read and commented on by the teacher. Individual students' paths through a particular mathematical terrain can be traced by analyzing the written records of their ways of thinking about problems and strategies for solving them. And teaching can be understood as a response to these student-constructed approaches. A second element of lesson design that is intended to support the collaborative construction of curriculum are teacher-led class discussion of students' conjectures about problem solving strategies and solutions. In examining the content of these discussions, it can be seen that the topic for consideration changes according to the ways in which students defend their conjectures and challenge others.

In order to examine what mathematics students were working on, we focused on a six-day period in a unit that was representative of work across the school year. We studied eight students who represented a range of ability and styles of work. Written work and spoken exchanges with teacher and other students were analyzed for content. A wide range of topics was found, and the interconnections among these topics in how they were handled was particularly striking. The research team also learned about the extent to which their own definitions of what work is associated with what topic is socially constructed and heavily dependent on one's mathematical and pedagogical experiences.

MATHEMATICS AND THE WORLD AROUND US

Ronald Lancaster

St. Mildred's–Lightbourn School, Oakville, ON [CAN]

A number of unique and unusual problems for use in school class-rooms were presented, with the topics ranging from highway traffic to the promotional strategies used by cereal companies to increase sales.

CURRICULUM CHANGE:
AN AMERICAN-DUTCH PERSPECTIVE

Jan de Lange

Freudenthal Instituut, Utrecht [NLD]

The Netherlands has experienced dramatic changes in mathematics education in the past decade. "Real world" mathematics curricula have been introduced nationwide both at primary and secondary levels. The changes are considered to have been successful, but associated problems include the need to change assessment procedures as well as teachers' attitudes. Now the Freudenthal Institute is collaborating with the University of Wisconsin at Madison in a Middle School Curriculum Project. Will "real world" mathematics succeed in the very different boundary conditions of the USA?

TRAINING TEACHERS OR EDUCATING
PROFESSIONALS? WHAT ARE THE ISSUES
AND HOW ARE THEY BEING RESOLVED?

Glenda Lappan

Michigan State University, East Lansing, MI [USA]

There are many persistent obstacles to making change in the teaching and learning of mathematics. In order to examine preservice teacher education programs and professional development programs for experienced teachers for the likelihood that they can help teachers make change, we need to build a framework of what teachers need to know and be able to do. In this paper we report such a framework put forward by the National Council of Teachers of Mathematics in the *Professional Standards for Teaching Mathematics* (PSTM). The writers of the PSTM identified four aspects of teaching that were judged to be so central to good teaching that they could be used to craft a framework, in the form of a set of standards, about what teachers need to know and be able to do. These four aspects of decision-making are choosing worthwhile mathematical tasks, orchestrating classroom discourse, creating an environment for learning, and analyzing teaching and learning.

The question for mathematics teacher educators that such a framework raises is "What do teachers need to know and be able to do to make pedagogically defensible decisions about each of the four aspects of the framework?" Knowledge of at least three kinds seems critical for teachers – knowledge of mathematics, knowledge of students, and knowledge of the pedagogy of mathematics. Yet, preservice and experienced teachers beliefs about each of these – mathematics, students, and teaching – is a significant obstacle to change. Interventions that hold promise in providing environments where teachers, whether preservice or inservice, examine their beliefs and consider alternatives include projects using hypermedia to provide powerful images of teaching, projects that use action research and actual classroom observation to promote reflection, and projects developing materials to help integrate mathematics and pedagogy in explicit ways.

The most promising interventions for helping teachers make changes in their instruction share three important characteristics: (1) They build on teachers' existing beliefs and knowledge; (2) They offer support for teachers that takes into account the realities of teachers' school situations; (3) They offer instruction and support that goes beyond a one-day or even one-week workshop, for example, an intensive summer experience with follow-up support during the year.

Note

This paper was written in collaboration with Sarah Theule-Lubienski.

Reference

National Council of Teachers of Mathematics. (1991). *Professional standards for teaching mathematics.* Reston, VA: NCTM

LE MIROIR INTÉRIEUR : UNE GENÈSE
DE L'IDÉE DE DISTANCE

Fernand Lemay

Université Laval, Québec [CAN]

Un « ingrédient » primordial de la géométrie paraît être la distance, notion que les dictionnaires usuels n'éclairent pas facilement et que les descriptions plus formelles asservissent aussitôt aux nombres réels.

Plutôt que de réclamer une définition stérile, on préférera relever certains défis primitifs qui la mettent en cause :

- Comment spécifier toutes et chacune des distances ?

- Comment reconnaître que des distances coïncident ici et là ?

Les problèmes de spécification et de comparaison de distances n'ont-ils pas de solution évidente ?

Le problème de la spécification se réduit bientôt à celui de la comparaison ou du transport, et ce dernier s'analyse en termes de translation ou de réorientation ou rotation.

La translation ne sera « sauvée » que par proclamation de l'axiome du parallélisme (avant d'échoir en catastrophe dans le contexte de la géométrie projective). Quant à la comparaison de distances dans des directions différentes, il semble bien qu'Euclide ait voulu contourner le problème dès le départ en se déclarant possesseur de cercles (qui sont des catalogues complets de distances « égales » de toutes les orientations).

Refusant la participation des nombres, nous nous sommes lancé sans relâche à la poursuite de la distance pour nous voir secouru par la relation harmonique, pour voir le cercle disparaître derrière l'idée de polarité et pour voir le grand Apollonius inspirer à von Staudt une redéfinition des coniques propre à regénérer le cercle (avant que Desargues et ses involutions ne rendent tout cela périmé).

Au moment de savourer la création d'une distance rénovée, les dieux grecs vengeront Apollonius en nous ravissant la victoire et en nous laissant seuls devant notre problème :

« Qu'est-ce donc que la distance ? »

WHAT IS DISCRETE MATHEMATICS AND HOW SHOULD WE TEACH IT?

Jacobus H. van Lint

Eindhoven University of Technology [NLD]

Quite often courses with the name "Discrete Mathematics" do not deserve that name. The subject is *not* the union of all subjects in mathematics that are not part of a calculus course but are necessary knowledge for students of computer science. It also happens quite often that a course in what I do consider to be discrete mathematics leaves the students with the impression that there is no structure in the subject. Each problem requires what appears to be an ingenious trick and a new problem also a new trick. This lack of structure is sometimes caused by choosing a too limited subset of topics from discrete mathematics as course material.

Discrete mathematics is concerned with discrete structures that are usually finite, but not always. It includes elementary number theory, combinatorial theory, finite groups, finite fields, finite geometries, and also newer areas such as coding theory. A course in discrete mathematics should be structured as a multigraph with, as independent sets, subsets of the following:

1. Objects: graphs, lattices, geometries, designs, codes, coverings, partitions, systems of sets, matroids;

2. Representations: addressing schemes, coding, (0,1)-matrices, (0,1)-sequences, graphs, diagrams, pictures, subsets of lattices;

3. Ideas: counting techniques, probabilistic techniques, (non)-existence methods, construction techniques, unification (e.g. matroids), optimization methods, max-flow, search techniques, symmetry;

4. Tools: algebra (matrix theory, groups, group rings, finite fields), elementary number theory, permutation groups, geometry, analysis (power series, Lagrange inversion).

Students should not only learn many applications but also to recognize situations in which a certain object from discrete mathematics is the *natural* tool to use. Most important is to get students to *enjoy* the subject by using applications that are surprising or ingenious, challenging problems, and recent applications such as satellite communications and the compact disc.

Let the students work on (homework) problems, preferably in groups of two or three, a few weeks *before* the relevant methods and theorems are treated. They often come up with (sometimes long and clumsy) solutions. The result is that in class they quite often immediately recognize that you are providing them with a *tool* that they desperately needed some weeks earlier.

Reference

Van Lint, J.H., & Wilson, R.M. (1992). *A course in combinatorics.* Cambridge, UK: Cambridge University Press.

THE PROFESSIONAL DEVELOPMENT OF TEACHERS THROUGH RECOGNIZING, DOCUMENTING AND SHARING THE WISDOM OF PRACTICE

Charles Lovitt

Curriculum Corporation of Australia, Melbourne [AUS]

The reform or growth agenda in mathematics is very similar across many countries. In Australia it is expressed in *A National Statement on Mathematics for Australian Schools.* The major thrust of this presentation is that there is within the teaching community a vast untapped resource of understandings and expertise about teaching and learning. Capturing and sharing this wisdom, is arguably the most productive pathway to successful implementation of the reform agenda.

The presentation briefly illustrated four captured classroom images, three presented on slides and one as a workshop activity. The four were titled;

1. Algebra walk;

2. Night and day, and time zones;

3. Problem solving task centers;

4. Crazy animals.

All of these have been collected from classrooms involved in the national MCTP (Mathematics Curriculum and Teaching Program), and are used within professional development networks to generate discussion about teaching and learning issues and to both create and illuminate the national reform agenda.

For each activity, I asked several questions in much the same way we would ask teachers at home:

1. Do you like them? "Is this the sort of activity you would like to see running in your classroom?" This question usually elicits an intuitive but superficial response. "It was neat – the kids liked it – it was fun".

2. Why do you like them? Digging deeper can expose the underlying reasons for apparent success in classrooms and highlight the vocabulary teachers choose to use to describe their beliefs about teaching and learning.

3. How should they be documented in order to capture the "spirit" of the learning environment for others? Documenting a dynamic classroom image is not easy. In many, many trials of documentation, teachers consistently failed to identify what it was that made the activity "great".

4. Where did these come from? Elements of these activities arise spontaneously in the cauldron of classrooms. Recognizing, capturing, codifying and refining them through networks of teachers is a process that can elevate these into works of art – the art of good teaching.

In summary, the reform agenda has a much greater chance of succeeding if systems recognize that teachers are practical experts, and that in their hands is the practical manifestation of learning theory and a very valuable resource.

INTUITION AND LOGIC IN MATHEMATICS

Michael Otte

Institut für Didaktik der Mathematik
Universität Bielefeld [DEU]

One important connection, psychologically well-established since the days of Descartes, is the fact that intuition and logic both serve the very same cognitive function, namely, to give certitude. Mathematics is seen as certain knowledge, as secure as human beings can hope to attain.

If we desire to distinguish logic from the empirical sciences, the question of how mathematical knowledge grows becomes predominantly important. To know is to generalize and mathematical generalization cannot be based on logic or inductive generalization. Mathematics then comes to be conceived of as substantialized human intuition. That mathematics is intuitive knowledge, or is an activity directly related to objects, already derives from the very fact that in mathematics one always has to discover everything by oneself. Only a person who already spent a lot of time intensively thinking in the same direction is able to understand the argument of a mathematical proof. Mathematics cannot be told because "what can be shown cannot be said" (Wittgenstein, *Tractatus* 4.1212). This renders it very fragile, as a thought experiment will demonstrate.

Imagine that I have found a proof of some mathematical theorem, which after having checked out the argument of the proof step-by-step is now intuitively completely clear to me.

> Suppose that a great authority questions my argument. [...] Just as before, I find that the argument appears to be correct; but this time I do not accept it as being correct. And there we have the difference between the two situations: in the first there is an act of acceptance as such, while in the second there is instead an act of questioning something that appears to be correct. (Stolzenberg, 1978)

By "an act of acceptance as such" is meant that the perception of the respective reality appears to the perceiver to be coincident with reality itself. It is this type of belief we call an intuition.

Mathematical intuition takes on various forms from Descartes to Kant and to Poincaré, whose lecture at the ICM in Paris in 1900 suggested the title of this paper. Cartesian intuition essentially meant to have apodeictic access to a known object; Kantian intuition focuses on the conditions for the construction of this object. There are, Kant believes, no objects to be known other than those we have constructed according to the the the rules of apodeictic certainty. With Poincaré intuition becomes specialized, retreating at the same time to the inner circles of human psychology. The mathematical spirit itself splits at the beginning of the 19th century. Analysis and synthesis seem to separate, the spirit of the so-called rigor movement of arithmetization evolves in contrast to the axiomatic approach.

DON'T LET TOMORROW BE THE PRISONER OF THE PRIMITIVITY OF YESTERDAY. RETHINKING WHAT THE COMPUTER PRESENCE CAN OFFER MATH EDUCATION

Seymour Papert

Massachussets Institute of Technology, Cambridge, MA [USA]

Critical part

The ideas about computers, computer science and computational thinking which have penetrated discussion on mathematics education come from a bygone epoch. New paradigms such as object orientation are seen as techniques to make computing less intellectually demanding rather than as rich conceptual models. Parallel processing is virtually ignored.

Constructive part

Computation has crossed a threshold that allows a new and more plausible shot at realizing the dream of giving young students access to a real mathematical culture of powerful ideas.

VERS UNE CONSTRUCTION RÉALISTE
DES NOMBRES RATIONNELS

Nicolas Rouche

Université catholique de Louvain, Louvain-la-Neuve [BEL]

Autrefois, les hommes manipulaient souvent les grandeurs pour faire des mesures. Dans la civilisation technologique d'aujourd'hui on utilise constamment des mesures, mais celles-ci sont faites par des instruments automatiques.

Depuis cinquante ou cent ans, les grandeurs ont disparu des mathématiques. Les nombres sont construits à partir des ensembles, et non plus à partir des grandeurs. De même les grandeurs ont disparu des enseignements secondaire et supérieur de mathématiques. On les retrouve en physique et, à l'état de traces, dans l'enseignement primaire.

On relève au cours du XXe siècle plusieurs propositions visant chacune l'enseignement des nombres dans un cadre axiomatique : en s'appuyant sur les naturels (Weber-Wellstein et Burkhardt), dans le cadre de la géométrie affine (Papy), en partant du concept de grandeur comme terme primitif (Steiner, Kirsch). D'autre part, Freudenthal déplace l'accent de la formulation axiomatique vers les *phénomènes* appréhendés à l'aide *d'objets mentaux,* la conceptualisation au sens habituel en mathématiques devant venir après.

Mais Freudenthal ne fait pas jouer un rôle clé dans l'enseignement aux *contradictions* que l'on rencontre inévitablement lorsqu'on se familiarise avec les phénomènes relatifs aux grandeurs et aux nombres. Ces contradictions sont à la fois un obstacle et une stimulation sur la voie de la théorisation (de l'abstraction). Exemples de telles contradictions :

- l'addition et l'ordre se rencontrent naturellement dans un domaine de grandeurs, mais la multiplication ne s'y trouve pas, au moins comme opération binaire interne ;

- la multiplication des fractions considérées comme opérateurs sur des grandeurs a le statut clair de composition des opérations, par contre l'addition de tels opérateurs est possible mais beaucoup moins naturelle.

Notre exposé a évoqué quelques-unes de ces contradictions et discuté du sort qu'on peut leur faire dans l'enseignement. Un exposé plus détaillé se trouve dans le livre : Rouche, N. (1992). *Le sens de la mesure, des grandeurs aux nombres rationnels.* Bruxelles : Didier-Hatier.

LES MATHÉMATIQUES SONT UN LANGAGE

Fritz Schweiger

Universität Salzburg [AUT]

Mathématiques et langage

Il y a beaucoup de travaux scientifiques qui s'occupent des relations entre mathématiques et langage. À cet égard, je pense aux mots-clés comme la linguistique mathématique, les langages d'ordinateur, la langue spéciale des mathématiques qui a développé un code symbolique remarquable, l'enseignement dans la langue maternelle ou une langue étrangère, les connexions entre l'apprentissage des mathématiques et celui d'une langue étrangère, les problèmes de communication dans nos classes.

Les mathématiques sont un langage

L'énoncé « Les mathématiques sont une langue (ou un langage) » n'est point très nouveau. Cet énoncé peut être considéré d'une manière métaphorique. C'est-à-dire qu'il faut poser les questions suivantes: Qu'est-ce que les mathématiques ? Qu'est-ce qu'une langue (ou le langage) ? Je considère les mathématiques comme une faculté humaine qui se base sur des facultés générales comme par exemple celles de compter et d'ordonner, de reconnaître et de produire des dessins et des symétries, d'utiliser des procédés récursifs et de construire des modèles. Je n'ose pas répondre à la seconde question, mais une analyse préliminaire des notions de langue et de langage semble légitime.

Sons, mots, énoncés et sens

Traditionnellement la linguistique s'occupe de l'analyse phonologique ainsi que de l'étude du lexique, de la syntaxe et de l'analyse sémantique. On peut appliquer ces moyens d'analyse aux textes mathématiques pour obtenir d'autres informations substantielles sur les mathématiques elles-mêmes. D'autre part, l'utilisation des mathématiques dans divers domaines culturels humains suggère que les mathématiques sont une amplification et un enrichissement du langage humain.

L'acquisition des mathématiques et du langage

Il me semble possible de comparer l'apprentissage des mathématiques à l'acquisition du langage soit de la langue maternelle soit d'une langue étrangère. Certaines recherches linguistiques contemporaines admettent l'existence d'un module-langage, responsable de la capacité humaine d'acquérir le langage. À mon avis, il existe de même un module-mathématiques qui se développe en interaction avec le module-langage. Par suite, on pourrait donc se demander si l'hypothèse d'un âge critique s'applique aussi à l'apprentissage des mathématiques.

MATHEMATICS: BEYOND GOOD AND EVIL?

Nancy Shelley

Canberra [AUS]

Polanyi writes of a "purposive tension" in which all living beings exist to make sense of the world around them. We each carry a number of realities that we have constructed to enable us to interact with the world as we encounter it, and the shapes of these have been influenced by our experience and the culture in which we grew up. At present the world faces a multiplicity of crises and there are stark differences between the realities of people's lives. These impinge upon us, more than ever before, through our interdependence. Any meaningful comprehension of our world, and attempt to locate our place in it, will come only through acknowledging realities.

From time to time, particular groups of people with common interests come together with the specific purpose of furthering the development of an understanding of the world along certain particular paths. Western mathematics is the product of the work of such a group and it constitutes a very elaborate model of reality built up over several centuries. It has become an extremely powerful construction having its beginnings in the common experience and culture of European men, with their "historically determined values built into it".

Western mathematics now plays a dominant role in western culture, while the logic which permeates it has become the basis of accepted rationality in western thinking. There are facets of the development of western mathematics, evident in western culture, which are associated with destructive features of that culture. Some of these, that quite consciously require mathematics to stand apart from human experience, have been selected as illustrations. Their effect upon mathematics education is also described. There as well, through the dominance that the culture of western mathematics has acquired, the model has been taken for the reality itself, and its inner consistency for truth. Western culture has become the dominant culture in today's world, along with the violence that pervades it and the militarism it espouses.

Logical argument is inadequate in considering these issues since it is part of the problem. Consequently the telling of a story has been employed, using other stories, word pictures, and poetry, to further encourage the reader (and listener) to ponder beyond the words and answer the question: is mathematics beyond good and evil?

MATHEMATICAL THINKING AND REASONING FOR ALL STUDENTS: MOVING FROM RHETORIC TO REALITY

Edward A. Silver

University of Pittsburgh, PA [USA]

Concern about the generally poor mathematical performance of students and the low participation rates in advanced mathematics courses, especially among students in economically disadvantaged communities, has led to calls for fundamental changes in the conduct of mathematics education in the United States, with the general goal of assisting more students to attain "high mathematical literacy". In *Thinking through mathematics,* Silver, Kilpatrick and Schlesinger (1990) proposed various forms of instructional practice that hold promise as vehicles for attaining the goal of mathematical thinking and reasoning for a larger percentage of students. A unifying theme for the many suggested forms of instructional activity is that mathematics be taught through activities that invite students to think, reason, explain, and justify, rather than simply to memorize and imitate. In this view, mathematics classrooms become communities of collaborative, reflective practice for students, within which students actively participate in legitimate forms of mathematical activity. The pedagogical implications of this view are substantial, especially as they relate to issues of teacher preparation, professional development and ongoing support.

Drawing on empirical evidence from school-based mathematics reform projects, such as QUASAR, and from theoretical notions found in the history and philosophy of science and mathematics (e.g. communities of practice) and in sociocultural theories of learning (e.g. assisted performance, legitimate peripheral participation), it is asserted that, in order to create such opportunities for students, communities of collaborative, reflective practice also need to be created for teachers. In such communities, teachers would be challenged to think deeply about and to participate actively in engaging the mathematics they are teaching. In these communities teachers would not only teach within their individual classrooms but also participate in larger forums of discussion about pedagogical practice and student performance. As with student communities of practice, the discourse in these teacher communities would be filled with observations, explanations, verifications, reasons, and generalizations and teachers would have opportunities to see, hear, debate, and evaluate mathematical explanations and justifications as well as pedagogical practice. The formation of such communities of collaborative, reflective practice for teachers would have as a natural consequence the realization of many aspects of the vision of professional practice portrayed in the *Professional standards for the teaching of mathematics* (NCTM, 1991).

References

National Council of Teachers of Mathematics. (1991). *Professional standards for the teaching of mathematics.* Reston, VA: NCTM.

Silver, E.A., Kilpatrick, J., & Schlesinger, B. (1990). *Thinking through mathematics.* New York: College Entrance Examination Board.

NEW APPROACHES TO THE MATHEMATICAL EDUCATION OF MINORITIES IN THE UNITED STATES

Uri Treisman

University of Texas at Austin [USA]

The environmental forces which shape special mathematics programs for minorities are rapidly changing. Some of these forces are demographic and political; others derive from contemporary reform movements in mathematics education. These forces and their interactions were examined, as were especially promising new strategies for increasing the participation of minorities in mathematics.

HUMAN AND UTILITARIAN ASPECTS OF MATHEMATICS

Thomas Tymoczko

Smith College, Northampton, MA [USA]

If I had to summarize this talk using the familiar distinction between pure and applied mathematics, I could say that when approaching mathematics, philosophers and educators make reciprocal mistakes. Philosophers exaggerate the importance of pure mathematics to philosophy while educators exaggerate the importance of applied mathematics to pedagogy.

However, I believe that the pure/applied distinction is misleading and I want to replace it with a contrast between utilitarian and humanistic mathematics. In the first part of this talk, I explained utilitarian mathematics as a constituent piece of such human endeavors as business and science. If philosophers began with utilitarian mathematics, they could answer the question of whether mathematical objects exist just as they answer similar questions about scientific objects or the objects of common sense.

In the second part of the talk, I looked for an account of pure mathematics. I argued that it *cannot* be described simply as the study of the universe of mathematical objects. Instead, mathematics includes a *point of view* on that universe. This is the essential thesis of humanistic mathematics – mathematics requires a human perspective.

In the third and final part of my talk, I suggested how attention to the humanistic dimension of mathematics could effect our teaching of it. In particular, I discussed the teaching of quadratic equations in secondary schools and showed how this might change by placing that topic in a more general mathematical context (including cubic equations) and in the historical context of discovery.

References

Dunham, W. (1990). *Journey through genius.* New York: Wiley.

Tymoczko, T. (1991). Mathematics, science and ontology. *Synthese, 88,* 221-228.

Tymoczko, T. (1986). Making room for mathematicians in the philosophy of mathematics. *Mathematical Intelligencer,* 8, 44-50

Tymoczko, T. (1985). *New directions in the philosophy of mathematics.* Boston: Birkhäuser.

FROM "MATHEMATICS FOR SOME" TO "MATHEMATICS FOR ALL"

Zalman Usiskin

University of Chicago, Chicago [USA]

In this century there have been two major developments in mathematics education, the teaching of more and more mathematics to more and more people, and the emergence of computer technology. The full paper uses an even longer historical framework as well as some recent work to suggest directions in which various branches of mathematics in school and society may be moving. It includes comments about literacy and the conditions required for mathematics to be learned by all.

Arithmetic

Between 1400 and 1900, "arithmetic for some" became "arithmetic for all", due to a societal need for the competence, the mathematical language and tools that made this competence a reasonable expectation, and technology that enabled this competence to be realized. In most places, paper and pencil skills still dominate class time. Yet in some countries long division and other complicated algorithms are disappearing from the curriculum. This exemplifies "arithmetic for all" becoming "arithmetic for some".

Algebra

Within the past five years, new technology has made the graphing of functions and data, and even curve-fitting and data analysis accessible to all. The cheap, user-friendly symbolic algebra calculator seems certain to come. These devices may decrease the necessity for people to learn much algebra. A technological world requires more mathematics for *some,* but less for *all.* Algebra is likely to become a subject for all, but it will not be today's school algebra.

Calculus

Calculus can be learned by all. Because today's technology enables calculus questions to be treated without today's school calculus, we must be careful that we do not lose calculus in school.

Geometry

The increasing accessibility of graphics means more attention to ordered pairs and triples, graphs of functions and relations, representations of graphs and networks, coordinates and transformations. Traditional work with polygons and circles is likely to decrease or be encountered by all students earlier.

Mathematical Reasoning

Because they can easily display examples, computers tacitly support using induction as a valid method of argument. Consequently, the population which learns deduction may decrease, despite the fact that deductive reasoning distinguishes mathematical thought and should be taught to all.

Summary

Today's technological advances make it likely that more mathematics than ever before will become part of everyone's education and everyday literacy. However, tasks that can be done more readily with technology are likely to be deemphasized in school. A more conceptual, more applied, and more visual mathematics will remain.

ABOUT THE APPRECIATION OF THEOREMS BY STUDENTS AND TEACHERS

Hans-Joachim Vollrath

Julius-Maximilians-Universität, Würzburg [DEU]

When theorems are taught in mathematics instruction students are expected not only to learn these theorems but also to know their importance in mathematics. It is traditional to evaluate a proposition by calling it "Lemma", "Corollary", "Theorem", or "Fundamental Theorem".

Teachers can express their personal appreciation explicitly by commentaries, such as: "This theorem is very useful for calculations of triangles", or: "This theorem is very interesting because it reveals a relationship between the sides of a triangle". But the importance of a theorem can also be implicitly expressed, e.g. by giving the theorem a name: "Pythagorean theorem", or "Mean value theorem". And teachers can express their personal appreciation implicitly by the way they deal with the theorem in mathematics instruction.

Explicit estimations are recognizable by the students; they ask for agreement, but can also invoke opposition. Implicit judgments allow the students more freedom for their own estimations. But the students can also be misled by the teacher's behavior.

Theorems can be judged with respect to knowledge, usage, culture, and beauty. Students tend to appreciate theorems primarily with respect to use, whereas teachers prefer judgments referring to knowledge. Students can only develop a valid impression of mathematics if they receive balanced teaching in which they can appreciate theorems as a concentration of knowledge and potential. But they also need an accented teaching in which they get the chance to distinguish between important and less important facts. They can only develop standards when they become acquainted with really outstanding results.

We understand the appreciation of a theorem as part of the metaknowledge that we want the students to develop in mathematics education. Therefore the students should get the chance to reflect upon theorems, and to talk about them. It is helpful to let them write an essay about an important theorem. Students should have the opportunity to discuss their assessment with other students and with their teacher, they should be willing to listen to reasons, to give reasons, and perhaps to change a personal assessment under discussion. Discussing assessments is a training method, but also a test of scientific culture. It can be seen as a contribution to "mathematical enculturation" (A.J. Bishop). According to A.I. Wittenberg's philosophy of mathematics education we can say: students and student teachers have the right to learn in which respects the theorems they are expected to learn are important.

DEVELOPING STUDENTS' PROBLEM-POSING ABILITIES BY DERIVING QUESTIONS FROM THEIR SURROUNDINGS, EVERYDAY MATERIALS AND OTHER THINGS

Marion Walter

University of Oregon, Eugene, OR [USA]

Textbooks give students the impression that all problems must be *given* to them. This surely undermines their confidence in their ability to pose problems. There are many ways to encourage students to pose problems (Brown & Walter, 1990). Many geometric and other notions, can be approached by encouraging students to pose problems about what they observe and visualize. Many slides and diagrams were used to illustrate how this may be done. For example, several street "brick" patterns were shown. Among various problems that might be suggested are: "In what way are some of these patterns related? How can such patterns be constructed? What other patterns can be made from the same selection of shapes?"

Slides of many other things in one's surroundings, such as shadows, hubcaps, and arrangements of fruit, can be used. We show how one can make use of diagrams as well as scrap materials to pose problems.

Once teachers model the activity of posing questions, students will suggest problems of their own. One can also start by asking students to visualize things. For example, visualize a square. Now visualize cutting off the corners – more and more. When does the shape become a regular octagon? How can you fold a square into a regular octagon? What problems can you think of? While engaging even in this first stage of problem posing it is worthwhile for the class to generate a list of useful questions. Such a list might include: How many? What do they have in common? Can it be done another way?

Once students get into the habit of posing problems, they will easily learn another stage of problem posing called the "What-If-Not?" technique. Students get more involved when they pose their own problems. They then clearly see the need to sometimes simplify and often clarify their own problems. Students will encounter problems that neither they nor we can solve and this needs to be considered.

References

Brown, S.I. and Walter, M. (1990). *The art of problem posing,* 2nd edition. Hillsdale, NJ: L. Erlbaum.

Walter, M. (September and December 1987). Mathematics from almost any-thing, parts I and II. *Mathematics Teaching, 120* and *121.*

Walter, M. (September 1989). Curriculum ideas through problem posing, *Mathematics Teaching, 128.*

SHORT PRESENTATIONS
AND ROUND TABLES

COMMUNICATIONS BRÈVES
ET TABLES RONDES

SHORT PRESENTATIONS AND ROUND TABLES

COMMUNICATIONS BRÈVES ET TABLES RONDES

The International Program Committee for ICME–7 was of the opinion that at a meeting like this one, where many participants may have difficulties in speaking or in listening to one or both of the official languages, 10-minute oral communications, though traditional, have almost no value. It was therefore decided that short presentations would only be allowed during the Congress in the form of posters, or videotapes, or computer software.

A total of 439 applications for short communications were accepted, including 377 poster presentations. The posters were subdivided into 43 sections – corresponding to the themes of the twenty-two Working Groups, sixteen Topic Groups and the five strands of the Miniconference on Calculators and Computers – and were on display throughout the Congress. Specific times were scheduled during which groups of presenters in turn were asked to stand by their posters in order to discuss with interested participants.

For each of the 36 short presentations using a videotape and the 26 others using a sample of software, two 1-hour sessions were scheduled (on different days).

Every participant received one copy of the Book of Abstracts of Short Presentations / *Recueil des résumés de communications brèves* containing summaries and schedules for every short presentation.

As an experiment, the Program Committee also decided to organize *round tables* in order to encourage participants making poster presentations on related topics to sit together to discuss them and engage in an exchange of ideas and information. Accordingly ten 1-hour round tables were arranged on the following topics: (1) *The character of mathematical reasoning*; (2) *Representational aspects of mathematics*; (3) *Conceptual errors and conceptual change*; (4) *Understanding mathematical understanding*; (5) *Teaching mathematics so as to be useful*; (6) *Mathematics and other subjects*; (7) *Mathematics and daily life*; (8) *Mathematical problem solving*; (9) *Writing and mathematics*; (10) *Teaching mathematics for creativity*.

PROJECTS AND WORKSHOPS

PROJETS ET ATELIERS

PROJECTS

PROJETS

Centre for Mathematics Education, the Open University

Members of the Centre gave short presentations about its innovative work. This involves providing distance learning materials to support the inservice training of teachers, particularly using video-recordings of classrooms. There was also an exhibition of study packs which provide supported self-study opportunities for teachers who wish to work at their own professional development. We are pleased to meet and share ideas with colleagues from a large number of other institutions.

Contact person: Barrie Galpin
Address: Centre for Mathematics Education, Open University,
           Milton Keynes, MK7 6AA,
           United Kingdom

Centre interdisciplinaire de recherche sur l'apprentissage et le développement en éducation (CIRADE)

Le CIRADE est un centre de recherche universitaire situé à l'Université du Québec à Montréal (UQAM) et qui regroupe des professeurs-chercheurs de cinq universités québécoises, intéressés à œuvrer dans une perspective multidisciplinaire et préoccupés par la recherche de solutions aux problèmes que posent les théorisations et pratiques éducatives actuelles. Des recherches conjointes sont également réalisées en concertation avec des enseignants issus d'écoles expérimentales. Le domaine d'expertise du CIRADE porte sur la problématique de la construction des connaissances et de l'appropriation de savoirs particuliers, systématisés (par exemple les mathématiques) ou liés aux processus interactionnels (par exemple les savoirs sociaux).

Pour information : Nadine Bednarz ou Richard Pallascio
Adresse : CIRADE, UQAM,
           C.P. 8888, Succ. A.,
           Montréal, QC, Canada H3C 3P8

389

Century Mathematics

Century Maths is a new and innovative mathematics resource for the 11-16 age range. Within the areas of number, algebra, shape and space, and handling data, it supplies a wealth of new ideas which are handled in an exciting way. The Century Maths texts are full of references to the use of Logo, databases, spreadsheets, graph-plotters, and graphic calculators. It is envisaged that children will grow up using these tools to support and encourage their mathematical thinking. Because Logo is central to the Century Maths scheme and philosophy, it seemed natural that children should use the Logo environment for all their computing needs. Therefore "Logo 2000", a set of three integrated microworlds, has been developed.

Contact person: Gareth Buckland
Address: Stanley Thornes Publishers Ltd., Old Station Drive,
          Leckhampton, Cheltenham, Glos., GL53 0DN,
          United Kingdom

Connected Mathematics Project

The Connected Mathematics Project is funded by the National Science Foundation for five years to develop a complete curriculum for grades six through eight for all students built on the Middle Grades Mathematics Project with influence from the Used Numbers Project and the Computer Intensive Algebra Project. Format is four- to six-week units emphasizing problem solving in number, geometry, probability, statistics, measurement, and algebra. Sixth grade is currently being tried in a formative mode with the seventh and eighth grades being written to be tried in 1993-95. Professional development centers are located in Queens, NY, Pittsburgh, PA, Mt. Pleasant, MI, Portland, OR, and San Diego, CA.

Contact persons: William M. Fitzgerald, Glenda Lappan, or
                 Elizabeth Phillips
Address: The Connected Mathematics Project,
          101 Wills House, Michigan State University,
          East Lansing, MI 48824, USA

"Equals" Programs

The "Equals" programs provide strategies and materials to encourage and involve all students, and particularly women and minorities, in problem-solving approaches to mathematics. The programs encourage all students to engage in thoughtful investigations and to pursue mathematics to higher levels of learning. "Family Math" creates family enjoyment of mathematics and teaches parents how to encourage their children in mathematics at home. The "Interactive Mathematics Program" has created four years of problem-based mathematics for all high school students. The curriculum integrates algebra, geometry, logic, statistics, probability, and other concepts in an interactive format that encourages expression and cooperation between students.

> Contact person: Sherry Fraser
> Address: "Equals", Lawrence Hall of Science,
> University of California,
> Berkeley, CA 94720, USA

Freudenthal Instituut

> Contact person: Jan de Lange
> Address: OW&OC, University of Utrecht, Tiberdreef 4,
> 3561 GG Utrecht, The Netherlands

The Calculus Consortium based at Harvard

We believe that the calculus curriculum needs to be completely rethought. Our project is based on the belief that the graphical, numerical and analytical aspects of calculus should all be emphasized throughout. We call this approach the "Rule of Three", and believe that a course built on this will make a much livelier calculus at any institution. We have written a single-variable text to support this concept; a multi-variable text is under preparation. The Consortium includes Harvard University, Chelmsford High School, Colgate University, Haverford College, Stanford University, Suffolk County Community College, University or Arizona, and the University of Southern Mississippi.

> Contact person: Herman O. Sudholz
> Address: Science Center # 325, One Oxford Street,
> Cambridge, MA 02116, USA

The International Cabri-géomètre Group

The Group was started at ICME–7. The aim of the group is to encourage discussion about the use of "Cabri-géomètre"-like software. The following issues and activities have been identified: changes which such software will have on the traditional classroom; small group work in the classroom; production of pedagogical material; use of Cabri to support research in mathematics education; investigation of fields outside the traditional mathematics in which geometry can be used as a modeling tool (e.g. physics, 3D-drawing, biology); use of Cabri to support mathematical research in geometry; integration of intelligent tutorial components. The Steering Committee of the Group is as follows : Nicolas Balacheff [FRA], Jeremy Kilpatrick [USA], Jean-Marie Laborde (main coordinator) [FRA], Nobuhiko Nohda [JPN], Iman Osta [LBN], Rosamund Sutherland [GBR].

Contact person : Jean-Marie Laborde
Adresse: LSD2–IMAG, BP 53X,
38041 Grenoble Cedex, France

Instituts de Recherche sur l'Enseignement des Mathématiques (IREMs)

Pour information : Rudolf Bkouche
Adresse : Université des Sciences et Techniques,
Bâtiment M1,
59655 Villeneuve d'Ascq, France

Mathematics Centre, West Sussex Institute

The Mathematics Centre initiates and promotes research and evaluates developments in the learning and teaching of mathematics. Our curriculum development research projects in mathematics focus on developing and encouraging good practice across the age and ability range, the use of technology in the learning of mathematics, and the nature and role of assessment. All the research is firmly rooted in the personal experiences of teachers and seeks ways of raising achievement in mathematics. This work has led to creative models for the professional development of teachers in order to contribute towards whole school improvement programs.

Contact person: Lesley West
Address: The Mathematics Centre,
West Sussex Institute of Higher Education,
Upper Bognor Road, Bognor Regis, West Sussex,
PO21 1HR, United Kingdom

Mechanics in Action

The display of project books and materials together with many examples of students' work provided a focus for much rewarding discussion. A strong emphasis on mechanics and mathematical modeling for students in the late secondary/tertiary systems was augmented by material aimed at "Using and applying mathematics" with younger students. Various activities were provided so the delegates could experience mathematics as a practical subject. Using the practical equipment, produced in collaboration with Unilab Ltd., provoked much interest. Two viewings/discussions were held of the video "Mechanics in action", the first of three stimulus videos produced by the Project.

Contact person: Julian Williams
Address: "Mechanics in Action",
University of Manchester, Oxford Road,
Manchester, M13 0PL, United Kingdom

National Center for Research in Mathematical Sciences Education (NCRMSE)

Research findings from the NCRMSE working groups on the learning/ teaching of whole number, models of authentic assessment, learning/teaching of algebra and quantitative analysis, learning/teaching of quantities, and learning/teaching of geometry, were presented. Materials from two projects associated with NCRMSE, The Cognitively-Guided Instruction (CGI) Project and the Maths in Context Project were also presented. Members of the working groups and projects were available to discuss findings and future plans with conference participants.

> Contact person: Donald Chambers
> Address: NCRMSE,
>   1025 W. Johnson Street,
>   Madison, WI 53706, USA

Réalisations des francophones de Belgique dans l'enseignement des mathématiques

Ce projet avait principalement pour but de faire connaître l'existence d'un rapport important intitulé « Perspectives sur l'enseignement des mathématiques dans la Communauté française de Belgique » (Bruxelles, 1990) dont un extrait du préambule intitulé « Une conception des mathématiques » a été mis en évidence. Le projet a aussi permis de montrer les publications de la Société belge des professeurs de mathématiques d'expression française et du Groupe d'enseignement mathématique de Louvain-la-Neuve destinées à la formation continue des enseignants.

> Pour information : Nicolas Rouche
> Adresse : Institut Mathématique,
>   2 chemin du Cyclotron,
>   1348 Louvain-la-Neuve, Belgique

School Mathematics Project (SMP)

The School Mathematics Project has worked in the field of mathematics curriculum development for over thirty years. Currently, its two main series are SMP 11-16 and 16-19 Mathematics. Chris Little spoke about secondary school assessment initiatives taken by SMP. Diana Sharvill led sessions on the role of graduated assessment in raising motivation among less able pupils and on the work of SMP's cross-curriculum group. Two members of the 16-19 Mathematics team gave presentations on "Graphic calculators for ten year olds" (Stan Dolan) and "Technology in the teaching of calculus" (Paul Roder).

Contact person: Chris Little
Address: School Mathematics Project,
            University of Southampton,
            Southampton, SO9 5NH, United Kingdom

Shell Centre for Mathematical Education

The display of the Shell Centre, Nottingham University showed a range of its recent research and development projects. The basic research on teaching and learning has led to the production of five new boxes of non-routine problem solving examples. Assessment has taken a prominent position in mathematics education world-wide and a collaborative project "Balanced Assessment for the Mathematics Curriculum" involving the universities Berkeley – Nottingham – Harvard – Michigan State is underway. The latest development in the I.T./Media line is "The World of Number", a package based on three videodiscs with associated interactive computer software and print materials.

Contact person: Professor Kath Hart
Address: Shell Centre for Mathematical Education,
            University of Nottingham,
            Nottingham, NG7 2RD, United Kingdom

Statistical Education Projects, Appalachian State University

Three projects supported by the National Science Foundation stress active approaches to learning and statistics as a problem-solving process. "Simulations in mathematics: probability and computing" (SIM-PAC) has developed computer simulation models for learning probability concepts. Materials include student activities (grades 9-12) and a teacher manual. "Statistics: leaders in North Carolina" (STAT-LINC) is developing a model for inservice teacher education in statistics. The project is built around 24 lead teachers. Events include two summer institutes for the lead teachers and workshops for middle and secondary school teachers. "Statistics: materials and activities for problem solving" (STAT-MAPS) is developing a secondary curriculum in statistics and the supporting materials based on eight categories of statistical problem solving.

Contact person: Mike Perry
Address: Department of Mathematical Sciences,
            Appalachian State University,
            Boone, NC 28608, USA

394

WORKSHOPS

ATELIERS

Association of Teachers of Mathematics Workshop

The workshop showed possible ways of working with children in the classroom. Through the use of Mathematical Activity Tiles and tiling generators, we demonstrated how one set of resources could be used to develop a wide range of concepts with children of any age or mathematical ability. Those who attended became involved with children in constructing polyhedra, making tiling patterns, making conjectures and discovering properties of polyhedra and tessellating polygons. They observed how children can develop a task to a point which is challenging at their level and which involves new learning as well as the consolidation of existing concepts.

Contact person: Michelle Selinger
Address: Association of Teachers of Mathematics,
           7 Shaftesbury Street, Derby, DE3 7YB,
           United Kingdom

Chaos

The idea of the Chaos Workshop arose from a travelling roadshow which included pictures from the "Frontiers of Chaos" exhibition. While these pictures attracted considerable interest, few people appeared to want to discover how they were generated. ICME-7 became a focus for the task of constructing a workshop in which visitors would be invited to work at ideas of chaos and fractals. Volunteers, including lecturers and primary school teachers, planned the workshop, deciding that there should be plenty of accessible activities using a variety of resources in addition to computers. The workshop was well attended and much enjoyed.

Contact person: Daphne Kerslake
Address: 4 Castle Close, Henbury, Bristol, BS10 7QU,
           United Kingdom

Story Games to develop Mathematical Thinking

The workshop consisted of three 90-minute sessions for a dozen eight year olds from a local day-care centre. This was an abridgment of a learning program normally lasting for several months. In the first session the children played a game (throwing dice and racing pawns) and grasped the idea of negotiating and obeying rules. In the second, the children constructed variants of the game (by drawing obstacles and by-passes). In the third session the children thought less about context, more of counting. Ewa Puchalska [CAN] acted as the teacher. Each session was followed by discussion with the Congress participants.

Contact person: Edyta Gruszczyk-Kolczynska
Address: ul. Czerniakowska 145 m.4,
00-453 Warszawa, Poland

MATh.en.JEANS

With MATh.en.JEANS, ordinary pupils do mathematics as mathematicians do, becoming productive not reproductive. Working in small groups with pupils from other schools, they explore subjects related to up-to-date mathematics. No hints are provided: teachers and mathematician(s) help them in creating the conditions of scientific debate (and methodological advice, documents, ...). Canadian and French pupils gave talks on the subjects they had discovered during the meeting: properties of 10-adic numbers, as infinite sequences of numerals written to the left, and as braids (involving unknotting, coding, ...).

Contact person: Pierre Duchet
Address: MATh.en.JEANS, Laboratoire LSD2–IMAG,
BP 53X, 38041 Grenoble Cedex, France

Using mathematical games in the classroom

The workshop, which housed a variety of classroom games, was introduced by a short paper, presented to Topic Group 7, offering a structure and a rationale for using games in the mathematics classroom. In the workshop nine people (from the U.K., Israel and the U.S.A.) gave short presentations of favourite games. Participants, who came from a wide range of countries and who were often actively engaged in similar activities, played the games and discussed the contribution these could make to classroom learning.

Contact persons: (1) Christine Shiu and (2) Gillian Hatch
Addresses: (1) Centre for Mathematics Education, Open University,
Milton Keynes, MK7 6AA, United Kingdom
(2) Didsbury School of Education,
799 Wilmslow Road, Manchester, M20 8RR,
United Kingdom

SPECIAL EXHIBITIONS AND MATH TRAIL

EXPOSITIONS SPÉCIALES ET SENTIER MATHÉMATIQUE

SPECIAL EXHIBITIONS

EXPOSITIONS SPÉCIALES

L'Esprit informatique

Comment présenter l'informatique sans parler de langage, sans parler « mécanique » ? Comment rendre accessible au grand public les rouages du fontionnement interne de cette science en création ? Cette exposition s'efforce de présenter, sous forme interactive et ludique, les concepts de base de l'informatique (codage binaire, algorithmes, logiques...) ainsi que des concepts qui font l'objet de recherches (automates, architectures parallèles, mémoires...). Complétée par du matériel informatique, elle a offert aux visiteurs, qu'ils soient néophytes ou savants, *le plaisir d'en savoir plus* à travers des objets à manipuler ou des jeux.

Pour information : Michel Darche
Adresse : « L'Esprit informatique », Centre-Sciences,
          CCSTI de la région Centre, 72 Faubourg Bourgogne,
          45000 Orléans, France

Horizons mathématiques

Comment faire se rencontrer les connaissances prémathématiques du grand public et les savoirs des mathématiciens ? Comment faire des mathématiques un objet culturel au même titre que la littérature, l'histoire, l'astronomie, le cinéma, la musique, etc. ? Depuis sa création, l'exposition « Horizons mathématiques » a montré que l'on pouvait apporter des réponses concrètes à ces questions. Avant Québec et ICME-7, plus de 50 pays avaient accueilli cette exposition interactive (présentée en langue française ou en version bilingue), ce qui montre que les mathématiques ont, de tout temps, traversé les cultures et les langues de tous les pays, au Nord comme au Sud.

Pour information : Michel Darche
Adresse : « Horizons mathématiques », Centre-Sciences,
          CCSTI de la région Centre, 72 Faubourg Bourgogne,
          45000 Orléans, France

Iberoamerican exhibition

Several Iberoamerican countries were invited to take part in this exhibition devoted to Art and Mathematics. From Spain, it included 656 photographs by Pilar Moreno about Geometry and shadows, as well as 40 photographs of mosaics from the Mosque of Cordoba and the Alhambra of Granada as examples of the history of group theory in Spain. From Portugal were shown the results of an activity carried out during the academic year 1991–1992 with pupils from 26 schools who studied various navigational instruments used in the routes that united Europe and America in the 15th–17th centuries. The exhibition also included one presentation entitled "Geoplano Aureo" by J.A. Dorta [ESP] and a display of musical instruments by a group of Uruguay teachers.

> Contact person: Rafael Pérez Gómez
> Address: Departamento de matemática aplicada,
>   Universidad de Granada, Campus de Fuentenueva,
>   18071 Granada, Spain

Le savoir-compter : l'école primaire et les mathématiques (1800 à 1920)

Recherche et conception : Louis Charbonneau, Charlotte Giguère et Paul Lavoie [CAN]

L'exposition *Le savoir-compter* visait à retracer les efforts déployés entre 1800 et 1920, au Québec comme dans la plupart des pays occidentaux, afin de rendre l'enseignement primaire accessible à tous. Rareté des maîtres, pénurie de livres, manque d'écoles, analphabétisme généralisé : voilà la situation scolaire au début du XIXe siècle. Des moyens ont alors été mis en œuvre afin de multiplier les écoles et de les pourvoir en maîtres, livres et matériel didactique de toutes sortes. En quelques générations, l'école a même réussi à généraliser un certain savoir mathématique autrefois regardé comme inaccessible. Cette exposition, constituée à partir de documents et d'objets appartenant à l'Université Laval, à divers organismes québécois ou étrangers ainsi qu'à des collections privées, a attiré plus de 2200 visiteurs durant le Congrès et les trois semaines qui ont suivi.

Sundials

This exhibition consisted of ten boards (size A1) containing over eighty photographs taken by Peter Ransom of some of the different types of sundials – vertical, horizontal, multiple, others – found mainly in Northumbria, England. One of the boards describes some of the theory behind the science of gnomonics and how it can be used in the mathematics classroom; another illustrates sundials from around the world. Also on display were reproductions of portable sundials, literature relating to the British Sundial Society and its publication "Make a sundial", and the publication that inspired the exhibition: "Mathematical tradition in the north of England".

Contact person: Peter Ransom
Address: 12 Annaside Mews, Leadgate,
             Consett, Co. Durham, DH8 6HL,
             United Kingdom

MATH TRAIL

SENTIER MATHÉMATIQUE

For the first time in the history of ICMEs, a "Math Trail" was designed on the occasion of ICME-7. This kind of activity, still relatively little known, aims to foster greater interest for mathematics in the general public. The math trail inaugurated at ICME-7 offers an opportunity to discover the history and architecture of Old Québec while on the way solving simple mathematical problems related to the environment. The day before the opening of ICME-7, Congress participants were invited to experiment the math trail, which brought them finally to the Musée de la Civilisation. On this occasion, a cocktail was offered and the museum remained especially open.

Un « sentier mathématique » a été créé à l'occasion d'ICME-7 – une première dans l'histoire des congrès ICME. Encore peu connu, ce genre d'activité s'adresse au grand public et vise à susciter un intérêt plus grand pour les mathématiques. Le sentier mathématique inauguré à ICME-7 fournit l'occasion de découvrir l'histoire et l'architecture du Vieux-Québec, tout en résolvant au passage un certain nombre de problèmes mathématiques simples reliés à cet environnement. La veille de l'ouverture d'ICME-7, les congressistes ont été invités à mettre à l'essai le sentier, qui les a finalement conduits au Musée de la Civilisation. À cette occasion, une réception leur a été offerte et le Musée est demeuré spécialement ouvert.

NATIONAL PRESENTATIONS

PRÉSENTATIONS NATIONALES

CANADIAN NATIONAL PRESENTATION

PRÉSENTATION NATIONALE CANADIENNE

Chief Organizer / *Responsable en chef* : Carolyn Kieran [CAN]

In a country the size of Canada, it is rather easy not to be aware of many of the wonderful mathematical endeavors going on outside of one's immediate geographical area — be it the school, the city, or even the province. Thus, the Canadian National Presentation allowed not only international participants at ICME-7, but also Canadians themselves, to have a brief glimpse at the variety of interesting mathematics education projects being carried out in Canada.

One of the highlights of the presentation was a display of Inuit teaching materials that focused on the geometrical interests and expertise of this group of native Canadians. Other interesting exhibits included: demonstrations of the computer algebra system, Maple, prepared by Waterloo Maple Software; the Benchmarks Project of the Toronto Board of Education dealing with new forms of assessment for elementary school mathematics; the multi-faceted work of the Canadian Mathematical Society and the Canadian Statistical Society; mathematics education research videos and material prepared by CIRADE (Centre interdisciplinaire de recherche sur l'apprentissage et le développement en éducation) of Université du Québec à Montréal; the video "Ten equations that shook the world", produced by the Atlantic Provinces Council on the Sciences; examples of exciting mathematical problems devised by the Canadian Mathematics Competition; and the description of the Niagara Falls Math Trail, accompanied by spectacular photos of this natural wonder. Various professional groups such as APAME (Association des promoteurs de l'avancement de la mathématique à l'élémentaire), AMQ (Association mathématique du Québec), GRMS (Groupe des responsables en mathématique au secondaire), MOIFEM (Mouvement international pour les femmes et l'enseignement des mathématiques), and CMESG (Canadian Mathematics Education Study Group / Groupe canadien d'étude en didactique des mathématiques), provided overviews of some of the mathematical projects they have recently innovated. In the area of publications, the exhibit included the journal *For the learning of mathematics*, published by David Wheeler [CAN], and the monograph *Current research on the teaching and learning of mathematics in Canada,* prepared by CMESG as part of its exhibit and available from Lars Jansson, Faculty of Education, University of Manitoba, Winnipeg, MN, Canada R3T 2N2.

Splashes of lively mathematical color were supplied by the posters on quadratic functions prepared by the students of Union High in Scarborough, Ontario, and by the mathematical drawings of elementary school students in Québec. Added visual interest was provided by posters of Canadian scenery, the flora and fauna, as well as by ongoing videos and slide shows of scenes of Canada and her people.

OTHER NATIONAL PRESENTATIONS

AUTRES PRÉSENTATIONS NATIONALES

A general invitation was extended to all nations represented in the International Commission on Mathematical Instruction (ICMI) to present a videotape during the Congress showing aspects of mathematics education in their countries. Brazil, Finland, Ireland, Taiwan, United Kingdom, and United States of America accepted the invitation, and each one was given three separate 30-minute periods to make its videotape presentation.

SPECIAL SESSIONS
SÉANCES SPÉCIALES

"PROBE": THE VALUE OF NATIONAL STUDIES OF MATHEMATICS EDUCATION FOR THE INTERNATIONAL COMMUNITY, DISCUSSED IN RELATION TO AN EXAMPLE FROM GERMANY

Organizers / *Responsables* : Hans Schupp & Hans-Georg Steiner [DEU]

This special session grew out of discussions among the members of a group of initiators in Germany who in 1989 had been asked by the Gesellschaft für Didaktik der Mathematik (GDM) to develop an outline and establish a writing team for a study on mathematics education in the Federal Republic of Germany. The crucial question was what features, problems, and experiences in this field should be exhibited so as to be valuable and useful for the international community.

The study was written with a view to being presented and discussed at ICME-7. In agreement with the International Program Committee, the presentation was embedded in the theme of this special session. Ken Clements [AUS] agreed to chair at the session and, together with Jeremy Kilpatrick [USA], to take the role of a discussant. Presenters were Hans Schupp, Werner Blum and Hans-Niels Jahnke [DEU]. All formed a panel together with the following members of the German initiative and editorial group: Christine Keitel, Hans-Georg Steiner, Rudolf Strässer and Hans Joachim Vollrath [DEU].

In his introductory presentation Schupp gave an overview of the genesis, the overall intentions, and the contents of the report, indicating that it had been published as a special issue (1992/7) of the international review and documentation journal *Zentralblatt für Didaktik der Mathematik* (ZDM) (Fachinformationszentrum Karlsruhe, D-W-7514 Eggenstein-Leopoldshafen 2, Germany). He explained that the steering committee quickly decided to confine the study to selected topics and related research perspectives and to describe institutional details only in so far as they were necessary to understand the research, thus offering a kind of "bouquet of themes". He pointed out that the writing was already well advanced when the East-German Democratic Republic was unified with the West-German Federal Republic, so that the report could not include the developments in the former GDR.

Part 1 of the report deals with the teaching and learning of mathematics within the German educational system, starting out with a short description of that system and its historical and recent development (I. Weidig), followed by contributions on themes like "Mathematical thinking in the primary school" (H. Winter), "Practical arithmetic in lower secondary classes" (H.J. Vollrath), "Curriculum developments relating to calculus teaching" (U.P. Tietze), "Mathematics teaching in vocational schools" (W. Blum, R. Strässer), "Teaching styles" (H. Maier, J. Voigt), "Grouping" (N. Sommer, U. Viet), "Intuition and rigor" (P. Bender, H.N. Jahnke).

Part 2 deals with teacher education, introduced by a critical historical and current review (C. Keitel), followed by special chapters on the importance of an educational viewpoint within the mathematical training of future teachers (E.C. Wittmann), and on experiences and problems with the practical second phase of teacher education as it is organized in Germany (F. Seeger, H. Steinbring).

Part 3, devoted to the didactics of mathematics, consists of a contribution about the development of its organization as a professional field (H. Griesel, H.G. Steiner) and a survey of research in didactics of mathematics in Germany (H.J. Burscheid, H. Struve, G. Walther).

After Schupp's overview, Blum reported on "Mathematics in vocational training and professional education", referring to the distinction between part-time vocational training and education known as the German "dual system" (a combination of classroom-type schooling and on-the-job training) and full-time vocational education in a great variety of forms. After characterizing the type and philosophy of mathematics taught within the related curricula, he exhibited as a general problem a dichotomy between the intentions and practices heading towards general education goals and those oriented towards professional training goals. A German-Austrian group is working on overcoming these discrepancies.

Jahnke's presentation related to the Bender-Jahnke chapter, which pursues the role of the German concept *Anschauung* (only inadequately translated by "intuition") throughout its history in philosophical and pedagogical-didactical discourse, thus going back to Pestalozzi, Kant, Herbart and others, who particularly connected it with the idea of "internal-mental intuition", understood as a productive power of the imagination. With the emergence of scientism and its influence on German Gymnasium teaching in the second half of the 19th century, the concept of *Anschauung* became pedagogically marginal and was discussed mainly as a component of the pair *Anschauung und Strenge* (intuition and rigor), keeping some strength however in connection to the elementary school. The chapter elaborates the meaning of mathematical rigor in science and in school, and explains the interrelation between intuition and rigor. The didactical consequences are brought out in three thoughtful theses.

In his reaction, Kilpatrick referred to the image of a "bouquet of themes" and characterized the selection as interesting and stimulating, indicating that, of course, many features were necessarily missing. He emphasized the great advantage of having the report in English and that he was very surprised to discover, though he was quite familiar with the German scene, how many things were new to him. He recommended that reports on mathematics education in a country should also be written by authors from other countries; some good examples already existed. Clements also under-lined how much he had learned from reading the study and put the question "what can be said about the relation between research and its use for practice?", which seemed a matter for criticism by mathematics teachers in Germany when he visited the country some years ago.

Some questions and remarks from the audience were directed to the panel. One participant from England reported that often in educational debates a foreign country is overly idealized, which does not seem to be a good basis for internationally learning from each other; maybe studies like the present one could serve as a more reliable source. A question was put concerning the evaluation by the unified Germany of the specific educational model and related experience in the former GDR. German panelists explained that the political and organizational changes (with far-reaching implications for individuals) happened so fast in East Germany that any stable basis for doing such an evaluation in cooperation with researchers from West Germany was missing, but a related study may be possible in some years. Another remark was concerned with increasing exchange and cooperation within the European Community in all domains of education, and particularly at the university graduation level.

"CROSSFIRE":
MATHEMATICAL COMPETITIONS – DO THE
BENEFITS OUTWEIGH THE DISADVANTAGES?

Organizer / *Responsable* : Edward J. Barbeau [CAN]

The 90-minute session included presentations by four panelists with interventions from a number of people in the audience. The panelists were: Peter J. Hilton [USA], Claudio Bernardi [ITA], Gilah C. Leder [AUS] and Anthony J. Gardiner [GBR].

After the first two panelists spoke, there was a brief space for audience participation before the last two were heard from. The following report is largely based on notes made by John Webb [ZAF].

Hilton established his credentials by recalling his chairmanship of the US Commission on Mathematics Instruction at the time the United States of America Mathematical Olympiad was established. While he felt generally positive about competitions in the schools, he was dubious about ones at the university level, particularly the Putnam competition. With emphasis on speed and efficiency, they require participants to submit to conditions no mathematician would dream of choosing. Important mathematical attributes, such as taste, depth, capacity for systematic thought and skill in asking questions, are not developed. Students may get the impression that mathematical problems "come down from the mountain on tablets" and may arrive in graduate school without a clear idea of how mathematics is done. On balance, competitions are beneficial in encouraging students to take up mathematics. Some of the problem books that have appeared have been stimulating and exciting. However, there must come a time to move beyond competition. As a humanist, he rejected the notion of individuals in competition; the authentic competition was with the domain, not with others.

Bernardi presented a balance sheet. On the negative side, competitions can foster excessive self-confidence, rivalry, and frustration among some participants. Their importance is overrated when only the top students are involved and they indicate only certain aspects of mathematical ability. Solving problems at speed is just one mathematical skill, one that not all good mathematicians share. It is possible to misinterpret competition results. Does the International Mathematical Olympiad really represent a fair comparison of participating countries, when these have differing curricula and success is conditional on training? However, these difficulties can be overcome. We should not assign too much importance to competitions, nor see their purpose as the early identification of genius or the selection of students for special training. We should focus on problem solving and not require too many prerequisites. They should be designed so that either all can take part or only the best; in Italy, the competitions have several rounds, the first involving ten per cent of the population and the final only 300 students. Competitions are a respite from dreary teaching. In summary, the aims of competitions are, most importantly, to stimulate the best students and give an idea of mathematical research, as well as to encourage a different view of mathematics and allow students to meet. They should stress the cultural value and beauty of mathematics.

Mary Barnes [AUS] spoke from the floor. She had heard nothing to indicate that there were any advantages to competitions. All of Hilton's criticisms applied at the junior levels as well. It is not acceptable to misrepresent mathematics at any level by insisting on a time constraint. Bernardi's goals can all be achieved in some other way, for example by math days, camps and classroom explorations. In reply, Hilton still felt that at the school level the stimulus offered outweighed the danger of misrepresenting mathematics. However, he was not happy to view them as a compensation for dreary teaching; rather, the teaching should be improved. Bernhard Neumann [AUS] reminded the audience that the oldest national competition, in Hungary, nurtured excellent research mathematicians. Peter Shiu [GBR], a member of the British Mathematics Olympiad committee, agreed with Hilton. Mathematics is a minority sport, but the young can be encouraged by such activites as teaching camps.

Leder discussed the multiple choice type of contest used in Australia. With 90% school participation, the Australian contest seems to have succeeded in making mathematics more than a minority sport. Recalling Hadamard's dictum that "the object of rigour is to legitimize the conquest of intuition", one might ask whether timed contests foster such a conquest. It is customary to penalize guessing; is this valid? The advantages of the multiple choice format is that it is an objective measure at different knowledge levels, covers a large domain in a short time, and can be scored easily. However, it assumes that the questions can be answered quickly, does not encourage guessing, conjecturing, testing, and problem posing. There are, according to Getzels, three types of problems: Type 1 requiring memorization, Type 2 requiring reason and Type 3 requiring imagination. Can this format do justice to all three? Some students do not perform well in such contests, especially girls. Therefore, one must not draw unwarranted conclusions about mathematical ability.

Gardiner drew attention to four groups of people: students, teachers, educationists, and those wishing to influence the teaching of mathematics, the last including organizers of certain mathematics competitions. Each of these groups has some interaction with the others, but the link between those wishing to influence and educationists is weak. A key question is how can competitions help teachers? Under what conditions? Within what time scale? It is not a criticism of the teacher to suggest that someone from outside can add spice to mathematical learning. However, some competitions might override the larger educational process. Competitions are too big to be left to the sidelines, and we have to make sure that their influence is beneficial. When we speak of competition, who competes against whom? or what? The proper competition is between participant and problem, and this can in itself provide incentive for students. Competitions can be effective in attracting students and teachers to mathematics. While there may be material rewards, it is important that the efforts of students should be recognized.

Mark Saul [USA] felt that it was important to challenge two assumptions of critics: competition is evil in and of itself; competitions are exclusive. Competition is natural, and preparing for it is not putting students into a boot camp. Students can be adversely affected in cooperative as well as competitive situations. Competitions can motivate teachers and make mathematics more fun in the classroom. Alexander Soifer [USA] quarrelled with the hypothesis that competitions misrepresent mathematics, but felt that high schools do. He himself disliked multiple choice and preferred an extended interaction between students and mathematics. While it may be excessive to play this game to adulthood, without competition there would be no mathematics. Paolo Toni [ITA], a secondary school teacher, reminded us of the three aspects of human nature, homo sapiens, homo faber, and homo ludens; competitions are for the third. Harley Flanders [USA] pointed out that the positive effect of the Putnam competition is well documented. Preparing for the Putnam does not replace regular undergraduate learning. Pat Hiddleston [MWI] expressed gratitude for the support given to developing countries by the Australian Mathematics Competition. John Egsgard [CAN] tried to enthuse his students with mathematics, but found that his good students were turned off by contests. Students look for a challenge that multiple choice contests do not provide. Their performance does not reflect their ability and there is a problem with distractors. They often get the message that they are no good and cannot do the problems. Bill Horton [USA] taught at a minority school in San Antonio that used to be looked down upon in his region. When his students started to participate in the Texan competition, something good happened. A mathematics club was formed, students worked collaboratively and developed a mathematics culture. While he did not reach everyone, it helped build bridges to other schools and his own students sometimes excelled. He has not seen anything work so well as competitions. Jarmila Novotna [CZR] is involved with team competitions in junior and secondary schools. The students learn how to work together. Saleha Habibullah [PAK], a teacher of statistics at a Lahore women's college, felt that in developing countries where competitions were scarce, textbook learning promotes a passive acceptance of facts. She began a statistics poster competition in Lahore to promote more active learning.

Peter Ransom [GBR] pointed out that life is competition, and that time pressures in the world can be real (such as at Bletchley Park during World War II or at Chernobyl). Competitions are voluntary; children are not forced to do them. Elizabeth Schwenk [USA] has a special concern about girls, who do not do well under competitive conditions and are discouraged by male winners. Competitions are "learning negative", and we must not be deceived into thinking we are selecting the best through them. Warren Page [USA] felt that it was naive to deny the competitive spirit. He extolled the modeling competition for North American undergraduates in which teams of three worked for a weekend on a real-world problem. There were many benefits for the students, and the winning papers may appear in journals.

The panelists were asked to make a few closing remarks. Gardiner pointed out that criticism is valid where public money is being used; however, criticism of competitions are often not appropriate since those involved are volunteers. Leder felt that, on the whole, there were many positive features to competitions. Bernardi suggested that neither competitions nor high school teachers misrepresent mathematics. Hilton remarked that the reward system in schools and academe is lousy, and applauded the modeling competition described by Page.

AWARDING OF HONORARY DEGREES TO JEAN-PIERRE KAHANE AND HENRY POLLAK

REMISE DE DOCTORATS HONORIFIQUES À JEAN-PIERRE KAHANE ET HENRY POLLAK

As ICME-7 was being held on its campus, Université Laval took the opportunity to confer honorary doctoral degrees on two personalities renowned for their work and their action in relation to mathematics education at the international level. The ceremony took place in presence of Dr. Michel Gervais, Rector of Université Laval, during a plenary session on the opening morning.

Jean-Pierre Kahane [FRA], professor at the Université de Paris-Sud, was awarded a doctoral degree in Science "honoris causa" (Mathematics). Université Laval wanted thus to pay tribute to his achievements as a leading researcher in pure mathematics and as a scientist strongly engaged in mathematical education. As President of the International Commission on Mathematical Instruction (ICMI) from 1982 to 1990, Professor Kahane has played an important role in the creation of the "ICMI Studies" series of publications.

On the other hand, a doctoral degree in Education "honoris causa" (Mathematics education) was conferred on Henry O. Pollak [USA], visiting professor at Teachers College of Columbia University and formerly from Bell Laboratories Inc. The recipient has distinguished himself by his research activities in applied mathematics as well as by his exceptional commitment over the last thirty years to improve mathematics education in schools and universities. Professor Pollak was Vice-President of the International Commission on Mathematical Instruction for many years and Chief organizer of ICME-4 in Berkeley 1980.

L'Université Laval a voulu profiter de la tenue d'ICME-7 en ses murs pour décerner des doctorats honorifiques à deux personnalités qui se sont illustrées par leurs travaux et leurs actions en rapport avec l'enseignement des mathématiques au niveau international. La cérémonie s'est déroulée en présence du docteur Michel Gervais, recteur de l'Université Laval, lors d'une séance plénière le matin de l'ouverture du Congrès.

Jean-Pierre Kahane [FRA], professeur à l'Université de Paris-Sud, a reçu un doctorat ès sciences « honoris causa » (mathématiques). L'Université Laval a voulu ainsi rendre hommage à ses réalisations à la fois comme chercheur de pointe en mathématiques pures et comme scientifique fortement impliqué dans l'éducation mathématique. À titre de président de la Commission internationale de l'enseignement mathématique (CIEM) de 1982 à 1990, le Professeur Kahane à joué un rôle important dans la création de la série de publications « Études de la CIEM ».

Pour sa part, Henry O. Pollak [USA], professeur invité au Teachers College de Columbia University et autrefois de Bell Laboratories Inc., s'est vu décerner un doctorat ès sciences de l'éducation « honoris causa » (didactique des mathématiques). Le récipiendaire s'est distingué tant par ses activités de recherche en mathématiques appliquées que par son engagement exceptionnel, durant les trente dernières années, pour améliorer l'enseignement des mathématiques dans les écoles et les universités. Le professeur Pollak fut membre du Comité exécutif de la CIEM pendant plusieurs années et responsable de l'organisation du Congrès ICME-4 à Berkeley en 1980.

TRIBUTE TO H.S.M. COXETER

HOMMAGE À H.S.M. COXETER

Organizer / *Responsable* : A.J. (Sandy) Dawson [CAN]

A special event held in conjunction with ICME-7 was a dinner and film presentation in honor of Dr. H.S.M. Coxeter, the noted Canadian mathematician. Professor Coxeter and his wife, Rien, were invited to Québec City for this event and were in attendance for much of the Congress.

A number of Coxeter's former students and colleagues travelled to Québec City to join in the tribute. Representatives of the ICMI Executive Committee, the Canadian National Committee for ICME–7, the Beatty Fund, the Canadian Mathematical Society and the Canadian Mathematics Education Study Group joined the Coxeters at a dinner, sponsored in part by an anonymous donor. After the dinner the guests moved to an open ICME session during which a short talk in honor of Professor Coxeter was given by his first doctoral student and longtime collaborator, Dr. William Moser of McGill University, Montréal.

Moser's tribute was followed by a showing of two films inspired by Coxeter's work, *Dihedral kaleidoscopes* and *Platonic solids,* the latter kindly made available by Michele Emmer [ITA]. Coxeter was actively involved in the preparation of *Dihedral kaleidoscopes* and can be seen on screen constructing the set-up for many of the film's sequences. He also appears as one of the geometry experts interviewed in the film *Platonic solids.*

At the conclusion of the film presentation, and with the encouragement of a most appreciative audience, which gave the Coxeters a standing ovation, Professor Coxeter made an impromptu presentation on some insights from his recent work with Escher drawings. The agility of mind and body, so evident as he mounted the stage to give this short talk, testified to Donald Coxeter's life-affirming passion for mathematics and its presentation in understandable ways. Everyone present joined in the wish that he may continue his work for many years to come.

A CELEBRATION IN MEMORY OF
CALEB GATTEGNO

À LA MÉMOIRE DE CALEB GATTEGNO

Organizer / *Responsable* : A.J. (Sandy) Dawson [CAN]

A film presentation, offered as a celebration in memory of Caleb Gattegno (1911-1988), was held on Friday evening, August 21, as part of the ICME-7 program. The event drew an audience in excess of 100 people. The core of the session was a showing of two Gattegno-inspired films, *Epi- and hypocycloids,* and *Folklore of mathematics: Trigonometry Parts 1 - 5.*

Prior to the showing and discussion of the films a short tribute to Caleb Gattegno was given by A.J. (Sandy) Dawson [CAN]. After sketching Gattegno's varied career and significant educational initiatives, he added:

> But above all Gattegno was a teacher and a student of education, a student of teaching and learning. He never lost contact with learners and schools. His focus was always on what was essential for learning to occur.

The *Folklore of mathematics* film was shown without introduction. Martin Hoffman [USA] led the discussion which followed this film. One comment was that the lack of sound on the film focused one's attention sharply on the visual aspects. Nancy Austin [USA] commented on her use of the film with twelve year olds. Arthur Powell [USA] then led the audience through a visualization activity in preparation for the viewing of the second film. This film, *Epi- and hypocycloids,* focuses attention on the dynamic generation of cycloids by means of rolling circles of different ratios. After a brief discussion of the impact of the film, it was shown a second time.

The session closed with Sandy Dawson expressing the hope that the audience had experienced, at least in a small way, both the manner in which Gattegno might have worked in interaction with learners, and the insightfulness of this creative educator who seized the essentials of a technology and used it to direct the learner's awareness to those features of mathematical situations that are crucial for learning to occur.

FILMS AND VIDEOS

FILMS ET BANDES VIDÉO

FILMS AND VIDEOS

FILMS ET BANDES VIDÉO

Organizer / *Responsable* : John Clark [CAN]

Thomas Banchoff [USA], Michele Emmer [ITA] and Jean-Michel Kantor [FRA] were each invited to present and introduce an hour of films and videos. Two of the other sessions were constructed as tributes to Professor H.M.S. Coxeter and the late Dr. Caleb Gattegno and are reported elsewhere in the Proceedings.

The following are some of the films and videos that were shown:

"Not knot" (The Geometry Center, University of Minnesota, USA)

"Dragon fold" (Marlin Motion Pictures, Toronto, Canada)

"Space-filling curves" (Marlin Motion Pictures)

"Platonic solids" (Key Curriculum Products, Berkeley, USA)

"Stella octangular" (Key Curriculum Products)

"Dance squared" (National Film Board, Montréal, Canada)

"Notes on a triangle" (National Film Board)

"Powers of ten" (IBM, USA)

"The hypercube: projections and slicing" (Thomas Banchoff, Providence, RI, USA)

"The hypersphere: foliation and projections" (Thomas Banchoff)

"Fronts and centers" (Thomas Banchoff)

"The eye of Horus: a math show" (Michele Emmer, Rome, Italy)

"Flatland" (Michele Emmer)

"Dihedral kaleidoscopes" (The Geometry Center, University of Minnesota, USA)

"Platonic solids" (International Tele-Film Enterprises, Toronto, Canada)

"Let's teach guessing" (Mathematical Association of America, USA)

"Similarity" (National Council of Teachers of Mathematics, USA)

"The theorem of Pythagoras" (National Council of Teachers of Mathematics)

"The drawing ball" (Júlianna Szendrei, Budapest, Hungary)

"Epi- and hypo-cycloids" (Educational Solution, New York, USA)

"Folklore of mathematics: Trigonometry" (Educational Solutions)

Films by Tom Apostol, the Consortium for Mathematics and its Applications (COMAP), and Children's Television Workshop, all USA, were also shown.

SPECIAL MEETINGS

RÉUNIONS SPÉCIALES

SPECIAL MEETINGS

RÉUNIONS SPÉCIALES

Meeting of representatives of national mathematics teachers associations.
  Organizer: John Egsgard [CAN]

Meeting of editors of mathematics education journals.
  Organizer: Gerhard König [DEU]

Meeting of school representatives and examiners for the International Baccalaureate.
  Organizer: Ruth Sweetman [GBR]

Business meeting of the International Organization of Women in Mathematics Education (IOWME /*MOIFEM*).
  Organizer: Gila Hanna [CAN]

Meeting of the Inter-American Committee on Mathematics Education (CIAEM/IACME).
  Organizer: Eduardo Luna [USA]

Meeting of the International Study Group on Mathematics Education in South-East Asia.
  Organizer: Lily Christ [USA]

Meeting of the International Study Group of Ethnomathematics.
  Organizer: Ubiratán D'Ambrosio [BRA]

Meeting of the Criticalmathematics Educators Group.
  Organizer: Arthur Powell [USA]

Information meeting about the Third International Mathematics and Science Study (TIMSS).
  Organizer: David F. Robitaille [CAN]

Information meeting about the Second International Assessment of Educational Progress (IAEP-2).
  Organizer: Nancy A. Mead [USA]

Information meeting about a comparative study of mathematics and science curricula in Iberoamerican States (IBERCIMA).
Organizer: Luis Hernández Encinas [ESP]

Meeting of national competitions organizers.
Organizer: Peter Taylor [AUS]

Information meeting about "The tournament of the towns".
Organizer: Peter Taylor [AUS]

Business meeting of the World Federation of National Mathematics Competitions.
Organizer: Peter O'Halloran [AUS]

"David Hilbert Awards" and "Paul Erdös Awards", sponsored by the World Federation of National Mathematics Competitions (WFNMC).
Organizer: Peter O'Halloran [AUS]

Presentation of the report: "Italian researches in mathematics education: historical roots and present trends".
Organizer: Nicolina A. Malara [ITA]

Skits on micro-inequities, sponsored by the Committee for the Participation of Women of the Mathematical Association of America.
Organizer: Fran Rosamond [USA]

SECRETARY'S CLOSING REMARKS

OBSERVATIONS FINALES DU SECRÉTAIRE

SECRETARY'S CLOSING REMARKS

OBSERVATIONS FINALES DU SECRÉTAIRE

Mogens Niss

Roskilde University [DNK]

ICME-7 has now come to an end. We have all – more than 3400 participants from 94 different countries – gained a rich variety of new experiences, new insights, new impressions. We have met old friends and made new ones.

So, we all know – now – what an ICME is, or what it can be, don't we? However, not all of us know exactly where ICME is located in the rather complex landscape of organizations, associations, institutions, conferences, and so forth which are behind all the acronyms that we love and hate: CIBEM, CIAEM, PME, LOC, TIMSS, IOWME, CME-EMS, WFNCM, UNESCO, ICME, ICOTS, ICASE, ICMI, CIEM, HPM, IMO, IOMSC, ICTMA, IPC, WMY2000, ISGEm, IMU, GA, SEAMS, EC, ICSU/CTS, IACME, ICMI Bulletin.

Now, what is an ICME "really"? ICME is the International Congress on Mathematical Education, of which this is the seventh:

ICME-1 (1969)   Lyon (France);

ICME-2 (1972)   Exeter (United Kingdom);

ICME-3 (1976)   Karlsruhe (Germany);

ICME-4 (1980)   Berkeley (USA);

ICME-5 (1984)   Adelaide (Australia);

ICME-6 (1988)   Budapest (Hungary);

ICME-7 (1992)   Québec (Canada);

ICME-8 (1996)   Sevilla (Spain);

ICME-9 (2000)   ?

Delegates are invited to send their evaluation comments on ICME–7 and suggestions for ICME–8 to Mogens Niss, Secretary of ICMI, IMFUFA, Roskilde University, P.O. Box 260, DK 4000 Roskilde, DENMARK; Fax: +45 46755065; Electronic mail: mn@mmf.ruc.dk. As can be seen from the list above, ICME–9, in 2000, will take place in a country yet to be chosen. Countries are invited and encouraged to submit bids to ICMI.

ICMEs are held on behalf of and under the auspices of (but not by) ICMI. What is ICMI then? It is the acronym for The International Commission on Mathematical Instruction, or the Commission internationale de l'enseignement mathématique (CIEM). ICMI, which was established in 1908, is appointed by the International Mathematical Union (IMU) but is autonomous in its work. In formal terms ICMI consists of the Executive Committee plus the General Assembly.

ICMI does other things besides holding congresses. In fact, it conducts a number of activities.

ICMI STUDIES

Past:

- *School Mathematics in the 1990s* (1986);

- *The Influence of Computers and Informatics on Mathematics and Its Teaching* (1986) (new edition under way with UNESCO);

- *Mathematics as a Service Subject* (1988);

- *The Popularization of Mathematics* (1990);

- *Mathematics and Cognition* (1990);

all published by Cambridge University Press.

Appearing soon:

- *Investigations into Assessment in Mathematics Education*;

- *Cases of Assessment in Mathematics Education*;

both published by Kluwer Academic Publishers (Dordrecht, The Netherlands).

In preparation:

- *Gender and Mathematics Education* (Discussion Document published in *ICMI Bulletin* 32 and *L'Enseignement mathématique, juin-juillet* 1992);

- *What Is Research in Mathematics Education, and What Are Its Results?*

Future plans:

- New perspectives on the teaching of geometry;

- The role of history in the teaching of mathematics;

- . . .

AFFILIATED STUDY GROUPS

- Psychology of Mathematics Education (PME);

- History and Pedagogy of Mathematics (HPM);

- Women and Mathematics Education (IOWME);

Guidelines for study groups are in preparation.

REGIONAL MEETINGS

- SEACME–6, 1993 (Sixth South East Asian Conference on Mathematical Education);

- IACME–9, 1995 (Ninth Meeting of the Inter-American Committee on Mathematics Education);

- . . .

Regional meetings are sponsored, but not held, by ICMI.

WORLD MATHEMATICAL YEAR 2000

- WMY2000, which is being held by the International Mathematical Union with collaboration of ICMI, among others, will be an n-dimensional activity (where n is big) the aim of which is to show and explain to the world what mathematics is and can do, and to demonstrate its place and function in human culture.

MATHEMATICS EDUCATION SOLIDARITY PROGRAM

In the first phase of the program as presented in the Presidential Address given to this Congress by Miguel de Guzmán, ICMI will

- produce guidelines,

- set up a Steering Committee (Chair: Jean-Pierre Kahane [FRA]),

- establish a basic administrative infrastructure.

Suggestions on and financial contributions to the Solidarity Program are welcome. Please contact the Secretary at the address above.

The ICMI Executive Committee met several times during this Congress to consider new initiatives for ICMI, the state of the organization, the ICMEs, ICMI Studies, Affiliated Study Groups, the ICMI Bulletin, the International Mathematical Olympiads, regional meetings, the development of the Solidarity Fund for Education in Mathematics, and relations to other communities and organizations. Also the General Assembly of ICMI had its quadrennial meeting here in Québec.

Allow me to make a few remarks of a personal nature. Mathematics Education is a growing practical and academic field. It is also growing when it comes to organizational variety. We should attempt to establish not uniformity but unity in our field. This means that we should emphasize that despite all variations and all differences in our methods and approaches, we concentrate our efforts on a common endeavor: We have been to this congress because

- we are convinced that mathematics education is essential to everyone in all segments of any society, and because

- it is very difficult to make mathematics teaching and learning achieve the goals we wish to set up.

So, we are here because we strive to understand and improve mathematics teaching, learning, application, and creation. Our approaches may well vary considerably and be subject to different perspectives, disagreement, and controversy, from which conflict may arise. This is inevitable, and not at all deplorable. We should, however, be cautious not to operate within too narrow a spectrum of interests, and not to form too closed and permanent subgroups or "clubs". Going too far in this direction would tend to tear our field apart. Again, this does not imply that discussion, disagreement and controversy should be avoided. On the contrary, these entail "voltage differences" from which dynamics and (hopefully positive) developments are derived.

Here, ICMI sees its role as being a unifying umbrella that provides stimulation and initiative, and as a catalyst for activities ranging from concrete and pragmatic day-to-day improvements of mathematics teaching and learning to philosophical and utopian speculation. The main trend in mathematics education during the last few decades has been to avoid the unjustified reduction of complexity in our field. Our goal should be to obtain a justified reduction of complexity.

This congress has provided us with an overwhelming richness of presentations and activities of all kinds. We have worked a lot, we have learned a lot, we have laughed a lot – but we haven't slept a lot. Personally, I believe that the most important point in a scientific congress is to provide a meeting place where participants can establish contacts and friendships, form working groups and generate the germs of research projects, some of which may join the forces of researchers from several different places.

New impulses, new insights, new knowledge are also important, very much so, but much of this can in principle be obtained by reading papers and books. The extraordinary – and sometimes exhausting – extent and intensity of formal and informal congress activities constitute one of the factors that has made ICME–7 such an important and unforgettable event to all of us who participated in it.

The evident success of this Congress is due to the efforts of a very large number of people, many of whom are invisible and unknown to the participants. It would have been well deserved here to thank every one of them personally. As this is not possible, allow me to take this opportunity to thank them all as a team. There are, however, a limited number of organizers to whom we should address our very special thanks. On behalf of the Executive Committee of ICMI – and, I am convinced, of every single delegate – it is my great pleasure to express our deepest gratitude and appreciation to three persons who have been the front runners at the forefront:

The Chair of the Local Organizing Committee, Professor Claude Gaulin, Université Laval;

The Chair of the National Committee, Professor Bernard Hodgson, Université Laval; and

The Chair of the International Programme Committee, Professor David Wheeler, Vancouver.

Please join me in expressing our warmest thanks to our three splendid colleagues and to the entire team behind ICME–7.

With these words I hereby declare the Seventh International Congress on Mathematical Education closed.

Avec ces mots, j'ai le plaisir de déclarer clos le septième Congrès international sur l'enseignement des mathématiques de 1992.

THANK YOU ALL.

SOCIAL AND CULTURAL ACTIVITIES

ACTIVITÉS SOCIALES ET CULTURELLES

SOCIAL AND CULTURAL ACTIVITIES

ACTIVITÉS SOCIALES ET CULTURELLES

EXCURSION DAY /
JOURNÉE D'EXCURSION

Following the tradition of past ICME congresses, a one-day excursion was organized on August 20 and gave participants an opportunity to relax and make new acquaintances. There was a choice of six excursions: A) Historic Québec and cruise on the St. Lawrence River; B) Historic Québec and a visit to a maple sugar shack; C) A rural excursion on Orléans Island and the Beaupré Coast; D) Sightseeing tour of the Charlevoix Region; E) Whale-watching in the Charlevoix Region; F) Excursion to Montréal.

Suivant la tradition des congrès ICME précédents, le 20 août fut jour d'excursion. Les participants et participantes eurent ainsi l'occasion de se détendre et de faire de nouvelles connaissances. Chacun avait le choix entre six excursions : A) Québec historique et croisière sur le fleuve Saint-Laurent ; B) Québec historique et excursion à la cabane à sucre ; C) Excursion champêtre à l'île d'Orléans et sur la côte de Beaupré ; D) Excursion touristique dans la région de Charlevoix ; E) Excursion aux baleines dans la région de Charlevoix ; F) Excursion à Montréal.

HAPPY HOURS /
RÉCEPTIONS

Daily "Happy Hours" provided excellent opportunities to meet new people and exchange ideas in an informal atmosphere. One of them was a reception offered by the Faculty of Education and the Faculty of Science and Engineering of Université Laval. During another one, sponsored by Sevillian authorities, Spanish representatives extended an invitation to all ICME-7 participants to attend the 8th International Congress on Mathematical Education (ICME-8) in Sevilla in July 1996.

Des réceptions ont fourni à chaque jour une excellente occasion de connaître de nouvelles personnes et ont favorisé l'échange d'idées dans une atmosphère détendue. L'une d'elles fut offerte par la Faculté des sciences de l'éducation et la Faculté des sciences et de génie de l'Université Laval pour souhaiter la bienvenue à tous. Lors d'une autre, commanditée par les autorités de Séville, les représentants espagnols ont cordialement invité les participants d'ICME-7 à assister au 8ᵉ Congrès international sur l'enseignement des mathématiques (ICME-8) à Séville en juillet 1996.

CULTURAL EVENING /
SOIRÉE CULTURELLE

On the last evening, following an informal outdoor party, a Cultural evening was offered to all participants. The program featured a selection of Québec artists and included a variety of activities: folk songs and dances, aerial ballet, classical music, humor, equilibrists act. The show was followed by dance with orchestra.

À la suite d'une réception informelle tenue en plein air, une Soirée culturelle a été offerte à tous les participants le dernier soir. Le programme a mis en vedette une sélection d'artistes québécois dans une variété de numéros : chansons et danses folkloriques, ballet aérien, musique classique, humour, équilibrisme. Le spectacle a été suivi de danse avec orchestre.

5 KM RUN–WALK /
COURSE–MARCHE DE 5 KM

For the first time in the history of ICMEs, a 5 km Run/Walk was organized on the campus of Université Laval, with the participation of nearly 450 people. The fastest times recorded were: 17 min 51 s (men), 21 min 34 s (women) and 22 min (youngsters). Some of those who preferred to take it easy and enjoy the nice surroundings took more than one hour. All participants were greeted by an enthusiastic crowd at the finish line.

Une première dans l'histoire des congrès ICME : l'organisation d'une Course/marche de 5 km sur le campus de l'Université Laval. Près de 450 personnes y ont pris part, les temps les plus rapides étant : 17 min 51 s (hommes), 21 min 34 s (femmes) et 22 min (jeunes). Certains ont préféré ne pas se presser et profiter de la beauté du site, prenant plus d'une heure pour compléter le parcours. Tous les participants ont été accueillis à la ligne d'arrivée par une foule enthousiaste.

MEETING OF THE "OLD HANDS" /
RENCONTRE DES « VIEUX ROUTIERS »

A special dinner was organized for the "old hands", i.e. the twelve persons who have participated in all ICMEs from ICME-1 (1969) to ICME-7: Josette Adda [FRA], Shmuel Avital [ISR], Jerry P. Becker [USA], Alan W. Bell [GBR], John C. Egsgard [CAN], Claude Gaulin [CAN], Geoffrey

Howson [GBR], Bernhard H. Neumann [AUS], Ruben Schramm [DEU], Hilary Shuard † [GBR], Hans-Georg Steiner [DEU] and Erich C. Wittmann [DEU].

Un diner spécial a été organisé à l'intention des « vieux routiers », c'est-à-dire les douze personnes qui ont participé à tous les congrès ICME, depuis ICME-1 (1969) jusqu'à ICME-7 : Josette Adda [FRA], Shmuel Avital [ISR], Jerry P. Becker [USA], Alan W. Bell [GBR], John C. Egsgard [CAN], Claude Gaulin [CAN], Geoffrey Howson [GBR], Bernhard H. Neumann [AUS], Ruben Schramm [DEU], Hilary Shuard † [GBR], Hans-Georg Steiner [DEU] and Erich C. Wittmann [DEU].

COMMITTEES AND SPONSORS

COMITÉS ET COMMANDITAIRES

INTERNATIONAL COMMISSION
ON MATHEMATICAL INSTRUCTION

COMMISSION INTERNATIONALE
DE L'ENSEIGNEMENT MATHÉMATIQUE

EXECUTIVE COMMITTEE / *COMITÉ EXÉCUTIF* **(1991-1994)**

President / *Président* : Miguel de Guzmán [ESP]

Vice-Presidents / *Vice-présidents* : Jeremy Kilpatrick [USA],
Lee Peng Yee [SGP]

Secretary / *Secrétaire* : Mogens Niss [DNK]

Members / *Membres* : Yuri L. Ershov [RUS],
Eduardo Luna [DOM],
Anna Sierpinska [POL]

Ex-Officio Members / *Membres d'office* : Jean-Pierre Kahane [FRA]
(Past President), Jacques-Louis Lions [FRA] (IMU President), Jacob
Palis [BRA] (IMU Secretary), J. H. van Lint [NLD] (IMU Represent-
ative on ICSU/CTS, the Committee on the Teaching of Science of the
International Council of Scientific Unions)

The International Commission on Mathematical Instruction (ICMI) is
a subcommission of the International Mathematical Union (IMU), whose
General Assembly elects ICMI's officers and other members of the Executive
Committee. ICMI has National Representatives from around 60 countries,
not all of which are IMU members.

La Commission internationale de l'enseignement mathématique (CIEM)
est une sous-commission de l'Union mathématique internationale (UMI),
dont l'assemblée générale élit les dirigeants et les autres membres du Comité
exécutif de la CIEM. Celle-ci a des représentants nationaux dans une
soixantaine de pays (pas tous membres de l'UMI).

MAJOR ICME-7 COMMITTEES

PRINCIPAUX COMITÉS D'ICME-7

NATIONAL COMMITTEE /
COMITÉ NATIONAL

John Berry
Michael Cassidy
Pierre De Celles
John C. Egsgard
Claude Gaulin
Gila Hanna
Carl Herz
Bernard R. Hodgson, chair / *président*
Lars Jansson
Carolyn Kieran
Thomas E. Kieren
Jean-Claude Méthot
Eric R. Muller
David F. Robitaille
Patricia K. Rogers
Rémi Vaillancourt
Charles Verhille
David Wheeler
Edgar R. Williams
Edward Zegray

EXECUTIVE COMMITTEE /
COMITÉ EXÉCUTIF

John C. Egsgard
Claude Gaulin
Bernard R. Hodgson
Carolyn Kieran
Eric R. Muller
David F. Robitaille, chair / *président*
Rémi Vaillancourt
David Wheeler

INTERNATIONAL PROGRAM COMMITTEE /
COMITÉ INTERNATIONAL DU PROGRAMME

Claudi Alsina
Willibald Dörfler
Rosemary Fraser
Geoffrey Howson (before / *avant* Jan. 1991)
Edward Jacobsen
Jeremy Kilpatrick
Lev Kudriatsev
Eduardo Luna
Eric R. Muller
Roberta Mura
Tibor Nemetz
Mogens Niss (since / *depuis* Jan. 1991)
Lee Peng Yee
David F. Robitaille
Anna Sierpinska
David Wheeler, chair / *président*

LOCAL ORGANIZING COMMITTEE /
COMITÉ D'ORGANISATION LOCALE

Executive / *Exécutif*
Claude Gaulin, chair / *président*
Bernard R. Hodgson
Monique Meilleur, executive assistant / *adjointe exécutive*
Edward Zegray
Dominique Houde, executive assistant until July 1991 /
adjointe exécutive jusqu'en juillet 1991

Other members / *Autres membres*
Julien Bouchard
Gilles Dionne †
Réal Dionne
Louis-Philippe Gaudreault
Richard Grenier
Lévis Lemire
Rivard Marois
Marcel Mius d'Entremont
Lucille Roy

453

Secretariat / *Secrétariat*
Monick Debroux
Ginette Lamontagne, secretary / *secrétaire*
Patricia Lorman
Eric R. Muller

Clerical support / *Personnel de soutien*
Diane Arseneault
Rosanne D. Bruneau
Charlotte Gélinas
Nathalie Paré

Graphic work / *Graphisme*
Elizabeth Ann Schofield

Equipment / *Équipements*
Francis Loubier
Rivard Marois, chair / *président*
Marc-André Pépin

Rooms / *Locaux*
Julien Bouchard, chair / *président*
Lyse Carrier

Accommodation / *Hébergement*
Louis-Philippe Gaudreault, chair / *président*
Monique Meilleur
Lucille Roy

Food services / *Services alimentaires*
Hervé-G. Morin, chair / *président*

Films and videos / *Films et bandes vidéo*
John Clark, chair / *président*

Educational materials exhibits / *Exposition de matériel didactique*
Thomas Déri, co-chair / *co-président*
Gilles Dionne †, local coordinator / *coordonnateur local*
Réal Dionne, local coordinator / *coordonnateur local*
Ginette Lamontagne
Bob Robinson, co-chair / *co-président*
Edward Zegray

Canadian presentation / *Présentation canadienne*
A. J. (Sandy) Dawson
Carolyn Kieran, chair / *présidente*
Israel Kleiner
Lise Paquin
John Poland

Exhibition / *Exposition* « Le savoir-compter »
Françoys Bédard
Louis Charbonneau, chair / *président*
Charlotte Giguère
Bernard R. Hodgson
Paul Lavoie
Mélanie Sainte-Marie

Autres expositions / *Other exhibitions*
Claude Gaulin
Lévis Lemire, chair / *président*
Richard Grenier
Pauline Lauzon
Ginette Leblanc
Richard Pallascio

Math Trail / *Sentier mathématique*
Dudley Blane, special consultant / *consultant spécial*
Denis de Champlain
Marcel Mius d'Entremont, chair / *président*
Louis-Philippe Gaudreault

Cultural evening / *Soirée culturelle*
Marie Gauvin Moisan, co-chair / *co-présidente*
Danielle Fiset, co-chair / *co-présidente*

5 km Run–Walk / *Course–marche de 5 km*
Marc Corcoran
Louis-Philippe Gaudreault, chair / *président*
Claude Levesque

Special collaborators / *Collaborateurs spéciaux*
Claudi Alsina
Diane Bédard
Noëlange Boisclair
Robert Caillibot
Charles Cassidy
Louise Chamberland
Françoise Cordeau
Guy Désilets
Jean Dionne
Thérèse Gadbois
Catherine-Ann H. Gauthier
Nancy Gélinas
Gilles Girard
François Grondin
Jean-Sébastien Hodgson
Louis-Philippe Hodgson
Marie-Isabelle Hodgson
Hélène Kayler
Raynald Lacasse
Caroline Lajoie
Hélène Laliberté
Céline Larochelle
Marie-Louis Lavertu
Lesley Lee
Jacques Lefebvre
Hélène Légaré
René J. Lemieux
François Lupien
Jean Lupien
Claudia Nieto
Nicole Pons
Luis Puig
François Rheault
Louise Roy
Anna Sierpinska

LIAISON COMMITTEE /
COMITÉ DE LIAISON

Michael Cassidy, co-chair / *co-président*
John C. Egsgard
Edward Zegray, co-chair / *co-président*

FUND-RAISING COMMITTEE /
COMITÉ DE FINANCEMENT

Governmental Grants / *Subventions gouvernementales*
John Berry
Claude Gaulin
Bernard R. Hodgson
Maurice Labbé
Rémi Vaillancourt, chair / *président*

Corporate Sponsorships / *Commandites privées*
Julien Bouchard
Jean-Marie De Koninck
Ron Fitzgerald
Marcel Jobin
Lévis Lemire
Guy-W. Richard
Edgar R. Williams
Edward Zegray, chair / *président*

SPONSORS /
COMMANDITAIRES ET PARRAINS

Agence canadienne de développement international /
    Canadian International Development Agency
Air Canada
American Mathematical Society (USA)
Association des promoteurs de l'avancement de la mathématique
    à l'élémentaire (Québec)
Association mathématique du Québec
Bell Cellulaire / *Bell Cellular*
Canon Tours, Inc. (Japan)
Casio Canada Ltée
Centre de recherches mathématiques, Université de Montréal
Conseil de recherches en sciences humaines du Canada /
    Social Sciences and Humanities Research Council of Canada
Conseil des ministres de l'Éducation (Canada) /
    Council of Ministers of Education, Canada
Conseil du Loisir Scientifique de Québec
Conseil national de recherches du Canada /
    National Research Council of Canada
Groupe canadien d'étude en didactique des mathématiques /
    Canadian Mathematics Education Study Group
Groupe des responsables en mathématique au secondaire (Québec)
Hewlett-Packard Canada Ltd.
Industrie, Sciences et Technologie, Canada /
    Industry, Science and Technology Canada
Janisse Inc.
Location d'autos Budget / *Budget Rent-A-Car*
Mathematical Association of America (USA)
Ministère de l'Éducation du Québec
Ministère de l'Enseignement supérieur et de la Science du Québec
Ministère des Affaires internationales du Québec
Ministère du Tourisme du Québec
National Council of Teachers of Mathematics (USA)
OE Inc.
Office du tourisme et des congrès de la Communauté urbaine de Québec
Quebec Association of Mathematics Teachers
Société mathématique du Canada / *Canadian Mathematical Society*
Société royale du Canada / *Royal Society of Canada*
Texas Instruments, Inc.
UNESCO
Université Laval

COMMERCIAL EXHIBITORS /
EXPOSANTS COMMERCIAUX

Addison-Wesley Publishing Company (USA)
Arlington-Hews, Inc. (Canada)
Cambridge University Press (UK)
Children's Television Workshop (USA)
Casio Canada Ltd.
Copp Clark Pitman Ltd. (Canada)
Diffusion et Promotion du Livre Universitaire (Canada)
Editions du Renouveau Pédagogique Inc. (Canada)
Élan informatique (Canada)
Fachinformations Zentrum Karlsruhe
      (Scientific Information Service, Inc.) (Germany/USA)
France Édition
Gaëtan Morin Éditeur (Canada)
Gage Educational Publishing Company (Canada)
Guérin / Lidec (Canada)
HBJ-Holt Canada
Hewlett Packard Canada Ltd.
Janson Publications, Inc. (USA)
Key Curriculum Press (USA)
Kluwer Academic Publishers (Netherlands/USA)
Lego-Canada Inc.
Mathematical Association of America (USA)
Mathematical Sciences Education Board (USA)
Mathpro Press
McGraw-Hill Ryerson Limited (Canada)
Modulor Éditeur (Canada)
Mondia Éditeurs Inc. (Canada)
National Council of Teachers of Mathematics (USA)
Nelson Canada
QED Books (UK)
Scott, Foresman & Co. (USA)
Soft Warehouse, Inc. (USA)
Texas Instruments, Inc.
University of Cambridge Local Examinations Syndicate (UK)
Waterloo Maple Software (Canada)
Wolfram Research, Inc. (USA)

PARTICIPANTS

PARTICIPANTS ET PARTICIPANTES

LIST OF PARTICIPANTS

LISTE DES PARTICIPANTS ET PARTICIPANTES

ABDOUS, M'hamed [CAN]
ABDUL HAMID, Hazimah [MYS]
ABDUL KHADHUR, A.A.Ali [KWT]
ABDULRAHMAN, Lyndamany [MUS]
ABDULRAHMAN, Rashid [MUS]
ABEL, Heinrich F. [DEU]
ABELE, Albrecht H. [DEU]
ABELE, Ursula E. [DEU]
ABELES, Francine [USA]
ABELES, Mieke [NLD]
ABERKANE, Younes [FRA]
ABRAMOVICH, Sergei [ISR]
ABRANTES, Paulo [PRT]
ACCASCINA, Giuseppe [ITA]
ADACHI, Kumiko [JPN]
ADAMS, Bennie A. [USA]
ADDA, Josette [FRA]
ADDINGTON, Susan [USA]
ADIE, Heather M. [AUS]
ADLER, Jillian Beryl [ZAF]
AFFLACK, Ruth H. [USA]
AFONSO-MARTIN, Maria Candelaria [ESP]
AHMED, Afzal [GBR]
AHRENS, Richard [GBR]
AHRENS, Susan [GBR]
AHUJA, Mangho [USA]
AIZPÚN LÓPEZ, Alberto [ESP]
AJOSE, Sunday A. [USA]
AKAHORI, Kanji [JPN]
AKAI, Toshiyuki [JPN]
AKHURST, William Thomas [AUS]
AKSU, Meral [TUR]
AL-KHALAF AL-SHEIK, Abdullah [KWT]
AL-QATTAN, Ibrahim H. [KWT]
ALAIN, Marcel [CAN]
ALAMOLHODAEI, Hassan [IRN]
ALBERS, Donald [USA]
ALBERT, Jeanne [ISR]
ALBERTI, Carla [ITA]

ALDAZ, Isaias [MEX]
ALDERFER, Charlotte S. [USA]
ALDERFER, Evan B. [USA]
ALDON, Gilles [FRA]
ALDRIDGE, Sharne Maria [AUS]
ALEXANDER, Bonnie [CAN]
ALEXANDER, David M. [CAN]
ALGABA DURAN, Encarnacion [ESP]
ALGABA DURAN, Santiago [ESP]
ALIBERT, Cendrine [FRA]
ALIBERT, Daniel [FRA]
ALIBERT, Micheline [FRA]
ALIBERT, Yann [FRA]
ALLAIRE, Richard [CAN]
ALLAN, George [CAN]
ALLAN, Janet E. [CAN]
ALLARD, Jacques [CAN]
ALLARD, Joane [CAN]
ALLEN, Amy [USA]
ALLEN, Hugh [CAN]
ALLEN, Jenni [GBR]
ALLISON, Desmond Michael [HKG]
ALLISON, Gisèle [HKG]
ALLODI, Mariarosa [USA]
ALM, Bengt [SWE]
ALM, Lena [SWE]
ALO', Richard [USA]
ALRO, Helle Klitgard [DNK]
ALSINA, Claudi [ESP]
ALVAREZ, Rosa [ESP]
ALVIN, Barbara [USA]
AMALBERTI, Robert François [FRA]
AMAMIYA, Masanori [JPN]
AMANO, Kasumi [JPN]
AMIT, Miriam [ISR]
ANDERBERG, Bewgt [SWE]
ANDERSON, Ann G. [CAN]
ANDERSON, Caroline Ida [USA]
ANDERSON, Christine E. [GBR]

ANDERSON, E. Earl [USA]
ANDERSON-WYCKOFF, Margaret [USA]
ANDZANS, Agnis [LAT]
ANGELI, Gianfranco [ITA]
ANGERS-TREMBLAY, Josée [CAN]
ANNICE, Clem [AUS]
ANTHONY, Glenda [NZL]
ANTIBI, André [FRA]
ANTONIUS, Sören [DNK]
ANTONIUS, Wedad [CAN]
ARAM, Saleh A. [YEM]
ARANDA PLATA, Antonio [ESP]
ARCAVI, Abraham [ISR]
ARDIZZONE, Maria Rosa [ITA]
ARIAS, José Elisfo [MEX]
ARITA, Eleanor [USA]
ARMSTRONG, Christine [GBR]
ARMSTRONG, Lee H. [USA]
ARMSTRONG, Peter Kenneth [GBR]
ARNOLD, Betty J. [USA]
ARNOLD, Gene W. [USA]
ARNOLD, Pip [NZL]
ARORA, Manmohan S [BHR]
ARRIERO VILLACORTA, Ma. Carmen [ESP]
ARSAC, Gilbert [FRA]
ARSENAULT, Diane [CAN]
ARSENEAULT, Micheline [CAN]
ARTIGUE, Michèle [FRA]
ARYA, Jagdish [CAN]
ARZARELLO, Ferdinando [ITA]
ASADA, Teruko [JPN]
ASAMI, Kayoko [JPN]
ASCOLI-BARTOLI, Maria Teresa [ITA]
ASHFORD, Marvin W. [USA]
ASHFORD, Stella R. [USA]
ASHOK, Robin [USA]
ASHOUR, Attia [EGY]
ASKER, Gunnar [SWE]
ASSELIN, Jacques [CAN]
ASTRUP, Thorvald [NOR]
ATKINS, Warren James [AUS]
ATWEH, William [AUS]
AUB, Elspeth [JAM]
AUB, Martin Richard [JAM]
AUDETTE, Julie [CAN]
AUDIBERT, Gérard P.A. [FRA]
AUDIN, Pierre [FRA]
AUGUST, John [USA]
AUGUST-ROTHMAN, Phyllis [ISR]
AUKEMA, Jan J. [NLD]
AUKEMA-SCHEPEL, Agneta [NLD]
AUSTIN, Nancy [USA]
AUTHIER, Hélène [FRA]
AVANZINO, Paula [USA]
AVITAL, Shmuel [ISR]
AWAD, Gilbert [CAN]

AWAGA, Hiroshi [CAN]
AYOUB, Ayoub B. [USA]
AZZALI, Evi [ITA]
AZZOLINO, Agnes [USA]
BABOLIAN, Esmail [IRN]
BACON, Lily [CAN]
BADEAU, Martin [CAN]
BADOIAN, Marty [USA]
BAGGETT, Patricia [USA]
BAILEY, Goldie [CAN]
BAILEY, Peter [GBR]
BAILEY, Robert [CAN]
BAILLARGEON, Serge [CAN]
BAILLE, Philippe [CAN]
BAJANI, Gurudas [IND]
BAKKER, Gert [NLD]
BALACHEFF, Nicolas [FRA]
BALBUENA, Luis [ESP]
BALDINO, Roberto Ribeiro [BRA]
BALL, Geoffrey R. [AUS]
BALL, Rita D. [AUS]
BALOGLOU, George [USA]
BANCHOFF, Thomas [USA]
BANDO CASADO, Trinidad [ESP]
BANKOV, Kiril [BGR]
BAÑOS POLGLASE, Blanca [ESP]
BAPTIST, Peter [DEU]
BARAK, Frank [USA]
BARAK, Marguerite [USA]
BARBEAU, Edward J. [CAN]
BARBIN-CHARLOT, Evelyne [FRA]
BARCHAM, Peter J. [AUS]
BARIL-VINCENT, Monique [CAN]
BARLOW, Alan [CAN]
BARNES, Judy M. [CAN]
BARNES, Mary S. [AUS]
BARNETT, Carne [USA]
BARNETT, Janet H. [USA]
BARRA, Mario [ITA]
BARRETT, Lida K. [USA]
BARRIÈRE, André [CAN]
BARROSO, Leônidas C. [BRA]
BARRY, Bill [AUS]
BARSHINGER, Richard [USA]
BARTLETT, Dawn N. [AUS]
BARTLETT, Steven P. [AUS]
BARTOLINI BUSSI, Maria [ITA]
BARTON, Bill [NZL]
BASARTE ANGUIANO, Pilar [ESP]
BASSO, Milene [ITA]
BATANERO BERNABEU, Maria Carmen [ESP]
BAUER, Carole A. [USA]
BAXTER, Carole [USA]
BAXTER, Jeffrey Peter [AUS]
BAZAN, Maria Chiara [ITA]
BAZIK, Edna [USA]

464

BAZZINI, Luciana [ITA]
BEAL, Susan R. [USA]
BEATTYS, Candice [USA]
BEAUDOIN, Danièle [CAN]
BEAUDOIN, Michel [CAN]
BEAUDOIN, Nicole [CAN]
BEAULIEU, Francine [CAN]
BEAULIEU, Hélène [CAN]
BEAULIEU, Liliane [CAN]
BEAULIEU-ROULET, Louiselle [CAN]
BEBOUT, Harriett C. [USA]
BECHARA-SANCHEZ, Lucilia [BRA]
BECKER, Jerry P. [USA]
BECKER, Joanne Rossi [USA]
BECKMANN, Astrid [DEU]
BECKMANN, Charlene [USA]
BÉDARD, Diane [CAN]
BÉDARD, Françoys [CAN]
BÉDARD, Isabelle [CAN]
BEDNARZ, Nadine [CAN]
BEERS, George S. [USA]
BEERS, Mary Leigh [USA]
BEEVERS, Clifford E. [GBR]
BEEVERS, Elizabeth A. [GBR]
BEGG, Andrew J.C. [NZL]
BEHFOROOZ, G. [USA]
BEJARANO DIAZ, Dolores [ESP]
BEKKEN, Otto B. [NOR]
BÉLAIR, Luc [CAN]
BÉLANGER, Alberte [CAN]
BÉLANGER, Patrick [CAN]
BÉLANGER, Yves [CAN]
BELL, Alan W. [GBR]
BELL, Dorothy [GBR]
BELL, Jean F. [USA]
BELL, Max [USA]
BELLEMARE, Marie-Luce [CAN]
BELLITTIERE, Daniel [USA]
BELLOT-ROSADO, Francisco [ESP]
BELSOM, Christopher G. [GBR]
BELYAZID, Fatima [CAN]
BEN-CHAIM, David [ISR]
BEN-CHAIM, Riva [ISR]
BENCIVENGA, Roberto [CAN]
BENJUMEA GONZALEZ, Carlos D. [ESP]
BENNETT, Sarah [CAN]
BERENJI, Mohammad Reza [IRN]
BERENSON, Hannah Grace [ISR]
BERENSON, Lewis [ISR]
BERENSON, Sarah B. [USA]
BERG, Gene [USA]
BERGGREN, Tasoula [CAN]
BERGSTEN, Christer [SWE]
BERGSTRÖM, Lars [SWE]
BERKOVITZ, Joseph [USA]
BERLIN, Donna F. [USA]

BERNAD GARCES, Elisa [ESP]
BERNARDI, Claudio [ITA]
BERNAT, Philippe [FRA]
BERNAT, Rolande [FRA]
BERO, Peter [SVK]
BERRY, Andrew [GBR]
BERRY, Christine [GBR]
BERRY, Elizabeth [GBR]
BERRY, John [CAN]
BERRY, John Stephen [GBR]
BERRY, Lisa [USA]
BERTHE, Daniel [FRA]
BERTIN, Christiane [FRA]
BERTNESS, Charles H. [USA]
BERTOLINI, Rinaldo [ITA]
BERZSENYI, George [USA]
BERZSENYI, Kay [USA]
BESSE, Chris [CAN]
BESSOT, Annie [FRA]
BESUDEN, Heinrich [DEU]
BESUDEN, Johanna [DEU]
BETZEL, Daniel [USA]
BETZEL, Elizabeth [USA]
BEZUSZKA, Stanley J. [USA]
BIBBY, John [GBR]
BICHARA, Jean Dominique [FRA]
BICHARA, Marie-Thérèse [FRA]
BICHO, Joaquim Mussuaho Luis Marungo
    [MOZ]
BICUDO, Irineu [BRA]
BICUDO, Maria A. V. [BRA]
BIDWELL, James K. [USA]
BIDWELL, Marilyn [USA]
BIEMBENGUT, Maria Salett [BRA]
BIGUERD, Ghyslaine [MTQ]
BILCHEV, Svetoslav [BGR]
BIRD, Elliott [USA]
BIRNIE, Susan [USA]
BIRON, Diane [CAN]
BISAILLON, Ginette [CAN]
BISHOP, Alan J. [AUS]
BISHOP, Diane [CAN]
BISSON, Diane [CAN]
BITTER, Gary [USA]
BITTER, Marie-Elise [NLD]
BJERRE, Erik [DNK]
BJÖRCK, Birgitta [SWE]
BJÖRCK, Göran [SWE]
BJORK, Elizabeth [USA]
BJÖRK, Lars-Eric [SWE]
BJÖRK, Ulla [SWE]
BJÖRKQVIST, Eivor [FIN]
BJÖRKQVIST, Ole [FIN]
BLANC, Paul [GBR]
BLANCO DEL CAN, Mª Concepcion [ESP]
BLANCO NIETO, Lorenzo [ESP]

BLANE, Dudley [AUS]
BLAZEY, Graham [AUS]
BLITHE, Thora Margaret [NZL]
BLOCK SEVILLA, David Francisco [MEX]
BLONDEL, Ezra [GBR]
BLUM, Werner [DEU]
BLUMENTHAL, Gladis R. [BRA]
BLUMENTHAL, José S. [BRA]
BOBANGO, Janet C. [USA]
BOBIS, Janette [AUS]
BOCKBRADER, Barbara [USA]
BODDY, Jean [USA]
BODIN, Antoine [FRA]
BÖER, Heinz [DEU]
BOERO, Paolo [ITA]
BOERYD, Bernt [SWE]
BOERYD, Birgitta [SWE]
BOHLIN, Roy M. [USA]
BOIERI, Paolo [ITA]
BOILEAU, André [CAN]
BOILY, Brigitte [CAN]
BOISCLAIR, Noëlange [CAN]
BOISVERT, Louise [CAN]
BOISVERT, Shelagh M. [CAN]
BOLDUC, François-Michel [CAN]
BOLES, Eugene [USA]
BOLES, Martha [USA]
BOLIVER, David E. [USA]
BOLIVER, E. Alene [USA]
BOLLETTA, Raimondo [ITA]
BOLON, Jeanne [FRA]
BONAR, Daniel [USA]
BONAR, Martha [USA]
BONILLA, Elisa [MEX]
BONOTTO, Cinzia [ITA]
BOOKER, George [AUS]
BOOKMAN, Jack [USA]
BOOTA, Albert I. [CAN]
BOPAPE, Mathume [ZAF]
BORBA, Marcelo C. [BRA]
BORG, Paul [NLD]
BOROVCNIK, Manfred [AUT]
BOROVCNIK, Waltraud [AUT]
BOROWCZYK, Jacques [FRA]
BOSWALL, Alberta [CAN]
BOSWALL, Graeme [CAN]
BOUCHARD, Jean [CAN]
BOUCHARD, Julien [CAN]
BOUCHARD, Michel [CAN]
BOUKHSSIMI, Driss [MAR]
BOULET, Geneviève [CAN]
BOULTON-LEWIS, Gillian M. [AUS]
BOURKE, Lex [AUS]
BOURKE, Wendy [AUS]
BOWERS, Craig S. [CAN]
BOWERS, Fred H. [USA]

BOWERS, Hazel G. [GBR]
BOWERS, Roger G. [GBR]
BOWERS, Sarah A. [GBR]
BOYCE, Elsa K. [USA]
BOYCE, Penny [AUS]
BOYCE, William E. [USA]
BOYÉ, Anne [FRA]
BRAATHE, Hans Jørgen [NOR]
BRADEN, Bart [USA]
BRADFORD, James C. [USA]
BRADFORD, Martha E. [USA]
BRADFORD, Richard [USA]
BRADSHAW, Carole M. [CAN]
BRADSHAW, John C. [CAN]
BRANDON, Paul R. [USA]
BRÁS DO ROSÁRIO, Maria Edite [PRT]
BRASSARD, René [CAN]
BREITEIG, Trygve [NOR]
BREKKE, Dale L. [USA]
BREWSTER, C. Stuart [USA]
BREWSTER, Renate [USA]
BRIAND, Joseph-Marie [CAN]
BRIEN, Christopher J. [AUS]
BRIGHT, George W. [USA]
BRILLANT, Michèle [FRA]
BRINKWORTH, Pauline [AUS]
BRINKWORTH, Peter Charles [AUS]
BRISEBOIS, Marcel [CAN]
BRITT, Murray Sarelius [NZL]
BRITTON, Sandra [AUS]
BROCHU, Carl [CAN]
BROCKMANN, Ellen Mary [USA]
BROCKMANN, K. [USA]
BROEKMAN, Harrie [NLD]
BROLIN, Hans [SWE]
BROLIN, Meiry [SWE]
BROOK, Michael [USA]
BROWN, Brenda [USA]
BROWN, Dawn [USA]
BROWN, Eillen [USA]
BROWN, Gary [USA]
BROWN, Ian C. [GBR]
BROWN, Jody D. [USA]
BROWN, Joseph G. [USA]
BROWN, Margaret L. [GBR]
BROWN, Marion [GBR]
BROWN, Ronald [GBR]
BROWN, Stephen I. [USA]
BROWN, Sue [USA]
BROWN, T. Grant [USA]
BROWNE, Richard A. [GBR]
BROWNING, Christine [USA]
BRUBAKER, Marvin L. [USA]
BRUCKLAND, Gareth H. [GBR]
BRUNEAU, Rosanne D. [CAN]
BRUNSON, Barry [USA]

BRUNSON, Pansy W. [USA]
BRUTLAG, Dan [USA]
BRYANT, Robert [USA]
BUENO, Ana Maria [BRA]
BUERK, Dorothy [USA]
BUNYA, Naruto [JPN]
BUONTEMPO, Alison [GBR]
BUONTEMPO, David John [GBR]
BURFORD, Frances O. [USA]
BURGUÉS, Carme [ESP]
BURJAN, Vladimír [SVK]
BURKHARDT, Hugh [GBR]
BURN, Robert P. [GBR]
BURNELL, John Gregory [NZL]
BURNETT, J. Dale [CAN]
BURNEY-VINCENT, Carole [CAN]
BURNS, Susan J. [GBR]
BURRILL, Gail [USA]
BURRILL, John C. [USA]
BURSCHEID, Hans J. [DEU]
BURSCHEID, Jugnid [DEU]
BURTON, Leone [GBR]
BUSEKIST, David [USA]
BUSHAW, Donald W. [USA]
BUSHAW, Sylvia [USA]
BUSSER, Elizabeth [FRA]
BUTEL, Carol. V. [NZL]
BUTLER, Douglas E. [GBR]
BYRKIT, Donald [USA]
CABALLERO, James B. [USA]
CABALLERO, Peggy D. [USA]
CABAÑAS SERNA, Angel L. [ESP]
CALLEJO DE LA VEGA, Maria Luz [ESP]
CALVO LEONOR, Mª Angeles [ESP]
CAMACHO TOSINA, Manuela [ESP]
CAMPBELL, Cleo [USA]
CAMPBELL, David M. [USA]
CAMPBELL, Gregory [USA]
CAMPBELL, Patricia F. [USA]
CAMPBELL, Sarah C. [USA]
CAMPÓN RODILLO, Petra [ESP]
CAMPOS, Tania M.M. [BRA]
CANATE, Humberto [USA]
CANNIZZARO BOLETTA, Lucilla [ITA]
CANTIN, Gino [CAN]
CANTORAL-URIZA, Ricardo [MEX]
CANTRELL, David [USA]
CAPÉRAÀ, Philippe [CAN]
CAPPO, Marjorie [USA]
CAPPONI, Bernard [FRA]
CARDINAL VON WIDDERN, Erika [DEU]
CAREY, Deborah [USA]
CAREY, Kathleen [USA]
CARL, Iris [USA]
CARLES ZARAGOZA, Pauli [ESP]
CARLSON, Ronald [USA]

CARMICHAEL, Jean-Pierre [CAN]
CARMINATI, Benedetto [ITA]
CARMINATI, Marco [ITA]
CARON, Chantal [CAN]
CARON, Renée P. [CAN]
CARPENTER, James E. [USA]
CARR, Alistair Robert [AUS]
CARR, Ron [CAN]
CARRAHER, David W. [BRA]
CARRIER, Lyse [CAN]
CARRIÈRE, Grégoire [CAN]
CARRINGTON, Anne [AUS]
CARSON, Virginia [USA]
CARSS, Marjorie [AUS]
CARTER, Jack [USA]
CARTER, Richard [USA]
CARVAJAL JUÁREZ, Alicia Lily [MEX]
CARVALHO, Dione Lucchesi De [BRA]
CASALS COLLDECARRERA, Mercedes [ESP]
CASAS-GARCÍA, Luis Manuel [ESP]
CASSIDY, Charles [CAN]
CASSIDY, Michael [CAN]
CASTAGNOLA, Ercole [ITA]
CASTELLO NORIA, Maria [ESP]
CASTERTON, Alina [CAN]
CASTRO, Encarnacion [ESP]
CASTRO GUTIERREZ, Fernando [VEN]
CASTRO-MARTINEZ, Enrique [ESP]
CAVALCANTI FERREIRA DE ARAUJO, Tereza C. [BRA]
CEDERBERG, Judith N. [USA]
CERQUETTI-ABERKANE, Françoise [FRA]
CESAR, Jean [FRA]
CESTARI, Maria Luiza [NOR]
CESTARI ZECCA, Marianne [NOR]
CHACKO, Indira [NGA]
CHALAIRE, Emily [USA]
CHAMBERS, Donald [USA]
CHANG, Ping-Tung [USA]
CHANKONG, Prateep [THA]
CHANKONG, Totsaporn [THA]
CHANNEL, Marea [USA]
CHAPMAN, Olive [CAN]
CHAPPELL, Michaele [USA]
CHARBONNEAU, Annik [CAN]
CHARBONNEAU, Louis [CAN]
CHARLEBOIS, Paul [CAN]
CHARLOT, Bernard [FRA]
CHAZAN, Daniel [USA]
CHEE, Liew S. [MYS]
CHEN, Dianna [USA]
CHEN, Susan [CAN]
CHEONG, May Lan [SGP]
CHERBULIEZ, Ariane [USA]
CHERKAS, Barry [USA]
CHERKAS, Sima [USA]

CHEUNG, Pak-Hong [HKG]
CHINN, Phyllis [USA]
CHINN, William G. [USA]
CHISSICK, Naomi [ISR]
CHIU, Sou-yung [TWN]
CHOATE, Jonathan [USA]
CHOE, Young-Han [KOR]
CHOUCHAN, Nicole [FRA]
CHOUINARD, Laval [CAN]
CHOVIN, Marie-Pierre [FRA]
CHRIST, Lily E. [USA]
CHRISTENSEN, Brad [FRA]
CHRISTIANSEN, Ibenmaj [DNK]
CHRISTOFFERSEN, Torben [DNK]
CHRISTOFFERSON, Stig [SWE]
CHROBAK, Michael [USA]
CHU, Tienchen [TWN]
CIANCONE, Tom [CAN]
CIRIANI, John [CAN]
CIRIANI, Lorna [CAN]
CITTADINO, Mary Jo [USA]
CIUPRYK, Fran [AUS]
CIUTAD, Jose M. [ESP]
CIVIL, Marta [USA]
CLAESSON, Peder [SWE]
CLAFFEY, Jim [AUS]
CLARK, John L. [CAN]
CLARK, Joyce [CAN]
CLARK, Megan June [NZL]
CLARKE, Barbara [USA]
CLARKE, David John [AUS]
CLARKE, Doug [USA]
CLAROU, Philippe [FRA]
CLAUSNITZER, Jim [USA]
CLEMENTS, Ken [AUS]
CLOSE, Gillian S. [GBR]
CLOSE, Sean [IRL]
CLOSS, Michael [CAN]
CNOP, Ivan [BEL]
CNOP, Tom [BEL]
COADY, Carmel [AUS]
COBB, Paul [USA]
COHEN, Arnold [USA]
COHEN, Gilles [FRA]
COHEN, Rina [CAN]
COHEN GOTTLIEB, Franca [BRA]
COHORS-FRESENBORG, Elmar [DEU]
COLLADA SANZ, Jesús [ESP]
COLLIGAN, J. Kevin [USA]
COLLINS, William J. [USA]
COLLINSON, Carole R. [GBR]
COLLINSON, Christopher D. [GBR]
COLLIS, Kevin F. [AUS]
COLOMBAT, Hubert [FRA]
COLÓN, Roberto [PRI]
COLUBI GÓMEZ, María José [ESP]

COLUCCI, Thomas [USA]
COMITI, Claude [FRA]
CONCEIÇÀO E ALMEIDA, Ema [PRT]
CONDE, Juan-Manuel [ESP]
CONFREY, Jere [USA]
CONNELLY, Ralph [CAN]
CONNORS, Wayne [CAN]
CONROY, John S. [AUS]
CONROY, Una [AUS]
CONSIGLIERE DEZEREGA, Lidia [CHL]
COOKSON, Connie [USA]
COONEY, Sara [USA]
COONEY, Thomas J. [USA]
COOPER, Alan [CAN]
COOPER, Martin [AUS]
COPLEY, Juanita [USA]
COPPE, Sylvie [FRA]
CORCOBADO CARTES, Juan Luis [ESP]
CORCORAN, Marc [CAN]
CORKISH, Peter [AUS]
CORNELIUS, Charmaine [USA]
CORNELIUS, Justine [USA]
CORNELIUS, Michael Leslie [GBR]
CORNELIUS, Neale [USA]
CORNELIUS, Patricia Anne [GBR]
CORNET, Jean-Rodny [HTI]
CORNU, Bernard [FRA]
CORNU, Brigitte [FRA]
CORRALÈS, Hermann [CAN]
CORY, Robert C. [GBR]
CÔTÉ, Benoît [CAN]
COUNTRYMAN, Joan [USA]
COUPLAND, Jonathan [GBR]
COURTADE, Geneviève [FRA]
COURTEAU, Bernard [CAN]
COUTURE, Isabelle [CAN]
COXETER, H.S.M. [CAN]
COXETER, Rien [CAN]
COZZENS, Margaret B. [USA]
CRAINE, Timothy V. [USA]
CRAWFORD, Kathryn P. [AUS]
CREMER, Peter [GBR]
CRESPO, Sandra [CAN]
CROSSAN, David Ian [NZL]
CROUSE, Fred [CAN]
CROWLEY, Mary [CAN]
CRUCIANI, Rosanna [ITA]
CRUMPTON, Sharon [USA]
CRUST, Rita [GBR]
CUCCINO, Barbara [USA]
CUISINIER, Ginette [BEL]
CUMMINGS, Andrew [USA]
CUMMINGS, Laura [USA]
CUNDY, David M. [GBR]
CUNDY, Wendy A. [GBR]
CUNHA LEAL, Francisco José [PRT]

CUNHA-LEAL, Leonor [PRT]
CUNNINGHAM, Robert F. [USA]
CUNNINGHAM, Roderick Bayne [GBR]
CUNNINGHAM, Trudy B. [USA]
CUNSOLO, Joseph [CAN]
CUOCO, Al [USA]
CUOCO, Marion [USA]
CURCIO, Frances R. [USA]
CZERNEZKYJ, Victor [AUS]
D'AMBROSIO, Beatriz S. [USA]
D'AMBROSIO, Ubiratan [BRA]
D'ARGENZIO, Carlo [ITA]
D'HALLUIN, Chantal [FRA]
DALIDA, John [USA]
DALLA TORRE, Paolo [ITA]
DALLAN, John [CAN]
DALMASSO, Juan Carlos [ARG]
DANIEL, Arthur [USA]
DANIEL, Jean-Claude [FRA]
DANIEL, Paule [FRA]
DASTOUS, Jérôme [CAN]
DAVENPORT, Linda [USA]
DAVIDSON, Luis [CUB]
DAVIDSON, Neil [USA]
DAVIES, Glyn [GBR]
DÁVILA-COATES, Grace [USA]
DAVIS, Brent A. [CAN]
DAVIS, Frank E. [USA]
DAVIS, Gary [AUS]
DAVIS, Philip [USA]
DAVIS, Robert B. [USA]
DAVIS, William J. [USA]
DAVISON, Chubbins [USA]
DAVISON, David M. [USA]
DAWSON, Sandra [CAN]
DAWSON, Sandy [CAN]
DAY, Lorraine [AUS]
DE AGUIAR, Maria C. [BRA]
DE BLOIS, Lucie [CAN]
DE BOCK, Dirk [BEL]
DE BRUYN, Ysbrand [CAN]
DE CAUSMAEKER, Marie-Louise [BEL]
DE CHAMPLAIN, Denis [CAN]
DE FLANDRE, Charles [CAN]
DE FRANCO, Thomas [USA]
DE GROOT, Ian Christie [CAN]
DE GROOT, Sheila [CAN]
DE KEE, Sonja [CAN]
DE KONINCK, Jean-Marie [CAN]
DE LA CRUZ, Yolanda [USA]
DE LA FUENTE ARAOZ, Victor [BOL]
DE LA FUENTE MARTOS, Miguel [ESP]
DE LAMADRID DE VAZQUEZ, Maria Ignacia [ARG]
DE LANGE, Jan [NLD]
DE LIEFDE, Peter [NLD]

DE MONICAULT, Gonzague Jean [USA]
DE ROO, Jean-Robert [CAN]
DE VALK, Stephan L. [NLD]
DE VILLIERS, Michael D. [ZAF]
DEBROUX, Monique [CAN]
DÉCARY, André [CAN]
DEGUIRE, Linda J. [USA]
DEITCHER, Rosalind [ISR]
DEL GRANDE, John [CAN]
DEL REGATO, John [USA]
DELANO, Richard [USA]
DELATTRE, Joëlle [FRA]
DELGADO OLIVEIRA, Maria José [PRT]
DELIERS, Mauricette [FRA]
DELIZ, Wilma [PRI]
DELORD, Robert [FRA]
DEMANA, Franklin [USA]
DEMBY, Agnieszka [POL]
DEMEY-VANHAMME, Monique [BEL]
DEMILL, Jacqueline [CAN]
DENIS, Gilles [CAN]
DENMAN, Theresa [USA]
DENNIS, David [USA]
DENT, Julie [USA]
DENTON, Brian H. [GBR]
DENTON, Pamela [GBR]
DENYS, Bernadette [FRA]
DEOKI, Parul V. [FJI]
DÉRAGON, Michel [CAN]
DÉRI, Thomas [CAN]
DESBIENS, Louise [CAN]
DESCHAMPS, Claude [FRA]
DESGRANGES, Katia [CAN]
DESHOUILLERS, Jean-Marc [FRA]
DÉSILETS, Guy [CAN]
DESLAURIERS, Denise [CAN]
DESMARAIS-ROY, Madeleine [CAN]
DESMEULES, Ghislain [CAN]
DESMOND, Nancy [USA]
DESROCHERS, Eddy [CAN]
DETWILER, Bettie C. [USA]
DEVITT, J. Stan [CAN]
DEWAR, Jacqueline [USA]
DEWES, Cathy [NZL]
DHOMBRES, Jean [FRA]
DIAZ, Enrique [ESP]
DIAZ GODINO, Juan [ESP]
DICKEY, Edwin M. [USA]
DIEFFENBACH, Robert M. [USA]
DIEGO, Fridrik [ISL]
DIESCHBOURG, Robert [LUX]
DIEZ FERNANDEZ, Adela [ESP]
DIEZ FERNANDEZ, Alice [ESP]
DING, Er-sheng [CHN]
DIONNE, Jean J. [CAN]
DIONNE, Jean-Paul [CAN]

DIONNE, Réal [CAN]
DIXON, Colin [GBR]
DOCKWEILER, Clarence J. [USA]
DOCTOROW, Gordon [CAN]
DOCTOROW, Roslyn [CAN]
DOIG, Brian [AUS]
DOLAN, Stanley William [GBR]
DOLBILIN, Nikolai [RUS]
DOLGAS, Margaret [USA]
DOLK, Maarten [NLD]
DOLL, Philip [AUS]
DOMENICO, Ettiène C. Guérios De [BRA]
DOMENICO, Fernanda Cordeiro Guérios de [BRA]
DONALDSON, Janice [AUS]
DONALDSON, Paul Bernard [AUS]
DONNELLAN, John R. [USA]
DONOGHUE, Eileen F. [USA]
DÖRFLER, Maria Mag. [AUT]
DÖRFLER, Willibald [AUT]
DORIER, Jean-Luc [FRA]
DORTA DIAZ, Jose Angel [ESP]
DOS REIS DE HERRERA, Isabel Julia [PER]
DOSSEY, Anne E. [USA]
DOSSEY, John A. [USA]
DOUMBIA, Salimata [CIV]
DOUSTAING, Louis [FRA]
DRAISMA, Frouke Buikema [MOZ]
DRAKE, Leslie M. [USA]
DRAKE, Pat [GBR]
DREYFUS, Tommy [ISR]
DRISCOLL, Mark [USA]
DROUHARD, Jean-Philippe [FRA]
DROUIN, Marjolaine [CAN]
DRUCK, Iole de Freitas [BRA]
DRUCKER, Jane E. [USA]
DUBÉ, Lilia [AUS]
DUBÉ, Vishwanath [AUS]
DUBIEL, Malgorzata [CAN]
DUBINSKY, Ed [USA]
DUBISCH, Joyce [USA]
DUBISCH, Roy [USA]
DUCKHORN, Patricia L. [USA]
DUCLOT, Bernadette [FRA]
DUFFIN, Janet M. [GBR]
DUGDALE, Sharon [USA]
DUMONT, Marcel [FRA]
DUNCAN, Allan G. [GBR]
DUNKLEY, Ronald [CAN]
DUPERIER, Jean [FRA]
DUPERIER, Michèle [FRA]
DUPLAIN, Carole [CAN]
DUPRAT, Brian [USA]
DURAND, Isabelle [CAN]
DURNIN, John [USA]
DUSTERHOFF, Marilane [USA]

EBEID, William [EGY]
EBERT, Christine [USA]
EDGE, Douglas [CAN]
EDGELL, Lucy [USA]
EDGELL JR., John J. [USA]
EDWARDS, Laurie [USA]
EGSGARD, John C. [CAN]
EHRLICH, Amos [ISR]
EHRLICH, Sara [ISR]
EID, Wolfram [DEU]
EISENBERG, Theodore [ISR]
EKSTIG, Kerstin [SWE]
EL BOUAZZAOUI, Habiba [MAR]
EL IDRISSI, Abdellah [CAN]
EL MOBARIK, Jihane [FRA]
ELEFTHEROPOULOS, Ioannis [GRC]
ELLERTON, Nerida F. [AUS]
ELLIS, Dormer [CAN]
ELLIS, Jill [NZL]
ELLIS, Susan [USA]
ELLWOOD, Mark [GBR]
ELLWOOD, William [NZL]
EMMER, Michele [ITA]
EMORI, Hideyo [JPN]
EMUDLUK, Susie [CAN]
ENGEL, Judith [USA]
ENGLUND, Tor [SWE]
ENGSTRÖM, Arne [SWE]
EPP, Susanna [USA]
ERBAN, Daniel [CAN]
ERNEST, Paul [GBR]
ERNESTAM, Arne [SWE]
ERNESTAM, Kerstin [SWE]
ERNIE, Kathryn T. [USA]
ERSHOV, Yuri [RUS]
ERSOY, Yasar [TUR]
ERVYNCK, Gontran [BEL]
ESCALONA FUENMAYOR, Maria Josefina [VEN]
ESCRIBANO-LOPEZ, Encarnacion [ESP]
ESCUDERO PEREZ, Isabel Maria [ESP]
ESLAVA TORO, Mª del Consuelo [ESP]
ESPEJO GIL, Concepción [ESP]
ESTEBAN, Julie [CAN]
ESTEBANEZ GARRIDO, Rosario [ESP]
ETTINGER, Pierre [FRA]
EVANS, Jeffrey T. [GBR]
EVANS, Michael W. [AUS]
EVANS, Warwick [GBR]
FABREGAS, Michèle [FRA]
FABREGAT, Jaime [ESP]
FÄGERLIND, Carl-Olof [SWE]
FAIRE, Mary [NZL]
FAIRHALL, Uenuku L.J. [NZL]
FALK DE LOSADA, Maria [COL]
FALSARELLI, Luiza Maria [BRA]

FANDRY, Norbert [AUS]
FANZONE, Patricia [CAN]
FARFÁN-MÁRQUEZ, Rosa Maria [MEX]
FARHLOUL, Abdelkrim [CAN]
FASANELLI, Florence [USA]
FAUVEL, John [GBR]
FAVILLI, Franco [ITA]
FAVRE, Pierre [CHE]
FAVRO, R.G. [USA]
FEDAII, Mohammad Reza [IRN]
FEE, Frederick [CAN]
FEGHALI, Issa [USA]
FELDMAN, Larry [USA]
FÉLIX DA SILVA SARAIVA, Manuel Joaquim
  [PRT]
FENDEL, Dan [USA]
FENDEL, Nina [USA]
FENTON, Claire [USA]
FERGUSSON, Andrew L. [AUS]
FERGUSSON, Barbara [AUS]
FERNANDEZ, Danièle [ISL]
FERNANDEZ DE CARRERA, Elena Teresita
  [ARG]
FERRES, Graham [AUS]
FERRES, Susan [AUS]
FERRI, Franca [ITA]
FERRINI-MUNDY, Joan [USA]
FERRUCCI, Beverly [USA]
FETTER, Anny [USA]
FEURZEIG, Wallace [USA]
FEY, James [USA]
FIELDS, Ewaugh Finney [USA]
FINLAY, Andrew [CAN]
FISCHER, Annelie [DEU]
FISCHER, Karin [DEU]
FISCHER, Walther L. [DEU]
FISET, Danielle [CAN]
FITALL, Patricia Rae [GBR]
FITZ SIMONS, Gail [AUS]
FITZGERALD, William [USA]
FLAKE, Janice [USA]
FLANDERS, Harley [USA]
FLANDERS, Jim [USA]
FLEISCHER, Gerhilde [DEU]
FLENER, Frederick [USA]
FLENER, Joen [USA]
FLIPPENS, Sara [USA]
FLORES, Alfinio [USA]
FLORES, Penelope [USA]
FLOWER, Jean [GBR]
FLOWER, Shena M. [GBR]
FLOYD, Teresa [USA]
FOLEY, Gregory D. [USA]
FONZI, Judith [USA]
FOOK, Leong [MYS]
FORBES, Sharleen Denise [NZL]

FORE, George E. [USA]
FORE, Sarah M. [USA]
FORESTER, Ruth I. [GBR]
FORGET, Luce [CAN]
FORGET, Raymond [CAN]
FORMAN, Ellice [USA]
FORMAN, Susan [USA]
FORTIN, Colette [CAN]
FORTIN, Jacques [CAN]
FORTIN, Michel [CAN]
FORTIN, Rolande [CAN]
FORTUNY AYMEMÍ, Josep Maria [ESP]
FOSTER, Robin [GBR]
FOUCHARD-DELSUC, Elisabeth [FRA]
FOURNIER, Alain [CAN]
FOXMAN, Derek [GBR]
FOXMAN, Ruth [GBR]
FRADETTE, Jean [CAN]
FRANCAVILLA, Marie [CAN]
FRANKENSTEIN, Marilyn [USA]
FRANKS, Douglas [CAN]
FRANSSON, Birgit [SWE]
FRANSSON, E. Robert [SWE]
FRASER, Sherry [USA]
FREEDMAN, Marvin [USA]
FREEMAN, Cindy [USA]
FRENCH, Graham [NZL]
FRENCH, Steve [NZL]
FRIEDLANDER, Alex [ISR]
FRIEDLANDER, Sara [ISR]
FRIEDMAN, Elisabeth Clare [USA]
FRIEDMAN, Lynn [USA]
FRIEL, Susan [USA]
FRIGON, Pierre [CAN]
FRY, Carol J. [USA]
FRYE, Shirley M. [USA]
FUEKI, Koji [JPN]
FUGLESTAD, Anne Berit [NOR]
FUJIEDA, Michiko [JPN]
FUJII, Toshiakira [JPN]
FUJIKAKE, Ayumi [JPN]
FUJIKAKE, Sumie [JPN]
FUJIMORI, Sadaharu [JPN]
FUJIMORI, Takako [JPN]
FUKUDA, Shoichiro [JPN]
FUKUDA, Yumi [JPN]
FULLERTON, Olive [CAN]
FULTON, John D. [USA]
FURINGHETTI, Fulvia [ITA]
GADANIDIS, George [CAN]
GADBOIS, Thérèse [CAN]
GAGATSIS, Athanassios [GRC]
GAGNÉ, Pascal [CAN]
GAGNON, Cédric [CAN]
GAGNON, Luc [CAN]
GALÁN PÉREZ, Mª Dolores [ESP]

GALBRAITH, Peter Lawrence [AUS]
GALINDO, Enrique [USA]
GALIZIA ANGELI, Maria Teresa [ITA]
GALLAGHER, Don [USA]
GALLO, Elisa [ITA]
GALLOU, Pierre André [FRA]
GALLOU-DUNIEL, Elisabeth [FRA]
GALPIN, Barrie [GBR]
GALPIN, Tricia [GBR]
GAMPER, Christiane [AUT]
GANGULI, Leela [GBR]
GANTER, Susan [USA]
GARANÇON, Maurice [CAN]
GARCIA ALVAREZ, Begoña [ESP]
GARCIA BLANCO, Mercedes [ESP]
GARCIA DEL MONTE, Julia [ESP]
GARCIA GARCIA, Maria Luisa [ESP]
GARCÍA GONZALEZ, María del Carmen [ESP]
GARCÍA-TELLO, Ma. Heréndira [USA]
GARDINER, Anthony [GBR]
GARFUNKEL, Solomon [USA]
GARRISON, Lionel [USA]
GARTON, Isabel [PRT]
GARTON, Karin Maria [PRT]
GATES, Carol S. [USA]
GATES, James D. [USA]
GATES, Peter [GBR]
GATTI, Mina [ITA]
GATTI, Sergio [ITA]
GATTUSO, Linda [CAN]
GAUDETTE, Modene [USA]
GAUDREAULT, Louis-Philippe [CAN]
GAULIN, Claude [CAN]
GAULIN, Louis-Marie [CAN]
GAUTHIER, Denis [CAN]
GAUTHIER, Lilian Solange [CAN]
GAUTHIER, Roger [CAN]
GAUVIN MOISAN, Marie [CAN]
GAVANT, Gail [USA]
GAVEGLIO, Giuseppe [ITA]
GEDDES, Keith [CAN]
GELFMAN, Emanuila [RUS]
GÉLINAS, Charlotte [CAN]
GÉLINAS, Mariette [CAN]
GÉLINAS, Nancy [CAN]
GENDREAU, Louis-M. [CAN]
GENDRON, Renée [CAN]
GENEST, Christian [CAN]
GEORGE, Glyn H. [CAN]
GEORGE, K.X. [TZA]
GEORGE, Rema [USA]
GERBER, Harvey [CAN]
GERETSCHLAGER, Robert [AUT]
GERETSCHLAGER-HAUPTMANN, Zita [AUT]
GERLING, Max O. [USA]
GERMAIN, Edith [FRA]

GERMAIN, Gilles [FRA]
GERVAIS, Jean-Jacques [CAN]
GIAMBRONE, Tom [USA]
GIAMMARIOLI, Caroline [CAN]
GIAMMARIOLI, Franco [CAN]
GIBBS, Richard [USA]
GIESSMANN, Ernst G. [DEU]
GIGANTI, Paul [USA]
GIGLIO, Louis [USA]
GIGUÈRE, Charlotte [CAN]
GILFEATHER, Mary [USA]
GILFILLAN, Andrew [GBR]
GILIS, Daniel [FRA]
GILLESPIE, Catherine Ann [GBR]
GILLESPIE, John A. [GBR]
GILLESPIE, Valerie Ann [GBR]
GILLETT, Robert C. [CAN]
GILLIES, John [AUS]
GILLIES, Roslyn [AUS]
GILLIS, Allan [CAN]
GILMER, Gloria [USA]
GIMENEZ, Joaquin [ESP]
GINBAYASHI, Ko [JPN]
GINBAYASHI, Mieko [JPN]
GINESTIER, Jean-Paul [CAN]
GIRARD, Gilles [CAN]
GIRARD, Laurent [CAN]
GIRARD, Louis [CAN]
GIRARD, Pascale [CAN]
GIROUX, Jacinthe [CAN]
GIRVAN, Doug [CAN]
GJONE, Gunnar [NOR]
GLACE, Diane [USA]
GLOVER, Hugh [ZAF]
GODDIJN, Aad [NLD]
GODMAIRE, Guy [CAN]
GOIFFON, Régis [FRA]
GOLDBERG, Dorothy [USA]
GOLDBERG, Joel [ISR]
GOLDBERG, Lester [USA]
GOLDBERG, Merilee D. [ISR]
GOLDEN, Thomas [USA]
GOLDENBERG, Paul [USA]
GOLDFINCH, Judy M. [GBR]
GOLDIN, Gerald A. [USA]
GOLDSTEIN, Colleen [ZAF]
GOMEZ, Cristina [COL]
GOMEZ, Pedro [COL]
GÓMEZ CASADO, Pilar [ESP]
GOMEZ DEL SOL, Julia [ESP]
GOÑI-ZABALA, Jesus Maria [ESP]
GONNOKAMI, Hiroaki [JPN]
GONZALEZ, Pierre-Louis [FRA]
GONZALEZ, Sarah [DOM]
GONZÁLEZ ALARCÓN, Gabriela P. [MEX]
GONZALEZ ALVAREZ, Nieves [ESP]

GONZALEZ CARMONA, Ana Rosa [MEX]
GONZALEZ GONZALEZ, Evaristo [ESP]
GONZALO, Marcos Rojo [ESP]
GOODSTEIN, Harvey [USA]
GORE, Henry A. [USA]
GOROFF, Daniel [USA]
GOROWARA, Christine C. [USA]
GOSSELIN, Patrice [CAN]
GOUGEON, Deborah [USA]
GRABINER, Judith [USA]
GRAF, Klaus-Dieter [DEU]
GRAHAM, Edward [GBR]
GRAHAM, Karen [USA]
GRANDES ARNAIZ, Begoña [ESP]
GRANDSARD, Francine [BEL]
GRANOVE, Dina Adelle [CAN]
GRANT, Irma [CAN]
GRANT, Theresa J. [USA]
GRANT MCLOUGHLIN, John [CAN]
GRAUMANN, Günter [DEU]
GRAVEMEŸER, Koeno [NLD]
GRAY, Lynne [USA]
GRAY, Shirley B. [USA]
GRAYSON, John [USA]
GREEN, David Robert [GBR]
GREEN, Walter [AUS]
GREENES, Carole [USA]
GREER, Brian [GBR]
GRÉGOIRE, Michèle [FRA]
GRENIER, Pierre [CAN]
GRENIER, Richard [CAN]
GREVHOLM, Barbro E. [SWE]
GREY SCOTT, Sarah [CAN]
GRIFFIN, Steven [GBR]
GRIFFITH, Gareth [CAN]
GRIFFITHS, Catherine E. [GBR]
GRIFFITHS, H. Brian [GBR]
GRIFFITHS, Rachel [AUS]
GRIGNON, Jean [CAN]
GRILLES RODRIGUEZ, Jesus Miguel [ESP]
GRIMISON, Lindsay A. [AUS]
GROMAN, Margaret W. [USA]
GRONDIN, François [CAN]
GRONINGER, Don S. [USA]
GRØNMO, Liu Sissel [NOR]
GROS EZQUERRA, Maria Jose [ESP]
GROULX, Pierre [CAN]
GROVES, Susie [AUS]
GRUGNETTI, Lucia [ITA]
GRUSZCZYK-KOLCZYNSKA, Edyta [POL]
GUALANDI-ACCASCINA, Vanna [ITA]
GUERIN, Frédéric [CAN]
GUÉRIOS, Henriette Cordeiro [BRA]
GUICHARD, Jacqueline [FRA]
GUICHARD, Jean-Paul [FRA]
GUIMARÃES, Henrique M. [PRT]

GUIN, Dominique [FRA]
GURNEY, Penelope J. [CAN]
GUTIERREZ, Angel [ESP]
GUTIERREZ, Isoline [ESP]
GUTIERREZ PEREZ, José [ESP]
GUZMÀN, Miguel de [ESP]
GUZMAN RETAMAL, Ismenia [CHL]
GYNNEMO, Ingemar [SWE]
HAAPASALO, Lenni [FIN]
HABIBULLAH, Saleha Naghmi [PAK]
HADAS, Nurit [ISR]
HADASS, Rina [ISR]
HADE, Lucette [CAN]
HAGBO, Anna Christina [DNK]
HAGELGANS, Nancy [USA]
HAGUEL, Marie-Jane [CAN]
HAHN, Corinne [FRA]
HAIMES, David [CAN]
HAIMO, Deborah T. [USA]
HAINES, Christopher R. [GBR]
HAINES, Margaret E. [GBR]
HÅKANSSON, Susie W. [USA]
HAKIM, Elizabeth [CHE]
HAKIM, Victor-Albert [CHE]
HÅKONSSOW, Erik [DNK]
HALL, James E. [USA]
HALL, Lucien T. [USA]
HALL, Nancy J. [USA]
HALL, Thelma [USA]
HALLEZ, Maryvonne [FRA]
HALLIDAY, Jan [NZL]
HAMBLETON, Kenneth [CAN]
HAMMOND, Michael [GBR]
HAMON, Gérard [FRA]
HAN SHICK, Park [KOR]
HANCOCK, Chris [USA]
HANES, Kit [USA]
HANNA, Gila [CAN]
HANNAH, John [NZL]
HANSON, Diane [CAN]
HANSSON, Doris [SWE]
HANSSON, Erik [SWE]
HARDING, Darlene [USA]
HARDY, Kenneth [CAN]
HARKER, Lorraine Josephine [AUS]
HARNASZ, Costel [GBR]
HARNISCH, Delwyn L. [USA]
HARPAZ-RUBIN, Yael [ISR]
HARRELL, Ronald [USA]
HARRIES, Helen [GBR]
HARRIES, Paul [GBR]
HARRIES, Ruth [GBR]
HARRIES, Tony [GBR]
HARRIS, Mary [GBR]
HARRIS, Pam [AUS]
HART, David [USA]

HART, Eric W. [USA]
HART, Kathleen [GBR]
HARTOG, Martin Dirk [USA]
HARVEY, John G. [USA]
HARVEY, Richard F. [GBR]
HARVEY, Wayne [USA]
HASEGAWA, Kenichi [JPN]
HASHIMOTO, Yoshihiko [JPN]
HASHIMOTO, Yoshihiro [JPN]
HASSAN, Bakr Ahmad [SAU]
HASTAD, Matts [SWE]
HATANO, Giyoo [JPN]
HATCH, Gillian Mary [GBR]
HATCHER, William S. [CAN]
HATEM, Moustafa Mohamed [EGY]
HATFIELD, Mary M. [USA]
HATORI, Asako [JPN]
HATTON, Joyce [GBR]
HAUANGARD, Stig [SWE]
HAWKINS, Anne [GBR]
HAWKSHAW, Morag [GBR]
HAWKSHAW, Robert [GBR]
HAWORTH, Anne Christina [GBR]
HAWORTH, James D. [GBR]
HAYES, Rebecca O. [USA]
HAYES, Roland M. [USA]
HAYNES, Maggie [NZL]
HAZAMA, Setsuko [JPN]
HAZEKAMP, Donald W. [USA]
HAZEKAMP, Lucille [USA]
HEARD, Terry [GBR]
HÉBERT, Michel [CAN]
HEBRON, John S. [CAN]
HEDRÉN, Rolf [SWE]
HEICKLEN, Susan [USA]
HEID, M. Kathleen [USA]
HEIDEMA, Clare [USA]
HEIEDE, Torkil [DNK]
HEIKKURINEN, Tooivo Ensio [FIN]
HEIKKURINEN, Tuulikki [FIN]
HEJNY, Milan [CZR]
HENDERSON, Annalee [USA]
HENDERSON, David W. [USA]
HENDERSON, Jenny [AUS]
HENDERSON, Ray C. [USA]
HENDERSON, Sharon [CAN]
HENDERSON, Shirley [USA]
HENGARTNER, Elmar [CHE]
HENGARTNER, Walter [CAN]
HENKIN, Ginette [USA]
HENKIN, Leon A. [USA]
HENNING, Herbert [DEU]
HENRION, Claudia [USA]
HENRY, Helen Mary [AUS]
HENRY, James Bruce [AUS]
HENRY, Michel [FRA]

HENSEL, Susann [USA]
HÉRAUD, Bernard [CAN]
HERBERT, Kristen [USA]
HERMAN, Eugene A. [USA]
HERMOSIN MOJEDA, Manuel J. [ESP]
HERNANDEZ ENCINAS, Luis [ESP]
HERNÁNDEZ HERNÁNDEZ, Teresa [AND]
HEROLD, Rosanne [CAN]
HERRINGTON, Anthony John [AUS]
HERSCHEL, Clem [USA]
HERSCHEL, Deborah [USA]
HERSCOVICS, Nicolas [CAN]
HERSHKOWITZ, Rina [ISR]
HIDDLESTON, George [MWI]
HIDDLESTON, Patricia [MWI]
HIGGINS, Daniel G. [USA]
HIGGINS, Joanna M. [NZL]
HIGGINSON, William [CAN]
HIGHET, Kristine [AUS]
HIGUCHI, Teiichi [JPN]
HILL, James D. [USA]
HILL, Linda C. [USA]
HILL, Rebecca E. [USA]
HILL, Shirley A. [USA]
HILLEL, Joel [CAN]
HILLMAN, Susan [USA]
HILTON, Peter [USA]
HIRAMA, Mariko [JPN]
HIROFUMI, Matsumoto [JPN]
HIROKO, Matsumoto [JPN]
HIROTA, Hitoshi [JPN]
HIRST, Ann Elizabeth [GBR]
HIRST, Keith Edwin [GBR]
HITCHCOCK, Anthony Gavin [ZWE]
HITOTSUMATSU, Shin [JPN]
HOBURG, Joan [USA]
HOBURG, Robert L. [USA]
HODGIN, Katharine W. [USA]
HODGSON, Bernard R. [CAN]
HODGSON, Brian [AUS]
HODGSON, Jean-Sébastien [CAN]
HODGSON, Louis-Philippe [CAN]
HODGSON, Marie-Isabelle [CAN]
HODGSON, Theodore Robert [USA]
HOFFER, Alan [USA]
HOFFER, Shirley A. [USA]
HOFFMAN, Martin R. [USA]
HOLMES, Peter [GBR]
HOLMES, Phyl C. [GBR]
HOLTON, Derek Allan [NZL]
HOMMA, Toshio [JPN]
HONDA, Shizue [JPN]
HOOGLAND, Kees [NLD]
HOOVER, James H. [CAN]
HOPKINS, Christine [GBR]
HORAIN, Yvette [FRA]

HORIBE, Hiroko [JPN]
HORIUCHI, Akira [JPN]
HORNE, Marj [AUS]
HORSMAN, Helen M. [CAN]
HORTON, William [USA]
HOSHINO, May [USA]
HOSKINS, James Dene [NZL]
HOSKINS, Judith Rosemary [NZL]
HOULE, Paul-Emile [CAN]
HOUSTON, Kerry [GBR]
HOUSTON, Patricia [GBR]
HOUSTON, Samuel Kenneth [GBR]
HOUSTON, Sarah [GBR]
HOWARD, Peter Thomas [AUS]
HOWSON, Geoffrey [GBR]
HOYLES, Celia [GBR]
HSU, Pao-Sheng [USA]
HU, Chiung-Lin [CHN]
HUA, Yang [TWN]
HUANG, Men-Fon [TWN]
HUARD, Jean-Luc [CAN]
HUBBARD, Ruth [AUS]
HUBER, Arla M. [USA]
HUDSON, Brian G. [GBR]
HUETINCK, Linda [USA]
HUGHES, Martin [GBR]
HUMAN, Piet [ZAF]
HUNDHAUSEN, Joan R. [USA]
HUNTER, Carolyn R. [USA]
HUNTER, Charles R. [USA]
HUNTER, Lawrie [JPN]
HUNTER, Robin [JPN]
HUNTING, Robert P. [AUS]
HURLEY, James F. [USA]
HUSSEIN, Mansour G. [KWT]
HUSSEIN, Rabab A. [KWT]
HYDE, Beverly [USA]
HYDE, Kendell [USA]
HYUN SUNG, Shin [KOR]
IACONO, John Robert [AUS]
IACONO, Rae Ellen [AUS]
ICHIJU, Ritsuko [JPN]
IDE, Fukiko [JPN]
IGNATZ, Donald R. [USA]
IIDA, Shinji [JPN]
IIZUKA, Yoshinori [JPN]
IIZUKA, Yutaka [JPN]
IKARI, Kuniko [JPN]
IKEDA, Toshikazu [JPN]
IKENO, Masako [JPN]
ILLAN GOMEZ, Inmaculada [ESP]
INAGAKI, Setsuko [JPN]
INDELICATO, Mary [USA]
INNES, Kathleen M. [CAN]
IRWIN, Kathryn Cressey [NZL]
ISHIDA, Mitsuko [JPN]

ISHII, Hideko [JPN]
ISHIKAWA, Masako [JPN]
ISHIKAWA, Natsu [JPN]
ISHIKAWA, Saneaki [JPN]
ISHIKAWA, Takeshi [JPN]
ISMAEL, Abdulcarimo [MOZ]
ISMAIL, Zaleha [MYS]
ISRAEL, Eliot [USA]
ITO, Junichi [JPN]
ITO, Yoshihiko [JPN]
IWABUCHI, Naoki [USA]
IWAKAMI, Ryokichi [JPN]
IWATA, Kazuo [JPN]
IWATA, Mieko [JPN]
IWATSURU, Chieko [JPN]
IZARD, Jan [AUS]
IZARD, John [AUS]
IZAWA, Shiori [JPN]
IZUMI, Kimozō [JPN]
IZUMORI, Hitoshi [JPN]
IZUSHI, Takashi [JPN]
IZUSHI, Yasuko [JPN]
JABLONKA, Eva [DEU]
JACKIW, Nicolas [USA]
JACKSON, Allyn [USA]
JACOBS, Judith E. [USA]
JACOBSEN, Ed [FRA]
JAEGER, Arno [DEU]
JAEGER, Doris [DEU]
JAEGER, Joachim [DEU]
JAGADISH, Mysore S. [USA]
JAGGER, Janet Margaret [GBR]
JAGGER, John B. [GBR]
JAHNKE, Hans Niels [DEU]
JAIME, Adela [ESP]
JAJI, Gail [ZWE]
JAKMAUH, Edward [USA]
JAKUBOWSKI, Elizabeth [USA]
JAMES, Agatha [LCA]
JAMES, David [USA]
JAMES, Jeannette [USA]
JANSEN, Huub M. M. [NLD]
JANSON, Barbara [USA]
JANSSENS, Dirk [BEL]
JANSSON, Lars C. [CAN]
JANSSON, Leonoor [CAN]
JANVIER, Bernadette [CAN]
JANVIER, Claude [CAN]
JAQUET, François [CHE]
JÄRNEK, Gunilla [SWE]
JARRATT, Catherine [USA]
JARRAUD, Pierre [FRA]
JAVAME GHAZVINI, Mohammad Javad [IRN]
JAVOR, Elisabeth [USA]
JAWORSKI, Barbara [GBR]
JAWORSKI, John [GBR]

475

JEAN, Roger [CAN]
JEANGROS, Nathalie [COL]
JEANGROS, Roland [COL]
JEANGROS, Santiago [COL]
JENNER, Dennis [GBR]
JENNER, Helen [GBR]
JENSEN, Robert [USA]
JERISON, Meyer [USA]
JERISON, Miriam [USA]
JIMBO, Katsuro [JPN]
JIMENEZ ADAN, Milagros [ESP]
JIMÉNEZ ALEIXANDRE, Maria Eugenia [ESP]
JIMENEZ JIMENEZ, Maria [ESP]
JIMENEZ JIMENEZ, Miguel Angel [ESP]
JOHANSSON, Ann-Margret [SWE]
JOHANSSON, Bengt I. [SWE]
JOHANSSON, Goeran [SWE]
JOHNSEN, Karl B. [NOR]
JOHNSEN, Veslemøy [NOR]
JOHNSON, Carolyn [USA]
JOHNSON, Howard C. [USA]
JOHNSON, Ivan [CAN]
JOHNSON, Jerry [USA]
JOHNSON, Karen A. [USA]
JOHNSON, Millie [USA]
JOHNSON, Phillip E. [USA]
JOHNSON, Sylvia [GBR]
JOHNSON, Todd [USA]
JOHNSON II, Arthur [USA]
JOHNSTON, Annette [AUS]
JOHNSTON, Betty [AUS]
JOHNSTON, Julie [USA]
JOHNSTON, Scott [AUS]
JOLICOEUR, Louise [CAN]
JOLLIFFE, Flavia [GBR]
JONES, Anthony J. [AUS]
JONES, Bev [USA]
JONES, Chancey O. [USA]
JONES, Eleanor [USA]
JONES, Graham Alfred [USA]
JONES, Lesley G. [GBR]
JONES, Leslie P. [GBR]
JONES, Marion Rose [USA]
JONES, Peter L. [AUS]
JONES, Sonia [GBR]
JONGSMA, Calvin [USA]
JÓNSDÓTTIR, Kristín H. [ISL]
JORDAN, Diana [USA]
JOSEPH, George Gheverghese [GBR]
JOUBERT, Maud [CAN]
JOURNAULT, Jacques [CAN]
JOZEAU, François [FRA]
JOZEAU, Marie-Françoise [FRA]
JUDSON, Jack [USA]
JUDSON, Phoebe T. [USA]
JUISTER, Barbara [USA]

JULIEN, Lucette [CAN]
JUNQUEIRA, Maria Margarida [PRT]
JUR, Barbara A. [USA]
JURASCHEK, Bill [USA]
JURDAK, Muna [LBN]
JURDAK, Murad [LBN]
KADER, Gary [USA]
KAELEY, Gurcharn S. [PNG]
KÅGESTEN, Owe [SWE]
KAHANE, Jean-Pierre [FRA]
KAHLIL, Therese [USA]
KAHN, Ann [USA]
KAISER-MESSMER, Gabrielle [DEU]
KAJIKAWA, Kumi [JPN]
KAJIKAWA, Toshiya [JPN]
KAJIKAWA, Yoshie [JPN]
KAJIKAWA, Yuji [JPN]
KAKIHANA, Kyoko [JPN]
KALDRIMIDOU, Maria [GRC]
KALIN, Robert [USA]
KÄLLGÅRDEN, Eva-Stina [SWE]
KALMIJN, Leonardus Johannes [NLD]
KALMIJN-KOEL, Sonja J. [NLD]
KAM, Irwin [CAN]
KAMETANI, Michiko [JPN]
KAMETANI, Yoshitomi [JPN]
KANAMARU, Ryohei [JPN]
KANEMITSU, Shigeru [JPN]
KANEOKA, Toshiko [JPN]
KANER, Peter Alan [GBR]
KANES, Clive [AUS]
KANTOR, Jean-Michel [FRA]
KANTOR, Tünde [HUN]
KANY-GRIGOZINSKY, Bat-Sheva [ISR]
KAPLAN, Rose K. [USA]
KAPUT, James J. [USA]
KAPUT, Susan [USA]
KARLSSON, Barbro [SWE]
KARLSSON, Sara [SWE]
KARLSSON, Sören [SWE]
KARLSTRÖM, Åsa [SWE]
KARLSTRÖM, Christer [SWE]
KASLOVÁ, Michaela [CZR]
KASTNER, Bernice [USA]
KATAGIRI, Shigeo [JPN]
KATAGIRI, Shizuko [JPN]
KATAOKA, Kei [JPN]
KATAYAMA, Yumiko [JPN]
KATO, Naoki [JPN]
KATSUNO, Motoshige [JPN]
KATSUSHIMA, Chizuko [JPN]
KATZ, Victor J. [USA]
KAUFMAN FAINGUELERNT, Estela [BRA]
KAUR, Berinderjeet [SGP]
KAWAMURA, Junichiro [JPN]
KAWAMURA, Katsuhisa [JPN]

KAWANA, Motoi [JPN]
KAYLER, Hélène [CAN]
KAZAMA, Kimie [JPN]
KAZIM, M. Maassouma [EGY]
KEITEL-KREIDT, Christine [DEU]
KELEMANIK, Grace [USA]
KELLOGG, Mary [USA]
KELLY, Brendan [CAN]
KEMP, Marian E. [AUS]
KENDALL, Mauray [USA]
KENDRICK, Eleanor [USA]
KENELLY, John [USA]
KENICHIROU, Urakawa [JPN]
KENNEDY, Johnelle [USA]
KENNEDY, Paul [USA]
KENNEY, Emelie [USA]
KENNEY, Margaret [USA]
KEOGH, Erica [ZWE]
KEPNER, Henry [USA]
KERANTO, Tapio Olavi [FIN]
KERDPRASOP, Kittisak [THA]
KERDPRASOP, Nittaya [THA]
KERNER, Immo O. [DEU]
KERSLAKE, Daphne [GBR]
KESTER-KINGSTON, Tina [CAN]
KEYNES, Harvey B. [USA]
KHANNA, Amil K. [FJI]
KHISTY, C. Jotin [USA]
KHISTY, Lena Licón [USA]
KHOLODNAJA, Marina [UKR]
KIBBEY, David [USA]
KIERAN, Carolyn [CAN]
KIEREN, Dianne [CAN]
KIEREN, Thomas E. [CAN]
KIERNAN, James F. [USA]
KIKUCHI, Isamu [JPN]
KIKUCHI, Tamako [JPN]
KILIAN, Hans [DEU]
KILIAN, Ursula [DEU]
KILLINGSWORTH, Trish [USA]
KILLION, Kurt [USA]
KILPATRICK, Carlene [USA]
KILPATRICK, Jeremy [USA]
KIMURA, Ishiko [JPN]
KIMURA, Toshiko [JPN]
KIMURA, Yuzo [JPN]
KING, James R. [USA]
KING, Lonnie Cecil Coke [ZAF]
KINNUNEN, Liisa [FIN]
KIRILLOV, Andréi [RUS]
KIRSHNER, David [USA]
KISSANE, Barry [AUS]
KIST, Patricia [USA]
KIST, Theresa [USA]
KITAGAWA, Setsuko [JPN]
KITAMURA, Kazue [JPN]

KITCHEN, Ann [GBR]
KITTO, Alison [ZAF]
KLAMKIN, Murray S. [CAN]
KLASA, Stanislas [CAN]
KLAWE, Maria Margaret [CAN]
KLEIMAN, Glenn [USA]
KLEINER, Israel [CAN]
KLEIVE, Inger [NOR]
KLEIVE, Per-Even [NOR]
KLEP, Joost [NLD]
KLIMAS, Florence E. [USA]
KLIMAS, Joseph J. [USA]
KLOTZ, Eugene [USA]
KLÜSENER, Renita [DEU]
KNIGHT, Genevieve [USA]
KNIGHT, Gordon H. [NZL]
KNIJNIK, Gelsa [BRA]
KNILL, George [CAN]
KNOCHE, Claudia [DEU]
KNOCHE, Ines [DEU]
KNOCHE, Ingrid [DEU]
KNOCHE, Norbert [DEU]
KNOSHAUG, Clayton [USA]
KNOSHAUG, Ivy [USA]
KNOSHAUG, Kristen [USA]
KOBAYASHI, Atsuko [JPN]
KOBAYASHI, Ichiro [JPN]
KOBAYASHI, Keiko [JPN]
KOBAYASHI, Ken [JPN]
KOBAYASHI, Michimasa [JPN]
KOBAYASHI, Mitsuko [JPN]
KOBAYASHI, Mitsuru [JPN]
KOCH, Laura Coffin [USA]
KOELLE, Ruth A. [USA]
KOENDERINK, Gerald [CAN]
KOENDERINK, Ms. [CAN]
KOENKA, Jack [CAN]
KOGI, Ichinose [JPN]
KOK, Douwe [NLD]
KOLDE, Rein [EST]
KOLESNIK, Michael [USA]
KOLLENVELD, Marian [NLD]
KOMMER, Manuel Maurice [NLD]
KONDO, Toshiji [JPN]
KÖNIG, Gerhard [DEU]
KONSTANTINOV, Nikolay [RUS]
KOOBURAT, Paktra [THA]
KORDIUK, Roman [CAN]
KORT, Edith [USA]
KOSS, Donald [USA]
KOSS, Roberta [USA]
KOSSEGI, Joanne D. [USA]
KOTA, Osamu [JPN]
KOTA, Setsuko [JPN]
KOTAGIRI, Tadato [JPN]
KOTANI, Ayako [JPN]

KOVACS, Zoltan [HUN]
KOYAMA, Masataka [JPN]
KOYAMA, Mikio [JPN]
KOZANECKI, Lucille [USA]
KOZAR, Evelyn [USA]
KRAINER, Konrad [AUT]
KRAUTHAUSEN, Günter [DEU]
KREIDT, Moritz [DEU]
KRINSKY, Eunice [USA]
KRIST, Betty J. [USA]
KRISTJÁNSDÓTTIR, Anna [ISL]
KRONFELLNER, Manfred [AUT]
KRULIK, Gladys [USA]
KRULIK, Stephen [USA]
KRUMMHEUER, Götz [DEU]
KRYSINSKA, Maria-Izabela [BEL]
KUCZMA, Marcin E. [POL]
KUENDIGER, Erika [CAN]
KUENDIGER, Till [CAN]
KUHN, Gabrielle [FRA]
KUHS, Therese [USA]
KUKU, Aderemi O. [NGA]
KUMAGAI, Koichi [JPN]
KUMAZAWA, Masaaki [JPN]
KUNIMOTO, Keiyu [JPN]
KUO, Yen-Wen [TWN]
KUPARI, Pekka Antero [FIN]
KURAI, Nobutada [JPN]
KURATA, Sylvia [CAN]
KURIHARA, Hideyuki [JPN]
KURINA, Frantisek [CZR]
KURTZ, David [USA]
KURTZ, Douglas S. [USA]
KUZNIAK, Richard [CAN]
KWAI MENG, Sin [SGP]
KWAN, Tjioe [USA]
LA BARRE, Robert [CAN]
LABELLE, Gilbert [CAN]
LABORDE, Colette [FRA]
LABORDE, Jean-Marie [FRA]
LABRIE, Jean-Marie [CAN]
LABROUSSE, Carole [FRA]
LABROUSSE, Jean-Philippe [FRA]
LACAMPAGNE, Carole [USA]
LACASSE, Raynald [CAN]
LACROIX, Christiane [CAN]
LAFLAMME, Sébastien [CAN]
LAFOREST, Jean-Claude [CAN]
LAFORTUNE, Louise [CAN]
LAGACÉ, Jacques [CAN]
LAHTI, Uno [SWE]
LAINE, Ilpo E. [FIN]
LAJOIE, Caroline [CAN]
LAKELAND, Robert [NZL]
LAKRAMTI, Ahmed [MAR]
LALANDE, Françoise [FRA]

LALIBERTÉ, Celyne [CAN]
LALONDE CARRIÈRE, Micheline [CAN]
LAMAGNA, Ed [USA]
LAMBATING, Julita [USA]
LAMBDIN-KROLL, Diana [USA]
LAMBERT, Carol S. [USA]
LAMON, Susan J. [USA]
LAMONTAGNE, Denis [CAN]
LAMONTAGNE, Ginette [CAN]
LAMPERT, Magdalene [USA]
LAMPHERE, Patricia [USA]
LANCASTER, Ronald [CAN]
LANE, Bennie R. [USA]
LANE, Jean [USA]
LANE, Josephine G. [USA]
LANGBORT, Carol [USA]
LANGDON, Nigel [GBR]
LANIUS, Cynthia [USA]
LAPOINTE, Gilles [CAN]
LAPPAN, Glenda [USA]
LARA-APARICIO, Miguel [MEX]
LARIDON, Paul Edward [ZAF]
LAROCHELLE, Céline [CAN]
LARSON, Dorine [CAN]
LARSON, Göran [SWE]
LARSSON, Monica [SWE]
LARSSON, Stig [SWE]
LASO DÍEZ, Emma [ESP]
LAURENCE, Lise [CAN]
LAURIN-BEAUDOIN, Ginette [CAN]
LAUZON, Pauline [CAN]
LAVAREDA LIMOÈS, José Maria [PRT]
LAVEAULT, Serge [CAN]
LAVERTU, Marie-Louis [CAN]
LAVOIE, Paul [CAN]
LAW, Chiu-Keung [TWN]
LAWSON, Alan M. [CAN]
LAWSON, Marilyn [CAN]
LAX, Anneli [USA]
LAZAR, Boris [FRA]
LAZARNICK, Sylvia [USA]
LAZRAQ, Aziz [MAR]
LE DEVEHAT, Yanick [CAN]
LEBLANC, Ginette [CAN]
LEBLANC, Mark [CAN]
LEBRÓN, Concepción [ESP]
LEBRÓN, M. Teresa [ESP]
LECHASSEUR, Marguerite [CAN]
LECOUTRE, Bruno [FRA]
LECOUTRE, Marie-Paule [FRA]
LEDDY, Frank [CAN]
LEDER, Gilah [AUS]
LEE, Beth [AUS]
LEE, Lesley [CAN]
LEE, Peng Yee [SGP]
LEES, Kevin [AUS]

LEESINSKY, Peter [CAN]
LEFEBVRE, Jacques [CAN]
LEFORT, Xavier [FRA]
LEGAULT, Lise [CAN]
LEGRAND, Daniele [BEL]
LEGRAND, Marc [FRA]
LEHMANN, Ingmar [DEU]
LEHRER, Richard [USA]
LEINBACH, L. Carl [USA]
LEINBACH, Patricia A. [USA]
LEINO, Anna-Liisa [FIN]
LEINO, Jarkko [FIN]
LEITZEL, James [USA]
LEMAY, Fernand [CAN]
LEMAY, François [CAN]
LEMIEUX-PROVENCHER, Fabiola [CAN]
LEMIRE, Lévis [CAN]
LEMOINE, Claudine [CAN]
LEMUT, Enrica [ITA]
LENART, Istvan [HUN]
LENCHNER, Edna [USA]
LENCHNER, George [USA]
LENTZ, Linda [USA]
LEON BAEZ, Ana Maria [ESP]
LEON BAEZ, Angeles [ESP]
LEON BAEZ, Antonia [ESP]
LEON MADERO, Lydia [MEX]
LEONARD, Susan [CAN]
LEPAGE, André [CAN]
LERMAN, Stephen [GBR]
LESH, Richard [USA]
LESLIE, Marilyn [USA]
LESSARD, Linda [CAN]
LESSARD, Sabin [CAN]
LESTER, Frank K. [USA]
LEU, Hsi-muh [TWN]
LEUNG, Frederick K.S. [HKG]
LEUNG, Jean [CAN]
LEUNG, Vincent [CAN]
LEVENBERG, Ilana [ISR]
LÉVESQUE, Louisiane [CAN]
LEVIN, Jutta [USA]
LEVITA, Asia [ISR]
LEVY, Azriel [ISR]
LEWIS, Deborah [USA]
LEWIS, Philip G. [USA]
LEWIS, Ronald S. [CAN]
LEWIS DULAC, Patricia [USA]
LIANG YI, Fong [CHN]
LIANTO, Jos [IDN]
LIBERMAN, Manhucia [BRA]
LIBESKIND, Shlomo [USA]
LICHTENBERG, Betty K. [USA]
LICHTENBERG, Donovan R. [USA]
LIDSTONE, Dave C. [CAN]
LIESJÄRVI-MÄKELÄ, Helena [FIN]

LIMA, Elon L. [BRA]
LIN, Fou-lai [TWN]
LINCHEVSKI, Liora [ISR]
LINCOLN, Clyde R. [USA]
LIND, Anja [DEU]
LIND, Brigitte [DEU]
LIND, Cora [DEU]
LIND, Detlef [DEU]
LIND, Ingemar [SWE]
LINDAHL, Göran [SWE]
LINDAHL, Kerstin [SWE]
LINDAU, Gertrude [USA]
LINDBERG, Lisbeth [SWE]
LINDENSKOV, Lena [DNK]
LINDH-MUNTHER, Agneta [SWE]
LINDQUIST, Mary [USA]
LINDQUIST, Paul [USA]
LING, Joseph M. [CAN]
LINGARD, Marc [USA]
LINGEFJARD, Thomas [SWE]
LINO, Sosa [USA]
LINUWIH, Susanti [IDN]
LIPSZYC, Joshua [CAN]
LITTLE, Chris T. [GBR]
LIU, Andy [CAN]
LIU, Yizhu [CHN]
LLINARES CISCAR, Salvador [ESP]
LO, Jane-Jane [USA]
LO MANTO, Ferdinando [ITA]
LOBB, Jill [AUS]
LOBB, Lawson [AUS]
LOCKHART, Deborah [USA]
LOGAN, Lindsay [GBR]
LOHSE, Heinz [DEU]
LONG, Eleanor M. [AUS]
LONG, Madeleine J. [USA]
LONG, Nigel [AUS]
LOPES, Ana Maria [PRT]
LOPES, Antonio José [BRA]
LÓPEZ-CHAMORRO, Maria Ascensión [ESP]
LORCH, Lee [CAN]
LÖRCHER, Gustav A. [DEU]
LORD, Kevin [GBR]
LORENZ, Dahlia [ISR]
LORENZ, Dan H. [ISR]
LORENZATO, Sergio A. [BRA]
LORMAN, Patricia [CAN]
LORRAIN, Anne-Marie [CAN]
LORTIE, Benoît [CAN]
LOSKA, Rainer [DEU]
LOTT, Johnny W. [USA]
LOUBIER, Francis [CAN]
LOUGHLIN, Julia [USA]
LOVE, Eric [GBR]
LOVITT, Annette L. [AUS]
LOVITT, Charles J. [AUS]

Lowman, Pauline [USA]
Lozano Leal, Mª Carmen [ESP]
Lozi, René [FRA]
Lucas, Carolyn D. [USA]
Lucas, William F. [USA]
Luckow, Anne [CAN]
Luedeman, John [USA]
Luengo Gonzalez, Ricardo [ESP]
Lukas, Jose F. [ESP]
Lum, Lois [USA]
Luna, Eduardo [USA]
Lund, Peter G. [AUS]
Lupien, François [CAN]
Lupien, Jean [CAN]
Luthuli, Dexter Vusumuzi [ZAF]
Luz Tavares, Wanda [VEN]
Lyness, Paul C. [USA]
Lyon, Betty [USA]
Lytle, Pat [CAN]
MacGregor, Mollie [AUS]
Machado, Silvia [BRA]
Machida, Shoichiro [JPN]
Macintyre, Thomas Gunn [GBR]
Mack, John M. [AUS]
MacKellar, Brenda [CAN]
Mackrell, Kate [GBR]
MacPherson, Joe [CAN]
Madsen, Anita [USA]
Maher, Carolyn A. [USA]
Maier, Eugene [USA]
Maier, Hermann [DEU]
Mailloux, Nicole [CAN]
Mäkelä, Heikki [FIN]
Maki, Daniel [USA]
Maki, Judith [USA]
Mäkinen, Jukka [FIN]
Makoshi, Abdullah [SAU]
Malara, Nicolina Antonia [ITA]
Malaret, Jesus Francisco [USA]
Malaty, George [FIN]
Malkova, Tatjana [RUS]
Mallet, Jacqueline [CAN]
Malm, Donald E.G. [USA]
Malm, Rebecca [USA]
Malone, John A. [AUS]
Mammana, Carmelo [ITA]
Mancini Proia, Lina [ITA]
Mandelbrot, Benoit B. [USA]
Manfredi Sanchez, Berta [ESP]
Manley, Don [GBR]
Manley, Richard [GBR]
Manley, Susan [GBR]
Mann, Giora [ISR]
Manon, Jon [USA]
Mansfield, Helen [AUS]
Mansilla, Carlos [ARG]

Maqsud, Muhammad [ZAF]
Marafioti Garnica, Antonio Vincente [BRA]
Marconi, Carla [ITA]
Marcotte, Ghyslain [CAN]
Marcoux, Angèle [CAN]
Margolinas, Claire [FRA]
Maria Flavia, Mammana [ITA]
Marion, Charles F. [USA]
Mariotti, Alessandra [ITA]
Marks, Rick [USA]
Marlie, Mogamat Faiz [ZAF]
Marois, Rivard [CAN]
Martin, David Charles [AUS]
Martin, Janet [USA]
Martin, Joan D. [USA]
Martin, Reg [AUS]
Martín Caño, Maria Agustina [ESP]
Martine, Alison [CAN]
Martínez Falcón, Norma P. [MEX]
Martínez Fernández, Pedro José [ESP]
Martinez Sanchez, Carlos [ESP]
Martinsson, Thomas [SWE]
Mary, Sheila [GBR]
Masanja, Verdiana Grace [TZA]
Mascarello, Maria [ITA]
Mashego, Teresa [ZAF]
Mason, Ralph [CAN]
Màté, Laszlo [HUN]
Matos, João Filipe [PRT]
Matos, José Manuel [PRT]
Matshaba, Lone L.B. [BWA]
Matsuda, Naoki [JPN]
Matsui, Mikio [JPN]
Matsui, Taiichi [JPN]
Matsumaru, Mitsuo [JPN]
Matsumiya, Tetsuo [JPN]
Matsuo, Yoshitomo [JPN]
Matsushita, Kayo [JPN]
Matsushita, Megumi [JPN]
Matsuura, Hiroshi [JPN]
Matsuzawa, Masao [JPN]
Mattatall, Peter J. [CAN]
Matthiasen, Jesper [DNK]
Mauk, Cherry C. [USA]
Mauk, Cynthia R. [USA]
Maurer, Stephen B. [USA]
Maurice, Louise [CAN]
Maury, Sylvette [FRA]
Mawyer, Farley [USA]
May, Lola [USA]
Mayes, Robert [USA]
Mayo, H. Elaine [NZL]
Mayo, Jacqueline [USA]
Mays, Marilyn [USA]
Mc Donald, Ian [CAN]

MC DONALD, Joanne [CAN]
MCARTHUR, David [USA]
MCARTHUR, Greig [AUS]
MCBRIDE, Maggie [USA]
MCCARTHY, Donald [USA]
MCCAUL, Marjorie [CAN]
MCCLEW, Edward Clifton [USA]
MCCLINTOCK, Edwin [USA]
MCCLINTOCK, Frances [USA]
MCCOY, Leah [USA]
MCCRAE, Barry J. [AUS]
MCDONALD, Margaret [AUS]
MCDONOUGH, Andrea [AUS]
MCDOUGALL, Gayle [CAN]
MCFARLANE, Felicia [LCA]
MCGEE, Ian J. [CAN]
MCGILL, Carol [USA]
MCHUGH, Richard [USA]
MCHUGH, Rosemary [USA]
MCINNES, Melanie [CAN]
MCINNIS, Linda [CAN]
MCKAY, Denis [CAN]
MCKILLIP, Carol S. [USA]
MCKILLIP, William D. [USA]
MCKILLOP, David W. [CAN]
MCLELLAN, Jan [AUS]
MCLEOD, Douglas B. [USA]
MCMASTER, Adrian Ronald [CAN]
MCNAIR, Rodney E. [USA]
MCNEAL, Betsy [USA]
MEECHAN, Robert C. [GBR]
MEEDER, Marja [NLD]
MEGGIATO, Sandra [ITA]
MEIER, Sherry L. [USA]
MEILLEUR, Monique [CAN]
MEIRA, Luciano de Lemos [BRA]
MEISSNER, Hartwig [DEU]
MÉNARD-GRISÉ, Gisèle [CAN]
MENDEZ, Zayra [CRI]
MENDICUTI, Teresa N. De [MEX]
MENDOZA GARCIA, Mercedes [ESP]
MENGHINI, Marta [ITA]
MERIL, Alex [GLP]
MERIL, Madame [GLP]
MERLO, Bruno [CHE]
MEROW, Craig B. [USA]
MERRI, Maryvonne [FRA]
MESHKANI, Ali [IRN]
MESQUITA, Ana L. [CAN]
MESSIER, André [CAN]
MESSIER, Denyse Gagnon [CAN]
MEYER, Gerrit [NLD]
MEYER, Walter [USA]
MICHAEL, Beverly K. [USA]
MICHAELS, Fahmy [AUS]
MICHEL-PAJUS, Annie [FRA]

MICHNOUICZ, Theresa C. [USA]
MIDDLETON, Jim [USA]
MIENTKA, Walter E. [USA]
MIESING, Daniel N. [CAN]
MIGNEAULT, Charles [CAN]
MILLER, Barbara A. [USA]
MILLER, David John [GBR]
MILLER, Jean [USA]
MILLER, Josephine Angela [GBR]
MILLER, Loretta Diane [USA]
MILLER, Mary Katherine [JPN]
MILLER, Richard [USA]
MILLER, Winnie [USA]
MILLMAN, Richard S. [USA]
MILLS, Elizabeth M. [GBR]
MILLS, Judith [GBR]
MILLS, Laurel [USA]
MILLS, Patricia [USA]
MILLS, Stuart E. [USA]
MILLSAPS, Gayle [USA]
MILLSAPS, Irene P. [USA]
MILNE, Ronald J. [USA]
MILTON, Ken [AUS]
MILTON, Yvonne [AUS]
MINACHIN, Victor [RUS]
MIRANDA, Isabel [ESP]
MITCHELL, Charles [USA]
MITCHELL, Christine H. [GBR]
MITCHELL, Robert J. [CAN]
MITCHELL, Wendy L. [CAN]
MITCHELMORE, Michael Charles [AUS]
MITSUMA, Kunio [USA]
MIUS D'ENTREMONT, Marcel [CAN]
MIYAKE, Akihiko [JPN]
MIYAMOTO, Ichiro [JPN]
MIYASATO, Akiko [JPN]
MIYASATO, Yasuhisa [JPN]
MIYAZAKI, Katsuji [JPN]
MIYAZAKI, Yuki [JPN]
MIYAZAKI, Yumiko [JPN]
MKANDAWIRE, Mymess [USA]
MKHONTA, Sibusiso Samuel [SWZ]
MOBERG, Margareta [SWE]
MOCHINAGA, Junko [JPN]
MOGENSEN, Arne [DNK]
MOGI, Isamu [JPN]
MOK, Ah-Chee Ida [HKG]
MOKANSKI, Joseph P. [CAN]
MOLAMPY, Alice [USA]
MOLANO-ROMERO, Antonio [ESP]
MOLDAVE, Cathy [USA]
MOLDAVE, Jay [USA]
MOLFINO, Maria Teresa [ITA]
MÖLLEHED, Ebbe [SWE]
MÖLLER, Herbert [DEU]
MOLONEY, Mihi Takotohiwi [NZL]

MONCECCHI, Gianfranco [ITA]
MONEY, Robert [AUS]
MONGEON, Diane [CAN]
MONTERO RODRIGUEZ, Ana Maria [ESP]
MONTGOMERY, Philip [USA]
MONZO DEL OLMO, Onofre [ESP]
MOORE, Brendan V. [GBR]
MOORE, David S. [USA]
MOORE, Mafori [USA]
MOORE, Nancy [CAN]
MOORE, Robert C. [USA]
MOORHOUSE, Nellie [CAN]
MORALES ALDANA, Leonel [GTM]
MORALES FIGUEROA, Bernardo R. [GTM]
MORALES GARCIA, Laura Maria [ESP]
MORANGE, Georges [FRA]
MORCILLO DELGADO, Angustias [ESP]
MOREIRA, Manuel R.F. [PRT]
MOREIRA, Maria Raquel [PRT]
MOREN, Elizabeth Belfort [GBR]
MORENO GÓMEZ, Pilar [ESP]
MORENO MARTÍNEZ, Ma Luisa [ESP]
MORENO MORENO, Maria del Mar [ESP]
MORGADO, Luisa Maria [PRT]
MORGAN, Alice M.W. [GBR]
MORGAN, Candia [GBR]
MORGAN, Ceri [GBR]
MORGAN, Flora I. [USA]
MORGAN, Lawrence A. [USA]
MORGAN, M. [CAN]
MORGAN, Patricia Margaret [GBR]
MORI, Koichi [JPN]
MORI, Masao [JPN]
MORI, Tomoko [JPN]
MORI, Yuichi [JPN]
MORIÉNA, Susana Mercedes [ARG]
MORIKAWA, Ikutaro [JPN]
MORIMOTO, Akira [JPN]
MORIN, Annie [FRA]
MORIN, Bernard [CAN]
MORIN, Hervé-G. [CAN]
MORISHITA, Hisayo [JPN]
MORIUCHI, Kazuki [JPN]
MORIYA, Seiji [JPN]
MORLEY, Ann Margaret [GBR]
MORLEY, Stephen [GBR]
MORO, Olga [ESP]
MORONY, Will [AUS]
MORRISON, Joan Scott [USA]
MORROW, Charlene [USA]
MORROW, James [USA]
MORROW, Lorna J. [CAN]
MORTON, Margaret James [NZL]
MOSON, Peter [HUN]
MOTTERSHEAD, Lorraine [AUS]
MOUNIER, Georges Marc [FRA]

MOURA, M. Eduarda B. [USA]
MOURA, Mr. [USA]
MOUSLEY, Judith Anne [AUS]
MOUZAS, Odysseas [GRC]
MUKHOPADHYAY, Swapna [USA]
MULDER, Fred [NLD]
MULLEN, Gail [USA]
MULLER, Alice [CAN]
MULLER, Eric [CAN]
MULLIGAN, Joanne [AUS]
MULRYAN, Catherine M. [IRL]
MUMFORD, Jeanette R. [GBR]
MUÑIZ, Lidia Dalmasi [DOM]
MUNOZ, Agustin [ESP]
MUÑOZ MORENO, Lucia [ESP]
MUNRO, John Eric MacKay [AUS]
MUNTHER, Roland [SWE]
MURA, Roberta [CAN]
MURAKAMI, Akiko [JPN]
MURAKAMI, Haruo [JPN]
MURAKAMI, Toshio [JPN]
MURPHY, Catherine M. [USA]
MURRAY, Hanlie [ZAF]
MURRAY, Michael [CAN]
NAEENI, S.M. Kazem [IRN]
NAGAI, Keiko [JPN]
NAGANO, Azuma [JPN]
NAGANO, Misuko [JPN]
NAGASAWA, Hiroko [JPN]
NAGATA, Chigusa [JPN]
NAGAYAMA, Yoshiki [JPN]
NAIR, Anand [GBR]
NAKAMURA, Yoshio [JPN]
NAKANO, Orie [JPN]
NAKANO, Toshiyuki [JPN]
NANTAIS, Nicole [CAN]
NARITA, Masahiro [JPN]
NASOETION, Andi Hakim [IDN]
NASSER, Lilian [GBR]
NASSRA, Reda Hassan [QAT]
NATSOULAS, Anthula [USA]
NAVA MONTES, Fredefinda I. [VEN]
NAVARRA, Giancarlo [ITA]
NEAL, Christine E. [GBR]
NEAL, David M. [GBR]
NEIL, Chalmers McPherson [GBR]
NEILL, Hugh [GBR]
NELSON, Glenn [USA]
NELSON, L. Ted [USA]
NELSON, Richard D. [GBR]
NEMETZ, Ibolya [HUN]
NEMETZ, Tibor [HUN]
NEMIROVSKY, Ricardo [USA]
NESHER, Pearla [ISR]
NEUBRAND, Michael [DEU]
NEUFELD, Carol [CAN]

NEUFELD, Eldon [CAN]
NEUFELD, Evelyn [USA]
NEUFELD, K. Allen [CAN]
NEUMAN, Dagmar [SWE]
NEUMANN, Bernhard Hermann [AUS]
NEUMANN, Dorothea [AUS]
NEUWIRTH, Erich [AUT]
NEVELING, Rolf J. [DEU]
NEVELING-WERBECK, Gisa [DEU]
NEWMAN, Richard [USA]
NEWMAN, Rochelle [USA]
NEWMAN, Vicki [USA]
NEYLAND, Jim [NZL]
NG, Fung Yee [HKG]
NICHOLLS, Gordon [CAN]
NICKEL, Lance [USA]
NICOL, Cynthia C. [CAN]
NIEDERDRENK-FELGNER, Cornelia [DEU]
NIETO, Claudia [COL]
NIKKEL, Dianne [CAN]
NILSSON, Ingemar [SWE]
NILSSON, Vivianne [SWE]
NINOMIYA, Hiroyuki [JPN]
NISBET, Steven [AUS]
NISHIMOTO, Yukie [JPN]
NISHIZAWA, Kiyoko [JPN]
NISS, Mogens [DNK]
NOBLE, Tracy [USA]
NOGUCHI, Mikako [JPN]
NOHDA, Nobuhiko [JPN]
NOJIMA, Junko [JPN]
NOLAN, Mary [USA]
NOLDER, Rita [GBR]
NOMACHI, Tadashi [JPN]
NORBERG, Hans [SWE]
NORDBLOM, Agneta [SWE]
NOREIGA, Emily [USA]
NOREM, Barbara [CAN]
NOREM, Philip [CAN]
NORIA JOVE, Montserrat [ESP]
NORMAN, F. Alexander [USA]
NORTHCUTT, Brita [USA]
NORTHCUTT, Robert [USA]
NORTON, David A. [ZAF]
NORTON, Elizabeth M. [ZAF]
NOVO FERNANDEZ, Fermin [ESP]
NOVOTNÁ, Jarmila [CZR]
NOZAKI, Akihiro [JPN]
NÜESCH, Peter Erich [CHE]
NUNES, Fernando [PRT]
NUNES, Terezinha [GBR]
NUTT, Jan [USA]
O'BRIEN, Gail M. [USA]
O'BRIEN, Thomas C. [USA]
O'DELL, Ruth D. [USA]
O'DONNELL, Carolyn R. [USA]

O'HALLORAN, Peter [AUS]
O'LANDER, Richard [USA]
O'SHEA, Donal [USA]
O'SHEA, Thomas [CAN]
O'SHELL, Anna [CAN]
OAKS, Ann [USA]
OBDEYN, Theo [NLD]
OBDEYN-DEGROOT, Elly [NLD]
OCHS, Phyllis L. [USA]
ODOM, Rebecca [USA]
OGAWA, Mitiko [JPN]
OHIA, Monte Rereamoamo [NZL]
OIKAWA, Hiroyuki [JPN]
OJEDA, Alfredo D. [VEN]
OKAMORI, Hirokazu [JPN]
OKETANI, Mikako [JPN]
OKUDA, Nobue [JPN]
OKUDA, Shogo [JPN]
OKUNO, Hiroshi [JPN]
OLAIZOLA, Inaqui de [MEX]
OLDHAM, Elizabeth E. [IRL]
OLIVE, John [USA]
OLIVEIRA, Agostino M. [PRT]
OLIVER, Dale [USA]
OLIVERAS, M. Luisa [ESP]
OLIVIER, Alwyn [ZAF]
OLLIVIER, Françoise [FRA]
OLOFSSON, Bo W. [SWE]
OLSON, Judith [USA]
OLSON, Marilyn [USA]
OLSON, Melfried [USA]
OLSON, Tanya [USA]
OLSON, Travis [USA]
OLSSEN, Kevin H. [AUS]
OLSTORPE, Kristina [SWE]
OLSTORPE, Roland [SWE]
OLSTORPE, Sofia [SWE]
ONION, Alice J. [GBR]
ONISHI, Mitsuko [JPN]
ONSLOW, Barry A. [CAN]
ONSTAD, Torgeir [NOR]
ONTIVEROS QUIROZ, Sofia Josefina [MEX]
OOSTERHOUT, Michael [BWA]
OOSTHUIZEN, Constance E. [ZAF]
OOSTHUIZEN, Wynand L. [ZAF]
OREY, Daniel [USA]
ORÍA DE CHOUHY AGUIRRE, Mª Margarita [ARG]
ORIOL, Jean-Claude L. [FRA]
ORMELL, Christopher Peter [GBR]
ORTIZ, Mirta [ARG]
ORTIZ CAPILLA, Maria Angeles [ESP]
ORTIZ-FRANCO, Luis [USA]
ORTOLLAND, Danielle [FRA]
ORTOLLAND, Emmanuel [FRA]
ORTOLLAND, Patrick [FRA]

OSAWA, Shigenori [JPN]
OSCARSSON, Edor [SWE]
OSCARSSON, Els-Marie [SWE]
OSER, Hans J. [USA]
OSHIO, Yoshiaki [JPN]
OSTA, Iman [LBN]
OTA, Minoru [JPN]
OTAKE, Kyoto [JPN]
OTAKE, Noboru [JPN]
OTANO CABO, Pilar [ESP]
OTSUKA, Kayo [JPN]
OTSUKA, Kenichi [JPN]
OTSUKA, Yoshinori [JPN]
OTTE, Michael [DEU]
OTTOSSON, Sven [SWE]
OUDADESS, Mohamed [MAR]
OUELLET, Anne-Marie [CAN]
OUELLETTE, Ginette [CAN]
OUTHRED, Lynne [AUS]
OWENS, Douglas T. [CAN]
OWENS, Faye [CAN]
OWENS, Kay Dianne [AUS]
OZAWA, Kenichi [JPN]
OZAWA, Yasuko [JPN]
OZAWA, Yoshiaki [JPN]
PAASONEN, Johannes [FIN]
PACE, John [USA]
PADILLA GONZALEZ, Alejandro [MEX]
PAGE, Warren [USA]
PAGNI, David L. [USA]
PAGNI, Terri [USA]
PAGON, Dusan [SLN]
PALIS, Gilda de la Rocque [BRA]
PALLASCIO, Richard [CAN]
PAÑOS ROCA, Josefa [FRA]
PAPERT, Seymour [USA]
PAPILLON, Vincent [CAN]
PAPPA, Konstandia [GRC]
PAQUET, Erik [CAN]
PAQUET, Solange [CAN]
PAQUIN, Lise [CAN]
PARAMORE, Eddie [USA]
PARÉ, Nathalie [CAN]
PARKER, Willard A. [USA]
PARRA SANDOVAL, Hugo E. [VEN]
PARSONS, Shirley [USA]
PARTRIDGE, Barry Douglas [AUS]
PARZYSZ, Annie [FRA]
PARZYSZ, Bernard [FRA]
PARZYSZ, Claire [FRA]
PARZYSZ, Elisabeth [FRA]
PASCUAL, José-Ramón [ESP]
PASCUAL SOLER, Teresa [ESP]
PATEMAN, Neil [USA]
PATKIN, Dorit [ISR]
PAULSSON, Kurt. A. [SWE]

PAULUS, Bob [USA]
PAULUS, Gloria [USA]
PAYAN, Charles [FRA]
PAZ FERNANDEZ, Maria Luz [ESP]
PEAD, Daniel A. [GBR]
PEARD, Robert [AUS]
PECAL, Michèle [FRA]
PEDERSEN, Jean [USA]
PEDERSEN, Katherine [USA]
PEDREIRA, Elaine [USA]
PEDREIRA MENGOTTI, Alicia [ESP]
PEET, Michael [GBR]
PEGG, John [AUS]
PEHKONEN, Erkki [FIN]
PEHKONEN, Leila [FIN]
PEIRIS, Anthony [CHE]
PEKRUL, Susan [CAN]
PELÉ, Colette [FRA]
PELED, Irit [ISR]
PELLEGRINO, Giuliana [ITA]
PELLEREY, Michele [ITA]
PELLERIN, Marianne [CAN]
PENALVA, Maria del Carmen [ESP]
PENCE, Barbara J. [USA]
PENGELLY, Helen [AUS]
PENN, Arthur W. [GBR]
PENN, Betn [USA]
PENN, Doreen M. [GBR]
PENN, Howard [USA]
PENNER, Leona [USA]
PENNIMAN, Paul K. [USA]
PÉPIN, Marc-André [CAN]
PÉPIN, Réjean [CAN]
PERCARIO, Zelinda [ITA]
PEREIRA DA SILVA, Ana Maria [PRT]
PEREIRA-MENDOZA, Lionel [CAN]
PERELLI, Maria Pia [ITA]
PERERO, Mariano [USA]
PEREZ FERNANDEZ, F.-Javier [ESP]
PEREZ JIMENEZ, Antonio [ESP]
PÉREZ-GÓMEZ, Rafael [ESP]
PERHAM, Arnold [USA]
PERHAM, Bernadette H. [USA]
PERKS, Patricia Anne [GBR]
PERL, Eliezer [ISR]
PERL, Hannah [ISR]
PÉROTIN, Catherine [FRA]
PERREAULT, Jean [CAN]
PERRIN-GLORIAN, Marie-Jeanne [FRA]
PERRY, Bob [AUS]
PERRY, Mike [USA]
PERRY, Sandra [USA]
PERSSON, Eva [SWE]
PERSSON, Gunilla [SWE]
PERSSON, Gunn [SWE]
PERSSON, Ingvar [SWE]

PERSSON, Sven-Olov [SWE]
PESCI, Angela [ITA]
PETOCZ, Dubravka [AUS]
PETOCZ, Peter [AUS]
PETRI, Janet [USA]
PHILIPPOV, George N. [GRC]
PHILLIPS, Alison Marie [AUS]
PHILLIPS, Brian Richard [AUS]
PHILLIPS, Elizabeth [USA]
PHILLIPS, Hilary J. [GBR]
PHILLIPS, Richard J. [GBR]
PICARD, Colette [CAN]
PICHARD, Evelyne [FRA]
PICHARD, Jean-François [FRA]
PICHETTE, Jean [CAN]
PIERLUIGI, Lucio [ITA]
PIETROCOLA, Norma Cristina [ARG]
PILLING, Josephine [GBR]
PIND, Pernille [DNK]
PIRIE, Susan E.B. [GBR]
PISARSKI, Marek [POL]
PITMAN, Allan [CAN]
POBLETE LETELIER, Alvaro Patricio [CHL]
POIANI, Eileen L. [USA]
POIRIER, Louise [CAN]
POIRIER, Maurice [CAN]
POITRAS, Louise-Andrée [CAN]
POLAND, John [CAN]
POLETTINI, Altair [USA]
POLETTINI, Valter J. [USA]
POLLAK, Henry O. [USA]
POLLARD, Graham Hilford [AUS]
POLLARD, Robyn [AUS]
POMPEU, Geraldo Jr. [BRA]
PONTE, João Pedro [PRT]
PONTILLE, Marie-Claude [FRA]
PONZA, Maria Victoria [ARG]
POPE, Lindsay [NZL]
PORRAS RUIZ, Agueda [ESP]
PORTEOUS, Joyce [GBR]
PORTER, Gérald J. [USA]
PORTUGAIS, Jean [CAN]
POSAMENTIER, Alfred S. [USA]
POTARI, Despina [GRC]
POU, Alacie [CAN]
POULIOT, Vincent [CAN]
POURKAZEMI, M. Hossein [IRN]
POUW, Hans [NLD]
POWELL, Arthur B. [USA]
POWELL, Beth [AUS]
POWERS-KUMP, Joanne [USA]
POZO LLORENTE, Teresa [ESP]
PRADE, Roland [SWE]
PRATT, David [GBR]
PRESMEG, Norma Christine [USA]
PRESTON, Vera [USA]

PRICE, Barbara [USA]
PRICE, Jack [USA]
PRICE, Justin J. [USA]
PRICE, Mike [GBR]
PROCUNIER, James W. [CAN]
PUCHALSKA, Ewa M. [CAN]
PURSER, Prue [NZL]
PUSTILNIK, Seymour W. [USA]
PUTKONEN, Hellevi [FIN]
PUTT, Ian John [AUS]
PUTTAYUK, Pasha [CAN]
QIU, Zong-Hu [CHN]
QUARTARARO, Philip [USA]
QUEDENFELD, Norma [USA]
QUICK, David [CAN]
QUICK, Debbie [CAN]
QUINN, Madge [UGA]
QUINONES, Esteban [PRI]
QUIROZ, Ana Lia [ARG]
QUTUB, Carol [USA]
RABONIWITZ, Stanley [USA]
RACINE, Michel [CAN]
RAHIM, Medhat [CAN]
RAJAN, Radha R. [USA]
RAJU, Louis V. [GBR]
RALSTON, Anthony [USA]
RAMASUBBAN, Rajaram [SGP]
RAMOS, Rosario Esther [ESP]
RAMSDEN, Helen Elizabeth [GBR]
RAMSDEN, Jenny Stephanie [GBR]
RANDHAWA, Bikkar S. [CAN]
RANSOM, Peter Howard [GBR]
RASMUSSEN, David [USA]
RASMUSSEN, Steven [USA]
RAUTENBERG, Cordula [DEU]
RAUX, Jacqueline [FRA]
RAYMOND, Claudine [CAN]
RAYMOND, Jean-Luc [CAN]
RAZAVI, Assadollah [IRN]
READ, Trevor [NZL]
RECIO, Tomás [ESP]
REDA HASSAN BAQER, Abdul Moayied
   [QAT]
REDDEN, Edward [AUS]
REDDEN, Michael George [AUS]
REDEKOPP, Reynold [CAN]
REED, Carlos [USA]
REED, Kevin F. [AUS]
REES, Robert A. [GBR]
REEVES, Howard [AUS]
REGAN, Shaila [USA]
REGGIANI, Maria [ITA]
REID, David [CAN]
REID, Maria A. [USA]
REID, Yolanda A. [USA]
REILLY, Barbara Joy [NZL]

REITER, Betty [USA]
REITER, Harold [USA]
REJALI, Ali [IRN]
REJTO, Margaret [USA]
RELICH, Joe [AUS]
RENÉ DE COTRET, Sophie [CAN]
RENSHAW, Peter D. [AUS]
REPO, Sisko [FIN]
RESEK, Diane [USA]
RESTIVO, Sal [USA]
RÉTHIER, Paul-Emile [CAN]
RETZER, Kenneth A. [USA]
RETZER, Wei [USA]
REYERO, Catalina [USA]
REYES CRUZADO, Angela [ESP]
REYNAUD-FEURLY, Josette [FRA]
REYNOLDS, Anne [USA]
REYNOLDS, Marion [GBR]
REYNOLDS, Peter [GBR]
RHEAULT, Benoît [CAN]
RHEAULT, François [CAN]
RHODES, Mary [CAN]
RHODES, Steve [ZAF]
RIBEIRO, Maria do Rosário [PRT]
RIBEIRO PÔLA, Marie-Claire [BRA]
RICARDO LOSADA, Ricardo [COL]
RICE, Mary T. [AUS]
RICHARD, Simone [CAN]
RICHARDS, Elizabeth Ann [AUS]
RICHARDS, John [USA]
RICHTER, Carita [SWE]
RICKETTS, Flauren [USA]
RICKEY, V. Frederick [USA]
RICO-ROMERO, Luis [ESP]
RIDGWAY, Jim [GBR]
RIEGO GAONA, Alejandrà [MEX]
RIEHS, Robert J. [USA]
RIFFEL, Anita Marie [CAN]
RIGGIO, Miguel Angel [BOL]
RIGHI, Bobby [USA]
RIINI, Mona [NZL]
RIINI, Sonny [NZL]
RILEY, Doug [USA]
RILEY-PFUND, Gay [USA]
RIPEAU, Pierre [CAN]
ROBERGE, Anne [CAN]
ROBERTA, Rizzo [ITA]
ROBERTS, Huw Gareth [GBR]
ROBERTS, Shirley [USA]
ROBERTS, Suzanne [NZL]
ROBERTSON, Wendy J. [AUS]
ROBINSON, Bob [CAN]
ROBINSON, Gillian [NZL]
ROBITAILLE, Claudine [CAN]
ROBITAILLE, David Ford [CAN]
ROBITAILLE, Rosanna [CAN]

ROCKEFELLER, Roger [USA]
ROCKHILL, Theron [USA]
RODER, Paul [GBR]
RODIGUEZ LIÑÁN, Marina [ESP]
RODINO, Luigi [ITA]
RODRIGUES DE OLIVEIRA LAVAREDA, Mª de
    Jesus [PRT]
RODRIGUEZ CORDOBES, Juan [ESP]
RODRIGUEZ POZO, Gracia [ESP]
RODRIGUEZ-REYES, Elicio [ESP]
ROELENS, Michel [BEL]
ROGALSKI, Marc [FRA]
ROGERS, Edward L. [GBR]
ROGERS, Leo F. [GBR]
ROGERS, Pat K. [CAN]
ROGERSON, Alan T. [AUS]
ROLDAN, Maria Myrna [GTM]
ROLPH, Cheryl B. [USA]
ROMBERG, Martha [USA]
ROMBERG, Thomas A. [USA]
ROMERO SANCHEZ, José [ESP]
ROMERO SÁNCHEZ, Sixto [ESP]
ROMIENS, Todd [CAN]
ROOS, Richard C. [ZAF]
ROS, Rosa M. [ESP]
ROSAMOND, Frances [USA]
ROSE, Barbara [USA]
ROSEN, Linda P. [USA]
ROSENFIELD, Steven [CAN]
ROSENQVIST, Birgit [SWE]
ROSENTHAL, Bill [USA]
ROSEVEARE, David [GBR]
ROSS, Kenneth A. [USA]
ROSSO, Cynthia [USA]
ROSSOUW, Lynn [ZAF]
ROTA, Carlotta [ITA]
ROTA, Elio [ITA]
ROTA, Filippo [ITA]
ROTHERY, Andrew [GBR]
ROTHMAN, Max [ISR]
ROUCHE, Nicolas [BEL]
ROUCHIER, André [FRA]
ROULET, Geoffrey [CAN]
ROUNCEFIELD, Mary [GBR]
ROUSHAM, Laurie [GBR]
ROUSSEAU, Julie [CAN]
ROUSSEL, Yves [FRA]
ROUTLEDGE, Joan [CAN]
ROY, André-Jean [CAN]
ROY, Louise [CAN]
ROY, Lucille [CAN]
ROY, Nancy [USA]
RUBENSTEIN, Rheta N. [USA]
RUBERU, Jathiratne [BRN]
RUBERU, Mallika [BRN]
RUDNICK, Jeannette [USA]

RUDNICK, Jesse A. [USA]
RUIZ, Ceferino [ESP]
RUIZ LOPEZ, Ma del Pilar [ESP]
RUNGE, Kathryn [USA]
RUNGE, M. Christine [USA]
RUPÉREZ-PADRÓN, José Antonio [ESP]
RUPPEL, Elizabeth [CAN]
RUSSO, Patti [USA]
RUSSOLO, Alessandra [ITA]
RUTH, Veronica Margaret [GBR]
RUTHVEN, Kenneth [GBR]
RYPKEMA, Koo J. [NLD]
SAAD, Germaine [USA]
SAARIMAKI, Peter [CAN]
SAENZ-LUDLOW, Adalira [USA]
SAHLBERG, Pasi [FIN]
SAINTE-MARIE, Mélanie [CAN]
SAKAGAMI, Eisho [JPN]
SAKAKI, Keiko [JPN]
SAKAKI, Tadao [JPN]
SAKAMA, Kayoko [JPN]
SAKAMA, Toshiaki [JPN]
SAKAMOTO, Masako [JPN]
SAKONIDIS, Haralambos [GBR]
SAKURAI, Seiko [JPN]
SALAZAR-LANGLEY, Cristina [USA]
SALDAÑA HERNÁNDEZ, Rocío [MEX]
SALGUERO, Manuel Luis [ESP]
SALLY, Paul [USA]
SALVOLINI, Luciano [ITA]
SAMPERIZ ESCANERO, Arturo [ESP]
SAMSON, Valérie [CAN]
SAMUELSSON, Christina [SWE]
SAMUELSSON, Jan [SWE]
SAMUELSSON, Lars [SWE]
SAN LUIS BUGALLO, Manuel [ESP]
SANCHEZ, Victoria [ESP]
SANCHEZ COBO, Francisco T. [ESP]
SANCHEZ GRANDE, José Manuel [ESP]
SANCHEZ SANCHEZ, Mª Carmen [ESP]
SANCHEZ-VASQUEZ, Gonzalo [ESP]
SANDEFUR, James [USA]
SANDER, Dick [USA]
SANDERS, Glenna E. [USA]
SANDERS, Susan E. [GBR]
SANDERS, Walter J. [USA]
SANDIN, Eva [SWE]
SANDIN, Peter O. [SWE]
SANDS, Bill [CAN]
SANGALLI, Arturo [CAN]
SANTOS, Madalena [PRT]
SANTOS, Vãnia Maria [USA]
SANTOS TRIGO, Manuel [MEX]
SANZ LERMA, Ines [ESP]
SATO, Katsuhiko [JPN]
SATO, Shuntaro [JPN]

SAUCIER, Danièle [CAN]
SAUL, Mark [USA]
SAVARD, Guy [CAN]
SAVOIE, Élise [CAN]
SAWADA, Daiyo [CAN]
SAWADA, Toshio [JPN]
SAWYER, Ted [AUS]
SAXE, Geoffrey [USA]
SAXENA, Subhash [USA]
SCALERA, Lucia [ITA]
SCANLAN, Anne [USA]
SCHAAFSMA, Willem [NLD]
SCHEAFFER, Richard [USA]
SCHELL, Vicki J. [USA]
SCHER, Daniel [USA]
SCHERER, Petra [DEU]
SCHERK, John [CAN]
SCHIELACK, Jane F. [USA]
SCHILLER, Barry [USA]
SCHILLINGER, George [USA]
SCHILLINGER, Jolene [USA]
SCHLAACK, Margaret [USA]
SCHLIEMANN, Analúcia Dias [BRA]
SCHLOMIUK, Norbert [CAN]
SCHMIDT, Siegbert [DEU]
SCHMIDT, Sylvine [CAN]
SCHMIDT, Victor E. [NLD]
SCHMITT, Carrie [USA]
SCHMITT, Lynn [USA]
SCHMITTAU, Jean [USA]
SCHNEIDER, Joel [USA]
SCHNEIDER, Maggy [BEL]
SCHOEMAKER, George [NLD]
SCHOENFELD, Alan H. [USA]
SCHOFIELD, Elizabeth Ann [CAN]
SCHRAMM, Ruben [DEU]
SCHROEDER, Bernie [USA]
SCHROEDER, Mary Anne [USA]
SCHROEDER, Thomas L. [CAN]
SCHULTZ, James E. [USA]
SCHULZ, Wolfgang [DEU]
SCHUMAKER, John A. [USA]
SCHUMANN, Heinz [DEU]
SCHUPP, Hans [DEU]
SCHUPP, Irmtreut [DEU]
SCHURING, Henk N. [NLD]
SCHURING, Henny [NLD]
SCHURLE, Arlo W. [USA]
SCHWARTZ, Judah L. [USA]
SCHWEIGER, Fritz [AUT]
SCHWENK, Elizabeth P. [USA]
SCHWINGENDORF, Keith [USA]
SCIMEMI, Benedetto [ITA]
SCIMEMI, Pietro [ITA]
SCOINS, Ron [CAN]
SCONIERS, Sheila [USA]

SCOTT, Heather Miranda [GBR]
SCOTT, Joy Frances [AUS]
SCOTT, Margaret Jean [AUS]
SCOTT, Patrick [USA]
SCOTT, Paul Raymond [AUS]
SCOZZAFAVA, Isa Di Fabio [ITA]
SCOZZAFAVA, Romano [ITA]
SCRUTON, Paul [GBR]
SCUDDER, Mary [USA]
SEARL, John Walter [GBR]
SEATS, Lee A. [USA]
SEEGER, Falk [DEU]
SEGAL, Joshua [USA]
SEKIGUCHI, Yasuhiro [JPN]
SELDEN, Annie [USA]
SELDEN, John [USA]
SELINGER, Michelle [GBR]
SELKIRK, Jennifer A. [GBR]
SELKIRK, Keith E. [GBR]
SELTER, Christoph [DEU]
SEMADENI, Zbigniew [POL]
SEMERIA, Severine [FRA]
SENDOVA, Evgenia [BGR]
SENK, Sharon L. [USA]
SENOO, Kiyonori [JPN]
SENTURIA, Jerome B. [USA]
SENUMA, Hanako [JPN]
SEPPÄLÄ, Reino [FIN]
SEQUEIRA, Michael [USA]
SERANT, Brigitte [FRA]
SERRANO-ROMERO, Luis [ESP]
SERRAZINA, Maria de Lurdes [PRT]
SERVÁN THOMAS, Maria Jesus [ESP]
SETIANINGSIH, Rini [CAN]
SETSURO, Kiyota [JPN]
SEVIC, Sybil [USA]
SFARD, Anna [ISR]
SHAFROTH, Chantal [USA]
SHAHVARANI-SEMNANI, Ahmad [IRN]
SHALABY, Ahmed [EGY]
SHAN-RANDHAWA, Harmeet [GBR]
SHAN-RANDHAWA, Sharanjeet [GBR]
SHANNON, Ann [GBR]
SHARP, Ann W. [USA]
SHARP, Karen [USA]
SHARVILL, Diana M. [GBR]
SHAUGHNESSY, Michael [USA]
SHAVER, Connie [CAN]
SHAW, Carl [CAN]
SHAW, Marian [CAN]
SHAW, Pamela Frances [AUS]
SHEALY, Barry E. [USA]
SHEATH, Geoff [GBR]
SHEATH, Pauline [GBR]
SHECKELS, Marie [USA]
SHEFFIELD, Linda [USA]

SHEFI, Yael [ISR]
SHELLEY, Nancy Jean [AUS]
SHELLY, Barbara [USA]
SHELP, Phillip [USA]
SHEPPARD, Evelyn [ATG]
SHER, Lawrence [USA]
SHIBANO, Hiroki [JPN]
SHIBATA, Kunie [JPN]
SHIBATA, Masanori K. [JPN]
SHIDA, Masao [JPN]
SHIENA, Steven [USA]
SHIGEMATSU, Keiichi [JPN]
SHIMIZU, Katsuhiko [JPN]
SHIMIZU, Senjo [JPN]
SHIMIZU, Shizumi [JPN]
SHIMIZU, Yoshinori [JPN]
SHIMOMACHI, Hisao [JPN]
SHINDO, Toshiaki [JPN]
SHINYA, Yamamoto [JPN]
SHIRA, Jack [USA]
SHIRLEY, Alberta [USA]
SHIRLEY, Lawrence [USA]
SHIU, Christine [GBR]
SHIU, Edward Man Kee [GBR]
SHIU, Peter [GBR]
SHOUKRY, Margaret [USA]
SHUARD, Hilary † [GBR]
SHULMAN, Bonnie J. [USA]
SHULTE, Albert P. [USA]
SHULTE, Joann C. [USA]
SIDDIQI, Jamil A. [CAN]
SIDDIQI, Rafat Nabi [KWT]
SIEGEL, Martha J. [USA]
SIEMON, Dianne E. [AUS]
SIERPINSKA, Anna [CAN]
SILAO, Dulce [AUT]
SILBERT, Bonnie [CAN]
SILBERT, Michael R. [CAN]
SILLANPÄÄ, Veikko [FIN]
SILVA, Antonio [CAN]
SILVA NUNO, Joaquim [PRT]
SILVER, Edward A. [USA]
SILVERMAN, Helene Joy [USA]
SIMARD, Christiane [CAN]
SIMAROV FERNANDEZ, M. Sagrario [ESP]
SIMONS, Dori [NLD]
SIMONS, Fred [NLD]
SINGH, Bhupinder [GBR]
SINGH, Europe K. [GBR]
SINGLETON, Mary K. [USA]
SINICROPE, Rose [USA]
SINKINSON, Anne [GBR]
SINNEMAKI, Jussi [FIN]
SIOUI, Claudine [CAN]
SISTAR-MAGRI, Carolyn [USA]
SIU, Heng [HKG]

SIU, Man Keung [HKG]
SIU CHAN, Fung Kit [HKG]
SKEATH, Ann R. [USA]
SKINNER, Penny [AUS]
SKOOGH, Brita [SWE]
SKOOGH, Lennart [SWE]
SKOVSMOSE, Ole [DNK]
SLAMMERT, Lionel [USA]
SLAVIT, David [USA]
SLOTTA, Olive A. [USA]
SLOYAN, Stephanie [USA]
SMALL, Lynne B. [USA]
SMART, Teresa [GBR]
SMET, Eddy [CAN]
SMID, Harm Jan [NLD]
SMIT, Cornelis P. [NLD]
SMITH, Anne W. [USA]
SMITH, Constance [USA]
SMITH, David A. [USA]
SMITH, Dorothy R. [USA]
SMITH, Duncan Alexander [CAN]
SMITH, Erick [USA]
SMITH, James L. [USA]
SMITH, Jennifer [USA]
SMITH, John Barry [CHE]
SMITH, Julien Clifford [ZAF]
SMITH, Pauline Leslie [GBR]
SMITH, Penny [ZAF]
SMITH, Therese [USA]
SNIDER, James [USA]
SNOW, Donald R. [USA]
SOBEL, Michele [USA]
SÖDERSTRÖM, Jan-Gustav [SWE]
SÖDERSTRÖM, Kerstin [SWE]
SÖDERSTRÖM, Ulf [SWE]
SOIFER, Alexander [USA]
SOIFER, Maya [USA]
SOLAR, Claudie [CAN]
SOLOMON, Avery [USA]
SONE, Hiroyuki [JPN]
SONE, Yurie [JPN]
SONS, Linda R. [USA]
SORMANY, Jacques [CAN]
SOUTHWELL, Beth [AUS]
SOUTHWOOD, Susan L. [GBR]
SOUVINEY, Randall [USA]
SOUZA DANTAS, Martha Maria [BRA]
SOWDER, Judith [USA]
SOWDER, Larry [USA]
SOYRING, Anselm [USA]
SPEIER, Patricia [USA]
SPEIER, Peter [USA]
SPIELBERG, Stephen E. [USA]
SPILIMBERGO, Francesca [ITA]
SPINADEL, Vera W. de [ARG]
SPIRIG, Franz [CHE]

SPIRO, Lea [ISR]
SPRAKER, John [USA]
SPRESSER, Diane M. [USA]
ST-PIERRE, Lise [CAN]
STAAL, Henk [NLD]
STAFFORD, Ann [USA]
STANBACK, Bessie [USA]
STARRITT, Alan J. [GBR]
STASTNA, Viena [CAN]
STEEG, Torben [GBR]
STEEL, Roslyn P. [AUS]
STEELE, Emilie [USA]
STEEN, Franklin M. [USA]
STEEN, Lynn Arthur [USA]
STEFFE, Leslie [USA]
STEFFE, Marilyn [USA]
STEIN, David A. [USA]
STEINBRING, Heinz [DEU]
STEINER, Erika-Luise [DEU]
STEINER, Hans-Georg [DEU]
STEMPIEN, Margaret [USA]
STEPHENS, Cynthia [USA]
STEPHENS, Jon [USA]
STEPHENS, Marie [USA]
STEPHENS, W. Max [AUS]
STERN, Jacques [FRA]
STERRETT, Andrew [USA]
STERRETT, Betts [USA]
STEWART, Bob [CAN]
STEWART, Jan [GBR]
STEWART, Patrick [CAN]
STICH, Mary [USA]
STICH, Philip [USA]
STOFBERG, François J. [ZAF]
STOKES, Victoria Burnard [AUS]
STORTZ, Clarence B. [USA]
STORTZ, Yvonne [USA]
STOUTEMYER, Karen [USA]
STRAESSER, Rudolf [DEU]
STRAIGHT, Joseph [USA]
STRANG, Tuula Kaarina [FIN]
STREEFLAND, Leendert [NLD]
STRNAD, Milena [SLN]
STRUMP, Anthony [USA]
STRUMP, Marion [USA]
STRUMP, Mary [USA]
SUCCI, Francesco [ITA]
SUDA, Chiyo [JPN]
SUDA, Hiroshi [JPN]
SUFFOLK, John A. [NAM]
SUGAWARA, Kazuko [JPN]
SUKTHANKAR, Neela [PNG]
SUKTHANKAR, Rahul [PNG]
SULLIVAN, Jillian C.F. [CAN]
SULLIVAN, Kevin [USA]
SULLIVAN, Peter [AUS]

SUMNER, Kip [CAN]
SUN, Wei [USA]
SUNDAR, Viji K. [USA]
SUNTER, Mary Julie [GBR]
SUNZUNEGUI DE IGLECIA, Elena [ARG]
SURGEY, Philippa Joy [GBR]
SURMAN, Pamela G. [AUS]
SUSUMU, Shintani [JPN]
SUTHERLAND, Rosamund [GBR]
SUTTON, John [USA]
SUZUKI, Shingo [JPN]
SVANEBORG, Vibeke [DNK]
SWAFFORD, Jane O. [USA]
SWAN, Malcolm B. [GBR]
SWANEPOEL, Jonathan [USA]
SWANK, Earl [USA]
SWARD, Marcia [USA]
SWEETNAM, Ruth K. [GBR]
SWEEZIE, Jean [CAN]
SWENSON, Carl [USA]
SWETZ, Frank [USA]
SWIFT, Jim [USA]
SWINSON, Kevan Victor [AUS]
SZCZEPKOWICZ, Andrzej [POL]
SZENDREI, Julianna [HUN]
SZENTIVANYI, Tibor [HUN]
SZETELA, Walter [CAN]
TADA, Minori [JPN]
TAHERIZADEH, Abdol Javad [IRN]
TAKAHASHI, Akihiko [USA]
TAKAHASHI, Shuichi [JPN]
TAKAHASHI, Susumu [JPN]
TAKAI, Fujie [JPN]
TAKAI, Kiyoshi [JPN]
TAKAMORI, Noriko [JPN]
TAKANO, Yoshiko [JPN]
TAKAO, Hiroshi [JPN]
TAKEI, Noriko [JPN]
TAKENOUCHI, Osamu [JPN]
TAKEUCHI, Masayo [JPN]
TAKEUCHI, Reiko [JPN]
TAKEUCHI, Taihei [JPN]
TAKEYA, Chie [USA]
TAKEYA, Makoto [USA]
TAKIMOTO, Reiko [JPN]
TALL, David [GBR]
TALOUMIS, Thalia E. [USA]
TANABE, Norio [JPN]
TANAKA, Hiroshi [JPN]
TANAKA, Masao [JPN]
TANG, Rui Fen [CHN]
TANIGUCHI, Noboru [JPN]
TANNER, Howard [GBR]
TARTRE, Lindsay A. [USA]
TASSÉ, André [CAN]
TATEYAMA, Kyoko [JPN]

TAVOUKTSOGLOU, Tom [CAN]
TAYLOR, Barbara [USA]
TAYLOR, Linda [USA]
TAYLOR, Lyn [USA]
TAYLOR, Peter C.S. [AUS]
TAYLOR, Peter D. [CAN]
TAYLOR, Peter James [AUS]
TEAGUE, Daniel J. [USA]
TECHAPIWAT, Patra [THA]
TEEGUARDEN, Janet E. [USA]
TEEGUARDEN, Sheryl [USA]
TEEGUARDEN, William [USA]
TEK HONG, Kho [SGP]
TEN HOVE, Juul [NLD]
TENNISON, Rosemary [GBR]
TEPPO, Anne [USA]
TER HEEGE, Hans [NLD]
TERLOUW, Pieter [NLD]
TETSURO, Yoshikawa [JPN]
TEXIER, Annie [FRA]
THALMARD, Thibaut [CHE]
THERRIEN, Denis [CAN]
THEULE-LUBIENSKI, Sarah [USA]
THIBAULT, Marie-France [CAN]
THIELE, Rudiger [DEU]
THOMAS, David A. [USA]
THOMAS, Dick [USA]
THOMAS, Gill Kaye [NZL]
THOMAS, Jan [AUS]
THOMAS, Lindsay [AUS]
THOMAS, Nancy J. [USA]
THOMAS, Robert [CAN]
THOMAS, Sally [USA]
THOMPSON, Alba [USA]
THOMPSON, Denisse R. [USA]
THOMPSON, Donald [USA]
THOMPSON, Lorraine [USA]
THOMPSON, Patrick [USA]
THOMPSON, Virginia [USA]
THORNE, Ann [USA]
THORNTON, Carol A. [USA]
THORSTAD, Ingrid Mary [GBR]
THULIN, Lennart [SWE]
TINGLEFF, Kirsten [DNK]
TINTO, Patricia Price [USA]
TIROSH, Dina [ISR]
TOBIN, Alexander [USA]
TOBIN, Evelyn Maria [NZL]
TOBIN, K.G. [USA]
TOBIN, Susan [USA]
TOKI, Osamu [JPN]
TOKINAGA, Akira [JPN]
TOLMIE, Julie Anne [AUS]
TOMINAGA, Yasuo [JPN]
TOMITA, Kouichi [JPN]
TOMITA, Makiko [JPN]

TOMITA, Shuichi [JPN]
TOMOKAWA, Hiroshi [JPN]
TOMPA, Klára [HUN]
TONI, Paolo [ITA]
TONKIN, Jan [AUS]
TONKIN, Wallace [AUS]
TONOJAN, Garnik [ARM]
TORBJÖRNSON, Lena [SWE]
TORGERSON, Frances L. [USA]
TORKILDSEN, Ole Einar [NOR]
TORKILDSEN, Valbjørg [NOR]
TORMO FERRER, Bienvenida [ESP]
TORRA, Monserrat [ESP]
TORRALBO RODRIGUEZ, Manuel [ESP]
TORREGROSA, David [ESP]
TORREGROSA GIRONES, German [ESP]
TORU, Sunahara [JPN]
TOURÉ, Salion [CIV]
TOUZEL, Timothy J. [USA]
TOWNSEND, Howard [USA]
TOWNSEND, Janet [USA]
TRAFTON, Patricia [USA]
TRAFTON, Paul [USA]
TRAVERS, Kenneth J. [USA]
TRAVIS, Betty [USA]
TREISMAN, Philip U. [USA]
TRI, Nguyen Dinh [VNM]
TRINICK, Tony [NZL]
TRUJILLO LARA, Manuel [ESP]
TSAMIR, Pesia [ISR]
TSASANE, Matseliso [ZAF]
TSATSANIS, Paula [CAN]
TSATSANIS, Peter S. [CAN]
TSUBOTA, Etsuko [JPN]
TSUBOTA, Kozo [JPN]
TSUCKERMAN, Vitaly V. [RUS]
TSUJI, Michiko [JPN]
TSUJI, Yoshio [JPN]
TSUKAHARA, Kumiko [JPN]
TSUYUKI, Shigeru [JPN]
TUNICA GROS, Cristina [ESP]
TUNIS, Harry [USA]
TUPPER, Gary A. [CAN]
TUPPER, Linda [CAN]
TURNAU, Stefan [POL]
TURNER, Jerome K. [CAN]
TYMOCZKO, Thomas [USA]
TZOULAKIS, Stavros [GRC]
TZUR, Ron [ISR]
UBUZ, Behiye [GBR]
UCHIMURA, Kazuo [JPN]
UEGAKI, Wataru [JPN]
UETAKE, Tsuneo [JPN]
UEWAKI, Masatsugu [JPN]
UGARTE, María Dolores [ESP]
UMAKOSHI, Misuzu [JPN]

UMAKOSHI, Youichi [JPN]
UMENO, Hajime [JPN]
UMENO, Yukiko [JPN]
UPSON, Thomas [USA]
URBANO SALVADOR, Ana Maria [ESP]
USHER, John Richard [GBR]
USISKIN, Karen [USA]
USISKIN, Zalman [USA]
USNICK, Virginia [USA]
UUS-LEPONIEMI, Markku [FIN]
UWIMANA, Alphonsine [CAN]
VAGI, Veronika [HUN]
VAIDYA, Arun M. [IND]
VAILLANCOURT, Rémi [CAN]
VALENTE, Sérgio [PRT]
VALIQUETTE, Philippe [CAN]
VALLECILLOS JIMENEZ, Angustias [ESP]
VALLS, Julia [ESP]
VAN ASCH, Bram [NLD]
VAN BRUMMELEN, Glen [CAN]
VAN DEN BRINK, Jan [NLD]
VAN DER WESTHUIZEN, Gert J. [ZAF]
VAN DER ZWAART, Pieter W. [NLD]
VAN DIEREN, Françoise [BEL]
VAN DORMOLEN, Joop [NLD]
VAN DYKE, Frances [USA]
VAN GAANS, Ms. [NLD]
VAN GAANS, Willem [NLD]
VAN GALEN, Frans [NLD]
VAN HEESWIJCK, Lutgarde [BEL]
VAN HOORN, M.C. [NLD]
VAN LEEMPUT, Guido [NLD]
VAN LINT, Jack [NLD]
VAN MAANEN, Jan A. [NLD]
VAN OERS, Bert [NLD]
VAN PINXTEREN, Peter [AUS]
VAN ZOEST, Laura R. [USA]
VANCE, Irvin E. [USA]
VANDAL, Éliette [CAN]
VANDEGRIFT, Judy [USA]
VANDERSTRAETEN, Godelieve [CAN]
VANG, Julie [USA]
VANHAMME-VAN ISACKER, Jacqueline [BEL]
VANHILLE, Bruno [FRA]
VASCO, Carlos E. [COL]
VASSILIEV, Nikolay [RUS]
VAZQUEZ DE TAPIA, Nelly [ARG]
VÁZQUEZ MANTECÓN, Teresa [MEX]
VEGA DE PADILLA, Maria Olivia [MEX]
VEILLET, René [FRA]
VELLARD, Dominique [CAN]
VELOSO, Eduardo M.S.S. [PRT]
VENHEIM, Rolf [NOR]
VERBEEK, John [NLD]
VERDE PÉREZ, M. Elena [ESP]
VERGANI, Teresa [PRT]

491

VERGNAUD, Gérard Michel [FRA]
VERHAGE, Heleen [NLD]
VERMANDEL, Alfred [BEL]
VERMEULEN, Dirk [CAN]
VERRIER, Claudine [FRA]
VERRIER, Francis [FRA]
VERRIER, Sylvie [FRA]
VERVOORT, Gerardus [CAN]
VIDAL SILVA, Maria Dolores [ESP]
VIEGAS, Filomena [PRT]
VIGIER, Noële [FRA]
VIGNEAULT, Denise [CAN]
VILLANI, Marcello [ITA]
VILLANI, Vinicio [ITA]
VILLAR ICASURIAGA, Maria Alicia [URY]
VILLAR LINAN, Trinidad [ESP]
VILLAR MARQUES DE SÁ, Antonio [BRA]
VILLAR MIRABAL, Ma. Emilia [ESP]
VILLAVICENCIO UBILLÚS, Martha R. [PER]
VILLENEUVE, Lina [CAN]
VINIK, Michael [USA]
VINNER, Shlomo [ISR]
VINSON, Mai [USA]
VIÑUALES-GAVIN, Ederlinda [ESP]
VIRDEFORS, Bo [SWE]
VITHAL, Renuka [ZAF]
VIZMANOS BUELTA, Jose R. [ESP]
VOIGT, Jörg [DEU]
VOISIN-ROUX, Monique [FRA]
VOIT, Gerard [USA]
VOIT, Kaihryn H. [USA]
VOLLRATH, Hans J. [DEU]
VOLLRATH, Ruth [DEU]
VOLMINK, John David [ZAF]
VON GLASERSFELD, Ernst [USA]
VON STERNBERG, Haydée [USA]
VORBROOK, Erwin [DEU]
WADA, Seisuke [JPN]
WAGNER, Linda [USA]
WAITS, Bert K. [USA]
WAIVERIS, Charles [USA]
WALKER, Dennis [GBR]
WALKER, Joan M. [GBR]
WALLACE, Clint [USA]
WALLACE, Martha L. [USA]
WALSH, Angela [GBR]
WALSH, Kathleen [USA]
WALTER, Marion [USA]
WALTON, Nancy [CAN]
WANBY, Göran [SWE]
WANBY, Karen [SWE]
WARMINGTON, Dana [CAN]
WARRINNIER, Alfred [BEL]
WASCHESCIO, Ute [DEU]
WATANABE, Kaeko [JPN]
WATANABE, Shin [JPN]

WATSON, Jane M. [AUS]
WATSON, Martha F. [USA]
WATSON-RHODES, Wanita [CAN]
WATT, Dan [USA]
WEBB, John H. [ZAF]
WEBB, Norman [USA]
WEBBER, Vicky [USA]
WEIDEMANN, Wanda [USA]
WEINKAMER, Erich [AUT]
WEINZWEIG, Avrum Israel [USA]
WEISER, Werner [DEU]
WEISKOPF, Joyce L. [USA]
WEISS, Asia Ivic [CAN]
WEISS, William [CAN]
WELLS, Deborah [USA]
WELLS, Rena S. [USA]
WELLS JR., Raymond [USA]
WELTON, John [CHE]
WENZELBURGER, Elfriede † [MEX]
WERNER, Judy [USA]
WEST, Beverly [USA]
WEST, Elizabeth T. [GBR]
WEST, James E. [USA]
WESTBYE, Øivind [NOR]
WESTEGAARD, Susanne K. [USA]
WHEATLEY, Grayson H. [USA]
WHEATON, Anita R. [AUS]
WHEATON, Neville K. [AUS]
WHEELER, David [CAN]
WHEELER, Trevor Edwin [NZL]
WHIPPY, Helen [USA]
WHITE, Alvin [USA]
WHITE, Arthur L. [USA]
WHITE, Harry [CAN]
WHITE, Jane [GBR]
WHITE, Myra [USA]
WHITNEY, Stephen [CAN]
WICK, Cathy [USA]
WIDMER, Connie Carroll [USA]
WIDMER, Firmin G. [USA]
WIEBE, Muffie [USA]
WIJERS, Monica [NLD]
WIKLUND, Staffan [SWE]
WILDER, Peter J. [GBR]
WILLIAMS, Douglas D. [GBR]
WILLIAMS, Edgar R. [CAN]
WILLIAMS, Floyd [USA]
WILLIAMS, Gwendoline [ZAF]
WILLIAMS, Honor Irene McLennan [GBR]
WILLIAMS, Julian S [GBR]
WILLIAMS, Steven [USA]
WILLIAMS, Susan [USA]
WILLIS, Donald [AUS]
WILLIS, Sue [AUS]
WILLIS, Vivienne [AUS]
WILLOUGHBY, Sali [USA]

WILLOUGHBY, Stephen S. [USA]
WILSON, Carolyn Q. [USA]
WILSON, Melvin R. [USA]
WILSON, Patricia S. [USA]
WILSON MEYER, Rochelle [USA]
WIMBISH, Joe [USA]
WINICKI, Greisy [ISR]
WINSTON, Bente [USA]
WINTER, Mary Jean [USA]
WIRSZUP, Izaak [USA]
WIRSZUP, Pera [USA]
WISBRUN, Hans [NLD]
WISMEIJER, Eduard [BOL]
WITTE, Marjolÿ [NLD]
WITTMANN, Erich Ch. [DEU]
WIZDA, Elaine [USA]
WOJCIECHOWSKA, Agnieszka [POL]
WOJCIECHOWSKA, Marzenna [SWE]
WOLF, Neli [USA]
WOLFENGAUT, Juri [RUS]
WONG, Chiu-Wing [HKG]
WONG, Ngai Ying [HKG]
WOOD, Leigh [AUS]
WOOD, Terry [USA]
WOODROW, Derek [GBR]
WOODROW, Patricia [GBR]
WOODS, Grant [CAN]
WOODS, Sheila [CAN]
WORRELL, Edward C. [USA]
WRIGHT, Bob [AUS]
WRIGHT, Graham P. [CAN]
WYCKOFF, Harry [USA]
WYNANDS, Alexander [DEU]
WYNANDS, Ursula [DEU]
WYNDHAMN, Gerd [SWE]
WYNDHAMN, Jan [SWE]
YAAKUB, Baiduriah [MYS]
YABUTA, Masayoshi [JPN]
YACKEL, Erna [USA]
YAMAGUCHI, Chisato [JPN]
YAMAGUCHI, Takeshi [JPN]
YAMANOSHITA, Hitofumi [JPN]
YAMANOSHITA, Toyoko [JPN]
YAMANOSHITA, Yuko [JPN]
YAMASHINA, Shiko [JPN]
YAMASHITA, Hajime [JPN]

YAMASHITA, Koji [JPN]
YAMAZAKI, Chikako [JPN]
YAMAZAKI, Koji [JPN]
YANAGIMOTO, Akira [JPN]
YANAGIMOTO, Tomoko [JPN]
YARMUKHAMEDOV, Sharof [UZB]
YASUYUKI, Miyata [JPN]
YERUSHALMY, Michal [ISR]
YOKOCHI, Kiyoshi [JPN]
YOSHIDA, Hajime [JPN]
YOSHIKAWA, Masaki [JPN]
YOSHIKAWA, Toshiko [JPN]
YOSHIOKA, Alan [CAN]
YOUNGKHONG, Danai [THA]
YRJÖNSUURI, Raija [FIN]
YRJÖNSUURI, Yrjö [FIN]
ZABULIONIS, Algirdas [LIT]
ZACK, Vicki [CAN]
ZAREMBA, Danuta [POL]
ZASLAVSKY, Claudia [USA]
ZASLAVSKY, Orit [ISR]
ZASLAVSKY, Sam [USA]
ZAWAIDEH, Tina [USA]
ZAWOJEWSKI, Judith S. [USA]
ZAWOJEWSKI, Lara K. [USA]
ZBIEK, Rose M. [USA]
ZECH, Linda [USA]
ZEGRAY, Edward [CAN]
ZEGRAY, Lucienne [CAN]
ZEHAVI, Nurit [ISR]
ZELLWEGER, Shea [USA]
ZEVENBERGEN, Robyn [AUS]
ZHANG, Dianzhou [CHN]
ZHI, Guan Cheng [CHN]
ZIEBKA, Janice [USA]
ZIEGENBALG, Jochen [DEU]
ZILLIOX, Joseph [USA]
ZIMMERMANN, Bernd [DEU]
ZIZI, Jacqueline [FRA]
ZORN, Paul [USA]
ZOUALI, Wafaa [CAN]
ZSEBY, Christa [DEU]
ZSEBY, Siegfried [DEU]
ZUBIAURRE, Lorea [ESP]
ZUCCO, Cathleen M. [USA]
ZWANEVELD, Bert [NLD]

DISTRIBUTION BY COUNTRY

RÉPARTITION PAR PAYS

Country / *Pays*	Total	Country / *Pays*	Total
Andorra / *Andorre* [AND]	1	France [FRA]	142
Antigua [ATG]	1	Germany / *Allemagne* [DEU]	85
Argentina / *Argentine* [ARG]	13	Greece / *Grèce* [GRC]	8
Armenia / *Arménie* [ARM]	1	Guadeloupe [GLP]	2
Australia / *Australie* [AUS]	182	Guatemala [GTM]	3
Austria / *Autriche* [AUT]	13	Haiti / *Haïti* [HTI]	1
Bahrain / *Bahreïn* [BHR]	1	Hong Kong / *Hong-Kong* [HKG]	11
Belgium / *Belgique* [BEL]	19	Hungary / *Hongrie* [HUN]	10
Bolivia / *Bolivie* [BOL]	3	Iceland / *Islande* [ISL]	4
Botswana [BWA]	2	India / *Inde* [IND]	2
Brazil / *Brésil* [BRA]	37	Indonesia / *Indonésie* [IDN]	3
Brunei Darussalam / *Brunéi Darussalam* [BRN]	2	Iran [IRN]	12
Bulgaria / *Bulgarie* [BGR]	3	Ireland / *Irlande* [IRL]	3
Canada [CAN]	543	Israel / *Israël* [ISR]	49
Chile / *Chili* [CHL]	3	Italy / *Italie* [ITA]	74
China / *Chine* [CHN]	8	Ivory Coast / *Côte d'Ivoire* [CIV]	2
Colombia / *Colombie* [COL]	9	Jamaica / *Jamaïque* [JAM]	2
Costa Rica [CRI]	1	Japan / *Japon* [JPN]	281
Cuba [CUB]	1	Kuwait / *Koweït* [KWT]	6
Czech Republic / *République tchèque* [CZR]	4	Latvia / *Lettonie* [LAT]	1
Denmark / *Danemark* [DNK]	16	Lebanon / *Liban* [LBN]	3
Dominican Republic / *République dominicaine* [DOM]	2	Lithuania / *Lithuanie* [LIT]	1
Egypt / *Égypte* [EGY]	5	Luxembourg [LUX]	1
Estonia / *Estonie* [EST]	1	Malawi [MWI]	2
Fiji / *Fidji* [FJI]	2	Malaysia / *Malaisie* [MYS]	5
Finland / *Finlande* [FIN]	28	Martinique [MTQ]	1
		Mauritius / *Île Maurice* [MUS]	2
		Mexico / *Mexique* [MEX]	22
		Morocco / *Maroc* [MAR]	5

COUNTRY / *Pays*	Total	COUNTRY / *Pays*	Total
Mozambique [MOZ]	3	Spain / *Espagne* [ESP]	164
Namibia / *Namibie* [NAM]	1	St. Lucia / *Ste-Lucie* [LCA]	2
Netherlands / *Pays-Bas* [NLD]	60	Swaziland [SWZ]	1
New Zealand /		Sweden / *Suède* [SWE]	96
Nouvelle-Zélande [NZL]	45	Switzerland / *Suisse* [CHE]	12
Nigeria / *Nigéria* [NGA]	2	Taiwan / *Taïwan* [TWN]	8
Norway / *Norvège* [NOR]	18	Tanzania / *Tanzanie* [TZA]	2
Pakistan [PAK]	1	Thailand / *Thaïlande* [THA]	7
Papua New Guinea /		Turkey / *Turquie* [TUR]	2
Papouasie-Nouvelle-Guinée [PNG]	3	Uganda / *Ouganda* [UGA]	1
Peru / *Pérou* [PER]	2	Ukrainia / *Ukraine* [UKR]	1
Poland / *Pologne* [POL]	9	United Kingdom /	
Portugal [PRT]	31	*Royaume-Uni* [GBR]	248
Puerto Rico / *Porto Rico* [PRI]	3	United States / *États-Unis* [USA]	970
Qatar [QAT]	2	Uruguay [URY]	1
Russia / *Russie* [RUS]	10	Uzbekistan / *Ouzbékistan* [UZB]	1
Saudi Arabia /		Venezuela [VEN]	6
Arabie Saoudite [SAU]	2	Vietnam [VNM]	1
Singapore / *Singapour* [SGP]	6	Yemen / *Yémen* [YEM]	1
Slovakia / *Slovaquie* [SVK]	2	Zimbabwe [ZWE]	3
Slovenia / *Slovénie* [SLN]	2		
South Africa /			
Afrique du Sud [ZAF]	31	Total	3407
South Korea / *Corée du Sud* [KOR]	3	Countries / *Pays*	94